COMPARATIVE LAW OF SECURITY A.

QUICK REFERENCE GUIDE

LAW AND PRACTICE OF INTERNATIONAL FINANCE

COMPARATIVE LAW OF
SECURITY AND GUARANTEES

AUSTRALIA
The Law Book Company
Brisbane * Sydney * Melbourne * Perth

CANADA
Carswell
Ottawa * Toronto * Calgary * Montreal * Vancouver

AGENTS:
Steimatzky's Agency Ltd., Tel Aviv;
N.M. Tripathi (Private) Ltd., Bombay;
Eastern Law House (Private) Ltd., Calcutta;
M.P.P. House, Bangalore;
Universal Book Traders, Delhi;
Aditya Books, Delhi;
MacMillan Shuppan KK, Tokyo;
Pakistan Law House, Karachi, Lahore.

LAW AND PRACTICE OF INTERNATIONAL FINANCE

COMPARATIVE LAW OF SECURITY AND GUARANTEES

By

Philip R Wood
BA (Cape Town), MA (Oxon)

Solicitor of the Supreme Court

Visiting Professor, Queen Mary
& Westfield College,
University of London

LONDON
SWEET & MAXWELL
1995

Published in 1995 by
Sweet and Maxwell Limited of
South Quay Plaza, 183 Marsh Wall,
London E14 9FT
Computerset by Interactive Sciences, Gloucester
Printed in Great Britain by
Butler & Tanner, Frome and London

Reprinted 1995

No natural forests were destroyed to make this product:
only farmed timber was used and re-planted

A CIP catalogue record for this book is
available from the British Library

ISBN 0 421 54320 5

To my wife Marie-elisabeth, my twin sons
John Barnaby and Richard,
my daughter Sophie and my son Timothy

PREFACE

This book is one in a series of six works on international financial law which, taken together, are the successor to my *Law and Practice of International Finance* which was published in 1980 and which was reprinted eight times.

The works now cover a much broader range of subjects, with substantial additions in the fields of comparative law, insolvency, security, set-off, payments, and title finance, as well as specialist subjects like netting, securitisations and swaps and derivatives. But the works have the same objectives as the original book. However great a gap there may be between the aim and the actuality, the objectives I have sought to achieve are to be practical as well as academic, to provide both a theoretical guide and legal source-book as well as a practitioner's manual, to be international, to provide serious comparative law information, to get to the point as quickly as possible, to simplify the difficulties, to find the principles underlying the particularity, to inform, and, most of all, to be useful.

The six works are separate but they are nevertheless related. Together the books are intended to form a complete library for the international banking and financial lawyer, as well as for specialists in related areas such as insolvency, leasing, and ship and aircraft finance. The topics covered by each volume are summarised on the inside of the front cover.

These books offer what I hope is a fundamentally new approach to comparative law in this area and, for the first time perhaps, provide the essential keys to an understanding of the world's jurisdictions, the keys to unlock the dark cupboard of financial law so that the light may shine in. These keys are not merely functional; they are also ethical and they are driven by history. The ideas are really quite simple, once discovered, but this should not obscure the difficulty of their application to the variety of circumstances. The core of the first book, entitled *Comparative Financial Law*, is a classification and snap-shot of virtually all the jurisdictions in the world – more than 300 of them – according to various financial law criteria. These criteria are developed in succeeding books in the series and applied to particular transactions. I believe that this also is the first time that a classification of this type has been done in this detail; but it has to be done because comparative law is no longer an academic luxury: it is a practical necessity if we are to have an orderly international legal regime.

My hope is that my voyage of discovery into what is really going on in world financial law will help to mitigate international legal surprises and legal risks and, in the wider context, that jurisdictions will be better equipped to make essential choices as to what their legal systems should achieve. This is particularly important in view of the fact that at least 30 per cent of the world's population live under legal systems which are still emerging and that the remainder live in jurisdictions divided into camps which often do not agree on basic policies. There is no reason why we should not agree on the basic policies: we do not have to have a muddle. The law is our servant, not our master. It must set us free, not tie us down. It must satisfy our sense of justice.

This book on the comparative law of security and guarantees is an attempt to sort out the (dangerous) international shambles which pervades this area of the law – an area which is of increasing importance in global financial transactions. Thus financial trading by a single institution can be collateralised on investment securities from 40 or 50 jurisdictions quite commonly. But jurisdictions differ diametrically in their attitude to security and I hope that this work will help to identify what the problems are so that we can do something about them. To achieve this, I have kept to the high road so that the points are not obscured by thickets of detail. The work also contains a comparative survey of the law of ship and aircraft finance. Ship finance in particular has played a major role in the development of the comparative law of security because the asset roams the world. In addition there is a study of guarantees and the like.

The books also contain lists of about 250 research topics in total which might be appropriate for further research and which I hope will be useful to prospective writers.

I am acutely conscious of the fact that, in writing about legal systems other than my own (which is England), I will often have committed some real howlers and I hope that my foreign colleagues will be tolerant of my ignorance. Obviously one must always confirm the position with competent local lawyers.

As regards style, I have endeavoured to be as economical as possible in these works. The citation is selective: there are now millions of cases and it is hopeless to try and list even a proportion of them. I am easily terrorised by footnotes and therefore, if material is good enough to go in the footnotes, it is good enough to go in the text: as a result there are no footnotes in these works. At least one does not have to read the text in two places at once. Table of cases and statutes seemed less sensible in a work endeavouring to cover hundreds of jurisdictions where there is an avalanche of names and numbers and dates and acts and statutes and decrees, and, in view of this, I decided to omit them.

I have endeavoured to reflect the law roundabout the middle of 1994 based on the international materials then available to me, although some subsequent changes were introduced in the course of publication.

Philip R Wood
One New Change
London

Request for Information

Works on the law in the jurisdictions of the world must rely heavily on information from private sources. With a view to improving the information in any subsequent editions there may be, I would be very pleased to receive papers of all kinds on subjects covered by this and other works in this series – seminar papers, essays, articles, client briefings by law firms, memoranda, notices of book publications, and the like. Material should be sent to me at the following address:

Philip R Wood
Allen & Overy
One New Change
London EC4M 9QQ

Fax: 0171 330 9999

ACKNOWLEDGEMENTS

I owe to many a debt of gratitude in the help they gave me in preparing this work.

I am grateful to many partners and colleagues at Allen & Overy and to secondees from foreign firms for their advice and assistance. The legal team from Morgan Guaranty Trust Company of New York at Euroclear in Brussels provided me with much advice and assistance on the operations of Euroclear. I owe a particular debt to the authors of the works listed in the bibliography and of a very large number of articles and books not listed in this book or in the bibliography without which it would not have been possible to write this book: if I have used their words, as I believe I often have, this is because they said it much better than I ever could. There are many others – practitioners, students, academics, bankers and others – who have contributed to this work in one way or another: it would be impossible for me to thank them all individually.

None of the above is of course responsible for the defects in this work.

I am most grateful to my secretary Sue Wisbey and to the Allen & Overy word processing department and checkers who laboured so magnificently to produce this work.

I am thankful to my publishers for their hard work and patience in bringing this work – and the other books in this series, to fruition and also for their support through all the years.

My brother John, my sister Melanie and my mother all encouraged me and were tolerant of my efforts.

My late father Leslie Wood, who was also a lawyer, first inculcated in me a fascination for the law while I was a boy in Northern Rhodesia, now Zambia.

Finally, I owe an enormous debt to my wife and children and can only express my affection for them by the token of dedicating this book to them.

CONTENTS

PART I: INTERNATIONAL SECURITY

PART II: SHIP AND AIRCRAFT FINANCE

PART III: GUARANTEES

PART IV: PREFERENCES

APPENDIX: CHECKLISTS, OUTLINES AND PRECEDENTS

ABBREVIATIONS

ABGB	Austrian General Civil Code
Art	Article
BA	Bankruptcy Act
BC	Bankruptcy Code
BGB	German Civil Code
BL	Bankruptcy Law
c	chapter (of laws)
CC	Civil Code
CCP	Code of Civil Procedure
CO	Code of Obligations
ComC	Commercial Code
Conflicts Restatement	Restatement of the Law, Conflict of Laws 2d, by the American Law Institute
Dicey	Lawrence Collins (general editor), *Dicey and Morris on the Conflict of Laws* (12th ed 1993) Sweet & Maxwell
EISO	Philip Wood, *English and International Set-off* (1989) Sweet & Maxwell
IA	Insolvency Act
ICSID	International Centre for the Settlement of Investment Disputes
IR	Insolvency Rules (England)
Mann, Money	FA Mann, *The Legal Aspect of Money* (5th ed 1992) Clarendon Press, Oxford
Ord	Order
PILA	Private International Law Act 1987 (Switzerland)
Restatement	Restatement of the Law by the American Law Institute
RSC	Rules of the Supreme Court (England)
s	section
Sched	Schedule
UCC	Uniform Commercial Code (United States)
ZPO	Code of Civil Procedure (*Zivilprozessordnung*)
Zweigert/Kötz	K Zweigert and H Kötz, *An Introduction to Comparative Law* (2nd ed 1987)

PART I

INTERNATIONAL SECURITY

CHAPTER 1

PRINCIPLES OF SECURITY

Security and insolvency

Secured creditors are super-priority creditors on insolvency. Security must 1–1
stand up on insolvency which is when it is needed most. Security which is
valid between the parties but not as against the creditors of the debtor is
futile. Bankruptcy laws which freeze or delay or weaken or de-prioritise
security on insolvency destroy what the law created. Hence the end is more
important than the beginning.

The objective of these chapters on security is to deal with the principles of
security internationally, but not the detail, so that the subject may be seen as
a whole.

Rationale of security

The main purposes and policies of security are as follows: 1–2

– protection of creditors on insolvency;

– the limitation of cascade or domino insolvencies;

– security encourages capital, e.g. enterprise finance;

– security reduces the cost of credit, e.g. margin collateral in markets;

– he who pays for the asset should have the right to the asset;

– security encourages the private rescue since the bank feels safer;

– security is defensive control, especially in the case of project finance;

– security is a fair exchange for the credit.

Main objections to security

The objections to security are mainly historical, but they resurrect and live 1–3
on. The hostility may stem from: debtor-protection stirred by the ancient
hostility to usurers and money-lending and now expressed in consumer

protection statutes; the prevention of false wealth, i.e. the debtor has many possessions but few assets – this is usually met by a requirement for possession (inefficient because not public) or registration; unsecured creditors get less on insolvency and this is seen as a violation of bankruptcy equality, although more often it is motivated by desire to protect unpaid employees and small creditors; security disturbs the safety of commercial transactions because of priority risks, e.g. the purchaser of goods; the secured creditor can disrupt a rescue by selling an essential asset, e.g. a factory.

Deep policies are involved, but choices have to be made. The international tendency seems to be to encourage security, but sometimes this is half-hearted, as where the secured creditors' rights are frozen on formal insolvency rescue proceedings.

Meaning of security

1–4 The essence of security is twofold:

- the creditor can force a sale of the property and use the proceeds to pay the secured debt ahead of other creditors;

- the debtor can insist on a release of creditor's rights of realisation on payment of the secured debt.

There is much confusing terminology: mortgage, pledge, charge, hypothecation, lien, fiduciary transfer, assignment. The confusion is often deepened by the old notion that security is a transfer of title by debtor to creditor and a re-transfer back when the secured debt is paid. But most jurisdictions distinguish absolute transfers and leases, e.g. sale and repurchase, finance leases. For title finance and its vulnerability to recharacterisation as security, see another work in this series of books on international financial law.

In the case of security proper, it is purely of historical interest to attempt to draw distinctions between, say, mortgages and charges on the basis that one is a transfer of property, the other is not: one cannot say that one is a 73 per cent transfer, another a 50 per cent transfer, a third a 3 per cent transfer. They are all security interests and classifications concentrating on the degree of proprietorial transfer miss the point. Other classifications are more important.

"False wealth" objection to security

1–5 The objection to "false wealth" is a foundation of limits on security in many countries, though being rapidly eroded as an inefficient ideology. False wealth or ostensible credit-worthiness arises when a debtor has many possessions but few assets, e.g. because he has mortgaged them, thereby alleg-edly encouraging false credit. This is met by public registration of security in many jurisdictions, but in those without a registration system for personal property, the result is that the secured creditor must have possession of the asset so as to take it out of the apparent ownership of the debtor – e.g. actual possession in the case of goods, or a complete transfer in the case of receivables (notice to the debtor), and registration of the investment securi-ties in the name of the secured creditor. Often these steps are impracticable. Also, possession is insufficiently public to meet the false wealth problem, if it is a problem. Because of the impracticality of creditor possession in most cases, the false wealth rule is fatal to general business charges (e.g. the float-ing charge), to non-possessory mortgages over inventory, goods and equip-ment, and to informal security over numerous receivables or securities. Other consequences of false wealth in the world's legal systems include the objection to the trust (divided ownership) in most jurisdictions outside the common law group.

Doctrine of specificity

The doctrine of specificity holds that a person may only sell or grant security over a specific identified and existing asset, not a future asset and not a generic class of assets. In the context of security, the objection to security over future or after-acquired assets stems partly from the desire to prevent a creditor from effectively taking security over a new asset for an existing debt since this is regarded as preferential. The doctrine is fatal to general floating charges over present and future corporate assets and to security over fung-ibles, like investment securities. The doctrine, too, is retreating in many advanced systems, and has virtually disappeared in others. This is because meticulous identification is often inconvenient, sometimes impractical, and always theoretical. The mischiefs it sought to contain can be addressed by better targetted policies.

1–6

Jurisdictional classification

One may rank jurisdictions according to whether a country is sympathetic or hostile to security:

1–7

- **Very sympathetic**: Most English-based common law countries and (to a lesser extent) Sweden, Finland and Norway (but not Denmark); most states in the United States, though with lesser enthusiasm than tra-ditional English countries.

- **Quite sympathetic**: Some Germanic countries, such as Germany, Japan, Netherlands, Switzerland, Scotland, South Africa.

- **Quite hostile**: Belgium, Luxembourg, most Latin American countries, Greece, Spain.

- **Very hostile**: Austria, France, Italy.

This ranking is based on a weighting of the factors listed below at para 1–10 *et seq*. It is bound to be impressionistic and unreliable. A country which is hostile to security is sometimes also hostile to title finance, e.g. retention of title, hire purchase, finance leases, receivables factoring and sale and repurchase. But the allowance of title finance in countries formally non-receptive to security is very marked and is transforming security law: this is because the traditional restraints on security are so inconvenient that courts the world over are content to sanction private ingenuity in avoiding them.

Jurisdictions without developed security

1–8   In addition, a few countries have little law on the grant of security, notably some fundamentalist Islamic states, agricultural or pastoral states without a commercial tradition, and states still emerging from communism.

China The concept of security appears undeveloped. Thus there are no developed rules regarding assignments of contracts or debts by way of security. But the laws of the Special Economic Zones (such as Shenzen) specifically recognise various kinds of mortgages, e.g. over buildings, goods and materials, marketable securities and the shareholdings in Sino-foreign joint ventures. And other enactments contemplate security. Thus the Enterprise Bankruptcy Law recognises the priority of mortgages: see Arts 28, 30, 32. Further, in the case of economic contracts in respect of matters not governed by Chinese law, international practice is to be followed: Civil Law Art 142; Foreign Economic Contracts Law Art 5. These provisions might apply in the case of security with a significant foreign element or in the case of recognition of foreign security. Because international practice is so various, the safest solution is perhaps for mortgages to comply with the lowest common denominator of legal systems, e.g. be in formal (notarised) form – if available – and stipulate a maximum amount. One could expect enforcement solely to be by public auction, perhaps judicially mandated. Giving publicity to a mortgage in a register seems problematic and pragmatic notifications should be considered.

Regulations of April 24, 1987 of the Bank of China set out the terms on which loans are made by the Bank of China to enterprises with a foreign investment. By Arts 16 and 17, the borrower will, if required, grant security.

Acceptable security includes house property, machinery and equipment, marketable goods in stock, foreign currency deposits, negotiable securities and other transferable rights and interests. The mortgage agreement must be duly notarised by a Chinese notary office.

Islamic countries Saudi Arabia is illustrative. The law there is still the   1–9
Shariah comprising The Koran and the sayings and deeds of Mohammed, as interpreted by the Hanbanli school of Islamic jurisprudence. Shariah law does not recognise mortgages of movables. But probably leases of goods are permitted if there is no obligation to pay interest.

But the **United Arab Emirates** enacted a commercial code in the early 1990s. And some Arab countries received a European system of law. Thus Algeria, Egypt and Syria received French law. But it is doubtful that Bahrain received English law, and Qatar did not do so. Pakistan, which is an Islamic country, has fully received English law.

Main issues

The main issues in relation to security are as follows: 1–10

— The **scope of assets** which may be mortgaged, e.g. the availability of floating charges or other general business charges over all assets of a corporate debtor; the availability of non-possessory chattel mortgages, of security over receivables without notification to the debtor, and of security over future or after-acquired property.

— The **perfection** of the security; whether the security must be publicly registered or protected by a public filing and whether the registration must be periodically renewed; whether the creditor must take possession of the asset or (in the case of debts) notify the debtor or (in the case of investment securities) be registered as the holder in the books of the issuer.

— The degree of **formalities** acting as a hindrance to the grant of security, notably whether the security must be notarised or in writing or in other formal form or can be created orally or informally by deposit of title deeds, share certificates or other indicia of ownership or paper representing the asset; whether the contents of the security document are prescribed.

— The scope of the **debt which may be secured**; whether there are any limitations on secured debt, such as exclusions for future debt (affecting current accounts, revolving loans and currency convertibles) or for damages (i.e. only liquidated sums); whether a maximum amount must be specified; whether foreign currency mortgages are possible; whether there are any limitations on interest; and whether junior priority debt secured on the same asset (a second mortgage) is possible.

— Any **limitations on the creditors** entitled to the security, e.g. domiciliaries or nationals only, or non-recognition of trustees holding security for several creditors, or restrictions limiting the grant of security to banks or other financial institutions.

— The scope of the **remedies** of the secured creditor, including any limitation of remedies, such as public auction only (as opposed to a private sale or temporary receivership or possession), compulsory grace periods on enforcement rights, or sale only to nationals or in local currency; and the costs of enforcement.

— Whether there are any **bankruptcy freezes** on enforcement of the security or a moratorium on secured debt; whether the insolvency administrator can use the secured asset or substitute security in the event of insolvency rescue proceedings.

— Whether the insolvency administrator of the debtor in an insolvency rehabilitation can raise **super-priority moratorium loans** to finance the rehabilitation but which prime existing security.

— Whether there are reasonable safe harbours in favour of the creditor against the security being avoided as a **preference** on insolvency and the length of the suspect period.

— Whether the secured creditor can check the debtor's **title** to the asset, e.g. whether the debtor owns the asset and whether there are any encumbrances over the asset.

— The certainty and predictability of the creditor's **priority** over competing interests, especially preferred creditors on bankruptcy, (e.g. taxes, employees, bankruptcy administration costs), attaching creditors, subsequent purchasers, subsequent mortgagees, liens (especially ships and aircraft); whether the creditor can claim subsequent accessories and fixtures; the creditor's position with regard to lessees, charterers and licensees of the asset.

— Whether the creditor may **restrict redemption** of the security, e.g. by a restriction on prepayments, or by prepayment penalties, or by insisting on the consolidation of mortgages (a doctrine which insists that the debtor redeem both mortgages or neither).

— Whether there are any **stamp duties** and other fiscal disincentives to taking security.

- The **recognition** by local insolvency law of foreign security which is invalid under local law but valid under the foreign law applicable to its creation.

- Whether the secured creditor is subject to any **liabilities** in relation to the secured asset, e.g. taxes, obligations on contracts and leases affecting the asset, preservation duties, environmental liabilities, duties to notify the interest to the issuer of shares.

Other points to check in taking security include: 1–11

- Whether the security violates any rules prohibiting a company from giving **financial assistance** in connection with the purchase of its shares, e.g. where an acquired company charges its assets to secure a bank loan made to the acquiror of the shares of the company to finance the acquisition.

- Whether the security conflicts with any **contractual restrictions** binding on the debtor, e.g. a negative pledge, pari passu clause or clause prohibiting disposals in the debtor's bank loan agreements or bond issues; whether there are any contractual restrictions in the asset itself prohibiting security, e.g. prohibitions on assignments in contracts or concessions.

- Whether a contract, lease or licence which is covered by the security can be **cancelled** on a default by the debtor in which event the secured creditor would be left with nothing.

- Whether a corporate debtor has the **power** to grant security and what **authorisations** are necessary.

- Where **insolvency proceedings** have been commenced against the debtor.

CHAPTER 2

UNIVERSAL BUSINESS CHARGES

Summary

2–1   A universal or general business charge is security over all of the present and
future assets of a corporate debtor, including its inventory and receivables.
Broadly, jurisdictions may be divided into six groups, namely those which:

— allow a universal registered floating charge, e.g. England;

— allow a more limited registered floating charge, e.g. Sweden;

— allow an unregistered fiduciary transfer up to 50 per cent as extensive as
the English floating charge, e.g. Germany;

— allow a form of notarial bond, e.g. South Africa;

— allow a registered business charge over specified assets only, e.g. industrial equipment, but not usually all inventory or receivables, e.g. France
and some Latin American countries;

— do not allow any general business charge, e.g. Austria.

2–2   But probably nearly all developed jurisdictions permit the following
security, if fixed:

— mortgages of land and buildings, usually registrable;

— possessory pledges of specific goods (impracticable if the debtor wishes
to use the goods);

— non-possessory mortgages of ships and aircraft;

— possessory pledges of specific negotiable instruments;

— security over specific contracts and receivables, provided that (in the
hostile countries) the debtor on the receivables is notified (which is
impracticable for general charges);

— security over specific investment securities, provided that (in the hostile
countries) the creditor is registered as the holder in the books of the
issuer.

The enhancing effect of the general floating charge or the general enter- 2–3
prise charge therefore is to allow security over:

- inventory, equipment and other goods which are left in the possession of the debtor;

- receivables, without notifying the debtors on the receivables;

- investment securities, without the creditor being registered as the holder;

- future assets;

- any assets without specifying or identifying them individually.

English-based universal floating charge: general

First in terms of coverage is the English-based floating charge. This is a 2–4
universal corporate security which can cover all kinds of property – including goods and receivables, even though non-possessory, i.e. the debtor can
continue to possess the assets. The floating charge can cover assets subject to
special security regimes, e.g. land, ship and aircraft, but priorities are weak
if the registration requirements for those assets are not followed, such as
dual registration in a separate land, ship or aircraft registry.

The arguments usually given to justify the monopolistic English floating
charge are as follows:

- The security is useful to finance new projects. The creditor generally pays for most of project, so it is not unreasonable that he should rank ahead. If he takes all, it is because he paid for all.

- Although most unsecured creditors are primed, in practice trade credi-tors continue to be paid until the position is really hopeless so that earlier trade creditors get out (and are often paid by the secured credi-tor's money).

- Since the bank feels safer, it is inclined to stay with the situation longer: this enhances the private rescue, which is seen as more effective than a judicial rehabilitation.

- The method of enforcement via a possessory receivership enables the business to be managed and kept going pending a sale (and at a time when the directors have had to stop trading because of fraudulent trad-ing rules).

- The comprehensiveness of the security enables the business to be sold as a whole: this ultimately preserves the business to the extent this is poss-ible.

The security is widely available in English-based jurisdictions. The classic description of the floating charge was by the always eloquent Lord Macnaghten in *Illingworth v Houldsworth* [1904] AC 355:

> "a floating charge . . . is ambulatory and shifting in its nature, hovering over and so to speak floating with the property which it is intended to affect until some event occurs or some act is done which causes it to settle and fasten on the subject of the charge within its reach and grasp".

See also *Governments Stock and other Securities Investment Co Ltd v Manila Railway Co* [1897] AC 81, 86, also Lord Macnaghten.

Main characteristics of floating charge

2–5 The main English characteristics of the floating charge are:

- It can cover future property, so there is no need to identify and mortgage each asset when it comes into existence. The grasp of the charge on after-acquired assets is not treated as preferential.

- It floats, so that the debtor can deal with the property in the ordinary course of business until the charge crystallises on a default. The debtor can collect his receivables and use the cash. The debtor can use raw materials to manufacture goods. The debtor can sell goods without any further consent of the creditor and the purchaser takes free of the charge.

- It requires the publicity of registration (because it is non-possessory and monopolistic). This deals with the "false wealth" problem.

- It is enforceable by the appointment of a "receiver" who is a possessory manager who can operate the entire assets subject to the charge. By a pragmatic legal device, the receiver is treated notionally as agent of the debtor company so that the creditor technically is not liable on his contracts although in practice he may be asked or expected to indemnify the receiver. Hence the business can be operated as a whole for the benefit of the creditor and, equally important, can be sold as a whole and hence its value will not be diminished by the piecemeal sale of individual assets or by a time-consuming public auction.

- It becomes a fixed charge on enforcement ("crystallisation").

There is considerable discussion in the cases and the literature as to precisely when a floating charge crystallises and whether it is possible to beat the potential priority of execution creditors and lienholders by an automatic crystallisation clause which automatically converts the charge into a fixed charge prior to an occurrence which might give another creditor priority. These considerations are usually somewhat academic because, apart from usually inconsequential lien creditors, floating charges are usually enforced long before creditors can get their execution orders and they are almost invariably crystallised by the appointment of a receiver.

Weaknesses of floating charges

The legal weaknesses of the floating charge are: 2–6

— It ranks after **preferential creditors,** e.g. value added tax (and other taxes in most non-English jurisdictions) and wages, because otherwise they would never be paid. This rule seems universal and applies in countries as disparate as Jamaica and Israel: Companies Ordinance 1983, s 354(c).

— Because it is monopolistic, it is subject to more stringent **preference** rules. In England, the charge is void if created when the debtor is insolvent during a longer suspect period (e.g. one year) except for cash or other consideration at the time of the creation of the charge. In other words, generally the money must be advanced at or about the time the security is created so that a creditor is vulnerable if he subsequently takes a floating charge for pre-existing debt. By the same reasoning, floating charges to secure guarantees are also vulnerable because a guarantee is not new money. But a floating charge can be "purified" by roll-overs of debt in a bank current account, as where payments in by the debtor reduce the overdraft and payments out restore it to its previous level. These payments out are treated as new money: see para 31–10 *et seq.*

— A garnishee or **execution creditor** who attaches an asset before the floating charge crystallises takes free of the charge (so to that extent the charge is not proprietary): see para 12–25.

— A third party creditor of the debtor who exercises a **set-off** prior to crystallisation against a debt he owes the debtor is entitled to keep his set-off, although in some cases he can exercise the set-off even after crystallisation provided both debts arose before he was aware of the crystallisation and satisfy the other requirements of set-off. This is discussed elsewhere in this series of works.

— The security ranks after **subsequent fixed charges** unless these are prohibited by the floating charge **and** the fixed chargee either has notice of the prohibition for which purpose notice of the mere existence of the floating charge is not notice of the prohibition: see para 12–24.

— **Possessory liens** arising prior to crystallisation rank ahead of the floating charge unless the lienholder had notice of the charge and of a prohibition against the creation of liens: see para 12–25.

— It may not be recognised abroad: para 13–26 *et seq*.

One of the practical effects of a floating charge is that the presence of the security will usually prevent the debtor from accessing other sources of finance and granting security for them. But obviously companies cannot raise money twice on the security of the same assets and it is possible for companies which do wish to raise secured finance from a variety of sources to do so by granting fixed and specific security or by title finance transactions and protecting the creditors in each case by junior subordinated featherweight floating charges. In practice, large companies borrow unsecured and protect the creditors with a negative pledge.

Impact of insolvency administration on floating charges

2–7   In England, changes to insolvency legislation in IA 1986 introduced a corporate rehabilitation procedure known as an administration involving the appointment of an administrator to run the company. Plainly there could not be both an administrator and a receiver in charge at the same time. The English determined to prioritise the floating charge, because otherwise it would have been negated by an administration. A universal floating charge enables the chargee to block the appointment of an administrator provided he appoints a receiver over the charge prior to the administration order which initiates a rehabilitation process. The chargee must be given notice of the petition for an administration but may have a very short time in which to act, e.g. two days. See IA 1986 ss 9 and 10.

Because an administration freezes the enforcement of security and some title finance, English financiers, when taking security over an asset, such as a land mortgage, sometimes resort to the "featherweight" floating charge in conjunction with their other security to enable them to block the administration and hence escape the freeze on the other security imposed by an administration. This charge contains no restriction on the debtor's ability to deal with the assets and will often permit prior charges since its purpose is not security, but the power to block.

A floating charge over *part* of the assets (unaccompanied by fixed charges covering substantially the rest of the assets) is insufficient to block an administrator (since there would be no conflict between two controllers of all the assets). The result is that partial floaters (e.g. over goods, securities or receivables) are weak by reason of the fact that an administrator can use the property as if not subject to the charge, need not make up its market value on sale and can charge his expenses as a priority claim: see IA 1986 ss 15 and 16, but subject to an "unfair prejudice" claim. The administration is peculiar to England, although Australia and Singapore have adopted parallel versions.

Jurisdictions adopting English floating charge

The English-style floating charge is available in most of the British Com- 2–8 monwealth or former British colonies except South Africa and its related jurisdictions (e.g. Botswana and Zimbabwe) and except Arabian Gulf states. Thus it is available in:

— the Dominions: Australia, New Zealand; common law Canada (though in modified form as a result of personal property security statutes based on the American UCC Art 9 in Ontario and provinces to the west of Ontario)

— former African colonies, e.g. Gambia, Kenya, Malawi, Nigeria, Sierra Leone, Zambia

— former Asian dominions, e.g. India, Malaysia, Pakistan

— island states, e.g. Bahamas, Bermuda, Brunei Darassalam, Cayman, Cyprus, Gibraltar, Hong Kong, Jamaica, Singapore

— others, e.g. Republic of Ireland and Israel.

Universal security in the United States

It is possible in the United States (except Louisiana) to create a general 2–9 enterprise security interest, the elements of which must often be perfected by filing under Art 9 of the UCC. The main differences, compared to the English-based floating charge are:

— the security interest is not subordinated to preferential creditors (administrative expenses, wages, taxes);

— the priorities as against competing claimants are different, but one should not make too much of these differences in practice;

— the grasp of the security interest over future property coming into existence in the suspect period for preferences is limited by BC 1978 s 547;

— although a receiver may be appointed as possessory manager, he cannot displace the powers of the directors;

— enforcement is subject to the automatic stay on bankruptcy under Chapter 11 of BC 1978.

Universal floating charges in non-English-based countries

2–10 Second in terms of coverage, ranking after the English-based floating charge, are non-English approximations. At least six non-common law countries have created a general floating charge by statute for commercial businesses or corporates:

> Finland: Enterprise Mortgage Law 24/8–1984
> Norway: 1986
> Scotland: 1961, now the Companies Act 1985
> Sweden
> Russia: Pledge Law of 1992, as amended by the new CC in force 1994

The chief difference compared to the English floating charge is that (apart from Scotland) none of the above is enforceable by possessory management through a receiver, but only by sale. The Scandinavian versions are available to all commercial enterprises, not just companies (as in England), and generally, do not cover assets which are subject to their own separate security regime, e.g. land and ships. The Swedish *foretagshypotek* does not cover cash in hand or at bank, corporate stock, assets not subject to execution and assets located outside Sweden. All of them must be registered publicly to be effective against creditors, except the Russian pledge which must be registered in a file kept by the bank (because of the absence of a public registry).

Argentina allows general floating charges for companies to secure issues of debentures and subject to conditions. This innovation was probably attributable to British investment in the early twentieth century. But foreign floating security to secure debentures on assets located in Argentina is not recognised there unless the debenture contract and the security are registered in Argentina. **Brazil** has something similar. It would seem that **Colombia** also permits a pledge of a commercial establishment, including inventory and receivables, but further investigation is required.

Fiduciary transfers in Germanic countries

2–11 Third in terms of coverage, ranking after the English-based floating charge and the non-common law equivalents, is the Germanic fiduciary transfer. This approaches the floating charge and has been developed by case law, although it does not achieve the all-embracing grasp of the English version. The original legal device employed was to treat the mortgage as a title transfer of the asset, conditioned on a re-transfer on payment of the debt, but this was clearly a convenient fiction and the fiduciary transfer is in commercial substance and legal characterisation a security interest. No physical delivery is required and the debtor remains in possession under the terms of a custody agreement (in Germany under BGB s 390).

The main countries concerned are:

Germany	– the *Sicherungsabtretung* for receivables and the *Sicherungsübereignung* for other assets
Indonesia	– based on pre-1992 Dutch law
Japan	– the *joto-tampo*: not much used
Korea (S)	– the *Yangdo Tambo*
Luxembourg	– *contrat fiduciaire* in favour of credit institutions, brought in by a Grand-Ducal Decree of 1983. The fiduciary transfer might be available outside the statute.
Netherlands	– codified as the *bezitloos pandrecht* in the 1992 Civil Code (notarial deed required)
Switzerland	– not much used.

The fiduciary transfer never caught on in Denmark or Italy, or in most Napoleonic countries, such as France, Belgium, Portugal and Spain. It may however be adopted in other German-influenced countries, such as Poland and the Czech and Slovak Republics.

The main differences when compared to the English floating charge are: **2–12**

– A varying degree of advance identification of assets is required which prevents generic security over "all future property" or "all future receivables". The transfer must be e.g. "all debts payable by [specified] debtors" or "all goods in a [specified] warehouse". The debtor must separate the transferred items from his property, e.g. by separate storing or marking or registration in special books or lists. The charge is therefore less comprehensive and more inconvenient. In England, by contrast, all that is necessary to identify the asset is that it should be possible to tell whether the asset is charged when the asset comes into existence and the charge bites: if all assets of a class are specified, then this test is satisfied.

– There is no remedy of possessory management through a receiver and hence one of the main business rationales of the floating charge is lacking. But a private sale is allowed unless the debtor resists.

– No registration is required, except for assets subject to their own security regimes, e.g. land, ships or aircraft, which must be mortgaged in the appropriate form. In Germany, if the debtor is a corporate enterprise, the debtor must state in the annex to its balance sheet the total amount of assets secured by pledges and other security interests, as well as the type and form of the security interest: HGB s 285. This would include the fiduciary transfer. Plainly there could be a significant gap between the creation of a security interest and its publicity in the accounts.

– The charge does not rank after preferential creditors except in the Netherlands.

2–13   Other points on the German transfer are:

– Future assets will be covered automatically if they are identifiable in accordance with the above principles, e.g. future goods which replace those in the specified warehouse.

– The fiduciary transfer can cover all present and future claims, not just those in existence. This is similar to the English floating charge.

– The rights of the debtor depend upon the agreement. Normally the debtor is permitted to work with and sell the secured assets in the ordinary course of business. This is identical to the English floating charge.

– Fiduciary transfers rank according to the time of creation. Second priority fiduciary transfers are possible: although subordinate creditors cannot obtain property rights, the desired result is achieved by allowing them rights of expectancy so that, if the prior claim is satisfied, the junior creditor automatically acquires full property rights to the assets or (on a realisation by the prior creditor) their proceeds.

– Creditors claiming under retention of title rank ahead of the fiduciary transfer: the debtor cannot transfer title to goods he does not own. The position is the same in respect of the English floating charge.

– The German tax authorities treat the transaction as in substance security, not ownership by the creditor, so that the creditor is not liable for taxes in respect of the assets concerned.

– Once the debt is repaid, the fiduciary transfer does not self-destruct automatically. The creditor must re-transfer title.

– Fiduciary transfers are subject to the normal rules avoiding preferential transfers.

2–14 Over-security   In Germany, the courts have applied the principle of *bonos mores* enshrined in BGB s 38 which is used to nullify security which defeats or endangers other creditors because of the excessive bargaining power of the secured creditor, which is an unfair tying contract and is over-restrictive of the debtor, and which represents "over-security": 150 per cent in the case of receivables.

Generally, German banks release security to the extent not needed by them to avoid the principle of fraudulently excessive security. The whole security is void, not just the excess. In Japan there is no principle of over-security as yet. This may be because the fiduciary transfer is not widely used.

The impact of the lack of publicity is exemplified by the following Dutch cases:

In *Erba v Amsterdamsche Bank NV* (NJ 1957, 514 and 1959, 581), a bank took comprehensive security from a textile company in difficulties so that the debtor no longer had any assets available to its creditors, but kept the appearance of creditworthiness. *Held* by the Hoge Raad: the bank would commit a tort if it knew or could have foreseen that on termination of the credit the *new* unpaid suppliers would be prejudiced *and* the bank had not taken care that those suppliers were paid or got their goods back. The bank would owe a duty to new suppliers who relied on the appearance of credit-worthiness since the bank took the profit from the re-sale of the goods by the debtor and also the value of goods as yet unsold which had not been paid for by the debtor. The security is not nullified but the bank is liable to pay damages to the injured creditor to the extent their loss is increased so that in effect the bank loses the proceeds. But a supplier might be guilty of contributory negligence if he sat back and continued to supply when the debtor had defaulted in payments. Further, the test is economic viability at the time the security is taken. But on the facts, the bank was not liable since it was found that, when the bank took the new security, it could not foresee that the debtor would fail.

In *Osby-Pannan AB v Las Verkoopmaatschappij BV* (NJ 1982, 443), a Swedish parent gave substantial credit to and took extensive security from its wholly-owned Dutch subsidiary. An unpaid supplier claimed damages in tort from the Swedish parents. The Hoge Raad applied the *Erba* test.

Netherlands practice The Dutch non-possessory pledge over moveables 2–15 is a good example of a hesitating step in the direction of the fully fledged non-possessory floating charge over moveables. The *bezitloos pandrecht* established by the new Civil Code in 1992 is similar to the old Dutch fiduciary transfer of title, still available in Indonesia. But now a notarial deed (or a private deed which is registered in a non-public register to record the time of the creation of the pledge) is required. The agreement must reasonably describe the assets but does not have to identify each of them separately. The normal practice for the pledgor is to produce a list of pledged assets at regular intervals or when requested by the pledgee. The pledge can cover future moveable assets and different forms are usually used for fixed moveable assets such as machines and current moveable assets such as stock. The pledgor is usually expressly permitted to work with and sell the pledged assets in the ordinary course of business. The pledge can cover both present and future claims so long as the claims are sufficiently determinable at the time the pledge is created: common practice is for the pledgor to fill in pledge forms and send them to the pledgee from time to time with regard to new debt. Second priority security is available. Security rights rank according to the time of creation. The security is not registered in a public register. On default as prescribed by the pledge agreement, the pledgee may call upon the pledgor to hand over the pledged assets to himself or to a third party, thereby converting the non-possessory pledge into a possessory pledge: *vuistpand*. This is a remarkable equivalent of the English floating charge crystallisation. But if the pledgor refuses, there is no possessory management by a receiver and an application to the court for sale must be made, although interim preservative sequestration orders are available whereby (theoretically) the pledged assets are delivered to a bailiff of the court who keeps the goods in custody until the end of the proceedings. Enforcement is by public auction unless the court authorises a private sale. Possessory liens rank ahead of the pledge and so do tax claims in respect of which the Inland Revenue has rights of attachment over the pledged assets on the tax payer's premises.

In the case of receivables, apart from the cumbersome regular pledge of a receivable which requires a deed and notice to the debtor owing the receivable, there is a silent pledge (*stil pandrecht*). This is also created by deed in form of a notarial act, or private document registered in a non-public register. The security does not have to be notified to the debtor for it to be effective on the pledgor's bankruptcy. However the only receivables which can be pledged are those which arise out of an existing legal relationship between the pledgor and its debtor, such as an existing contract, so that if it is desired to pledge future receivables the pledgor must actually pledge them each time by a fresh deed which is somewhat inconvenient. As under English law, the pledge will not catch receivables which have to be earned by the bankrupt in order to generate them after the onset of insolvency proceedings: para 4–13. The pledge is enforceable without court interference by notifying the debtor and collecting the receivable.

South African notarial bond

2–16   Fourth – after the English-based floating charges, the non-common law equivalents, and the German fiduciary transfer – is the notarial bond developed by South African jurisdictions. This form of general non-possessory security is apparently not favoured because it loses priority to a purchaser without notice – although this has not been a disincentive in other jurisdictions. The jurisdictions include: South Africa; Botswana; Zimbabwe.

In all three countries, the bond must be registered in the Deeds Office.

If specified articles are mortgaged, such as stock in one particular warehouse, the bond is termed a special mortgage. A business may mortgage the whole of its assets, stock-in-trade, book debts, goodwill, etc., in which case the notarial bond is a general mortgage. In Botswana only specific movables can be hypothecated – not movables generally.

Notwithstanding any prohibition in the bond itself, while the debtor is solvent he is able effectively to alienate the mortgaged property, to the prejudice of the mortgagee, to a purchaser who takes free unless he has notice of the notarial bond. This is not greatly different from other jurisdictions embracing the floating charge or fiduciary transfer. But once the debtor is made insolvent, the notarial bondholder obtains preference over unsecured creditors in respect of all moveables covered by a bond which are then still in the debtor's possession. In Natal, 1932 legislation gave notarial bonds of movables the legal effect of a pledge with improved priority and this was extended to the whole of South Africa by the Security by Means of Movable Property Act 57 of 1993.

Countries with restricted business charges

Fifth in line are countries which permit restricted business charges created 2–17 by commercial enterprises, typically over loose machinery and equipment, but sometimes extending to business goodwill and intellectual property, such as patents and trademarks.

Although there is much variation, the chief characteristics of the group are, in general:

– The chattel mortgage must be registered and is ineffective against creditors without registration. Registration may be at a special registry, or at the commercial registry or at the land registry.

– Only the chattels specified in the enabling legislation can be covered. These typically comprise agricultural assets – to be expected in virtually all countries, and not surprisingly in the agricultural South American republics – and also industrial machinery and implements used on the business premises. Identification is crucial and the asset must be particularised in the public register. Often the asset cannot be removed from its specified location, except in the case of vehicles.

– Receivables usually cannot be charged without notice to the debtor on the receivables.

- Because of the insistence on identification (the doctrine of specificity) the spread of the security to floating raw materials and inventory and to future assets (goods or receivables) is uncommon, though not unprecedented, in this group.

- In the main, the formalities for the creation of the security, the scope of the debt which may be covered and the enforcement remedies are anti-creditor. These topics are examined later.

- In many cases, the security is available only in favour of specified creditors, such as local credit institutions, thereby inhibiting not only inter-company security and margin collateral for market dealings but also security in favour of foreign institutions.

- Land mortgages may be expanded to include chattels used closely in connection with land or buildings, without necessarily being permanently fixed to the land, e.g. Denmark.

- Traditional real property mortgages and *possessory* pledges over specified existing goods, debts, contracts, intellectual property and securities continue to be available.

The countries include (with qualifications):

- **Europe**: Belgium, Denmark, France, Italy, Luxembourg and Spain

- **Far East**: the Philippines, Thailand and Taiwan

- **Latin America**: many countries, including Argentina, Brazil and Mexico.

Examples follow.

2–18 **Belgium** Belgium is some way away from the floating charge concept: the *nantissement de fonds de commerce* (1919) is limited in scope. Assets which can be pledged are: goodwill, and the name; trademarks and patents; supply contracts; tangible assets, such as raw materials, industrial and commercial furniture and equipment, and 50 per cent of the value of goods in stock; securities, receivables and cash if so provided (Decision of November 6, 1970, para 1971, 1200); immovables, even if already subject to a prior mortgage (Decision of May 26, 1972, JT 1972, at 625).

The pledgor must not diminish the assets – a somewhat unrealistic requirement so far as the pledgor is concerned. The security was originally designed to help small businesses. But there is no right of receivership, only court-ordered public auction. The *nantissement* must be registered. The security can be granted only in favour of financial institutions.

Amongst the priority claims ranking ahead of this charge, apart from the legal costs for the maintenance of the pledged assets, one may include the privilege of the insurer for payment of insurance premiums during the previous two years relating to the pledged assets (Art 23 of Law of June 11, 1874), the privilege of a lessor for payment of rent if the lease agreement pre-dates the pledge of the business (Cassation, June 11, 1982), and the privilege of the unpaid vendor of professional or industrial equipment, if he deposits the invoice with a registry of commerce within 15 days of delivery of the equipment: Arts 20 and 23 of the Law on Privileges and Mortgages, Art 546 of the Bankruptcy Law, Cassation May 29, 1964, November 10, 1967, September 28, 1972 and May 7, 1987. Where a warrant is granted over the same assets by way of fixed security, then the first in time prevails: Cassation, November 19, 1992.

France In France the Dailly Act of 1981 allows charges over *bordereaux* 2–19 (lists of commercial invoices) to avoid the *huissier* problem under CC Art 2075: see para 4–6. A Law of January 18, 1951, allows charges over machinery and equipment (very limited). The *nantissement de fonds de commerce* allowed under law of March 7, 1909, specifically excludes stocks (inventory) and receivables and accounting books but covers: equipment; the trade name, patents, trademarks, goodwill; lease rights.

The general charge must be filed within 15 days with the Registrar of the Tribunal of Commerce and is null and void if not registered. Registration secures priority over bona fide purchasers. The pledge must be in writing but need not be made by notarial deed. Competing pledges rank in priority according to the order of date of registration. The pledge is valid for a period of 10 years from the date of registration. The pledgee's only right of enforcement is sale pursuant to court order by public auction – no private sale and no rights of foreclosure or possessory management. The pledgor can dispose of individual assets unless the pledgee can prove that the disposal has or will result in a material decrease in the value of the security. The pledge ranks after liens which arise by operation of law, such as tax and social security liens and the unpaid vendor's lien, provided that the latter has been duly registered. Partly because of the limit of the security and partly because of the fate of the security in the event of insolvency proceedings (the *redresssement judiciaire*) the security is very weak and is sometimes taken primarily as a defensive measure.

France also has special provisions for various non-possessory chattel mortgages, e.g. for crude oil and industrial manufactured goods (which are not very useful) and a purchase money chattel mortgage: para 3–7.

Italy In 1994, Art 46 of a Banking Law introduced a limited enterprise 2–20 charge. The Article provides that medium term and long term loans by banks to enterprises may be secured by the *privilegio speciale* on movable goods not registered in public registers. The *privilegio* may relate to:

(a)   existing and future equipment, concessions and produced goods of the enterprise;

(b)   raw materials, semi-manufactured goods, stock, finished goods, fruit, livestock and goods;

(c)   goods purchased with the loan;

(d)   credits (including future credits) from the sale of goods mentioned in (c).

The *privilegio*, on pain of nullity, must be in a written deed. The deed must exactly describe the goods and the credits over which the *privilegio* has been established, the creditor bank, the debtor and the chargor, the loan amount, the loan terms and the amount of the loan which is secured by the *privilegio*. Note the adherence to the doctrine of specificity – generic descriptions of the goods by class are evidently insufficient.

The enforceabilty of the *privilegio* against third parties is subject to the registration of the deed in the register referred to in CC Art 1524, second paragraph.

The *privilegio* must be published by notice in the *Foglio Annunzi Legali*. The notice must disclose the relevant particulars of the registration. The registration and its publication must be made in the offices that have authority in the place where the head office of the financed enterprise is located.

The *privilegio* regulated by this Article has the priority stated in CC Art 2777, last paragraph. It does not override the priority of other interests whose certain date is before the registration date.

Having regard to CC Art 1153, the *privilegio* may be enforced against third parties that have rights concerning the same goods acquired after the registration referred to above.

If enforcement against the purchaser of the goods is not possible the *privilegio* will take effect on their price. [Original translation kindly provided by Mr Fabio Recine.]

2–21   **Luxembourg** A Grand-Ducal Decree of 1937 established the pledge of a whole business – the *gage sur fonds de commerce*.

This pledge comprises in particular: the business name and goodwill; office equipment and other fittings, cars and trucks; patents, trade marks, copyrights and similar rights; leasehold and similar rights; goods in stock, but only up to 50 per cent of their value.

The pledge cannot cover receivables (but, unlike Belgium, these can probably be covered by a fiduciary transfer).

The pledge is created by a public deed or a deed under private seal, and must be registered within 15 days with the registrar of mortgages in whose district the business is located. Registration lapses after 10 years unless renewed. It can be granted only to authorised banks, credit institutions, notaries and brewers (a strange, but no doubt justifiable, list) who must have a special licence which specifies the conditions of the pledge.

Priority between pledges is determined by the date of registration. The pledge can secure future debts. Enforcement is by court-ordered auction and cannot be effected by private sale.

Spain In Spain an Act on Chattel Mortgages and Pledges without Delivery 2–22 of Possession of 1954 and a Regulation of 1955 established non-possessory chattel mortgages and pledges which must be registered.

The **mortgage** can cover the following assets: commercial establishments, the place where the business is carried on, including all movable property located in the premises and necessary to carry on the business, e.g. machines, furniture, tools and other instruments for production and work, provided they are fully paid for (unless the security is for the purchase price) and are in permanent use for the purposes of the business, plus business names, logo and intellectual property rights, plus commodities and raw materials intended for use in the business (the debtor must maintain these in the amount referred to in the mortgage and only replace them as they are used); certain vehicles, including train carriages; aircraft; industrial machinery which must be kept at the place in which it was mortgaged; intellectual and industrial property rights.

The mortgage covers rights against third parties arising after creation of the mortgage and arising in connection with the mortgaged property, e.g. (apparently) rentals, royalties and the like.

The **pledge** may only be created over those assets specifically listed in the law, namely: fruit, crops, animals and agricultural machinery; certain machinery and fittings; stocks; artistic and historic collections.

The mortgage must be formalised in a public deed to be valid and the pledge must similarly be by public deed or in some cases may be by a document authenticated by a stockbroker. It must be registered to be valid. Registration of a mortgage expires after six years. The mortgage must be payable in Spanish currency. Second priority chattel mortgages are not available. In certain cases the mortgage is limited to two instalments of interest plus accrued current interest.

Priority ranks from the date of registration. But both the mortgage and the pledge rank after labour costs under the Workers Statute so that there could be a significant erosion of the value of the security. As well as labour costs, the *pledge* also ranks after (a) debts for seeds, cultivation and harvesting and (b) rent for the last 12 months under the lease of the land and premises where the pledged property is located.

Enforcement is by court order and public auction, i.e. no private sale. But extra-judicial notarial proceedings instead of a court order are available if so provided in the mortgage.

Countries with no general business charge

2–23 Sixth in rank are those countries which have no general business charge of any kind. These include, in Europe, Austria and Portugal and, elsewhere, scattered countries still adhering to the traditional Napoleonic view (e.g. Egypt, Haiti, Lebanon and Syria) and a few largely agricultural Latin American countries, such as Paraguay. As to undeveloped security laws in legally emerging states and Islamic jurisdictions, see para 1–8 *et seq*.

CHAPTER 3

LAND AND CHATTEL MORTGAGES

Mortgages of land

It is presumably true that land and buildings may be mortgaged in all devel-   3–1
oped jurisdictions recognising private ownership of property and it is not
proposed to deal with the topic any further, other than a few remarks.

Almost invariably the mortgage must be registered at a land registry.
Dual registration may be required, as in English-based systems where corporate charges over land must also be registered at the companies registry.

The land mortgage will generally cover buildings and also assets firmly
fixed to the land, such as machinery concreted in. It is interesting to note
that some countries, which otherwise object to non-possessory chattel mortgages, extend land security to movable business assets used in connection
with the land, such as machinery and tools, as in, for example, Denmark
and Mexico. In Switzerland movable property which constitutes accessories
to real estate can be normally mortgaged with the real estate, provided the
chattels are "locally and by their normal destination" related to the real
estate: CC Art 805. Thus the furnishings of a hotel qualify as accessories:
BGE 104 III 31.

The old form of antichrèse in the civil countries conferring security over
the income from land is now obsolete. This gives the creditor the right to
receive the income from real estate, but the creditor cannot force a sale of
the real estate to pay his debt and suffers the disadvantage that he is responsible for the maintenance of the real estate and the payment of any related
charges unless (it may be) otherwise agreed. It is little used in the countries
which contemplate it, e.g. countries in the Franco-Latin group such as
Argentina, Belgium and France.

Possessory pledges of chattels

The possessory pledge, derived from the Roman *pignus*, whereby the credi-   3–2
tor has possession of the goods is probably available in all developed com-

---

mercial jurisdictions: there is no concealment of the mortgage and hence a registration requirement is unusual.

Outside trade finance, the possessory pledge is of little value in practice because businesses normally need to be able to use the assets and hence to have possession. The goods pledge is mainly used to secure short-term trade finance, e.g. goods (commodities, metals) located in an independent warehouse; and, more importantly, letter of credit export/import finance where the financing bank takes control of the bill of lading or other documents of title representing the goods.

The creditor may have constructive possession which removes from the debtor the actual opportunity to dispose of the goods, e.g. key of the cage (silo, warehouse); cage controlled by creditor's keeper; attornment to the creditor by independent warehousekeeper who holds the goods; or delivery to the creditor of the documents of title (bills of lading, negotiable warehousekeeper warrants). Because the debtor has neither possession nor the right to possession, there is no false wealth objection. For an English review, see *Dublin City Distillery Ltd & Docherty* [1914] AC 823, HL.

In English-based jurisdictions the pledge is preserved if the creditor delivers the goods to the debtor under a trust receipt to allow a sale so that the debtor can sell the goods and use the proceeds to repay the finance: *Re David Allester Ltd* [1922] 2 Ch 211, *Official Assignee of Madras v Mercantile Bank of India Ltd* [1935] AC 53, PC. Of course the pledgee has poor priority if the pledgor fails to account for proceeds . The loss of possession is usually fatal in mainly Franco-Latin jurisdictions, e.g. Belgium.

Non-possessory chattel mortgages

Generally

3–3   The availability of non-possessory chattel mortgages shows great division between jurisdictions – because of the concealment from creditors or false wealth (met in many permitting jurisdictions by public registration requirements).

Apart from consumer security, the main corporate uses are security over:

— large equipment, e.g. industrial machinery;

— ships and aircraft (registered mortgages are allowed probably by most maritime and aviation nations) and other transport conveyances;

— inventory and raw materials – the security must float if it is to be of any use;

— agricultural mortgages over farm machinery, crops, etc. These are allowed in most countries, but are not of much interest internationally. Often (especially in Latin America) they are limited to short-term finance, e.g. 180 days.

Classification of jurisdictions

Apart from the various forms of general business charge discussed above,   3–4
the jurisdictions in descending order of sympathy to non-possessory chattel
mortgages are:

1. Common law jurisdictions (more than 70 English-based states and most US states). These have liberal attitudes to corporate chattel mortgages, usually registrable. But in many English-based jurisdictions (not the US) chattel mortgages are impracticable for individuals because of restrictive bills of sale legislation (substantially liberalised in some Australian and Canadian territories to enhance consumer security) which does not apply to companies. The consumer void is filled by hire purchase.

2. Germanic "fiduciary transfer" countries: Germany, the Netherlands, Indonesia, Japan, S Korea, Switzerland: para 2–11 *et seq.*

3. Countries allowing non-possessory chattel mortgages, invariably registrable, over the list of chattels specified in the statute, notably identified industrial machinery, plant and equipment, which must often be kept at a named location. These countries include Denmark, the Philippines, Taiwan and Thailand and a number of Latin American countries, e.g. Argentina, Brazil, Chile, Colombia, Costa Rica, Ecuador (perhaps), Guatemala, Honduras, Mexico, Panama, Peru and Uruguay. In the Latin American group, often the mortgage is subject to formalities (public deed) and prescribed contents.

4. Countries with virtually no non-possessory chattel mortgages (except sometimes agricultural assets, ships and aircraft) for example:

    Europe Austria, France (apart from the *nantissement* and other isolated mortgages, France allows only a purchase money chattel mortgage), Hungary (perhaps), Portugal, Scotland (except for the English-based floating charge)

    Latin America Dominican Republic, El Salvador, Nicaragua

    Elsewhere Egypt, Lebanon, Syria, and no doubt many other French-influenced countries

Objecting countries may partially fill the gap by vendor/lessor title "security", such as finance leases, hire purchase and retention of title, though often with hesitation.

Country survey

3–5   A few illustrations may be given.

Argentina Apart from the agrarian pledge, other farming security, vehicle mortgages and floating charges securing issues of debentures, registered pledges (Decree-Law 15348 of May 28, 1946, as amended and decree 8572 of July 28, 1960) may cover any chattels but only in favour of: (a) the State, (b) associations of industrialists, (c) merchants and industrialists to secure the price of merchandise sold, and (d) registered loan establishments. The registered pledge may be a specific pledge covering specific articles of any nature, or a floating pledge, covering merchandise and raw material in general to secure obligations of not more than 180 days. The floating pledge covers the original articles and also those manufactured from them. The floating pledge contract may be assigned by endorsement, which must be recorded if it is to be valid against third parties.

3–6   **Brazil** Under Decree Law 413 of January 9, 1969, the debtor may issue documents of credit, recordable in the real property registry, known as "industrial credit cedulas" giving a pledge, chattel mortgage (*alienacao fiduciária*) or mortgage of industrial buildings and constructions, raw materials, machinery, products, vehicles and other items used in industrial enterprises to secure industrial credits.

Non-possessory chattel mortgages are regulated by Law 4728 of July 14, 1972 (Art 66). The mortgage must be evidenced by a written document which must be registered in a special registry.

Corporations can issue debentures with a general floating lien on their assets. There are special provisions for agricultural security.

Denmark Non-possessory chattel mortgages over identified chattels, registrable at the local court of the domicile of the debtor, are permitted: Registration Act. There may be appreciable stamp duties. The assets must be individualised or specifically listed and the security cannot generally cover a class of assets such as "inventory".

3–7   **France** There is a registrable non-possessory pledge of machinery and equipment (Law of 1951 as amended) but only in favour of the person who lends the money to buy the equipment.

Italy has limited non-possessory chattel mortgages. But a registered non-possessory lien can be created over machinery in favour of the seller or the bank which financed the purchaser: CC Art 2762. The security is limited to three years. Unhappily, the security becomes invalid if the machinery is moved to a location outside the territorial jurisdiction of the court in which the lien is recorded – this jurisdiction is a province of Italy or part of a province. If the machinery is returned, e.g. after repairs, the lien is automatically reinstated. However Italy introduced a restricted enterprise charge in 1994: see para 2–20.

The Philippines Non-possessory chattel mortgages must be recorded in the Chattel Mortgage Register in the Office of Register of Deeds of province in which the mortgagor resides at the time of making the mortgage or, if residing outside the Philippines, in the province in which the property is situated. If the property is situated in a province other than that in which the mortgagor resides, the mortgage must be recorded in both provinces.

Taiwan A non-possessory mortgage can be created over the chattels speci- 3–8
fied in Art 4 of the Chattel Secured Transactions Act, e.g. machinery, equipment, tools, raw materials, semi-finished products, finished products and vehicles.

Thailand There is no general non-possessory chattel mortgage. But specific movables may be subject to non-possessory chattel mortgages under special legislation, e.g. the Machinery Registration Act (BE 2514 (1971)) which allows mortgages of specified types of industrial machinery defined in the Act and regulations. In relation to machinery, there are various rules limiting the ability of the mortgagor to move the machines. Where removal is allowed, then re-registration must be effected in the new province.

Venezuela Non-possessory mortgages may be placed on: (1) business enterprises or stock in trade; (2) motorcycles, automobiles, passenger vehicles, freight vehicles, locomotives, railroad cars and other equipment; (3) aircraft; (4) industrial machinery; (5) intellectual property rights (copyrights, literary property, patents and industrial property); and (6) vessels: Law of Chattel Mortgages and Pledges without Delivery of December 20, 1972, Law of August 24, 1983.

CHAPTER 4

SECURITY OVER CONTRACT DEBTS

Introduction

4–1 The type of intangible movables eligible as collateral are legion and include:

- Ordinary contract debts, such as commercial receivables for the supply of goods or services, bank deposits, mortgage loans, unsecured loans and other financial credits, guarantees, and hire moneys payable under charterparties and equipment rental agreements: see below

- Negotiable instruments, such as bills of exchange, promissory notes, and negotiable bearer bonds: para 4–7

- Investment securities, such as registered debt securities, debentures and corporate stocks and shares (sometimes not evidenced by documents – "dematerialised"): para 6–1 *et seq*

- Insurance policies: para 22–1

- Intellectual property rights: para 7–1 *et seq.*

Categories of contract debt

4–2 This class of intangible movables includes:

- Commercial receivables for the supply of goods and services

- Financial credits, such as bank deposits, loans and guarantees, sometimes secured

- Hire moneys payable under charterparties and equipment hire agreements.

The security is used primarily over: specific large contracts, e.g. supply contracts, to finance the contract or as part of project finance (usually notified to the debtor); portfolios of contracts, e.g. equipment leases or home mortgage loans, as in securitisations; and revolving commercial receivables.

Objections to security over contract debts

Unquestionably amongst all the intangible movables, the deepest dividing   4–3
gorge between jurisdictions is exhibited by the different attitudes to the
efficacy of security over contract debts on insolvency.

Objections in hostile states appear to stem from four main sources:

1. The traditional hostility to the concealment of the security and the
   appearance of wealth.

2. The desire to protect the debtor from a change of creditor – who might
   be hostile.

3. Possibly, the fear that trading in claims might lead to the financing of
   litigation by those not interested in the dispute and hence a multiplicity
   of litigation clogging the courts and pursued only for the personal gain
   of the financier, as opposed to the personal distress of the original
   creditor. This objection was expressed in the old English torts of cham-
   perty and maintenance.

4. The historic fear that a man may be oppressed into assigning his
   income, his means of survival, maintenance for himself and his family.
   This family-orientated anxiety can be, and often is, met in civil code
   countries by prohibiting the assignment of wages.

Classification of jurisdictions

Two main groups may be discerned. The first group does not require a   4–4
"possessory" pledge, but the second group does.

Countries not requiring a "pledge" This group facilitates credit on the
security of contract debts. A charge or assignment of a contract debt is effective against the assignor's creditors as soon as the security is created, even if
notice of the assignment has not been given to the debtor. Notice is desirable
to inform the debtor that he is to pay the assignee (although often the
assignee financier may be content for the debtors to pay the assignor who
then accounts to the assignee), to determine priorities between successive
competing assignees, and to prevent the debtor from varying the contract or
acquiring new defences, such as set-offs, against the assignee. But if the
assignor becomes bankrupt, the security assignment is effective. It is not
necessary for the chargee to take possession of any document evidencing the
debt, and the chargor can be permitted to continue to collect the proceeds.

This group includes the following countries:

England and most, if not all, the English-based jurisdictions, including India and Israel (Assignment of Obligations Law) except (often) in the case of individuals by reason of the "reputed ownership" clause in the Bankruptcy Act (abolished in England in 1986).

Austria
Belgium (since 1994)
Czech and Slovak Republics (it seems)
Germany: BGB s 398 *et seq*
Liechtenstein
Netherlands
South Africa
Switzerland: see CO Art 167
United States (except Louisiana)

Note that Japan unexpectedly does not fall into this group.

The common law group requires public registration or filing to perfect some corporate security assignments as against creditors: para 9–34 *et seq*. The Germanic group does not in the case of a fiduciary assignment. In the English-based group, the ability of the chargor to use the proceeds freely and to deal with the receivables in the ordinary course of business may convert the security into a floating charge with a less satisfactory priority and other disadvantages. In English-based countries, a general assignment of all present and future trade receivables by an individual (not companies) is usually void: this debtor-protection rule was introduced by BA 1913 and continued ever since. It never applied to companies and so is unimportant.

4–5 **Countries requiring a "pledge"** In many states in the Franco-Latin group and some others, security over receivables must, if it is to be valid on the pledgor's bankruptcy or against his attaching creditors, be notified to the debtor in prescribed form (in France, Belgium and Luxembourg by a *huissier* or bailiff) or accepted by him in a formal way (in France by an *acte authentique*). If notice is given late in the suspect period, the security may be voidable as a preference.

Usually the creditor must also take possession of any documents evidencing the debt, and must prohibit the debtor from receiving the proceeds (because this gives him possession, thereby destroying the possessory pledge).

The formal notification process is impracticable in the case of bulk charges and is generally inconvenient. It means that the assignment must identify each receivable, instead of a generic description. It also usually rules out assignments of future debts in advance and general charges over the revolving commercial receivables of a company. The doctrine of specificity, coupled with the "notice to debtor" rule, prevents these. For commercial reasons, a business may not wish to have it known that it has assigned its receivables – the debtor may be confused as to whom he is to pay and the assignment may damage the business relationship.

These rules result from the imposition on security over intangible moveables of the concept of the possessory pledge of goods, i.e. the pledgee must have total possession to constitute valid security against creditors. This possession is abstract and notional. The need for possession is based on the objection to false wealth deceiving creditors. For example, in *Benedict v Ratner*, 268 US 353 (1925) the US Supreme Court held that it was a fraud on creditors to permit the assignee to continue to receive the proceeds of an assigned debt: this proposition has since been abolished by the UCC. The weakness of solving the false wealth problem by "possession" is that creditors cannot easily ascertain whether notice has been given to debtors or that the pledgee has got the documents: public registration is needed to meet this priority, if indeed it is really worth the trouble.

The pledge rule (subject sometimes to exceptions) applies in the following 4–6 countries, amongst others.

Chile Notice must be given to the debtor by an officer of the court or a notary public. The debtor must notify personal defences against the assignor within three days, but retains defences arising from the title assigned.

France, Luxembourg The assignment must be notified by a sheriff (*huissier*) or accepted by the obligor in an authentic deed: CC Art 1690. The rule applies in many other jurisdictions using the French code, e.g. the **Dominican Republic, Egypt, Haiti, Lebanon, Morocco and Syria**.

However, in France, the Dailly Act of 1981 (Law of January 2, 1981, as amended in 1984) seeks to simplify the pledging of receivables in order to facilitate the factoring of receivables and pledges of receivables to raise finance: they can be pledged by single delivery of a list specifying the receivables (*bordereau*) in favour of a credit institution (which can include foreign banks). The procedure is formalistic, e.g. the instrument must bear a specified title and refer to the 1981 Act and must clearly identify the receivables. Notice to the debtors is not necessary for the efficacy of the assignment on the pledgor's insolvency. If a creditor sells an asset to the assignor subject to a reservation of title clause, then that creditor has priority over the assignee of the receivable under the Dailly Act on a resale by the assignor. Future claims not arising out of existing contracts can be covered, but there must be a degree of certainty that they will arise: hence the ability to pledge future receivables is weak. There is also a restricted exception in favour of securitisations.

Belgium a business debt represented by an invoice can be pledged by endorsing the invoice. This was to facilitate commercial financings. The debtor must be notified of the pledge by registered letter. In addition the pledge can only be made to approved credit institutions. But Belgium abolished *huissier* notification in 1994.

Italy   CC Art 2800. It is doubtful that an outright fiduciary assignment under CC Arts 1260–1267, subject to a proviso for reassignment on payment of the secured debt, avoids the notification requirement.

Japan CC Art 467. The notice to or consent by the obligor must be certified by a notary or a certified post-marked certificate (*Kakutei hizuke*) to fix the date. Similarly in **S Korea** (CC 450 II).

The rule applies in **Portugal** and **Thailand** and seems to apply in a number of Latin American jurisdictions, such as **Colombia, Costa Rica, Ecuador, El Salvador, Honduras, Nicaragua, Uruguay** and **Venezuela**, but **Guatemala** permits certain non-notified assignments of commercial credits if the assignment is registered at the Commercial Registry. The position in **Spain** and certain Spanish-influenced jurisdictions, like **Argentina** and the **Philippines**, appears unclear. The position in **Denmark, Greece** and **Norway** is worth checking.

Negotiable instruments

4–7   Exceptionally, in those countries which require notice to the debtor to validate an assignment as against the assignor's creditors, the security is usually possible without that notice if the debt is represented by a negotiable instrument or (sometimes) by other acceptable packaging (insurance policies, debt invoices, debt securities) which is deposited and therefore pledged with the creditor. Because the debt is wrapped up in an instrument, the dispossession of the original creditor who deposits the instrument with the financing creditor overcomes the objection based on the appearance of false wealth. The policy of the protection of the debtor was overtaken by a stronger policy of the need to finance mercantile transactions, notably by negotiable instruments.

Nevertheless, generally in the "pledge" countries, the hostility to the assignment of receivables is so strong and the intent to prevent evasion by the use of negotiable instruments so powerful that the conferment of the privilege of negotiability is significantly restricted when compared to countries which do not have the "pledge" rule, e.g. nominative negotiable notes cannot bear interest except as a lump sum. This can be seen by a comparison of the Geneva Conventions on negotiable instruments, inspired by civil code countries, with English-based bills of exchange legislation.

In "non-pledge" countries it is often the case that a non-possessory charge over a negotiable instrument must be protected by public registration, as under the US UCC.

Income-producing property

An outstanding question in those countries which require a possessory   **4–8** pledge of a receivable if the assignment is to be valid on the mortgagor's bankruptcy is whether this rule also applies to the income accruing on income-producing property which is mortgaged, such as rentals from a lessee of mortgaged land, charterhire, freight or passenger moneys from a hirer of mortgaged equipment, dividends or interest due from the issuer of mortgaged securities, royalties from a licensee of charged intellectual property rights, and so on. The value of the asset will normally be greatly reduced if the security does not also carry the income, and the formality of notification may increase the expense and documentation required for effective security.

Either the income is treated as an accessory to the mortgaged asset and therefore covered by the security without further formality, or the income must be separately and specifically assigned and the formal notice given to the debtor liable on the contract.

By way of example, countries in the "notice to debtor" group arrive at different solutions as to whether freight earned by a ship is deemed part of the mortgaged vessel or whether it must be separately assigned to the mortgagee. The solutions show a bewildering variety.

In **England** freight in the course of being earned belongs to the mortgagee as from the time he enforces his mortgage by taking possession: *Keith v Burrows* (1877) 2 AC 636. It does not need to be separately assigned, although it commonly is.

Turkey applies a similar rule: freight belongs to the mortgagee as from the date of filing of a forced sale demand.

In **Belgium** freight is treated as an accessory to the mortgage and in **Spain** the freight of the last voyage is an accessory.

But in **Greece** and **Italy** freight is not an accessory and must be separately assigned and the appropriate assignment formalities observed. In **France**, assignments of freight for more than one year must be registered to be valid against third parties. Assignments of charterhire must be notified in the prescribed manner to the charterer if the assignment is to be effective on the insolvency of the shipowner-assignor.

Prohibitions on assignment

4–9   The financing of contracts and receivables is inhibited if the debtor and creditor on the receivable have agreed that the creditor may not assign the benefit of the receivable and this is effective against an assignee of the receivable. If a company wishes to assign a large number of its commercial receivables, it is impracticable for the chargee to examine the terms of each contract debt individually; but if he does not do so, he runs the risk that he has security over nothing.

It seems to be generally true in the Germanic group, the common law group and the Franco-Latin group that assignments contrary to a contractual prohibition on assignments are ineffective. This reflects either a desire to protect the debtor, or a policy in favour of freedom of contract.

The English solution is to construe the prohibition on assignments as narrowly as possible. Although a clear prohibition on an assignment will nullify an assignment contrary to the contractual term (*Linden Gardens Trust Ltd v Lenesta Sludge Ltd* [1993] 3 All ER 417, HL), case law indicates that a prohibition on an assignment will not restrain a trust of proceeds and (in the context of leases) a prohibition on assignment will not prevent an assignment of part, nor will it prevent a mortgage as opposed to an absolute sale. The policy of the law is to encourage the free marketability of assets (and hence their availability for security) as opposed to the freeze effect of restrictions. A prohibition may not stop a floating charge over the debt, but might catch the crystallisation of the charge: this would be a matter of construction.

The United States is the only country which has been found which overrides certain contractual prohibitions on assignments. Article 9 of the Uniform Commercial Code – an Article which does not apply in Louisiana – renders any prohibition of assignments (or on assignments without the consent of the debtor) ineffective with respect to an account or general intangible: s 9–318(4). For the technical meaning of these terms, see para 9–16 *et seq.* The objective is to facilitate receivable financings.

An assignment of the benefit of a contract is to be distinguished from an assignment of the obligations: the latter is a novation and presumably the law everywhere requires the consent of the beneficiary of the obligation since the identity of the obligor is of the essence of the value of the obligation.

Cancellation clauses in contracts

4–10   If a creditor has security over a contract and the counterparty can cancel the contract on the default or bankruptcy of the debtor, the creditor will have security over nothing at the very time he needs the security. This affects executory contracts, e.g. supply or transportation contracts in relation to project finance, and ship charters. The protections available to the creditor are:

— The creditor can negotiate a direct agreement with the counterparty entitling the creditor to keep the contract on foot provided he performs in place of the debtor. This is only realistic for large contracts justifying negotiated agreements, not small commercial receivables.

— In a few states, notably Canada, France and the United States, bankruptcy law provisions nullify certain cancellation clauses operating on insolvency. These rules are generally too unpredictable to protect an assignee since they depend on the willingness of the insolvency administrator to perform. They are examined in another work in this series on financial law.

— A universal bankruptcy rule prohibits the removal of vested assets from the bankrupt estate, e.g. accrued debts. This does not help for executory contracts.

Secured and guaranteed debts: sub-mortgages

Where a contract debt over which security is granted is itself secured, then it **4–11** is necessary to transfer the security or the guarantee for the debt. In England an assignment of a debt implies the assignment of any security for the debt even though not expressly mentioned: see *Patrick Bills v Tatham* (1891) 1 Ch 82, CA. If a mortgage debt is transferred without mentioning the mortgage, then the transferor holds the mortgage as trustee for the transferee who must enforce in accordance with the directions of the transferee who is the sole beneficial owner: see *Morley v Morley* (1858) 25 Beav 253.

It seems to be universally the case that the assignment of a debt secured by some security also transfers the security by way of accessory as a necessary implication. However in countries which do not recognise the trust (see para 8–21), the assignment of a debt which is secured by a registered mortgage must also be registered in the mortgage registry if it is to be effective on the bankruptcy of the assignor. For example, it seems that this rule prevails in the following countries in the case of ships and this may be indicative of the usual position in relation to registered security over other assets:

Belgium
Greece (notarial deed)
Italy
Japan (plus notice to the debtor)
Panama (notarial deed)
Spain (notarial deed and notice to the debtor)

It appears that registration of an assignment of a mortgage in the mortgage register is not necessary in order to validate the assignment of a ship mortgage on the assignor's bankruptcy in Denmark, Finland, Norway or Sweden.

Under the US Uniform Commercial Code, if a secured party assigns a perfected security interest, no filing under Art 9 is required in order to continue the perfected status of the security interest against creditors of, and transferees from, the original debtor: s 9–302 (2). However the new security interest will require perfection by the appropriate method. Prudent practice in all cases is to assign the benefits of any security and guarantees specifically by way of security. In England there are various provisions as to the transfer of secured mortgages, the observance of which is desirable, but not necessary, for the efficacy of the assignment on the bankruptcy of the assignor: see, e.g. the Law of Property Act 1925 s 114 providing for transfers of land mortgages.

Formalities

4–12 For the question of whether security assignments need to be in ceremonial form, e.g. by way of deed or notarised, see para 8–1 *et seq*. In England the security assignment of an unsecured debt can be made orally but naturally it is desirable to reflect the terms of a security agreement in writing. Under the US Uniform Commercial Code, security interests within Art 9 must usually be in writing.

Security over future debts

4–13 The question here is whether it is possible to create security over future debts, merely by identifying them, e.g. debts which may become owing in the future by a particular debtor to the assignor, or debts of a particular type such as future home mortgage loans.

In countries within the Germanic and Franco-Latin groups, i.e. nearly all countries except those in the English-based common law group, the doctrine of specificity applies in varying degrees and may prevent the assignment of a future debt. The doctrine of specificity holds that, in order to transfer any property, it is necessary specifically to identify the property: the degree of specificity varies a great deal, ranging from detailed particularisation of the debtor and the debt to information sufficient to identify the debt. Because the debt has to be specified in this way and usually the obligor indicated, the classical view leads to the conclusion that it is not possible to create security over future debts.

This doctrine of specificity in this context appears to have three roots. The first is a general vague instinct that one cannot transfer an asset unless one identifies the asset. The second is that, if one created security over a future asset now to cover an existing debt, then this in effect would be creating security for pre-existing debt when the asset came into existence: this is treated as potentially a voidable preference. Finally, there may be a prejudice against debtors granting security over all of their future receivables and thereby either destroying their means of livelihood or diluting the cushion available to unsecured creditors.

One cannot explore the twists and turns of the application of this doctrine, except to record that it appears to be on the retreat, e.g. in countries like Luxembourg and Belgium.

The **English** dropped the doctrine, so far as it prevented security over   4–14
future property, in two fundamental House of Lords cases.

> In *Holroyd v Marshall* (1861) 10 HL 191, the owner of a mill gave a mortgage of machinery and agreed that subsequent machinery to be later installed would also be security for the loan. Later the debtor did install further machinery. *Held*: The new machinery became subject to the security as soon as acquired without any new act, even though it covered a pre-existing debt, and the asset was adequately identified. It was clear that the subsequently acquired machinery was covered by the original agreement.
>
> In *Tailby v Official Receiver* (1881) 13 AC 523, the debtor assigned all future book debts by way of security. *Held*: the security caught the future debts as soon as they came into existence without any further new act. This case is one of the foundations of the floating charge over book debts.

It is obvious that the need for identification cannot be at the root of the objection to security over future assets since the above two English cases show that it is perfectly possible to identify future assets generically. It would seem that the hostility to security over future assets probably stems in great part from the desire to restrict security and also the desire to prevent future property being caught up as security for pre-existing debt.

In the **United States** Art 9 of the UCC allows security over personal property to cover after-acquired collateral (s 9–204 (1)), but it limits the attachment of a security interest in the case of consumer goods. The policy of the latter consumerist provision was to protect a necessitous consumer from encumbering all his present and future assets. The same policy is expressed in the provision in English-based Bankruptcy Acts applying only to individuals (not companies) preventing an individual from giving a general assignment of all his future trade receivables. The section was first introduced by the English Bankruptcy Act 1913 s 14 as a direct response to the *Tailby* case, and it thereafter found its way into many British Commonwealth countries.

4–15   In **England,** a security assignment will even catch debts coming into existence after the bankruptcy: see *Re Lind* [1915] 2 Ch 345; *Re Irving, ex p*
Brett (1877) 7 Ch D 419. The contrary case of *Collyer v Isaacs* [1881] Ch D
347, CA, is considered to be wrong.

However there is an important and necessary English exception: the
security does not grasp on to the future receivable if the bankrupt estate
must earn the receivable to bring it into existence, e.g. by carrying out building works to earn the price. This is because assets of the bankrupt would be
unfairly depleted if the post-bankrupt estate, at the cost of the general body
of creditors, carried out work in order to earn the debt and that resulted
merely in the debt being swept into the security net of the secured creditor.

> In *Wilmot v Alton* [1897] 1 QB 17, CA, a theatrical costumier contracted to
> supply dresses to a company for a ballet and to keep them in repair for twelve
> weeks. She subsequently charged the benefit of this contract to Wilmot as
> security for an advance. The dresses were duly supplied to the company under
> the contract but before any moneys became payable under it the costumier
> became bankrupt. *Held:* since the moneys were due only at the end of the
> twelve weeks and since repairs still had to be carried out, the debt belonged to
> the bankrupt estate. See also *Drew & Co, v Josolyne* (1887) 18 QBD 590.

> Contrast *Re Davis & Co, ex p Rawlings* (1889) 22 QBD 193, CA; money due
> under a hire agreement was payable in instalments over a period of time. The
> owner assigned the instalments as security for an advance. Notice of the assign-
> ment was given to the debtor. The assignor later became bankrupt. *Held:* the
> assignee of the instalments was entitled in priority to the trustee in bankruptcy.

For the US position, see para 11–15.

4–16   In **Germany,** and perhaps other Germanic states such as the Netherlands,
some degree of identification is often required, e.g. the security can cover
debts due from a particular debtor but cannot cover all future receivables
owing to a company.

In the Franco-Latin group, the attitude to security over future assets
ranges from non-acceptance to a grudging acceptance. In both **Belgium** and
Luxembourg there is a controversial tendency to permit charges over future
property but subject to restrictive identification rules. A Luxembourg Law
of June 1, 1929 on the pledging of securities gives express authority to
secure future obligations of the debtor and to pledge future security. In **Italy**
a future receivable may be pledged provided it is identifiable and, if notified
to the potential third party debtor, becomes effective as soon as the debt
arises. See also para 3–7. In **France** however security over future assets is
generally not available, subject to limited exceptions, because of the emphasis placed on the publicity necessary for security.

However, it appears to be universally true that if a debt arises directly out
of an asset so that it really is accessory and part of the asset itself, such as

dividends on shares or interest on a bond, then this is not treated as a future non-assignable asset within the above rules: para 6–14.

Permissible secured debt

As to the scope of the debt which may be secured, e.g. future debts such as revolving loans, the need to state a maximum amount, whether a foreign currency security is possible, whether there are limitations on interest, and whether junior priority debts can be secured on the same asset, see chapter 8. **4–17**

Permissible secured creditors

There may be limitations on the creditors entitled to the security, e.g. domi- **4–18** ciliaries or nationals or the non-recognition of trustees or restrictions limiting the grant of security to banks or other financial institutions: para 8–3 *et seq*. Apart from non-recognition of trustees in most civil code coun- tries, creditor restrictions in the case of the assignment of ordinary debts or contracts are rare, but in the case of general business charges which include contract debts there often are limitations on the grant of the security to financial institutions, e.g. as in Belgium.

Liabilities of secured creditors

Secured creditors who have possession of an asset generally have duties to **4–19** take reasonable care of the asset and this is so in all developed legal systems. A secured creditor who has given notice to the debtor of the assignment to him so that he is to all intents and purposes the owner of the debt is, in a sense, in possession and may be subject to these responsibilities. Section 9–207(1) of the American UCC is typical in codifying the duty by providing that a "secured party must use reasonable care in the custody and preserva- tion of collateral in his possession". In the case of debts and contracts there is little for the assignee to do other than to collect payments, but presumably reasonable care might include duties not to waive or vary the contract or to terminate it so as to diminish the claims and possibly duties in exceptional circumstances to preserve the assigned rights.

Preferences

Any security is subject to the usual rules as to the avoidance of preferential **4–20** transfers made in the suspect period: see chapters 30 to 32. The main areas of risk are security for pre-existing debt, security for a guarantee which has a gift element or is a transaction at an undervalue, and assignments of debts as part of a bulk transfer.

Enforcement remedies

4–21   The remedies available for enforcement of the security, e.g. foreclosure, sale and possessory management through a receiver, are considered generally in chapter 10. Contrary to the normal rule that foreclosure is not permitted – in the sense that a mortgagee cannot take over the mortgaged property himself on a default except (sometimes) with a court order – it seems to be generally accepted as a matter of course, though often without legal analysis, that this is not an infringement of the ban on foreclosure: a creditor who has security over a simple debt can collect the debt and apply it towards the secured loan. He does not have to sell the debt. This is clearly sensible since the basis of the ban on foreclosure is that the mortgagee may be subjected to an intolerable temptation to take over the property for himself and further there may be questions of valuation which can only really be settled by a sale. On the other hand, in the case of a debt the money payable by the debtor on the debt is already ascertained. There are no valuation uncertainties, nor, normally, any temptation to acquire the mortgaged property for oneself with consequent risk of abuse.

The following topics are reviewed elsewhere:

— Grace periods on enforcement: para 10–15 *et seq*

— Bankruptcy and rehabilitation freezes on the enforcement of security: chapter 11

— The right of an insolvency administrator to use the collateral or to substitute collateral: chapter 11.

Priorities

4–22   The general priority rules are summarised in chapter 12. The main priority questions in this context will include:

— the priority of preferential creditors, e.g. taxes and wages;

— the ability of an insolvency administrator to raise a super-priority moratorium loan ranking ahead of the existing security;

— competing mortgagees and purchasers of the same asset;

— lienholders over the asset (unusual in this context);

- sales by an agent or broker contrary to instructions (again unlikely to arise in this context);

- the priority of future advances made by a first mortgagee when a second mortgage is in place;

- set-off. The ability of a debtor on receivables to set off against an assignee or a chargee is reviewed elsewhere in this series of works.

As to consolidation, see para 8–19. As to marshalling, see para 10–17 *et seq.*

Conflict of laws

This topic is reviewed in chapter 13. See especially para 13–20 *et seq.*

CHAPTER 5

ASSIGNMENTS OF DEBTS BY CREDITOR TO DEBTOR: "CHARGE-BACKS"

Illustrations of charge-backs

5–1 A charge-back is an assignment, by way of security, of a debt by the creditor to the debtor liable on the debt. The transaction is conceptually difficult and it may therefore be useful to give examples, commencing with those where the transaction is easier to visualise.

1. **Insurance policies** An individual takes out an endowment insurance policy from an insurance company. The insurance company is the debtor on the policy and the insured individual is the creditor. The individual insured wishes to raise money on the security of the policy and so he asks for a loan from his insurance company. The insurance company makes a loan to the insured individual and the insured individual deposits his policy back with the insurance company and executes a mortgage over the policy in favour of the insurance company in order to secure the insurance company's loan. In this transaction, a creditor – which is the individual insured – has created a mortgage in favour of the debtor – which is the insurance company – over a claim which the debtor owes the creditor (the policy). Instead of a mortgage by transfer of the policy back to the insurance company, the insurance company could instead have relied on a right to set the loan off against the policy when it matured. In that case, the individual would not transfer his asset by way of mortgage back to the insurance company.

2. **Debentures** A company has invested in unsecured registered debentures issued by a bank. The bank is the debtor liable to pay the debentures and the company, as holder of the debentures, is the creditor. The company wishes to borrow money from the bank and the bank requires security. Accordingly the company creditor deposits the debenture certificates with the bank and executes a fixed charge in favour of the bank over those debentures in order to secure the loan. The company creditor has created a charge-back, in favour of the debtor bank, over a debt (the debentures) owed by the debtor bank to the company creditor. Instead of a charge by way of security assignment by the company back

to the bank, the bank could instead have relied on a right to set the loan off against its liability on the debenture. In that case the company would not assign its asset by way of security back to the bank.

3. **Certificates of deposit** A company holds negotiable certificates of deposit issued by a bank and representing deposits placed with the bank. The bank is the debtor in respect of those deposits and the company, as holder of the certificate of the deposit, is the creditor. The company creditor wishes to borrow money from the bank and the bank requires security. The company creditor accordingly deposits the certificates of deposit with the bank and executes a pledge agreement. The company holder of these certificates of deposit, as creditor, has created, in favour of the bank as debtor, a pledge over an obligation owed by the debtor bank to the creditor holder. Instead of a pledge of the certificate of deposit, the bank could instead have relied on a right to set the loan off against the deposit evidenced by the certificate of deposit. In that case the company would not transfer its asset by way of pledge back to the bank.

4. **Bank deposits** The transaction is the same as in the previous example except that the deposits are not evidenced by a certificate of deposit or other writing. A customer charges, or assigns its rights in the deposit, back to the bank by way of security for a loan by the bank owing by the customer. This transaction is more difficult to visualise because there is no document which one can see being mortgaged back from the creditor to the debtor. But in terms of theory this transaction and all the other transactions described above involve debts or liabilities owed by a debtor to a creditor and in each case the creditor has created security over the claim back to the debtor. It should not matter how the debt is packaged or wrapped – whether it is represented by a negotiable instrument or a debenture certificate or an insurance policy or whether it has no documentary wrapping at all. This is because the underlying property is broadly the same in each case, i.e. a debt claim constituting an intangible movable.

Distinction between charge-backs and set-offs

There is a distinction between set-off and the creation of security. Although the substantive commercial effect is often the same, one is peas, and the other beans.   5–2

In the case of set-off, one debtor-creditor simply sets off the claim owed to him against the claim he owes. There is no transfer or security interest of any kind.

In the case of a charge-back, one party transfers an interest in the debt he is owed back to his debtor by way of security. This may be a pledge, mortgage, assignment or charge, depending on the type of debt, but, regardless of the form or the legal vernacular, the effect is to transfer or create a proprietary interest in the debt.

There is a third protective device, known as a flawed asset. In the case of a flawed asset, a debtor agrees with his creditor that the debt owed by the debtor is not payable at all, unless some event happens, such as the payment by the other party of the debt he owed the debtor. Flawed assets have been used where set-off might not be available, and are widely employed where there is a chain of debtor-creditors, such as in the case of bank loan sub-participations. The limitations of flawed assets are discussed elsewhere in this series on international financial law.

Although the commercial effect of each transaction is broadly the same, they are legally very different and attract their own disparate legal consequences.

For example, if the parties choose not to rely on set-off but prefer to take a specific security interest, then they will be subject to the rules of law and the commercial implications of taking security. Some of the differences between set-off and security might include, e.g.:

—   Registration or filing of charges or security interests: chapter 9. It is doubtful that a charge over a bank deposit is a charge over a "book debt" requiring registration under English-based corporate charge registration systems. If a charge-back fails for want of registration, then the assigned debt swings back and set-off may still be available in which event no harm is done.

—   Compliance with contractual negative pledge covenants prohibiting borrowers and others from taking security

—   Freezes on enforcement of the security on bankruptcy or an insolvency rehabilitation proceeding: chapter 11

—   The scope of remedies available to a secured creditor: chapter 10

—   Duty of a mortgagee to safeguard the mortgaged property: para 4–9

—   Priority rules for security: chapter 12

—   Exclusion from voting on insolvency proceedings to the extent the creditor is secured

—   Conversion of the security into a floating charge if the depositor has a right of free withdrawal.

In addition, the chargor may take the risk of loss of set-off on the insolvency of the chargee in special situations too complex to review here, but illustrated in *Re City Life Assurance Co Ltd, Grandfield's Case* [1926] 1 Ch D 191.

Set-off as protection

If set-off is an adequate protection, the commercial and financial com- 5–3
munity would not need an additional security device by the creation of
actual security.

Under English law in most cases a right of set-off, backed by appropriate
contractual devices, will afford protection to the party desiring the set-off.
Thus, insolvency set-off is available on the insolvency of the counterparty:
IR 1986, r 4.90. Set-off can be exercised against an intervener, such as an
attaching creditor, assignee or undisclosed principal, provided (sometimes)
that there is a contract to set-off and provided the claims intended for set-off
were incurred (even if not due) before the party claiming the set-off has
notice of the intervener. A set-off can be insulated in the event of a rehabilitative administration order or company voluntary arrangement under IA
1986. These and other aspects of set-off are reviewed in another volume in
this series of works on financial law.

But in some cases, set-off requires complex contractual provisions to
ensure that the remedy is available and these may be inconvenient and
cumbersome, for example:

1. **Reimbursement liabilities** A bank issues a guarantee or letter of credit
    to a third party beneficiary customer. The customer is liable to indem-
    nify the bank if the third party calls the guarantee. The bank takes a
    deposit from its customer as "cash cover" in case the letter of credit or
    guarantee should be called. The bank owes the blocked deposit to the
    customer; the customer owes the bank a contingent reimbursement
    liability – two mutual claims which one would expect to be eligible for
    set-off. Because of the technicalities of the rule against double-proof
    there are situations where the reimbursement liability of the customer
    may not be eligible for set-off against the deposit if the customer should
    become insolvent. The position is explained at para 25–15. The risk –
    which is for practical reasons usually small – can be avoided altogether
    by a stipulation in the agreement or letter of credit that the beneficiary
    must call on the guarantor before filing a proof in the insolvency of the
    debtor who is guaranteed.

2. **Collateral security** If a customer gives collateral security to a bank by
    charging a bank deposit to the bank as security for a loan made by the
    bank to a third party, then there would be no set-off between the loan
    and the deposit on the insolvency of the customer because of the

absence of mutuality. This too can be met by contract. The mutuality can be established if the customer guarantees the third party credit on the basis that his liability under the guarantee is limited to the amount of the deposit plus interest thereon: the bank can then set off the guarantee liability against the deposit: the criss-cross claims are mutual on the customer's insolvency.

3. **Secured syndicated loans** In a secured syndicated loan, the borrower may open a proceeds account with one of the banks in which proceeds of a venture being financed are deposited. The proceeds bank is debtor to the borrower in respect of the deposit and the borrower is the creditor. The borrower charges all its assets to the syndicate of banks as security for the loan by fixed and floating charges and creates a fixed charge over the deposit. So far as the proceeds bank is concerned, this is a charge-back to itself. If the customer were to become insolvent, there might be no set-off as between the liability of the proceeds bank to the borrower in respect of the deposit and the liability of the borrower to the proceeds bank in respect of the loan because the borrower has charged the benefit of the deposit to the other banks, thereby destroying mutuality. Various means are available to deal with this: for example, any excess recovered by banks over and above that recovered by the proceeds bank could be returned to the proceeds bank under a pro rata sharing clause which typically provides for the sharing of unequal recoveries by one bank amongst all the banks. Or it could be agreed that the proceeds bank can set off against the assignee banks.

5–4   Common cases where charge backs or set-off are peculiarly germane include:

–   A client pays a margin deposit to his broker or to a clearing house in a securities or financial market to cover price swings and his broker or clearing house becomes a debtor to the client in respect of the margin deposit.

–   A bank has a floating charge granted by a customer which crystallises over credit balances owed by the bank to the customer, thereby operating as an assignment by way of fixed security back to the bank.

–   A bank mortgagee realises its security and holds the proceeds as part of its general funds and hence as debtor to the mortgagor.

–   A bank mortgagee of a portfolio of securities holds proceeds of sale as debtor to the customer on a switch of investments by the customer or holds interest or dividend proceeds received on the securities.

In all these cases, the document should build in a contractual set-off as a protection to preserve the set-off – if a charge-back is not available.

But a large bloc of important states does not permit insolvency set-off except in very limited cases and in many jurisdictions (contrary to the English position) it is difficult, if not impossible, to protect a set-off against attaching creditors: these include many members of the Franco-Latin groups such as France, Belgium, Spain and most Latin American countries. In these situations, charge-backs are essential.

In many cases, a prohibition on charge-backs or set-off could be cured by restructuring the transaction. The party giving the security deposits the money with a third party bank and then assigns the benefit of the resulting deposit claim to the creditor desiring security. Here, there is no assignment by creditor back to debtor but rather a simple security assignment of a debt owed by a third party to the assignor, not by the debtor to the assignor. However this requires the involvement of a third party and there may sometimes be commercial, tax, regulatory and other reasons militating against that involvement in particular cases.

Theoretical objections to charge-backs

Charge-backs have met with some judicial hostility in England and Austra-   5–5
lia. One reason given is that if a creditor assigns a debt by way of security back to the debtor, then there must of necessity be a merger and the debt would simply disappear or be released.

But the courts have held in England that there is no merger if the debtor does not intend there to be a merger, e.g. where an acceptor of a negotiable instrument has acquired the instrument on which he is liable or where a mortgagor has acquired his own land mortgage before selling it on. In the case of a charge-back, clearly the parties do not intend a merger because a merger would involve the forfeiture of the mortgagor's property to the mortgagee and would lead to a foreclosure before the mortgagor had defaulted.

Another reason given is that a debt is merely a right to sue, and therefore, if the creditor assigns this right back to the debtor, the transaction is invalid since the debtor cannot sue himself. The answer to this is that debts are not merely rights to sue. They are a form of property; they are assets. Claims can be sold, bequeathed and dealt with as with any other form of property. Banks do not label the asset side of their balance sheet containing their portfolio of loans as "Rights to sue". Nor should it matter that a chief characteristic of the asset is suspended in that the debtor cannot sue himself during the course of the security. The temporary inapplicability of the right to sue is not a fatal destruction of the essence of the asset. In other contexts, debts do not cease to be property when the right to sue is barred, as where the debtor is entitled to sovereign immunity or some stamp duty has not been paid.

The secured party is not prejudiced by the inability to sue himself – he does not need to.

International reception of charge-backs

5–6   In **Australia** the courts have resolutely refused to permit charge-backs; see, e.g. *Broad v Stamp Duty Commissioners* [1980] 2 NSWLR 40; *Estates Planning Associates (Aust) Pty Ltd v Stamp Duty Commissioners* (1985) 16 ATR 862; and in other cases since. These original cases may have been influenced by the fact that in Australia stamp duty is usually payable on mortgages, but not on set-off, and the courts may have strained to help the taxpayer by finding that a mortgage was void and finding instead that the parties could set off. See also *Esanda Finance Co Ltd v Jackson* (1993) 11 ACLC 138 (S Ct of S Australia).

In **England**, in *Re Charge Card Services Ltd* [1986] 3 All ER 289, the court said that it was "conceptually impossible" for a creditor to grant security over a debt owed by the debtor back to the debtor. This decision created sufficient uncertainty to destroy the predictability which is vital to a mortgage, even though the previous English authority in favour of charge-backs was substantial and, because some of it was appellate, overrode the first instance *Charge Card* decision. The details of the decisions are reviewed in Wood, *English & International Set-Off* (1989) Sweet & Maxwell, para 5–134 *et seq*.

> For example, there are at least five insurance company cases (including an Australian decision) where the insured mortgaged his policy back to the insurance company. The courts had no objection to the transaction: *Re Jeffery's Policy* (1872) 20 WR 857; *Sovereign Life Assurance Co v Dodd* [1892] 1 QB 405; *Re National Benefit Assurance Co Ltd* [1924] 2 Ch 339; *Hiley v The People's Prudential Assurance Co Ltd* (1938) 60 CLR 468 (High Court of Australia); *Re City Life Assurance Co Ltd, Grandfield's Case* [1926] 1 Ch D 191.

> There are at least two cases in which charge-backs were specifically upheld and were essential to the decision in the case. Both of these were appellate decisions: *Re Jeavons, ex p Mackay* (1873) LR 8 Ch App 643 (1873) LJ (NS) Bankruptcy 68 (charge on patent royalties); *Webb v Smith* (1885) 30 Ch D 192, CA (sale proceeds owing by auctioneers to principal).

> There are in addition a number of other cases in which charge-backs of various types of claims, ranging from bank deposits to dividends on shares, have either been contemplated or arguably been accepted without demur, e.g. *Re Hart, ex p Caldicott* [1883] Ch D 716, CA; (bank deposit); *Commercial Bank of Australia Ltd v Wilson* [1893] AC 181, PC (bank deposit); *Re City Equitable Fire Insurance Co (No 2)* [1930] 2 Ch 293, AC (insurance premiums); *Swiss Bank Corp v Lloyds Bank Ltd* [1981] 2 All ER 449, HL [1980] 2 All ER 419; *Re*

General Exchange Bank, Re Lewis (1871) 6 Ch App 818 at 821 (proceeds of sale of shares); *Hague v Dandeson* (1848) 2 Ex 742 at 746 (dividends).

In *Welsh Development Agency v Export Finance Co Ltd* [1992] BCLC 148, and *Re Bank of Credit and Commerce International SA* (1994) Ch D, the court opined that *Charge Card* was incorrect, but these remarks were obiter and are not binding precedents.

In both **Bermuda** and **Hong Kong** legislation has been adopted to nullify   5–7
the effects of the *Charge Card* decision.

In Hong Kong, s 15(a) of the Law Amendment and Reform (Consolidation) Ordinance provides:

> "For the avoidance of doubt, it is hereby declared that a person ('the first person') is able to create and always has been able to create, in favour of another person ('the second person') a legal or equitable mortgage or charge over all or any of the first person's interest in a chose in action enforceable by the first person against the second person and any mortgage or charge so created shall operate neither to merge the interest thereby created with, nor to extinguish or release, that chose in action."

In Bermuda, the Charge and Security (Special Provisions) Act 1990 provides:

> "Any charge purportedly created, or any security purportedly given, by a creditor in favour of a debtor over a debt due or to become due to that creditor from that debtor, for the purpose of securing any obligation of that creditor to that debtor, shall be valid and enforceable by that debtor to the same extent as if the charge had been created or security given, as the case may be, over that debt in favour of a person other than that debtor. This Act applies to any charge purportedly created or security purportedly given before or after the coming into operation of this Act."

A comparable provision is found in the Property (Miscellaneous Provisions) Law 1994 of the Cayman Islands.

Charge-backs have been sanctioned in common law **Canada**: see *Re Cen-*   5–8
tury Steel & Boiler Ltd (1981) 36 NBR (2d) 490, CA (New Brunswick) (lessee's security deposit paid to lessor) and *Clarkson v Smith & Goldberg* (1925) 58 OLR 241 (Ontario appeals) (bank deposit represented by cheque).

It seems that many **United States** common law jurisdictions permit charge-backs. But some US courts seem to have vacillated in the same way as the English courts as to whether a debtor may be an assignee of a debt he owes, particularly in the absence of a CD or other evidentiary paper, and as to the applicability of the public filing requirements. In *Re CIL Co*, 71 Bankr 261 (Bankr D Or 1987), the security over a deposit account failed because the depositor retained unfettered control of the account, thereby destroying a pledge. But a charge-back now seems to be accepted in the main US jurisdictions; thus a charge-back over a deposit account was upheld in the New York case of *Gillman v Chase Manhattan Bank NA*, 534 NE 2d 824 (NY 1988). If the bank has sufficient control over the account and free withdrawals are prevented, the security is good: *Duncan Box & Lumber Co v Applied Energies Inc*, 270 SE 2d 140 (W Va 1980). A frequent practice in those jurisdictions adopting the Uniform Commercial Code is for security over a bank account to be constituted by a pledge of a certificate of deposit issued by the bank and deposited back by the customer. The advantage of this arrangement is that a certificate of deposit is thought to fall within the definition of "instrument" within s 9–105(i) of the UCC (Texas, Florida and South Carolina decisions have so held) so that no UCC filing is required: the pledge is perfected by possession.

5–9   Apart from non-conforming provisions in California and Hawaii, Art 9 of the UCC does not apply to a "transfer of an interest in a deposit account" with exceptions in relation to proceeds: s 9–104(1). A deposit account is defined in s 9–105(c) to mean "a demand, time, savings, passbook or like account maintained with a bank, savings and loan association, credit union or like organisation, other than an account evidenced by a certificate of deposit". Precautionary filings are sometimes made where the claim assigned back to the debtor is not represented by an "instrument" – which is indeed the practice followed in England.

In California, Art 9–302(g)(i) of the Californian version of the UCC – a provision which is non-conforming – states that a security interest over "a deposit account" maintained with the secured party is perfected "when a security agreement is executed". Article 9–302 excludes a "security interest in a deposit account" from the necessity to file a financing statement to perfect the security interest.

> For reviews of US law, see Dwight L Greene, "Deposit Accounts as Bank Collateral", 39, *Drake L Rev* 259 (1989–1990), and Alvin C Harrell, "Security Interests in Deposit Accounts" 23 *UCC LJ* 153 (1990)

5–10   In **France** there are two types of pledge of a bank account by the customer back to the bank, although it is believed that these are untested in the courts:

(a) Pledge of an operating account (*nantissement de compte en cours de fonctionnement*). Pursuant to such an agreement, the customer pledges an account with the bank to the bank, the balance of which may vary from time to time. The inconvenience of this arrangement is that the pledge may be subject to the formalities of Art 2075 of the French Civil Code which requires notification to the bank by notarial deed of the pledge plus notification to the tax authorities and payment of a nominal fee.

(b) Pledge of cash (*nantissement d'espèces*). Pursuant to this agreement the customer pledges an account with the bank to the bank, and the pledged account is blocked, precluding the customer from withdrawing the credit balance. It is uncertain whether this form of pledge is subject to the requirements of Art 2075 of the Civil Code.

There are special rules in each case as to the application of Art 2074 of the Civil Code which require that the amount of the underlying obligations secured be stated in the document which establishes the pledge.

It is probably the case that **Belgium** and **Luxembourg** adopt the French attitude to these pledges.

It is understood that the consensus of legal opinion in Germany, the Netherlands, Norway, Sweden and Italy is that a depositor may charge back its deposit to the bank. In Germany and Sweden no registration is required. A relevant Italian decision is the Court of Cassation decision No 1380, 1977.

CHAPTER 6

SECURITY OVER INVESTMENT SECURITIES

General principles

Types of investment security in summary

6–1 One may attempt a functional classification of investment securities by dividing them into three categories:

— the degree of documentation of the security;

— the identity of the issuer;

— the type of investment security.

Documentation of investment securities

6–2 The degree to which an investment security is packaged or wrapped up in paper has a bearing upon its legal treatment. For example, an investment security may be a negotiable bearer security which is transferable by delivery without any writing: these are mainly debt securities but bearer shares are common — at least outside English-based countries where there have historically been stamp duty and other disincentives to bearer shares. Second in degree of completeness of packaging are certificated securities, whether registered or unregistered, e.g. shares represented by a share certificate and debentures represented by debenture certificates. Finally there are dematerialised securities which are not represented by any certificates or receipts or other paper. The objective of dematerialising securities is to reduce paperwork and administration. Instead of giving the holder a certificate evidencing his holding, the holder's rights are represented by an entry in a register maintained by an agent on behalf of the issuer. For this reason they are often called "book entry securities". The trend commenced with government bonds and has been extended on many stock exchanges to ordinary corporate securities.

The main implications of the packaging in the context of charges over securities are several. First, the manner of transfer depends upon the packaging, e.g. transfer by delivery in the case of negotiable bearer securities and by assignment in other cases. Secondly, in those countries adhering to the false wealth rule whereby a mortgagee must have full possession of the asset charged, possession is given either by taking physical possession of the negotiable security or, in the case of certificated securities, by taking possession of the certificates themselves, accompanied by registration of the holder as the holder of the securities in the books of the issuer. Thirdly, priority rules differ somewhat. A holder in due course of a negotiable security has more or less perfect priority, unless it is forged. A chargee who is registered as the holder of a certificated security has a good priority but is more vulnerable if he does not obtain the certificates. The holder of a dematerialised security has no document to take hold of; hence the priority rules cannot hinge upon the possession of the evidential documents and must be decided by the rules applicable to the registration system. Fourthly, and finally, the validity of a security transfer usually depends upon the lex situs of the security in the developed jurisdictions. The lex situs of a negotiable bearer security is commonly where the bearer security is actually situated, whereas the location of a certificated security will usually be where the register is kept (if there is one), and this will also be the position with regard to dematerialised securities. There appears to be a large measure of international consensus on these points.

A sub-classification within this classification is to divide securities into those which are registered and those which are not registered in a register maintained by or on behalf of the issuer. This has similar implications for the manner of transfer, perfection, priorities and lex situs. A separate class is formed by those securities which are kept with custodians who may also operate a book entry system, but in this case the custodians are not agents of the issuer but rather are agents of the holders of the securities.

Identity of issuer

Securities may be issued by governments or state entities, ordinary com- 6–3
panies or by trustees of a unit trust – which is an Anglo-American form of collective investment scheme.

The identity of the issuer is clearly crucial to the value of the collateral since his solvency or otherwise depends upon whether the chargee will be paid at all. Questions of immunity may arise in relation to governmental securities. In the case of corporate securities, note that in France debt securities may not be accelerated by reason only of the insolvency of the debtor on the security: see Art 37 of the Decree-Law of 1985 (the French Bankruptcy Act).

Type of investment security

6–4   The securities may be debt securities, equity shares (voting or non-voting, preferred or common) and may be secured or unsecured, guaranteed or unguaranteed; they may be junior debt or senior debt; they may be convertible; they may be warrants to subscribe for securities; they may be an interest in fungible securities deposited with the custodian; they may be listed or unlisted or dealt in on an over-the-counter market or a non-marketable security. Debt securities may or may not be constituted by a trust deed with a trustee to look after the interests of the bondholders.

In practice, the main division is between debt securities and equity securities: the latter carry a vote and a right to a dividend. A holder of equity securities may incur the responsibilities of an equity holder, e.g. notification duties, liabilities for unpaid calls, liabilities springing from voting control, especially on the insolvency of the issuer, and a restriction on the identity of the holders of equity securities in particular businesses, e.g. banks and other critical enterprises: para 6–20.

Use of charges over investment securities

6–5   In this section, the term "charge" will be used instead of "security interest" or "mortgage" in order to prevent confusion between investment securities and security over these investment securities. The term "charge" can be used conveniently in order to cover whatever terminology is preferred locally, e.g. security interest, pledge, hypothecation, mortgage or whatever.

Charges over investment securities are of immense importance in international finance, mainly because of the marketability and ease of valuation of the collateral and also the facility with which investment securities can be made available, usually with a minimum of formality and fuss – in sharp contrast to, say, mortgages of land. This obviously results from the nature of the property.

Typical illustrations of the use of charges over investment securities are: margin collateral in organised markets, e.g. in the commodities, futures and option markets, where participants must deposit security in order to cover their exposures to counterparties or to clearing houses (commonly called "initial margin" and "variation margin" to cover fluctuations in prices); collateral for the exposures of banks in payment systems; collateral for the exposures of banks to their own central banks who have advanced funds to cover open positions at the banks; collateral for ordinary loans; mortgages over the shares of one-ship companies and, in project finance, the project vehicle; and charges over investment securities which are part of a general enterprise charge over all or a significant portion of the assets of a company.

International availability of charges

It seems that charges over investment securities are available in all of the   6–6
developed jurisdictions and no exceptions have been found. Charges can be constituted which are valid on bankruptcy of the debtor and against the debtor's attaching creditors although in some cases there are greater formalities to be observed than in others and erosions of priority and enforcement. By contrast, a non-possessory chattel mortgage and general enterprise charges are often simply not available at all.

Restrictions on charges

Restrictions on the creation of charges over investment securities may spring   6–7
from three main sources. First, there may be restrictions by the terms of the investment security itself. This will be unusual since investment securities are intended to be freely marketable. The most common examples are the shares of private companies which in many jurisdictions are subject to various restrictions in their constitutional documents. The directors may have an unfettered right to refuse to register transfers, there may be pre-emption rights in favour of other shareholders, and there may be specially onerous formalities in relation to transfers, e.g. notarisation, so as to discourage marketability.

In the case of private or closely-held companies, there may be a shareholders agreement governing transfers. For example, in the typical project finance structure, the shareholders regulate their rights by a joint venture agreement. Commonly a shareholder who, for example, does not supply the required funds to the project vehicle, loses his vote on his shares and dividends and may be subject to forcible sale to the other complying shareholders – the "withering interest". Any creditor taking a charge over the shares would normally be subject to these restrictions as an assignee. In appropriate cases shareholders may require chargees of the shares to agree to be subject to the contract.

Secondly, charges may be restricted by regulatory law. Thus in the United States margin regulations made by the Federal Reserve Board under the authority of the Securities and Exchange Act 1934 limit the amount of credit that may initially be extended on any security, e.g. to 50 per cent of the price. The margin regulations apply to equities and convertible bonds but not debt or US official securities: see Regulations T and X. The objects of these regulations are to control the purchase of securities on credit in order to prevent the diversion of credit to speculative securities transactions and to protect the investing public from overreaching themselves.

Under local law, banks and insurance companies may by official guide-line or regulation be restricted from granting charges.

In most countries in Europe and the common law world, but not the United States or Canada, a company may not give financial assistance for the purpose of acquiring its own shares.

Finally, the debtor granting the security may be subject to a contractual restriction e.g. a negative pledge or a prohibition on disposals in its credit agreements.

Charges over the shares of a private company must be considered to be particularly weak, e.g. because of the problems of valuation and marketabi-lity. If the shares are those of a subsidiary company in a group, consider-ation may be given as to whether it is appropriate by contract to restrict the activities of the subsidiary, e.g. by requiring that all transactions are at arm's length, that there are no borrowings except as approved, no capital expendi-tures, no acquisitions, and no other businesses and other typical credit cov-enants designed to protect the value of the subsidiary.

Perfection of charge

6–8 The methods of perfection of the charge against creditors of the debtor generally appear to follow the pattern established for charges over debts, that is, some countries require the attributes of a possessory pledge while others are content with non-possessory security.

Countries which require a possessory pledge do so in order to meet the "false wealth" objection and also to protect commercial dealings against unpredictable secret priorities. Hence the chargee must publicise his security so far as possible by full possession. In the case of a negotiable instrument, this means that the chargee must take actual physical delivery of the instru-ment or do so through an independent custodian or agent. In the case of other investment securities, the possession has to be artificial or abstract. In the classical form, the creditor must take possession of any certificates or other evidences of the securities and must also have himself registered as the holder of the securities in the books of the issuer. Note that this is different from registration or filing in a public register of security interests generally. In the case of dematerialised securities, he must be registered as the holder in the books maintained by the issuer. Sometimes registration is in a special pledge register and sometimes all that is necessary is that the pledgee is inscribed in the register, e.g. as in Belgium and the Netherlands. The difficulty here is that often the registrar cannot by law or custom or inclination record notice of dealings on the register other than full transfers on sale. This is particularly true of share registers and has been a problem in the United States where one of the required methods of perfection of a security interest over investment securities is by registration in the books of the issuer.

Countries which require a possessory pledge include the Germanic and Franco-Latin jurisdictions and also, surprisingly, the United States, at least in the case of dematerialised book entry securities, called "uncertificated securities" under Art 8 of the Uniform Commercial Code. But it can be expected that there are many derogations from this strict Roman position in the interests of the convenience of commerce. One may take an example from a conservative Roman jurisdiction, Scotland:

> In *Guild v Young* (1884) 22 SLR 520, the debtor transferred shares by way of security. The debtor then became bankrupt. The creditor successfully applied to the company for registration of himself as the holder. *Held*: the creditor had a valid security during the period between the execution of the transfer and its registration because the debtor had done all he needed to do to pass the title and the creditor could get registered at any time. Hence, Scotland recognised the secret security.

France The position in France is illustrative of a system which adheres to 6–9 the old possessory pledge but has moved on to dematerialisation. A Law of January 3, 1983 required that shares in public companies (SA) are no longer represented by share certificates, whether or not they are quoted on a stock exchange, but rather by an inscription in an account – a book entry. A pledge of shares can be writing without notarisation but must contain a description of the shares and the number of the shares which are to be pledged. The pledge must be registered in the company's books: the shares pledged are transferred to a special account opened in the name of the pledgor but indicating that the shares have been pledged and identifying the pledgee. The pledgee receives an acknowledgement (*attestation de gage*) and the pledge is valid as against creditors as from its registration in the special account. Assuming the pledge is commercial, the pledgee can have the shares sold publicly eight days after notification of its intention to enforce the pledge given to the debtor. Provision for a private sale is void. In the case of pledges of shares in private companies, a draft of the pledge document must be sent to the company and each of the shareholders for their approval in accordance with French company law: it is not sufficient that shareholders merely give their consent in writing to the pledge and the pledge agreement. Once entered into, the pledge must be notified to the company by a bailiff in order for the security to be effective as against creditors and other third parties.

6–10 **English-based states** By contrast, the English-based common law systems do not generally require a possessory pledge and it is perfectly possible to create a charge over securities without handing over any certificates and without the chargee being registered in the books of the issuer. Of course the chargee has a poorer priority: he is liable to be primed if the debtor transfers the securities to somebody else who takes the transfer without notice of the earlier charge and gets himself registered first. But often chargees are content to rely on the integrity of the chargor not to cheat in this way. The "false wealth" argument is seen as so inconvenient in relation to securities that the English-based system of corporate registration of charges does not generally apply to charges over securities. If they are caught at all, it is because they are unintentionally captured by some other technical head of registration e.g. if the charge is a floating charge (as it might be where there are rights of free substitution), if the charge is over "book debts" (most unlikely, even in relation to financial instruments charged by a financial company), or if the charge is given to secure an issue of debentures.

Germanic group As to the Germanic group, those countries which adopt the fiduciary transfer generally allow this technique in relation to investment securities as well and therefore avoid the need for the possessory pledge, e.g. Germany, the Netherlands, Switzerland, Japan and South Korea, but not Austria or Italy: para 2–11 *et seq.*

6–11 **United States** The general position in the United States under Art 8 of the Uniform Commercial Code is that in the case of certificated investment securities (which are defined) the debtor must transfer them to the secured party or his nominee and hand over any certificates by physical delivery. But it is not necessary for the secured party to be registered as the holder of the securities in the books of the issuer. Alternatively notice may be given of the security interest to a third party authorised to control and transfer the security, i.e. a custodian of the security. Perfection by filing is ineffective. In the case of uncertificated investment securities, e.g. book entry securities, perfection is by registration of the security interest with the issuer of the security or a registered transfer to the secured creditor as if he were the owner. Again, perfection by filing is ineffective. Note that Art 8 differs between states and has not been adopted by all states. Where the old 1972 Art 9 applies (Art 8 was introduced in 1977) investment securities will either be "instruments" (these are mainly negotiable instruments and negotiable securities) – where perfection is by possession, subject to temporary automatic perfection – or they are "general intangibles" – where perfection is by central filing. Revisions to the above were proposed in 1994: see para 9–24A.

Disadvantages of non-registration In those countries which do not require 6–12 a full possessory pledge, the disadvantages to the chargee of not being registered as the holder of the securities include: communications, financial statements and dividends are sent to the chargor; the chargee may lose priority, e.g. if the chargor obtains duplicate certificates or has the original certificates and gives good title to a bona fide purchaser; the voting rights are exercisable by the chargor (which may be desired in any event); and the mechanics of a forced sale are more cumbersome, because the chargee is not already on the register and therefore will have to go through some process to transfer to a purchaser.

In common law countries it is usual for charged securities to be registered in the name of a nominee company of the chargee bank or broker. The nominee company holds the charged securities on trust for the secured creditor. The split of the legal holder and the creditor entitled to the debt does not give rise to legal problems in common law jurisdictions because of the recognition of the trust: it is the beneficial interest which is covered by the charge.

Substitution rights

A person who charges a portfolio of securities often wishes to be able to deal 6–13 with the securities which are subject to the charge in order to take advantage of market opportunities. This is especially the case with securities deposited by way of margin. It is generally agreed that the chargor may substitute securities provided that the value of securities is maintained at a specified level of coverage over the secured debt.

Under classical doctrine in "possessory pledge" jurisdictions, the ability of the debtor to deal with the secured property generally means that the pledge is lost because the pledgor has dominion over the pledged property: this is fatal to the pledgee's possession. This is not so in English-based common law countries, although the right of substitution may convert the fixed security into a floating charge which is generally registrable and suffers other disadvantages: see para 2–6. In other words the chargee does not lose his security but has a security enjoying a lower rank and a greater vulnerability.

A jurisdiction which strains against these unhappy results will characterise the right of substitution as a right of the chargor to sell the investment securities but always subject to the charge which is only released when the new securities are substituted. In other words, the chargor does not have the freedom to deal which converts the fixed charge into a floating charge, and does not have dominion over the securities which destroys the possessory pledge because he can only procure a release of existing securities by depositing new securities. The pledge jumps from one set of securities to another. Such a jurisdiction will also strain to find that the substituted charge is not a new charge to secure a pre-existing debt, but is merely a substitution which does not result in any improvement of the creditor's position so long as the collateral value is not increased on the substitution. Security for pre-existing debt is often treated as a voidable preference if created during the suspect period. It is believed that Belgian case law tends to this conclusion. Common law courts outside England have on occasion construed the right of substitution as converting fixed security into a registrable floating charge which, if not registered, is void as against the creditors and liquidator of the chargor, e.g. Singapore.

Accessories and future securities

6–14   A charge over an asset should cover accessories to the asset which are really part and parcel of the asset itself. Typical accessories to investment securities are dividends and interest payable on the securities, securities issued in right of the securities (such as bonus and rights issues), exchanges, securities on conversion, securities issued pursuant to warrants and capital redemptions.

It is thought that it is universally recognised in the developed jurisdictions that these accessories are covered by the original security, even if not so provided. They are not future assets subject to the doctrine of specificity preventing charges over future non-identified assets. They are not subject to the avoidance of preferences constituted by the grant of security for pre-existing debt. But the proper course in all cases is to make it clear in the security document that these accessories are covered by the charge. Problems can still arise:

> In *Re Mathews*, 29 UCC Rep Serv 684 (4th Cir 1980), the pledgee bank had possession of the original shares and did not have to be registered as the holder of the shares in the books of the issuer in order to perfect the security interest. There was a stock split and the pledgee did not obtain possession of the newly-issued shares which of course went to the pledgor as the holder of record. *Held*: on the pledgor's bankruptcy, the newly-issued shares belonged to the pledgor and not to the pledgee.

As to the use of proceeds, it is usually provided that dividends and the like are paid over to the pledgor until a default. If any capital redemptions are paid to the pledgee before the secured debt has matured, then there should be a procedure for the crediting of these proceeds to an account and the grant of security over that account. This is somewhat more complex when the pledgee is a bank in which event the bank must either rely on a right of set-off or it must be possible for the pledgor to create a charge-back of the debts owed by the bank back to the bank: see para 5–1 *et seq*. The American Uniform Commercial Code s 9–207(2)(c) requires the application of proceeds in reduction of the secured debt unless they are paid to the pledgor.

Voting rights

Investment securities generally carry voting rights at some stage or another. 6–15 For example, equity securities carry normal voting rights as a shareholder. Debt securities may carry voting rights to vote on compositions or alterations and creditors may have voting rights in bankruptcy or rehabilitation proceedings. Inevitably therefore the secured creditor may be bound by a majority vote, even if he is a dissenting minority, and this may affect the value of his security.

If the chargee is registered in the books of the issuer as the holder of security, then he will be entitled to vote as the holder of record in the normal case. He may grant a proxy to the chargor. If on the other hand the chargee is not registered as the holder, the chargor will be entitled to vote. The security agreement should deal with the exercise of voting rights. Typically it will be provided that the chargor can vote until an event of default but will not exercise voting rights in such a way as to diminish the value of the securities. The security agreement may go into more detail, e.g. by dealing with voting on take-overs or insolvency. The power of the chargee to vote the securities may give rise to some unfortunate consequences: see para 6–22 *et seq*.

Fungible securities

Many investment securities nowadays are no longer represented by certifi- 6–16 cates with a specific number, but rather are fungible, i.e. it is not possible to distinguish one security of the same class from another. Under traditional rules of universal application, if a party has a right to return equivalent securities and in the meantime to deal with the securities transferred to him as if they were his own, he must inevitably acquire the property in the securities and the transferor loses his property: this is an absolute transfer, not a transfer by way of security. The mortgagor loses title.

This reasoning has been used in the development of title finance transactions as a replacement for collateral over investment securities in order to avoid the inconveniences of mortgage law. The most common examples are stock lending and repos. The essence of the difference is that in each case the "secured" creditor obtains title to the securities, not a limited security interest. These transactions are reviewed elsewhere in this series of books.

Statute may intervene to admit fungibility. See the discussion in relation to Euroclear securities at para 6–46 *et seq.*

Formalities

6–17　The question of the formalities necessary to create a charge, e.g. whether mere writing is sufficient or whether some more ceremonial form is required, e.g. deed or notarisation, is reviewed at para 8–1 *et seq.*

In English-based countries, charges over investment securities can be created informally without writing. A mere deposit is sufficient. The main disadvantage is that a court order is required for a sale, but otherwise the chargee has security which is valid on the bankruptcy of the chargor: see *Harrold v Plenty* [1901] 2 Ch 314.

> In *Stubbs v Slater* [1910] 1 Ch 632, 638, CA, the debtor handed over to the brokers a certificate together with a transfer executed by the debtor in blank. Cozens-Hardy MR said: "Now what is the effect of that? I am astonished that there should be any doubt about it . . . the whole transaction was a mortgage."

In the United States normally writing is necessary for Art 9 security interests, but in Art 8 states, where the secured party has possession no writing is necessary for the security agreement although naturally security agreements are normally reduced to writing.

Outside the Anglo-American jurisdictions, i.e. in the Germanic, Franco-Latin and mixed jurisdictions, one can only record a tendency to reduce the formalities away from the ceremonial notarisation normally required for mortgages.

However there is one important continuing factor in these countries: the doctrine of specificity may require that the securities concerned must be specifically particularised and identified, e.g. by the number of the certificates. For this doctrine, see para 1–6. A jurisdiction which holds to this view would be conservative and more investigation is needed. In common law jurisdictions it is usually sufficient to identify the securities generally: all that is necessary is to be able to ascertain which securities are included and which securities are not, e.g. "all securities of which you hold the certificates" or "all our Barclays Bank equity shares".

Permissible secured debt

As to the debt which may be secured, see para 8–3 *et seq*. This concerns 6–18
such matters as whether a future debt can be secured (current accounts, revolving debts, multicurrency debts, new money on a rescue); whether a maximum amount must be specified; whether foreign currency mortgages are possible; the coverage of the security for interest, e.g. usury laws limiting interest to a maximum rate, capitalised interest, penalty interest, maximum back interest, and post-insolvency interest; second priority security; and third party collateral security. For restrictions on redemptions and for premiums and penalties, see para 8–14 *et seq*.

Permissible secured creditors

For a discussion of creditors who may be secured creditors, see generally 6–19
para 8–20 *et seq*. This relates to such matters as whether a trustee may hold a security for beneficiary creditors, and whether the creditors who may take charges are limited to credit institutions. Limitations of the chargee to credit institutions seem rare in the case of investment securities: where these restrictions apply, they seem to apply only to non-possessory chattel mortgages and general business charges.

Permissible securities

It may not be possible for foreigners to obtain a charge over restricted 6–20
securities, e.g. equity securities of defence industries, newspapers and media, natural resource companies, landholding companies, or "public interest" institutions such as banks, insurance companies and investment dealers. For example, the UK Banking Act 1987 imposes tiered controls on those who may be shareholders in banks. These restrictions will ordinarily apply to equity shares, not debt securities – which do not confer control – but it would be a matter for examination of the detail of the prescription to ascertain whether the prohibition affects secured creditors as opposed to beneficial owners. The question may be determined according to whether or not the chargee controls voting. In any event a restriction may limit the persons to whom the securities may be sold on an enforcement and hence affect the marketability of the collateral.

Liabilities of secured creditor generally

6–21   The list of responsibilities of a chargee over investment securities seems to be rather longer than one would expect. It is true that the chargee does not have to repair or feed or water or insure the property but some liabilities remain.

Liabilities on the securities

6–22   If the chargee has security over partly-paid shares, then the chargee may be liable for unpaid calls on the insolvency of the issuer of the shares, but only if the chargee has been registered as the holder.

Duty to take care of charged property

Most charges over other assets are non-possessory, e.g. a mortgage of land or a ship or an aircraft, or a general enterprise charge, such as a floating charge. But a charge over investment securities is often possessory in the artificial sense since the chargee may become registered as the holder of the securities.

There is a general rule, codified in the United States and in civil code states and established by a case law in English-based common law states, whereby a pledgee must take reasonable care of pledged property in his possession.

For example, s 9–207(1) of the Uniform Commercial Code provides that a "secured party must use reasonable care in the custody and preservation of collateral in his possession. In the case of an instrument . . . reasonable care includes taking necessary steps to preserve rights against prior parties unless otherwise agreed." A pledgee who fails to exercise reasonable care does not lose his security interest but he may be held liable for losses arising from his failure (s 9–207(3)) and, although the pledgee cannot disclaim his obligation to take ordinary care, the parties can define in the security agreement the standards by which ordinary care is to be measured (see s 1–102(3)) and the agreement will be upheld provided the standards prescribed by the parties "are not manifestly unreasonable".

6–23   Thus, a chargee may be required to use reasonable care in relation to voting, transmitting communications, or exercising rights in respect of the securities, e.g. conversion rights before the conversion period expires or warrant rights before the warrant period expires.

In *Waddell v Hutton*, 1911 SC 575 (a Scottish case), it was held that a mortgagee of shares will be liable in damages to the mortgagor if he declines to take up a rights issue without communicating with the mortgagor and if the shares become worth more than the issue price.

In *Traverse v Liberty Bank & Trust Co*, 5 UCC Rep Serv 535 (Mass Super 1967), a pledgee bank failed to convert debentures convertible into $78,000 worth of common stock prior to the termination of the conversion privilege after which the debentures were worth $25,000. *Held*: the pledgee bank was liable to the pledgor. The pledgee's personnel did not read the debenture terms and the note teller responsible for the collateral did not know what convertible debentures were. See also *Grace v Sterling, Grace & Co*, 30 AD 2d 61, 289 NYS 2d 632 (1st Dept 1968) (pledgee liable on similar facts). There are other US cases to the same effect.

Pledgors have sometimes complained that the pledgee should have sold securities when there was a very sharp fall in the market. These claims have usually been based upon the pledgee being a broker or other institutional advisor in relation to the securities and have generally failed. Several US cases have held that a pledgee is not responsible for a decline in the value of the pledged instruments and that an obligation to sell the collateral because of a serious and notorious market decline would be to shift the investment risk from the borrower to the lender: see, e.g. *Tepper v Chase Manhattan Bank*, 376 So 2d 35 (Fla Dist Ct App 1979).

In *Nelson v National Bank of Scotland*, 1936 SC 570 (a Scottish case) it was held that an assignee in security of shares owed a duty to the debtor to sell no more of the shares than were necessary to liquidate the debt or at least to keep the over-sale within reasonable bounds and to return the rest of the shares in kind.

In **England** if a creditor having a charge over securities uses the securities to pledge to somebody else for the broker's own debt, then the secured creditor is not entitled to recover his secured debt: *Ellis Co's Trustee v Dixon-Johnson* [1925] AC 489.

A security agreement should deal with the responsibilities of the chargee to take care of the charged property and deal specifically with duties to exercise rights in respect of the securities, consideration being given to the usual restrictions on exculpation clauses.

Notification duties

In the case of equity voting securities, the beneficial owners may have duties 6–24 to notify the issuer of the securities of their holdings and this duty may extend to chargees who have voting control. The object of these rules is generally to enable a company to know the identity of its shareholders. Non-compliance may result in freeze orders on voting, receipts of dividends and rights to transfer the security. Thus there are notification duties in relation to 3 per cent holdings in public companies under the British Companies Act 1985 s 198, and, at the request of the issuer, in relation to all securities under s 212 of the Act. In the United States there is a 5 per cent notification threshold for beneficial holdings of equity securities registered under the Securities and Exchange Act 1934, subject to an exclusion for certain pledgees, and a 10 per cent test under s 16(a) of the 1934 Act in relation to certain equity securities.

Liability of controllers

6–25 If a party has voting control of a company then it may incur liabilities in relation to the company if the company becomes insolvent, notably if that party interferes in management so as to become a director and hence incurs the liabilities of a director. Under s 15 of the US Securities Act of 1933, controllers are liable for misstatements in registration statements (prospectuses), subject to a due diligence defence.

If a chargee has voting control, the company may become a subsidiary for the purposes of corporate, tax and accounting law – see, e.g. the British Companies Act 1985 s 736.

Insider dealing

6–26 If a chargee obtains price-sensitive information from the chargor and acts on it by selling the securities or if the chargee assists the chargor to sell the securities on the basis of the information, the chargee may be liable for aiding and abetting the offence of insider dealing Insider dealing is dealt with elsewhere in this series of works.

Preferential transfers

6–27 A chargee of investment securities is subject to the usual rules regarding preferential transfers granted by an insolvent debtor in the suspect period or intended to prefer a creditor.

The main areas of risk in relation to the charges over investment securities are:

– where the security is granted to secure a guarantee which has an element of gift or is a transaction at an undervalue and therefore potentially voidable;

- security given for pre-existing debt, especially variation margin in markets, i.e. extra security called for by a clearing house or a broker to cover increased exposures of the clients on market dealings by reason of fluctuations in market rates; and

- where the securities are part of a bulk transfer.

See chapters 30 to 32.

Enforcement remedies

The enforcement remedies available to a secured creditor are reviewed briefly in chapter 10, e.g. foreclosure, sale, and possessory management through a receiver.   6–28

The secured creditor may be required to comply with securities regulation on a sale, e.g. if there is an offer or sale to the public. If a large holding of equity securities is involved, then in England the provisions of the Take-over Code may come into operation, e.g. a compulsory offers for all the equity securities of the company by a person who acquires 30 per cent of the company. The following topics may also be relevant:

- Freezes on the enforcement of security under bankruptcy and rehabilitation rules: chapter 11

- Compulsory grace periods before enforcement action may be taken: para 10–15 *et seq*

- Rights of an insolvency administrator to substitute collateral on a rehabilitation proceeding: chapter 11.

Priorities

Priorities are reviewed generally in chapter 12. The following priority contests should be borne in mind: 6–29

- The priority of the security over preferential creditors, e.g. employee wages and taxes

- The ability of the insolvency administrator to raise super-priority moratorium loans priming existing security

- The priority of the security over prior and subsequent mortgagees and purchasers or optionholders. The basic rule for negotiable instruments is that a holder in due course has an absolute priority, provided that the instrument is not forged or materially altered. In the case of certificated securities, priorities tend to depend upon first in time, displaced by a bona fide purchaser or mortgagee who acquires the legal estate without notice and for value, and (unusually) displaced by first to register or file in a public bureau. In England, it is not possible for companies to record equitable mortgages on the share register (although there is some case-law dealing with the situation when they in fact do so), but a creditor may obtain a stop notice which involves a court affidavit served on the company and which obliges the company to give eight days notice to the mortgagee of any proposed transfer so that the mortgagee has time to block it by applying to the court: see RSC 50, r 11. This is an extremely cumbersome process.

— Unauthorised sales by agents or brokers

— The priority of future advances made by a first mortgagee over a second mortgage: para 12–21 *et seq*

— Set-off by the issuer of debt securities. Generally debt securities will contain a prohibition on the exercise by the issuer of set-offs. In the case of negotiable securities, normally an issuer cannot raise set-offs against holders in due course.

— Liens arising by operation of law. That can be significant in relation to securities, notably a vendor's lien (arising in clearing systems), a custodian's lien, an issuer's lien (not usually permitted by listing rules), and a broker's lien.

As to consolidation, see para 8–19, and as to marshalling, see para 10–17 *et seq.*

Conflict of laws

For a short review of the principle conflict of laws issues, see chapter 13.

Security interests over securities deposited with custodians

Reasons for depositories

6–30   The main purposes of depositing securities with a depository are:

— To reduce the risk of loss or theft, especially in the case of negotiable securities. A thief of a negotiable security can confer good title on a holder in due course. The use of a depository reduces insurance costs.

- To delegate to the depository the duty (a) to collect payments on the securities, e.g. by presenting them for payment at the offices of the paying agents, and (b) to exercise voting rights as instructed by the depositor.

- To facilitate transfers. If transferor and transferee both use the same depository, a security can be transferred from one account to the other in the books of the depository without physical delivery. Physical delivery is expensive, cumbersome, dangerous and generally impracticable. There would be a paperwork crisis. In a depository system, the physical securities can stay where they are – in the vault – and need not be moved. It is also easier to arrange payment against transfer, thereby mitigating the risk that the seller transfers title and the buyer becomes bankrupt before payment of the price. In practice, this is now the most important reason for the use of custodians.

Summary of types of claim against depository

Probably most investment securities are deposited with custodians, very often on the basis that they are fungible, i.e. the custodian need not return the identical securities, but rather equivalent securities. The question then arises as to how the owner of the securities can create a security interest over them and the nature of the right which is the subject of the security interest.   6–31

The claim against the custodian might be:

- a proprietary claim for specific securities;

- a proprietary claim for a share in a pool of securities, but not specific securities;

- a non-proprietary debt claim.

The nature of the claim depends upon:

- whether the jurisdiction recognises the trust;

- whether the securities are fungible;

- whether the custodian has the right to use the securities as his own, subject to a duty to return equivalent securities.

Summary of legal aspects

By way of summary, in most civil code jurisdictions, the trust is not recognised and it is not possible to pledge a proprietary interest in fungibles (because the doctrine of specificity requires that an asset transferred or   6–32 pledged must be specifically identified, e.g. by the number of the certificates). Therefore, the claim of the depositor against the custodian is at best a debt claim and, if it can be pledged at all, must be transferred and perfected by the mode applicable to the pledge of debt claims, e.g. formal notification of the pledge to the custodian in Napoleonic countries and Japan. For a list, see para 4–5 *et seq.* This has been changed by statute in some jurisdictions.

In common law jurisdictions, the trust is recognised and it is possible to transfer an interest in a pool of fungible assets. Hence the claim of the depositor against the custodian is a proprietary claim and is transferred and perfected by the mode applicable to charge over interests under a trust.

In all countries, if the custodian has the right to use the deposited securities as his own, subject to a duty to return equivalent securities for cash, then the depositor has transferred the property to the custodian and has only a debt claim.

Wherever the depositor has only a debt claim, he is exposed to the insolvency of the custodian and cannot claim the securities he deposited in kind ahead of the other creditors of the custodian. He can only claim as an unsecured creditor for his loss. This affects the value of the asset as suitable risk-free collateral.

There can be, and often is, a chain of custodians, stacked in tiers. For example, the depositor, such as a pension fund, deposits securities with his bank in London who deposits them with a custodian operating an international clearing system, such as Euroclear in Brussels who deposits them with a sub-custodian in the country of the currency, e.g. a French bank who deposits them with a custodian operating a local clearing system, namely SICOVAM in France.

If the original depositor at the head of the ladder pledges his "securities", the key question is the nature of the asset he is pledging. There is also the subsidiary question of whether he, and therefore the pledgee, run the risk of the insolvency of a sub-custodian; this is no greater than the risk that depositors accept on routine bank accounts.

The final piece to be added to the jigsaw is the type of investment security. They may be (a) negotiable securities payable to bearer and transferable by delivery, (b) certificated securities represented by a certificate where the holder is registered as the holder in a register of the securities maintained by or on behalf of the issuer, or (c) uncertificated or "dematerialised" securities where the holder does not have a certificate but his ownership is recorded in a register maintained by or on behalf of the issuer.

6–33   In summary, the type of security affects how it is pledged and the manner of perfection of the pledge. In civilian countries, the pledgee must take possession of negotiable securities and must be registered as holder, or noted as pledgee, in the books of the issuer in the case of ordinary transferable securities and take possession of any certificates. In some Germanic countries, the non-possessory fiduciary transfer is available. In English-based countries, possession or registration is not necessary for the validity of a pledge on the bankruptcy of the pledgor, but sometimes (and unusually) the publicity of possession is replaced by the publicity of registration or filing: para 9–34 *et seq*.

If the pledgor has the right to deal in or substitute securities, this may destroy the pledge in civilian countries or convert it into a registrable floating charge in English-based countries. This aspect has already been considered: para 6–13.

It will therefore be seen that the presence of custodians greatly increases the complications and, in order to analyse the relationships, it is necessary to review the comparative legal theory in relation to:

— bailment to or custodianship of securities and the trust;

— fungibility;

— transfers of ownership to a custodian by conferring a right to use the property as its own.

Ownership of securities held by custodians

Trust recognition As frequently noted in this series of works, a fundamental   6–34 distinction between common law and civil code jurisdictions is the attitude to the trust. Under a trust, the legal holder (the possessor, or nominal or registered holder) is a trustee and the real owner is the beneficiary. On the insolvency of the trustee, the securities belong to the beneficiary who can insist on their return in full. In most civil code countries, the securities are deemed to belong to the trustee and so go to his creditors. The effect is that the true owner or beneficiary is expropriated and left with a mere debt claim against the custodian which is usually valueless. The securities can also be attached by judgment creditors of the custodian, i.e. the trust is invalid against the trustee's creditors.

To avoid this, in civilian countries, negotiable securities held by the custodian must be physically segregated and marked as belonging to the true owner and registered securities must be registered in the name of the beneficial owner (not the custodian) in the books of the issuer of the securities (or the beneficial ownership noted), unless there is a statute disapplying the rule.

Often the solvency risk of the custodian is not crucial since they are often banks or other credit-worthy institutions: most pledgees are willing to take the risk of leading banks, e.g. where they take a security interest over an ordinary bank deposit. But the characterisation of the rights of the investor is fundamentally important for the mode of transfer or charge of the investor's interest. If the investor is merely a creditor of the custodian who does not hold in trust for him, then transfers and charges must comply with the rules applicable to transfers and charges of debts as opposed to negotiable securities. In some countries, e.g. France, Luxembourg, Japan and South Korea, notice (often in prescribed form) of the transfer or charge is required for the validity of the transfer or charge of a debt against the creditors of the transferor or chargor: para 4–4 *et seq*. The transaction fails on the insolvency of the transferor or chargor and the debt goes to his creditors. Attaching creditors of the transferor or chargor can ignore the transaction and attach the claim. A charge is therefore useless, unless the formality is complied with. Whether these rules applicable to debts would be applied to debt claims against custodians is a matter for further research, but it is believed that there is little case law and so reduced predictability.

6–35 **Forms of trust of securities** In common law countries, the trust is highly flexible. Securities may be held by the holder in trust in three main forms:

1.   The custodian holds specific identifiable securities in trust for each holder, e.g. bonds numbered 1 to 100 in trust for investor A.

2.   The custodian holds specific identifiable securities in partitioned shares for each holder. Thus if a custodian holds 100 bonds for 20 holders, each holder may have a one-twentieth share of each specific bond. This form is unusual.

3.   The custodian holds the securities as a pool for all holders. A unit trust for investors is an analogy. No holder has a specific interest in any specific security, but only a pro rata share of the pool. If the custodian becomes insolvent, the securities must be sold and each holder receives his pro rata share of the proceeds. The custodian holds those proceeds in trust so they do not go to the custodian's creditors. This arrangement is common for fungible securities.

The result, therefore, is that the claim which is pledged is a proprietary interest under a trust – a general intangible. These claims may be charged in English-based countries (writing is usually required under equivalents of the Law of Property Act 1925 s 53), and the charge would not normally require registration unless it is a floating charge or a charge to secure an issue of debentures: para 9–34 *et seq*. The proprietary claim is clearly not within the registrable head of "book debts" – it is not a debt. The perfection requirements under the American UCC Arts 8, 9 and the new Art 8A and under the Canadian Personal Property Security Acts are different.

Statutory custodian trusts

Some civil code countries have statutes which effectively give depositors a   6–36
proprietary claim for securities held by custodians so as to protect investors
against the insolvency of the custodian and to facilitate transfers. Two of
these statutes are:

– The Belgian Royal Decree No 62 of November 10, 1967 "Facilitating
   the Circulation of Securities in favour of all members of a *Caisse Inter-
   professionale de Depots et de Virements de Titres NV*" (CIK) which
   includes the Euroclear System. Pledges over Euroclear Securities are
   dealt with at para 6–46 *et seq* below.

– The Luxembourg Grand-Ducal Decree of February 17, 1971, which
   applies to Cedel and which is similar to the Belgian Decree.

The establishment of central depositories to hold fungible securities on
trust for the depositors who have a proprietary claim for the securities is
now widespread in a large number of countries which otherwise could not
permit the proprietary claim, either because of non-recognition of the trust,
or because fungibility destroys ownership (by reason of the doctrine of specificity requiring securities to be specifically segregated and marked for
which purpose they have to be specifically identified by number and name.

Thus Germany has a system of co-ownership of a collective mass of fun-   6–37
gible securities which fall within the definition in the Custody Act 1937
(*Depotgesetz*) and which are deposited with central depositories. This is
known as *Sammelverwahrung* (which must be agreed to by the depositor in
writing and which is the most usual form) and is distinguished from *Sonder-
verwahrung* (specific deposit) where the custodian must segregate and mark
specific securities as belonging to the depositor, and from *uneigentliche Verwahrung* (irregular deposit) where the depositor agrees in writing that the
custodian will have title to the securities in which event he has merely an
unsecured non-proprietary claim for the return of equivalent securities.

Dematerialised securities issued by public bodies in Germany and evidenced by book entry in a register kept by an official body in Germany are
transferable and capable of pledge in the same way as bearer securities kept
in safe custody by German banks and are protected against the bankruptcy
of the accounting bank in the same way as securities which have been
deposited under the safe custody system. This applies only to securities of
the German bodies concerned and does not apply to unregistered issues of
other German issuers or to foreign issuers.

Austria has a similar system to the German *Depotgesetz* under the Aus-   6–38
trian *Depotgesetz* 1969. By *Depotgesetz* 1969 s 23 the depositor has a

priority claim in the bankruptcy of the custodian bank if the depositor's rights are infringed by unlawful act, e.g. alienation or encumbrance of the securities or negligent administration, provided the depositor performs any unperformed obligation on his side (e.g. payment of fees) within one week of notification.

Other schemes, similar or dissimilar, include:

– the Netherlands *"Necigef"* created by the Securities Giro Act 1977 for bearer securities;

– the Danish *VaerdipapirCentralen* for Danish securities;

– the Korea Securities Depository Corporation for certain South Korean securities (but the securities must be held in the name of the real owner and there appears to be no fungibility regime);

– securities deposited with authorised Portuguese financial intermediaries pursuant to Arts 78 and 79 of the Securities Code;

– stock exchange schemes in Argentina and Brazil.

Some Latin American countries (which otherwise do not recognise the trust) have enacted special statutes whereby property deposits with banks for safe custody are held in trust, e.g. Venezuela.

6–39   Central depositories in common law countries do not generally need special statutes to confer the proprietary remedies on insolvency, even if the securities are fungible. Examples are the US Depository Trust Company, the Singapore Central Depository (Pte) Ltd and The Canadian Depository for Securities Ltd, although sometimes there is special legislation governing the duties of the depository.

But, apart from these special statutes, the general rule in the civil countries is that lack of recording in the name of the true beneficial owner in the books of the issuer and any fungibility destroy the true owner's ownership on the custodian's bankruptcy – fungibility because, as discussed below, it is then impossible to identify the true owner's specific property. This is the general position in, for example, Argentina, Belgium, Chile, Denmark, Indonesia, Korea, Luxembourg, Mexico, the Netherlands, Portugal and Venezuela.

Fungibility

6–40   Securities are fungible if they have exactly the same terms, e.g. as to interest, redemption, covenants, events of default and voting rights.

Securities of the same issue are usually fungible, even if they are numbered. Securities of different issues can be fungible, even though the issue dates are different, provided their terms are the same. Thus they must have the same redemption date.

If the custodian can treat the securities as fungible then there is less administration in segregating specific securities and allocating them to a specific investor and a security can be transferred by a mere book-entry in the books of the custodian. In view of the vast number of securities now dealt in, fungibility is essential. But some consequences of fungibility are:

— If the **custodian can use the securities as his own**, subject to replacement, the investor's ownership may be replaced by a debt claim against the custodian and the investor takes the risk of the custodian's insolvency: see below.

— In some civil code states which adhere to the doctrine of specificity, fungibility is fatal to the investor's **ownership** because it is no longer possible for the custodian to mark the specific securities as belonging to the investor so that the "false wealth" doctrine is contravened, nor is it possible to transfer securities without identifying them. The investor then becomes a creditor of the custodian and he loses his proprietary *in rem* claim. Therefore, the claim must be pledged by the mode applicable to debt claims, e.g. formal notification to the custodian as debtor in many Napoleonic countries. Apart from that, there is often no method of pledging an unidentified asset so that the pledge is impossible. The pledgor would have to recover the securities from the custodian if they are negotiable and give possession of them to the pledgee, or, if they are registered securities, the pledgee would have to be registered as the holder of (or his pledge noted against) specific securities in the register maintained by or on behalf of the issuer. Belgian and Luxembourg statutes override these problems in the case of Euroclear and Cedel so that fungibility does not destroy ownership or prevent transfers: each investor has a proprietary share in the securities pro rata. Austria, Germany, Denmark and the Netherlands have similar statutes which apply only to a defined class of securities.

— If securities are **partly redeemed** by the issuer, the investor must have some agreement with the custodian as to whose securities are deemed to be redeemed. This could be pro rata or, more commonly, determined by drawings by lot by the custodian.

— If securities are **lost, destroyed or counterfeit**, then the loss must also be apportioned amongst the depositors. In England, in the absence of agreement, the loss is shared pro rata: *Gill and Duffus (Liverpool) Ltd v Scruttons Ltd* [1953] 2 All ER 977 (bags of chestnuts burst in a ship and became commingled); *Spence v Union Marine Ins Co Ltd* (1868) LR 3

CP 427 (obliteration of identification marks on goods on board ship). Euroclear and Cedel provide for losses to be apportioned pro rata.

Custodian has right to use securities as his own

6–41 It seems to be the case in most developed legal systems that the beneficiary loses his proprietary in rem interest if the custodian can use the securities as his own, e.g. by borrowing them or selling them, even if the custodian must substitute equivalent securities or replace them with cash. The right of the custodian to treat the securities as his own property is inconsistent with the investor's ownership.

This principle has been established in common law countries in two main contexts.

The first line of cases is where a farmer deposits his grain with a silo owner or miller on terms that the custodian can use the grain as his own on the basis that he either returns equivalent grain or money. The farmer loses his property ownership in the grain and becomes a creditor of the miller. See, e.g. *South Australia Insurance Co v Randell* (1869) LR 3 PC 101; *Lawlor v Nicol* (1898) 12 Man LR 224 (Manitoba); *Chapman Bros v Verco Bros* (1933) 49 CLR 306; *Farnsworth v Federal Commissioner of Taxation* (1949) 78 CLR 504. But the farmer does not lose the property merely because the custodian has a right to substitute: *Mercer v Craven Grain Storage Ltd.*, March 17, 1994, HL.

6–42 The second line of cases is where an agent collects proceeds of sale or revenues on behalf of his principal and is allowed to credit the moneys to his own account without segregation and use them as his own, provided he accounts to his principal for an equal amount. The agent is debtor to his principal and does not hold the benefit of the bank account in trust for his principal. See, e.g. *Henry v Hammond* [1913] 2 KB 515; *Neste Oy v Lloyds Bank PLC* [1983] 2 Lloyds LR 152. The same principle has been established by numerous cases in relation to deposits with banks (who are debtors to their depositors), subscription moneys for securities, proceeds of sale under title retention clauses, and landlord caution moneys. The copious English and American case law also shows that, even if the custodian or sub-custodian can convert the proprietary claim into a debt claim, his authority to do so terminates as soon as the depositor or custodian or sub-custodian stops business or becomes judicially insolvent, because this must inevitably determine the right of whoever is holding the securities to deal with them as his own. Thereafter he holds the securities, and any claims for proceeds not yet received, in trust for the ultimate depositor. The case law is further discussed elsewhere in this series of works.

The point usually arises in relation to fungible assets, such as grain, metal, commodities, money – or equivalent securities – because they lend themselves to substitution.

One may remark parenthetically that there seems no reason in principle in England why the parties should not agree that the beneficiary does not lose ownership so long as no substitution has taken place and that the trust will fix on to replacement securities immediately on substitution by the custodian: consider the grain case *Mercer v Craven Grain Storage*, March 17, 1994, HL.

However, if the investor loses ownership by virtue of this rule, then he is a 6–43 creditor of the custodian and exposed to the insolvency of the custodian; purchasers of the securities from the custodian acquire good title since the custodian is authorised to dispose of them; and (more importantly in our context) sales and charges over the investor's rights against the custodian must comply with the rules applicable to assignments or charges of contract debts – like assignments of bank deposits.

Hence the agreement with the custodian must not give the custodian rights of use or substitution of the securities in favour of the custodian personally. It is not fatal, at least in common law countries recognising trusts, that the custodian can substitute securities with those of other beneficiaries, so long as they are not the custodian's, since a trust of a fungible or fluctuating pool of assets in pro rata shares for the investors without segregation of identifiable securities to specific investors is possible. A similar result has been achieved by the Belgian and Luxembourg statutes in favour of Euroclear and Cedel.

If the custodian deliberately removes the investor's securities without the investor's consent, the investor in common law countries has a right to trace the securities, including any money into which they are converted, as an in rem claim, except into the hands of a bona fide purchaser for value without notice. The tracing remedy – which defeats the custodian's insolvency – is not available in many, if not most, civilian jurisdictions.

Pledges over securities

The effect of these rules can be summed up as follows. 6–44

Common law countries In common law countries, if the depositor has a proprietary claim under a trust against his immediate custodian for a share in non-specific fungible securities, then this should be characterised as an intangible movable which is located for the purpose of private international law at the office of the custodian where the securities are primarily recoverable, and which can be assigned by way of security. In English-based countries, possession is not necessary and it is suggested that there should not usually be a requirement for the registration of corporate charges, unless the right to deal converts the charge into a floating charge or the charge is to secure an issue of debentures. Note that the depositor is not transferring the specific securities, but rather his beneficial ownership under a trust of fungible securities – one does not see through the trust. If the securities are fungible, one is clearly not charging specific securities because it is impossible to point to any security as being subject to the charge. The analysis might be different if the securities are not fungible, but specific.

If the securities have been deposited by the custodian with a sub-custodian, the analysis is similar. The custodian has either a proprietary claim or a debt claim against the sub-custodian, depending on the application of the rules discussed above, but, whatever it is, this is the claim which the custodian holds on trust for the depositor. The asset pledged is still the depositor's beneficial interest under the trust of the claim held by the custodian against the sub-custodian.

For the position under revisions to the UCC in the United States proposed in 1994, see para 9–24A.

6–45   **Civil code countries** In traditional civil code countries in the absence of a statute, the pledge must be a possessory pledge. In the case of negotiable securities, the depositor must either obtain the securities from the custodian and give possession of them to the pledgee, or the custodian, who must be independent of the pledgor, must acknowledge to the pledgor that he holds the securities for the benefit of the pledgee, segregate them accordingly and mark them as belonging to the pledgee. If the securities are registered securities, the pledgee must either be registered as the holder of the securities in the register kept by or on behalf of the issuer or (if so allowed) have his pledge noted in that register, and, in both cases, must take possession of any certificates evidencing the securities. Clearly these steps are impracticable in many cases, especially if the securities are with sub-custodians, and impossible if the securities are fungible.

In the case of the Germanic fiduciary transfer countries, this dispossession should not be necessary.

If on the other hand, the depositor's claim is a debt and not a proprietary claim against the custodian, then that claim must be pledged by the manner applicable to debt claims: in many Napoleonic countries and Japan (but not the Germanic countries) this may require abstract dispossession of the pledgor by formal notice in prescribed form given to the custodian as debtor.

Where the securities are with sub-custodians, then the relevant method must be followed – either actual possession or registration of the title to the securities, or assignment of a debt claim against the custodian.

That, at least, is the classic civilian position. Needless to say, collateral over securities would be impossible if this traditional view were insisted upon. Hence there are numerous statutory and other relaxations and it is proposed to examine one of the most important of these by way of illustration – Euroclear.

Pledges over securities with Euroclear

Euroclear System

The Brussels branch of Morgan Guaranty Trust Company of New York,   6–46 through its Euroclear Operations Centre located in Brussels ("MGT"), acts as a depository for eligible securities, including euro-debt securities, such as eurobonds and euronotes, and also equities. Many are negotiable securities payable to bearer but the System includes global, domestic, registered and dematerialised securities. As at December 31, 1993, the total value of securities deposited with MGT was US$1,471 billion. As at that date, there were more than 2,500 depositors, called participants.

The corporate structure for the Euroclear System is as follows:

– Euroclear Clearance System plc ("ECS PLC") is an English public company owned by 124 financial institutions. This company owns the rights to the Euroclear System.

– Euroclear Clearance System Société Cooperative ("ECS Coop") is a Belgian cooperative owned as to 87.5 per cent by ECS PLC and as to the 12.5 per cent by the participants. ECS PLC has granted ECS Coop a licence to use the rights pertaining to the Euroclear System.

– ECS Coop has in turn appointed MGT as operator of the system.

– In acting as operator of the Euroclear System, MGT acts as principal (a *commissionaire* of the ECS Co-op under Belgian law). The custodian of the securities is Morgan Guaranty Trust Company of New York through its Brussels office. ECS Coop is not the depository, nor is ECS PLC. The rights of the depositor-Participants are solely against MGT. A depositor wishing to use the depository services of MGT-EOC is bound by the Terms and Conditions Governing Use of Euroclear (revised as of December 1, 1982) and by supplemental Operating Procedures ("Euroclear Terms and Conditions").

Some of what is said in this section about the Euroclear System applies in a general, but not identical, way to Cedel founded in 1972, located in Luxembourg and owned by about 100 financial institutions. Cedel is governed by the Luxembourg Grand-Ducal Decree of February 17, 1971, which is similar to the Belgian Royal Decree discussed below. There are numerous detailed differences.

Belgian position apart from statute

6–47 Belgian law generally follows the "false wealth" rule, adheres to the doctrine of specificity, and usually requires possessory pledges of securities. But the case law erosions are significant. Taking these points in turn:

– Belgian law requires that securities in the reputed ownership of a person are treated as belonging to him on bankruptcy. Hence Belgium does not recognise the **trust** whereby securities held legally by a depository may be owned beneficially by the depositor. If the trust is not recognised, the claim against the custodian is a debt claim which must be assigned. The formal *huissier* notification to debtors of assignments under CC Art 1690 was abolished in 1994. As a lesser matter, if the depository becomes insolvent, the securities belong to the bankrupt estate of the depository and are used to pay his creditors.

– Apart from special statutes Belgian law generally adheres to the **doctrine of specificity** for non-fungible securities whereby the securities belonging to each depositor must be specifically identified, e.g. by the number of each certificate. This prevents fungibility and results in the inconvenience that the depository cannot pool securities of the same issuer which have the same terms (e.g. as to interest, redemption, covenants, events of default and voting rights), but must allocate specific securities to specific depositors. Transfers must be by physical delivery of specific securities, not by book entry.

– Belgian law usually requires that a security interest over securities must be a **possessory pledge**, i.e. the pledgee (or his agent) must have physical possession of negotiable securities and, in the case of registered securities, must be registered as pledgee of the securities (or his pledge registered) in the books of the issuer: see the Law of May 5, 1872, as modified by Royal Decree No 300 of March 30, 1936.

Belgian Royal Decree No 62 of November 10, 1967

6–48 To enable Belgium to establish a proper depository and clearance system for securities, the Belgian Royal Decree No 62 of November 10, 1967, was passed. The original impetus of the Royal Decree was to facilitate the transfer of securities kept with professional intermediaries (such as brokers) which, until then, had to be transferred by physical delivery. This was unsafe, expensive and slow and put Belgium at a competitive disadvantage. But this would be avoided if securities could be credited to an account with the broker or other intermediary without any need to identify them by their individual serial numbers and to transfer them by mere book-entries in the books of the custodian. This meant that the securities had to be fungible which would have destroyed the depositor's ownership, so the legislature resolved to give the depositor the same proprietary rights as he would have had if the securities had been identified and segregated. The result was a statute which also enabled Belgium to host a depository and clearance system for the new eurobond markets.

As amended by laws of April 10, 1973, December 4, 1990 and August 6, 1993, this Decree ("the 1967 Decree") in effect:

– gives proprietary rights to securities deposited with a qualifying depository in favour of the depositors so that the depositor is not a mere creditor of the depository: see Arts 10 and 13;

– provides that the proprietary rights are not invalidated by the securities being treated as fungible, so that the depository can pool all fungible securities and the depositors have co-proprietary rights in the notional pool of the same securities pro rata (see Arts 4, 10 and 13). If securities are lost, then the rights of the co-proprietors abate pari passu: see Art 10;

– provides for the constitution of commercial pledges by the establishment in the books of the depository of a special account to which the pledged fungible securities are credited, without specifically identifying them by their certificate numbers (Art 5).

In order to have the benefit of these provisions, the securities must either   6–49
be deposited with a special Belgian company, Caisse Interprofessionelle des Dépôts et de Virements de Titres ("CIK"), or an "affiliate" of the CIK, and the depositor with an affiliate must agree to the fungibility regime. A depository satisfying prescribed qualifications becomes an affiliate by making appropriate application. MGT is such an affiliate. Depositors agree to the fungibility regime under the Euroclear Terms and Conditions. MGT opens a Securities Clearance Account and a Cash Account in the name of the depositors and the securities are credited to the Securities Clearance Account.

The effect therefore is that participant depositors have co-proprietary rights pro rata to their deposited securities. The claims are not debt claims and are transferred by book entry without further formality.

On the insolvency of MGT as depository, the securities would not go to the creditors of MGT, nor can those securities be attached by creditors of

MGT: see Art 9. Of course, bank depositors are creditors of the bank, and hence inevitably take the insolvency risk of their banks (subject to deposit protection schemes). They are generally content to do so and this is not a problem with leading banks. The principal importance of the characterisation in the present context is the nature of the property which is being charged and its location. Conceptual characterisation is important because it dictates the method of obtaining a security interest.

Nature of the interest of depositors

6—50 Each depositor has a proprietary interest, shared with other depositors of the same security, in all the securities of that class deposited with MGT. MGT is obliged to deliver securities of that class to the depositors, subject to the Euroclear Terms and Conditions. These securities need not be the specific securities originally deposited, so long as they are equivalent securities. The depositor's entitlement is recorded by naming him in the books of MGT as the holder of a Securities Clearance Account.

Hence the depositor's interest is a shared co-proprietary interest in a mass of fungible securities which is realised by an obligation on MGT to deliver that mass to the depositors pro rata and which is evidenced by entries in the depositor's Securities Clearance Accounts. For conflict of law purposes, this asset should be characterised as a registered intangible movable.

Pledges over securities held in the Euroclear System

6—51 As mentioned, any security interest over securities held in the Euroclear System is a security interest over the co-proprietary rights of the pledgor-depositor against MGT, as evidenced by the entry in his Securities Clearance Account. The pledge is not over the securities themselves. This must inevitably be the case since it is not usually possible to identify any specific security which is the subject of the pledge. Hence the procedures for obtaining possessory pledges of specific securities should not apply.

The conflicts of laws rules of many developed nations, including England, generally give paramountcy to the law of the situation of the property in determining whether one can, and how, one transfers the property, e.g. by the creation of a security interest. Intangible property can have no physical habitation, and so its location must be artificial or abstract. It is thought that this location is in Belgium. The obligation to deliver is owed by a custodian in Belgium and is primarily enforceable there. The account is located in Belgium. It is immaterial that the securities may be physically located in vaults abroad or being transported in a security van. The Euroclear Terms and Conditions are governed by Belgian law and the Decree which establishes the property interest is a Belgian statute.

Hitherto, market participants (other than MGT in its capacity as banker for the System) have pledged securities held in the Euroclear System securities outside Art 5 without using a special pledge account. Instead the pledgor has executed an ordinary security agreement and instructed MGT to transfer the securities concerned into the name of the pledgee who must also be a participant. The pledgee therefore appears as a transferee and as the owner of the securities, although it is clear that, as between pledgor and pledgee, the transaction is a security transaction and not a sale.

It is difficult to see what else a pledgee could possibly do to get better possession of the claim against MGT or to disposses the pledgor. Nevertheless this transaction is sometimes viewed with unease perhaps because these co-proprietary rights are unfamiliar to Belgian law and are a creature of the Royal Decree, and because the ordinary law of commercial pledge does not clearly apply to a pledge of a proprietary interest in fungibles.   6–52

In any event the Royal Decree itself provides a specific method in Art 5 of creating security interests. As mentioned, this involves the opening of a special pledge account in the books of MGT to which the pledged securities are transferred. This is how the debtor is dispossessed. Article 5 states that the charge constituted by the inscription of the securities (identified solely by nature, not number) in the special account is valid against third parties without other formality. If one wants certainty, there it is. It would therefore seem prudent to adopt the Art 5 procedure.

Luxembourg law also requires a possessory pledge of securities. But the Grand-Ducal Decree benefiting Cedel permits a pledge to be perfected if the securities are transferred, without being identified by number, to an account designated in the books of the depository as pledged.   6–53

But to return to Belgium. The security agreement should ideally grant the security over the co-proprietary rights, credited to the special pledge account, not the securities themselves. But usually it will be clear what is meant.

In any event, it seems clear that the formalities for the creation of security over debts and other contract claims do not apply. In accordance with CC Art 1690 a security assignment of a debt is valid against creditors of the assignor by the execution of the pledge agreement and, since 1994, no *huissier* notification to the debtor is required for validity on the assignor's bankruptcy. However, to be valid against the debtor (which, in the context of the Euroclear System, would be MGT), the assignment has to be notified in writing to, or recognised by, the debtor. The recognition by the debtor is not subject to any particular form: it may be evidenced by its books and records or by other documents issued by the debtor, such as statements of accounts. But this is irrelevant because the claim of participants against MGT, as indicated by credits to a securities clearance account, are not mere debt claims, but are co-proprietary claims.

A possible alternative method of creating a pledge without taking the securities out of the Euroclear System would be for the depositor to transfer his securities absolutely to an external custodian and to pledge that claim (which could be proprietary or a debt claim in accordance with the principles discussed above). See para 6–44.

Euroclear sub-custodians

6–54   A majority of the securities are not in fact physically deposited with MGT in Brussels but are located with sub-custodians abroad. Often the sub-custodians have deposited the securities with local clearing systems so that there are tiers of custodians with MGT as head custodian, the foreign depository as sub-custodian and the foreign depository system as sub-sub-custodian.

The reason that foreign sub-custodians are used is usually that the securities are denominated in the currency of the country of the securities and it is convenient to have the securities situated locally so that they can be presented to local paying agents for payment. Alternatively, regardless of the currency, the paying agents may be located outside Belgium.

The initial question is the nature of MGT's rights as depository against sub-custodians. These could be proprietary rights and debt claims as discussed above, depending on local rules as to reputed ownership, fungibility and the ability of the depository to use the securities as its own.

The Royal Decree is purely a Belgian decree and cannot create proprietary rights over securities situated abroad. Hence the rights against sub-custodians in relation to these securities will often be governed by the law of the place where the sub-custodian or the securities are situate.

6–55   It is understood that MGT have obtained legal opinions that MGT would, as depository, have proprietary rights to the securities deposited with sub-custodians and sub-sub-custodians by reason of the adoption of the necessary procedures to take the securities out of the reputed ownership of the sub-custodians, where this is required.

MGT obviously cannot warrant that it would have proprietary claims against sub-custodians. It is not realistic for pledgees to check the position specifically on each occasion, but many depositors may not be concerned with the credit risk on sub-custodians by reason of the status of the sub-custodians.

Further, it is understood that in certain cases MGT has been advised that creditors of MGT would not be able to attach the benefit of securities deposited with sub-custodians for a debt owed by MGT. In other words they are not treated as assets of MGT as the beneficiary, but rather as the assets of the ultimate depositors. This is hardly a major issue in the case of a leading bank.

In any event, it seems clear that the Euroclear assets which are being pledged by the depositor within the Euroclear System are the co-proprietary rights which are located in Belgium and created by the Royal Decree. The pledged assets are not the securities themselves. Hence any requirements for possessory pledges of the securities themselves according to the lex situs or physical or registered location of the securities should not apply. One does not see through the "trust" to the ultimate securities located with sub-custodians.

One reason that one does not see-through the co-proprietary rights against MGT to the actual securities is that the actual securities are not identified because of the fungibility system so that one could not point to a particular security located in a vault in Japan, Italy or Spain as being the subject of the pledge. Therefore, the situation of the pledged property should remain in Belgium for transfer purposes and not where the securities are actually located and it is that asset which is pledged, not the securities.

Other matters

Other matters to be considered in relation to Euroclear relate to security   6–56
generally. They include:

– Whether a **pledgor's right to deal** with pledged securities or rights of substitution would affect the pledge: para 6–17

– The procedures for creating security over **cash proceeds** from the securities, e.g. interest payments, redemption payments and sale proceeds. *Huissier* notification to MGT is not necessary for validity on bankruptcy. Consider whether the Art 5 pledge also catches payments on the securities as accessories (it ought to, but proceeds may be credited to a special account with MGT which must be properly pledged as an ordinary bank deposit).

– The existence of the MGT lien

– **Liens of sub-custodians**

– **Priorities** against subsequent mortgagees and subsequent transferees

– The risk of **loss** of securities and its effect in abating the securities available for the pledge. MGT limits its responsibility under the Euroclear

Terms and Conditions for sub-custodians and is not liable for their insolvency.

- **Formalities.** Notarisation not required in Belgium

- **Debt which can be secured.** In Belgium, the maximum amount secured should be stated. Explicit statement that interest is secured. No interest limit, unless abusive of weaker party (Criminal Code Art 494, CC Art 1907). Mention penalty interest expressly – increase not to exceed $\frac{1}{2}$ per cent p.a. (CC Art 1907.3). No capitalisation of interest unless overdue for at least one year except for current accounts (CC Art 1154). For Belgian pledgors, post-insolvency interest is recoverable but only if collateral is sufficient. Future debts can be secured if determined or determinable, but usually no objection to revolving credits. Pledge must not be indefinite in time, so stipulate fixed time limit for pledges to secure future debt or revolving credits. Secured debt may be in foreign currency. Second priority and third party pledges are allowed.

- **Trustee for security:** not recognised in Belgium

- Bankruptcy freezes on corporate rehabilitation: UK administration (1986), US Chapter 11 (1978), French *redressement judiciaire* (1985), Australian administration (1992), Irish examinership (1990), Canadian commercial reorganisation (1992). Not for Belgian debtors

- No Belgian official consents required

- No Belgian stamp duties or documentary taxes on these transactions

- Repos: note Belgian statutory recognition in Art 23 of the Law of January 2, 1991. Tripartite documentation with MGT is available.

- Application of fraudulent preference and similar doctrines, mainly under bankruptcy laws of pledgor's jurisdiction. Usually new money for contemporaneous security is purified. Main risks are security for pre-existing debt (note top-up collateral) and guarantees supporting security (to extent of "gift" or undervalue element in the guarantee). Chapters 30 to 32.

- Super-priority moratorium loans. No risk in Belgium. But note US Chapter 11 and particularly French *redressement* – forced substitutions possible in both cases. Mainly a question for bankruptcy laws of pledgor's jurisdiction.

- Financial assistance for purpose of acquiring one's own shares: pledgor's jurisdiction. Usually prohibited in English-based systems and under EU Directive. Attacked by conventional preference doctrine in the US under BC 1978 s 547.

– Contractual restrictions, notably negative pledges, borrowing ratios, anti-disposal clauses

– **Filing** and other perfection requirements, e.g. English-style registration of corporate floating charges and charges over book debts; US UCC Arts 8 and 9; Canadian Personal Property Security Acts.

– **Enforcement procedures.** Judicial public auction is common in civil code countries, but less usual for securities and Belgian court can authorise private sale. Private sale/possessory receivership available in Anglo-American countries.

– Any priority of preferential creditors on local bankruptcy of debtor? Employees, taxes, etc. do not rank ahead of Art 5 pledge in Belgian insolvency.

CHAPTER 7

SECURITY OVER INTELLECTUAL PROPERTY

Types of intellectual property

7–1 Intellectual property is the umbrella term used to describe the various legal rights which protect creative and inventive ideas. They give protection to product designs, manufacturing techniques, product names and publicity materials, amongst other things. They can greatly enhance the value of the product and are often the key to the profitability of a business. This section is mainly descriptive of the English position and does no more than provide a few pointers: the subject is a complex one.

The UK rights fall within five main categories, which are briefly summarised below.

Patents Patents protect inventions. The invention must be new, not be obvious, and capable of industrial application. It must involve an inventive step. The patent will be useless as a security if it is set aside.

Patents are registered at the United Kingdom Patent Office and its equivalent throughout the world. Patents usually last for 20 years. During that time, it is only the owner of the patent or its licensees who can exploit the invention. The patent will be infringed by the unauthorised manufacture, sale or importation of the process or products covered by the patent.

7–2 **Copyright** Copyright protects original literary, artistic, musical and dramatic works, sound recordings, films, broadcasts, and cable programmes. The work must be recorded in some material form, whether on paper, in a computer programme, on film or otherwise. Copyright only protects the expression of a particular idea, and not the idea itself. There is no protection if the work is not original. A work is original if it was independently created by the author, and required a certain amount of skill and care to produce.

In the United Kingdom, there is no register in which copyright works are recorded. Instead, in broad terms copyright automatically protects all original works of the types listed, from the date when they are first recorded in a material form.

Copyright in literary, artistic, musical and dramatic works lasts for the life of the author plus 50 years (extended to 70 years under an EC harmonisation directive). Copyright in sound recordings and films lasts for 50 years from when they are made, unless they are released before the end of that period, when the copyright will expire 50 years after the year in which they are released. Copyright in a broadcast or cable programme expires 50 years after the broadcast was made or the programme was included in a cable programme service.

Trade marks Trade marks can be registered or unregistered. If they are   7–3
registered and remain valid, the registration lasts for as long as the renewal fees are paid. If they are unregistered, they are protectable only if they enjoy reputation and goodwill. In England, unregistered marks are protected by an action for passing-off. Other countries may have the equivalent in the form of an action for unfair competition.

Registered marks are infringed by the unauthorised use of the same or a similar mark on the same goods or services as those for which the mark is registered. Unregistered marks are misused and give rise to an action for passing-off if the user makes a misrepresentation that products sold under the mark belong to the proprietor.

Designs Designs can be registered or unregistered. Registered designs protect products which appeal to the eye and last for a maximum of 25 years. They are infringed by reproduction and sale of the registered design. There is no need to prove copying.

Unregistered designs last for a maximum of 15 years. Very broadly speaking, they cover industrial designs. They are infringed by copying or dealing with an infringing article. Licences of right are available to third parties after the first five years.

Confidential information/trade secrets It is possible to prevent misuse of   7–4
confidential information. The owner of the information must show that it is genuinely confidential, that it was given to a third party under terms of confidence and that it is being misused by that person or someone else who knows he is not entitled to it.

Obtaining world-wide protection in these rights is exceedingly expensive. There is no such thing as a world-wide intellectual property right. Patents, registered designs and registered trade marks can be applied for in most countries. But prior disclosure anywhere in the world prevents registration of a patent anywhere. There is an extensive international legal regime in the form of international conventions which, amongst other things, set minimum requirements for intellectual property protection and create a number of international registration procedures. There is a European Patent Convention.

Use of security over intellectual property

7–5 The most common uses of security over intellectual property include specific assignments of intellectual property rights, and charges or assignments of intellectual property rights as part of a general enterprise charge, e.g. a fixed and floating charge in English-based countries.

The security may be given by the owner of the property right or alternatively by a licensee of the property right in which case the licensee assigns the benefit of his rights under the licence. The position regarding cancellation of licences on the insolvency of the licensee or abandonment of the licence by the owner's insolvency representative is discussed elsewhere in this series of works. A security over a licence which can be cancelled on the licensee's insolvency is valueless.

It may also be necessary to create security over physical materials derived from the property right, e.g. computer programs, inventions, films and computer codes. The agreement might also deal with access, e.g. to computer codes.

The efficacy of the security over the rights can be crucial, e.g. where the property right is essential to the continuance of the owner's business, e.g. a trade mark or patent.

Availability

7–6 It seems that it is possible in many developed countries to create security interests over patents which are valid on bankruptcy and against attaching creditors although there is wide divergence in the methods of perfection and of course the position on bankruptcy. But in numerous countries it is not possible to create security over trade marks and copyrights. The objection to security in trade marks is that the whole business must be transferred with the mark since they cannot be separated, as in Germany and Italy. In Taiwan the Trade Mark Law prohibits pledges of trade marks. There are various provisions in the United Kingdom designed to prevent trafficking in trade marks and to ensure that marks are used in relation to goods.

See Kaufman, Simensky and Bryer, "International Law on Security Interests in Intellectual Property," 3 *Journal of International Banking Law* 120 (1991).

Apart from the above, the main restrictions on the grant of security include limitations springing from the property itself, e.g. non-assignability clauses in licences, non-assignability of personal contracts of services, and general contractual restrictions, e.g. negative pledges or anti-disposal clauses in the owner's credit documents.

As already mentioned, the doctrine of specificity in some countries means that it is not possible to grant security over future assets since it is not in such a case possible to identify them with sufficient particularity.

Perfection of security

The methods of perfecting the security so as to constitute security as against   7–7
the bankruptcy trustee and attaching creditors follows the usual lines. In those states which have a strong policy against false wealth and hence a need for the publicisation of non-possessory security, a possessory "pledge" is necessary. In the case of intangible moveables, such as intellectual property rights, this possession can only be artificial or abstract and is usually constituted by the secured creditor being registered as the holder of the right, e.g. in the patent or trade mark registry (in France security interests in a motion picture must be recorded at the National Centre of Cinematography) – or sometimes registered in a special pledge register – and taking possession of any documents evidencing the right. Of course, the position depends upon whether the right is a registered or unregistered right. Publicity by dispossession is the classical view in the Franco-Latin states and also in the Germanic states, but the position may not be insisted upon in all of them. Thus, notably in the Germanic states, it may be possible to use the fiduciary transfer which does not require registration of the secured creditor and which is not registrable in a local register. However in the English-based countries, security can be created over these rights which is effective on bankruptcy and against attaching creditors without registration at the intellectual property registrar, although the holder of the security has a less satisfactory priority as against other purchasers and mortgagees of the property rights, unless he is registered. See, e.g. the Patents Act 1977 ss 32 and 33.

In English-based systems requiring registration of corporate charges at a company's registry, the security generally has to be registered within 21 or 30 days of the creation of security if it is to be valid against the liquidator and creditors of the company. In the United States, UCC Art 9 does not apply to copyrights and the like but instead there is a federal system. If the property right is not governed by the federal system, then the right is a "general intangible" within the UCC Art 9 and a security interest is perfected by central filing, usually. See chapter 9 *et seq*.

Dual registration may be required – once in the register of the right and once in some mercantile or companies register.

Accessories

7–8 Often a security interest will cover accessories to the right, e.g. royalties payable and any licences: assign these specifically. See generally, para 4–8 *et seq*. Consideration should be given to the creditor's interest in any insurances relating to the property, e.g. loss or destruction of the property covered by the right.

Formalities

For the formalities generally necessary for the creation of a security interest in the various countries, see para 8–1 *et seq*. This covers such matters as whether a ceremonial form is essential to the validity of the security on bankruptcy, e.g. deed or notarisation. A deed is not necessary in English-based countries for validity but notarisation may be necessary in Franco-Latin and Germanic countries, except for the Germanic fiduciary transfer.

Permissible secured debt

7–9 As to the question of what debt may be secured by a security interest over these rights, see generally para 8–3 *et seq*. This covers such topics as whether the security interest can secure future debt, e.g. revolving loans, whether a maximum amount must be specified, whether a foreign currency security interest is possible, and various limitations on interest.

Secured creditors

The question of whether there are any limits on permissible secured creditors is discussed at para 8–20 *et seq*. As mentioned, the convenience of a security trustee is not available in most civil countries. Nationality restrictions on the secured creditor should be considered.

Liabilities of secured creditor

7–10 The normal rule for any form of pledged property where the creditor has an element of possession or rights over the property is that the pledgee must take care of the pledged property: see the discussion at paras 4–19 and 6–22 *et seq* in relation to other assets. The security agreement should deal specifically with the responsibilities of the secured creditor, the standard of care expected and in particular the position regarding infringement actions. Often the courts can apportion infringement damages between owners and licensees, and licence agreements commonly deal with the situation expressly.

Preferential transfers

As to when the grant of security may be a voidable preference on the insolvency of the debtor, see chapters 30 to 32. The main areas of risk are security for guarantees which have an element of gift and may therefore be a transaction at an undervalue, security given for pre-existing debt, and a general security which is a bulk transfer.

Miscellaneous

The following topics are studied elsewhere: 7–11

- the enforcement remedies generally available to a secured creditor: chapter 10
- bankruptcy and rehabilitation freezes: chapter 11
- compulsory grace periods on sale: para 10–15
- right of the insolvency administrator to substitute collateral in rehabilitation proceedings: chapter 11
- the main priority contexts: chapter 12. The position as regards licensees and sub-licensees is of particular importance.

Conflict of laws

This topic is discussed generally in chapter 13. The validity of a security is initially determined by the lex situs of the assets in most developed countries and in the case of intellectual property rights which are registered, the lex situs ought to be the jurisdiction where the register is kept. They are national rights and so the situs ought to be the jurisdiction which creates the rights.

CHAPTER 8

FORMALITIES FOR SECURITY AGREEMENTS; SECURED DEBT; SECURED CREDITORS

Formalities

8–1 Formalities for security agreements include such matters as notarisation, deed, writing, and witnesses.

The objectives are: to prevent fraud (e.g. to prove that the transaction is security not sale, to establish authentication of authorities and signature, to evidence the terms); to impress on the debtor the seriousness of transaction for the debtor (debtor-protection); to improve the collection of documentary taxes; and to secure publicity via notarised public deeds (to mitigate the false wealth objection). Amongst these objections, one surmises that the desire to protect the debtor – to convey to him the enormity of what he is doing by means of high ceremony – is the deepest motive.

Hence the formality is typically necessary for the admissibility of the document as evidence, i.e. judicial enforcement. This is shown in the case of many civil code countries by quicker enforcement for notarised agreements. Notarisation is an executive authenticated act not requiring further proof and has presumptions of validity.

The disadvantages of these formalities include inconvenience and expense, e.g. they are impracticable for frequently changing margin collateral. Notarial fees can be high, especially if calculated on a scale according to the amount of the secured debt. Further, it has been found that a rule dedicated to suppress fraud becomes an instrument of fraud because non-compliance with a formality enables debtors to avoid the transaction on a pure technicality.

8–2 The intensity of the formality varies according to the asset which is the subject of the security. In the case of land mortgages, notarisation is required in most civil countries, but common law countries only require writing or may allow the security to be created by mere deposit of title deeds. Nevertheless even here land mortgages are usually in the form of a deed for technical reasons, e.g. this facilitates a private sale and hence corresponds to the civil notarial act which confers an executive or enforceable title. England requires writing for land mortgages by the somewhat pre-Cambrian Law of Property (Miscellaneous Provisions) Act 1989 which thereby prevented informal land mortgages by deposit of title deeds.

As to other collateral, the Franco-Latin group, mainly the French and Spanish countries, generally require notarisation for some assets, e.g. mortgages of ships and aircraft, but in other cases writing is a minimum for admissibility in evidence, and notarisation is highly desirable to avoid delays in court enforcement (because an unnotarised transaction has to be proved in evidence). The common law group, as well as Germanic and Scandinavian countries, do not usually require notarisation or deeds, but sometimes writing is required in non-common law countries, and there is much variation.

One can only illustrate by a few examples. In England a debt can be charged over the telephone, but in France the security requires a notarial deed or a registered private contract notified to the debtor, subject to exceptions, e.g. under the Dailly Act of 1981. Switzerland requires assignments of receivables to be in writing: CO Art 165. English security over investment securities or goods can be created by a mere deposit of the certificates or bill of lading, but in Spain pledges of goods must be set out in a public deed or other public document formalised before an authenticating officer to be valid against third parties.

Permissible secured debt

The issue here is the scope of the debt which may be secured.   8–3

Future debt

If a mortgage cannot secure future debt, this prevents security for current accounts and revolving credits, even if the total amount outstanding remains the same; loans convertible into other currencies by a roll-over; and the addition of new rescue money when a debtor is in financial difficulties.

The objections to tacking on future debt seem to originate from a prejudice against security, the protection of impecunious debtors, and the preservation of assets for unsecured creditors. Sometimes future debt is seen as inhibiting second priority mortgages (this conflicts with the first objection). A roll-over of debt may purify security for pre-existing debt and this is seen as preferential. There may be uncertainty as to the amount secured (though this can be met by the "maximum amount" mortgages).

Probably all developed countries allow security for bank current accounts. Future interest, costs and increases in exposures on market contracts are generally not treated as future debt. Most countries appear to allow security for revolving debt, with common law and Germanic jurisdictions the most flexible. There may be greater reluctance in France and some Latin American countries.

The hazard can be avoided (inconveniently) by making the credit available to a newly-formed subsidiary under the guarantee of the parent which gives the security over the assets for the guarantee. The problem is sometimes dealt with in countries like the Netherlands by the pledgor filling in "pledge forms" and sending them to the pledgee at regular intervals as future debts arise.

Maximum amount mortgages

8–4 There is no objection in many English-based common law countries (including Australia, Israel and New Zealand) to security for an unnamed amount – it is not necessary to state the maximum amount secured as a caution to other creditors nor is it necessary for this amount to be registered. The security can be for all present and future moneys owing to the creditor. But a maximum amount appears to be a requirement in most other developed jurisdictions, including the Germanic, Scandinavian, French and Latin groups. In the Republic of Ireland, since 1990, company registered charges must specify a maximum amount.

The purposes of the maximum amount are: publicity to other creditors of the amounts secured; the encouragement of second mortgages; and (conversely) the protection of impecunious debtors.

The disadvantages are that a maximum amount: inhibits new money, particularly rescue money; inhibits the capitalisation of interest; involves guesswork as to future financing requirements or potential exposures on market contracts; and creates uncertainty for mortgages for foreign currency credits which have to be expressed in local currency.

If there must be separate limits for interest and costs, those have to be estimated. Both can be substantial, especially in countries requiring judicial enforcement leading to long delays.

If the maximum is exceeded, then the expense and inconvenience of a new mortgage is required. The new mortgage may be primed by existing liens or second security.

Usually however the parties can agree any maximum limit and so leave room. But debtors might resist this because a huge amount disclosed on a register might damage their credit unnecessarily.

Foreign currency mortgages

Sometimes (independently of exchange controls) mortgage debts have to be   8–5
expressed in local currency even though the loan itself is denominated in a
foreign currency. If the value of the local currency were to decline relative
to the currency of the loan, the lender might find himself unsecured for the
difference.

One solution is to ensure that the maximum sum secured is large enough
to cover foreseeable fluctuations in exchange rates or alternatively to require
the borrower to provide additional security in the event of a decline, i.e. a
maintenance of value provision (which is of limited value in practice).
Another is to index the local currency amount to the rate of exchange for
the foreign currency of the loan. This revaluation technique is permitted in
France, Italy and Luxembourg. The validity of these devices depends on the
jurisdiction but plainly the absence of a foreign currency mortgage is out of
keeping with the modern world. The rule is usually not insolvency-related
or debtor-protective, but derives either from the legal tender rules designed
to sanction and protect the national currency, or, more simply, from the fact
that the law is out-of-date.

The following are among the countries which may require recordation of
some classes of mortgage in local currency, at least in the case of certain
registrable mortgages (which may include land, ships, aircraft). But the position is thought to be subject to rapid development and this list may be more
than usually inaccurate. Further, it is believed that these rules will not
usually apply to charges over investment securities or contracts or debts, as
in Belgium.

Argentina (sometimes)	Luxembourg (sometimes)
Austria	Mexico
Belgium	Philippines (usually)
Ethiopia	South Africa
Germany	Spain (sometimes)
France	Switzerland (surprisingly)
Italy	Thailand (CCC s 708)
Japan (sometimes)	Venezuela

Sometimes the rule is relaxed if the mortgage is foreign, as in Germany and
Greece.

A related question is whether a judicial sale of an asset may be conducted   8–6
in a foreign currency. One suspects that there will be greater international
objections to this, but data are needed. England allows an admiralty court
sale of a ship in foreign currency. In Greece the public auction of ships and
aircraft may be conducted in a foreign currency by virtue of a 1987 measure

designed to discourage sales abroad to escape Greek exchange controls: Civil Proc Art 1012 para 5.

Whether foreign currency sale proceeds can be repatriated depends on local exchange controls.

Interest and usury

8–7   In many commercial countries, usury laws still limit the rate of interest which may be levied and may also inhibit the capitalisation of interest or the charging of interest on interest. Interest penalties for late payment are everywhere subject to varying degrees of legal hostility.

Usury laws are briefly reviewed in another work in this series. Apart from extortionate credit, England has had no usury laws as such since 1854. As to other countries, Belgium is a useful illustration because it is a highly commercial jurisdiction, which nevertheless has traces of former anti-usury attitudes. In general there is no limit on the interest which can be secured on a mortgage, but the interest must be referred to specifically and, as mentioned below, the interest secured is limited to an amount equal to three years back interest: Art 9, Law of October 25, 1919. Interest may not be charged to the extent that the creditor takes an unfair advantage of the weakness, the needs or the ignorance of the debtor to stipulate an abnormally high interest rate: Criminal Code Art 494, which corresponds roughly to the English objection to extortionate credit bargains. In the case of late payment, CC Art 1907.3 prohibits an increase of interest by more than one-half per cent per year on the principal outstanding. The pledge agreement must explicitly mention default interest. CC Art 1154 prohibits the accrual of interest on interest producing capital unless the interest has been due for at least one year, but this prohibition does not apply to current accounts. There is a similar provision in Germany.

8–8   An additional anti-usury feature in some countries is a limit on the period of back-interest which can be covered by the security. This limitation is probably particularly inflamed by the traditional antipathy to interest. The expiry period can be unrealistic in those states where mortgage enforcement can take years and can have an unfortunate impact on the debtor since the creditor might be incentivised to enforce sooner rather than later. Based on indicative ship and aircraft mortgages, the following are examples of countries which have relatively short periods for recoverable interest:

Two years: Argentina, Egypt, Italy, Panama

Three years: Belgium (Art 6 of Law of October 25, 1919), France (usually), Greece, Luxembourg, Mexico (CC Art 2915)

These limitations do not apply in most English-based jurisdictions: interest recovery is subject to the normal limitation periods, e.g. six or 12 years. Portugal has five years (CC Art 489).

Post-insolvency interest

Under developed bankruptcy laws, interest accruing after the commencement of insolvency proceedings is generally not claimable – at least if there is no surplus. If the security is insufficient, the issue is whether the creditor can take non-claimable post-insolvency interest out of the proceeds of the security first and then claim for uncovered principal or whether he must appropriate only allowable claims to the security in which event he has no claim for post-insolvency interest. In England, the creditor cannot take non-provable interest out first, so that he cannot increase his allowable claim in this way: *Re William Hall (Contractors) Ltd* [1967] 2 All ER 1150. This is also the position in Belgium (BA Art 451.2) and the Netherlands. 8–9

Damages

Whether a mortgage may secure a damages or other unliquidated claim is a matter for investigation. There is generally no objection in English-based states. The question may arise in those states which require stated mortgage amounts or an executive (notarised) title which contemplates debt which is liquidated and certain. 8–10

Second priority security

It is generally the case that, where security is available, the security can be a second priority security ranking after a first security, i.e. it is possible to create double security over the same asset. But it should not be assumed that this is always the case. Panama does not allow a second mortgage of an aircraft. In Spain it is understood that a registered non-possessory chattel mortgage is not available over property which has already been mortgaged. This conceptual obstacle seems rare, but may result from the archaic idea that a mortgage is an absolute transfer of property which is retransferred on payment of the secured debt so that it is not conceptually possible to transfer it to another person as junior mortgagee. Similarly, it is difficult to conceptualise a junior possessory pledge since only one person can have possession at a time. 8–11

Third party security

8–12 No case has been encountered where the grantor of the security cannot give the security for the debt of another, as opposed to the grantor's own debt. If there were such a case, presumably the objection could be met by arranging for the grantor to guarantee the third party's debt and to give the security as security for the grantor's obligations under the guarantee. The guarantee could be limited to the security. The security document should contain protective clauses of the type found in a guarantee, e.g. waivers of defences and a non-competition clause. Generally the security is subject to similar preference attacks as apply to guarantees: see para 31–3 *et seq*.

Scandinavian "owner's mortgage"

8–13 An idiosyncratic system exists in Scandinavian countries whereby a mortgage can be made available for a series of successive mortgages. In Finland, under the owner's mortgage (*omnistajankiiunitys*), as the debtor repays the loan, he is subrogated to the mortgagee's security and may then reissue the mortgage for a new loan having the priority of the original mortgage. If the loan is partially paid, the debtor may use his subrogated security as a second mortgage ranking after the first mortgagee's rights. The owner's mortgage is documented by a loan agreement, the mortgage itself, and a promissory note for the mortgage sum. It appears that an unsecured judgment creditor can attach the benefit of the owner's subrogated security and hence secure the priority of the security ahead of other unsecured creditors. A similar owner's mortgage is available in Sweden – *agarehyptek*.

Restrictions on redemption

8–14 A hostility to restrictions on the debtor's right to pay off the secured debt and to redeem the security is debtor-protective. In English parlance these restrictions are generally called clogs on the equity of redemption, or, as one typist felicitously expressed it, a "dog" on the equity of redemption.

Restrictions on prepayment

8–15 A secured creditor may wish to impose a restriction on prepayment in order to preserve his investment, e.g. in case interest rates should fall below the agreed fixed rate, or to protect himself against breakage costs, e.g. because he has funded the mortgage loan by a fixed interest deposit from a third party so that if the mortgage loan were prepaid at a time when interest rates had sunk, he would suffer a loss equal to the shortfall between the rate he can obtain on re-lending the prepaid mortgage debt elsewhere and the rate he is obliged to pay on the fixed term funding deposit.

In the case of secured loans in England the equitable rule that any stipulation which restricts or clogs the equity of redemption is void, will not usually affect prepayment restrictions. A restriction on the right of prepayment will not be void unless it is unconscionable or oppressive.

In *Multiservice Bookbinding v Marden* [1979] Ch 84, a mortgage loan to a company was repayable by instalments and irredeemable for ten years. Principal and interest were payable in sterling indexed to the Swiss franc (thereby in the event substantially increasing the borrower's liability). *Held*: the prohibition on redemption was not unfair and unconscionable. The debtor was not a young, inexperienced or ignorant person.

In common with other developed systems, English law distinguishes between commercial contracts, where the sanctity of contract is upheld, and contracts with those of weak bargaining power who require special protection, a distinction which is espoused by the Consumer Credit Act 1974 and the Unfair Contract Terms Act 1977.

A secured corporate loan may be perpetual and irredeemable:

In *Knightsbridge Estates Trust Ltd v Byrne* [1939] Ch 441, CA; affirmed by the House of Lords on a different ground [1940] AC 613, a mortgage was made irredeemable for a period of forty years. *Held*: in the circumstances this was not a clog on the equity of redemption since the provision was not unfair or unconscionable nor inconsistent with or repugnant to the contractual or equitable right to redeem. Mere unreasonableness is not enough. This result is confirmed by the Companies Act 1985 s 193.

The position in other creditor-oriented countries may be similar, e.g. as in 8–16 Germany. In Israel the Pledges Law of 1967 allows the debtor to redeem a pledge provided that the debtor pays the creditor interest until the original due date or for the next six months, whichever is earlier. But this right does not apply if the parties have otherwise agreed or in the case of a pledge securing a series of debentures.

However in other jurisdictions, particularly those in the Franco-Latin camp, it seems that the debtor may have a right of clearance of all mortgages by offering the purchase price and thereby effectively forcing an undesired prepayment of the loan. In France see Civil Code Arts 2167, 2181–92. There appears to be a similar rule in Italy.

8–17 Premiums on prepayments A related question is whether the lender may require a premium calculated on the amount of the prepayment. The purpose of the premium is to discourage prepayments and also to compensate the lender for the loss of the investment. Occasionally success fees are met, notably in debt restructurings and project finance: these are a proportion of the proceeds in excess of the secured debt and are intended to give the lender a share of the profits.

Fixed premiums and success fees are to be distinguished from compensation clauses commonly found in eurocurrency loan agreements whereby, in the event that the borrower prepays, the borrower must compensate the lender for any losses on account of funds borrowed in order to maintain the loan. Such losses may be encountered if the rate of return which the lender could obtain on the amount prepaid is less than the rate which the lender is paying on moneys borrowed by the lender, e.g. in the London interbank market, in order to fund the loan.

8–18 In the case of secured loans, similar principles apply under English law to premiums as apply to a collateral advantage given to a mortgagee, namely, it must satisfy the requirements (1) that it is not unfair and unconscionable; (2) that it is not in the nature of a penalty clogging the equity of redemption; and (3) that it is not inconsistent with the right to redeem: *Kreglinger v New Patagonia Meat and Cold Storage Co Ltd* [1914] AC 25 at 61, HL. A premium will not therefore be struck out unless it is unfair and unconscionable (not merely unreasonable): *Multiservice Bookbinding v Marden* [1979] Ch 84, [1978] 2 All ER 489; contrast *Cityland and Property (Holdings) Ltd v Dabrah* [1968] Ch 166. [1967] 2 A11 ER 639 (where the original loan was to be repaid at a substantial premium which was held unconscionable).

Bonuses and premiums have met with varying judicial treatment in some of the older cases on secured loans. Sometimes bonuses and premiums have been upheld except where they are payable solely on a default: see *Booth v Salvation Army Building Association Ltd* (1887) 14 TLR 3.

> In *Cato v Cato* (1972) 116 Sol Jo 138, a promissory note provided that on default the defendant should be liable to pay (inter alia) an attorney's fee of fifteen per cent of the amount due. *Held*: although the 15 per cent may not have been a penalty in the United States, it was a penalty in England and irrecoverable.

Consolidation

8–19 Consolidation is the right of a secured creditor who holds two mortgages over separate assets from the debtor to insist that the debtor redeems both and not one only. The object is to ensure that the debtor does not pick and choose between safe and unsafe mortgages and is a creditor-oriented rule. A creditor does not have this right under English law but he can contract for it and the contract is effective outside the consumer context: s 93 of the Law of Property Act 1925.

Permissible secured creditors

Summary

Restrictions on who may take security are of three main types: 8–20

– non-recognition of trustees holding security for several creditors or exclusions of foreign trustees who cannot be supervised by the home state

– nationalistic rules excluding foreigners from having any interest in key national or defence assets, such as land, ships, aircraft or equity holdings in sensitive local companies: para 6–20. Sometimes the rules allow the foreign creditor to take security but require enforcement sales only to nationals

– restrictions allowing the grant of security only to local credit institutions.

Trustees

Where the security is given to secured creditors, e.g. a syndicate of banks, it   8–21
is useful for a trustee to hold the security for the common benefit of the creditors.

It is often otherwise impracticable to grant security to each individual creditor in bond issues or other financings involving numerous creditors. Other advantages are: there can be common monitoring, enforcement, covenants and insurance; the trustee can hold the documents of title; and the trustee is the legal holder of the property and hence can be authorised to deal with it without involving numerous bondholders; and the orderly application of proceeds of realisation amongst the creditors is facilitated and controlled. If payments must be made to the trustee, he can distribute pro rata to the creditors. Creditors can transfer their claims by novation (so that commitments to lend can be transferred) and new creditors can be added by accession without the need to grant new security in their favour. The trustee is the holder of the security and it is only necessary that he should be able to determine who the beneficiary creditors are when the time comes to distribute the trust property. Additional assets can be added to the trustee's security without the need to vest the security in each creditor separately.

Various other advantages of trustees are examined in another work in this series in a chapter on trustees for bond issues.

8–22   The legal mechanics of the mortgage trust in Anglo-American countries are as follows. The debtor covenants to pay the creditor and gives to the trustee a parallel covenant to pay. The security is granted to the trustee to secure that parallel covenant and the trustee holds the security for the benefit of the creditors pro rata. Although there are two covenants to pay, the debtor does not pay twice: rather, the agreement provides that the debtor must pay the creditors direct until, say, an event of default occurs, whereupon all future payments must be made to the trustee direct who holds those payments on trust for the creditors.

Since the trustee is not the beneficial owner, if the trustee becomes insolvent, he is simply replaced (the court will compel this, if the trustee refuses) and the beneficiary creditors remain entitled to their property: they are not creditors of the trustee and the trust property does not fall into the trustee's insolvent estate. If the trustee wrongfully diverts the trust property, the beneficiaries have the right to trace it into whosoever hands it may come other than a bona fide purchaser for value without notice. It is their property.

A trustee for security is recognised in common law jurisdictions. It is not generally recognised in others, e.g. not in France, Greece or Thailand, although there is some patchy acceptance. The hostility to the trust stemming from Roman law might have been partially based on the objection to the appearance of ownership and hence potential fraud of creditors on insolvency – false wealth.

8–23   It is understood that approximations of the mortgage trustee are to be found also in the following countries but the precise ambit of the concept varies.

Europe: Finland, Liechtenstein (trust fully received), Luxembourg (for bond issues, since 1972), the Netherlands, Norway, Switzerland

Latin America: Argentina (Law No 8875 of 1912), Brazil, Peru (Law 23407 of May 28, 1982) – in all these cases the trust is for debenture issues and the trustee must be a bank. Also Mexico (business trusts since 1926), Panama and Venezuela (only authorised credit institutions may be trustees)

Elsewhere: Japan (codified law of trusts, the Code of Trusts, based on Anglo-American principles), Philippines, South Africa

Financial institutions

Sometimes if a state is otherwise hostile to a particular form of security, it **8–24** may be prepared to allow the security in favour of local financial institutions. One reason is a realistic acceptance of the fact that, as chief suppliers of credit, banks are entitled to security and that business development would be hindered without it. Another is that the legislators can regulate, monitor or control their home banks and hence protect the public against what they see as possible abuse. The pattern is typical of the Franco-Latin group and appears rare in the common law, Germanic and Scandinavian jurisdictions which have a more liberal attitude towards security.

Examples of security which can only be granted to financial institutions are:

— The **Belgian** *nantissement de fonds de commerce*, a form of restricted business pledge discussed at para 2–18. Similarly a pledge of an invoice enjoying comparatively relaxed formalities can only be given to a bank or approved credit institution: para 4–6.

— In **Haiti**, certain non-possessory industrial and agricultural mortgages over movables are available in favour of certain Haitian development banks.

— The **Luxembourg** *gage sur fonds de commerce* can be granted only to licensed banks, credit institutions, notaries and brewers: see para 2–21. The *contrat fiduciaire* may only be granted to credit institutions but it is possible that it is available outside the enabling statute to non-credit institutions.

— In **Peru**, industrial or mercantile pledges can be granted to the Industrial Bank of Peru: Legislative Decree 202 of June 12, 1981.

— In **Venezuela**, the Chattel Mortgages Law Art 19 provides that chattel mortgages can only be validly given to Venezuelan government entities, certain approved foreign financial institutions, and Venezuelan financial institutions and insurance companies.

CHAPTER 9

PUBLIC REGISTRATION OF SECURITY

Registration of security generally

Objectives of registration

9–1 The main objectives of registration systems for security are:

- the avoidance of false wealth;
- predictability of priorities;
- improvement of ownership title.

These may be reviewed in turn.

No false wealth Public registration is notice to unsecured creditors, especially for non-possessory security, so as to avoid the appearance of false wealth and to protect expectations of pari passu payment. Security registration is non-comprehensive in this respect because other non-secured assets can disappear on bankruptcy otherwise than by reason of security, e.g. the cancellation of profitable contracts, loss of claims by set-off, the forfeiture of leases of land and goods, and the repossession of assets subject to vendor/lessor "security" or title finance, e.g. retention of title in finance leases.

9–2 **Priorities** Registration can order priorities as against subsequent purchasers and mortgagees (always for land, ships, aircraft; sometimes for other assets, e.g. UCC Art 9, British Companies Act 1989) e.g. security interests rank in the order in which they are entered on the register notwithstanding actual notice of a prior unregistered security interest. The object of fixing priorities in this way is to abolish factual disputes as to whether a person has knowledge of prior interests or would have had such knowledge if he had made reasonable enquiries.

There seems little doubt that registration derived impetus from a motive quite different from the objection to false wealth – normally, the desire of secured creditors to protect their priority against competing purchasers and mortgagees. In other words, secured creditors allied themselves with unsecured creditors for separate reasons, but with a unity of result. This helps to explain why the American Art 9 of the UCC is both a "false wealth" system and a priority system.

Title Registration can be a guarantee of ownership title. This is rare, except in relation to land, and, sometimes, ships and aircraft. English registered land carries a state guarantee. In British Columbia, Alberta and Saskatchewan, the Torrens land registration system effectively guarantees the registered title, while in Manitoba and Ontario there is both a Torrens system and an unguaranteed system for the registration of land deeds. Registration of ships and aircraft is in most countries only evidence of title, but not conclusive: see para 15–21 *et seq*.

Disadvantages of registration

Registration has a number of disadvantages. First, it can lead to burdensome formality and hence expense and delay. Then, registration may invite extraterritorial conflicts and a resulting increase in the risk of a creditor inadvertently losing his security because of a foreign registration requirement which he cannot reasonably be expected to check. It results in loss of privacy and is intrusive. Governmental expense is engaged. The government of the day is often tempted to use the registration system as a source of revenue by insisting that documents must be stamped with a documentary tax before they are accepted for registration.   9–3

But the most pertinent disadvantage is that the nullity of non-registered transactions or of transactions which fail because they do not technically contain all the prescribed particulars, operates as a heavy penalty for non-compliance. The punishment may exceed the crime. In effect, the property granted to the secured creditor is taken away from him and used to pay the unsecured creditors of the bankrupt. In short, this hostility to secret property rights is another symptom of the hostility to false wealth, an ideology which has led to unconscionable results in other fields, i.e. the expropriation of one man's property to pay another man's debts. This proposition led to the civilian non-recognition of the trust and the civilian rejection of secret ownership. The Anglo-American systems dispensed with the reputed ownership doctrine on bankruptcy, but continue to adhere to it with vehemence in the case of security, as evidenced by the public registration of personal property security. The advantage of publicity is that those countries were able to develop extraordinarily wide and flexible forms of security because nobody could object that they did not know. But now the desirability of all-embracing registration should be re-examined, even if the result of the re-examination is that the original policy is adhered to. Financial statements do not publicise the catastrophic collapse of values if the company becomes bankrupt – they assume a going concern basis. This collapse is often much more cataclysmic than the impact on creditors of this or that unpublished charge over some assets which are taken away by a sale on insolvency.

9–4   In any event, registration systems can be excessive if they attempt to cover ephemeral assets having a short life, e.g. debts and most commercial goods; small assets where the security does not materially prejudice unsecured creditors; multitudinous assets, e.g. consumer goods, where the expense and trouble of a registration system outweigh the need to protect creditors against secret security and false wealth; assets subject to very short-term security, e.g. goods in the course of sale or margin collateral in organised markets; and swiftly-changing assets, e.g. receivables and securities. Margin collateral in organised markets may be called for daily or even more frequently. Securities in portfolios may be constantly bought and sold. A registration system should not attempt to record too many complicated interests, such as fixtures or the rights of tracing claimants.

If a jurisdiction requires registration over all these assets, then it is prioritising the policy of protecting unsecured creditors and of enlarging the debtor's estate against the conflicting policy of protecting secured creditors and facilitating security.

Registration by asset and by debtor

9–5   Broadly speaking, there are two types of registration, registration by asset and registration by debtor. Registration by asset involves the indexing of assets in an ownership register and not debtors and is practical only for land and those goods which are large and easily identifiable, not too multitudinous and not ephemeral, such as ships or aircraft. The method is obviously inappropriate for debts or investment securities. Registration by debtors is convenient if there is a commercial or companies registry where security can be entered on the enterprise's public file. It is not appropriate for consumer credit.

Constitutive effect of registration

9–6   It is invariably the case that lack of registration invalidates the mortgage if the mortgagor is bankrupt or as against attaching creditors since the main object of registration is not so much to order priorities as to forestall the secret lien prejudicing creditors. A mortgage which is void on bankruptcy is useless. Hence registration is constitutive of the security, that is, the act which constitutes the security and without which there is no security.

There are degrees of constitutive effect. In some states, if the mortgage is not registered, the mortgagee get nothing and the mortgage is totally invalid as between the parties, as well as against creditors. This is true of aircraft mortgages (and, one expects, perhaps other chattel mortgages) in, for example Chile, Ethiopia, Finland, France, Greece, Italy, S Korea, Norway, Portugal, Spain and Sweden, although even here in some cases the mortgage may have effect solely between the parties.

One result of this absolute avoidance is that, if the mortgage is registered in the suspect period prior to bankruptcy, it is treated as created at the time of registration and hence is subject to avoidance, even though the mortgage was actually executed prior to the suspect period.

Alternatively the absence of registration may not invalidate the security as between the parties prior to the insolvency of the debtor (this is so in England and American UCC states), but the mortgage is liable to be postponed to subsequently registered mortgages or purchasers, as in the case of British ships and of personal property security under Art 9 of the US Uniform Commercial Code, even though the subsequently registered mortgagee knew of the prior unregistered mortgage. The effect is that, if the creditor realises his security before the bankruptcy of the debtor, he may be able to keep the proceeds to pay off the secured debt.

Renewal of registration

In many countries the registration of the mortgage has to be renewed perio-   9–7
dically to preserve its effect. The main object of this may simply be forcibly to clear the register of obsolete entries (most debtors will want to clear their entries in any event) or, more seriously, to impose a prescriptive limitation on mortgages which the legislator thinks should be stale.

The effect is to introduce yet another complication. Renewal is not a thorn in the side of the mortgagee if the expiry period is longer than the life of the longest usual mortgage, in which event renewal is merely a good housekeeping rule.

It is generally the case that renewal continues the perfection and priority of the original mortgage and does not amount to the recreation of the mortgage which might fall within the suspect period prior to bankruptcy and hence be vulnerable to avoidance (because it is a new mortgage for pre-existing debt), but it should not be assumed that this is always the case. For example, the Mexican 10-year renewal of aircraft mortgage registrations confers priority only from the renewal date: CC Art 2930.

Examples of countries requiring renewal of registration in relation to aircraft (which may be indicative of other assets) include the following:

Country	Years
Argentina	7
Finland	10
France	10
Italy	20
Luxembourg	10
Panama	4 – no extension possible
United States	5 for personal property security to be filed under Art 9 of the UCC; 10 in some states
Uruguay	5

England and the numerous English-based states do not require renewal. The following states also do not require renewal of aircraft mortgage registration (which may again indicate the general attitude).

Europe:	Germany, Malta, Norway, Sweden, Switzerland
Middle East:	Israel, Turkey
Far East:	Philippines, Taiwan
Latin America:	Guatemala, Peru, Venezuela

The above information is based on the Hames/McBain aircraft survey cited in the bibliography.

Place of registration

9–8   Ideally registration should be at a clearly defined place, e.g. a central register in the debtor's country of incorporation. Registration for tangible and intangible movables may, for example, be at the companies registry, the commercial registry, a deeds registry in the locality of the debtor (Philippines, South African jurisdictions), or a special local or central filing office for security interests (American UCC states). Land, aircraft and ship mortgages may have their own special registers and, in such a case, dual registration is sometimes required – both at the special registry and at the corporate registry (as is the case with many English-based states). Centralised national registration is probably the most convenient, except perhaps for small assets or consumer security, or for large federal countries, like the United States. Local registration is dangerous for movable assets if they have to be re-registered in a new locality, e.g. as in Italy, the Philippines, and American UCC states.

Registration of particulars or security document

9–9   In the US UCC states and in the English-based systems, only particulars of the security appear on the file, although in English-based systems the charge itself must be submitted for checking and return. In many other cases, particularly countries in the Franco-Latin group, the security document itself is registered publicly or full details of the debt contract must be filed. Other systems think that this offends privacy. It certainly increases the paper which the filing office must maintain and results in inefficiency and delay: computerisation is more difficult and searches are slower.

In some systems the registrar has a quasi-judicial function: he reviews the documents to see if they comply. This is particularly true of land and ship registration. In others, his function is ministerial only, i.e. to file the form. This avoids bureaucratic delays and interference by the registry.

Conclusivity of registration

It is essential for predictability and continuity that the registration system should be reliable and, ideally, state guaranteed, so that it can be relied on by third parties. It is also germane whether the accuracy of search certificates provided by the registration authority is guaranteed. It is to be expected that practice differs. The English land registration system for registered land is state guaranteed. Ontario and British Columbia have compensation funds for errors in the registry under their Personal Property Security Acts: see Ontario, s 44; BC ss 69 (2), 52–53.   9–10

Extraterritoriality of registration

Registration often has extraterritorial effect by catching security created by foreign companies over property which comes into the territory of the registration state. In other words, registration is intended to protect local creditors. Multiple foreign registration is most likely to affect movables (ships, aircraft, vehicles, other goods and chattels), universal business charges over all the assets of an enterprise, and assets having a fictional location, such as debts, contracts, and securities. The result may depend upon whether the action is brought in the registering state or in another state. If an action is brought in the courts of the state which requires registration, then those courts are likely to treat the local registration statute as mandatory. If, on the other hand, the action is brought in foreign courts, they may be more inclined not to give extraterritorial effect to the foreign registration rules since they may see it as none of their business to protect the unsecured creditors of a foreign state.   9–11

For example, in **Switzerland** the Federal Court has held that a retention of title over goods validly created under German law was not valid when the goods were brought to Switzerland for lack of registration of the clause in the Swiss Register: BGE 106 II 198. For the position in the United States and English-based countries, see below.

Hence in order to protect collateral against local creditors, a mortgagee may be required to investigate whether registration of his charge is required in numerous jurisdictions, notably (as appropriate and having due regard to the class of asset):

— Where the debtor is incorporated.

— Where the debtor has an established place of business or principal office.

— Where the debtor does business.

— Where the asset is located. In the case of intangible movables, a notional location must be ascribed to the asset, e.g. contract receivables or bank deposits may be located where the debtor is. Ships, for this purpose, are generally located at their port of registry.

— Where the asset may arrive.

International attitudes to registration

9–12   There are broadly three camps:

— Countries which object to non-possessory security and therefore have not developed a comprehensive registration system for personal property, e.g. many countries in the Franco-Latin group. But the episodically-allowed security over personal property is usually subject to registration.

— Countries which are sympathetic to security over personal property and have therefore installed a registration regime, e.g. most states in the United States, and most English-based jurisdictions.

— Countries which are quite sympathetic to security but have not bothered to set up a registration system for personal property security. These are primarily the Germanic "fiduciary transfer" countries, e.g. Germany, Japan, the Netherlands and Switzerland.

9–13   The general result is as follows for corporate security:

— Mortgages of **land, ships and aircraft** almost invariably have to be registered, sometimes dual registered locally, and (in the case of ships and aircraft) sometimes registered in more than one country.

— Fixed non-possessory security over **goods** almost invariably has to be registered (but not if possessory), except in the case of the Germanic fiduciary transfer in the countries concerned.

— Fixed non-possessory security over **negotiable instruments** usually has to be registered (but not if possessory) but there are exceptions.

- Fixed security over **ordinary receivables** and contracts either has to be notified to the debtor in prescribed form .(para 4–5), or registered, whether or not notified to the debtor (e.g. in the US UCC states and in English-based countries, subject to exceptions). But the Germanic fiduciary transfer is not registrable in the countries concerned.

- Fixed security over **transferable investment securities,** such as debentures and equity shares, which are not negotiable instruments, are often not registrable anywhere (subject to exceptions), but (a) in many civil code countries the security must be completed by registration of the creditor as holder of the securities in the books of the issuer, (b) in the US there are special rules for certificated and uncertificated securities, and (c) registration is required in English-based countries if the charge over the investments is a floating charge and in certain other cases as well.

  assumes legal charge

- **Floating security** has to be registered, except in the Germanic fiduciary transfer countries.

- There are special rules for **intellectual property rights, goodwill** and various minor assets, such as security over uncalled capital.

Article 9 of the US Uniform Commercial Code

Generally

Article 9 of the US Uniform Commercial Code is an ambitious attempt to provide a unified codification of rules for the public registration of security interests in personal property (broadly, all assets except land) and also a set of priority rules. Although there are individual state variations, the Code has been enacted in the following States: **9–14**

- 49 US states
- District of Columbia
- Guam
- N. Mariana Islands
- Virgin Islands (US)

Louisiana (which is a French-based jurisdiction) has enacted the Code, except for Art 9. No part of the Code has been enacted by Puerto Rico. The first generally accepted version of the Code was the 1962 version. Amendments were made in 1972 and further amendments in 1977 (relating mainly to security over investments – a new Art 8). Some states still retain the older versions which are ignored in this review. Further, many states brought in non-uniform variations of the Official Text, notably California. Further revisions to Arts 8 and 9, relating primarily to investment securities, were proposed in 1994: see para 9–24A.

The aim of UCC Art 9 is to provide a unified structure for virtually all security over personal property, i.e. all property other than land, so that it extends to all tangible movables (goods) and intangible movables (debts, securities, negotiable instruments) and sometimes to fixtures. Like other registration systems, Art 9 adopts the "false wealth" view by insisting that a non-possessory security interest must be publicised to creditors if it is to be effective on the bankruptcy of the debtor and against subsequent attaching creditors of the debtor. The main features compared to other registration systems are that Art 9 codifies priority rules, as well as ensuring publicity for bankruptcy purposes; and applies to all transactions intended to create security interests in personal property and fixtures, e.g. reservation of title to goods, finance leases and hire purchase. It also applies to the sale of certain receivables, even if not intended to create a security interest. Hence Art 9 recharacterises certain forms of title finance as security.

Definitions

9–15　It is important to grasp the definitions:

1. **Goods**

   Goods includes all things which are movable at the time the security interest attaches (tangible personal property) or which are fixtures. Goods are further subdivided into:

   – **Consumer goods** – goods used or bought for use primarily for personal, family or household purposes, e.g. a television set or furniture.

   – **Equipment** – goods used or bought for use primarily in business.

   – **Farm products,** e.g. crops, livestock or their products, if possessed by a debtor engaged in farming.

   – **Inventory** – (1) goods held for disposition including raw materials, and (2) goods not held for disposition, namely materials used or consumed in a business, such as fuel and containers to package goods.

   – **Fixtures** – goods which have become so related to particular real estate that an interest in them arises under real estate law.

2. **Indispensable paper**   9–16

This term does not appear in the Code as such, but covers paper which is either negotiable or often dealt with as if negotiable, subdivided as follows:

– **Document** – a document of title, e.g. bills of lading, warehouse receipts.

– **Instruments** – usually a negotiable instrument (draft, cheque certificate of deposit, note), or an investment security, e.g. stocks, bonds and a note secured on land (even though a land mortgage is not covered by Art 9).

– **Chattel paper** – a writing which evidences both: (1) a monetary obligation and (2) a security interest in specific goods (or a lease of specific goods). An example is where a manufacturer sells a machine to a business debtor under a conditional sales contract. That is a security agreement over "equipment". The manufacturer then transfers the benefit of the contract to his bank either outright or to secure a loan. The conditional sales contract is chattel paper.

3. **Intangibles**   9–17

This asset is a pure intangible, that is, intangibles not evidenced by an indispensable writing, and is subdivided as follows:

– **Account** – any right to payment for goods sold or leased or for services rendered which is not evidenced by an indispensable writing (instrument or chattel paper) i.e. the ordinary commercial account receivable.

– **General intangibles** – any personal property (including things in action) other than: goods, accounts, chattel paper, documents, instruments, and money, i.e. purely intangible collateral which is not an account. Examples are goodwill, literary rights and rights to performance, and (usually) copyrights, trademarks and patents.

4. **Proceeds**

This includes whatever is received upon the sale, exchange, collection or other disposition of collateral or proceeds, e.g. cash or a cheque or a trade-in car.

For revisions relating to investment securities proposed in 1994, see para 9–24A.

Transactions subject to Art 9

9–18   Article 9 applies:

1. To any transaction which is intended to create a security interest in personal property or fixtures: s 9(102)(1)(a). "Security interest" means an interest in personal property or fixtures which secures payment or performance of an obligation: s 1–201. "Personal property" (goods, documents, instruments, general intangibles, chattel paper, accounts) and "fixtures" are defined above.

2. To any sale of accounts or chattel paper. This extension to non-security is to avoid problems of distinguishing between transactions intended for security and those not so intended.

Hence, the Article applies to various vendor/lessor title financing transactions if intended to create security and subordinates form to substance. It will therefore catch the following if intended to create security – conditional sales, reservation of title to goods, finance leases of goods and hire purchase of goods. Inevitably there are grey areas and in such a case the prudent creditor should file. For a discussion of the distinction, see the review of title finance in another book in this series on international financial law.

Generally a subordination agreement does not create a security interest unless so intended, nor do negative pledges, nor do the subrogation rights of a surety: *Canter v Schlager*, 358 Mass, 789, 267 NE 2d 492 at 499 (1971). There are special provisions regarding the security interest of a collecting bank in items in the collection process, and special rules for bulk transfers.

9–19   Article 9 does not apply to (see Art 9–104):

1. security interests to the extent they are subject to any statute of the United States, e.g. aircraft and copyrights;

2. nonconsensual liens;.

3. interests in real estate (except fixtures);

4. transactions not involving ordinary commercial financing; transactions which do not customarily serve as commercial collateral, such as an assignment of wage claims, sale of accounts or chattel paper as part of a sale of a business, assignments for collection, a right represented by judgment, a right of set-off, or transfer of a tort claim;

5. certain commercial financing transactions, such as rights under life insurance policies and deposit accounts because such transactions are adequately covered by existing law;

6. certain governmental borrowings.

A transaction, although subject to Art 9, may also be subject to a local consumer statute regulating small loans, retail instalment sales and the like, e.g. the Uniform Consumer Credit Code.

Attachment of a security interest

Attachment is when a security becomes effective against the debtor. Perfec-   9–20
tion is when the security becomes effective against creditors of the debtor and other third parties, e.g. on his bankruptcy.

A security interest attaches when it becomes enforceable against the debtor with respect to the collateral. Attachment occurs (usually) as soon as all of the following events have taken place (unless explicit agreement postpones the time of attaching):

– there is an appropriate agreement that a security interest attach; and

– value is given, e.g. the loan is made; and

– the debtor has rights in the collateral, e.g. he acquires the goods.

The formal requisites of a security agreement are usually that it is in writing unless the collateral is in the possession of the secured party, it creates or provides for a security interest, it is signed by the debtor, and contains a description of the collateral whether or not it is specific, provided it reasonably identifies what is described. Hence writing is usually required unless the debtor hands over possession of the collateral.

Perfection of security interests

Subject to exceptions, in general after perfection the secured party is pro-   9–21
tected against subsequent creditors of the debtor, e.g. attaching creditors, and the debtor's insolvency. The security interest also has strong priority against subsequent purchasers and mortgagees of the collateral.

A security interest is perfected (i.e. protected from creditors of the debtor and enjoying priority against transferees) when it has attached and when all of the applicable steps required for perfection have been taken. These steps are one of the following:

1. Filing a financing statement to give public notice of the security interest.

2. Filing or registration, etc., pursuant to statutes other than the UCC. Examples are:

    (a) Statutes or treaties of the United States which provide for registration or filing, e.g., aircraft, copyrights.

(b) State certificate of title acts (for perfection of security interests by notation on the certificates) covering automobiles, trailers, mobile homes, boats, farm tractors, and the like.

In these cases suitable alternative systems for giving public notice of a security interest are available.

3. The secured party taking **possession** of the collateral (pledge). A debtor not in possession, it is said, puts third parties dealing with him on notice that his interest or property may be subject to an encumbrance.

4. In some cases no additional steps beyond attachment are necessary. This is sometimes called **automatic perfection.** Examples are certain consumer transactions, assignments of isolated accounts, and certain temporary or short-term transactions.

If the above steps (filing or possession) are taken before the security interest attaches, it is perfected at the time when it attaches (agreement, value given, debtor has rights in the collateral). For revisions relating to investment securities proposed in 1994, see para 9–24A.

Perfection by filing

9–22   **Types of collateral perfected by filing** Generally, most types of collateral either may or must be perfected by filing under Art 9: goods (including fixtures), chattel paper, negotiable documents, accounts, and general intangibles. However, filing is not effective to perfect a security interest in money or instruments. This is because of their negotiable quality: bona fide transferees of negotiable instruments must get good title. For revisions relating to investment securities proposed in 1994, see para 9–24A.

Filing is by a financing statement in a form which sets out details of the parties and a description of the collateral, but not the security agreement itself. There is no need to refer to after-acquired property or future advances in the financing statement, or to proceeds.

A financing statement may be filed before a security agreement is made or a security interest otherwise attaches.

Place of filing Filing may be central or local. The principal advantage of state-wide filing is ease of access and the avoidance of scattered searches. On the other hand, most credit inquiries about local businesses, farmers and consumers come from local sources so that some transactions may be locally filed, e.g. farm and consumer collateral and land-related collateral (timber, minerals, fixtures).

Proper presentation for filing of a financing statement constitutes filing and gives constructive notice from the time of presentation, not from the time of indexing.

Renewal of filing A filed financing statement is usually effective for a period of five years from the date of filing. A succeeding continuation statement may be filed by the secured party within six months prior to the expiration of each five-year period.

Perfection by possession

A security interest in (1) letters of credit and advices of credit, (2) goods, (3) instruments, (4) money, (5) negotiable documents, or (6) chattel paper may be perfected by the secured party's taking possession of the collateral (pledge). A security interest in money or instruments (other than instruments which constitute part of chattel paper) can be perfected only by the secured party's taking possession, except in certain instances where such collateral may be automatically perfected and where proceeds are involved.   9–23

A security interest in accounts and general intangibles cannot be perfected by possession since possession is not possible.

Possession may be by the secured party himself or by an agent on his behalf. Notice of the secured party's interest to an independent bailee is sufficient. The debtor or a person controlled by him cannot qualify as such an agent for the secured party since the collateral is then effectively in the possession of the debtor.

In some instances a secured party in possession of certain collateral (e.g. instruments, negotiable documents) may temporarily release the collateral to the debtor. The security interest remains perfected (for a temporary 21-day period) without filing. No useful purpose would be served by cluttering the files with records of very short term transactions. An example is the release of an instrument so that it can be sold or exchanged or the release of a note so that it can be presented for payment.

For revisions relating to investment securities proposed in 1994, see para 9–24A.

Summary table of perfection requirements

The perfection requirements may be summed up as set out below: 9–24

Type of collateral	Methods of perfection
Equipment (mainly goods used in business)	Central filing or possession
Inventory (mainly stock-in-trade)	Central filing or possession

Type of collateral	Methods of perfection
Goods in the possession of a bailee for which a negotiable document has not been issued	Issuance of a document in the name of the secured party or notification to the bailee of the secured party's interest (no attornment or acknowledgement by bailee required) or filing appropriate for the type of goods involved
Goods in the possession of a bailee for which a negotiable document has been issued	Central filing as to the document or possession of the document or temporary automatic perfection (e.g. 21 days) as to the document
Instruments (mainly negotiable instruments and negotiable securities)	Possession or temporary automatic perfection
Negotiable documents (mainly documents of title to goods)	Central filing or possession or temporary automatic perfection
Money (actual cash)	Possession
Chattel paper (mainly a security interest in specific goods, e.g. a finance lease)	Central filing or possession
Letters of credit	Possession
Accounts (mainly ordinary commercial receivables)	Central filing, but if assignor is foreign, notification to account debtors. Automatic perfection of assignment of less than significant part of accounts of any debtor
General intangibles (mainly intangibles, such as goodwill)	Central filing, but if assignor is foreign, notification to account debtors
Security interest of collecting bank in collection item	Automatic perfection
Proceeds of the above (e.g. money, instruments, chattel paper, deposit account, or accounts)	Usually automatic perfection if security interest in original collateral perfected. Otherwise by filing. 10–day period of temporary automatic perfection.

Type of collateral	Methods of perfection
Certificated investment securities (Art 8)	Transfer to secured party or to nominee plus certificates (e.g. physical delivery without necessity for registration of security in name of secured party) or notice of security interest to third party authorised to control and transfer the security. Perfection by filing ineffective.
Uncertificated investment securities (Art 8)	Register security interest with issuer of security or registered transfer to secured creditor as if he were the owner. Perfection by filing ineffective.
Aircraft, copyrights, etc	File or register under applicable Federal statutes

This summary does not cover consumer goods; farm equipment, products, accounts and intangibles; vehicles; watercraft; fixtures; accessions and accessories; consignment of goods for sale; property of a transmitting utility; Art 2 security interests; assignments of a beneficial interest under a trust or decedent's estate or for the benefit of all creditors of the transferor. It is essential to note that there are inter-state differences.

For revisions relating to investment securities proposes in 1994, see para 9–24A.

Revised Art 8: investment securities

In 1994 Art 8 of the UCC regarding investment securities was revised and this involved changes to Art 9. At the time of writing the changes had not yet been adopted by the various states.   9–24A

The changes were necessitated because most securities in the US are now held by custodians so that trades are completed not by delivery of certificates or registration of the transfer on the records of the issuer or their transfer agents, but by computer entries in the records of clearing corporations and securities intermediaries. One depository in New York – the Depository Trust Company – holds 60 to 80 per cent of all publicly traded US shares through its nominee Cede & Co so that the great majority of trades can simply be effected in the books of DTC as common depository. The 1978 Art 8 did not deal effectively with this indirect holding system, and so changes were appropriate. The basic concepts of the direct holding system are retained, but a revised Part 5 of Art 8 covers holdings through a securities intermediary – calling them a "security entitlement" with respect to a financial asset. The securities intermediary must maintain a sufficient quantity of financial assets to satisfy the claims of all entitlement holders and these financial assets are the beneficial property of the holders and are not subject to the claims of the intermediary's general creditors.

Consequential changes are made to Art 9 security interests over certified and uncertified securities and the new security entitlements.

The revised Art 9 rules continue the long-established principle that a security interest in a security represented by a certificate can be perfected by a possessory pledge, but also allows security interests by agreement between the debtor and secured party without any requirement for "transfer", "delivery", or the like.

The perfection methods for security interests in investment securities are set out in revised s 9–115(4). The basic rule is that a security interest may be perfected by "control", defined in s 8–106. As explained in a prefatory note to the revisions, in general, obtaining control means taking the steps necessary to place the lender in a position where it can have the collateral sold off without the further cooperation of the debtor. Thus, for certificated securities, a lender obtains control by taking possession of the certificate with any necessary endorsement. For securities held through a securities intermediary, the lender can obtain control in two ways. First, the lender obtains control if it becomes the entitlement holder, that is, has the securities positions transferred to an account in its own name. Secondly, the lender obtains control if the securities intermediary agrees to act on instructions from the secured party to dispose of the positions, even though the debtor remains the entitlement holder. Such an arrangement suffices to give the lender control even though the debtor retains the right to trade and exercise other ordinary rights of an entitlement holder. It seems to follow that the English-based unregistered equitable charge without notification is not adopted and there is a preference for a degree of the possessory pledge concept.

Except where the debtor is itself a securities firm, filing of an ordinary Art 9 financing statement is also a permissible alternative method of perfection. However, filing with respect to investment property does not assure the lender the same protections as for other forms of collateral, since the priority rules provide that a secured party who obtains control has priority over a secured party who does not obtain control.

Subject to exceptions, the revisions retain the basic conflicts rules described in para 9–31 for certificated and uncertificated securities, but, subject again to exceptions, the perfection of a security interest and the priority of a security interest in a security entitlement or securities account are governed by the local law of the securities intermediary's jurisdiction (new s 9–103(d)) which will usually be the law specified as governing the agreement between the securities intermediary and its entitlement holder or, if none, the office of the intermediary when the securities account is specified to be kept – but not the jurisdiction where any certificates are physically located or where the issuer is organised: s 8–110(e). There are different rules for security interests granted by debtors who are brokers or securities intermediaries – the law of the debtor's location in certain cases.

The revisions contain a new definition of "investment property" to include securities, whether held directly or through intermediaries, and commodity futures which are henceforward excluded from the definition of goods, instruments and general intangibles, and which are covered by the new set off rules as regards the creation, perfection and priority of security interests.

Comparison of the US UCC and English-based corporate systems

The general perfection requirement of the UCC is similar in many respects   9–25
to the English-based corporate system in its emphasis upon publicity of non-possessory security and its exemption for possessory security. Thus:

– In the case of ordinary **goods**, whether they are equipment or inventory, the secured creditor must either have a possessory pledge (actual possession of the goods or constructive possession through holding a negotiable document of title or possession through a bailee) or the secured creditor must file. Ditto English-based corporate systems.

– In the case of **receivables** and other intangible movables which are not negotiable (whether they are actual accounts or general intangibles), the secured creditor must file. This corresponds roughly to the English-based requirement for the registration of charges over "book debts". Both the UCC and English-based corporate systems abandon the traditional concept in many civil code countries that a pledge of a receivable is publicised by giving notice to the debtor – creditors cannot ascertain this. But the United States preserves the traditional idea of a "possessory" pledge of receivables by allowing perfection if the assignor is foreign (when notice must be given to the account debtor to take the debt completely out of the possession of the assignor). As a further difference, the United States also accepts that isolated assignments of accounts and general intangibles should not have to be perfected by filing.

– Both systems recognise that possession of a **negotiable instrument** is a non-registrable pledge, but the English-based system is none too clear on this.

– Both systems exclude filing of security over some investment securities, but the technicalities have to be watched. This is subject to the proposed 1994 UCC revisions: para 9–24A.

– Both systems provide for filing of mortgages over **aircraft** and **ships**. The English system requires such registration so that registration is dual. The US system is federal.

– Both systems provide for filing of security interests over **copyrights**, etc. The US system is federal.

Choice of law and perfection in multiple state transactions

9–26   Under s 1–105(1), the parties may by agreement determine the law that governs their relationship, so long as the transaction "bears a reasonable relation" to the jurisdiction the law of which is selected. Failing such specification of a particular law by agreement, a court in a Code state may apply its own law (the Code) to transactions "bearing an appropriate relation" to the state. Generally US courts will follow general conflict-of-laws principles and apply the law of the place having the most significant relationship with the transaction.

Choice-of-law principles have limited application to secured transactions. The reason is that most disputes concerning secured transactions are not as between the debtor and the secured party, but instead concern claims to the collateral as between the secured party and third persons.

The conflict of laws provisions in relation to perfection of security interests are set out in s 9–103 of the UCC and are broadly as follows.

9–27   **Goods, documents and instruments: lex situs** In the case of "ordinary goods" (generally most goods other than mobile goods and minerals), "documents" (generally documents of title to goods) and "instruments" (mainly negotiable instruments and negotiable securities), perfection and the effect of perfection or non-perfection are governed by the law of the jurisdiction where the collateral is when the "last event" occurs on which is based the assertion that the security interest is perfected or unperfected. The "last event" is the last to occur of (a) the collateral is in the possession of the secured party or the debtor has signed a security agreement, (b) the secured party has given value, e.g. made the loan, and (c) the debtor has rights in the collateral. This rule adopts the internationally accepted lex situs rule for security over goods and negotiable instruments.

There are also special rules (a) for goods covered by a certificate of title, and (b) where goods are bought in one state subject to a security interest at the time of sale, but where it is understood by the parties to the secured transaction that the goods are to be kept in a different state.

Accounts and general intangibles: usually law of debtor In the case of   9–28
"accounts" (generally, any right to payment for goods sold or leased or for services not evidenced by an "instrument" or "chattel paper" but excluding vessel charter hire) and "general intangibles" (mainly such items as good-will, patent rights and the like), the law (including the conflict of laws rules) of the jurisdiction in which the debtor (the party granting the security inter-est, not the debtor on the receivable) is located governs the perfection and the effect of perfection or non-perfection of the security interest. Location of the debtor is the debtor's place of business or, if more than one, his chief executive office (not place of incorporation). However, if the debtor is located in a non-UCC jurisdiction and if that jurisdiction does not provide for perfection by filing or recordation in that jurisdiction, the law of the state in which the debtor has its major executive office in the United States governs. If the debtor is a foreign air carrier, it is deemed located at the designated office of the agent upon whom service of process may be made. If the debtor is located in a jurisdiction which is not part of the United States or Canada, then a security interest in accounts or general intangibles for money due or to become due may be perfected by notification to the account debtor.

If the chief office is in a UCC state, then the security interest must be per-fected by filing. It follows that a floating charge created by an English com-pany, for example, over accounts, need not be registered in a UCC state if it is registered in the place where the company has its chief executive office provided that this is not in a UCC state. An assignment of charter hire by an English or Liberian ship-owning company also need not be registered in the United States in any event if notice is given to the charterer.

Mobile goods Mobile goods include trailers, rolling stock, aeroplanes, ship-   9–29
ping containers, construction machinery and the like. The same rules apply as for accounts except that the security interest cannot be perfected by noti-fication to the debtor. There are special rules when the mobile goods are covered by a certificate of title, such as cars.

Chattel paper Chattel paper is a writing which evidences both a monetary obligation and a security interest in or a lease of specific goods other than a charterparty in respect of a vessel. If the security party takes possession of the chattel paper, then the rules as to goods apply. If the interest is non-possessory, the rules as to accounts apply except that the security interest cannot be perfected by notification to the account debtor.

9–30 Debtor changes location to another state Where the state in which to perfect a security interest is that of the location of the debtor, with respect to accounts, general intangibles and mobile goods, the Code covers the case where the debtor changes location (moves his residence, office or chief executive office to another state). A security interest perfected in the former state of location remains perfected normally for four months after the debtor moves.

9–31 Investment securities: law of issuer The law (including the conflict of laws rules) of the jurisdiction of organisation of the issuer governs the perfection and the effect of perfection or non-perfection of a security interest in uncertificated securities. Hence Delaware law will apply to security over stock issued by a Delaware corporation, even if its principal office is in New York.

There is a similar provision in s 8–106 that applies the law (including conflict of laws rules) of the jurisdiction of organisation of the issuer with respect of such matters as the registration of transfer, pledge or release of an uncertificated security, i.e. dematerialised securities.

Where the security is a certificated security, the law of location of the certificate governs perfection, because a certificated security is an instrument.

For the proposed 1994 revisions, see para 9–24A.

9–32 Minerals: place of mine There are special rules for security interests created by a debtor who has an interest in minerals or oil or gas before extraction and which attaches as extracted or which attaches to an account resulting from the sale of minerals at the wellhead or minehead. The perfection and the effect of perfection or non-perfection of the security interests are governed by the law (including the conflict of law rules) of the jurisdiction where the wellhead or minehead is located. In the case of a UCC state, the place to file is the real estate records of the country where the wellhead or minehead is located.

Canadian registration systems

9–33 Alberta, British Columbia, Manitoba, Ontario, Saskatchewan and the Yukon Territory have enacted Personal Property Security Acts based on Art 9 of the US Uniform Commercial Code. Like the US version, registration often applies to all transactions which have the effect of security. But there are substantial divergences of detail. The system in the remaining common law provinces is based on the English system – Newfoundland, New Brunswick, Nova Scotia, and Prince Edward Island and also the Northwest Territories. Quebec has a French-based system of security – but substantially modified.

English-based registration of company charges

Charges by companies

The traditional English requirements for the registration of charges created   9–34
by companies are normally contained in the local Companies Acts.

Registration commonly applies to:

– charges by companies incorporated in the jurisdiction; and

– charges on property in the jurisdiction created by, or acquired by, a company incorporated outside the jurisdiction which has an established place of business (or, in some countries, simply a place of business) in the jurisdiction. This extra-territorial limb is discussed below.

Registration applies only to companies, not individuals or partnerships. The only security interests created by individuals which require registration are certain non-possessory chattel mortgages under bills of sale legislation. General assignments of all commercial receivables by individuals are usually void under bankruptcy acts. Agricultural or vehicle charges may have a separate regime.

Country illustrations

Countries with a traditional English requirement for registration of com-   9–35
pany charges (but sometimes with a 30–day, not 21–day, registration time limit, subject to extension for foreign charges) include the following, by way of illustration:

> **Australia** (a modified regime); **Bermuda** (Companies Act 1981 Part V; priority is based on the date of registration, not date of the charge; no time period for registration; applies to Bermuda companies and companies with an "established place of business" in Bermuda); **Cayman Islands** (Companies Law s 51); **Cyprus** (Companies Law s 90); **England** (Companies Act 1985 s 395 *et seq*, as amended); **Hong Kong** (Companies Ordinance s 80 (more nebulous test of local "place of business" for foreign companies, not "established place of business")); **India** (Companies Act 1956, as amended (30 days)); **Ireland (Republic of)** (Companies Act 1983 s 99 as amended); **Israel** (Companies Ordinance 1983 Arts 164, 178(a)); **Jamaica** (Companies Act (based on UK 1948 Act)); **Kenya** (Companies Act, Laws of Kenya Chapter 486, based on UK 1948 Companies Act); **New Zealand** (Companies Act s 102. NZ companies and companies with "established place of business" in NZ); **Nigeria** (Companies and Allied Matters Decree 1990 s 197); **Pakistan** (Companies Ordinance 1984 s 121 *et seq*); **Singapore** (Companies Act ss 131–141). One surmises that similar provisions

are likely to prevail in most of the 70 or so English-based jurisdictions, though common law Canada has its own systems.

Charges requiring registration

9–36   Not all charges require registration – only those listed in the section. The basic list first appeared in England in 1908. The Companies Act 1929 added unpaid calls on shares, ships and aircraft, and goodwill, patents, trade-marks, copyrights – and licences under these rights. Hence the list was absorbed into numerous former British colonies throughout the world before the great independence movement commencing with the Indian sub-continent in 1947 and gathering momentum in the 1950s and 1960s. It is believed that the list remains in those colonies which remain British, e.g. Gibraltar and the Cayman Islands.

The usual charges requiring registration are:

1.   Charges to secure any issue of debentures

2.   Charges on uncalled share capital of a company or on calls made but not paid (but not on the shares themselves under this head)

3.   Non-possessory charges on goods, but not possessory pledges of the goods or of the documents of title to the goods. The scope of this head is somewhat technical in many jurisdictions and would, for example, include fixtures and crops if separately charged, but not goods in foreign parts or at sea. This head often (but not always) includes ships and aircraft, in which event there is a double registration requirement – both at the Companies Registry and at the ship or aircraft registry.

4.   Charges on land anywhere or any interest in land. Dual registration in a lands registry is often also required

5.   Charges on "book debts" of a company, but (often) not the deposit of a negotiable instrument to secure a book debt. Giving notice to the debtor is not enough (since creditors cannot ascertain this). This cur-ious term "book debts" has been defined judicially to mean "debts aris-ing in a business in which it is the proper and usual course to keep books and which ought to be entered in the books": *Official Receiver v Tailby* (1886) 18 QBD 25, 29, affirmed sub nom *Tailby v Official Receiver* (1888) 13 AC 523, HL. Broadly the term includes business receivables, but probably does not include debt securities held as invest-ments. Charges on bank deposits are probably not included, but this is not absolutely certain: see *Re Brightlife* [1986] BCLC 418. An export credit insurance policy is not a book debt: *Paul & Frank Ltd v Dis-*

count Bank (Overseas) Ltd [1967] Ch 348. A lien on sub-freights created by a company under a time-charter in favour of the owner is a charge on a book debt: *Re Welsh Irish Ferries Ltd* [1985] 3 WLR 610. This inconvenient case was negated in Britain in the Companies Act 1989 (section not yet in force) but may still be persuasive in other English-based countries.

6. Floating charges of a company. This could catch floating charges on a part of the assets of a company, e.g. shares, even though a fixed charge on shares is generally not registrable

7. Charges on various intangibles, notably goodwill, intellectual property rights and licences of those rights. Registered designs were included in the English list in the Companies Act 1989.

"Charge" includes any form of security interest, other than one arising by   9–37
operation of a law, such as a possessory lien. But there must be a security interest, and hence rights of set-off, finance leases, hire purchase agreements, retention of title, sale and repurchase, sale and leaseback, and recourse factoring agreements and other forms of vendor/lessor title financings are not registrable if properly drafted so as not to confer a security interest in law. Form prevails over substantial commercial effect. Unlike Art 9 of the US Uniform Commercial Code, the traditional English registration does not extend the meaning of charge to include transactions having the commercial effect of security.

In summary, the effect of the traditional English approach is that all   9–38
security created by companies is registrable, except

— charges over shares or debt securities held as investments (unless the charge is a floating charge or is to secure an issue of debentures);

— liens arising by operation of law, such as a repairer's or vendor's lien;

— possessory pledges of goods or of the documents of title to goods;

— transactions which are not security interests in legal form, e.g. retention of title, factoring of receivables, forfaiting, sale and repurchase, financial leases, hire purchase, sale and leaseback, and set-off;

— various miscellaneous items, such as (sometimes) charges on insurance policies, and (probably) charges on bank deposits.

For a comparison with Art 9 of the US UCC, see para 9–25.

Time for registration

9–39   The charge must be registered at the Companies Registry within 21 days of its creation (sometimes 30), with an extension for charges executed abroad. Late registration can be permitted by the courts if, amongst other things, non-registration was inadvertent, but case law disallows late registration if the company is insolvent or insolvency proceedings have commenced and is in any event on terms that late registration does not prejudice prior rights, e.g. of those who took charges in reliance on a clean register. In England, under the Companies Act 1989 (sections not yet in force) it is no longer necessary to obtain the court's permission to register out of time, but the statute applies the case law rules and preferential transfer rules to late registration.

If a charge is not registered, it is void against the insolvency representative and creditors. But the secured debt becomes immediately repayable on demand so that there is an incentive on the debtor to help regularise the situation. The usual practice is to re-execute the charge, and register that.

Only prescribed particulars of the charge appear on the public file, not the whole charge. In most jurisdictions, the certificate of the registrar that the charge has been duly filed is conclusive, even if the particulars were defective. This is designed to ensure absolute certainty. Unhappily, conclusivity was removed in England by the Companies Act 1989 (section not yet in force), so that defective particulars are fatal.

The submission of the prescribed particulars to the Registrar satisfies the registration requirement, even if not entered on the file until later or at all.

A significant difference between the traditional English approach and UCC Art 9 is that the English method does not set up a priority system and is intended purely to act as a caution to other creditors dealing with the company to obviate secret security. Its only effect upon priorities is that registration can operate as constructive notice to third parties, i.e. deemed notice of particulars required to be registered (*Wilson v Kelland* [1910] 2 Ch 306) and therefore may affect ranking in those cases where priorities depend upon whether the subsequent creditor had notice of the prior interest. The "deemed notice" rule was modified in England in the Companies Act 1989 (section not yet in force) in a manner which is somewhat obscure.

Extraterritoriality of English-based registration

9–40   Companies Act registration is usually required not only if the debtor-chargor is locally-incorporated but usually also if the chargor is a foreign company and if (a) the chargor has an established place of business locally at the time of the creation of the charge, and (b) the property is or subsequently comes into the territory.

The location or property is probably determined by ordinary location rules, e.g. where they are for goods and negotiable instruments, where they are registered for registered securities and where the debtor is for ordinary receivables.

Thus, if a foreign company actually has an established place of business in England, it is immaterial that the company has failed to register the branch at the Companies Registry as required so that the creditor does not know of the branch and hence of the registration requirement: *NV Slavenburg's Bank v Intercontinental Natural Resources Ltd* [1980] 1 WLR 1076 (unregistered charge created by Dutch company on oil in tank in England was void). Since it is usually impracticable to ascertain whether or not a foreign company does have an established place of business locally (for which purpose probably some fixed abode may be required although it should not be forgotten that a foreign company trading through an agency locally may have any established place of business locally by virtue of the agency), charges created by foreign companies which may affect property locally, e.g. ships coming into the jurisdiction or assignments of contracts where the debtor is located locally, might have to be filed at the Companies Registry in order to comply with the statutory requirements. Precautionary registrations are common. If there is no registered branch of the company locally, the particulars will not appear on a public file. If the relevant provisions of the Companies Act 1989 come into force, registration will be required only if the foreign company has a registered place of business in England and if various rules about the location of the property in England are satisfied.

In some states (such as Australian states) with similar registration requirements, a more tenuous nexus may crystallise registration, e.g. doing business in that state.

An Australian example of a case where a charge in another state was defeated by failure to comply with local registration rules is *Luckins v Highway Motel (Caernarvon) Pty Ltd* (1975) 133 CLR 164:

> A company incorporated in Victoria gave a floating charge over all its assets. The company had no place of business in Western Australia but its bus tours passed through Western Australia and incurred debts there in respect of meals, camping expenses and the like. A judgment creditor seized a bus in Western Australia. *Held* by the High Court of Australia: even if the charge over the bus was valid on the ground that the bus was in Victoria when the charge was created, the validity of a charge over a chattel depended on its situs; Western Australia required registration of all charges created by foreign companies "carrying on business" in Western Australia. The court held (a) that the company was carrying on business in Western Australia in connection with its bus

tours because touring expenses were incurred there, (b) that the registration provisions of Western Australia were mandatory, and (c) that therefore the charge on the bus was void and the unsecured creditor could take the bus ahead of the debentureholder.

CHAPTER 10

ENFORCEMENT OF SECURITY

Summary of obstacles to enforcement

The international obstacles to enforcement include: 10–1

- enforcement may be subject to the delay and formalisation of court-ordered public auction as opposed to a private sale and (sometimes) weakened by the absence of adequate preservation orders;

- the absence of possessory management through a receiver; compulsory grace periods before the creditor can enforce;

- realisation only by the insolvency administrator if the debtor is finally bankrupt so that there is a delay;

- stays on enforcement if the debtor has commenced a formal rehabilitation procedure;

- costs of enforcement, including court, custodial, legal and auctioneer fees (a hefty percentage in some countries);

- a requirement that the creditor deposit security with the court in the form of cash or a bond;

- sale only in local currency;

- exchange control restrictions on the repatriation of the sale proceeds to a foreign creditor.

Compulsory delays in enforcement are intended to be debtor-protective and probably stem originally from traditional anti-usurer attitudes and the desire to protect individuals. In the corporate context this approach bears re-examination. Mature credit institutions, which are subject to official supervision and popular pressures, do not generally enforce until the position is hopeless when there is no point in waiting. Delays and costs increase the interest and cost burden on the debtor, as well as prejudicing the creditor if he is undersecured. Volatile assets, such as securities, goods and foreign currency receivables, may lose value if there are delays. An example is margin collateral. Often the fall in values is a cause of the insolvency.

Goods may perish. Finally, some assets require special (and expensive) preservation, e.g. ships and aircraft.

Methods of enforcement

10–2   In English-based jurisdictions, an exceptionally flexible array of enforcement remedies is available to the secured creditor under a properly drafted security document. These include private sale, taking possession temporarily to collect the income, and taking possession through a receiver to operate the asset or the business covered by a floating charge. Flexible enforcement remedies are also available in common law United States. In both cases, the remedies are self-help.

By contrast, in most other jurisdictions, the secured creditor is generally limited to public auction, usually only after a court order. These jurisdictions historically have given priority to the protection of the debtor by insisting on judicial monitoring of enforcement and by a public sale designed to prevent a collusive sale by the mortgagee. Hence, judicial protectionism.

In the English-based jurisdictions, abuse by the mortgagee is controlled by the imposition of duties of fair realisation. Since the English espouse freedom of contract, these duties can be eroded by contractual terms, subject to consumer credit legislation and the application of statutory or common law doctrines of unfair or unconscionable contract terms, e.g. *Bishop v Bonham* [1988] 1 WLR 742, CA (mortgagee must exercise reasonable care to obtain a proper price). But the mortgagee must take reasonable care in the sale. Thus he may be liable if the particulars of sale fail to state that planning permission had been obtained for the erection of flats: *Cuckmere Brick Co Ltd v Mutual Finance Ltd* [1971] Ch 949. He may be liable if he sells specialist music equipment and fails to obtain specialist advice or advertise in popular music publications: *American Express International Banking Corpn v Hurley* [1985] 3 All ER 564.

One may consider the various remedies in more detail.

Foreclosure

10–3   Foreclosure is an absolute transfer of the mortgaged property to the mortgagee without a sale. Because there is no test of value and a possible temptation to the creditor, this remedy is universally controlled or even prohibited. Forfeitures without court order are almost invariably invalid. In

England foreclosures require a court order and such orders are rare: the court usually orders a sale. Foreclosure has been abolished in the **Republic of Ireland**.

But the prohibition on foreclosure does not usually apply to receivables: the mortgagee can collect them and apply them towards the secured debt without court order. There can be no abuse because the proceeds are already money and therefore the creditor cannot take more than he should. This is no more harmful than applying the proceeds of sale of land. This is the position in, e.g. England, Germany, Luxembourg and Spain (CC Arts 486 and 507) except pledges of bills of exchange.

A partial exception to the bar on foreclosure arises from the frequent rule that, if the sale is by public auction, the creditor can himself bid at the auction. There is no risk of foreclosure abuse because of the publicity of the auction and the ability of third parties to bid.

The mortgagee may sell the asset to a company owned by the mortgagee so as to continue to control the asset (in the hope of an upturn), yet be insulated by the veil of incorporation from the risk of the asset. If at a proper price, this is probably not a foreclosure requiring a court order in England, but may be elsewhere. These sales are very frequent, as where a bank sells to a company controlled by the bank to hold the property and manage it.

> In *Twe Kwong Lam v Wong Chit Sen* [1983] 1 WLR 1349, a mortgagee arranged for the property to be sold by public auction. There was only one bid – that by a company owned by the mortgagee and his family. *Held*: there was no fixed rule that a company in which the mortgagee was interested could not buy the mortgaged property, but there was an onus on the mortgagee to show that the price was reasonably fair in the circumstances. See also *Farrar v Farrars Ltd* (1888) 40 Ch D 395, CA.

Possessory management and receivers

Generally English-based jurisdictions generally permit a mortgagee to take   10–4
possession of the secured asset and to collect the income from the asset. When the secured debt is repaid, the creditor surrenders possession, i.e. possession is not an absolute foreclosure. Possession may be taken directly by the creditor or (more usually) by appointing a receiver who is technically the agent of the mortgagor. This type of possessory management is different from a custodial possession by the creditor to protect the asset pending sale.

Purposes of possession A mortgagee may wish to take temporary possession of the secured asset for a variety of reasons, for example: to manage the asset because the debtor has ceased trading, e.g. because of fraudulent trading objections which compel the directors to cease business; to keep the asset earning (ship) or to keep the business together and trade out of the difficulties; to keep contracts and leases alive by performing them (unless they contain termination clauses operating on mortgagee enforcement); and, in the case of ships and aircraft, to move the asset to a favourable enforcement jurisdiction where there are less obstacles in the form of prior liens, delayed proceedings, exchange controls, limits on the sale currency, right only to arrest but not "merits" jurisdiction, high security for costs, excessive court costs, or insolvency stays on enforcement.

10–5 **Risks of possession** But there are disadvantages of possession. The creditor incurs the liabilities of an owner to third parties, e.g. for environmental pollution or damage caused by the chattel (hence insurance is important). The creditor is liable to the debtor for negligent losses, but some contracting out is possible. Thus, in the foundation English case of *White v City of London Brewery Co* (1889) 42 Ch D 237, a mortgagee in possession of a public house was held liable for losses in letting the pub as a house tied to a particular brewer when he should have let it as a free house. Damages result if possession is wrongful or premature. Finally, in the case of ships, aircraft and other assets whose operation must be officially licensed, the mortgagee or his representatives may need to obtain the necessary certificates to operate the asset or conduct the business. It may be possible to do so through a specialised manager, but this factor generally rules out the remedy in the case of, say, financial institutions where the official authorisation is generally cancellable on actual or threatened insolvency.

The appointment of a receiver to manage the asset, as opposed to mortgagee himself going into possession, may help cure some of the above problems because, under English law at least, the receiver can be constituted as agent of the debtor (until winding-up of the company) so that the secured creditor is not liable for his contracts or for his negligent acts or omissions: see IA 1986 s 44. They are treated as liabilities of the debtor himself – leaving the third party with a mere unsecured claim against the debtor which is often worthless. This remarkable state of affairs is grounded on two strong English policies – the protection of secured creditors and the intense resistance to big pocket liability, i.e. fixing responsibility on the receiver and hence on the bank or other institution who may have appointed him and expressly indemnified him unless the receiver is really seriously at fault. In practice however banks appointing a receiver are generally expected to indemnify him for liabilities properly incurred by him personally. Further, administrative receivers are, in England, personally liable on contracts entered into by them, in carrying out their functions: IA 1986 s 44. Case law amplifies whether a receiver can cause the company to break its contracts.

Method of appointment of receivers If the security document contains the   10–6
necessary powers, no court order is necessary for the mortgagee to appoint a
receiver or to take possession. A receiver in respect of a floating charge can
be appointed immediately in writing. He does not have to consider all relevant matters, or the interests of the debtor: *Shamji v Johnson Matthey
Bankers Ltd* [1991] BCLC 36. The mortgagee can take possession of a ship
at sea by simply giving notice to the mortgagor, the crew and the charterer
with or without appointing a manager. The powers of the directors to manage the business are suspended: *Moss SS Co Ltd v Whinney* [1912] AC 254,
HL.

Country survey Countries which allow this remedy of possessory manage-   10–7
ment (with or without variations) include the English-based states and most
states in the US (although the directors cannot be dispossessed), but the
remedies have caught on only episodically elsewhere. For example, because
of the desire to promote the foreign financing of its merchant fleet, the
Greek Legislative Decree No 3899/58 gives the mortgagee of a duly
recorded and notarised preferred mortgage of a Greek flag ship an
additional power of possessory management and sale without court order if
so provided in the mortgage. This also applies to Greek flag aircraft. A similar amendment was introduced in Panama in 1984 for naval mortgages:
ComC Art 1527 A. The ability in other countries, such as Norway and
Spain, for the court to appoint a manager to operate a vessel is purely a protective measure designed to safeguard the vessel while in the custody of the
court and is not to be equated with the English power to continue trading
the vessel. Although Norway, Finland and Sweden have a statutory floating
charge, this does not confer powers of management. Scotland has receivership only for the floating charge. The Germanic fiduciary transfer does not
confer powers of possessory management. Generally the remedy is only
rarely available in civil code countries or in Scandinavia, including countries
otherwise sympathetic to security, e.g. Germany, Japan and Sweden.

According to surveys of ship and aircraft mortgages (cited in the bibliography), the remedy of possessory management is not available in the following countries in relation to ships or aircraft or both and this is likely to
indicate the general attitude:

Europe:	Belgium, Denmark, France, Germany, Italy, Luxem-bourg, Portugal, Spain
Scandinavia:	Finland, Sweden
Latin America:	Argentina, Bolivia, Brazil, Chile, Colombia, Costa Rica, Guatemala, Mexico, Peru, Uruguay, Venezuela

Elsewhere: Egypt, Ethiopia, Japan, South Africa (generally – not just ships and aircraft), Taiwan, Thailand.

Judicially ordered public auction vs private sale

10–8   A public auction under judicial supervision is intended to protect the debtor. Generally a court order is required in those numerous jurisdictions which limit the realisation remedies of the mortgagee to this sole method. The court order results in delay and cost (extra burden on both parties). Public auctions are not necessarily the best way of obtaining a good price.

A private sale permits a rapid disposal of the asset without delays or court costs. But there are risks for the creditor. Thus, there are no protections on the price. The mortgagee should obtain expert valuations and conduct the sale reasonably. Then, the sale may not be recognised in other jurisdictions. This is especially important for ships and aircraft where a certificate of deletion may be required for the purchaser to re-register elsewhere. In the case of ships, the British shipping authorities do not require to see a certificate of deletion. Next, in the case of ships and aircraft, the sale may not scrape off lienholders, e.g. maritime liens. The selling creditor might therefore be liable under the sale agreement to the purchaser. Further, a private sale by agreement and after the mortgage was given in those jurisdictions requiring judicial public auction but allowing a port-mortgage agreement may be set aside as a voidable preference if in the suspect period, e.g. as in Venezuela. Finally, because of title risks to the purchaser, purchasers may pay less.

Public auction procedures

10–9   Court-driven public auctions inevitably lead to delays. In the Hames/McBain survey of aircraft enforcement proceedings covering some 60 countries (cited in the bibliography), delays of between one and five years were frequently cited.

Judicial protectionism is evidenced in many countries by elaborate formalism in the auction process which is hardly conducive to a quick and opportunistic sale. Thus in some countries, the court must fix a minimum estimated value of the asset and, if that estimate is not met on first auction, other auctions have to follow. This appraisal, generally referred to an expert or more than one, inevitably leads to more delay. It may also form the basis of judicial costs and bond security.

In Italy, for example, the initial auction price of a ship is the expert's estimate of the value of the ship and, if no offers are made at that price, the judge reduces it by 20 per cent until reduced to 40 per cent when the judge orders a sale by private treaty. In Spain, three surveyors, one nominated by each of the mortgagor and the mortgagee, and the third by the judge, must survey and value a ship prior to the court-ordered public auction. In Mexico, there is also a staged system of auctions. At the first auction, the sale can go ahead at two-thirds of the valuation and at the second auction a further 10 per cent can be deducted if the court so allows.

Private sale countries

Countries which allow a private sale, if so agreed in the security document, include the English-based states, most states in the United States (subject to a "commercially reasonable" test in the Uniform Commercial Code), and sometimes Greece (in the case of preferred ship and aircraft mortgages), Panama (for ships: C Com Art 1527), South Korea, Norway (for ships – Enforcement Act s 188), the Philippines (CC Art 1306), Switzerland (if the debtor is bankrupt) and Taiwan (Chattel Secured Transactions Act, Art 18, subject to restrictions). In Germany the fiduciary transfer allows a private sale unless the debtor resists and this may be true in the other "fiduciary transfer" countries, e.g. Japan and Switzerland. But otherwise the general rule in non-common law states is judicial auction, but subject to the exceptions mentioned below. **10–10**

Judicial sale countries

Countries which require a court order for realisation or public auction or both for (possibly indicative) ship or aircraft mortgages include the following (although there may be exceptions for certain types of assets and although the creditor can usually bid at the auction). **10–11**

Europe:	Austria; Belgium; Denmark (summary bailiff sale sometimes allowed); Finland (summary sale available); France; Germany; Iceland (summary sale available); Italy; Luxembourg (court may order private sale); Malta (possibly private sale of ships and aircraft since this area of law is based on English law); Norway (perhaps); Portugal; Spain (extrajudicial notary auction available); Sweden (Execution Code 1982 c 12); Switzerland (private sale if debtor bankrupt);
Latin America:	Argentina; Bolivia; Brazil; Chile; Colombia; Costa Rica (staged auctions); Ecuador; Guatemala; Mexico (staged

auctions); Panama (staged auctions, but private sale of ship allowed); Peru (but mortgagor can appoint third party, e.g. bank, as seller); Uruguay; Venezuela;

Elsewhere: Egypt; Ethiopia; Israel; Japan (see CC Art 387, Civil Execution Law Art 181–188); South Korea; South Africa; Thailand; Turkey.

In some countries, the mortgagor can waive the right to judicial evaluation prior to sale or fix the minimum appraisal value in the mortgage itself which is then taken as the basis for the judicial auction. Whether the latter is of much use in practice might be questionable where the default has been exacerbated by a general collapse in asset values.

Further, in the Germanic countries, a transferee under a fiduciary transfer can usually sell privately – a noted advantage over the pledge.

Quick summary procedure

10–12   In some countries, the formalism of a judicial auction is replaced by a summary enforcement procedure which short-circuits the normal court process. Thus in Finland and other Scandinavian countries, mortgages can usually be enforced by a summary procedure by order of a subordinate court official, but if the debtor challenges the enforcement on grounds which are not merely shadowy a full judicial trial is necessary. Similarly in Israel enforcement through the Executive Office is available by virtue of the Pledges Law of 1967 for certain types of property as a quick proceeding, e.g. for registered pledges of movable property. It may be that summary procedures are more widely practised than might appear from the law digests.

Post-mortgage agreement to private sale

10–13   It is commonly the case in the "judicial public auction" group that the mortgagor can agree to a private sale after the mortgage has been entered into so that, if the mortgagor accepts that the position is hopeless, he can allow a private sale to side-step the cumbersome court procedures. The object of this post-mortgage stipulation is to protect the debtor in his initial negotiations for the credit when his bargaining power is weaker. **Belgium** and **Israel** are examples of countries which allow a post-mortgage agreement to a private sale and in practice it is believed that debtor consent is common. But elsewhere, even this post-mortgage agreement is prohibited, e.g. Egypt and perhaps other traditional Napoleonic countries.

Forced sale of liquid assets

One suspects it may often be the case that, although a state may insist on a   **10–14**
judicially supervised public auction as the mandatory remedy for assets
which are not prone to ready valuation, such as land and (to a lesser extent)
ships and aircraft, this right may not apply to assets having a readily ascertained market value, such as quoted securities. But whether this is a safe
generalisation requires detailed research.

Grace periods on enforcement rights

Related to the question of the degree of protection afforded to the debtor by   **10–15**
limits on the remedies of the secured creditor is the attitude to compulsory
grace periods before enforcement and controls on the type of default which
justify enforcement.

As regards the acceleration of secured loans, the English courts will not
(outside the consumer context) grant relief against cancellation of the credit
if the agreement provides that payment is to be made promptly on the due
date and the payment is late, even only a day late: see, for example, *The
Angelic Star* [1988] Lloyds Rep 122, CA (acceleration of shipping loan).
The rationale is that the debtor is free to negotiate a grace period if he
wishes and it is not for the court to substitute its own view of an appropriate
grace period. The accent is on certainty and freedom of contract. If the court
can substitute its own views, the mortgagee runs risks of substantial
damages for premature enforcement – should he have waited a week, 10
days, a fortnight, a month? Although statute (the Law of Property Act
1925) imposes grace periods for certain mortgage enforcements, these can
be, and usually are, excluded by contract, and if a charge states that the
chargee can appoint a receiver if the loan is not paid on demand, it means
what it says. The debtor is given time to obtain the money on the assump-
tion that he has it in his bank, i.e. no more than a few hours: *Cripps (Phar-
maceuticals) Ltd v Wickenden* [1973] 2 All ER 606; *Moore v Shelley* (1881)
8 App Cas 285, 293, PC. Consumers are protected by special consumer
legislation – the Consumer Credit Act 1974. By contrast, Canadian case law
shows more indulgence to the debtor: see *Ronald Elwyn Foster Ltd v Dun-
lop Canada Ltd* [1982] 1 SCR 726, which resulted in extensive litigation as
to what was a reasonable period of time. As from 1992, Canadian bankruptcy law imposed a 10-day freeze on enforcement which gives the debtor
the ability to apply for a rehabilitation proceeding which freezes enforcement: para 11–23 *et seq.* The position is similar in the US under the UCC.

Outside English-based countries, grace periods on enforcement are common. Apart from debtor protection, one reason may be that, if the only

method of enforcement is a judicial public auction, grace periods to the debtor are neither here nor there in the context of the delays involved in a court-driven enforcement process.

In Switzerland mortgages are enforced by service, through a debt collection authority, of a payment order requiring payment within one month. In Spain a ship mortgagee cannot enforce unless a judicial or notarised demand has been served on the mortgagor and he has failed to pay for three days. Even then, if the vessel is loaded and ready to sail, the arrest can be postponed, but subject to adequate security being given as required by the court. In Denmark, notice of a sale of a mortgaged ship must be given six weeks prior to the sale. In Italy a court order for the sale of a ship cannot be applied for until 30 days have elapsed from the seizure of the ship and not later than 90 days thereafter. Whether these grace periods apply to other assets is a matter for investigation.

Efficacy of events of default

10–16　As to the defaults which justify enforcement, the English courts leave that to the parties (outside consumer credit), although it is probably true to say that in practice enforcement is a last resort and so usually occurs when the position is hopeless and the mortgagor has stopped paying.

This combination of commercial liberalism and pragmatism is not shown everywhere and legislation is to be found in many jurisdictions which limits the defaults which justify enforcement. In Continental European countries, the use of events of default is controlled by general concepts of good faith entrenched in the Code, as in Germany, or a concept of abuse of rights, as in France. Sometimes the legislature is more specific. For example, s 258 of the Norwegian Maritime Code provides that, apart from the due date agreed in a mortgage, a debt secured by a mortgage on the ship entered in the Register of Ships falls due when: "(1) the ship is lost or scrapped, (2) the mortgagee's security is materially impaired in consequence of damage to the ship, (3) the ship loses its nationality, (4) a compulsory or necessary auction takes place, (5) bankruptcy proceedings or public composition proceedings are commenced against the owner of the ship or against the debtor, and (6) material default is made in the obligation to pay interest or instalments of the principal sums or to maintain or to insure the ship as agreed." If the agreement contains provisions whereby the debt matures otherwise than on these grounds then such provision may be set aside in whole or in part if it would be unreasonable or clearly contrary to proper business practice to rely on it.

In some civil code countries there is effectively a short stay on enforcement in the event of bankruptcy by reason of the fact that the creditor must notify his secured claim to the administrator and the administrator has the right to redeem the security. Hence, the creditor is delayed during the grace period during which the administrator must make up his mind.

Countries which give this right to the administrator include Belgium, Italy (sometimes – see BA Art 53), Luxembourg and possibly some other members of the Franco-Latin group. In Denmark the trustee must approve a sale in the case of non-possessory chattel mortgages but if he has not taken any steps to have the assets sold by enforcement sale within six months of the date of the declaration of bankruptcy, the mortgagee may demand the sale. In the Netherlands a court can order a cooling-off period of one month, extendible for a further month, during which security rights may not be enforced.

Marshalling

Marshalling applies where a debtor mortgages one asset to a senior creditor   10–17
and another asset to the senior creditor and also a junior creditor. If the senior creditor realises out of the asset on which he is solely secured, there is more for the junior creditor on the other asset. If the senior creditor realises out of the asset on which they are both secured, the junior creditor is disappointed and receives less.

Marshalling allows the junior creditor to take over the senior creditor's sole security pro rata if the senior creditor disappoints him in this way. The effect is not just to protect the junior creditor but to favour the junior creditor at the expense of the insolvent estate. Marshalling is available to a junior creditor under English law, but the law protects the senior creditor by allowing him to choose which asset to realise first: he does not have to look to the sole security first. Various forms of marshalling appear to exist in American common law states.

CHAPTER 11

SECURITY AND REHABILITATION PROCEEDINGS

General

Introduction

11-1 This chapter is drawn from sections in another work (on the principles of international insolvency) in this series of books on financial law and, for the convenience of the reader, summarises aspects relevant to the impact of rehabilitation proceedings on security.

This chapter focuses solely on security and does not deal with the jurisdiction of the courts to order a rehabilitation proceeding, with eligible debtors, with stays on legal proceedings or title finance or set-off or contract rescission, or with reorganisation plans or with the general policy background to those proceedings. The reader is referred to the other work for these aspects.

The main questions are whether the rehabilitation proceeding stays the enforcement of security or otherwise interferes with the security, e.g. by allowing the insolvency administrator to substitute the collateral or by subordinating the security to the expenses of the proceeding.

Rescue proceedings and private restructurings

11-2 Corporate rescue proceedings designed to resuscitate debtor companies in distress are a feature of modern insolvency law in many industrialised countries.

The alternative is a private consensual debt restructuring (work-out) agreed between creditors, or more usually by bank creditors. The pros and cons of formal rehabilitation proceedings compared to work-outs are summarised elsewhere in this series of works. The main advantages of formal proceedings are a statutory freeze on individual creditor enforcements and a power to bind dissentient creditors. The main disadvantages are that the public declaration of insolvency normally devastates a business, that the freeze can prejudice creditor protections and that formal proceedings are costly. Formal rehabilitation proceedings have a low rate of success – often around a mere 10 per cent of those initiated. Many experienced practitioners in this field agree that the private restructuring is much faster, safer and cheaper than a formal proceeding and that a formal proceeding is a last resort to be used only if there is absolutely no alternative. Nevertheless, these proceedings are now pervasive and their potential impact on security can be major.

Classification of proceedings

One may in outline classify the various forms of present-day proceedings 11–3 into the following groups:

— Voluntary compositions

— Traditional compositions and moratoriums

— Corporate rehabilitation proceedings

The first two are little used in those countries which have them and hence it is mainly the corporate rehabilitation proceedings which are of interest. Nevertheless, the first two groups may briefly be described prior to a more detailed review of corporate rehabilitations. Country surveys of compositions and moratoriums are to be found elsewhere in this series of works.

Voluntary compositions

These are compositions which are either voluntary or operate without the 11–4 benefit of a freeze on legal proceedings or security enforcement actions by creditors. They include corporate schemes of arrangement and individual deeds of arrangement with creditors in England and other English-based countries, such as Australia, Singapore and New Zealand. The English-based schemes of arrangement under companies legislation (in Britain now under s 425 of the Companies Act 1985) do not impose an initial freeze on proceedings, let alone the enforcement of security, and so are virtually ineffective as an insolvency proceeding (although sometimes they can be implemented behind the curtain of bankruptcy or rehabilitation proceedings, as in the case of the English administration). Other compositions are ineffective because they require unanimous creditor approval (Swedish *ackord*).

Traditional compositions and moratoriums

Preventive composition proceedings These are widespread and are usually 11–5 little used or rarely successful. One reason for this in some countries is that the composition must offer a minimum immediate payment to creditors. It is generally found that the debtor's position is hopeless and the threshold payment unattainable. This is the case, for example, in Austria, Brazil, Denmark, Italy, Norway and Sweden. The thresholds vary from 25 per cent to 40 per cent for immediate payments with, sometimes, a sliding scale upwards for delayed payments. The debtor is generally in no position to make any payments at all, let alone payments of that order – which far exceed the normal dividends on a liquidation (zero to 20 per cent in the usual case). Alternatively, as in Belgium and Luxembourg, the debtor must show that his insolvency resulted from misfortune and not mismanagement – something which only courts which are exceptionally sympathetic to debtors find convincing.

The usual pattern is that a petition for composition stays creditor executions and bankruptcy petitions, but does not freeze the rights of preferential creditors or secured creditors, nor does it prejudice title finance, set-off, contract cancellations or lease forfeitures: hence the debtor loses assets which might otherwise be used in the rehabilitation process. In other words, the procedures are primarily distributive in an order which reflects the bankruptcy hierarchy and are intended to result in a writing-down of debt or a sale so that the debtor can start again.

Although the debtor's management often remains in possession, any transaction of significance usually has to be approved by a supervisor or by a creditor committee.

The debtor presents his composition plan, usually in consultation with a creditors committee or a supervisor, and the plan is voted on by unsecured creditors. The majorities vary from 50 per cent to 80 per cent or more and sometimes the majorities required increase according to the degree that debts are written down, e.g. Norway. The composition must generally be approved by the court to give it judicial force and to bind dissentient creditors. Normally this homologation is conditional on equality of treatment between unsecured creditors of the same rank and the prior payment in full of preferential creditors (such as taxes and employees), although here and there the rules recognise the fact that it may be desirable to pay off small creditors in full.

These compositions may be preventive in that they precede bankruptcy as an alternative to bankruptcy or they may be suspensive by suspending bankruptcy proceedings which have already begun.

Moratoriums These are often limited in time. Some are short breathing-spaces, e.g. the 1982 Austrian preliminary procedure – five weeks – which stays the enforcement of security, and the Danish suspension of payments (up to 12 months). Others are much longer, e.g. the Belgian and Luxembourg *sursis de paiement* – three years; the Dutch *surséance van betaling* – three years; and the Italian *amministrazione controllata* – two years.

Secured creditors are not effected under the English company voluntary arrangement under IA 1986, under the Italian judicial composition (*concordato preventivo*) in BA 1942, under the Luxembourg controlled management (*gestion controllé*) and the preventive composition (*concordat préventif á la faillite*), the Netherlands judicial composition (the *akkoord*) or the Swedish *ackord*.

Corporate rehabilitation proceedings

Examples of proceedings

Modern forms of corporate rehabilitation impose a freeze on creditor proceedings and also significantly impinge on creditor rights including security rights. The rationale of the disturbance of creditor rights is that the rights are merely delayed and are reinstated if the rescue is successful so that the creditors, it is said, lose nothing. However, these rescue proceedings have had a very low rate of success, e.g. 10 per cent, so that this rationale appears to be more difficult to justify.   **11–6**

They include: **mild proceedings**, such as:

- In **Australia** the voluntary administration and deed of company arrangement under the Corporate Law Reform Act 1992

- In **Britain**, an administration under IA 1986

- In the **Republic of Ireland**, an examinership under the Companies (Amendment) Act 1990

- In **Japan**, the Corporate Rehabilitation Law of 1952, based on the pre-1978 US Bankruptcy Act of 1898 Chapter X as amended and introduced at the suggestion of the Occupation authorities. The Bankruptcy Law of 1923 was based on German ideas. See Brooke Schumm III "Comparison of Japanese and American Bankruptcy Law", *Michigan Year Book of International Legal Studies* 291 (1988).

- In **Singapore** the judicial management introduced by the Companies (Amendment) Act 1987 and largely based on the British administration under IA 1986, but limited to 180 days. As in Britain, floating chargees have blocking powers.

- In **Spain**, the suspension of payments under the Suspension of Payments Act of 1922.

Tough proceedings, such as:

- In **Canada**, the commercial reorganisation proposal under the Bankruptcy and Insolvency Act 1992 and the older but tougher Companies' Creditors Arrangement Act dating from the 1930s. Both are federal.

— In **France** the *redressement judiciaire* under the Law of January 25, 1985

— In **Italy**, the extraordinary administration of 1979 (*amministrazione straordinaria*), a dirigist statute dispensing with the rule of law

— In **New Zealand**, the statutory management under the Corporations (Investigation and Management Act) 1989

— In the **United States**, Chapter 11 of the Bankruptcy Code of 1978 which is a federal statute.

This section discusses some of the main issues relevant to security and compares the approach in Britain, the US, France, Japan, Australia and Canada. A fuller treatment and details of other countries is found elsewhere in this series. All the proceedings stay legal proceedings and final bankruptcy petitions and the question here is the impact they have on security.

Impact on security interests generally

11–7 **Attitude to security** It has already been seen that jurisdictions fall into four main groups as regards their attitude to security as a protection against insolvency – (1) those very sympathetic to security (e.g. English-based countries, Sweden); (2) those fairly sympathetic (e.g. Germany, Netherlands, Japan, Switzerland, United States), (3) those quite hostile (e.g. Belgium, most Latin American countries, Spain) and (4) those very hostile (e.g. Austria, France). These attitudes tend to be reflected in rehabilitation statutes in that the sympathetic jurisdictions surrender the benefits of security more grudgingly, while those initially hostile to security have in any event subordinated the role of security as a creditor-protection and therefore lose little by subordinating it further on rehabilitation.

Stays on enforcement If there is a stay on the enforcement of security, the main points to be considered are the period of the stay and whether the stay is limited to assets essential to the continuing business which are idiosyncratic (not securities, cash or ordinary commodities). The alleged object of the stay is to keep the business together while the rehabilitation is allowed to work, e.g. by preventing the mortgagee sale of the main factory, computer equipment, or an essential patent or unfinished inventory. But the effect of excessive interference in the security is to deprive the creditor of the benefit of the security: the whole purpose of security is that it should be available on the insolvency of the debtor and therefore, if the jurisdiction destroys the security when it is most needed, the value and utility of security itself is demoted. Accordingly jurisdictions have to decide whether they desire the advantages of security or whether they prefer the draconian rehabilitation procedure, although middle courses are possible, e.g. a stay on enforcement for a limited period.

The stay causes problems for perishable assets; volatile assets, such as securities, commodities and foreign currency deposits, especially margin collateral for market dealings; ships, aircraft and other assets which are in need of special protection or which could attract an "assets" bankruptcy jurisdiction just because they happen to be there or which can be spirited away to avoid a surprise attachment; liens covering small assets not essential to the business; income-earning assets if the debtor can use the income, e.g. rent from land and equipment leases, dividends and interest on securities, recoveries on receivables, royalties and intellectual property rights (the income may have been essential to service the creditors' interest); and possessory pledges and liens since the security is lost if possession must be surrendered.

Other factors Other factors are: (1) a stay results in the erosion of security if   **11–8**
it falls in value or if interest continues to pile up – the period of the stay is germane; (2) whether the debtor can use the secured assets for the purpose of the continuing business and the powers which the creditor has to preserve the asset; (3) whether the debtor can substitute alternative secured assets in order to retain some essential asset; (4) whether a plan can bind dissentient secured creditors to an extension of the maturity of the debt or a reduction in amounts or a change of currency; (5) whether the security is primed by the costs of the administration (liabilities incurred in continuing the business, super-priority loans, employees, taxes) so that the creditor's security is eroded and its value highly unpredictable; (6) whether security expressed to cover after-acquired property such as a floating charge over all present and future assets or an aircraft mortgage over engines subsequently replaced, can catch assets acquired by the debtor post-commencement; (7) the degree of protection given to secured creditors against unfair prejudice; (8) whether cash collateral can be taken away in the interests of financing the business; (9) whether post-commencement interest continues to run and can be added to the secured debt.

A common problem is whether a creditor who has security over investments or receivables violates a stay if he receives payment on the assets from the third party and applies it to the secured debt: this would be a violation of the US stay in BC 1978 s 362.

Plainly, there can be many degrees of interference, ranging from a short freeze on enforcement to total expropriation.

English administration

11–9   **Summary** In an English administration, the petition stays the enforcement of security without administrator consent or court leave: IA 1986 ss 10 and 11. There is no time limit, although in practice the position is contained by court guidelines which support secured creditors. This freeze applies not only to mortgages and the like but also ships, aircraft, liens and (probably) the collection by the secured creditor of assigned receivables. These liens include unpaid vendor liens, probably possessory liens (including liens on cheques being collected) and the statutory rights of an airport to detain aircraft leased to the debtor for unpaid airport charges: *Re Paramount Airways Ltd* [1990] BCC 130.

The courts have signalled adherence to the traditional English support of security and title finance by stating that an administrator should normally give consent to enforcement and repossession, unless substantially greater loss would be caused to others, since an administration for the benefit of unsecured creditors should not be carried on at the expense of those with proprietary rights: the guidelines were laid down by the Court of Appeal in the landmark decision of *Re Atlantic Computer Systems plc* [1990] BCC 859. Leave to enforce was refused in *Re Meesan Investments Ltd* [1988] 4 BCC 788 because the administrator had nearly completed a satisfactory sale.

The administrator can dispose of the property charged with the leave of the court, e.g. to obtain a more advantageous realisation. The object of this is to facilitate a sale of the business, or a segment of the business, as a whole and thereby to secure a better price: this might be prejudicial if, say, a creditor had a mortgage over the factory or over some essential intellectual property right. The secured creditor is entitled to the net proceeds plus a top-up for any shortfall below market value as determined by the court: IA 1986 s 15.

An administration does not suspend post-order interest and so this can continue to be covered by the security, although the forced stay causes extra interest to eat into the value of the security.

The secured creditor is not prevented from accelerating the secured debt by reason of the order and is not therefore relegated either to the original terms of the loan or to a moratorium on payments, nor can he be if a voluntary arrangement is instituted behind the protective curtain of the administration since voluntary arrangements cannot affect secured creditors.

The secured creditor is not bound to accept substitute security or alternative adequate protection so that his rights are more or less intact. Fixed security is not primed by ordinary preferential creditors or expenses of the administration. The court can sanction a lifting of the freeze in its discretion.

A secured creditor can make an "unfair prejudice" application to the court under IA 1986 s 27.

If the security is margin collateral or other security in an organised market, it may be exempt from the stay on security under the provisions of Part VII of the Companies Act 1989 applying to certain recognised investment exchanges and clearing houses, amongst others. These provisions recognised the paramount importance of protecting the integrity of markets.

Blocking power of universal chargee But a remarkable feature of the English   **11–10** approach is that, in choosing whether to support the rights of the holder of a universal floating charge to manage the business through a receiver for his own benefit as against the rights of unsecured creditors on a rehabilitation, the English decided to support the holder of the floating charge. The reason for this is that the universal floating charge has been shown to be a highly effective method of saving a business when compared to other rescue proceedings and indeed the administration procedure was not modelled on the US Chapter 11, but rather on the equivalent for unsecured creditors of a floating charge receivership. The administration can be blocked by the holder of a floating charge who has security (fixed or floating) over "substantially the whole" of the assets of the company if he appoints an administrative receiver (broadly a private manager of the security) prior to the making of an administration order – the chargee must be notified of the petition for the administration to give him time to block: IA 1986 s 9. Five clear days are required, but this can be abridged: *Re A Company No. 00175 of 1987* (1987) 3 BCC 124. The security must not be subject to avoidance. The theory is that it is not possible to have two persons managing the business of the company – the administrator and the chargee's receiver – the chargee's receiver takes precedence. As a result of this blocking power, banks and other creditors often take "featherweight floaters" over all the assets of a company which can be subordinated to other third party charges without losing their blocking vitality – so that the debtor is not restrained from raising fresh secured finance.

The holder of a floating charge is usually well-advised to block, although this is not necessarily so, e.g. because the chargee wishes to freeze liquidation petitions, but can control the administrator by virtue of the administrator's need for fresh funds from the chargee. But blocking is usually desirable because, if the security is a floating charge, it can more or less be wiped out on administration. See IA 1986 s 15. In the case of a floating charge not used to block, the administrator can deal with the property charged as if it were not subject to the security (e.g. lease it, dispose of it, create prior charges over it to secure new loans) but, if the property is disposed of, the priority of the charge traces through to property directly or indirectly representing the charged property. Unlike fixed security, the administrator need not make up the sale proceeds to market value. The creditor is left with an "unfair prejudice" application under IA 1986 s 27. The administrator's contracts and expenses are a prior charge on the property so that the security is diminished if the administrator trades at a loss: IA 1986 s 19. The overall effect is that partial floating charges, e.g. over receivables or inventory or portfolios of securities, are weak, because they cannot block unless accompanied by fixed charges so that substantially all the company's property is charged. This seems regrettable because partial floating charges were extremely useful. The English have therefore guillotined the partial floating charge but glorified the comprehensive charge. On the other hand, administrators can be expected to reflect cautiously before they embark on a course which might erode security, because of the risk of liability. Whether a floating charge would extend to assets of the company acquired after the administration order is undecided.

The English stay on security is odd. This is because companies which borrow secured are usually small companies, property companies or single-project companies which give full fixed and floating charges over all their assets: hence the banks can defeat the administration and there would be no point in freezing the security. The effect therefore is to freeze isolated security, notably charges over investment securities or liens or over equipment where the need to realise quickly is more pressing, and the need to preserve the assets for the business less convincing. In the light of English financings, the stay therefore seems somewhat ideological. In practice, administrators have readily consented to realisations and the practical effect may not be as serious as the statute envisages.

US Chapter 11

11–11   Under the US Chapter 11 in BC 1978 the position is markedly different and much more complicated. Initially the effect of the bankruptcy petition is to stay the enforcement of security without the consent of the court for "cause", e.g. that the debtor has no equity in the property. The creditor will usually satisfy the second test of "no necessity" if there is no reasonable possibility of a rehabilitation within a reasonable period, e.g. less than a year : see *US Association of Taxes v Timbers of Inwood Forest Associates Ltd*, 484 US 365 (1988) *and* the property is not necessary to an effective Chapter 11 organisation, or where the property is depreciating in value. See BC 1978 s 362(a)(4).

The security must not be capable of avoidance.

11–12   **Adequate protection** Rather than allowing relief from the stay, the court may order the creditor to be given adequate protection of its security interest, e.g. additional liens or cash payments to match the fall in value. The basic protection given to secured creditors is that they must receive indubitably adequate protection for their security.

The House Report indicated that the concept of adequate protection is derived from the Fifth Amendment protection of property interests and from a policy that secured creditors should not be deprived of the benefit of their bargain, so that if the secured creditor does not get the exact collateral (because, like a factory, it is needed for the debtor's business), he must get the equivalent in value. Case law shows that the creditor has adequate protection if he is over-secured (to the extent of the cushion) or has a recoverable guarantee from a third party, but not usually if the guarantee is unsecured. The US Supreme Court established in the *Timbers* case above that, if the creditor is under-secured, the creditor is entitled to cash payments (or the equivalent) if his collateral is decreasing in value, that he is not entitled to compensation for loss of the ability to reinvest proceeds from a foreclosure, and that the creditor should be granted relief from the stay if the property is not necessary for an effective reorganisation which is feasible and in prospect.

Debtor's use of collateral The debtor in US Chapter 11 can obtain permission to obtain credit that is secured by an equal or superior lien on the encumbered property if this is the only way credit can be obtained.   **11–13**

The debtor can use collateral for which purpose a distinction is made between cash and non-cash. Cash collateral includes cash, negotiable instruments, documents of title, securities, deposit accounts and the rents, income and proceeds of other collateral: s 363(a). Non-cash will therefore include, for example, inventory, machinery, equipment and real estate.

The debtor may also request emergency use of its cash collateral prior to a final hearing, subject to the likelihood of adequate protection being available on the final hearing in order to avoid a cessation of the business and to protect the value of the business: s 363(c)(2). Court approval is required for the use of cash or cash equivalents in which a creditor has a security interest. The debtor can use non-cash collateral without that approval in the ordinary course of business (s 363(c)(1)) but subject to "adequate protection", such as additional liens or cash replacements, in the absence of which the creditor may have grounds to apply for foreclosure. The object of using cash collateral is that the debtor needs cash to survive and would immediately collapse if, say, its cash balances at the bank were removed. Naturally any dissipation of the cash or securities would render security over these items quite useless. Generally the courts have recognised the importance of adequate protection; see, e.g. *Re CF Simonin's Sons Inc*, 28 Bankr 707, 10 BCD 343 (Bankr EDNC 1983); *Re Greenwood Building Supply Inc*, 23 Bankr 720, 7 CBC 2d 659, 9 BCD 907 (Bankr WD Mo 1982). For example, if the debtor can borrow 80 per cent of accounts receivables or inventory (which both turn into cash collateral as they are realised), that ratio must be maintained for fresh post-commencement advances which must be covered by replacement receivables and inventory, but there have been cases where this principle has not been honoured.

There is case law on how to value the collateral – usually on the higher going concern basis: receivables and inventory generally collapse in value on a liquidation. There is also complex case law on whether a mortgagee of real estate is entitled to post-petition rents and hotel revenues: see *Butner v United States*, 440 US 48, 99 S Ct 914, 59 L Ed 2d 136 (1979). Generally rents can be protected under state law, but hotel revenues are usually treated as after-acquired property which belongs to the estate: the effect therefore is that the secured creditor loses the post-petition income from the hotels, e.g. *Re Sacramento Mansion Ltd*, 117 Bankr 592 (Banker D Col 1990).

If certain conditions are met, the debtor may sell encumbered property free of the lien so that the lien attaches to the proceeds of sale.

An under secured creditor will not be entitled to adequate protection for time lost during which his enforcement rights are stayed.

11–14 **Priority** BC 1978 s 507(b) provides that, to the extent that the trustee has given adequate protection to the interest of a holder of a claim under ss 362 (relief from automatic stay), 363 (relief from ability to trustee to use, sell or lease property of the debtor in which a third party has an interest) or 364 (superpriority security for post-petition loans which prime existing security) that proves to be inadequate (and such claims were secured on the property of the debtor), the secured creditor's claim has complete priority, including priority over administrative expenses, employees and taxes. The secured creditor's absolute priority is intended to be preserved.

11–15 **Post-commencement property** Without court approval, a floating lien on accounts receivable, inventory and the like will not extend to property acquired after the commencement of the case. The effect of BA 1978 s 552 is that a security interest cannot cover post-commencement property, but can cover the proceeds, product or rents which arise post-commencement out of pre-petition collateral, e.g. the sale of inventory. Thus the following have been held not to be caught by a security interest if received post-commence-ment: refund of state unemployment taxes; proceeds of crops planted after commencement; gate receipts from a car race-track; hotel room revenues; and the proceeds of sale of products made from materials purchased post-petition.

> In *Re Cleary Brothers Construction Co*, 9 Bankr 40, 1 CBC 2d 989 (Bankr SD Fla 1980), the trustee rented a crane to a third party. The crane was subject to a security interest in favour of a creditor. *Held*: the rents belonged to the debtor's

estate and were not caught by the security interest. The creditor had not taken an assignment of the rents.

Contrast *Re Slab Fork Coal Co*, 784 F 2d 1188 (4th Cir 1986): the creditor had a security interest over a long term coal supply contract. The debtor continued to supply coal to the buyer post-petition. *Held*: the post-petition proceeds of sale belonged to the creditor since they were proceeds of pre-petition collateral.

Post-petition interest Post-petition interest is not covered by the collateral if the creditor is under secured: BC 1978 s 506(b). If he is over-secured, post-petition interest may accrue but may not be paid during the pendency of the case and the accrued interest becomes part of the secured creditor's claim to be treated under the plan.

Plan As regards the plan, the general scheme is that secured creditors retain   **11–16** their liens to the extent of the allowed amounts of their claims (any unsecured portion being treated as an unsecured claim) and this is so even if the collateral is transferred to another entity. Each holder must at least receive deferred cash payments up to the allowed amount of the claim having a present value equal to the value of the collateral. Of course if the plan takes months or years to formulate, the secured creditor has to wait (asset erosion, interest pile-up). The security is valued on a projected use/ going concern basis at the time of the plan: BC 1978 s 1111(b).

The secured creditor is not primed by administration expenses or preferential creditors except to the extent of the super-priority lien for debtor financing referred to above, which is subject to adequate protection.

There are special provisions in BC 1978 s 1110 applying to aircraft and to ships. The general effect of this section is that the holder of certain security interests in aircraft operated under a Civil Aeronautics Board Certificate or a US flag vessel can take possession unless the trustee, with the courts' approval, agrees to perform all future obligations and (generally) to cure past defaults. Hence there is an effective 60-day stay. Note that the protection does not avail foreign carriers or foreign ships so that a flag ship of a foreign entity can be subject to the general stay if the foreign entity becomes subject to a US Chapter 11. The 1994 amendments to the section should be considered.

French *redressement judiciaire*

In France security must be regarded as virtually worthless or at least highly   **11–17** unpredictable.

Initially, as in the case of England and the United States, the proceeding operates as a stay on enforcement of security, unless the repossession is justified by the continuation of operations.

Post-order interest is not recoverable except for loans or deferred credits of one year or more.

But most crushingly the security is subject to post-order administration expenses and to bankruptcy preferential creditors – employees, taxes and the like. The administrator can, with judicial approval, raise new loans priming all security: 1985 Law Art 40. By Art 40(2) the order of ranking of post-opening creditors is: (1) certain wage claims; (2) legal expenses; (3) loans granted by credit establishments and claims resulting from the forced continuation of contracts pursuant to Art 37 (which nullifies cancellation, acceleration and forfeiture clauses in contracts arising by reason of the insolvency); (4) certain sums advanced in accordance with the Labour Code; and (5) all other claims according to their rank, including secured claims. Hence the secured creditor can never know what his security is worth.

11–18   Apart from this, the rights of the secured creditor depend upon whether the security is a possessory pledge, a non-possessory security, or a mortgage of land and buildings. In all cases the court may order substitution of security if the plan provides for a continuation. If the plan provides for a general assignment to another entity, it is unclear if possessory pledges can go with it. In other cases the secured creditor receives the sale proceeds allocated by the court, subject to claims of higher rank.

Creditors cannot accelerate claims by reason of the proceedings (1985 Law Art 37) and further the secured debt may, as part of the plan approved by the court, be subject to a moratorium on debt service. Although the court cannot reduce the secured debt, the effect of a moratorium and the absence of post-proceeding interest have a similar effect. If the asset is sold, the proceeds receivable are discounted to reflect the fact that the particular creditor is achieving an advantage denied to other creditors.

If the enterprise goes into judicial liquidation, the secured creditors' rights of realisation revive.

There appear to be no special protections for aircraft or ships. But in the case of a liquidation, creditors with a retention of title clause and credit establishments to whom the debtor assigned professional debts (i.e. trade receivables) can enforce their rights and are not subject to the proceedings.

Priorities

11–19 In the case of liquidation, security ranks as follows:

1. employees have a super-priority over all security interests;

2. possessory pledgees and retention of title claimants have first priority over the property, subject only to employees;

3. post-opening creditors rank ahead of all security, except that in (2) – these are as itemised above;

4. general real property security interests and then special real property security interests;

5. special personal property security interests, subject to (1) and (2) above, and to tax claims, and then general personal property security interests;

6. general personal property security interests in the order in CC Art 2101;

7. pre-opening unsecured creditors.

Japanese corporate reorganisation Once the Japanese reorganisation has   11–20
commenced, official auction sales and the enforcement of an enterprise hypothecation are suspended, as are the enforcement of tax claims (with a one-year extendable maximum for tax claims): CRL Art 37(1). But the court can lift the suspension: CRL Art 37(5). A pre-ruling suspension is available only if there is no "likelihood of inflicting unreasonable losses on the creditors": CRL Art 37(1). This may approximate to the English judicial hostility to stays on security.

By Art 123 interest on secured claims is limited to one year but this does not apply to debentures.

Apart from this, secured creditors form a separate voting class for the purposes of approval of the reorganisation plan and high majorities are required to postpone security rights (75 per cent) or to reduce security rights (80 per cent). If the secured creditors do not approve the plan as a class, then the court can nevertheless approve the plan, but only if the security is maintained over any asset to be transferred to a new company, or if the asset is sold, or if its fair price is paid to the security-holder, or if other "fair and equitable protection" is given to the holder.

Australian company arrangement

Background In the Corporate Law Reform Act 1992, Australia adopted a   11–21
mild corporate rehabilitation statute comprising a voluntary administration and deed of company arrangement. The procedure stays security enforcement for a very short period comparatively (up to 60 days), but, like the British administration but unlike the Canadian BIA of 1992, does not stay the universal floating charge.

11–22   **Automatic stay** The main effect is to stay the exercise of rights against the company and property owned, possessed, used or occupied by it. The stay affects all unsecured creditors, secured creditors (with some exceptions) and others. Enforcement procedures and winding-up petitions are stayed.

A fully secured creditor can continue to enforce a security if the enforcement commenced before the appointment of the administrator or if it is commenced during a 14-day period, commencing from notice of the appointment of the administrator to the secured creditor: s 441A. A security over perishable property may be enforced: s 441A. Other secured creditors may only enforce their security if the enforcement process had commenced before the appointment of the administrator but this is subject to a power of the court to order, on the application of the administrator, a restraint on the continued enforcement of the security, subject to adequate protection of the creditor: s 441D. Also, in some circumstances a person holding a fixed or specific security over, for example, land, who has progressed the enforcement of the security to the point of exercising a power of sale of that property, may complete that process.

The administrator may not dispose of property subject to a charge otherwise than in the ordinary course of the company's business, or with the written consent of the chargee, or with the leave of the court; although the leave of the court may not be given unless the court is satisfied that arrangements have been made to adequately protect the interests of the chargee: s 442C.

If the charge is in the nature of a floating charge, subject to those limitations and the superior powers of the person who is entitled to and who is enforcing the charge, the administrator may deal with the company's property which is subject to that charge as though it continued to be a floating charge: s 442B. Additionally, in the case of the company's assets which are subject to a floating charge, the administrator's right of indemnity for administrative expenses out of those assets will enjoy priority to the claims of the chargee subject to exceptions. Hence the partial floating charge appears to be very weak, as in Britain: see para 11–10.

The stay continues for a period anticipated, in many cases, to be not longer than 35 days, but which may be extended by order of the court in a complex or large administration. There are provisions for voting on a creditor arrangement.

Canadian creditors arrangement and commercial reorganisation

11–23   In Canada, there are two parallel rehabilitation proceedings (1) the older and tougher Companies' Creditors Arrangement Act, dating from the 1930s, intended originally for publicly-held corporations with public debt and now used by the courts as a draconian reorganisation statute for everybody, and (2) the commercial reorganisation under the Bankruptcy and Insolvency Act 1992 (ss 50–66), amending the Bankruptcy Act 1949, previously significantly amended in 1966. Both statutes are Federal. The BIA was to be reviewed by a Parliamentary Committee in 1995.

The BIA evidenced a marked shift from a creditor-orientated bankruptcy procedure to the fashionable debtor-orientated rehabilitation and was probably intended to help employees and small businesses, while the CCAA may be regarded as more suitable for larger businesses. But, apart from the very wide automatic stay in the BIA (up to six months), the Act does not appear as tough as the US Chapter 11.

The CCAA is an open procedure with few formal rules. On the one hand, this allows flexibility. On the other hand, it creates unpredictability and much therefore depends on whether or not the signals from the courts are protective of creditor rights and recognise the tendency of reorganisations to fail in most cases.

Automatic stay There is a limited stay on filing of a proposal notice for the   **11–24** commercial reorganisation procedure under BIA 1992. On the filing of a definitive proposal or a proposal notice by an insolvent person under the BIA then (amongst other freezes):

(a) No creditor has any remedy against the insolvent person's property nor may any creditor commence or continue any action, execution or other proceeding for the recovery of a claim payable in bankruptcy.

(b) Except with respect to the use of, or dealing with, assets that would significantly prejudice the secured creditor, a provision in a security agreement between the insolvent person and a secured creditor will be ineffective that provides, in substance, that on insolvency or default under the security agreement the insolvent person ceases to have such rights to use or deal with the assets secured under the security agreement. Possibly these stays will prevent creditors from perfecting security during the time periods provided for under statutes such as Ontario's Construction Lien Act, Mortgages Act or Personal Property Security Act.

(c) No person may terminate or amend any agreement or claim any accelerated payment under any agreement with the insolvent person by reason only of the insolvency of the person or the filing of a proposal notice or proposal.

The stay does not prevent a secured creditor who took possession of the   **11–25** secured assets for the purpose of realisation before the proposal notice or proposal was filed from dealing with those assets or prevent a secured creditor who gave a realisation notice to enforce its security more than 10 days before filing of the proposal notice or definitive proposal from realising on its security: s 69. But the debtor could beat the realisation by filing a proposal notice in the 10-day period which is therefore a warning period for the debtor.

The court may lift the stay in respect of a creditor if it is satisfied that the creditor is likely to be significantly prejudiced by the continuance of the stay or that it is otherwise equitable to lift the stay: s 69.4.

There are provisions for voting on proposals. Secured creditors of a class that rejects the proposal at a creditor meeting are free to deal with their security as provided for in their security agreement and need not comply with the requirement for 10 days prior notice of enforcement in Part XI of the Act: s 69.1(6). Secured creditors of a class to whom the proposal was not made need not comply with the 10 days' notice requirement before realising their security: s 69.1(5).

Under the CCAA, the stay is discretionary, but broad. Courts have limited relief from the stay, prevented the termination of contracts with the debtor, required suppliers to continue to supply (on normal trade terms but without the US priority), and extended the stay to secured creditors. The CCAA stay is typically for 60 to 90 days, but some stays have lasted up to two years while a plan is prepared. Hence the CCAA may be preferred for larger companies.

CHAPTER 12

SECURITY AND PRIORITIES

List of main priority questions

12–1 The subject of priorities is complex, largely because of the sheer number of possible competing interests. This section can do little more than indicate the main priority contests and summarise in skeletal form some basic approaches. The chief competing claimants include:

- **Preferential creditors** on bankruptcy, e.g. for taxes and wages: para 12–5

- **Prior attaching creditors** who attached or levied execution over the collateral prior to the grant of the security. Whether these rank prior may depend on whether the secured creditor had notice, but this is not always the case.

- **Subsequent attaching creditors** after the grant of the security. If these rank ahead, the security is weak or useless since the purpose of security is to stand up against unsecured creditors. The priority of subsequent attaching creditors over properly-constituted security is unusual, but not unprecedented.

- **Prior mortgagees** of the asset or its proceeds

- **Subsequent mortgagees** of the asset or its proceeds

- **Prior purchasers** of the asset (or those with an option to purchase)

- **Subsequent purchasers** of the asset (or those with an option to purchase)

- **Beneficiaries under a trust** of the asset or its proceeds held by the debtor as trustee, e.g. retention of title sellers entitled to the proceeds

- **Principals** who have given possession of the asset or the documents of title or evidence of ownership (land deeds, bills of lading, bills of sale, warehouse receipts, certificated securities) to their agent, such as a broker.

- **Unpaid sellers** of the asset to the debtor who have a retention of title clause 12–2

- Holders of a prior **lien** over the asset

-   Holders of a **subsequent lien** over the asset, e.g. a possessory repairman's lien, a maritime lien or an unpaid vendor's lien. For maritime and aviation liens, see chapter 20. For the priority of liens over floating charges, see para 12–25.

-   Second secured creditor claiming to rank ahead of **future advances** made to the debtor by the first secured creditor: para 12–21

-   **Prior lessees,** charterers and licencees of the asset, e.g. a lessee of land, the charterer of a ship or the licencee of a patent. The principles are discussed in relation to ship mortgages and may be of general application: see para 20–17 *et seq.*

-   **Subsequent lessees,** charterers and licencees of the asset: see para 20–19 *et seq* in relation to ship mortgages

-   Owners or mortgagees of assets (a) to which the collateral is attached as a **fixture or accession** such as materials incorporated in a building or an engine fitted to an aircraft, or (b) into which the collateral is **commingled** or processed, such as glue incorporated in chipboard. This is a large and fascinating subject – but, despite its attractions, too large for further attention here, unfortunately.

-   Holders of **prior contractual restrictions** on the grant of security, e.g. a negative pledge in a loan agreement

-   Debtors with a **set-off** against a secured receivable. The position with regard to the exercise of set-off by debtors against assignees is discussed in another work in this series.

12–3   Priorities are more complicated in common law countries than most civil code countries by reason of the common law recognition of the trust (so that one person may be the apparent owner and another the real owner) and – which is much the same thing – by reason of the wider acceptance of ownership or security without a complete transfer of possession, e.g. delivery of goods or notification of an assignment to a debtor.

Where a secured creditor's priority is not legally cast-iron, he sometimes has to rely on contractual restrictions imposed on the debtor and hence on the debtor's observance of the restrictions. Examples are prohibitions on further mortgages, disposals or leases of the collateral. Often this reliance by creditors is well-founded, but unhappily not always so.

Some of these priorities are often more properly characterised as matters of initial title or ownership to the secured asset, as opposed to matters of priority, but there is much overlap. Outside land, title is difficult to check in the case of goods and most receivables and securities.

The detail of the position in the world, and even the position in a single jurisdiction, is too complicated to admit a summary of all the rules for all assets. Only some selected comments will be made. In practice, priorities cause far fewer problems than is often imagined, probably because (a) responsible debtors do not mortgage assets they do not own, (b) they abide by contractual restrictions (e.g. on disposals and further mortgages) designed to protect the creditor's priority, (c) creditors recognise that they are liable to be primed by the most frequent subsequent interest, the retention of title supplier, and (d) there are registered priority systems for important assets, like land. The preoccupation with priorities may reflect a jurisdiction's historical experience of fraud or, perhaps, a fear of fraud or a low opinion of one's fellow-beings.

Priority of security on bankruptcy and against attaching creditors

If a security interest fails altogether on bankruptcy or against an attaching 12–4 creditor, this is not a priority matter: the security is futile since the very object of security is that it should be a protection against insolvency. A secured creditor who must realise before the onset of insolvency is subject to the whims of fortune and has no predictability. Some US states prioritise the liens of certain attaching creditors over even a prior perfected security interest.

Priority creditors on bankruptcy

In the hierarchy of bankruptcy priorities of unsecured debts, certain prefer- 12–5 ential debts rank first, typically expenses of the insolvency administration, taxes, employees' wages and benefits and (in the case of individuals) various miscellaneous claims, such as sickness and burial expenses. A crucial matter is whether the security ranks ahead of all unsecured creditors, including these priority creditors, so that the secured creditor is a super-priority creditor who is effectively outside the bankruptcy to the extent he is secured. In many countries these priority creditors rank after fixed security, e.g. English-based jurisdictions (there being a different rank for floating charges), the Netherlands and Sweden. In the United States, this is generally true: thus the Federal tax lien ranks after a prior-perfected security interest under UCC Art 9.

But, in a sizeable group of jurisdictions, the priority creditors rank ahead of all security. Where this is the case, the security is hopelessly unpredictable because the mortgagee can never know in advance how much the priority creditors will add up to and hence how much he must deduct from his security. This is the position in France under the *redressement judiciaire* and apparently in some Latin American countries, e.g. Argentina (BA s 265) and Colombia. In Spain it seems that employee wages rank ahead of security. Sometimes the preferential creditor has access to the proceeds of the security only if the free assets are insufficient.

It is generally the case that certain priority creditors whose debts relate to the secured asset itself will enjoy priority over the mortgagee. Examples are court or other costs incurred to preserve the asset and prior maritime and aircraft liens.

General priority rules for competing purchasers and mortgagees

12–6 Although the detail is insuperable, some general principles of priority between competing purchasers and secured parties may be discerned.

These may be summed up by the rule that the first in time is first in right, except as modified by

— first to register;

— first to acquire a better title for value without notice – the English "bona fide purchaser" rule; and

— estoppel of the party who is first in time, e.g. where the first in time induced the second in time to believing there was no prior interest, as where the prior creditor leaves documents of title with the mortgagor, or with an agent, and thereby clothes them with authority to sell or mortgage to an innocent third party.

First in time, first in right

12–7 The basic priority rule is that the first title-holder ranks before the second in order of time. Thus a purchaser of the asset who buys before the mortgage ranks before the mortgagee. A first mortgagee in point of time ranks before the second. But this fundamental rule is eroded by major exceptions.

Priority by registration

12–8 **Generally** Registration systems for ownership and security seek to overcome the uncertainty, expenses and delay inherent in ascertaining the ownership of an asset and of the existing encumbrances and third party interests in the asset. Purchasers and mortgagees of large and costly assets, such as land, aircraft and ships, need legal certainty: those with prior interests are not abandoned but can protect themselves by noting their interests on the register, where permitted.

Registration of ownership title Registration of ownership title by asset can   12–9
confer varying degrees of title predictability, ranging from conclusivity of
the register, with or without a state guarantee, through to prima facie or
weak evidence of title. High degrees of conclusivity are more commonly
found in relation to land registration systems, and registration of ships and
aircraft is generally only evidence of title, not conclusive. Registration of
ownership title is not practical in relation to ephemeral assets, such as ordinary goods, or most intangible assets, such as receivables. The public expense
of a registration authority, the private expense and inconvenience, and the
complexity would never justify such a system.

Land registration Many states prioritise the need for the stability, predicta-   12–10
bility and safety of the ownership of land by registration of title. Nevertheless, because the range and scope of possible interests in land are so various
and the history often so complicated, few registration systems record everything and some areas of risk remain for mortgagees.

In England, the old system of laboriously investigating title to land by an
examination of the history of the dealings in the land as evidenced by the
title deeds back to a 15-year "root" of title, coupled with some help from
protective priority rules or from registers for charges and the like, has been
substantially replaced by a land registration system whereby registration of
absolute title is a state guarantee of the ownership of the legal title. But there
are numerous interests which do not have to be registered but will bind a
mortgagee. Apart from a jumble of inconsequential interests, such as rights
of sheepwalk and the liability to repair the chancel of a church, the most
important exceptions in practice are (a) the rights of persons in actual occupation (such as the ownership rights of wives and the interests of lessees) or
in receipt of the rents and profits, save where enquiry is made of such person
and the rights are not disclosed, and (b) leases at a rent for a term not
exceeding 21 years.

In Australia, most land has been brought under the Torrens System of
title registration which is a more complete registered record of the title and
which is state guaranteed. The Torrens System has been adopted in British
Columbia, Alberta and Saskatchewan, while in Manitoba and Ontario there
is both a Torrens System and an older unguaranteed system for the registration of land deeds.

Priority of mortgage registration Where a mortgage registration system   12–11
indexed by reference to assets is in force, such as land, ships and aircraft
registers, the registration of the mortgage is often conclusive as to the prior-

ity of the mortgage against subsequent purchasers and subsequent mortgagees. This can be stated as a general rule and no exceptions have been found. It is often also true in relation to many registration systems for non-possessory chattel mortgages, e.g. in Spain.

12–12 **Mortgages registered on same day** In some countries mortgages registered on the same day rank equally (at least in the case of either ship or aircraft mortgages or both), e.g. Finland, France, Greece (subject to exceptions), Portugal (CC Art 492) and Sweden.

Examples of countries which divide up the legal day and which rank certain mortgages according to the time of registration include (in the case of ship or aircraft mortgages or both) England and English-based states, Argentina, Belgium, Chile, Guatemala, Israel, Malta, the Netherlands (since 1992), Panama, South Africa, Spain, Taiwan and Thailand.

12–13 **Advance registration** Because of the inevitable time gap between the creation of a mortgage and its registration or (in the case of ships and aircraft) where the mortgage is created in a foreign jurisdiction away from the home registry, the safety of the mortgagee is facilitated if he can file a priority notice which gives him priority for a mortgage created in the priority period, e.g. 14 days. This is possible for registered land and aircraft in England, and is generally true under the American UCC and the Ontario Personal Property Security Act of 1989.

12–14 **Registration by debtor** Where registration is against the debtor, as opposed to registration by asset, the priority effect is often less strong. This is partly because usually registration is primarily designed to protect unsecured creditors against the appearance of false wealth rather than to establish priorities between secured creditors. This is generally true of English-based registration systems for company charges: here registration is notice to third parties only if the subsequent mortgagee or purchaser of the same asset actually knew of the registration or is deemed to know of it on the ground that prescribed entries on the company's file at the Company's Registry constitute notice to all the world. By contrast, Art 9 of the US Uniform Commercial Code and the Canadian versions attempt an elaborate priority system for security interests in personal property.

The general position under Art 9 is that a secured creditor who is the first to file or perfect his security interest (as to which, see para 9–14 *et seq.*) ranks ahead of all subsequent purchasers and mortgagees of the collateral and of the proceeds of the collateral, but subject to wide exceptions. The main non-consumer, non-farm exceptions relate to (a) bona fide purchasers of goods from a business seller who has granted a security interest over those goods, (b) purchase money security interests, e.g. lenders financing new assets and retention of title suppliers, (c) certain purchasers in good faith of chattel paper, instruments and negotiable documents which are covered by a prior security interest (as to these terms, see para 9–15 *et seq*), (d) persons holding certain possessory liens (e.g. a repairman's lien) or a vendor's lien in some cases, and (e) collecting bankers. These exceptions are not unexpected and perhaps reflect approaches elsewhere in a general way, although the detail varies greatly. There are complex rules in Art 9 concerning fixtures attached to land, accessions to goods, and goods which are processed or commingled where there is competition between security interests and purchasers. Revisions proposed in 1994 (see para 9–24A) set out new priority rules for investment securities.

Bona fide purchaser doctrine

One of the most important exceptions to the "first in time, first in right" rule   **12–15**
– at least in England and many English-based systems – is that a person ranks prior if he (a) acquires the asset for value or takes a security interest over the asset for value, (b) in each case without notice at the time of the prior security interest (usually meaning actual notice, but in the case of land the notice he should have had if he made reasonable enquiries) and (c) he obtains a better title than the prior security-holder. The rationale is that the prior mortgagee should not upset a subsequent purchaser or mortgagee who acts in good faith and acquires a more convincing title, notably where the prior mortgagee's security is secret. The basic rationale is that, if a mortgagee takes a secret security, he has no one to blame but himself if another innocent party is misled into thinking the asset is unencumbered and that party in good faith gets a non-secret security by better title.

This better title is often referred to in English-based jurisdictions as the legal title, as opposed to the equitable title. In the case of **land,** the better title is being registered or (in an unregistered system) taking possession of the title-deeds. In the case of **goods,** the better title is taking actual possession when the security-holder has merely a non-possessory security – an unusual situation since generally non-possessory chattel mortgages have to be registered. Thus in England a subsequent bona fide pledgee of goods takes ahead of a prior non-possessory mortgagee of the goods: *Joseph v Lyons* (1884) 15 QBD 280. A similar principle has been enunciated in Switzerland by the Federal Supreme Court: BGE 49 II 340. In the case of **investment securities,** the better title is being registered as the holder where the security-holder is not so registered. In the case of **debts,** the better title is giving notice to the debtor because that is the means of effectively taking complete possession. In the case of **negotiable instruments and bearer bonds** the better title is taking possession as a holder of a bearer instrument or as indorsee of a nominative instrument.

This doctrine is generally not applicable in civil systems which require a full possessory pledge for all assets – the equivalent of the English legal mortgage or charge, i.e possession of goods, notice to debtor of an assignment of a receivable and registration of the pledgee as holder of the investment securities. If the pledgee does not acquire the full "possessory" title, he has no pledge and accordingly subsequent purchasers and pledgees who do obtain a possessory pledge inevitably rank ahead. Whether they would rank ahead if they knew of the prior unperfected pledge is a matter for investigation.

Prior and subsequent purchasers and mortgages

12–16   Where the debtor sells an asset to a purchaser and then mortgages the asset (which he no longer owns), this is a matter of title. Where the debtor mortgages the asset to the creditor and then sells it to a purchaser or mortgages it to another mortgagee, this is a matter of priorities.

Land The basic English position is that, as between purchaser and mortgagee, one applies the rules of first in time, first in right, overridden by bona fide transferee for value of a better title (the legal estate) without notice, overridden by a disposal authorised by the otherwise successful transferee, or overridden by registration. In practice most land in England is registered with absolute title which is state guaranteed so that both ownership and "best title" mortgages are determined conclusively by the "first to register" rule. There is a system of preserving priority by advance notices entered on the register. The position elsewhere is often determined by registration.

12–17   **Goods** The mortgage may be a possessory pledge or a registered non-possessory mortgage in which event registration is crucial to the ordering of priorities.

When a person grants security over goods he does not own, the basic English rule is that of *nemo dat quod non habet*, i.e. he who has no title can give no title.

Accordingly, if a debtor grants a mortgage over goods to a creditor and the debtor does not own the goods, the creditor gets nothing and his mortgage fails. Apart from a commercially unimportant exception protecting purchasers in a recognised *market ouvert* (ancient fairs where, it appears, stolen consumer goods were often offered for sale) – which has been abolished in England but may still apply in other English-based jurisdictions – the main exceptions to the rule that a non-owner of goods can confer no title on a fixed mortgagee apply to mercantile agents, sellers and buyers who are in possession of the goods even though they have no title: see the Factors Act 1889 ss 2 and 8 and the Sale of Goods Act 1979 s 25. Hence the English protections are primarily of importance in the context of dealers holding goods with the consent of the owner where the dealer grants a mortgage over the goods to a good faith mortgagee. These rules are not a major inroad on the *nemo dat* principle.

Where the owner of the goods grants a mortgage over them, without giv- **12–18** ing up possession to the secured creditor, and then sells to a third party purchaser, the international consensus appears to favour the good faith purchaser – probably because the mortgagee should not have left the goods with the debtor. In **England**, the purchaser acquires good title if he can bring himself within the bona fide purchaser doctrine and gets actual possession of the goods.

In **France**, the purchaser in good faith takes free of a prior mortgage because possession is equivalent to title: "*En fait de meubles, la possession vaut titre*": see CC Art 2279.

In **Germany, the Netherlands** and **Japan** the purchaser in good faith takes free of the security, but in Germany in particular there is a very low threshold of notice and purchasers may be expected to make enquiries or to assume that there is a fiduciary transfer.

In the **United States**, subject to conditions, a buyer from a business seller who buys in good faith and without notice that the sale is in violation of a term of a security interest of a third party takes free of the security interest, even if he knows of the security or it is perfected: UCC s 9–307(1). But as between competing security interests in the same collateral, the first to file or perfect has priority, subject to exceptions: s 9–312(5)(A). The main exception is a special priority in favour of the "purchase money security interest", such as a lender financing new goods or a retention of title supplier. His priority is based on the policy that he provides new money and a new asset to the debtor and so his security interest should rank prior to existing security interests.

Ships and aircraft are governed by special registration rules akin to those applying to land. The "goods" rules are important for aircraft engines by reason of the common airline practice of substituting engines from other aircraft.

Receivables Apart from registration priority rules, the priority of successive **12–19** assignments of receivables often depends upon the date upon which the debtor is notified of the assignment. This is the rule in England and displaces the principle of the priority of the "bona fide purchaser" and the "order in time" rules: *E Pfeiffer Weinkellerei GmbH & Co v Arbuthnot Factors Ltd* [1988] 1 WLR 150. The second assignee cannot secure priority by being the first to give notice if he took his assignment when he knew of the earlier assignment. In Switzerland assignments rank according to the date of the assignment, not the date of notification to the debtor on the receivable.

In those countries which require notice to be given to the debtor in order to validate the assignment as against creditors of the assignor, the first to give the prescribed notice ranks prior, e.g. as in France, Luxembourg and Italy. As to France, see Civ August 29, 1849, DP 1849 1.973; as to Italy, see CC Art 1265. In France, if the second assignee knew of the first assignment when he took his assignment, but is the first to notify formally, several lower courts have found in favour of the first assignee, e.g. Trib civ Seine, January 5, 1905.

In American UCC states, the position is complex. The old American rule was that the first assignee had priority, but this was much modified by state law and by the UCC. Under the UCC, as between competing security interests in the same collateral, generally the first to file or perfect has priority: s 9–312(5)(a).

12–20 **Negotiable instruments** There is an overriding need for the marketability of negotiable instruments, such as promissory notes and bearer-bonds and hence the priority of a good faith holder for value ranks ahead of all other prior or subsequent purchaser or mortgagees, and ranks ahead even if the mortgage was granted to him by a thief of the instrument. Hence the basic international position is that a payee or indorsee of a negotiable instrument in possession of the instrument or the bearer of a bearer negotiable instrument will obtain a good title against all other purchasers, mortgagees or lienors if the holder took the instrument before it was overdue, in good faith, for value and without notice of any defect in the title of the person who negotiated it. See, e.g. the English Bills of Sale Act 1882 s 29. This is also generally true under Art 9 of the US Uniform Commercial Code: see s 9–309.

This principle overrides, for example, any rule that notice to the debtor is required to validate an assignment of a debt, any rule that a non-owner cannot confer title, the rights of any prior or subsequent purchaser or mortgagee, and any right of the debtor on the instrument to have it set aside for fraud, misrepresentation or duress. The one exception is if the instrument is itself a forgery or has been materially altered: here the instrument becomes a nullity.

Although undecided, it is considered that corporate registration of company charges in English-based systems will not constitute deemed notice to a holder.

Future advances

A first secured creditor may make a further advance after another creditor   12–21
has taken a second mortgage over the same asset: the question is whether
the further advance ranks ahead of the second mortgage. First mortgages
usually prohibit second mortgages and so the question will arise only if the
debtor ignores the prohibition or there is no prohibition.

The basic English rule is that, if the future advance is legally obligatory,
the first secured creditor has priority over a subsequent secured creditor as
to the future advance regardless of any knowledge or notice of the intervening interests. If the future advance is optional or voluntary (not legally
obligatory), the first secured creditor has priority over a subsequent secured
creditor only if the future advance is made by the first secured creditor without notice of the intervening interest. But the English position is complex:
see s 94 of the Law of Property Act 1925 and s 30 of the Land Registration
Act 1925.

The US UCC gives an improved priority to the first secured party. Generally a perfected secured creditor has priority with respect to the future
advance even if it is not legally committed. See s 9–312. The justification is
that he should not have to check the file each time he makes a subsequent
advance, nor should he have to prove that technically he was bound to lend.

Priority of floating charges

The English-based floating charge has a lesser priority than a fixed charge.   12–22

Preferential creditors These rank prior, e.g. certain taxes and employee
benefits and liquidation expenses, otherwise the preferential creditors would
often not be paid: IA 1986 s 40, s 175. This erosion of the security can be
mitigated by converting as much as possible of the security into a fixed
security over those assets which are more or less permanent or where it is
not overburdensome to require the debtor to seek a consent to the release of
the security when he wishes to dispose of the asset concerned, e.g. land and
buildings, shareholdings in subsidiaries, other investments, vehicles and
capital equipment, major contracts and intellectual property rights. This
hardening of the security cannot in principle apply to inventory dealt with in
the ordinary course of business or to raw materials. Theoretically the fixed
charge could apply to bank accounts into which the company's receivables
are paid, but the charge is not fixed if the company has the free use of the
bank account to pay its creditors because in that case it has the right to deal
with the secured asset free of the charge which is the essence of the floating
charge. Banks in England, Ireland, Australia and other countries hope to

forestall this result by establishing a separate account for new moneys paid in which are frozen for, say a day or a week prior to transfer to the operating account in the hope that the restrictions on the separate account will be enough to preserve the fixed charge over that account. There is substantial English case law on whether or not the right of the company to use receivables once paid into its bank account converts the charge over the receivables into a floating charge. The general tendency of the case law was that it did until the case of *Re Bullas Trading Co Ltd* [1994] BCC 36 where it was held that the charge on the receivables was fixed (because the company could not deal with them) but the charge on the bank account was floating (because the company had a free right of withdrawal). This discussion is reminiscent of the vicissitudes which followed the US Supreme Court decision in *Benedict v Ratner*, 268 US 353 (1925) holding that any dominion of the pledgor over pledged assets destroyed the pledge. The dispute was ultimately resolved by Art 9 of the UCC.

In England, the old trick of defeating the preferential creditors by converting the floating charge into a fixed charge automatically on default prior to liquidation has now been defeated by legislation – the test is whether the charge was fixed or floating when it was created. But these techniques may still be available elsewhere.

12–23 **Retention of title** Generally retention of title creditors rank ahead of English-based floating charges since a charge over property of the debtor cannot grasp property not belonging to the debtor. This is also the case with the Swedish floating charge and the German fiduciary transfer.

Purchasers Purchasers of assets from the company prior to crystallisation take free of the floating charge since the chargee authorised the company to deal in those assets, assuming they did not actually know of any restriction on sales.

12–24 **Mortgagees** If the chargor creates a subsequent fixed charge having already created a floating charge then the fixed charge will rank ahead of the floating charge even if the subsequent fixed mortgagee had notice of the prior floating charge: *Re Hamilton's Windsor Ironworks* (1879) 12 Ch D 707. The company also has apparent authority to create a prior floating charge over a part of the assets: *Re Automatic Bottle Makers Ltd* [1926] Ch 412, CA. But a subsequent floating charge over the identical assets will be postponed to the existing floating charge: *Re Benjamin Cope & Sons Ltd* [1914] 1 Ch 800. In order to prevent this, floating charges invariably contain express prohibitions against the creation of subsequent fixed or floating charges over the assets and the rule is that if a subsequent chargee has notice of this restriction, then he is bound by it: *Wilson v Kelland* [1910] 2 Ch 306;

English and Scottish Mercantile Investment Co Ltd v Brunton [1892] 2 QB 700, CA. The restriction on the grant of other charges is generally filed with the particulars in the charges registry at the companies register so that it is likely that those dealing with the company and taking fresh security will have searched at the companies registry and seen the restriction. However it is probably the case that if they do not make a search and nevertheless take the charge they are not on notice of the restriction because it is not one of the prescribed particulars. They will only be on constructive notice if in the particular circumstances they should have made all such reasonable enquiries as they should have made before taking their security – a rule which generally applies only in relation to land. As at the time of writing, changes to this rule in England effected by the Companies Act 1989 were not in effect.

Attaching creditors A completed creditor's execution takes priority over an   **12–25** uncrystallised floating charge: *Evans v Rival Granite Quarry Ltd* [1910] 2 KB 979, CA. But if the charge crystallises before the creditor has completed his execution by selling the assets which have been seized, the floating charge ranks ahead: *Re Opera Ltd* [1891] 3 Ch 260, CA. Similar principles apply to garnishee orders and, with some modifications, Mareva injunctions: *Cairney v Back* [1906] 2 KB 746; *Cretanor Maritime Co Ltd v Irish Marine Management Ltd* [1978] 3 All ER 164. There is detailed case law in relation to the priority of the landlord's right of distress for unpaid rent.

Lien creditors A lien creditor – whether his lien arises by contract or otherwise – such as the holder of a vendor's lien or a carrier's lien, takes priority over a floating charge which has not crystallised when the lien arises. In *George Barker (Transport) Ltd v Eynon* [1974] 1 All ER 900, the court held that a contractual lien in a transport agreement takes its priority from the date when the contract was entered into, not when the lorry driver took possession of the goods concerned so that the lien beat the crystallisation of the floating charge. Perhaps liens could be prevented by registration of a prohibition against liens at the companies registry, provided that the lien-holder had notice of the restriction before he acquired his lien.

Set-off A creditor of the debtor can set off as if there were no floating charge over the debt he owes. Crystallisation operates as a fixed assignment of the debt to the chargee and this may affect set-off. Set-off is reviewed in another work in this series.

Chapter 13

SECURITY AND CONFLICT OF LAWS

Main issues

13–1   It has already been seen that jurisdictions fundamentally disagree as to the availability of security as a protection against insolvency. Some jurisdictions allow comprehensive fixed and floating charges over all the present and future assets of a corporate debtor and others severely restrict the security to real property and to special assets, such as ships and aircraft.

There are potentially a large number of separate issues involved. The private international law of security interests is infinitely more complicated than the ordinary contractual conflicts which seem elementary and routine by comparison. This is because the number of issues is a multiple of contract issues. Apart from ordinary contract, one also has to consider the conflicts rules applying to bankruptcy, the conflicts rules applying to proprietary transfers, and the conflicts rules applying to priorities, quite apart from jurisdiction and remedies – in each case in relation to different properties, e.g. land, goods, debts and investment securities. Any attempt to summarise is therefore hopeless and all one can do is to identify a few of the key issues, perhaps sketch in a framework, perhaps fix in place some starting-blocks.

13–2   Some of the issues which the practitioner will bear in mind in taking the security may be listed as follows:

– **Powers and authorisations** of the debtor granting the security

– **Formalities**, e.g. whether notarisation is required: see para 8–1 *et seq* and para 13–4

– **Validity of security**, i.e. whether the asset can be subject to the security of the type concerned, e.g. a non-possessory chattel mortgage or an assignment of a future debt

– **Permissible secured debt**, e.g. whether the security can cover a future debt or can secure an unlimited amount without stating a maximum: see para 8–3 *et seq*

– **Trustees**, i.e. whether a trustee will be recognised as the mortgagee. See para 8–20 *et seq*. See also the Hague Convention on Trusts of 1986.

- **Permissible secured creditors,** i.e. whether there are any rules restricting the grant of security in favour of local credit institutions: see para 8–20 *et seq*

- **Perfection and registration,** e.g. whether a possessory pledge is required and whether the security fails for lack of local registration

- **Preferences,** e.g. whether the security is liable to be set aside on the insolvency of the debtor as a fraudulent preference: see chapters 30 to 32

- **Remedies,** e.g. whether the security-holder can enforce his security by private sale, possession, or receivership or must resort to a public auction: see chapter 10

- **Priorities,** e.g. priority of the security against subsequent mortgagees, lienholders and purchasers. This is too large a subject to review in any detail and can only be touched on.

- **Priority of preferential creditors,** i.e. rules whereby taxes, wages and other priority claims rank ahead of the security: see paras 12–5 and 13–32

- **Freezes,** i.e. stays on the enforcement of the security mandated by the home forum's bankruptcy law: see chapter 11 and para 13–30

- **Forced substitutions,** i.e. rules allowing the insolvency administrator to substitute the security: see chapter 11.

- **Contractual aspects of security,** e.g. the effect and interpretation of representations, covenants, and the like

- **Documentary taxes,** e.g. stamp duties payable on the security agreement. The conflict of laws on stamp duties is examined elsewhere in this series of works.

Categorisation of issues

In relation to the conflict of laws affecting security, the best way to   **13–3** approach the subject is to distinguish the character or nature of the issues. Four main categories may be observed as follows:

1. Contractual aspects of the security, governed by ordinary contract conflict of laws

2. "False wealth" aspects of the security, governed by the conflict of laws rules relating to bankruptcy. This relates to the question of the degree of publicity required of a security interest, whether by way of a possessory pledge, registration or otherwise. This topic is generally treated in the literature as belonging to the question of the validity of security

but the matter is almost exclusively determined by the attitude to false wealth.

3. Priorities, e.g. between mortgagees and purchasers of the same assets. These are governed neither by the private international law relating to contracts nor that relating to bankruptcy but by a collection of rules which depend on the particular priority contest.

4. Other bankruptcy rules, e.g. bankruptcy freezes on enforcement and preferential transfers. These are bankruptcy issues and are determined by the private international law relating to bankruptcy and not contract conflicts.

Contractual aspects of security

13–4   The contractual aspects of the security should be governed by the normal private international law rules relating to contracts, e.g. the 1980 Rome Convention on the Law Applicable to Contractual Obligations. These are examined in detail in another work in this series of books on financial law. For example, these rules should govern the law applicable to the following matters: whether an agreement exists at all (consent, offer and acceptance or unilateral agreement), any requirement for consideration or cause, voidability because of undue influence, misrepresentation or mistake; formalities, such as writing or notarisation; powers and authorities of the debtor; interpretation of the agreement, e.g. meaning of the terms, the intended currency and the scope of the liabilities covered; performance, such as where payments have to be made and by when they must be made, the appropriation of partial payments, the performance of the covenants, the meaning and effect of representations and warranties and whether or not an event of default has occurred; limitation and prescription; and evidence and procedure. Where the Rome Convention of 1980 applies, the parties are free to choose the governing law to determine these matters in accordance with the Convention. Note the exclusion in the Convention for matters of public policy or mandatory statute (Arts 7 and 16) and note the exclusion for questions governed by the law of companies, including winding up (Art 1(2)). See Dicey Rule 185.

The public policy exception, which is applied by all developed states, is generally now regarded restrictively in the leading nations. Matters which may fall within the public policy head in states which take a more serious view about these matters include: usury, acceleration on an event of default without reasonable cause (even though strictly in accordance with the contract), restrictions on rights of redemption and prepayment, exclusion clauses e.g. protecting the secured creditor against negligence on enforcement, and appropriation of partial payments.

Formalities, e.g. whether in writing or a notarisation, should in principle be determined concessionally either by the law of the place where the security agreement is entered into or by the law governing the security agreement. See Art 9(1) of the 1980 Rome Convention. But by Art 9(6) of the Rome Convention, a contract the subject matter of which is a right in immovable property is subject to the mandatory requirements of form of the law where the property is situated if by that law those requirements are imposed irrespective of the country where the contract is concluded and irrespective of the law governing the contract.

False wealth and publicity

False wealth is the principle which requires a security interest to be publi-   **13–5** cised either by a possessory pledge or by registration or filing in a public bureau. The doctrine is intended to protect unsecured creditors and should be determined by the bankruptcy conflict laws which are examined elsewhere in this series of works. The general rule is that bankruptcy courts apply their own law which is regarded as a matter of overriding and mandatory public policy, subject to increasingly wide exceptions based upon comity and the more civilised rules of contractual conflicts, and subject to the practicalities of the situation i.e. that bankruptcy courts cannot in practice enforce their laws extraterritorially in most cases.

This question will arise where a secured creditor takes a non-possessory chattel mortgage but the home forum of the debtor requires a possessory pledge, where the secured creditor takes an unnotified assignment of a debt but the home forum of the debtor insists that assignments of receivables must be notified to the debtor who owes the receivables if they are to be valid on the bankruptcy of the assignor, where the secured creditor takes a charge over investment securities without being registered as the pledgee in the books of the issuer, but the home forum of the debtor requires that pledges of investment securities must be so registered in order to dispossess the debtor; and where the secured creditor gives the debtor a degree of dominion over the collateral (e.g. the right to deal in securities or to deal in the goods or to use raw materials or to sell inventory or to use a bank account into which receivables are paid) and this destroys the possessory pledge in the home forum.

All of these rules are intended to publicise the security to unsecured creditors, although there may be an unspoken secondary motive, i.e. to protect debtors from their own impecuniosity or to defeat the money-lender.

Most international collisions on security result from this doctrine of false wealth.

13–6 Where security has to be registered in a public bureau, then one must simply interpret the registration statute to see whether it has extraterritorial effect. Commonly registration statutes which are indexed by reference to debtors (as opposed to registration systems indexed by reference to assets, e.g. land ships and aircraft) require a registration in the jurisdiction of the debtor's place of incorporation or principal place of business, subject to wide exceptions, particularly in the case of moveables where filing may follow the moveable in order to protect creditors locally dealing with that moveable. As noted at para 9–11, these registration statutes often have extraterritorial effect.

In the absence of a registration statute, one can expect courts to apply similar concepts if they require the publicity of a possessory pledge, i.e. the matter is intended to be protective of all unsecured creditors of the debtor, whether local or foreign, who can prove in the bankruptcy, and therefore these courts may hold that they should apply their home law where the debtor's principal place of business or place or incorporation is located, as opposed to the lex situs of the asset concerned. They will only apply the lex situs law if it is abroad because of considerations of comity or because of the practicalities of the situation, i.e. they cannot give sway to their orders extraterritorially.

Hence, if the asset is located within the bankruptcy jurisdiction of the home forum, the courts may well apply the home law and insist on a possessory pledge. If the asset is abroad, then the home forum may still seek to apply its own rules as to possession in order to protect all creditors, but this is affected by various considerations. Firstly the home forum may consider that it is none of its business to protect foreign creditors and to see that security interests are publicised to them as well, even though they have a right to prove locally. This seems sensible and reasonable. Secondly, they may be susceptible to the demands of comity. Thirdly, as mentioned, there are the practicalities of the situation.

13–7 Looking at the matter from the point of view of the foreign forum away from the home forum of the bankrupt debtor, if the asset is located within the foreign forum's jurisdiction one can expect that foreign forum to apply its own rules regarding the degree of publicity needed to protect local creditors.

The Rome Convention of 1980 evidently does not apply to these matters: see p 10 of the Giuliano-Lagarde Report. In any event public policy and mandatory rules of law are overriding by virtue of Arts 7 and 16 and questions governed by the law of companies, including winding up, are excluded by Art 1(2).

Two qualifications may be added to the above. First, some purely contractual aspects may have a false wealth resonance, e.g. the formality of a public deed may also have a publicity function. Secondly, some of the false wealth rules are not intended merely to protect unsecured creditors but are debtor-protective, e.g. restrictions on security for future advances, or security covering future unspecified assets. The presence of these motives will tend to increase the intensity of the attitude of the debtor's home forum to the rules.

Priorities

Priority rules should be governed, not by bankruptcy conflicts nor indeed by contractual conflicts in the main, but by their own set of rules applicable to the priority contest in question. Apart from the protection of unsecured creditors, one of the objectives of the false wealth doctrine is the protection of commerce against secret interests, but this is not a bankruptcy doctrine and should not be governed by bankruptcy rules, even though it is an emanation of the false wealth view.   13–8

Priorities relate to such matter as priorities between successive mortgagees and purchasers of the mortgaged assets, the rights of beneficiaries under a trust, the ability of agents to grant unauthorised security over collateral deposited with them, the position of lessees of land, ships and aircraft, the position of licensees of intellectual property rights; fixtures and the doctrine of confusion; and the ranking of future advances made by a first secured creditor over the mortgage of a second creditor.

Each of these disputes attracts its own considerations and all that one can say is that situs and governing law are likely to have much greater sway that lex fori. But the potential disharmony, divergence and endless complication is exhibited by the international disarray in relation to the priorities of maritime liens as against a ship mortgage, which shows just how greatly states differ in the emphasis which they give to the protection of property, the protection of capital providers, the protection of small creditors and the protection of commerce.

These priority matters are quite separate from bankruptcy priorities, i.e. whether the security interest is an in rem interest ranking ahead of other creditors and whether preferential creditors have a special privilege. The latter are pure bankruptcy matters governed by bankruptcy conflicts.

Other bankruptcy rules

There are a variety of other issues which should be determined in accordance with bankruptcy conflicts. These include: bankruptcy freezes on enforcement in order to aid a rehabilitation; the ability of the insolvency   13–9 administrator to substitute collateral; the ability of the distressed company to prime existing security by a super-priority moratorium loan; the disgorge of fraudulent preferences made by an insolvent debtor in the suspect period; and prohibitions on the giving by the company of financial assistance for the purpose of the acquisition of its own shares.

Impact of title registration

13–10   The ordinary contracts conflicts rules are modified by title registration, e.g. for land, ships, aircraft, intellectual property rights and the like, because, if a registration statute prescribes eligibility requirements for mortgages, e.g. special formalities, limitations on permitted secured debts, requirements for specific terms and limitations on secured creditors, then the mortgage cannot be registered, and if it cannot be registered there is no mortgage. In this way a minor requirement which could be decided by ordinary conflicts rules is turned into a fundamental policy rule. This situation cannot arise in relation to notice registration or filing systems, e.g. Art 9 of the US UCC.

Impact of lex situs

13–11   The lex situs of the collateral is of peculiar importance in this area. For example, it affects the choice of law for contractual matters in the absence of an express choice. The lex situs is a factor to be taken into account and in the case of land is likely to be conclusive. The lex situs affects the false wealth doctrine because courts may be particularly diligent to protect local creditors dealing with the assets. The lex situs may also affect priorities, e.g. between successive mortgagees or between a mortgagee and a purchaser because the situs is where the transaction took place. The lex situs will also affect arrest jurisdiction because the asset is within the jurisdiction, and it will affect bankruptcy jurisdiction: most countries assume discretionary jurisdiction to bankrupt debtors if there is an asset within the jurisdiction.

The lex situs for land and goods does not present problems since they have a physical habitation. The same applies to negotiable securities which are treated like chattels. Lex situs is infinitely more complicated in the case of contract debts and investment securities: see para 13–20.

Enforcement of bankruptcy policies by home forum

13–12   It might happen that a creditor abroad enforces his security and pays himself out of the proceeds in circumstances where, in the eyes of the home forum of the debtor, the security was invalid or the enforcement was frozen or premature. In such a case the home forum has to resort to indirect methods to enforce its views, e.g. by equalisation (obliging the foreign creditor to bring into account the excess receipt which he received from abroad before he can claim in the local insolvency) and, if the foreign creditor is subject to the home jurisdiction, orders to disgorge the excess or an injunction or, finally, contempt of court penalties. These indirect methods are discussed elsewhere in this series of works.

Land mortgages

Generally all matters regarding land mortgages are lex situs, e.g. formalities,   **13–13** registration, permissible secured debts, permissible secured creditors, priorities, remedies, bankruptcy freezes and the like. This flows from the practical consideration that land mortgages must usually be registered in a register and therefore must comply with local law and because it is generally futile for a foreign court to express a view which will be ignored by the local court where the land is.

It therefore appears to be accepted amongst the developed nations that if a mortgage has not been properly constituted in accordance with the law of the country where the land is, then a foreign court will regard the security as invalid.

> In *Waterhouse v Stansfield* (1852) 10 Hare 254, a debtor in England mortgaged land in British Guiana to a creditor. The mortgage did not observe Guianan formalities and was ineffective there. The debtor became bankrupt in England. *Held*: the mortgage was void.

Similarly it was held in 1939 in Argentina that an English mortgagee of royalties from oil wells in Argentina was invalid since the Argentine formalities were not observed.

On the other hand if the foreign mortgage over the foreign land is effective where the land is, the English courts will recognise that mortgage.

> In *Re Somes, ex p De Lemos* (1896) 3 Mas 131, the English bankrupt had charged a mine in Venezuela to a creditor. The creditor realised his security and proved for the unsecured shortfall in England. *Held*: the creditor did not have to account for the proceeds of his security, i.e. the charge was treated as valid. Obviously.

On the other hand, a foreign court may strain to give effect to a mortgage   **13–14** if it takes a liberal attitude to mortgages but the home forum does not, and the mortgage is destroyed on an apparent technicality. For example, the foreign court, particularly if it is an English court, may treat the invalid mortgage as an agreement to create a mortgage and insist that the debtor create a properly constituted mortgage by an order for specific performance – though this will be too late if the debtor is already bankrupt. If the mortgage has already been realised and the proceeds are within the jurisdiction of the court, then again the court may be able to give effect to its own views of mortgages because here the security has been transferred from land into proceeds.

> In *Re Anchor Line (Henderson Bros) Ltd* [1937] Ch 483, an English incorporated company granted a floating charge over all its assets to a Scottish bank. The charge was registered in England. The charge over the land was ineffective under Scots law, as it then was. The company went into liquidation in England. *Held*: the proceeds of sale of the Scottish land was subject to the equitable charge in favour of the bank.

Validity of security over goods

13–15   It has been seen that jurisdictions differ greatly in their attitude to non-possessory chattel mortgages, with some states allowing them (usually subject to registration in the English-based states but not in Germanic states espousing the fiduciary transfer) while others are hostile to this form of security (France, Italy and others).

Different rules may apply to the type of goods in question as follows:

1. **Stationary goods** In the case of stationary goods, many countries apply the law of situation of the goods to determine whether a security interest was validly created. See below.

2. **Goods in transit** One might refer to these as movable movables: they include goods being transported, e.g. imported goods, and goods which are habitually globe-trotting, e.g. shipping containers. Where goods are in transit and their location is casual or unknown, it is thought that **English-based states** will tend to apply the proper law of the security interest, but there is little case law on the matter: Dicey Rule 118. Some states apply the law of the country of destination, e.g. **Belgium, Germany, Portugal** (CC Art 4612) and **Switzerland**: Art 101 of the Private International Law Act of 1987: "Acquisition and loss by legal transaction of real rights in goods in transit are governed by the law of the country of destination". But in the case of Germany, the lex situs will apply if the goods in transit are located in Germany when the security is created and it is invalid under German law. **Spain** applies the law of the place from which the goods are sent and this was the solution adopted

by the Hague Convention of 1958 on the law governing the transfer of title in the international sale of goods. It seems that **Argentina** may apply the law of the domicile of the owner. The question does not appear to have arisen frequently, at least in England, no doubt because goods the subject of international sales are often represented by bills of lading and many countries recognise possession of a bill of lading as conferring a valid possessory pledge of the goods. These rules may be affected by registration statutes for non-possessory chattel mortgages. Further, if a bankruptcy supervenes and the goods are within the jurisdiction, one suspects that countries hostile to non-possessory chattel mortgages might dishonour the validity of a mortgage valid by the lex situs.

3.   **Ships and aircraft** The international tendency is to test the validity of a mortgage over these ambulatory chattels according to the law of the flag since the lex situs may be wholly arbitrary. See chapter 19.

Validity of security over stationary goods

Apart from goods in transit and apart from ships and aircraft, the consensus   **13–16** of developed systems is that the question of whether a mortgage of tangible movables must be possessory to be valid against creditors depends upon the law of the place (and possibly the conflict of law rules of the place) where the goods happen to be when the transfer is made. The lex situs is generally upheld in Anglo-American jurisdictions and in civil code jurisdictions, e.g. Belgium, France, Germany Italy (Art 22 of *Disposizioni sulla lege in generale*), Luxembourg, the Netherlands, Sweden and Switzerland.

See the English case of *Cammell v Sewell* (1860) 5 H&N 728; s 252 of the US Conflicts Restatement, and Rabel, *The Conflict of Laws*, chapter 56, pp 70–75.

Therefore if a non-possessory mortgage is invalid in a foreign country where the goods are when the mortgage is created, then, on the home bankruptcy of the debtor, the mortgage should be treated as invalid even if a non-possessory chattel mortgage is valid in the home forum.

> In the English case of *Inglis v Robertson* [1898] AC 616, a London wine merchant bought whisky from a Scottish seller. The whisky was stored in a warehouse in Scotland. The London buyer hypothecated the whisky as security for a loan. The London hypothecation was invalid under Scots law because notice had not been given to the Scottish warehousekeeper. The Scottish seller, not having been paid, arrested the whisky. *Held*: the Scottish seller's title prevailed because the goods were situate in Scotland and therefore Scottish law applied.

13–17   If a non-possessory mortgage is valid abroad where the goods are when the mortgage is created, then, on the home bankruptcy of the debtor, the home forum ought to treat the mortgage as valid if the goods stay abroad, even if a non-possessory mortgage is invalid at home. But this would have to be investigated. Sometimes the home forum of the debtor will have a registration statute which may avoid the foreign security for lack of home registration, but this is not always the case, e.g. the Germanic fiduciary transfer or goods released under an English trust receipt.

If the home forum invalidates the foreign mortgage, the secured creditor may be able to enforce abroad where the goods are. The home forum must then resort to indirect means of enforcing its views, e.g. equalisation or injunction and recovery action or penalties against the secured creditor if he is subject to the jurisdiction.

13–18   If the security over the goods was validly created in another state and the goods are moved to the state where the bankruptcy commenced so that at the time of the commencement of the bankruptcy the goods are located in the home forum state when the debtor who created the security is bankrupted, then it can be expected that states which generally recognise non-possessory chattel mortgages will recognise the valid creation of the security under the original lex situs before the goods were moved to the home forum, but subject to any home registration statute.

> Thus in a Netherlands decision of 1978 (NJ 1981, 16 Court of Appeals, The Hague), a security interest was created over groundnuts in Georgia in the United States in accordance with the UCC. The groundnuts were transported to the Netherlands. *Held*: the security was similar to the Dutch fiduciary transfer and should therefore be recognised.

But it is also to be expected that, if the home forum state does not permit non-possessory chattel mortgages, it may decline to apply the law of the original lex situs which does, on the ground that the "false wealth" principle, which requires the publicity of possession, is a mandatory bankrupt policy intended to protect unsecured creditors. This is probably the position in France. See Venturini, *International Encyclopaedia of Comparative Law*, Vol III, chapter 21, Pt VI, s 39, n 244. In the French case of *Ste Heinrich Otto*, Cass civ January 8, 1991, D 1991 IR, 40, the court applied French bankruptcy law to overturn a retention of title clause.

13–19   **Priorities** If a mortgage is validly created in one jurisdiction and the goods are then moved to another jurisdiction, priority problems may arise while they are in the new state, e.g. the possessor of the goods may mortgage them again or sell them. The new lex situs of the goods should decide whether or not the new mortgagee or purchaser acquires good title. Note that this is a matter of priorities, not validity against unsecured creditors.

> A leading case on the subject is the Canadian case of *Century Credit Corporation v Richard* (1962) 34 DLR (2d) 291: A sold a motor car in Quebec to B, a resident of Quebec, under a conditional sale contract which provided that the title would remain in A until the price was paid. A conditional sale contract of this sort is similar to a mortgage in commercial substance. Before the price was paid, B took the car to Ontario without A's knowledge or consent and sold it in Ontario to C, a resident of Ontario, who had no notice of A's rights in the car. The law of Ontario required conditional sale contracts to be registered, but the law of Quebec did not. *Held*: A's reservation of title, which was valid by the law of Quebec, must be recognised by Ontario because the reservation of title transaction was entered into in Quebec. The court upheld the Quebec validity even though the contract was not registered in Ontario. On the other hand Ontario had a statute whereby a person in possession of goods who had agreed to buy them could give good title to a bona fide purchaser of those goods and therefore B could pass a good title to C as a bona fide purchaser under the lex situs which was Ontario. See also *Winkworth v Christie, Manson & Woods Ltd* [1980] Ch 496 (England).

This case is a classic illustration of the distinction between the recognition of a title acquired under the original lex situs (even though that title would not be recognised in the state where the goods happen to arrive) and the overriding of that title by dealings at the new lex situs. There is much Canadian case law on the topic, mainly concerning motor vehicles driven from one province to the next: see Dicey Rule 120.

Validity of security over intangible movables

Generally Intangible movables cover a wide variety of assets including con- 13–20
tracts, concessions, shares and other securities, receivables, charterparties, insurances, moneys in a bank account and intellectual property rights.

Being intangibles, these items have no physical situation and have to be given a fictional site. The usual English rules for situs are (see Dicey Rule 113):

- **contract debts:** usually where the debtor resides or has his principal office or, in the case of branches, where the branch is located at which the debt is primarily recoverable (even though the debt may by contract be payable abroad)
- **letters of credit:** where it is payable against documents
- **debts under seal:** usually where the deed is. This normally applies also to mortgages of land under seal.

- **negotiable instruments:** where the instrument is, e.g. the bearer bond

- **transferable (but not negotiable bearer) shares in companies:** usually where the company shareholder register is on which transfers are usually recorded.

The lex situs of fungible securities deposited with a custodian ought to be the office of the custodian where the securities account is kept: paras 6–44 and 6–51 *et seq*.

13–21 **Contract debts** It has been seen that there is much divergence between the degree of publicity required to validate a security interest over debts as against the attaching creditors and the bankruptcy trustee of the debtor: para 4–4 *et seq*. In the mainly Franco-Latin group, but also Japan, the security is invalid against creditors unless it is notified to the debtor owing the receivable in prescribed form. In the English-based countries, notice to the debtor is not necessary, but a corporate charge over "book debts" must be registered to be valid on insolvency. The US UCC adopts both filing and notice to debtor, according to the circumstances: para 9–24. The Germanic group requires neither.

The home forum should also apply its own registration statute. But, apart from this, there is no agreement as to whether the degree of publicity, i.e. where a possessory pledge is required, should be determined by the law governing the debt which is subject to the security, or the law of the fictional situs of the debt, which will often be the law of the debtor.

13–22   Outside bankruptcy, the Rome Convention of 1980 Art 12 establishes that the validity of an assignment and the form of notice is determined by the proper law of the debt assigned and not by the situs of the debt. The Giuliano-Lagarde Report on the Convention notes that the proper law of the debt governs, inter alia, "the procedures required to give effect to the assignment in relation to the debtor". But this is subject to overriding public policy (see Arts 7 and 16), which presumably includes bankruptcy policies, and in any event the Convention applies to contractual obligations and not to "questions governed by the law of companies . . . such as the . . . winding up of companies".

The English courts have applied the situs to the effect of attachments and garnishments of a debt in order to mitigate the risk that the debtor on the claim might have to pay twice – once to the attaching creditor and again to his original creditor in a foreign country: see Dicey Rule 124. The same risk arises on bankruptcy because if, the bankruptcy forum declines to recognise the charge on the debt, the debtor might be obliged to pay the secured creditor as assignee in one jurisdiction and the bankruptcy trustee in another. It seems unclear whether in England the proper law or the situs law of the debt should determine whether it is necessary for the security to be a "possessory" pledge (notice to the debtor, possession of any document evidencing the debt, control of proceeds). The safest solution is to comply with the proper law, the lex situs and, if different, the law of the debtor on the receivable.

In the case of the French rule requiring formal notification for validity, **13–23** German and Swiss decisions have determined the applicability of this requirement in accordance with the law of the debt assigned. However if the debtor who owes the debt is in France and the assignor becomes bankrupt, the French courts insist on the formal notification so that, if it is not duly effected, local creditors can attach the debt and ignore the assignment and the assignment would be invalid on the assignor's bankruptcy in France. The French position is derived from the fact that the notification rule is designed not only to protect unsecured creditors against false wealth, but also to protect the debtor who owes the receivable. It is understood that the Japanese conflicts position, if the debtor who owes the assigned receivable is located in Japan, is the same.

Priorities Where a debt is successively mortgaged or assigned, the priorities **13–24** ought to be determined by the governing law of the debt assigned. Article 12 of the 1980 Rome Convention is silent on the matter. In any event this is not a bankruptcy matter to be decided by bankruptcy conflicts. The application of the law governing the debt assigned will give the same answer for all parties and is the law to which parties would naturally look. Hence if a debt is governed by English law, then the priorities between successive assignees depend upon the first to give notice to the debtor, assuming that when he took his assignment he was not on notice of the previous assignment.

Investment securities

In the case of investment securities the familiar division is that between **13–25** states which require a possessory pledge, i.e. possession of negotiable instruments or registration of the pledge in the books of the issuer, and those which do not require full legal possession.

Apart from registration in a public bureau, the competing laws are those of the governing law of the investment security, the law of the debtor and the lex situs of the investment securities. The competition is likely to be between the law of the insolvent debtor because the degree of possession is a bankruptcy rule for the protection of unsecured creditors and the more tolerant lex situs. A progressive court ought to follow the lex situs: see para 13–20.

Recognition of floating charges

13–26   **Charge not recognised by home state** Where a floating charge is created by a
company in a jurisdiction, which does not recognise a floating charge, over
assets located in another country which does recognise the charge, the
charge ought to be valid over those assets. But this has not always been the
result. The Scottish case of *Carse v Coppen*, 1951 SC 233 is illustrative:

> A company registered in Scotland with assets and a branch office in England
> granted a floating charge in English form over all its assets including those
> located in Scotland. At the time the floating charge was utterly repugnant to
> Scots law (but now the floating charge has since been legislated into Scots law).
> The liquidator conceded that the charge would not be effective over property
> situate in Scotland but he sought the court's guidance as to whether the charge
> was effective over assets of the company in England. *Held*: the charge was anal-
> ogous to a universal assignment whose validity is governed by the laws of the
> domicile of the corporation. The Scottish court refused to uphold it.

13–27   **Charge not recognised where assets are situate** The question here is whether
a floating charge created by a company in a jurisdiction where it is valid will
be recognised as a valid charge in that jurisdiction in respect of assets in
other countries which do not recognise the floating charge. So far as English
law is concerned, an English floating charge operates at the minimum as an
agreement to charge: this in English law constitutes a valid equitable security which bites on the property sought to be covered as soon as it comes into
existence. It creates rights in rem and not merely in personam. Hence the
English courts have given effect to their own floating charges even though
the floating charge was invalid under the foreign lex situs where the property was located. Thus in *British South Africa Co v De Beers Consolidated
Gold Mines Ltd* [1910] 2 Ch 502, reversed on other grounds [1912] AC 52,
the court held that an English floating charge created by an English company amounted to an agreement to charge land abroad which was a valid
security over that land. This decision was followed by *Re Anchor Line
(Henderson Bros) Ltd* [1937] Ch 483:

> An English company owning property in Scotland executed a floating charge in
> Scotland in favour of a bank in Scotland over all of its assets. The charge was
> duly registered in England. The company went into liquidation. *Held* by the
> English court: the proceeds of sale of the property situate in Scotland were pay-
> able to the debentureholder notwithstanding that Scots law (then) did not
> recognise the charge.

The English courts have not upheld their floating charge in respect of
foreign assets in all cases.

In *Re Maudslay Sons & Field* [1900] 1 Ch 602, an English company charged all its assets to an English debentureholder. A receiver was appointed on a default. English creditors crossed to France and attached debts owing to the English company from a French debtor. Under French law the charge was invalid because assignments of debts had to be in writing, registered and formally notified to the debtor. *Held*: the English court would not restrain the French attachment by the English creditors. To do so would have given French creditors an advantage over the English creditors.

The next question is whether a floating charge created by a company in a   **13–28** jurisdiction where the floating charge is recognised will be treated as valid by other jurisdictions in relation to assets within their territory. The charge may fail over these foreign assets for a variety of reasons.

If the floating charge is over foreign land situate within the local bankruptcy forum, the mortgage of the land should be tested by the lex situs and may fail if the prescribed formalities for the creation of a mortgage over land have not been observed, e.g. notarial deed plus registration in the local land registry.

If the floating charge is over foreign goods situate within the local bankruptcy forum, the charge may fail on the ground that the local forum of the lex situs objects to non-possessory chattel mortgages.

If the floating charge is over a debt owed by a debtor situated in the local bankruptcy forum, the charge may fail on the ground that future property cannot be charged, that the local forum requires notice to be given in prescribed form to the debtor who owes the receivable, and on the ground that the law of the situation of the debtor governs this issue: see para 13–23.

In all cases the charge may fail on the ground that the debtor's free right of disposition until the charge crystallises negates the effectiveness of the charge: giving free dominion to a debtor may be held to destroy a possessory pledge.

Recognition of receiver Another question is whether a foreign court will rec-   **13–29** ognise the right of a receiver and manager to sue in the foreign courts so as to get in the assets covered by the floating charge. The proper characterisation of a receiver in respect of a floating charge is an officer of the company and not a trustee in bankruptcy so that his powers should depend upon the law of the place of incorporation. This appears to have been accepted in a 1939 Argentine case where an English receiver was recognised as agent of the English company in an Argentine insolvency proceeding, but in that case the debtor had expressly consented to the receiver's agency powers.

Previously, courts in the United States were reluctant to confer recognition on a receiver, partly because of a common rule in the United States whereby even court-appointed receivers were not permitted to maintain an action in the United States if local creditors are prejudiced.

But these earlier decisions have not always been followed in the United States. It is likely that a receiver appointed under a floating charge would not be recognised as a "foreign representative" for the purposes of ancillary insolvency relief in aid of a foreign court under the US BC 1978 s 304 (discussed elsewhere in this series of works). But in at least two US decisions, receivers were recognised in the US: *Clarkson Co v Rockwell Int'l Corp*, 441 F Supp 792 (ND Cal 1977) (Canadian receiver over floating charge permitted to sue in California); *Hammond Screw Machine Co v Sullivan*, 580 F Supp 24 (ND Ill 1984) (Illinois court refused to allow set-off of claims acquired by the defendant after the appointment of a receiver).

An **Ontario** court has recognised an English receiver.

> In *Re C A Kennedy & Co Ltd* (1986) 14 OR (2d) 439, an English borrower gave an English bank a floating charge over all its assets including a debt due from an Ontario company. An unsecured Canadian creditor of the English borrower sought to attach the Canadian debt ahead of the receiver of the English bank. The question for the court was whether it would recognise the right of the receiver to sue for the Canadian debt. *Held*: the effect of the floating charge was to create an equitable assignment of the debt. Priorities depended upon the lex situs of the debt. The court would recognise the receiver appointed in the foreign jurisdiction.

Possibly **Belgium, Malta** and **Panama** will recognise the rights of a mortgagee taking possessory management of a ship if he is entitled to do so under the law of the mortgage (generally the flag state): see *Maritime Law*, International Bar Association (1977–83) Kluwer.

Freezes on enforcement and interference with security

13–30   Where the bankruptcy laws of the home forum of the debtor freeze the enforcement of security, this will plainly bind assets within the jurisdiction and will be treated as a mandatory rule. Whether it binds foreign assets depends on the scope given to the statute. There appears to be no express limitation to territorial assets in the case of the English administration (which usually however applies only to British companies), the US Chapter 11 or the French *redressement judiciare* but the Japanese corporate reorganisation is limited to assets located in Japan.

If a foreign jurisdiction declines to give effect to the home forum's freeze, the home forum has indirect methods of obtaining a remedy, namely, equalisation (in the sense that the creditor cannot prove without bringing his existing receipts into account), injunction against a creditor who is subject to the jurisdiction, action for recovery of realisation proceeds against a creditor who is subject to the jurisdiction, and the imposition of contempt of court or other penalties. These are reviewed elsewhere in this series.

Similar principles should apply to other interferences with the security. Thus under the US Chapter 11, existing security can be displaced or substituted under the "adequate protection" rules. Under the French *redressement* the asset covered by the security can be substituted and the property sold. Presumably these jurisdictions will treat these rules as mandatory and may regard them as having extraterritorial effect, subject to comity and the realities of the situation.

Foreign attitude to home forum freeze Where the debtor's home forum   13–31
freezes the enforcement of security over assets located abroad or purports to allow the insolvency administrator to substitute security or allows the administrator to sell the security, the foreign local forum should always ignore the home forum if the home forum's bankruptcy proceedings are not recognised in the foreign local forum. The question only arises if they are recognised.

If the bankruptcy proceedings at the foreign home forum are recognised, it is tentatively suggested that the English courts should apply the lex situs of the assets covered by the security to determine these matters: land is situate where it is, shares where the issuing company is incorporated or where the registry is kept, goods where they are situate, negotiable instruments where they are situate, ordinary debts where the debtor is or where they are primarily recoverable (bank deposits being located where the branch of the depositee bank is located), debts under seal where the instrument is, and so on. If the asset is located within the territory of the foreign home forum, then the English courts may recognise the freeze or substitution or sale imposed by the rules of the foreign home forum, but not if the asset is situate externally.

Under the English comity provision in s 426 of the Insolvency Act 1986 the court must give assistance to corresponding courts in the designated countries, but this is expressly subject to the rules of private international law and may therefore not apply to override the above propositions. Section 304 of the US Bankruptcy Code of 1978 is not so limited and expressly enables the court to enjoin any judicial proceedings to enforce a lien against the property of the foreign estate, but subject to the guidelines set out in s 304(c).

Priority of preferential creditors

It has been seen that in some countries preferential creditors (usually bank-   13–32
ruptcy costs, taxes and employee wages) rank ahead of security. This is universally true of the floating charge, but conflicts may technically arise if,

say, an English court characterises a German fiduciary transfer (which ranks before preferential creditors in Germany) as in substance a floating charge (which ranks after preferential creditors in England). Another example concerns the partial floating charge which in an English administration can be primed by prior-ranking post-order expenses of the administrator. The assets concerned may, e.g. be a portfolio of securities which are situated abroad.

In a French *redressement*, the preferential creditors, including the post-order expenses and contracts, rank ahead of all security, including fixed security. In the US Chapter 11, preferential creditors do not rank ahead but the security can be primed by a super-super-priority "debtor-in-possession" loan, subject to adequate protection of the secured creditor.

Again the first question is whether the home forum treats these rules as having extraterritorial effect over security located abroad. If it does, it may treat the rules as being mandatory bankruptcy policies, but subject to comity and subject to the practicalities.

Where the home forum crams down security by priming it by preferential creditors, a foreign local forum may well apply the lex situs to determine the matter so that the state which has the situs can apply its priority rules. If the principal creditor in the home forum is the home taxman, it seems unlikely that the foreign local forum will recognise this subordination of security located abroad within the territory of the foreign forum.

PART II

SHIP AND AIRCRAFT FINANCE

CHAPTER 14

SHIP AND AIRCRAFT FINANCE: INTRODUCTION

It is worth treating ships and aircraft together. They are both expensive   14–1
chattels used for transportation. They both wander the world, one on the
waters, the other in the air. They therefore both are the most experienced
travellers of the world's legal systems.

Ship finance generally

Legend, Justinian, and hence everybody else, say that the origins of customary codes for ship finance are to be found in the traditional sea law of the
island of Rhodes. However, English admiralty law, which has played a
significant role in the development of international maritime law, took its
genesis from the laws of Oleron, a small island off the mouth of the
Charente in the Bay of Biscay. A written version of the laws survives from
1266 although the original was probably of greater antiquity.

The laws of Oleron expressly acknowledged the possibility that a master
of a vessel could pledge his ship to a lender in return for an advance and no
doubt this customary transaction formed the origin of the now obsolete
security transactions of bottomry and respondentia whereby a master of a
ship could, for the purpose solely of obtaining supplies or repairs necessary
to enable the vessel to return to its home port, pledge the vessel by means of
a bottomry bond or pledge the cargo by means of respondentia. The liens
were of doubtful value because the lienholder lost the right to be repaid if
the ship or cargo was lost. In any event modern communications have rendered these methods of raising money on the security of a vessel obsolete
since the funds for necessaries can now be supported by the credit of the
owner as opposed to the credit of the vessel.

However, it was many hundreds of years before maritime jurisdictions
developed a proper system of registered ship mortgages. British and Continental European developments took place mainly in the nineteenth century,
but it was only in 1920 that the United States, finding itself after the First
World War with a fleet of ocean-going vessels with a value in excess of

$3 billion, decided to put its admiralty law on a proper footing so as to attract private investment by strengthening ship mortgage security which under American state law was practically worthless.

Aircraft finance generally

14–2 Aircraft mortgages tread in the path of ship mortgages. The vulnerable chattel mortgage is bolstered up by statutes allowing for registered aircraft mortgages. Borrowings from ship registration legislation is everywhere apparent. Sometimes the legislators have seen fit to make some improvements.

The techniques of financing aircraft and the documentation are similar in many respects to ship mortgages, as are private international law aspects. However while the one-ship company is common, the one-plane company is not. Many airline companies are owned by governments. Further, aircraft are often financed not on the security of mortgages but by financial leases.

Another difference flows from the importance of spare parts in aircraft financing, especially engines. Airlines may substitute engines or take engines on lease. These items of equipment can form a substantial proportion of the cost of an aircraft and hence of the security, but many legal systems are unsuccessful in bringing these separate pieces within the scope of effective charges. The 1958 Geneva Convention made a somewhat unrealistic stab at the matter.

Finally, a large proportion of the world's merchant fleet of ships is registered under flags of convenience in curious jurisdictions – mainly Liberia, Panama and Cyprus. But aircraft tend to fly the national flag.

Security structures for shipping loans: generally

14–3 The usual security structure for a shipping loan comprises a number of elements:

— A mortgage of the vessel: see below

— An assignment of earnings, such as hire from a charter-party, out of which the loan is to be repaid: chapter 21

— An assignment of insurances: chapter 22

— An assignment of compensation for any requisition for hire or for title

— Sometimes, in the case of a one-ship company, a pledge on the shares of the company to give the lender the alternative of selling the company instead of the vessel on a default. The lender may wish to do this to preserve a beneficial charter which could be terminated by the charterer if the ship were sold.

Fleet mortgages

The loans may be secured on several ships owned by the same company or,   **14–4**
more commonly, by several one-ship companies. Shipowners often arrange
for ships in their fleet to be owned by separate companies in order to isolate
the financial risk associated with each ship and to forestall the sister-ship
action whereby one ship can be arrested for the debts of another (New York
taxicabs do the same). In such a case each shipowning company will guarantee the loan to the borrowing company and secure the guarantee by a mortgage on its ship.

Care should be taken to ensure that the guarantees are not liable to be
avoided on the grounds that the guaranteeing companies received no
corporate benefit for their guarantees or that the guarantees are transactions
at an undervalue voidable on insolvency. See para 31–3 *et seq*.

One-ship companies are more than usually vulnerable to the lifting of the
veil of incorporation on insolvency by treating all the one-ship companies as
a single enterprise and merging all their assets and liabilities, notably if they
have been run as a single enterprise with excessive commingling and without regard to corporate formalities. This topic is discussed elsewhere in this
series of works on financial law.

Financial leases

Sometimes (in order to take advantage of tax concessions or for other   **14–5**
reasons) the financing may take the form of a financial lease of the ship. The
elements are:

– The lender makes a loan to a shipowning company specially formed for
  the purpose.

– The owning company charters the ship under a demise charter to the
  "real" owner. The demise charter is in substance a financial lease and the
  hire is sufficient to repay the loan plus interest.

– The demise charterer may then charter the vessel under an ordinary
  operating charter to a charterer.

– The demise charterer assigns the benefit of the sub-charter and earnings
  from the ship to the owner by way of security for the demise charterer's
  obligations under the demise charter.

– The loan to the shipowner is secured by a mortgage on the vessel, an
  assignment to the lender of the demise charter, plus insurances, requisition compensation and a further assignment of the operating sub-
  charter.

— Because the demise charter is the source of debt service, its terms may approximate a take-or-pay contract under which the hire is payable in all eventualities and the demise charterer will, in its acknowledgement to the lender of notice of the assignment, agree with the lender not to raise, as against the lender, set-offs and counterclaims that could be raised as against the owning company, e.g. for failure to comply with the charter-party.

Financial leasing is discussed in another book in this series of works.

Security structures for aircraft loans

14–6 The security structures for aircraft finance are similar to those for ships, except that, as mentioned, insulation by one-ship companies is less commonly followed in the airline industry, and financial leasing is a preferred form of financing, largely because of the wider availability of tax incentives. In addition, there may be a mortgage of spare parts, such as engines which may be subject to the normal rules applicable to non-possessory chattel mortgages: para 15–28 *et seq*.

CHAPTER 15

SHIPS AND AIRCRAFT: REGISTRATION OF TITLE AND MORTGAGES

Registration of title

Generally

Ships and aircraft are chattels. But they have such national importance (for   15–1
national defence and for employment) that most nations provide a system of
registration of title to ships and aircraft flying their flag. The legal objects of
registration are to capture the craft for the state (and thereby to confer
jurisdiction) and to enhance the ability to finance the craft (by a system of
registered mortgages). For a craft to be registered, it must be eligible as to
type and ownership. Non-eligibility may prejudice a mortgage.

The consequences of title registration include:

- The ship or aircraft becomes subject to the jurisdiction of the flag state in
  such matters as administrative regulations pertaining to safety, seaworthiness and airworthiness, crewing, employment regulations, pollution prevention, load lines, tonnage measurements, maritime
  conventions, and the like and to the criminal code of the flag state in
  respect of offences committed on board.

- The flag state is obliged to accept international obligations for its flag
  craft. Examples are treaty obligations and responsibility for international wrongs.

- The craft benefits from the diplomatic protection afforded by the flag
  state to its nationals. In times of war, owners may re-flag to gain the protection of a strong state, as at the time of the wars involving Iraq, Iran
  and Kuwait in the 1980s.

- Registration is evidence of title (but in many states such evidence is not
  conclusive).

- Trading preferences, e.g. only flag ships can trade or fish coastal waters
  (cabotage) or carry flag cargo.

- Requisition by the flag state, even without compensation, is less likely to be capable of question in foreign municipal courts. The comparative law of expropriations is reviewed elsewhere in this series of works.

Registration of title to ships generally

15–2   Generally, in times of war and peace merchant ships have an obvious strategic and economic importance and it is not surprising that states should impose their nationality, as evidenced by the ship's flag, on their merchant fleets.

Article 5(1) of the 1958 Geneva Convention on the High Seas (which some states consider to be generally declaratory of established principles of international law) imposes a duty on Convention States to register ships:

> "Each State shall fix the conditions for the grant of its nationality to ships, for the registration of ships in its territory, and for the right to fly its flag. Ships have the nationality of the State whose flag they are entitled to fly. There must exist a genuine link between the State and the ship; in particular, the State must effectively exercise its jurisdiction and control in administrative, technical and social matters over ships flying its flag."

In fact, country of flag and country of registration are not necessarily the same thing: for example, ships registered with ports in certain British Commonwealth countries can still fly the Red Ensign. Sometimes dual registration of owner and charterer are permitted. But country of flag and country of registration are generally coincident.

Eligible vessels

15–3   The vessel must satisfy certain characteristics before it is eligible for ship registration. Many jurisdictions limit registrability to ships over a certain size, such as 15 or 20 tons (to avoid the expense, inconvenience and overcrowding of the register with small craft) and exclude non-ocean-going vessels. The ability of the vessel to move under its own propulsion is a common criterion and may disqualify certain types of off-shore drilling rigs, pontoons, and barges which are towed, but not necessarily storage vessels. In some countries, hovercraft are assimilated to the registration requirements for ships: see, e.g. the United Kingdom Hovercraft Act 1968. Under s 33 of the Norwegian Maritime Code hovercraft and off-shore constructions for drilling for oil or gas or for the production or storage of such resources can, amongst other maritime properties, be registered and enjoy the benefits of the Code.

In Britain under the Merchant Shipping Act 1894 ss 1, 3 and 742, as amended, every description of vessel "used in navigation" and not propelled by oars can be registered, subject to certain exemptions such as ships not exceeding 15 tons and employed solely on rivers and coasts of the United Kingdom, and lighters, barges and other like vessels used exclusively in non-tidal waters. The words "used in navigation" will usually exclude non-sea-going vessels, uncompleted ships and ships which are lost, actually or constructively. As to oil rigs, see Summerskill, *Oil Rigs: Law and Insurance* (1979).

Eligible shipowners

The other usual qualification for national registration is based upon the nationality of the ownership of the vessel and it is here that one finds the greatest differences in international practice. Many countries regard their merchant fleet of such significance and strategic importance that they will grant the benefit and protection of their flag only to nationals. This creates no difficulty in the case of individuals but, where a corporation incorporated locally is concerned, other tests have had to be developed to determine whether the shipowner is truly a national of the state concerned. **15–4**

There are two broad groups:

(1) States which merely require that the owning company is locally incorporated and has its principal place of business locally, but do not require that the directors or shareholders are nationals. This is the pattern found in the main British registries.

(2) States which require that, not only is the company local, but also a majority of the directors and shareholders must be nationals. This is the pattern followed by, for example, France, Norway and specially the United States. But wide exemptions are often granted.

> For example, in Greece, only Greek citizens and Greek companies owned as to 50 per cent by Greek citizens are allowed to register and own more than 50 per cent of a Greek vessel. However, as an exception, a foreign corporation which is controlled by a majority of Greek citizens, irrespective of whether it has its central office or a branch in Greece, can register and own a vessel under Greek flag if so provided specifically for that vessel by a joint decision of three Ministers issued under Legislative Decree 2687/53: re investment and protection of capital imported from abroad. The decree has constitutional force (Art 107 of the Constitution of 1975). Many Greek flag ships are in fact owned by Liberian or Panamanian companies.

Flags of convenience

In contrast to these various national restrictions are the "open register" states. Notwithstanding the "genuine link" required by the 1958 Geneva **15–5**

Convention, these are states which accept on their register ships owned directly by foreign nationals, thereby giving rise to the somewhat derogatory term "flags of convenience". It does not follow that safety and construction standards are dispensed with (owners, lenders and insurers set their own standards), although it is more difficult for those states to exercise regulatory controls over non-nationals.

The main reasons for flagging out to a convenience flag have been:

- reduction of costs, e.g. no crewing by nationals at high rates or no minimum complements and manning scales; annual fees or tonnage taxes; initial registration fees; build and safety standards;

- avoidance of national restrictive practices (national building and repairs);

- neutrality and freedom from political control, economic sanctions and blockades, e.g. the Panama register was used by US liners at the time of US prohibition enabling them to serve alcohol on board to passengers; and by owners trading with Britain in the Second World War to avoid the US neutrality acts;

- confidentiality of beneficial ownership (bearer corporate shares);

- low taxation;

- no restrictions on the upper age of the ship.

Liberia (since 1948) and Panama (mid 1920s) are the pre-eminent states offering flags of convenience. Others with relaxed ownership qualifications were originally Costa Rica, Honduras (since the United Fruit Company transferred its entire fleet to Honduran registry) and Uruguay and now include such territories as Vanuata, the Republic of the Marshall Islands, Bahamas, Hong Kong, the Cayman Islands, Cyprus, Barbados, Bermuda, Gibraltar, Isle of Man, Netherlands Antilles and even Kerguelen. A large proportion of the world's fleet is registered in Liberia, Panama and Cyprus.

Liberia ceased to be an open register state in the wide sense in 1975 since a corporate owner of a Liberian ship must be a Liberian corporation, subject to official dispensations. However, there are no requirements as to the nationality or residence of the directors or shareholders or as to the domestication of the principal corporate office. In the result Liberian shipowners are almost invariably brass-plate companies. The position in Cyprus is similar. But in Panama the owner may be foreign.

There are some offshore international registers: Germany, Japan and Norway have these.

For a summary of registration requirements, see *The Official Guide to Ship Registries* (3rd ed, 1994) International Ship Registry Review.

Division of ship into shares

Many maritime jurisdictions divide their ships into shares, originally so as   15–6
to facilitate the spreading of the cost of financing the purchase and operation of the vessel amongst several persons. An Italian vessel is divided into
24 shares, a British ship into 64 shares and Liberian vessels into 100 shares.
Panamanian ships are not divided into shares. Division into shares has
ceased to have any practical importance since ships are generally owned by
corporations and the financing of a share of a ship is now virtually unknown
in the international markets.

Registration of ship demise charterers

Some jurisdictions permit registration of demise charterers in their national   15–7
registries instead of the owner and also the registration abroad of demise
charterers of vessels whose title is registered locally. Under a demise or
"bareboat" charterer, the charterer leases the ship for its full useful life on
terms that he is entirely responsible for crewing, maintaining, insuring and
operating the vessel.

It appears that registration of the demise charterer is permitted, subject to
conditions, in, e.g. Britain (since 1994) Germany, France, Spain, Liberia,
Panama, Vanuatu, Mexico, Philippines, Antigua, Togo and St Vincent, but
not Britain, Italy or the Netherlands. One object is to permit cheaper bareboat flag crews.

Bareboat registration gives rise to possible confusion as to whether bareboat registration (charterer flies his flag) or the suspended owner registration covers matters often referred to the flag, e.g. mortgage validity, lien
availability and priority, requisition recognition, applicability of conventions as to arrest, liens, safety, liability and other matters, regulatory jurisdiction, forced deregistration if the bareboat terminates prematurely (the
stateless ship) and ability to procure deregistration if the charterer defaults
or the owner terminates.

Registration of title to aircraft: Chicago Convention of 1944

The Chicago Convention of 1944 on International Civil Aviation lays out   15–8
the basic rules for international civil air transport, e.g. as to flight over the
territory of contracting states, rules of the air, and airport charges, and constitutes the International Civil Aviation Organisation. Most countries have
ratified the Convention so that it is almost global. The Convention applies
only to civil aircraft.

The rules as to the nationality of aircraft are contained in Arts 17 to 21:

> "17 Aircraft have the nationality of the State in which they are registered.
>
> 18 An aircraft cannot be validly registered in more than one State, but its registration may be changed from one State to another.
>
> 19 The registration or transfer of registration of an aircraft in any Contracting State shall be made in accordance with its laws and regulations."

Article 20 deals with nationality and registration marks and Art 21 with exchange of registration details between the contracting states.

Eligible aircraft

15–9   Eligible aircraft will usually comprise commercial aircraft, and may extend to balloons and airships, helicopters, gliders and satellites, but not usually hovercraft (which tend to be treated as ships). There is no statutory definition in the United Kingdom. The Japanese Aviation Law of 1952 applies registrability to aeroplanes, gliders, helicopters, balloons and others prescribed by Cabinet Order. The Netherlands registers "any machine that can derive support from the reactions of the air". France registers "all devices able to fly up or circulate in the air".

Eligible aircraft owners

15–10   Typically there are nationality requirements as to the location of the corporate owner, its directors and (sometimes) its shareholders.

In the **United Kingdom** an aircraft shall not fly in or over the UK unless it is registered in some part of the Commonwealth or in a Chicago Convention country or in some other country having a bilateral agreement with the UK permitting such flight, subject to minor exceptions: Air Navigation Order 1985 Art 3. Eligible owners are similar to those in relation to British ships under the Merchant Shipping Act 1988, mainly citizens of the Commonwealth and the Republic of Ireland, bodies incorporated in some part of the Commonwealth and having their principal place of business in any part of the Commonwealth and (if the Civil Aviation Authority so agrees) persons residing or having a place of business in the United Kingdom.

In the United States, broadly there must be 75 per cent voting control by US citizens and two-thirds of the officers must be US citizens, but the position is complex. Registration is in Oklahoma City. Japan requires 66 per cent of the votes and directorate, and France a majority. In the Netherlands there are no requirements as to the nationality of directors or shareholders. The latest requirements in these countries should be checked.

Registration of aircraft charterers

As to registration of operators, the split of operator and owner is common.   15–11
The United Kingdom allows registration of qualified demise charterers and the owner's name does not appear on the register: Air Navigation Order 1985 Art 4(5). The owner need not be qualified. In the United States there are complex rules, but broadly buyers under conditional sale agreements and finance leases with an option to purchase can be registered. In the Netherlands, a lessee can be registered.

Registration of ship and aircraft mortgages

Generally

One of the objects of registration of title was to permit registration of mort-   15–12
gages and thereby to enhance the ability to finance the national fleet.

Almost universally, registration has replaced the requirement that a chattel mortgage may be constituted only by the lender taking actual or constructive possession of the chattel. This is impracticable because the owner wishes to use the ship or aircraft – not the bank. The object of registration is to override the "false wealth" problem with the non-possessory chattel mortgage and to improve priorities against subsequent purchasers and mortgagees. In some countries the result was achieved by assimilating the ship to real property for security purposes. Some ship mortgage statutes were simply copied from land mortgage legislation, as in Sweden. Other states neatly resolved the objection to the non-possessory chattel mortgage by reclassifying a ship as an immovable, e.g. Japan and Peru.

As mentioned, the main object of mortgage registration is to ensure that the mortgage is effective on the bankruptcy of the owner. A mortgage is useless if it fails on insolvency. The need for registration is based on publicising the mortgage to creditors on the basis of the proposition that if a debtor has many possessions but no assets – because he has mortgaged them – he induces creditors to give him false credit: see chapter 9.

Aspects of registration dealt with elsewhere include:

– dual registration at a corporate register and at a shipping registry, e.g. in England and Panama;

- periodic renewal of registration: para 9–7;

- form of registration – prescribed particulars or whole mortgage: para 9–9;

- extraterritoriality of registration: para 9–11;

- whether registration is constitutive of the mortgage: para 9–6.

Floating charges

15–13   Universal floating charges are possible in English-influenced countries, Scotland, Finland, Norway, Sweden, Russia and the United States: para 2–1 *et seq.* Generally, mortgages of ships and aircraft have to be constituted and perfected by the statutory method, but in the English-influenced countries non-perfection by registration in the title register does not affect the validity of the floating charge over the craft, although the floating charge has poor priority against subsequent purchasers and mortgagees and is primed by registered mortgages, even if the registered mortgagee knew of the prior floating charge. The Scandinavian floating charge does not bind those assets which are subject to a special regime, e.g. land and ships.

Registration of ship mortgages

15–14   No case has been found where a non-possessory mortgage of a ship which is not publicised in some manner is effective on insolvency although sometimes the mortgage may be effective between the parties (which is usually futile).

In Britain, a ship mortgage by a company must be registered at the Companies Registry and also at the ship registry. If it is not registered at the Companies Registry it fails on insolvency. If it is not registered at the ship registry, it loses priority to a subsequent mortgagee of the same vessel who registered his mortgage even though the subsequent mortgagee knew of the prior unregistered mortgage: see s 33 of the Merchant Shipping Act 1894, as amended, and *Black v Williams* [1895] 1 Ch 408.

In the United States a mortgage which does not fulfil the formalities necessary to create a preferred mortgage is usually invalid on insolvency, is primed by maritime liens and loses the benefit of the admiralty jurisdiction.

In most states, registration is constitutive of the mortgage. Thus in Greece an unregistered title to a mortgage may give rise to certain rights *in personam* but it is not a lien or encumbrance on the vessel: Art 197 of the Private Maritime Code.

In some countries, as an extra publicity measure the mortgage must also be endorsed on the ship's certificate kept on board. This is not a British requirement, and is tiresome when it applies. Liberia dropped this formality in 1986 – previously the vessel's certificate had to be flown to the nearest Liberian consul.

Mortgages can often be registered abroad by a provisional registration, e.g. at a foreign Panamanian consulate or at the Greek consulate in London. The registration is then transferred to the main home register. The procedures should guarantee that the provisionally registered mortgage will not be primed by a registration of another mortgage at the main register, but this is not always the case. The proper and safest course is to register initially at the home register.

Registration of aircraft mortgages

Aircraft mortgages follow on from ship mortgages and for the same reasons.   **15–15** Again a possessory pledge of an aircraft is impracticable, because it is the airline which wishes to use the aircraft, not the bank: the result is that most commercial jurisdictions permit non-possessory aircraft mortgages but subject to registration.

Registration may be either in the title register of the aircraft or in a special mortgage register for aircraft. Some countries, notably in the traditional English group, do not have a special registry for aircraft mortgages (Britain does) but require registration under the system of registration of company charges (para 9–34 *et seq*) or under individual bills of sale registration for individuals. These countries include:

Australia	Jamaica
Cyprus	New Zealand
Hong Kong	Nigeria
Ireland	Pakistan
Israel	Singapore

Some countries without a developed system of commercial law do not countenance aircraft mortgages, e.g. Saudi Arabia. The position in China seems unclear.

But, surprisingly, some legally developed states will not permit a non-pos-   **15–16** sessory chattel mortgage even of aircraft. These states include:

Austria

Belgium. But the *gage sur le fonds de commerce* discussed at para 2–18 may offer succour, although this can only be created in favour of approved financial institutions.

Quebec. But the Special Corporate Powers Act permits the creation of non-possessory security by a trust indenture providing for the issue of debentures.

Thailand

Turkey

Nevertheless in these refusing countries it may and often is possible to resort to title financing, e.g. a finance lease or conditional sale. South Africa introduced registered mortgages of aircraft only in the early 1990s.

Priorities of registered mortgages generally

15–17 The main priority risks for mortgages of ships and aircraft relate to the following:

— ineligibility of the ship or aircraft for title registration: para 15–18 *et seq*

— forfeiture of the ship or aircraft, e.g. for smuggling: para 15–19

— general preferred creditors on insolvency, e.g. the priority of general unpaid employees wages taxes and insolvency administration costs: para 12–5

— super-priority insolvency loans to the insolvency administrator to finance a rescue proceeding

— the shipowner has no title (prior purchasers): para 15–21

— subsequent purchasers: para 15–23

— prior and subsequent mortgagees: para 15–26

— prior lienholders for maritime and general liens: para 20–8 *et seq*

— subsequent lienholders, notably maritime and aircraft liens: para 20–8 *et seq*

— prior and subsequent charterers: para 20–7 *et seq*

— accessories, e.g. a third party's equipment or engines fixed to the ship or aircraft: para. 15–28 *et seq*

— prior contractual restrictions, e.g. a negative pledge

– the priority of future advances made by the first mortgagee over a subsequently created second mortgage: para 12–21.

Ineligibility for title registration

If it is shown that registration was improperly procured and that the craft   **15–18**
was not in fact eligible, registration of title may be lost. The question then is whether the mortgage goes with it.

In the United States it has been held that recordation of a mortgage on a vessel which is incapable of being documented will not allow the mortgage to be perfected: *The Susana*, 2 F 2d 410, 1924 AMC 1389 (4th Cir 1924).

On the other hand, s 11 of the Norwegian Maritime Code provides that registered rights in ships that are entered into the Register of Ships may not be contested upon grounds that the ship did not fulfil or no longer fulfils the conditions for registration.

In the United Kingdom, the Air Navigation Order 1985 Art 4(17) provides that, if the owner is unqualified, the title registration is void except for registered undischarged mortgages. Deregistration from the nationality register does not affect the rights of mortgagees registered in the aircraft mortgages register: Mortgaging of Aircraft Order 1972 Arts 9 and 12.

Forfeiture

Many maritime jurisdictions reserve the right to forfeit a vessel in certain   **15–19**
circumstances which are considered serious enough to justify the removal of the privileges of the national flag, e.g. smuggling or a change of nationality. For example, in Britain a change of nationality which removes the character of a British ship can result in forfeiture: Merchant Shipping Act 1894 s 71. But in certain cases, a mortgage is not affected: Merchant Shipping (Registration, etc.) Act 1993 s 6(4). A ship owned by a qualifying British corporate owner can be condemned as prize if the shareholders are alien enemies, i.e. the veil of incorporation is pierced: *The St Tudno* [1916] P 291.

Section 102(4) of the Liberian Maritime Law provides: "the interest of a mortgagee in a vessel registered under this Title shall not be terminated by a forfeiture of the vessel for a violation of any law of the Republic of Liberia, unless the mortgagee authorised, consented, or conspired to effect the illegal act, failure, or omission which constituted such violation".

In the United States an aircraft carrying illicit goods may be forfeited. The mortgagee's right to proceeds is not available as of right, but only fairness. In the United Kingdom an aircraft carrying illegal drugs is liable to forfeiture even if the airline knew nothing of the drugs: *Commissioners for Customs & Excise v Air Canada*, *The Times*, June 15, 1990, CA.

Title of owner: prior purchasers or owners generally

15–20 A basic requirement of any mortgage is that the mortgagor should have good title to the asset which is the subject of the mortgage. However, ship and aircraft registration systems have never achieved the protective perfection obtained by land registration. Title to chattels is more vulnerable and more difficult to prove than title to land. Further, many ships and aircraft spend most of their operating life travelling from one jurisdiction to another. All sorts of dealings may take place abroad and foreign courts may apply their own rules as to the priority of transfers.

Title of shipowners

15–21 The initial risk is that the mortgagor does not own the vessel. Most title registration systems do not guarantee title but are only prima facie evidence of title. This is broadly the case for ships in Australia, England, Finland, Germany, Israel, Japan, Malta, Spain, Taiwan and Turkey. Apparently ship registration is conclusive proof of title or is state-guaranteed in Denmark, Greece, Norway, Thailand and Venezuela.

In English-based jurisdictions, one encounters the ancient principle of English law that he who does not have title cannot confer title: *nemo dat quod non habet*. British ships are transferred by a bill of sale which itself has to be registered; in other respects, ships are goods within the Sale of Goods Act 1979. Therefore if the seller of the ship over which the buyer is to grant a mortgage to the lender does not own the vessel, e.g. because title is retained by the former seller to him, then, as ships are chattels and as registration in Britain is only evidence of title and not conclusive, the real owner may be entitled to procure the de-registration of the ship from the register, leaving the lender with a mortgage on nothing. There are only a few specialist exceptions: para 12–17.

> In *McLean v Grant* (1840) 3 NBR 50, CA, a builder sold an unregistered vessel, but the sale was cancelled because the purchaser could not pay. But the purchaser in possession registered the vessel in his name. *Held*: the registration was obtained by fraud and was void. Title remained in the builder.

> In *Robillard v The St Roch & Charland* (1922) 62 DLR 145, a registered vendor sold to a purchaser who registered. The vendor held the vessel on behalf of another person and was not entitled to sell. *Held*: the purchaser's title was obtained by fraud and was void.

In some countries this is less likely to happen because of rules sympathetic to buyers which hold that somebody who leaves a third party in possession of his goods and therefore with apparent ownership cannot divest a purchaser who did not know of the prior title. This is common in Franco-Latin countries.

Norway is one of the few countries where the state guarantees the registered ship particulars in certain cases. Under s 18 of the Norwegian Maritime Code the registrar has powers to correct erroneous ship entries but under s 37 any person suffering inculpable loss because of an error in registration is entitled to compensation from the state in the circumstances prescribed in the section, e.g. where he has relied on a registration certificate.

Title of aircraft owners

As to aircraft, registration of title is said to be conclusive proof of ownership   15–22
in Norway and Portugal. But these countries are exceptional and in most countries registration of title to aircraft is prima facie evidence which can be upset by a showing of fraud, a prior lien (such as a seller's lien) or by the *nemo dat* rule in common law countries (one who has no title can give no title) or by the rule that a person who is not a bona fide acquirer of the best available title (the legal title, such as possession) for value loses priority to a person who is such an acquirer. See para 12–15 *et seq* for a discussion. A state guarantee of registered aircraft title is even more unusual, but in many countries an administrative remedy may lie against the registration authorities for negligent errors in the record.

As an illustration, according to the Hames/McBain survey cited in the bibliography, in the following countries registration of title to aircraft is prima facie evidence of title, but is not conclusive. But "prima facie" evidence varies from strong evidence to very weak evidence. For example, in the United States, the Federal Aviation Act states that aircraft registration is not evidence of ownership, and in Germany aircraft registration is said to be very weak evidence of title.

Australia	Iceland
Belgium	Israel
Cayman Islands	Japan
China	S Korea
Colombia	Malta
Cyprus	Mexico
Denmark	Norway
England	Peru
Finland	South Africa
France	Sweden
Germany	Taiwan
Guatemala	Venezuela

Subsequent purchasers

15–23   The usual effect of ship and aircraft mortgage registration is that the registered mortgage is valid against subsequent purchasers of the ship or aircraft
from the owner. The purchaser is taken to be on notice of the public registration of the mortgage and cannot complain if he does not search in the flag
state.

The two principal risks for the mortgagee are: fraud, and de-registration
of title, taking the mortgage with it. Both appear to be quite small risks in
practice.

As to **fraud**, a fraudulent shipowner might forge de-registration papers
and thereby procure the discharge of the mortgage on the register or might
change the name to that of a registered ship. The cases involving shareholders who procure replacement share certificates from a company with a
view to defeating a mortgage might provide helpful guidelines on this point.
Ultimately no system can be complete proof against fraud.

15–24   As to **de-registration of title**, a change of ownership can occur (a) when a
newbuilding is transferred from the building state to the flag country, (b)
where there is a private sale of an existing ship or aircraft, or (c) where there
is a forced sale by court order, e.g., at the instance of a maritime lienholder.
In some jurisdictions there is a possibility that the de-registration will also
lead to a de-registration of mortgages noted on the register and that the
local procedures for publicising the de-registration or obtaining the consent
of the mortgagee are weak, ineffective or absent altogether, particularly in
the case of ships.

In the case of the transfer of a ship newbuilding from the construction
state to a foreign flag, the technical risk of loss of priority as a result of an
intermediate dealing in favour of a third party remains a possibility in many
jurisdictions. The risk, which is probably not a serious commercial risk, was
sought to be covered by the 1967 Brussels Convention on Maritime Liens
and Mortgages which never came into force.

A private sale will almost invariably not result in the loss of the mortgagee's priority: it is probably everywhere the case that a purchaser is subject to a properly registered mortgage.

In the case of transfers to a new registry or new ownership, a certificate of
deletion from the old registry is commonly required. The original registry
will also usually require the consent of the mortgagee for a deletion from the
register. Thus s 72 of the Liberian Maritime Law states "the certificate of
registry of a vessel subject to a preferred mortgage shall not be accepted for
surrender without the consent of the mortgagee". The position is similar in
the United States (whose legislation formed the basis of the Liberian code).
Britain does not require a certificate of deletion from the original registry.

Greek law gives limited honour to previous flags by providing that a foreign mortgage on a ship which acquires the Greek flag remains valid, provided that under the law of the preceding flag the mortgage was recorded by an entry in a public register and provided the mortgage was subsequently registered in the Greek register of mortgages within 60 days after the registration of the ship in Greece: Art 20 of the Legislative Decree 3899/58.

The British merchant shipping legislation, which is in the process of consolidation, protects if a ship is deregistered.

Where a creditor, such as a maritime lienholder, seizes a mortgaged vessel   **15–25** and seeks a judicial sale, the ideal is that the procedural rules of the enforcing court should require that both the foreign mortgagee and the foreign registry are notified of the proposed sale in good time. Such notification is a requirement in, for example, Germany. However, in many countries including, it seems, Japan and many British jurisdictions, such as Singapore, Australia and Canada, no notice need be given (although in practice it usually is) and it is up to ship mortgagees to keep themselves informed as to what is happening to the ship. In Britain, see the 1988 and 1993 amendments to Merchant Shipping Act 1894 preserving undischarged registered mortgages. If a vessel is sold without the mortgagee knowing, he loses his right to bid at the auction and, if he fails to file his claim in the distribution of the proceeds in time, he may also lose his right to participate. In practice, mortgagees often find out in good time when something is amiss. Similar rules may apply to aircraft.

The 1967 Brussels Convention on Maritime Liens and Mortgages (which was never adopted but which may represent the law in some Scandinavian countries and Germany) provided in Art 3 that no Contracting State is to permit the de-registration of a vessel without the written consent of all holders of registered mortgages and "hypotheques". However it permitted an exception in the event of the forced sale of the vessel in a contracting state in which case the mortgages attach not to the vessel but are transferred to the proceeds of sale.

Prior and subsequent mortgages

Most ship and aircraft registration statutes establish a system of priorities   **15–26** which depend upon the order of registration rather than confusing unpredictable doctrines of reputed ownership, actual or constructive notice of prior interests and the like.

The priority of registered mortgages generally ranks according to the date of registration as opposed to the date upon which the mortgage is created, e.g. for ships in Denmark, Liberia, the United States, Italy, Norway, Sweden and Britain.

One difference concerns the ranking of mortgages created on the same day. Many states prescribe that the order of *time* of registration governs for ships or aircraft or both, e.g. England and many English-influenced states, Argentina, Belgium, Chile, Guatemala, Israel, Malta, the Netherlands (since 1992), Panama, South Africa, Spain, Taiwan and Thailand. But in some cases, mortgages registered on the same day have equal priority. Examples for ships or aircraft or both are Finland, France, Greece (subject to exceptions), Norway, Portugal (CC Art 492) and Sweden. Article 21 of the Greek Legislative Decree No 3899/58 provides that recordations on the same date have equal priority. It is said however that the difficulty in Greece is reduced where the first mortgage includes a provision to the effect that the owner may not encumber the vessel further without the prior written consent of the first mortgagee. The ship mortgage registrar should in practice refuse to record a second mortgage that is unaccompanied by such a consent.

Under s 23 of the Norwegian Maritime Code, acquisitions of rights that are registered rank in priority before those that are not registered. Those that are registered on the same day have equal rank unless otherwise stipulated in the mortgage deeds. However as an exception, s 24 provides that an earlier right ranks prior to a later right if this is acquired by contract (loosely translated) and if the acquiring party knew or ought to have known about the earlier right at the time when his right was entered in the Journal. This is quite different from British maritime law where the time order of registration of ship mortgages is conclusive as to priority.

Prior liens

15–27   A more serious risk in practice is the presence of prior maritime liens which can surface after the ship has been sold and mortgaged to a mortgagee unaware of the lien. As will be seen later, many maritime liens are secret in the sense that they do not have to be registered and they travel with the vessel into whosoever hands she may come until scrapped off by a forced judicial sale (not a private sale). Similar rules apply to aircraft.

The reality of this risk is demonstrated by the English case of *The Bineta* [1966] 2 Lloyd's Rep 419:

> On the sale of a yacht, the new owner was registered but the seller retained possession of the yacht since the purchaser had not paid the price in full. The seller then resold the yacht to another purchaser in exercise of the statutory right of sale conferred on an unpaid vendor in possession. *Held*: the new purchaser was entitled to an order declaring him the owner of the yacht and entitling him, as against the original purchaser, to be registered as such.

Section 109 of the Liberian Maritime Code requires the mortgagor to disclose prior liens and encumbrances upon pain of penalties – for what that is worth.

Aircraft spare parts generally

An acute problem in relation to aircraft is the availability of a mortgage of spare parts, notably spare engines. The problem is exacerbated by the fact that airlines often pool engines and agree to provide spare engines to each other. As a result, a series of questions arise.

15–28

Removed engines If an engine is removed from the aircraft for repairs, does the mortgage still cover the detached engine? In states which do not object to non-possessory chattel mortgages, this is not a difficulty. For a review of non-possessory chattel mortgages, see para 3–3 *et seq.*

15–29

Spare engines

Can spare engines located in a store be subject to a non-possessory chattel mortgage even though they are not attached to the aircraft? Again, states which allow non-possessory chattel mortgages will allow this mortgage. As to other states, fortunately, a number of countries which object to non-possessory chattel mortgages specifically authorise the mortgage of spare parts, provided, for example, they are identified, kept in a specified place (where a public notice of the mortgage is exhibited) and recorded in the aircraft mortgage register. This conforms with the requirements of the 1948 Geneva Aircraft Convention: para 19–23 *et seq.* Thus France, Greece and Guatemala are amongst the states which are generally hostile to non-possessory chattel mortgages, but which will allow a mortgage of spare parts, generally on the Geneva terms.

15–30

But the following countries do not contemplate separate mortgages of spare parts unless the mortgage can be brought within the scope of some other permitted type of chattel mortgage, such as an industrial pledge of machinery: para 3–3 *et seq.*

Argentina	Italy
Bolivia	S Korea
Brazil	Luxembourg
Chile	Mexico
Denmark	Peru
Finland	Uruguay

In the **United States,** spare parts mortgages can be recorded at the Central

Registry in Oklahoma City. A floating charge is possible under the UCC. A change in location invalidates the perfection of mortgages filed at the FAA Registry so a UCC filing is also desirable but even this is not always adequate since the FAA Registry in many cases pre-empts UCC filings.

In the **Netherlands**, a mortgage on present and future spare parts is possible subject to a degree of specificity under the fiduciary transfer (para 2–11 *et seq*) but the mortgage is not recorded in the Aircraft Record kept for Geneva purposes.

15–31　　In **England,** a mortgage of existing spare parts (but not future parts on this register) can be registered in the aircraft registry as part of an aircraft but not separately. A floating charge cannot be registered (Mortgaging of Aircraft Order 1972) but can and must be registered at the Companies Registry. An MAO mortgage benefits from deemed notice, priority notice, and priority by order of registration and so has a better priority – although in both cases priority against attaching creditors and the insolvent estate is confirmed. Dual registration is required for companies – at the aircraft registry and also the Companies Registry. As to future spare parts, although the aircraft register may in practice refer to mortgages of future spare parts, it is doubtful that this benefits from the MAO protections, although a future mortgagor who actually searches the register will be on notice. But all this is not problematic since non-possessory chattel mortgages by English companies are permitted provided they are registered at the Companies Registry within 21 days of their creation. This is also the case in many English-based states.

In **France**, spare parts can be mortgaged if they are identified and their location specified in the mortgage. No statutory aircraft mortgage is possible on spare parts alone, but a registered non-possessory pledge is possible (not on the aircraft register). Registration must be renewed every five years with maximum of 10 years.

Mortgage over replacement engines

15–32　If a replacement engine owned by the mortgagor is installed on the mortgaged aircraft, is the engine automatically covered by the original mortgage as an accessory or is some new act required to perfect the extension of the mortgage to the replacement engine? Assuming the engine belongs to the airline and is not mortgaged to a third party, it seems that many countries will treat the new engine as covered by the mortgage without any new registration or other act, provided that the original mortgage was expressed to extend to the subsequently installed engine:

England (see *Holroyd v Marshall* (1862) 10 HL Cas 191) and related
countries
France (treated as an accessory)
Italy
S Korea
Luxembourg
Netherlands (treated as an accessory)
Peru
Sweden
Switzerland

Priority of mortgage over replacement engines owned by third party

If the replacement engine belongs to a third party, such as another airline or   15–33
a lessor of an aircraft and its engines, is the third party subject to the mortgage on the aircraft on which the engine is installed? If the engine is treated
as an accession, then it may become part of the mortgaged property and
subject to the mortgage. If it is not an accession, then one would have to
apply the ordinary priority rules applicable to chattels: see para 12–17.

Priority of mortgage over replacement engine mortgaged to third party

If the replacement engine is already subject to a mortgage in favour of   15–34
another creditor (because it comes from a pool of spare parts mortgaged to
the other creditor or is taken from an aircraft mortgaged to another creditor), does the other creditor lose priority to the mortgagee of the aircraft on
which the replacement engine is installed? This is a priority question which
admits of many solutions and is too specialist to be dealt with here, other
than to flag the question.

CHAPTER 16

SHIPS AND AIRCRAFT: ASPECTS OF THE MORTGAGE AND COUNTRY SURVEYS

Formalities for ship and aircraft mortgages

16–1 Ship and aircraft mortgages tend to be formal documents. The formal requirements may include deed, notarisation and legalisation, stemming mainly from doctrines designed to prevent fraud: para 8–1.

The incidence of stamp duties and other documentary taxes on the ship and aircraft mortgage should not be forgotten. There are no UK stamp duties on ship or aircraft mortgages.

Other aspects of documentary prescription include:

— identification of debtor or creditor;

— identification of the ship or aircraft;

— identification of the debt: para 8–3 *et seq*;

— execution by both parties or mortgagor only.

Restrictions on secured debt

16–2 Aspects of the debt which may be secured are reviewed at para 8–3 *et seq*. Relevant issues include:

— the ability to secure future debt, e.g. current accounts and revolving loans;

— the necessity to state the maximum amount secured;

— foreign currency mortgages;

— usury limits on interest;

- whether the mortgage can secure post-insolvency interest;

- whether the mortgage can secure claims for damages;

- the availability of third party security;

- the Scandinavian owner's mortgage;

- limitations on prohibitions on prepayments.

Restrictions on secured creditors

There may be limitations on the identity of the creditor entitled to receive   16–3
the mortgage. The main limitations were reviewed elsewhere and are as
follows:

- A trustee of the security is not recognised. In this event, the mortgage
  must be registered in the name of each syndicate bank and bondholder:
  para 8–20 *et seq.*

- The mortgage may only be granted to a national: US ships are an
  example.

- The mortgage may only be granted to designated financial institutions:
  para 8–24.

None of these restrictions apply in England.

Country survey of ship mortgages

Generally

This section examines selected aspects of the formal requirements of ship   16–4
mortgages in five jurisdictions for illustrative purposes, namely Britain (and
its related jurisdictions, like Cyprus), Liberia, Panama, Greece and Norway.
These are the main registries for merchant fleets. The United States is not
covered since, in general, foreign mortgagees of US vessels are not permitted, subject to exceptions. It must be borne in mind that ship mortgage law
was primarily a nineteenth century development and a concentration on

procedural and formal matters is much in evidence. These formalities are not to be ignored if the lender seeks a good mortgage.

It is advisable to check well in advance what documents will be required for title and mortgage registration, to clear the form of mortgage with the registration authority, to ensure that all taxes and levies in relation to the vessel and the owner have been paid, and (often) that a firm of notaries has been engaged to notarise the documents. Consular legalisation may also be required if the mortgage is entered into abroad.

British ship mortgages

16–5   The first English ship mortgage registration statute was enacted in 1825. Registered mortgages of British ships are now covered by the Merchant Shipping Act 1894 as amended ("MSA").

Countries still operating wholly within the MSA include the Channel Islands, Cayman Islands, Gibraltar, Hong Kong, Bermuda and numerous small British or ex-British islands. The position regarding Australia, Canada and New Zealand should be checked. A number of countries formerly part of HM Dominions have enacted their own maritime legislation though this is often based on the MSA with local adaptations. These countries include the Bahamas, India, Pakistan, Singapore and Cyprus.

16–6   **Prescribed form** British-related jurisdictions are exceptional in requiring ship mortgages to be in a prescribed form. There are two such forms: "Account Current" and "Principal Sum and Interest". Although many mortgages are intended to secure a specific loan, it is the account current form which is commonly used. This is because the Principal Sum and Interest form secures precisely that and no more: a properly advised mortgagee will wish to secure other moneys as well, e.g. sums expended to protect the security such as insurance premiums which the mortgagee may have to pay in order to ensure that the insurances do not lapse. A non-complying unregistered mortgage is valid against creditors but loses priority to a complying registered mortgage. New forms were introduced in Britain in 1994: see the Appendix.

16–7   **Deed of covenants** The prescribed form is generally accompanied by an ancillary document known as a deed of covenants which sets out various provisions which one would expect to find in a ship mortgage, such as assignments of earnings, insurances and requisition compensation, covenants as to repair, insurance and operation, events of default and powers of enforcement. There is no objection to this: *The Benwell Tower* (1895) 8 Asp

MLC 13. In Britain, the deed of covenants is not required to be registered at the port of registry (but see below for Companies Act registration) but in certain other related jurisdictions, such as Cyprus, it must be registered in addition to the prescribed form.

Formalities The mortgage should be a deed, i.e. executed under seal.

Mortgage registration The mortgage is registered by presenting it at the port   16–8
of registry. Priority ranks according to the time of production to the registrar. There are provisions for advance priority notices in 1993 Regulations. A copy of the mortgage is not retained nor is the mortgage endorsed on the certificate of registry retained on board the vessel: this is not a document of title. This is in contrast to many other maritime codes, and fails to satisfy Art 12 of the 1926 Brussels Convention on Maritime Liens and Mortgages: para 19–8.

Registration under the Companies Act 1985 is also required within 21 days of the creation of the mortgage if the mortgage is created by a company incorporated in England (s 395) or, if the ship is "property in England", by a company incorporated outside England but having an established place of business in England. A ship is not property in England merely because it is registered there and is possibly not property in England merely because she from time to time trades in England waters. But the safe course is to register if the owner has a branch in England. If not duly registered, the charge is void against any creditor and the liquidator of the company. Since Companies Act registration requirements apply to most charges, any assignments of earnings should be registered, but assignments of insurances may be exempt in the normal case: see *Paul & Frank Ltd v Discount Bank (Overseas) Ltd* [1967] Ch 348. Only short particulars of the property charged remain on the company file. Changes to the regime for registration of mortgages by foreign companies are effected by the Companies Act 1989 but are not yet in force. See generally, para 9–34 *et seq.*

Secured debt An idiosyncrasy of the British-related form is that the amount   16–9
secured does not have to be stated in the mortgage. If the account current form is used all that is necessary is that it is possible to ascertain the amount owing by reference to the books of account of the mortgagee. Secrecy is preserved. There is no need to state a maximum amount. The mortgage can secure further debt and foreign currency debt. The mortgage can secure capitalised interest, as well after as before judgment. Outside the consumer context, there are no usury limits, except from legislation concerning extortionate credit bargains. As to post-insolvency interest, see para 8–9. For the latest British form (introduced in 1994), see the Appendix.

16–10 **Secured creditors** No official consents are required in the United Kingdom to mortgage a British ship to a foreign bank. Mortgage trustees are recognised and need not be nationals.

Fishing vessels There are special rules in MSA 1988 for fishing vessels.

Transfer of mortgages Transfers of mortgages can be registered, but failure to register the transfer does not affect the validity of the transfer on the insolvency of the transferor: *The Two Ellens* (1871) LR 3 A&E 345, 355.

Liberian ship mortgages

16–11 **Generally** Liberian ship mortgages are governed by the Liberian Maritime Law, Title 22 of the Liberian Code of Laws of 1956 as amended. The last major amendment was in 1986. Although there are significant differences of detail, the original Law was almost a direct copy of the United States Ship Mortgage Act of 1920 as amended and indeed s 30 of the Law states that, in so far as it does not conflict with any other provisions of the Title, the non-statutory general maritime law of the United States is adopted as the general maritime law of Liberia. The Liberian registry is effectively a US off-shore registry to escape the rigours of national flags (tax, national crewing, operating restrictions) and operated with great efficiency by American representatives.

16–12 One of the leading text-books on American maritime law (Gilmore and Black, *The Law of Admiralty* (2nd ed, 1975)) alludes to certain provisions of the old US Ship Mortgage Act as follows: "outdoes the worst of the old-fashioned state chattel mortgage acts," "procedural niceties," "a horribly botched job", "idiotic statement", "the fun is just beginning", "statutory merry-go-round", "customary genius for complication", "makes no kind of sense", and "up to the usual standard in maritime legislation". It must be said however that, provided the formalities are observed, Liberian registration procedures are efficient and safe and it is thought that Liberian admiralty law, if indeed it follows American law, provides considerably better protection to mortgagees than many other codes, particularly in the area of remedies.

Perhaps one reason that the American Act was so contorted was that the form of the American legislation was partly dictated by constitutional divisions between state and Federal legislative competence. Indeed it was only in 1934 that the American Act was declared constitutional: *Detroit Trust C v The Thomas Barlum*, 293 US 21,55 S Ct 31, 1934 AMC 1417 (1934).

If certain of the formalities are not literally complied with, then the mortgage loses its status as a preferred ship mortgage. This means in practice that it would fail on insolvency, would not attract the admiralty *in rem* jurisdiction, and would be postponed to all maritime lienholders (even though they knew of the mortgage).

There appears to be very little Liberian case-law on their own law which is hardly surprising since few Liberian ships call on Monrovia or get arrested there. One therefore turns to American case-law for authority, although presumably the American cases will not necessarily be considered binding on a Liberian court.

Chapter 3 of the Title sets out the requirements for a Liberian mortgage.

Recordation Section 100(1) states that a sale, mortgage or assignment of   **16–13** mortgage of any vessel shall not be valid against any person other than the mortgagor and persons having actual notice thereof unless the instrument is recorded in the relevant office of the Commissioner or an appointed agent. In practice mortgages are recorded at the office of the Deputy Commissioner in New York. Mortgages are recorded by time in the order of their reception: s 100(2). If all the conditions are satisfied and subject presumably to other rules of law applicable to mortgages generally, then according to s 107 the preferred mortgage is to constitute a maritime lien upon the mortgaged vessel in the amount of the outstanding mortgage indebtedness secured by the vessel.

The mortgage must bear an apostille issued by a competent authority of a state party to the Hague Convention of October 5, 1961, as amended, or must have been acknowledged or must be submitted with such other proof of due execution as may be required by regulation: s 103. In practice this requires a notarised acknowledgement of the authority and execution in prescribed form: Maritime Regulation 3.103.

Whole vessel The mortgage must cover the whole of the vessel: see s 101, and para 16–15 below. The mortgagor must disclose prior encumbrances on pain of penalties: s 109.

Secured debt The mortgage must state the interest of the mortgagor in the   **16–14** vessel, the interest mortgaged, and its amount and date of maturity: s 101(2).

In *Merchants National Bank of Mobile v The Ward Rig No 7* (1981) AMC 1930, the court held, in the case of a US mortgage under the Ship Mortgage Act of 1920, that a minor discrepancy in the maturity dates (four days longer than stated in the mortgage) did not invalidate the mortgage or preclude proper documentation.

Written proof must be furnished to the Commissioner or the Deputy Commissioner of the amounts and dates of any documents or evidence of debts in support of the mortgage: s 105. Often the loan agreement or the notes are attached to the mortgage itself.

A mortgage can secure revolving credits and future advances and is not extinguished by full repayment "provided that an advance or other value is given at a later time pursuant to a commitment existing at the time the Mortgage is recorded". A commitment remains a commitment for this purpose even if "a subsequent event of default or other event not within [the mortgagee's] control" relieved him from the obligation: s 106A(1). In the case of future advances and repayments, the maximum amount of the mortgage must clearly stipulate "whether the amount is the maximum amount that may be outstanding at any one time or is the aggregate of all possible advances". These provisions do not allow new money not agreed in the original loan agreement, e.g. for a restructuring: a new mortgage would have to be recorded.

The mortgage may secure foreign currency debt and there are detailed provisions for currency conversions allowed by the loan agreement: s 106(B).

The mortgage may secure such interest as may be agreed, including fluctuating rates: s 108.

16–15 **Maritime property only** There must be a separate discharge for non-maritime property. "A mortgage which includes property other than a vessel shall not be held a Preferred Mortgage unless the mortgage provides for the separate discharge of such property by the payment of a portion of the mortgage indebtedness": s 106(2).

The reason for this opaque requirement is traceable to the United States constitutional limitation of the Federal admiralty jurisdiction to civil causes of admiralty and maritime jurisdiction. This does not include non-Admiralty foreclosures. If non-maritime property were included in an entangling alliance with maritime property the Admiralty jurisdiction would have been extended beyond the constitutional confines. For some reason the Act was not adapted to Liberian conditions on this point.

It was held in the United States in relation to the Ship Mortgage Act of 1920 that a percentage must be fixed: it is not adequate to state specific sums which are apportioned to the assets secured by mixed mortgages: e.g. $5 million for the vessel and $4 million for the land: *The Emma Giles*, 15 F Supp 502, 1936 AMC 1146 (DMd 1936). Sometimes it is stated that "the discharge amount for the separate property covered by this mortgage is 99.99 per cent of the total amount of this mortgage". However it is perhaps not clear whether a court would construe the section to mean that an apportionment of 99.99 per cent of the total amount as the discharge amount for the non-maritime property would leave only 0.01 per cent of the indebtedness secured by the vessel. For this reason many Liberian mortgages now contain language on the following lines:

"Notwithstanding anything in this mortgage to the contrary, this mortgage shall not cover property other than the vessel as that term is used in Section 106(2) of Chapter 3 of Title 22 of the Liberian Code of Laws of 1956 as amended."

In *The R Lenahan*, 10 F Supp 497, 1935 AMC 513 (ED Pa 1935), it was   **16–16**
held that freight is part of the vessel and therefore does not require a separate discharge. Some practitioners set out the assignments of earnings and insurances in separate documents and thereby hoped to avoid the question. But in *Re Levy-Mellon Marine*, 1987 AMC 472 (Bankr WD La 1986), the court held that earnings from freight and charter-hire were not part of the vessel within the US 1920 Act and that a preferred ship mortgage could extend to these, but must be explicitly included in the mortgage.

The mortgage does not have to be endorsed on the vessel's document: s 116. This obviates the previous obstacle that the ship's document had to be flown to the nearest Liberian consul except on first issue in the case of a transfer to Liberian registry.

To ensure that there is an official public record of the encumbrance on board the vessel, s 110 provides that upon recording of a preferred mortgage two certified copies of the mortgage must be delivered to the mortgagor who must keep one copy on board "and cause such copy and the document of the vessel to be exhibited by the master to any person having business which may give rise to a maritime lien or to the sale, conveyance or mortgage of the vessel". Retention of the copy on board is not a condition precedent to the preferred status of the mortgage: *The Oconee*, 280 F 927 (ED Va 1921).

No waiver of preferred status The mortgage must not stipulate that the   **16–17**
mortgagee waives the preferred status thereof: s 101. Few mortgagees would be that supine but care has to be taken with subordinations and permissions for the creation of prior liens: see *Crofton Diesel Engine Co Inc v Puget Sound Nat Bank of Tacoma*, 205 F 2d 950, 1953 AMC 1359 (9th Cir 1953), and *The Henry W Breyer*, 17 F 2d 423, 1927 AMC 290 (DMd 1927); *Cantieri Navali Ruiniti v M/V Skyptron*, 802 F 2d 160 (5th Cir 1986).

In *International Paint Co v M/V Mission Viking*, 637 F 2d 382 (5th Cir 1981), a US mortgage provided that no provision in the mortgage constituted a waiver of the preferred status as given by the US Ship Mortgage Act of 1920. Another clause prohibited the owner from incurring any liens on the vessel except in respect of (among other things) crew's wages and current operations aggregating not more than $100,000 provided the owner discharged them within 15 days. *Held*: the mortgagee had not waived its statutory priority.

16–18   **Date of mortgage** Perhaps the mortgage must be dated on or after the date of the registration of the title of the vessel. In the United States it has been held that recordation of a mortgage dated prior to a vessel's documentation will not perfect the preferred lien: *Re Empire Shipbuiding Co*, 221 F 223 (2d Cir 1915).

> But in *Merchants National Bank of Mobile v The Ward Rig No 7* (1981) AMC 1930, the court was more flexible. The US mortgages and the application for documentation were executed and delivered to the US Coast Guard on the day that the mortgagor bought the vessels. Two days later the Consolidated Enrolment and licence was issued for each vessel. *Held*: the vessels did not cease to be "vessels of the United States" within the US Ship Mortgage Act during the period between the time they were sold and the time they were documented and, although the mortgages were signed during that period, they were entitled to preferred status.

16–19   **Enforcement remedies** As to enforcement, s 112(1) provides that a preferred mortgage may be enforced in Liberia by an admiralty suit *in rem*. US case law is divided on whether the comparable US provision excluded a self-help private sale. Section 112 also permits enforcement by admiralty suit "or otherwise" pursuant to the "procedure of any foreign country in which the vessel shall be found for the enforcement of ship mortgages constituting maritime liens on vessels documented under the laws of said country". It is arguable that this may contemplate the English possessory management. Shortfalls are recoverable from the mortgagor in any court of competent jurisdiction: s 112(3).

16–20   **Maritime liens** Maritime liens attach to the proceeds of sale. Liens ranking prior to the mortgage are pre-recording liens, tort damages, certain tonnage taxes and fees, crews' wages, general average, salvage, and costs: s 113. The lien for necessaries contemplated by s 114 does not rank ahead of the preferred mortgage.

Miscellaneous There is apparently no objection to granting the mortgage to a trustee. Liberian corporate law is based on New York law. There appears to be no corporate bankruptcy law in Liberia.

Panamanian ship mortgages

16–21   Panamanian formal registration requirements afford a contrast to both the British and the Liberian methods but illustrate Franco-Latin systems. The law is to be found mainly in the Code of Commerce Arts 1512 to 1526, as amended by Law No 14 of May 27, 1980 and Law No 43 of November 8, 1984. Because Panama is a major flag, statute has introduced mortgagee protections not found in other Latin American systems.

Article 1515 of the Panamanian Code of Commerce, as amended in 1984, provides for a naval mortgage which must be presented at the Public Registry to be effective against third parties and creditors. The maximum principal must be stated, but the maximum covers in addition interest, costs and currency fluctuations. The mortgage can cover future claims, revolving credits, roll-overs on currency conversions, guaranteed amounts and floating interest. See also Arts 1513B and 1513C. The maximum Panamanian interest limit is disapplied. Article 1527 permits an extra-judicial sale subject to 20 days' notice. Article 1527A (inserted in 1984) permits possessory management by the mortgagee "if it deems it convenient for the protection of the credit".

Provisional registration can take place in Panama or at a Panamanian **16–22** consulate abroad (New York, Los Angeles, London, Barcelona, Genoa, Venice, Hamburg, Singapore, Piraeus, Yokohama and others). The procedure has been improved to ensure that a mortgage which is the subject of preliminary registration abroad will have the effect of permanent registration, thereby conferring power upon the mortgagee to exercise all his rights under the mortgage, for six months after preliminary registration if within that time the mortgage deed is protocolised and filed for permanent registration at the Public Registry at Panama City through a lawyer admitted to practice in the Republic: see Law No 14 of May 27, 1980; Art 1512 of the Code of Commerce, as amended. If executed abroad, the mortgage may be in any language and can be in a private document (although the signatory must be authenticated by a notary public) but a permanently registered mortgage must be translated into Spanish. The mortgage may secure any currency.

The mortgage should be dated after the owner acquired title and preferably after at least provisional registration.

Transfers of a mortgage must be registered if they are to be valid: C Com Art 1514 as amended.

There are no nationality requirements and the owner may be Panamanian or foreign.

Greek ship mortgages

Generally Greek ship mortgages are governed primarily by the Greek Code **16–23** of Private Maritime Law and the Mortgage on Ships, Legislative Decree 3899/58 ("MSLD"). The Civil Code and the Code of Civil Procedure contain pertinent general provisions.

In Greece there are basically two types of ship mortgage: the ordinary mortgage and the preferred mortgage. The difference between an ordinary mortgage and a preferred mortgage lies mainly in the remedies available in Greece. The MSLD was passed with a view to improving the security of mortgagees and liberalising freedom of contract by shaking off pro-debtor restrictions. Under the MSLD a mortgage can expressly confer additional remedies allowing the mortgagee to take possession and run the vessel for his own benefit and of private sale without public auction. If it is "stipulated that the mortgagee shall be entitled to assume the management of the ship as from the time when his claim becomes due and payable", the mortgage is a preferred mortgage. The term "preferred" is to be distinguished from the use of the same term in Liberian and American maritime parlance where, as has been seen, a preferred mortgage is one which qualifies for admiralty in rem jurisdiction and takes precedence over certain maritime liens to which it would otherwise be subject.

16–24 **Formal requirements** According to Art 197 of the Code of Private Maritime Law the ship mortgage shall come into existence as from its due registration in the mortgage register of the district in which the ship is registered. In order to qualify as a preferred mortgage the following requirements must be complied with:

1. If the mortgage is entered into in Greece, it must take the form of an agreement executed before a notary public. If abroad, it must be executed in accordance with the formalities required either in Greece or in the foreign country concerned. But in all cases it must be executed by both parties: Art 2 MSLD. An ordinary mortgage may be made by a unilateral declaration before a notary public and does not have to be a contract. The mortgage must be in Greek – at least for enforcement purposes.

2. The mortgage must contain the name and nationality of the ship owner, recitals as to the title document of the vessel, the vessel's name, its international call letters, its official number and port of registry, the dimensions and tonnage based on the official measurement, the type of propulsion power and the engine power.

3. The mortgage must contain the name of an agent to receive service of process residing in the place where the mortgage records are kept. If no such agent is appointed then service may be made on a local court official. It is obviously in the interests of the mortgagee to appoint an agent since otherwise the vessel could be sold by public auction, e.g. at the instance of a maritime lienor, without the mortgagee knowing about it.

4. A preferred mortgage lien is constituted only on the whole of the vessel.

5. The mortgage must state its maturity and also the amount secured. This may be a global figure but is commonly split between an amount for principal, an amount for interest and an amount for expenses, e.g. payment of insurance premiums and enforcement costs: see Art 1306 of the Civil Code and MSLD Art 12. For enforcement purposes, it is desirable that terms of the entire claim should be publicised in the mortgage. This means either attaching a translation of the loan agreement or setting out the financial terms in the mortgage itself. It is possible for a Greek mortgage to secure an account current within the stated maximum amount.

Recordation The recording of a mortgage can be effected only at the port   16–25
where the vessel is registered. The competent authorities to register a vessel are the Harbourmaster's offices at any central Greek port and the Greek Consular Harbourmaster's in London, New York and Kobe. When a vessel is registered abroad, the foreign Consular Harbourmaster forwards all the documents to the Harbourmaster of a Greek port, usually Piraeus, for the transcription of the vessel and of the mortgages in the register kept there. The foreign register is closed. In the case of an existing vessel it is only possible to register in Greece: there is no provision (as there is in the British system) for registration abroad.

An advantage of foreign registration of new acquisitions is that it is not necessary for the vessel to be cleared through Greek customs as would be the case with local Greek registration. The objection to customs clearance is that the bill of sale is required to be deposited with the authorities and naturally the seller is not prepared to give it up until he has been paid. This clearance is not required when the vessel is registered abroad and can be done on transcription. However administrative procedures have eased the clearance difficulty.

The registrar must cause details of the mortgage to be noted in the mortgage book which the master must carry on the vessel. This can be made by local harbour or consular authorities upon the request of the registrar if the vessel is in foreign waters. The master must carry on board a copy of every mortgage agreement constituting a lien on the vessel and this, together with the mortgage book, must "upon request be exhibited by the master to the parties having a legal interest therein". It seems that a failure to endorse the mortgage in the mortgage book kept on board does not prejudice the preferred status of the mortgage. This is in line with Art 12 of the 1926 Brussels Convention which absolves the mortgagee from responsibility for omission, mistake or delay in the endorsement.

16–26 **Official consents** Apart from the joint Ministerial Decision and the cable order from the Ministry authorising the Greek Harbourmaster to effect registration, no Greek governmental consents are required to enable a foreign bank to take a mortgage on a Greek vessel. However there are special rules for passenger ships.

Trustees and agent banks The trust is not recognised in Greece. Hence bondholders secured by a mortgage registered in the name of a trustee would not be treated as having a proprietary *in rem* interest on the trustee's insolvency: para 8–20 *et seq*. In the case of syndicated loans, it is not sufficient to register only the agent bank as holder of the mortgage: all the banks must be registered as mortgagees.

Norwegian ship mortgages

16–27 Generally the law relating to Norwegian mortgages is contained in the Norwegian Maritime Code dated July 20, 1893, as amended, including amendments by an Act of December 20, 1974. Reference to statutory provisions is taken from the translation of the legislation by Per Gram published by Nordisk Skibsrederforening, Oslo 1976. The Norwegian Maritime Code is a helpful example because the other Scandinavian maritime codes are similar in may respects on account of the co-operation between the Scandinavian countries in legal matters.

In practice many Norwegian mortgages are based upon a standard form of ship mortgage deed which is adapted to meet the circumstances of the case: see the Appendix.

16–28 **Formalities** Section 15 of the Code provides that a document presented for registration must be written in Norwegian, Danish, Swedish, English or German and "must be so legible and clear that no doubt arises as to how it should be noted".

A mortgage deed must be attested by a lawyer, certain public servants or two witnesses and the attestation must expressly confirm that the signature has been made or acknowledged in the presence of the witnesses and must confirm that the signatory is more than 20 years of age.

According to s 256 mortgages on ships cannot obtain legal protection unless the registered document evidencing the right specifies the subject matter of the mortgage (so that the mortgaged vessel must be properly identified, usually by name and call signal) and also records the amount of the mortgage debt or the maximum sum thereby secured. The amount may be stated either in Norwegian or foreign currency.

By s 255 a contractual mortgage on a ship can only obtain legal protection by registration of the right in accordance with Chapter 2 of the Code.

A mortgage may be issued to a trustee or to an agent for a syndicate of banks.

A shipowner may issue a mortgage for a specified maximum amount due on, say, two weeks' notice and then, by declaration of deposit, use the mortgage to secure all present and future debts owing by the owner to a particular lender: para 8–13.

UK aircraft mortgages

The UK Mortgaging of Aircraft Order 1972 provides that any mortgage **16–29** (not including a floating charge) of any aircraft registered in the United Kingdom may be registered in the Register of Mortgages maintained by the Civil Aviation Authority, including a mortgage of the aircraft together with any store of spare parts for the aircraft: Arts 3 and 4. Unregistered mortgages are still possible but a registered mortgage (even if taken in knowledge of the unregistered mortgage) takes priority over an unregistered mortgage. The ranking of successive mortgages depends upon the order of registration. Additional registration would also be required under s 395 of the Companies Act 1985 where applicable: para 9–34 *et seq*. Foreign language mortgages must be accompanied by a certified British translation: Art 6.

There is a helpful system of priority notices. A proposed mortgagee can register a priority notice and, provided he registers his mortgage within 14 days, the mortgage is deemed to have priority from the time when the priority notice was registered: Art 5.

However, a registered mortgage has no priority over any possessory lien in respect of any work done on the aircraft on the express or implied authority of any person entitled to the possession of the aircraft, nor does it have priority over any statutory right to detain the aircraft.

Transfers of mortgages must be notified (Art 8(1)), but it is for investigation whether non-compliance affects the validity of the transfer on the transferor's insolvency.

CHAPTER 17

COVENANTS IN SHIP AND AIRCRAFT MORTGAGES

Generally

17–1   A modern ship mortgage generally contains warranties as to ownership and title, eligibility for title registration, the validity and priority of the mortgage, the absence of liens and other encumbrances and as to the seaworthiness of the vessel. There are comparable warranties in the case of aircraft mortgages. Other warranties on usual lines are usually found in the loan agreement. These are discussed in another volume in this series of works on financial law.

Apart from covenants as to insurances and earnings, which are discussed separately below, and corporate covenants, some or all of the following covenants (which are set out in outline form only) are commonly included in Liberian, Panamanian and Greek mortgages and in British deeds of covenants, but with modifications according to the flag.

Aircraft covenants are similar. A summary of aircraft covenants in a financial lease is to be found in another work in this series in the chapters on title finance.

List of typical covenants

17–2   The shipowner covenants:

(1)   To **maintain the mortgage** as a valid first priority mortgage, to keep on board a copy of the mortgage and the certificate of registry with details of the mortgage endorsed thereon, to exhibit the same to those interested, and to post notices in the chartroom and the master's cabin detailing the mortgage and stating that neither the owner, the charterer, or the master of the vessel or any other person has any authority to create, incur or permit to be imposed upon the vessel any lien whatsoever, except for current crew's wages or salvage. The requirement that a copy of the mortgage be kept on board and details of the mortgage be noted on the certificate of registry reflects Art 12 of the 1926 Brussels Convention on Maritime Liens and Mortgages and the

municipal law of jurisdictions such as Liberia, the United States and Greece. Prominent notices on board the vessel notifying the existence of the mortgage and withdrawal of authority to create liens are in any event helpful.

(2)   To **maintain the registration of the vessel** under the flag of the state concerned, and to ensure that nothing is done or omitted whereby the registration may be forfeited or imperilled.

(3)   **Not to change the name or port** of registration or documentation of the vessel.

(4)   To ensure that the vessel is **operated** in conformity with all applicable laws and regulations (e.g., safety regulations).

(5)   To keep the vessel in good and seaworthy **repair**, fair wear and tear excepted, and in such condition as entitles her to the specified classification with the specified classification society.

(6)   Not to make any substantial **change in the structure**, type or speed of the vessel.

As to the prohibition on structural changes, some maritime codes require re-registration in the event that the vessel is substantially altered: see, e.g. the Liberian Maritime Code s 73 and the British Merchant Shipping Act 1894 s 48.

(7)   **Not to sell,** assign or otherwise dispose of the whole or any part of the   17–3
vessel, her earnings or insurances, not to pool earnings, and not to grant options or pre-emption rights. Pooling of earnings with those of other ships owned by one-ship owners in the same group may depreciate the value of the security, give rise to priority problems on enforced sale and the risk of insolvency consolidation on insolvency on account of commingling of assets. In some jurisdictions the sale of the vessel by the mortgagor without the mortgagee's consent is forbidden by statute. A disposal to a non-qualified owner may imperil the title registration.

(8)   To keep the vessel free of any **lien** or other encumbrance, except for salvage and current crew's wages. Section 35 of the British Merchant Shipping Act 1894 provides that a second mortgagee cannot enforce without the consent of the first mortgagee except under the order of a court of competent jurisdiction. In Panama it seems that a second mortgagee may enforce his mortgage even though the first preferred mortgagee does not wish to enforce. It seems that the position is the same in Greece.

17–4 (9) To **pay all liabilities** which may give rise to liens in respect of or claims enforceable against the vessel.

(10) Not to place the vessel in the hands of any **repairer** or other person who may be entitled to exercise a lien or right of retention unless such person has first waived such rights, or unless the claim so secured would not exceed a stated sum. As to the prohibition on leaving the vessel in the hands of repairers, unpaid repairers in possession of the vessel may be entitled to retain the vessel ahead of the mortgagee: para 20–16. In the United States unpaid repairers have a maritime lien even if they lose possession.

(11) Not to create or permit to subsist any **mortgage**, charge, encumbrance or other security interest over the whole or any part of the vessel, her earnings or insurances. In secured loans (unless there is a proper subordination agreement), the clause should prohibit second-ranking security because:

– a second mortgage is restrictive of management of a default or a restructuring, e.g. if the senior creditor wishes to lend new money and add it to the existing security and the junior creditor can veto this. By withholding his consent, the junior creditor might attempt to harass the senior creditor into paying out the junior creditor;

– the junior creditor may have an independent right of enforcement at an inopportune time.

Where second mortgages on the vessel are allowed, it is customary for senior and junior mortgagees to enter into a co-ordination deed whereby the junior mortgagee subordinates his debt. Subordination agreements are discussed elsewhere in this series of works.

17–5 (12) Not to let the vessel on demise **charter** for any period or on time or consecutive voyage charter (a) for any period which exceeds, or which, by virtue of any optional extension could exceed, six months' duration, or (b) on terms whereby more than one month's hire is payable in advance, or (c) at less than a commercial rate having regard to prevailing rates, or (d) to any affiliate or related person.

Control over other charters is principally designed to prevent depreciation of the security by adverse charters, e.g. a charterparty where a large amount of hire is payable in advance and is paid to the shipowner thereby leaving the mortgagee with a non-earning asset. The control also prohibits long or insider charters to which the mortgagee may be subject if he enforces. The rights of a charterer as against a mortgagee are considered at para 20–17 *et seq.*

A mortgagor of a British ship can charter the vessel as he wishes provided that the charter does not materially impair the security: *The Heather Bell* [1901] P 143. There is much case law which is of relevance if the owner breaches the covenant since improvident charters are not binding on a mortgagee: para 20–19 *et seq.*

Where demise charters are permitted, the mortgagee should obtain express covenants from the demise charterer, (1) that it will carry out the mortgage covenants because the demise charter in effect removes possession and control of the vessel from the mortgagor who is therefore in a weak position to procure performance of the covenants, and (2) that its rights in respect of the demise charter are to be subject to the mortgage, e.g. ability to terminate the charter on enforcement. The demise charterer should assign the benefit of its interest in the insurances so that the mortgagee scoops up all the proceeds of insurances and should also assign sub-charters and earnings (the master will sign bills of lading as employee of the charterer, not the owner).

A special risk of demise charters is that in many jurisdictions maritime creditors of other vessels owned by or demise chartered to the charterer can enforce their claims against other vessels demise chartered to the same charterer. The result is that the mortgagee carries the credit risk of other maritime creditors of the demise charterer and some of these claims may prime the mortgage.

Insurers' consent may be required to a demise charter because this is a change of the ship operator.

(13) To **perform all charterparties** and other contracts of employment which may be entered into with respect to the vessel.

(14) To ensure that the vessel does not engage in any **trade which is illegal**   17–6
or which may render the vessel liable to confiscation, seizure, detention or destruction. A covenant against smuggling plus diligent efforts to police it, can improve the mortgagee's ability to obtain the benefit of the proceeds of sale after a forfeiture – where this is not available as of right. Trading with the enemy legislation may throw risks on to banks from the legislating state, e.g. the United States.

(15) To ensure that the vessel does not trade in any territorial waters where her safety may be imperilled or in any **war zone.**

(16) To ensure that the vessel is **managed** solely by a specified manager.

(17) To give the mortgagee **full information** regarding the vessel, her employment, the position and engagements, copies of classification certificates and survey reports, information as to casualties, copies of the ship's log and particulars of towage and salvages.

(18) To notify the mortgagee forthwith if a **major casualty** occurs, if the

vessel is arrested, detained, seized, condemned, compulsorily acquired or requisitioned for title or use, or if a lien is exercised in respect of the vessel.

(19) To obtain the **release** of the vessel within 14 days if she is seized, condemned, arrested or detained.

(20) To provide additional security or prepay the loan proportionately if the appraised value of the vessel sinks below a prescribed percentage of the amount of the loan, e.g. 125 per cent. A maintenance of value clause is solely a trigger clause for event of default. It is unlikely to be specifically enforceable. The debtor may have no additional collateral. Any additional collateral provided in the suspect period may be voidable as preferential security for pre-existing debt. The clause is sometimes used too late (margin erodes rapidly on default, e.g. default interest, operating costs, enforcement costs and delays, e.g. years).

(21) Not to carry on any **business** other than owning and operating the ship.

(22) Not to **lend money** or grant credit or give guarantees.

(23) To maintain **corporate existence** and not merge.

(24) Not to **borrow money** other than under the bank's loan agreement.

CHAPTER 18

DEFAULTS AND ENFORCEMENT OF SHIP AND AIRCRAFT MORTGAGES

Generally

The enforcement of an aircraft or shipping mortgage is usually expensive, **18–1** time-consuming and difficult. The main areas for consideration are:

- recognition of the mortgage: para 9–1 *et seq*
- restrictions on events of default: para 18–2
- compulsory grace periods prior to enforcement: para 10–15
- priority of other creditors who, because of the insolvency, go unpaid, e.g. maritime or aircraft liens and preferential creditors on insolvency: para 12–5
- bankruptcy freezes on enforcement under rescue statutes: chapter 11
- exclusive right of the insolvency administrator to sell: para 10–16
- consolidation of commingled one-ship companies: this topic is examined elsewhere in this series of works
- problems of jurisdiction
- obsolete enforcement procedures and inordinate delays in some jurisdictions, during which the custodial and insurance costs must be paid: para 10–1 *et seq*
- costs of enforcement and security bonds required to be posted by the creditor to the court
- the "ready to sail" rule which prevents the arrest of a ship which is ready to sail: para 18–17
- disputes with charterers and cargo-owners: para 20–17
- the need to obtain a final judgment before the ship or aircraft is sold: para 18–18
- sale only in local currency
- exchange controls on repatriation of the proceeds

- sovereign immunity of the mortgagor or potential governmental inter-ference, e.g. refusal to provide a certificate of deletion to enable the pur-chaser to register abroad

- sale of national craft only to nationals, in order to preserve the national fleet for emergencies. (Note the restrictions on mortgagee sales of US vessels to foreigners: s 9 of the Shipping Act of 1916 as amended in 1989 by Public Law 100–710).

- lender liability, e.g. responsibility for the vessel or aircraft, shadow directors and equitable subordination. These latter topics are reviewed in another work in this series of books.

Events of default

18–2   The events of default in a ship or aircraft mortgage will be on similar lines to those described for unsecured loan agreements, (e.g. non-payment, non-compliance with covenant, breach of representation, cross-default, creditors processes, insolvency and the like) except that additional events of default are usually added which are attuned to the security. In particular it is usually also a default if:

- The vessel or aircraft is an actual, constructive, agreed, arranged or com-promised total loss. This event of default enables the mortgage to acce-lerate the loan and to apply the insurance proceeds in reduction of an accrued obligation. In the case of fleet mortgages, the total loss of one ship will not usually occasion a general default: the insurance proceeds may instead be deposited in a collateral account as security in place of the ship.

- The country of the flag of the vessel or aircraft becomes involved in hos-tilities or civil war unless the owner transfers the vessel or aircraft with the prior consent of the mortgagee to another flag acceptable to the mortgagee.

- Trading with the enemy legislation or embargoes applicable to the mort-gagee which prohibit transactions with the owner or its charterer.

- Any circumstances arise which imperil the security created by the mort-gage.

- (In the case of ships) there is a change in the ownership of the shares of the shipowner (significant where reliance is placed upon the managerial skills of the owners).

Under English law, a ship mortgagee has power to exercise his rights as a   **18–3**
secured creditor where the owner jeopardises the security, e.g. where the
mortgagor fails to repair the ship so as to make it incapable of performing a
chartered voyage (*De Mattos v Gibson* (1868) 4 De G & J 276) or where he
allows the ship to be burdened by maritime liens for an unreasonably long
time (because such conduct indicates that the owner is financially distressed
and the liens might rank in priority to the mortgage: *The Manor* [1907] P
339).

Section 258 of the Norwegian Maritime Code furnishes an example of
municipal limitations on freedom of contract. This section provides that,
apart from the due date agreed in a mortgage, a debt secured by a mortgage
on the ship entered in the Register of Ships falls due when "(1) the ship is
lost or scrapped, (2) the mortgagee's security is materially impaired in consequence of damage to the ship, (3) the ship loses its nationality, (4) a compulsory or necessary auction takes place, (5) bankruptcy proceedings or
public composition proceedings are commenced against the owner of the
ship or against the debtor, and (6) material default is made in the obligation
to pay interest or instalments of the principal sums or to maintain or to
insure the ship as agreed". If the agreement contains provisions whereby the
debt matures otherwise than on these grounds then such provision may be
set aside in whole or in part if it would be unreasonable or clearly contrary
to proper business practice to rely on it.

A mortgage may be liable in damages to the mortgagor if he wrongfully
arrests or takes possession, e.g. *The Maxima* (1878) 4 Asp MLC 21.

Restrictions on events of default

In England there are no restrictions on the events of default. If the mortgage   **18–4**
provides for immediate enforcement, there are no compulsory grace
periods. For grace periods elsewhere, see para 10–15.

Enforcement remedies: summary

The main enforcement remedies internationally are:

— Foreclosure, i.e. the acquisition of absolute ownership by the mortgagee

— Sale. This may be a private sale or a compulsory judicial public auction

— Possessory management, either directly by the mortgagee or through a
  receiver.

These remedies are discussed generally in chapter 10, but some special remarks applicable to ship and aircraft mortgages may be made here.

Express enforcement remedies

18–5 The following express powers of enforcement are commonly inserted in ship mortgages (the remedies in aircraft mortgages are similar). On a non-payment, the mortgagee is entitled immediately:

1. To take possession of the vessel.

2. To collect the earnings of the vessel, to institute proceedings, to compromise claims and to give a good receipt for the earnings on behalf of the owner.

3. To collect the insurances, to compromise claims, to institute all such proceedings as the mortgagee in its discretion thinks fit and to permit the brokers through whom collection is effected to retain their usual brokerage.

4. To discharge, release or compromise claims in respect of the vessel which may give rise to charges or liens on the vessel having priority over the mortgage or which are or may be enforceable by proceedings against the vessel.

5. To sell the vessel by public auction or private contract, with or without advertisement, for cash or on credit and upon such terms as the mortgagee deems fit, and at any public auction or private contract, with or without advertisement, for cash or on credit and upon such terms as the mortgagee deems fit, and at any public sale to purchase the vessel and to set off against the purchase price the mortgage debt; power to deregister the vessel.

6. To manage the vessel and to do all such things as the owner could do, including insurance, maintenance, repair, chartering and operation.

7. To appoint a receiver who is to be the agent of the owner and who is to be solely responsible for the receiver's actions and remuneration.

It is agreed (a) that the mortgagee is not liable for any losses sustained by reason of the exercise of these powers, (b) that any purchaser or other person dealing with the mortgagee is not concerned whether the mortgagee's power of sale has arisen and (c) that the receipt of the mortgagee is to effectively discharge the purchaser or other person who is not to be concerned with the application of the proceeds of sale.

Enforcement remedies will in England and, perhaps, in many other countries, be primarily a matter for the lex fori because they are procedural.

Sale

Jurisdictions vary as to whether the mortgagee can sell privately or must go **18–6** through a prescribed judicial auction procedure (with or without judicial supervision), whether there must be a minimum price, whether the vessel can be sold on credit, whether the mortgagee can bid (and, if he does, whether he can set off his mortgage debt against the price) and so on. The delays in public auctions can run to years and the costs can be astronomical. For a list of states insisting on judicial auction and those allowing a private sale in the case of ships and aircraft, see para 10–8 *et seq.*

Whatever the local rules, the advantage of a judicial sale is that the court order will generally give a clear title, free of all prior claims, which will usually be recognised internationally.

The disadvantages of a private sale of a ship are:

– Maritime liens may survive a change in ownership and be enforceable against a purchaser from the mortgagee who is innocent of knowledge of such claims: para 20–4. Standard sale conditions usually require a seller to indemnify the purchaser against these risks.

– A private seller may run the risk of being found liable to the owner for the difference between the price actually realised and a reasonably obtainable price: see, e.g. *Gulf & Fraser Fisherman's Credit Union v Calm C Fish Ltd* [1975] Lloyd's Rep 188.

– If the flag state does not recognise a forced private sale, the purchaser may not be able to obtain a certificate of deletion from the registry necessary for the re-registration of the vessel in the new flag state. Evidence of deletion from a foreign register is not necessary to obtain registration under the British maritime flag, but under 1993 legislation the registered owner is bound to take reasonable steps to terminate the foreign registration. But in the case of aircraft, the 1944 Chicago Convention (which most states have ratified) requires that an aircraft cannot be validly registered in more than one state: para 15–8.

These factors may result in practice in a lower price or a more difficult sale.

As to England, s 35 of the Merchant Shipping Act 1984 as amended in **18–7** 1993 (the legislation is in the process of consolidation) confers upon every registered mortgagee of a British ship express power to sell the security and give an effectual receipt for the purchase money. A subsequent mortgagee requires the consent of the court to sell the ship unless every prior mortgagee has agreed to sell. The sale may be by public auction or by private treaty. The remedy is available to mortgagees whether or not the deed of covenants contains a power of sale, but if the deed limits the power of sale, the mortgagee can only sell in accordance with that limitation. For example, where a deed provided for sale only at public auction and the mortgagee sold by private treaty, the mortgagee was held liable in damages to the mortgagor.

> English ship mortgage enforcement proceedings through the courts are commenced by issuing a writ *in rem* against the vessel claiming payment of the outstanding debt. When the writ is issued the bank should apply for the arrest of the vessel which is effected by the Admiralty Marshall. The mortgagee should then apply to the court for permission to pay off and repatriate the master and the crew if they are still on board and for an order subrogating the mortgagee to the maritime lien of the crew for the wages. During the arrest, the mortgagee will be responsible for the court costs of maintaining the arrest but these expenses are a high priority claim against the sale proceeds. The Marshall does not insure the vessel so the mortgagee should see that this is done. Fourteen days after the service of the writ, the mortgagee can apply to the court for sale pendente lite since a vessel is a wasting asset and should be sold as soon as practicable. The courts may then make a sale order whereby the Admiralty Marshall sells the vessel by private treaty. The Marshall instructs London brokers to place a valuation upon the vessel and to advertise the vessel for sale in the maritime press. Sealed bids are submitted on the terms of the Marshall's standard sale and purchase contract. The Marshall accepts the highest bid provided that this is not less than the valuation which is kept secret. If the valuation is not attained then the Marshall discloses the valuation and applies to the court for permission to sell at a lesser figure: all interested parties may be represented at the hearing. The vessel is sold "as is and where is" without any warranties. The bill of sale executed by the Marshall contains a certificate "that the effect in English law of this judicial sale is that the ship above particularly described has been freed from all liens, encumbrances and debts whatsoever up to [the date of the sale]". English Admiralty sales are generally recognised universally. Any claims against the vessel are then transferred to the fund in court representing the sale proceeds and the mortgagee should then, on obtaining final judgment, apply to the court for determination of the priority of claims and payment of sums due to the mortgagee. A ship may be sold for foreign currency: *The Halcyon the Great* [1975] 1 Lloyds Rep 518. [This summary and that in para 18–9 are based on Martin Watson, "Aspects of Ship Financing in the United Kingdom", *Current Issues in Ship Financing* (Nelson ed, Practising Law Institute, 1981) p 213.]

Possession

18–8   The taking of possession of the security for a temporary period (to be distinguished from the taking over of the title) is in practice an important remedy because it enables the mortgagee to operate the vessel, to sail her to a jurisdiction more amenable to his interests for enforcement if the owner should be uncooperative (or has stopped trading) or to complete a voyage. Possession in order to keep a charter alive is often unhelpful in practice. The default may have occurred precisely because the charter rate failed to cover operating expenses and debt service. The remedy is also useful where the owner has ceased trading because of fraudulent trading rules in which event the mortgagee will wish to take possession to preserve the safety of the vessel. For a list of countries allowing possession in relation to ship and aircraft mortgages, see para 10–7 *et seq.*

In England a mortgagee of a ship can take possession of the vessel himself on a   **18–9** default or if the security is imperilled. The right arises at law regardless of any express provision in the deed of covenants. The method of taking possession may be actual, when the mortgagee will dismiss the master, and then, if the master agrees, reappoint him in which case the master acts thereafter as agent of the mortgagee. It has been held that the appointment of a new ship's husband constitutes a sufficient act of constructive possession, i.e. an act clearly indicating an intention to assume the rights of ownership: *Beynon v Godden* (1878) LR 3 Ex D 263. If actual possession is impossible, e.g. because the ship is at sea, then notice to the mortgagor and the charterer is enough: *Rusden v Pope* (1868) LR 3 Ex 269. If the owner resists entry into possession, then the mortgage should commence mortgagee enforcement proceedings in England and apply to the court for the arrest of the vessel.

From the date when the mortgagee takes possession, all expenses incurred in operating the ship from that date are payable by the mortgagee (ranking prior to the mortgage debt) and the mortgagee is entitled to receive all the earnings of the ship due to the mortgagor after the time of possession and unpaid including earnings assigned to a third party under an assignment entered into by the mortgagor even if made prior to the registration of the mortgage unless the mortgagee had notice of the assignment: *Wilson & Wilson* (1872) 41 LJ Ch 423. However a mortgagee in possession is liable to the mortgagor for any losses sustained through any imprudent use of the ship by the mortgagee: *Marriot v Anchor Reversionary Co* (1861) 30 LJ (Ch) 571, *The Calm* C [1975] 1 Lloyds Rep 188 (Br Columbia CA). It is essential for the mortgagee in possession to check that the insurances are in place since the mortgagee in possession has the same liabilities in tort as the true owner and may be personally responsible, e.g. for crew negligence or oil pollution. The prudent course is to place the vessel with professional ship managers. If the vessel is carrying cargo, and the mortgagee wishes to remove the vessel to a favourable enforcement jurisdiction, it is desirable to come to an agreement with the cargo interests as to the disposition of their cargo. If this is not done then in some jurisdictions the cargo interests may have prior claims for loss of or damage to the cargo which might entitle them to arrest the vessel. Where agreement cannot be reached, it is usually possible for the mortgagee to obtain court orders for the unloading and disposition of the cargo.

18–10   The English position with regard to aircraft is considered to be similar. But possession directly is usually out of the question because the operator needs an air carrier's licence and other permissions.

Possessory management is a peculiarly English remedy readily available in English-influenced jurisdictions. It is unusual elsewhere. But in Greece, Legislative Decree No 3899/58 gives the mortgagee of a duly recorded preferred mortgage the additional right of possession if so provided in the mortgage. Similarly in Panama since 1984: ComC Art 1527A. Some countries, like Spain, allow limited operation of the vessel while it is in the custody of the court but only under the supervision of a court official. Norway does not allow the mortgagee to take possession but the mortgagee can apply to the court to appoint a manager to provide for the proper operation, maintenance and insurance of the vessel. These are primarily custodial remedies.

The English receivership is similar to possession, except that in the case of receivership the mortgagee takes possession through an agent who is deemed to be the agent of the owner. This receiver is not to be confused with a trustee in bankruptcy. *Re Edderside* (1887) 31 SJ 744 is an example of a case where a receiver of a British ship was appointed.

Arrest jurisdiction

Jurisdiction generally

18–11   Jurisdictional rules are of the greatest importance in relation to ship and aircraft finance for the obvious reason that ships and aircraft can end up in practically any state in the world and the mortgagee may become involved in enforcing his rights there.

The three stages in the process must be separated:

— What courts will have jurisdiction to enforce the mortgage?

— If the courts have jurisdiction, what law will they apply to decide such matters as the validity of the mortgage and its priority over other claims, e.g. maritime liens or attachments by unsecured creditors?

— After the law which will be applied to decide the issue in question has been ascertained, what are the substantive rules of the applicable legal system?

Jurisdiction clauses

18–12   A jurisdiction clause in a ship or aircraft mortgage should give non-exclusive jurisdiction to named courts, and (where appropriate) appoint an agent for service of process or comply with Art 17 of the European Judgments Convention. The clause should also confer jurisdiction on the courts of any country where the ship or aircraft happens to be when the action is commenced or where the craft is arrested. Whether the courts will accept this arrest jurisdiction would be a matter for procedural rules, including applicable conventions.

Bases of maritime jurisdiction: summary

There are four basic regimes governing maritime jurisdiction over ships: 18–13

- *In rem* jurisdiction which confers jurisdiction over a ship within the jurisdiction *and* over the owner for the payment of the loan, but only up to the value of the ship

- Attachment jurisdiction over the ship which is provisional only and does not of itself confer jurisdiction over the debtor to determine the claim for the debt itself

- Jurisdiction under the rules of the Brussels Arrest Convention of 1952

- Jurisdiction under the European Judgments Conventions.

In addition, insolvency jurisdiction may be invoked. Often this can be based on the presence of local assets. Insolvency jurisdiction is reviewed elsewhere in this series of books.

In rem jurisdiction over ship and debtor

The first solution is the *in rem* jurisdiction which confers jurisdiction over a   18–14
claim arising in respect of a ship merely because the vessel is within territorial waters. Here it is not necessary that the courts also have jurisdiction over the borrower himself, although strictly the claim may only be enforced against the ship. However if the owner appears in the action, as is usually the case in order to secure the release of the ship, then he is deemed to have submitted to the jurisdiction *in personam* and any judgment can also be enforced against his other assets; see *The Prinsengracht, Financial Times*, July 24, 1992. This is characteristically the common law solution. But in the Australian case of *Shell Oil Co Ltd v The Ship "Lastrigoni"* (1974) 48 ALJR 295, it was held that *in personam* jurisdiction must also be available if a ship is to be arrested for a maritime claim secured by a maritime lien.

Another group of countries allows jurisdiction for all contract claims (not just maritime claims) if the debtor has an asset within the jurisdiction – the "toothbrush" jurisdiction. The claim is not limited to the toothbrush or, in our case, the ship. The general jurisdiction may be discretionary – as in Japan. These countries include Germany, Japan, South Africa, Scotland and jurisdictions in Scandinavia.

18–15   The upshot is that countries which allow jurisdiction over ship and debtor if the ship is physically within the jurisdiction include:

> England: Supreme Court Act 1981 s 20.
> Most English-based countries, e.g. Canada. See, e.g. *The Kosei Maru* (1979) 94 DLR (3d) 658, where a Canadian court took jurisdiction over enforcement proceedings by Japanese mortgagees against a Japanese ship arrested in Canada.
> Germany
> Japan
> Netherlands
> Norway
> Scotland
> South Africa
> Sweden

As mentioned, England limits the claim to the vessel within the jurisdiction. If the borrower chooses not to appear in the action, e.g. to secure bail, and is prepared to lose the ship rather than submit, then the lender's claim for enforcement will be limited to the vessel itself. In practice, a walk-away by the owner is rare.

Attachment jurisdiction over ship but not debtor

18–16   The second solution, characteristic of many countries in the Franco-Latin group, is to allow attachment of the vessel in order to prevent her from sailing away and thereby frustrating a judgment. But the attachment is only a provisional arrest *(saisie conservatoire)* and is not in itself sufficient to ground jurisdiction to try the merits of a claim. Instead the court remits the case to a foreign court having *in personam* jurisdiction to try the merits and holds on to the ship pending the judgment, unless adequate security is given.

In personam jurisdiction means that the court must have jurisdiction over the defendant to enforce the loan and the security. This aspect of jurisdiction is discussed in another volume in this series of works. Typical circumstances conferring *in personam* jurisdiction are: the borrower does business locally; the borrower has his principal place of business within the jurisdiction; (in some civilian countries) the lender is a national of the country of the courts or is resident or domiciled there; or the "toothbrush" jurisdiction just discussed. If the ship is in a foreign port with which neither the lender nor the borrower has any connection, then the case has to be tried in another competent court. That court's judgment must then be capable of enforcement in the state of the arresting court.

Countries which allow provisional arrest, but not merits jurisdiction, on the basis solely of the presence of the ship include Denmark, France and Italy.

"Ready to sail" rule

Historically some states, mainly in the Franco-Latin group such as France, have been hostile to the arrest of ships but have sought rather to protect the interests of cargo-owners so as to promote freedom of navigation. Thus Art 215 of the French Code of Commerce expressly prohibits arrests in order to obtain execution of a judgment when a vessel is "ready to sail" and this also applies to provisional arrests. The interests of cargo owners are placed ahead of the interests of those financing the vessel and other creditors. Similar rules are found in other countries which are influenced by the French Code, e.g. Spain, Japan, Italy and Argentina (ComC Art 870). 18–17

Final judgment necessary

A serious obstacle to enforcement in some countries (e.g. Italy) is that a creditor must get a final judgment against the debtor before the ship can be sold: this can disastrously delay the sale while the mortgagee in effect bears the cost of preserving the vessel (court preservation costs are almost invariably a prior claim on the proceeds). In English jurisdictions and in the United States a prompt judicial sale is available without waiting for determination of all claims. The claims simply attach to the proceeds. 18–18

Enforcement of foreign judgments

The enforcement of foreign judgments for debt claims and the European Judgments Conventions are described in another work in this series. 18–19

In England, a judgment creditor who obtains a final judgment against a shipowner for a pecuniary sum (which is not a fine or penalty) by a proceeding *in rem* in a foreign admiralty court can bring an action *in rem* in the English admiralty court to enforce the decree of the foreign court if it is necessary to complete the execution of that judgment, provided that at the time of the vessel's arrest she is still the property of the judgment debtor: see Dicey Rule 40.

In *The Despina GK* [1983] 1 All ER 1, a vessel was arrested in a Swedish port by cargo owners for cargo lost at sea. The vessel was released after the ship-owners put up security. The Swedish court ordered the shipowners to pay a specified sum. Only part of that sum was paid. *Held*: the cargo owners could arrest the vessel when it entered an English port.

In *Simpson v Fogo* (1860) 29 LJ Ch 657, a mortgaged British ship was attached by creditors in New Orleans, which did not recognise non-possessory chattel mortgages. The New Orleans court sold the ship to another British subject. The mortgagees brought action in England to enforce their mortgage. *Held*: the New Orleans judgment was *in personam* and did not bind persons not parties to the action, and therefore did not bind the mortgagees.

Brussels Arrest Convention of 1952

18–20   The Brussels Convention of 1952 relating to the Arrest of Sea-going ships sought to improve the international mess regarding the arrest of ships. The Convention applies to any vessel "flying the flag of a Contracting State in the jurisdiction of any Contracting State": Art 8(1).

18–21   **Ratifying states** The Convention has been ratified or acceded to by (amongst others and sometimes with reservations) Algeria, Belgium, Costa Rica, Great Britain and Northern Ireland, Egypt, Germany, France, Greece, Haiti, Nigeria, Paraguay, Portugal, Spain, Yugoslavia and certain present or former overseas territories of France and Britain. Other countries, though not adhering formally to the Convention, have nevertheless used it as a model for domestic legislation, e.g. Japan, Lebanon and Tunisia. Among important maritime states which have not adhered to the Convention are the United States and Norway but, as we shall see below, the *in rem* jurisdiction is nevertheless available in certain non-ratifying states. Panama and Liberia have not ratified.

The United Kingdom implementation of the 1952 Arrest Convention is presently contained in ss 20 and 21 of the Supreme Court Act 1981. These provide that the Admiralty jurisdiction of the court may be invoked by an action *in rem* against the ship in question in respect of "any claim in respect of a mortgage of or charge on a ship or any share therein": s 20(2)(c). The jurisdiction applies to all mortgages and charges, whether registered or not and whether legal or equitable, including mortgages and charges under foreign law: s 20(7).

The Convention overrides the European Judgments Conventions: see Art 57 of the European Judgments Convention and *The Deichland* [1990] 1 QB 361, CA.

Arrest jurisdiction Article 2 of the Convention provides: "A ship flying the   **18–22**
flag of one of the Contracting States may be arrested in the jurisdiction of
any of the Contracting States in respect of any maritime claim, but in respect
of no other claim." A maritime claim includes a claim arising out of "the
mortgage or hypothecation of any ship": Art 1(1).

Further, Art 8(2) provides: "A ship flying the flag of a non-Contracting
State may be arrested in the jurisdiction of any Contracting State [in respect
of a maritime claim]or of any other claim for which the law of the Contracting State permits its arrest." It follows therefore that the courts of a Contracting State can arrest vessels at the instance of the mortgagee even though
the vessel flies the flag of a non-Contracting State.

In the Convention "arrest" is used in the sense of a prejudgment attachment ("the retention of a ship by judicial process to secure a maritime
claim" (Art 1(2)) and does not of itself confer jurisdiction to determine the
merits. However, the Convention expressly provides in Art 7(1):

> "The Courts of the country in which the arrest was made shall have jurisdiction
> to determine the case upon its merits if the domestic law of the country in which
> the arrest is made gives jurisdiction to such Courts, or . . . if the claim is upon a
> mortgage or hypothecation of the ship arrested." [See Art 7(1) for the other five
> cases in which merits jurisdiction is available.]

Article 5 provides that in the case of mortgages, hypothecations and certain other maritime claims: "The Courts or other appropriate judicial authority within whose jurisdiction the ship has been arrested shall permit the
release of the ship upon sufficient bail or other security being furnished."

The amount of the bail or security is to be determined by the court if the
parties do not agree.

Procedure The arrest has to be under judicial supervision: Art 4. Many   **18–23**
states require the arresting creditor to post a bond to indemnify the owner if
the arrest is unjustified. This procedural aspect, as with other matters of
procedure, is left to the law of the Contracting State: Art 6.

Exclusion of benefits from non-contracting states Article 8(3) provides: **18–24**

> "Nevertheless any Contracting State shall be entitled wholly or partly to
> exclude from the benefits of this Convention any Government of a non-Con-
> tracting State or any person who has not, at the time of arrest, his habitual resi-
> dence or principal place of business in one of the Contracting States."

Two of the benefits of the Convention are (1) the right to arrest and (2)
the ability of the court to adjudicate upon the merits pursuant to Art 7(1). If
therefore the claimant is from a non-Contracting State, he may be left with
non-Convention law if a contracting state has adopted the exclusions.

As an illustration, one may review how this might affect an American mortgagee seeking to arrest a Norwegian-owned and documented vessel in France. (This example is based on Kriz, Duke LJ 671 (1963) and 70 (1964).) The United States and Norway are not parties to the Convention. Therefore one falls back on non-Convention French law since the American mortgagee is not entitled to the Convention benefits. If the vessel is "ready to sail", the mortgagee cannot arrest provisionally: Art 215 of the French Code of Commerce. If the vessel is not "ready to sail", the French courts can under the ordinary law provisionally arrest the vessel even though no French court is available to adjudicate upon the merits: *Petrico v Rogenaes*, Court of Appeal, Alger, February 13, 1923, 2 Rev Dor 518 (1923). In this situation Art 7(2) provides:

> "If the Court within whose jurisdiction the ship was arrested has no jurisdiction to decide upon the merits, the bail or other security given in accordance with Article 5 to procure the release of the ship shall specifically provide that it is given as security for the satisfaction of any judgment which may eventually be pronounced by a Court having jurisdiction so to decide; and the Court or other appropriate judicial authority of the country in which the arrest is made shall fix the time within which the claimant shall bring an action before a Court having such jurisdiction."

Article 7 (4) goes on to provide that if "the action or proceedings are not brought within the time so fixed, the defendant may apply for the release of the ship or of the bail or other security". Hence the French court may remit jurisdiction to a more suitable forum after bail has been set and the vessel released. The position in Italy is understood to be similar.

18–25   **Assignments to secure jurisdiction** The claimant cannot evade the provisions of the Convention excluding its benefits in the case of non-residents, etc., of a Contracting State by assigning the claim to a resident. Article 8(5) provides:

> "When a maritime claim is asserted by a third party other than the original claimant, whether by subrogation, assignment or otherwise, such third party shall, for the purpose of this Convention, be deemed to have the same habitual residence or principal place of business as the original claimant."

18–26   **No multiple arrests** Once the claimant has arrested once and the ship has been released upon security being given, he cannot arrest the vessel in another jurisdiction, e.g. because he thinks he will obtain more favourable treatment there. The creditor therefore relies on the security given to the court. Article 3(3) of the Convention provides:

> "A ship shall not be arrested, nor shall bail or other security be given more than once in any one or more of the jurisdictions of any of the Contracting States in

respect of the same maritime claim by the same claimant; and, if a ship has been arrested in one of such jurisdictions, or bail or other security has been given in such jurisdictions either to release the ship or to avoid a threatened arrest, any subsequent arrest of the ship or of any ship in the same ownership by the same claimant for the same maritime claim shall be set aside, and the ship released by the Court or other appropriate judicial authority of that State, unless the claimant can satisfy the Court or other appropriate judicial authority that the bail or other security had been finally released before the subsequent arrest or that there is other good cause for maintaining that arrest."

Sister-ship actions The sister-ship action *in rem* which is available for certain maritime claims may not be available for mortgages or hypothecations under the Convention. Under the sister-ship action, subject to various exceptions, "a claimant may arrest either the particular ship in respect of which the maritime claim arose, or any other ship which is owned by the person who was, at the time the maritime claim arose, the owner of the particular ship, event though the ship arrested be ready to sail": Art 3(1). To attach a sister-ship the mortgagee would have to obtain a judgment *in personam* and then enforce it against the vessel pursuant to an ordinary order for execution.   **18–27**

European Judgments Conventions

Generally These Conventions, summarised elsewhere in this series of works, provide for compulsory jurisdiction in civil and commercial matters at the courts of the defendant's domicile but subject to wide exceptions including the ability to contract out under Art 17. Judgments within the Conventions must be recognised and enforced by the courts of contracting states. Each contracting state can continue to apply its own rules as to provisional measures, such as a prejudgment arrest: Art 24.   **18–28**

Mortgage registration By Art 16(3) in "proceedings which have as their object the validity of entries in public registers, the courts of the Contracting State in which the register is kept" shall have exclusive jurisdiction which cannot be overridden by a contractual choice by the parties. Because the Article overrides consent, the Article is construed restrictively: *Sanders v Van der Putte* [1978] 1 CMLR 331 (European Ct). Article 16(3) presumably would apply to the validity of ship and aircraft title and mortgage registration in a public register or in a register for company charges. It seems unlikely that it would apply if the mortgage was not registered at all, but   **18–29**

rather such matters as whether the registered particulars are adequate or submitted in time or properly renewed.

18–30   *In rem* jurisdiction It seems that the *in rem* merits jurisdiction of the English courts over ships is available only under the Brussels Arrest Convention if the case is within the European Judgment Conventions (defendant domiciled in a Convention country): see *The Deuchland* [1989] 3 WLR 478, CA. This is because Art 3 of the European Judgments Conventions vetoes UK jurisdiction based upon "the presence within the United Kingdom of property belonging to the defendant", but Art 57 of the European Judgments Conventions preserves the Brussels Arrest Convention. Nevertheless provisional and protective measures are preserved by Art 24 of the European Judgments Conventions. Further the additional jurisdictions are also available under the European Judgments Conventions, e.g. if the defendant is domiciled locally or has submitted to the jurisdiction under Art 17 of the European Judgments Conventions.

18–31   **Multiple proceedings** Article 21 of the European Judgments Conventions provides that where proceedings involving "the same cause of action are brought in the courts of different Contracting States, any court other than the court first seized shall of its own motion decline jurisdiction in favour of that court". It is doubtful that an arrest in another jurisdiction while the case is being tried elsewhere is stopped by this provision since the arrest is preservative within Art 24. See also *The Nordglimt* [1988] QB 183.

Jurisdiction to arrest aircraft

18–32   It is believed that, in many cases, the jurisdiction to arrest aircraft will be similar to that pertaining to ships. But there is no equivalent of the Brussels Ship Arrest Convention of 1952.

Apart from minor exceptions, the *in rem* ship jurisdiction of the English courts does not apply to aircraft: see the Supreme Court Act 1981 s 20. The courts have jurisdiction on the normal grounds, including an express jurisdiction clause. A Mareva injunction can be obtained to prevent the aircraft leaving the jurisdiction prior to judgment: for an aircraft case, see *Allen v Jambo Holdings Ltd* [1980 1 WLR 1252.

Many US states allow prejudgment attachments for clear money demands to preserve the property. this may confer jurisdiction on the merits if there are other minimum contacts. Conservatory arrests are often available, as in France and the Netherlands.

Everywhere the mortgagee is liable for damages if the attachment is wrongful.

Rome Aircraft Convention of 1933

The purpose of the Rome Convention on the unification of certain rules   18–33
relating to the precautionary arrest of aircraft is to prevent the arrest of
aircraft where the arrest would seriously interfere with state services (such
as post) or disrupt commercial traffic.

The Convention restricts the rights of creditors and owners and accord-
ingly has been ratified by only a limited number of states. These include:
Algeria, Finland, Haiti, Mali, Mauritania, the Netherlands, Niger, Senegal,
Sweden and Zaire.

The restriction on arrest does not apply if the arresting party is relying
upon "an immediately enforceable judgment already obtained by ordinary
process, or upon any right of seizure equivalent thereof": Art 2(1). The
effect therefore is to restrict prejudgment arrests and not post-judgment
execution.

CHAPTER 19

RECOGNITION OF FOREIGN SHIP AND AIRCRAFT MORTGAGES

Applicable law

19–1   The validity of a mortgage of a chattel is usually governed by the law of the place where the chattel happens to be when the mortgage is created, but where the chattel is ambulatory, then possibly one looks to the law of the most significant relationship to the transaction: para 13–15. In the case of ships and aircraft, the law of the place where the chattel happens to be when the mortgage is created is obviously inappropriate as the dominant legal system: the craft may be on international waters or in international airspace. Subject perhaps to any valid choice of law by the parties, the validity and effect of the mortgage should be governed by the law of the flag. Indeed reference to the laws of the flag has been called the "most venerable and universal rule of maritime law" *Lauritzen v Larsen*, 345 US 571 (1953). Many jurisdictions in fact regard the law of the flag as decisive and this is the solution adopted by international conventions.

As to the law governing the validity of a mortgage, the possible choices are between:

— The law of the flag—the most stable

— The lex situs of the ship when the mortgage was created. This is the most evanescent, but is useful as an additional ground for validating a mortgage.

— The law of closest connection on centre of gravity principles or the law expressly chosen.

A distinction is to be observed between the law applicable to the proprietary transfer created by a mortgage (and the publicity needed to validate the mortgage on the debtor's insolvency) and the law applicable to the contractual terms, e.g. the terms of the secured debt. The topic is discussed generally in chapter 13.

Meaning of recognition

The main purpose of a mortgage is valid security on the bankruptcy of the   **19–2**
mortgagor and against his attaching creditors. However other questions are
involved, e.g.:

–   priority of the mortgage against general priority creditors, e.g. insol-
    vency administration costs, taxes and employees wages: para 12–5 *et
    seq*

–   priority of the mortgage against super-priority loans in rescue proceed-
    ings: chapter 11

–   bankruptcy freezes on enforcement: para 10–15.

Recognition of foreign ship mortgages

Flag law Apart from applicable conventions, few states appear now to refer   **19–3**
to situs or governing law. The following decide validity by the flag:

> Argentina (subject to reciprocity) – Shipping Act No 20,094 Art 600
> Denmark
> England
> Finland
> France
> Germany (*Reichsgericht* February 9, 1900, RGZ 45,276)
> Israel
> Italy
> Japan
> Taiwan – Conflict of Laws Act Art 10(3)
> United States

But in the case of England and common law United States, it is possibly
the case that, if the mortgage is invalidated by flag law, the courts might give
the mortgage effect if it is valid by the lex situs when the mortgage was
created or by the governing law (law of closest connection).

Non-recognition It has been said that the following jurisdictions do not rec-   **19–4**
ognise foreign ship mortgages at all, but this requires investigation:

–   Natal – *Re SS Mangoro* (1913) 34 Natal LR 67, but the other South
    African seaboard provinces evidently do recognise foreign ship mort-
    gages
–   Thailand (apparently)
–   Turkey (unless the flag is that of a 1926 Brussels Convention
    country).

As to **Venezuela**, foreign vessels are not subject to attachment except for debts contracted in Venezuela for the benefit of those vessels, so that effectively it is useless to attempt to enforce a foreign ship mortgage in Venezuela: CC Art 621.

19–5 **England** The English courts will probably uphold a foreign mortgage as valid if it is valid under flag law, but if it is invalid under flag law, the courts may possibly seek to uphold it if it is valid by the law of the situs or by its governing law.

> In *The Colorado* [1923] P 102, an English supplier of necessaries to a French ship arrested her in an English port. The ship was subject to a French mortgage deed ("hypotheque"). *Held*: the question of the rights created by the mortgage must be determined according to French law as the contract was made there though the question of priorities must be decided according to English law since priorities are a matter for the lex fori. As a result the French mortgagee had priority. See also *The Arosa Kulm* [1959] Lloyds Rep 212.

> In *The Pacific Challenger* [1960] 1 Lloyd's List Rep 99, American suppliers of bunkers to a Liberian flag ship claimed that a Liberian mortgage granted to an American bank was invalid because of alleged defects regarding the affidavit of good faith and endorsement of the mortgage on the ship's certificate of registry kept on board. *Held*: the court applied Liberian law and upheld the mortgage.

An interesting case where the English courts leant over backwards to give some effect to a foreign security where the mortgage failed for want of registration is *The Angel Bell* [1979] 2 Lloyd's Rep 49:

> The case had complicated facts and was mainly concerned with the right of a mortgagee to the proceeds of an insurance policy. The mortgagees had been granted a Panamanian mortgage over a Panamanian vessel. The mortgage had been provisionally registered in London. The mortgage was not forwarded to Panama and registered permanently there within six months as required by Panamanian law. *Held*: the mortgage was governed by Panamanian law and was therefore invalid. However the court seemed to indicate that a mortgage over a foreign flag ship may be governed by English law, as in the case of foreign land, and had it been so governed it would have created a valid contract to create a mortgage which was a valid equitable mortgage although perhaps not conferring rights in rem against the ship until perfected under flag law.

19–6 **France** A leading case in France is *The Wang Importer*, Court of Appeal, Rennes, February 6, 1962 (1962) DMF 475:

> The court seemed to acknowledge that the validity of a United States mortgage was to be determined in accordance with United States law. The court appointed three American lawyers as experts to determine whether a preferred mortgage executed in New York on an American flag vessel was valid under US law.

United States The United States amended its legislation in 1954 to extend   19–7
the maritime jurisdiction to foreign mortgages. The initiative for the amendment arose from the fact that after World War II the United States Government owned a large fleet of vessels built during the war which it then
proceeded to sell off to aliens, generally in return for purchase-money mortgages. There were serious questions whether the American Admiralty courts
had jurisdiction to foreclose a mortgage on a foreign flag vessel, but the
doubts were removed by an amendment to the 1920 Act in 1954 which in
effect recognised a mortgage validly executed in accordance with the laws of
a foreign nation under the laws of which the vessel is documented and duly
registered in accordance with such laws in a public register either at the port
of registry of the vessel or its principal office. It is believed that this was
inadvertently omitted from the 1989 Act replacing the 1920 Act and it
needs to be investigated if the omission has been rectified. See 46 USC
s 31301(6)(b).

> In *The Aruba*, 139 F Supp 327, 1955 AMC 1143 (D Canal Zone 1955), the
> court held that the 1954 section was applicable to a 1949 mortgage on a
> Panama-flag vessel held by a Swiss bank.

Since then there have been a number of cases where the American Admiralty courts have looked to the law of the flag to determine validity, e.g. *State
of Israel v M/V Nili*, 435 F 2d 242 (5th Cir 1970).

Brussels Convention of 1926 The answer given by the 1926 Brussels Con-   19–8
vention relating to Maritime Liens and Mortgages as regards recognition of
mortgages is set out in Art 2 which provides as follows:

> "Mortgages, hypothecations, and other similar charges upon vessels, duly
> effected in accordance with the law of the Contracting State to which the vessel
> belongs, and registered in a public register either at the port of the vessel's
> registry or at a central office, shall be regarded as valid and respected in all the
> other contracting countries."

This Convention was acceded to by only 19 countries, including Argentina, Belgium, Brazil, Denmark, Finland, France, Hungary, Italy, Monaco,
Poland, Portugal, Rumania, Spain, Syria and Turkey. It will be noted that
this list does not include the United Kingdom, the United States, Japan,
Canada, the Netherlands and Russia. Norway and Sweden (amongst others)
have adapted their maritime law to the 1967 Brussels Convention.

The 1967 Brussels Convention, which, never came into force but which   19–9
may reflect Scandinavian law, set out a somewhat longer list of requirements for recognition as follows:

> "Mortgages and 'hypotheques' on sea-going vessels shall be enforceable in Con-
> tracting States provided that:

(a) Such mortgages and 'hypotheques' have been effected and registered in accordance with the law of the State where the vessel is registered;

(b) The register and any instruments required to be deposited with the registrar in accordance with the law of the State where the vessel is registered are open to public inspection, and that extracts of the register and copies of such instruments are obtainable from the registrar; and

(c) Either the register or any instruments referred to in paragraph (b) above specified the name and address of the person in whose favour the mortgage or 'hypotheque' has been effected or that it has been issued to bearer, the amount secured and the date and other particulars which, according to the law of the State of registration, determine the rank as respects other registered mortgages and 'hypotheques'."

The requirement for a statement of the amount secured reflects civilian thinking on mortgages and would have disqualified the British account current form of mortgage. This is one reason that common law countries on the British standard did not ratify the Convention.

Recognition of aircraft mortgages

19–10 **Generally** It is to be expected that as regards the recognition by one state of a foreign aircraft mortgage, countries will adopt similar rules as those applying to the recognition of foreign ship mortgages. However international co-operation has played a more important role: the 1948 Geneva Aircraft Convention recognising rights in aircraft has achieved much wider adoption than the corresponding 1926 Brussels Maritime Convention.

The choice lies between recognising a foreign mortgage if it is valid by the law of:

— the flag (nationality);

— the place where the aircraft was physically located when the mortgage was created (lex situs);

— the law of the closest connection (centre of gravity).

For a comment on these, see para 19–1.

19–11 **Applicable law** The 1948 Geneva Convention adopts the law of the flag and this principle is adopted by many states, including:

Argentina (but the mortgage must also comply with Argentine law: CC Art 3129)
Austria: International Private Law Act Art 33
Belgium (but it is possible that, on bankruptcy, the courts may apply

Belgian law to invalidate the mortgage if the aircraft is in Belgium. Belgium does not permit non-possessory aircraft mortgages)

Brazil

England (probably, but possible validation by situs or governing law, if invalid by flag)

France

Greece

Iceland (probably)

Korea (S): the Conflicts of Law Act 1962 Art 2 provides that the law governing the validity of a real right is the local law of the place of the subject matter of that right, but Art 44 applies the nationality law to ships. Hence it is probably the case that the courts will follow the same rule for aircraft as they do for ships

Luxembourg (probably)

Peru

Portugal (probably)

Spain

Switzerland

Taiwan – Law Governing the Application of Laws in Civil Matters involving Foreign Elements Art 10

Apart from any applicable conventions, it appears that amongst the countries which might apply the lex situs when the mortgage was created are Chile (or possibly the flag), Germany (ordinary conflict rules for chattel mortgages) and Uruguay.

Non-recognition It is said that foreign aircraft mortgages will not be recog-   **19–12**
nised at all in Thailand.

In Venezuela by the Chattel Mortgage Law a chattel mortgage must comply with Venezuela law as to form and content to be enforceable: this may disqualify a foreign mortgage by reason of a formalistic technicality, e.g. lack of notarisation. The position appears to be similar in Argentina.

Geneva Aircraft Convention of 1948

General

The Geneva Convention of 1948 on the International Recognition of Rights   **19–13**
in Aircraft was promoted in order to give as much security as possible to lessors and lenders financing these expensive pieces of equipment.

Contracting States

19–14   The Convention has achieved much wider acceptance than the corresponding Brussels Convention on ship mortgages. Although the current position should be checked by the practitioner, it is believed that the contracting states include:

North America: United States, but not Canada

Europe: France, Greece, the Netherlands, Portugal, Switzerland, Germany and Luxembourg, but not the United Kingdom, Ireland, Spain, Austria or Turkey

Scandinavia: Denmark, Norway, Sweden and Iceland, but not Finland

Latin America: Argentina, Brazil, Chile, Mexico, Ecuador, El Salvador, Haiti and Paraguay, but (apparently, although this should be checked) not Colombia or Venezuela

Africa: Mali, Mauritania, Niger, Algeria, Ivory Coast, Tunisia, Cameroon, Egypt, Gabon, Rwanda, Chad, the Libyan Arab Republic, Zimbabwe and the Central African Republic, but not South Africa, Kenya, Nigeria or Zambia

Middle East: Kuwait, but not Saudi Arabia, the United Arab Emirates, Bahrain or Israel

Asia and Pacific: Pakistan, Bangladesh and Thailand, but not India, Sri Lanka, Japan, China, Australia, New Zealand, Malaysia, Hong Kong or Singapore.

It is easy to see that there are still significant gaps. The main omissions are:

— Many English-influenced states. But these are very ready to recognise foreign security interests in any event. Britain regarded the Convention as too restrictive

— A few states hostile to security generally, e.g. Austria

— States without a developed commercial and insolvency law, e.g. some Arabian Gulf States.

Because Mexico reserved on the priority of fiscal claims and certain crew claims, it is probable that Mexico has not properly adhered as a contracting state. This at least is the US view.

A state may denounce its adherence, effective six months after notice to the International Civil Aviation Organisation: Art XXII. Presumably a denunciation will rob a creditor of the recognition protection he thought he had.

Aircraft covered

The Convention does not apply to "aircraft used in military, customs or police services" and hence applies only to civil aircraft: Art XIII. By Art XVI:

19–15

> "the term 'aircraft' shall include the airframe, engines, propellers, radio apparatus, and all other articles intended for use in the aircraft whether installed therein or temporarily separated therefrom".

The term "aircraft" is not defined and whether such odd craft as airships would be included is a matter of conjecture.

Rights protected

Article I(1) of the Convention provides:

19–16

> "(1) The Contracting States undertake to recognise:
>   (a) rights of property in aircraft;
>   (b) rights to acquire aircraft by purchase coupled with possession of the aircraft;
>   (c) rights to possession of aircraft under leases of six months or more;
>   (d) mortgages, hypotheques and similar rights in aircraft which are contractually created as security for payment of an indebtedness [but with a limit of three years unpaid interest: see Article V];
> provided that such rights:
>   (i) have been constituted in accordance with the law of the Contracting State in which the aircraft was registered as to nationality at the time of their constitution; and
>   (ii) are regularly recorded in a public record of the Contracting State in which the aircraft is registered as to nationality."

Points to note on this are:

19–17

(1) The Convention does not validate these rights. To be recognised, they must be constituted in accordance with the law of the national registry. Hence if the registration state does not permit these rights, there is nothing to recognise. In this connection Art II(3) provides:

> "A Contracting State may prohibit the recording of any right which cannot validly be constituted according to its national law."

(2) Although commentators differ, the better view is that the valid constitution of the rights is determined by the domestic law of the recording state, not including its conflict of laws. This enhances certainty. If on the other hand a contracting state's conflict rules are included, then if, for example, flag state F will under its conflict rules recognise a mortgage as having been validly constituted under the law of a non-flag state NF, even though not validly constituted under the internal law of flag state F, the mortgage is protected by the Convention if duly recorded in flag state F. In any event, each contracting state cannot apply its own conflict rules when called upon to recognise a mortgage recorded in another contracting state (e.g. lex situs of the aircraft when the mortgage is created) but must look to the law of the flag state.

(3) The law of the flag determines validity, not the lex situs of the aircraft and not the governing law of the mortgage. It is immaterial that the mortgage was not registered in a non-flag contracting state, e.g. on the basis of a rule that mortgages by entities doing business locally must be registered, so long as the mortgage is valid and registered in the flag state. This side-steps the problems of multiple international registration.

19–18   (4) The protected rights include ownership by a lessor (so as to facilitate lease financings), hire purchase, conditional sale agreements, title retention, mortgages, leases of more than six months and the right of a sub-lessor against a head lessor. They do not cover:

- liens not created by agreement, such as statutory liens for airport services or possessory liens for repairs (see para (1)(d));
- options to purchase without possession of the aircraft;
- short-term leases (since these are not usually financing leases);
- (probably) floating charges since para (1)(d) appears to contemplate only fixed security.

Other rights are permitted if the law of a contracting state so provides, but they rank after the recorded rights. Article I(2) provides:

"Nothing in this Convention shall prevent the recognition of any rights in aircraft under the law of any Contracting State; but Contracting States shall not admit or recognise any right as taking priority over the rights mentioned in paragraph (1) of this Article."

Thus, a Contracting State can recognise unrecorded mortgages and can recognise a variety of other liens, but they must be subordinate to recorded rights.

19–19   (5) The requirement for recording of the property interest attacks the creation of hidden security interests since the contracting states will not recognise unrecorded rights as ranking prior to recorded interests.

(6) The reference to "indebtedness" in Article I(1)(d) is not limited to loans, but may evidently include a purchase money credit, a guarantee, or the debt of another. Contracting states therefore ought to recognise the flag state's views as to:

   – security for future debt, e.g. revolving loans. Thus France should recognise a US revolving loan flag mortgage even though France does not permit a mortgage to secure future advances: para 8–3;

   – the need to state a maximum secured amount: para 8–4;

   – foreign currency mortgages: para 8–5.

   Whether this Convention overrides the flag state's view as to usury, penalty interest, capitalised interest or post-insolvency interest seems unclear. Note the limit to three years unpaid interest: Art V.

(7) Contracting States ought to recognise the flag state's views as to formalities, e.g. notarisations, deed, legalisation, degree of identification of the debtor, creditor and aircraft, and execution by one or both parties.

(8) Contracting States ought to recognise the flag state's views as to the availability of security over future and after-acquired property.

(9) The Convention does not cover security assignments of charterparties, earnings, insurances or requisition compensation. These must comply with non-Convention applicable law.

   All recorded rights must be centralised in the same record: Art II(1). This facilitates searches. But the nationality register required by the 1944 Chicago Convention need not be the same as the register where Geneva rights are recorded.

   There are various provisions in Art III as to the taking of copies or extracts. If local law so provides, the filing of a document for recording has the same effect as a recording: Article III(3). This was intended to cover those jurisdictions where there is a gap between lodgement of the document and its entry on the register.

Effects of recording

Article II(2) provides: 19–20

> "Except as otherwise provided in this Convention, the effects of the recording of any right mentioned in Article I, paragraph (1), with regard to third parties shall be determined according to the law of the Contracting State where it is recorded."

Third parties include creditors, e.g. general creditors on insolvency and attaching creditors. Presumably the effects of recording also govern such matters as whether the recording is deemed notice to third parties, the priority ranking of successive recordings, and whether the mortgage is effective against prior and subsequent attaching creditors.

By the last paragraph of Article I(1):

> "The regularity of successive recordings in different Contracting States shall be determined in accordance with the law of the State where the aircraft was registered as to nationality at the time of each recording."

Meaning of recognition

19–21 Recognition and effects against creditors are broad terms. They ought to include the following:

— The priority in accordance with flag law of the mortgagee's or lessor's rights on the insolvency of the owner or the lessee or their attaching creditors so that the aircraft does not go to unsecured creditors of the mortgagor or lessee

— The priority in accordance with flag law of the mortgagee's or lessor's ownership against general priority creditors (insolvency costs, employees wages, taxes), other aircraft claimants and super-priority moratorium loans. The Convention limits priorities under the flag law in this respect: para 19–29. Hence France and other countries should exclude their usual priority of preferential creditors.

— The validity in accordance with flag law of bankruptcy freezes on the enforcement of mortgages and the repossession of leased aircraft, e.g. as in France, Canada and the United States. Accordingly, the flag state can apply its bankruptcy freezes, but ought not to apply its freeze to another flag state which does not have a freeze. But it is arguable that freezes are part of sale proceedings which by Art VII (1) are determined by the law of the contracting state where the sale takes place.

It seems unlikely that the Convention overrides fraudulent preference rules: but see Art VI giving limited recognition to evasion of creditors by a debtor.

Persons protected

19–22 Article XI provides:

> "The provisions of this Convention shall in each Contracting State apply to all aircraft registered as to nationality in another Contracting State."

The Convention therefore does not apply if the state where the aircraft is registered or the state called upon to recognise the right are not contracting states. Thus contracting states are not called upon to recognise a British or Japanese mortgage. But it is immaterial that the mortgagee is not a national of the flag state of the aircraft. Thus a British or Japanese bank can benefit if they enforce in a contracting state a mortgage recorded in another contracting state.

Further, only some of the provisions apply to matters within the flag state itself. If an aircraft is registered in a contracting state, that contracting state need only apply Art II and III (mainly procedural provisions about the central record), IX (non-recognition of non-permitted transfers) and IV (dealing with the priority of salvage and preservation expenses, unless these operations have been terminated within its own territory). It follows that, for example, an enforcement within the flag state does not have to abide by the minimum standards in Art VII.

Spare parts

Because spare parts of an aircraft, especially engines, may well form a very   **19–23** substantial portion of the total cost of the aircraft, special protection is required. Article X sets out details for the recognition of chattel security over spare parts. But the protection is fussy and restrictive and reflects a compromise between states hostile and sympathetic to security. Article X(1) provides:

> "(1) If a recorded right in an aircraft of the nature specified in Article 1, and held as security for the payment of an indebtedness, extends, in conformity with the law of the Contracting State where the aircraft is registered, to spare parts stored in a specified place or places, such right shall be recognised by all Contracting States, as long as the spare parts remain in the place or places specified, provided that an appropriate public notice, specifying the description of the right, the name and address of the holder of this right and the record in which such right is recorded, is exhibited at the place where the spare parts are located, so as to give due notification to third parties that such spare parts are encumbered.
>
> (2) A statement indicating the character and the approximate number of such spare parts shall be annexed to or included in the recorded document. Such parts may be replaced by similar parts without affecting the right of the creditor."

By Article 10(4):

> "the term 'spare parts' means parts of an aircraft, engines, propellers, radio

apparatus, instruments, appliances, furnishings, parts of any of the foregoing and generally any other articles of whatever description maintained for installation in aircraft in substitution for parts or articles removed".

19–24   In broad terms, spare parts are within the Convention rights on the following terms:

(a) The law of the Contracting State must extend recorded security rights in aircraft to spare parts, i.e. it is left to local law to decide whether security over spare parts can be created and recorded. If local law does not permit a non-possessory chattel mortgage, there is nothing to record and nothing to recognise.

(b) The spare parts must be stored in a place specified in the record: this reflects the civilian view about specificity.

(c) Appropriate public notice must be exhibited at the specified place: this is to publicise otherwise secret security interests to overcome "false wealth" and safeguard priorities.

(d) The central records must reflect the inclusion of spare parts within the security and indicate their character and number. This is a problem for spare parts subsequently acquired. It is not necessary to designate each part, only the total number of spare parts stored. Replaced similar parts can be covered.

   Even though the protection is expressed to apply to spares only so long as they remain in the specified place, it seems that parts originally part of the aircraft sent away for repair can be within the scope of the Convention. This is because Art XVI includes in the definition of aircraft "all other articles intended for use in the aircraft whether installed therein or *temporarily separated therefrom*" so that they are still considered to be part of the aircraft. Note that the definition of spare parts in Art X(4) includes those "in substitution for parts or articles removed."

19–25   Unsecured creditors seizing spare parts can obtain limited priority of one-third of the net sale proceeds over a mortgagee if local law so provides: see Art X(3). This reflects a bias in some states in favour of unsecured creditors.

A recorded right cannot extend to spare parts alone but only if the aircraft itself is mortgaged: see the opening language of Art X(1).

A general charge, such as a floating charge, over spare parts will usually not be covered, either because the parts are unidentified or because they are not stored in a specified place. Whether or not the Article is in any event limited to fixed security merits further investigation.

Judicial sale

The Convention provides in Art VII for only one method of enforcing a   **19–26**
right in an aircraft, namely, a judicial sale (since the Article refers to "proceedings"), and sets out detailed minimum standards for the notification
and publication of the sale. For a discussion of the suitability of judicial
sales, see para 10–8 *et seq*.

The date and place of the sale must be fixed at least six weeks in advance
and the executing creditor must give at least one month's prior public notice
of the sale where the aircraft is registered as to nationality and concurrently
notify the recorded owner and the holders of recorded rights in the aircraft.
Hence there are compulsory grace periods – unsuitable for aircraft. Apart
from those minimum standards, the "proceedings of a sale of an aircraft in
execution shall be determined by the law of the Contracting State where the
sale takes place": Art VII(1).

The minimum standards do not apply to spare parts covered by Art X.
These spare parts are sold in execution in accordance with the law of the
contracting state where the sale takes place: Art X(3) applying Art VII(1).

If the sale of the aircraft is not made in accordance with the prescribed   **19–27**
rules:

(a) The consequence of failure is determined in accordance with the law of
the contracting state where the sale takes place. But there is an overriding mandatory requirement that a party damaged by contravention of
the minimum requirements can require the sale to be annulled in six
months: Art VII(3). A purchaser must therefore be sure that the formalities are complied with or he is liable to be divested of his aircraft.

(b) No transfer of the aircraft from the nationality register or the record of
a contracting state to that of another contracting state may be made
unless all holders of recorded rights have been satisfied or consent to the
transfer: Art IX.

An executing creditor cannot achieve a sale of an aircraft or spare parts
covered by Art X unless all rights having priority over his claim are covered
by the proceeds of sale or are assumed by the purchaser: Art VII(4). One
result of this is that a junior mortgagee cannot himself compel a sale unless
he stands to recover.

Another result is that, if there is a fleet mortgage, a second mortgagee   **19–28**
over one aircraft could not force a sale unless the bidder made a minimum
bid for the whole debt secured on all the aircraft. This is not unfair since a
second mortgagee should not be able to partition the debt between the aircraft and thereby prevent the first mortgagee from recovering shortfalls on

one aircraft out of surpluses on another. He should be left to whatever rights of marshalling are available to him if the senior mortgagee sells the junior mortgagee's aircraft and hence saddles it with the entire debt.

Where an unsecured creditor executes, contracting states may limit the amount claimable by the holders of the prior rights over spare parts (but not the aircraft) to two-thirds of the proceeds of sale in certain circumstances, so that effectively these unsecured creditors can look to one-third of the sale proceeds. This provision was inserted to encourage local business to give credit to airlines and reflects sympathy for the small unsecured creditor: Art X(3).

Priority rights

19–29   The Convention severely limits the claims which can rank ahead of the Article I rights and thereby subordinates numerous claims which under the laws of many states would rank ahead of chattel mortgages, especially costs of the insolvency administration, taxes, crew wages and liens of charterers, suppliers and repairers. The privileged claims are:

1. **Costs** First on the list are certain costs "legally chargeable under the law of the Contracting State where the sale take place, which are incurred in the common interest of creditors in the course of execution proceedings leading to a sale": Art VII(6). In some countries, these costs are enormous – said to be 6 per cent in Argentina, for example.

2. **Salvage and preservation expenses** Second in rank are compensation for salvage and "extraordinary expenses indispensable for the preservation of the aircraft" if they "give rise, under the law of the Contracting State where the operations of salvage or preservation are terminated, to a right conferring a charge on the aircraft": Art IV(1). The Convention does not create these privileges since that is left to local law. The privileges rank in inverse order of time. The preservation expenses must be both extraordinary (in the sense of not being routine) and indispensable and therefore undoubtedly do not include the cost of repairs for wear and tear but they probably include cost of safeguarding the aircraft or moving it to a secure place. The salvage and preservation privileges expire within three months unless noted on the register and unless certain other steps are taken. Hence the prior claims can remain unrecorded and secret but only temporarily.

3. **Tort liability** The mortgagee's priority may be reduced by liability for injury or damage to persons or property on the surface in the contracting state where the sale of a mortgaged aircraft takes place, except, in most cases, where the liability is adequately insured: see Art VII(5).

Broadly, contracting states may optionally provide that security holders over the aircraft (and other aircraft under a fleet mortgage) may not claim more than 80 per cent of the sale price of the aircraft sold so as to leave 20 per cent for those unsecured tort victims. The object is to give the victims a source of payment, especially in the case of fleet mortgages. The provisions are of little practical importance since the privilege cannot apply if the aircraft is adequately insured. But they are a further example of unsecured creditors potentially ranking ahead: see also the prior claim of unsecured creditors against spare parts discussed above.

4. **Violations of local law** By Art XII:

> "Nothing in this Convention shall prejudice the rights of a Contracting State to enforce against an aircraft its national laws relating to immigration, customs or air navigation."

It follows that a contracting state can impose a first lien on an aircraft for violation of its smuggling rules and its air traffic rules. The sacred lien for crews wages and the profane lien for taxes are not privileged (although Mexico has reserved on these items). Possessory repairers liens are subordinated – a major UK objection. All other rights permitted by the law of a contracting state are subordinated to the above privileged rights and to the recorded rights.

Judicial sale confers clear title

Article VIII provides: 19–30

> "Sale of an aircraft in execution in conformity with the provisions of Article VII shall effect the transfer of the property in such aircraft free from all rights which are not assumed by the purchaser."

It follows that in the event of a public sale all liens and mortgages are scraped off and instead attach to the proceeds of sale. The aircraft is purged. The purchaser of the aircraft on a forced sale can therefore be reasonably sure of getting a good title. This facilitates a sale and forms an incentive to judicial rather than private sale. The sale transfers only the aircraft and does not destroy any unsatisfied claim for the loan originally secured on the aircraft.

Transfer of aircraft subject to consent of recorded right-holders

Article IX of the Convention faces the difficulty sought to be dealt with by   19–31
the failed 1967 Brussels Convention on Ship Mortgages, i.e. that a ship could be transferred from one register to another without a mortgagee necessarily knowing. Article IX provides:

"Except in the case of a sale in execution in conformity with the provisions of Article VII, no transfer of an aircraft from the nationality register or the record of a Contracting State to that of another Contracting State shall be made, unless all holders of recorded rights have been satisfied or consent to the transfer."

This does not of itself prevent a transfer to the nationality register or record of a non-Contracting State, such as the United Kingdom or Japan, so that if a creditor executes his sale in a Contracting State privately or without complying with the minimum requirements of the Convention, the purchaser can register in a non-Contracting State if he is otherwise eligible for registration. However, the 1944 Chicago Convention, which most states have ratified, provides in Art 18 that an aircraft cannot be validly registered in more than one state so that the UK should not register an aircraft sold privately if the flag state – which is a Geneva Contracting State – declines to deregister.

CHAPTER 20

MARITIME AND AIRCRAFT LIENS

Generally

Until fairly recently maritime liens were perhaps more important than they   20–1
are now in practice – at least in the case of large ships – because the amounts
secured by maritime liens are often very much less than the huge sums
advanced to fund the construction or purchase of vessels and because some
of the more serious lien claims can be covered by insurance. However, the
exercise of maritime liens is a major irritant to an effective and speedy disposal of a vessel on a default since the lienors will, by seizing the ship,
prevent her from being employed or from sailing to a jurisdiction where a
sale may be facilitated. Tedious battles may then ensue before the vessel can
be sold or, if a sale is allowed, before the proceeds can be distributed.

The maritime lien was developed to enable an injured party to secure
himself on the vessel itself for his claim by seizing the vessel by an action in
rem. If no such right were available to secure claims for collision, loss of life
or necessaries supplied to the ship in foreign parts or for assistance given to
a vessel when encountering perils of the sea, then the person suffering the
damage or incurring the expense might be faced with insuperable problems
of recovery. The owner may be situate abroad and of uncertain financial
standing. The courts might not have jurisdiction or be particularly
approachable. In the meantime, the vessel, often the only asset of any worth
available to satisfy the claim, might have slipped out of the jurisdiction.

However maritime liens are strictly security devices of the past to meet
short-term credit needs: they have now come into sharp conflict with the
interests of the providers of long-term credit on vessels such as bank mortgagees and lessors. Jurisdictions can be classed into those which favour the
capital-provider and those which favour the short-term creditor, with many
degrees in between.

Characteristics of maritime liens

Maritime liens are extraordinary legal creatures. Some of the differences   20–2
when compared with ordinary security rights may be mentioned.

Secrecy Maritime liens are secret: they do not usually have to be registered
and their existence does not usually depend upon possession.

20–3   **Priorities** Contrary to normal principles of priorities amongst secured creditors, the liens sometimes rank in the inverse order of their creation (subject
to numerous exceptions). The theory is that the later lienor, such as a salvor
or crews' wages, is preserving the value of the vessel for all earlier liens and
so should have first bite. This has sometimes been called the "beneficial service theory". Another, "the proprietary interest theory", holds that a prior
lienor who does not immediately arrest the vessel has become fictionally a
part-owner and impliedly consents to the creation of subsequent liens. This
theory is more appropriate to tort liens.

20–4   **Indelibility** They are indelible: they cling on to the ship, even if the ship is
bought by a purchaser who has no notice of the lienor and would not have
had notice even if he had made enquiries (the French *droit de suite*). Unless
previously paid, they can only be scraped off the ship by an in rem action
against the ship by an admiralty court and until then are good against the
world. However, the indelibility of the lien may be restricted by the common law doctrine of laches whereby a lienholder loses his lien if he
unreasonably delays to the prejudice of others. In civil code countries the
lien is particularly evanescent: unless enforced by legal process within a
limited time, such as one year or before the commencement of the next
voyage, it never comes to life. Under the British Maritime Conventions Act
1911 s 8, there is a two-year limitation period on salvage and collision
claims. Hence liens can pollute clean title on transfers and threaten the
safety of sales.

Inchoate Maritime liens are said to be "inchoate". They are devoid of any
legal consequences until they are enforced by a proceeding *in rem*.

Classes of lien

20–5   Not all the claims which have a right against a ship are strictly maritime
liens, namely, those which arise out of maritime transactions. Some are
rights created by statute while others are liens available at general law in
respect of ships and other chattels alike. From the mortgagee's or lessor's
point of view, the result is the same: somebody has a claim against the ship
which might rank prior to the mortgage. Although the list set out below is
not exhaustive and is certainly not generally applicable in all states, the
main classes of claims against a ship (some of which are not strictly
maritime liens) might include the following:

– **Court costs** These are costs which arise from the care and operation of
the vessel while she is in the custody of the court. The costs of arrest and

enforcement will usually be included. Inevitably protective costs to produce proceeds in the general interests of creditors must come first.

– **Seaman's wages** The seaman's claims for his wages have been described romantically as "sacred liens, and so long as a plank of the ship remains, the sailor is entitled, against all other persons, to the proceeds as security for his wages": *The John E Stevens*, 170 US 113, 118, 18 S Ct 544 (1898), per Justice Gray. The lien may also cover social insurance contributions and injury and repatriation expenses. Seamen enjoy universal affection. They are paid in arrears and an unpaid seaman might disembark.

– **Salvage** This is the compensation which is owed to the persons who voluntarily assist in saving a ship or her cargo from peril. Life salvage is compensation for saving a life from a vessel. The lien is an incentive. Salvage remuneration is usually covered by the hull insurance policy. Liens for wreck removal are in a similar category.

– **General average** General average is the ancient principle of shipping law 20–6 (certainly known to the Greeks and probably also to the Phoenicians) whereby a loss or expenditure incurred for the benefit of the venture as a whole must be spread rateably amongst the parties who participate in the venture. Thus if the vessel is in difficulties in a storm and the master jettisons some of the cargo in order to save the vessel, then it is fair that each other cargo-owner and the shipowner himself should contribute to the cost of the jettisoned goods: all benefited from the sacrifice of one of the co-ventureres. The principles of general average are embodied in the York-Antwerp Rules. Since insurance is available, the lien seems less justifiable.

– **Tort claims** These are claims arising from a defect of the vessel or the negligence of those employed on board the vessel, e.g. collision damage, personal injury and pollution. The lien is to protect involuntary victims. The liability is usually insurable.

In *The Bold Buccleugh* (1851) 7 Moo PC 267, the Bold Buccleugh ran down the plaintiff's vessel. Before proceedings in the Admiralty court were taken, the ship was sold to a purchaser without notice of the incident. *Held*: the lien operated against a bona fide purchaser for value. It related back to the time when it attached. The lien was lost only by negligence or delay, neither of which was proved in this case.

– **Necessaries and other contracts** These are claims for fuel, necessaries, supplies, wharfage, stevedoring and the use of a dry dock. This lien covers claims for breach by the owner of a charterparty, and claims for damage to cargo. The charterer's lien appears to exist only in the US.

20–7　　– **Bottomry and respondentia** These security devices are now obsolete: para 14–1.

　　　　– **Repairer's lien** This is the lien which a repairer has over the ship so long as the repair bill is not paid. The lien reflects the improvement of the asset and enhances safety. In many countries (but not the United States) the lien is lost as soon as the repairer gives up possession. In some states (e.g. England) the lien does not confer a right of sale.

　　　　– **Vendor's lien** This is the lien which a vendor has for the unpaid purchase price of goods sold and may therefore be available both to ship-builders and sellers of second-hand vessels. Like the repairer's lien, it is usually a possessory right and is lost when possession is lost. The lien protects the vendor against the insolvency of the buyer. In England, the lienor has a statutory right of sale under the Sale of Goods Act 1979: see, e.g. *The Bineta* [1966] 2 Lloyd's Rep 419. A similar rule may apply in relation to aircraft.

　　　　　　In the Swedish case of *Beech Acceptance Corpn v Travelair*, Norrkoping 1974, Travelair was the registered owner of an aircraft. Beech had retained title as seller. Travelair became bankrupt. *Held*: Beech could recover the aircraft even though Travelair was the registered owner.

　　　　– **Port dues** Port authorities may have statutory liens on a vessel for unpaid port dues, removal of wrecks and the like. Pilotage dues are in the same category. These liens reflect views about the public interest.

Priorities between liens and mortgages generally

20–8　There is great diversity amongst seafaring nations as to which of these liens should take precedence over the rights of the mortgagee. Although practically everybody with a view on the matter seems to agree that court costs, master's and seaman's wages, salvage, general average contributions and collision liability must come before the mortgagee, there is no such agreement on liens for necessaries or for supplies (such as fuel), liens for breach of contract (such as breach of charterparty) and possessory liens, notably those in favour of repairers. Often the difference is attributable to the general orientation of the jurisdiction – whether pro-creditor or pro-debtor. Some of the reasons for the differences are economic and political. A country with a strong and vocal shipbuilding and ship repairing industry may succeed in persuading the legislator that the public interest is best served by protecting their rights ahead of the claims of those who finance ships. Countries with powerful maritime suppliers groups may also be successful in urging the superiority of their claims.

In practice the mortgagee will everywhere be subject to some prior liens, notably wages and tort claims, e.g. for collision. The main issue then is whether the mortgage is primed by the dangerous liens (such as the cost of repairs or fuel or damages for breach of charterparty) or for uninsurable liens (such as massive liabilities for oil pollution). One may broadly group jurisdictions as follows:

1.   Pro-creditor, e.g. England, Germany, Scandinavia, the Netherlands, Panama (C Com Art 1507)

2.   Pro-debtor, e.g. France, Greece and indeed all the countries either expressly adopting the 1926 Brussels Convention on Maritime Liens and Mortgages, or, if not, adopting the principles. But in Greece Ministerial Decisions approving a preferred mortgage can limit the prior liens to those recognised by Greek law, thereby excluding the priorities in Art 2(5) of the 1926 Convention (necessaries) and cargo or baggage damages in Art 2(4). The United States is in this group.

The two Brussels Conventions are summarised at paras 20–11 and 20–14 and the position with regard to the governing law of liens at para 20–28 *et seq.*

Subrogation to lienholder

If a person pays off a lienholder, he may be subrogated to the lien. Or he   **20–9** may take an assignment of the lien. The comparative law detail of the liens eligible for subrogation or assignment is too complex for summary: see Tetley, *Maritime Liens & Claims* (1985) chapter 27. In England, a lender can be subrogated to the lien for crews wages if he pays them pursuant to court order: *The Vasilia* [1972] 1 Lloyds Rep 51. French and US law appears to be liberal on subrogation to maritime liens.

England

In England, usually in domestic cases without a foreign element, claims   **20–10** ranking prior to a mortgage would include:

—   Court and enforcement expenses

—   Master's and crew's wages (*The Feronia* (1868) LR 2 A&E 65); master's disbursements (namely, those incurred by the master by virtue of his general authority and in the ordinary course of his employment for which he can pledge the owner's credit), but not other necessaries: *The Mary Ann* (1865) LR 1 A&E 8. The lien for master's disbursements is virtually obsolete and is not as wide as the US or French lien for necessaries.

— Salvage: *The Veritas* [1901] P 304

— Collision damage: *The Aline* (1839) 1 Wm Rot 111. The tort victim is an involuntary creditor.

— Possessory liens (such as the repairer's lien). These are not strictly maritime liens, do not confer a right of sale and, unlike under American law, are lost if possession is lost. There is much English case law.

1967 Brussels Convention countries

20–11   The 1967 Brussels Convention sank before launch and never came into effect but is of interest because (it is believed) the principles were absorbed into the law of a number of important maritime states, notably Denmark, Finland, Germany (HGB s 574), Norway and Sweden (although this should be checked). The main changes effected to the 1926 Brussels Convention sprang from a wish to reflect the increasing importance of long term credit and its claim to priority in the pecking-order, and the decreasing role to be played by credit which could find support only in the ship itself. Nowadays a master can get instructions from home and the owner can arrange for money to be advanced through his bank. Comprehensive agency networks can cope with local credit demands. Suppliers can more easily rely on the credit of the owner instead of the ship. The ship is therefore not required as security. Hence the Convention suppressed the claims of the suppliers of necessaries and demoted them below the mortgagee. The master's contracts were no longer sacrosanct.

20–12   Article 5 of the Convention provided that the maritime liens set out in Art 4 were to take priority over registered mortgages and "hypotheques". Article 4 provided:

"The following claims shall be secured by maritime liens on the vessel:
(i) Wages and other sums due to the master, officers and other members of the vessel's complement in respect of their employment on the vessel;
(ii) Port, canal and other waterways dues and pilotage dues;
(iii) Claims against the owner in respect of loss of life or personal injury occurring, whether on land or on water, in direct connection with the operation of the vessel;
(iv) Claims against the owner, based on tort and not capable of being based on contract, in respect of loss of or damage to property occurring,

whether on land or on water, in direct connection with the operation of the vessel;

(v) Claims for salvage, wreck removal and contribution in general average.

The word 'owner' mentioned in this paragraph shall be deemed to include the demise or other charterer, manager or operator of the vessel."

Although at first sight the prior tort claims could be dangerous for a mortgagee, many will usually be covered by insurance.

Article 5 then went on to state that no other claim is to take priority over these maritime liens or over mortgages and "hypotheques" which were effected and registered in a public registry in accordance with local law and which satisfied certain documentary requirements except that, pursuant to a somewhat controversial Art 6(2):

"In the event that a lien or right of retention is granted in respect of a vessel in possession of:
(a) a shipbuilder, to secure claims for the building of the vessel, or
(b) a ship repairer, to secure claims for repair of the vessel effected during such possession,
such lien or right of retention shall be postponed to all maritime liens set out in Article 4, but may be preferred to registered mortgages or 'hypotheques'. Such lien or right of retention may be exercisable against the vessel notwithstanding any registered mortgage or 'hypotheque' on the vessel, but shall be extinguished when the vessel ceases to be in the possession of the shipbuilder or ship repairer, as the case may be."

In implementing the Convention, Norway ranked the possessory liens of a shipbuilder or ship repairer ahead of mortgages: Norwegian Maritime Code s 247.

United States

In the United States the list of liens is longer than that in England. In purely **20–13** domestic cases, generally speaking, all maritime liens, including service liens and liens for breach of contract of carriage created prior to the filing of the preferred mortgage rank ahead. Subsequent court costs, seaman's wages, salvage, maritime tort claims, general average and wages of certain stevedores rank ahead. Subsequent contract claims generally rank after the mortgage. Preferred maritime liens are defined in the Ship Mortgage Act, 46 USC s 31301(5) and the maritime lien law is codified in ss 31341 and 31342.

As to the priorities of US liens on foreign ships, a protectionist rule, initially enacted in 1954 and revised in 1989, provides that a mortgage on a foreign vessel is to be subordinate to maritime liens for repairs, supplies, towage and the use of dry dock or marine railway provided in the United

States: 46 USC Chapter 313. The 1954 version of this rule to similar effect was transported to the Philippines: Presidential Decree 1521 s 15.

1926 Brussels Convention countries

20–14   The attitude of pro-debtor countries, which favour current creditors over the capital-provider, is exemplified by the 1926 Brussels Convention on Maritime Liens and Mortgages.

Article 3 of the Convention provides that the mortgages, hypothecations, and other charges on vessels referred to in Art 1 (that is mortgages and hypotheques which are effected and registered in a public register in accordance with the law of the Contracting State) rank immediately after the secured claims specified in Art 2. Article 2 provides as follows:

> "The following give rise to maritime liens on a vessel, on the freight for the voyage during which the claim giving rise to the lien arises, and on the accessories of the vessel and freight accrued since the commencement of the voyage:
>
> (1) Law costs due to the State, and expenses incurred in the common interest of the creditors in order to preserve the vessel or to procure its sale and the distribution of the proceeds of sale; tonnage dues, light or harbour dues, and other public taxes and charges of the same character; pilotage dues, the cost of watching and preservation from the time of the entry of the vessel into the last port;
>
> (2) Claims arising out of the contract of engagement of the master, crew, and other persons hired on board;
>
> (3) Remuneration for assistance and salvage, and the contribution of the vessel in general average;
>
> (4) Indemnities for collision or other accident of navigation, as also for damage caused to works forming part of harbours, docks and navigable ways; indemnities for personal injury to passengers or crew; indemnities for loss of or damage to cargo or baggage;
>
> (5) Claims resulting from contracts entered into or acts done by the master, acting within the scope of his authority, away from the vessel's home port, where such contracts or acts are necessary for the preservation of the vessel or the continuation of its voyage, whether the master is or is not at the same time owner of the vessel, and whether the claim is his own or that of ship-chandlers, repairers, lenders, or other contractual creditors."

The Convention reserves the right of Contracting States to confer certain other prior liens, principally, those in favour of authorities administering harbours, lighthouses and the like and those in favour of public insurance associations in respect of crew insurance claims.

The United Kingdom did not ratify this Convention because (amongst other things) it required contracting states to create and recognise maritime liens in favour of necessaries men.

Supplier's lien

This is the lien of supplier of necessaries to the vessel, of which fuel is usually the most costly. Countries which rank this lien ahead of the mortgage include many 1926 Brussels Convention countries, Japan, Malta, Spain and Turkey.   20–15

Often the lien is available only in respect of supplies for the last voyage, and may be limited to supplies authorised by the master as opposed to the owner, and hence may be rare.

Countries which rank this lien after the mortgage include Argentina, Greece, Israel and Panama.

Repairer's lien

This is the lien of a repairer of the vessel and is almost invariably a possessory lien—except in the United States. In other words, the lien is available if the ship is in yard or dock or otherwise in his possession. Once the repairer redelivers the vessel, he loses his lien.   20–16

This possessory lien is widespread and ranks ahead of the mortgage in the following countries by way of example:

Argentina
England and the many countries basing their maritime law on English law
Denmark
Finland
Israel (but a registered mortgage has priority)
Japan (possibly)
Portugal (CC Art 592)
Scotland
South Africa
Sweden
Thailand (but the lien must be registered)

The lien is not available in the following countries:

Germany
France
Greece

Italy
Philippines (unless acquired prior to recordation of the mortgage)

Charters and cargo-owners generally

20–17   On an owner's default, a mortgagee must usually deal with charterers of the vessel, as well as cargo-owners. The main protections available in one country or another to a charterer or cargo-owner are:

— a charterer's lien for breach of the charterparty by the owner (probably almost exclusively a US lien): para 20–18;

— inability of the mortgagee to arrest the ship if the ship is "ready to sail": para 18–17;

— right of the charterer to block a sale before the end of the current voyage (so that the cargo can be delivered);

— right of the charterer to prevent a sale which would involve a breach of the charterparty: para 20–19;

— bankruptcy freezes on the cancellation of contracts with a bankrupt owner: these are reviewed in another volume in this series of works;

— mortgagee liability in tort for interfering with the goods of the cargo-owner (he cannot simply throw them overboard).

In practice, it is usually necessary to complete the voyage to off-load the cargo and avoid cargo disputes. Consider the ability to off-load cargo at an intermediate port, and liability for discharge, warehousing and insurances.

Charterer's lien

20–18   American law confers an automatic lien over the vessel in favour of a charterer whose charter has been wrongfully terminated: *The Oceano*, 148 F 131 (SDNY 1906). But generally this contract claim ranks after preferred mortgages: see *Rainbow Line, Inc v M/V Tequila*, 341 F Supp 459 (SDNY 1972). This lien appears to be almost exclusively American.

In England no such lien arises automatically but many charters expressly create such a lien. The enforceability of that lien will depend upon normal principles of security law, e.g. whether the charge has been duly registered. The point was raised in *The Panglobal Friendship* [1978] 1 Lloyd's Rep. 368, CA in interlocutory proceedings, but the case was settled. However in

The Lancaster [1980] 2 Lloyds Rep 497, the court held that a lien clause of this type merely conferred on the time charterers a right to postpone delivery of the ship to the owners. But see *Re Welsh Irish Ferries Ltd* [1985] 3 WLR 61 where it was held that a corporate owner's lien on sub-freights was registrable at the Companies Registry as a charge and was void for non-registration. This case is scheduled to be overridden by the Companies Act 1989 (section not yet in force).

The safe course is for the mortgagee to check through any existing charterparty before he takes his mortgage and to obtain waivers from the charterer of his rights in the event of a default. Naturally many charterers are unwilling to do this.

Cancellation of charterparty

If current rates are low, the mortgagee may hope to sell the ship with the 20–19 charter, but the charterer may be looking for an opening to terminate. If on the other hand rates are high, the charterer may wish to preserve his charter notwithstanding the sale of the vessel. The presence of the low-rate charterparty will reduce the value of the vessel, especially if it is long-term. In both cases the question is whether the charter is an in rem right clinging to the ship or merely an in personam contract with the shipowner, not binding on the mortgagee.

The problem is complicated by the fact that courts and statute-makers have had an ambivalent approach to the ship as, on the one hand, being merely a chattel but, on the other hand, enjoying some of the legal characteristics of real estate. In chattel law, generally speaking, a contract of hire is with the owner. It does not attach to the chattel. If the owner repudiates the lease, the lessee is left with a mere right of damages against the owner. If the owner sells, the lessee may claim that the contract is personal and he cannot be obliged to deal with a new owner. On the other hand, in the case of land a mortgagee may be bound by leases entered into prior to the mortgage or entered into with his consent. The lessee cannot be dislodged on a sale. Nor can the lessee repudiate merely because the owner sells the freehold.

Where the mortgagee on a default wishes to sell the ship with the benefit 20–20 of a favourable charter, usually the charterer could terminate if the charter expressly or impliedly prohibits vicarious performance by the new owner. A method of preserving the charter where, as in Sweden and many other countries, a sale would usually allow the charterer to cancel, is for the lender to take a charge over the shares of the owning company (usually non-objectionable in the case of one-ship companies) thereby conferring power on the lender to sell the shares rather than the vessel on a default. In practice the difficulty arises with less frequency because the inadequacy of the charter-hire is often the cause of the default.

The converse position is where the charterer wishes to keep his charter alive as against the purchaser from the mortgagee.

The English law position is that where the charterparty was entered into before a mortgage was granted, then the charterer can obtain an injunction restraining the mortgagee from exercising his rights under the mortgage in such a way as to interfere with the performance of the charter. But the mortgagee must have actual knowledge of the charterparty at the time he took his mortgage: for this purpose constructive notice, i.e. knowledge which would have been obtained after reasonable enquiry, is not sufficient. However, if the shipowner is unable to perform the charterparty, e.g. because the shipowner is insolvent, then the mortgagee cannot be restrained by the charterer. This principle was first laid down in *De Mattos v Gibson* (1858) 4 De G & J 276, and was affirmed in *Swiss Bank Corporation v Lloyds Bank* [1979] 2 All ER 853 (subsequently reversed by the House of Lords on the facts).

20–21   Where the charterparty is entered into after the mortgage is granted, the mortgagee is not entitled by exercising his rights under the mortgage, whether by taking possession, or selling, or arresting the ship in a mortgagee action in rem, to interfere with the performance of the contract. Interference with the contract constitutes a tort against the charterer whose remedies against the mortgagee in respect of the tort are (a) an injunction restraining the mortgagee from interfering, (b) an order for the release of the ship from any arrest at the instance of the mortgagee; and (c) further or alternatively, damages. The reason that the mortgagee is thus subject to the charterparty is based on the proposition that an owner is entitled to deal with the ship, including employing her under a contract with a third party, in the same way as he would be entitled to do if the ship were not mortgaged. However, there are two important exceptions: (1) the owner is not entitled to deal with the ship in such a way as to impair the security of the mortgagee, e.g. by entering into an improvident or speculative charterparty, and (2) the charterer is without remedy against the mortgagee where the owner is unwilling or unable to perform the charterparty. These principles were established in *The Myrto* [1977] 2 Lloyds LR 243 where the supporting decisions are cited.

In practice the position from the point of view of a mortgagee is not as serious as it might at first seem. The reason is that the enforcement of the mortgage will usually have arisen from an insolvency or insolvency will result from an acceleration of the loan. The court may then be able to infer that the owner would be unable to perform the charterparty. The charterer is left with a claim against the vessel which, under English law, is primed by the mortgagee.

In many countries, e.g. Greece, the charterer can prevent a mortgage sale until the end of the current voyage.

Oil pollution

Oil pollution may achieve maritime lien status under the head of tort   20–22
damage caused by the vessel. The potential liabilities are vast and difficult to insure in full and so could, if ranked prior to a mortgage, completely devastate the security.

The following may be relevant:

1. **Liability for common law trespass or nuisance.** This is usually based on fault.

2. **International Convention on Civil Liability for Oil Pollution 1969 and 1984 Protocol.** This established strict liability of shipowners for oil discharge in coastal waters. There is a limit on liability (so that it is insurable). The Convention has been ratified by (inter alia) Denmark, France, Norway, Sweden, the United Kingdom, but not the United States or Saudi Arabia (where liability is strict without limitation). It applies only to persistent oil (not other chemical substances). Liability is fixed on owners (not demise charterers) but can include operators. Note the UK Oil Pollution (Compulsory Insurance) Regulations 1981.

3. **International Convention on the Establishment of an International Fund for Compensation 1971.** This establishes a compensation fund for excesses over 1969 Convention limits.

4. **Tovalop and Cristal.** Tovalop is the Tanker Owners Voluntary Agreement concerning Liability for Oil Pollution under which tanker owners agree to reimburse national governments for coastline spills and are insured with protection and indemnity clubs.

5. **International Convention for the Prevention of Pollution from Ships 1973 and 1978 Protocol** (MARPOL). This covers requirements for crude oil washing, segregated ballast tanks and clean ballast tanks. Governments are to supply adequate reception facilities. There are reporting and investigation duties.

6. **US statutes.** In the US, the principal statutes are the Oil Pollution Act of 1990, the Comprehensive Environmental Response, Compensation and Liability Act (CERCLA) which also applies to marine spills of hazardous substances other than oil, and numerous state statutes.

Aircraft liens generally

20–23 **Generally** The law on aircraft liens takes its inspiration from maritime liens, but these liens are in practice less important than maritime liens for two reasons. The first is that creditors of airlines tend to rely more on the credit of the airline company than such an inconvenient asset as an aircraft which is not an attractive asset to attach. Secondly, a large number of countries have ratified the 1948 Geneva Aircraft Convention which severely limits the liens which can rank ahead of a mortgage: para 19–29. These are broadly limited to enforcement costs, salvage and preservation expenses (which must be noted on the register in three months) and tort liability for injury or damage to persons or property on the surface caused by the aircraft. Contracting states may optionally provide that security holders over the aircraft (and other aircraft under a fleet mortgage) may not claim more than 80 per cent of the sale price of the aircraft sold so as to leave 20 per cent for these unsecured tort victims. This optional regime is a classic instance of a compromise between states which favour the secured creditor and those which seek to preserve the position of unsecured creditors – in this case, an involuntary unsecured creditor. But the teeth of these tort provisions are blunted since the privilege cannot apply if the aircraft is adequately insured.

One can expect that the types of lien which might be available include:

- judicial custodial and enforcement costs
- crews' wages
- preservation expenses
- suppliers
- repairers
- salvage
- charterers
- vendors
- airport dues
- aircraft taxes.

20–24 In England, there is no *in rem* right to proceed against aircraft in the same way as maritime liens, except for minor exceptions, e.g. the salvage of aircraft: see the Supreme Court Act 1981 s 20. But possessory liens of repairers and statutory rights of detention (e.g. for unpaid airport charges and navigation services) have priority over aircraft mortgages: Mortgaging of Aircraft Order 1972.

As to the possessory repairers' lien, the following countries rank this ahead of the mortgagee, unless the 1948 Geneva Convention applies:

England and many English-based countries (most of which have not ratified the 1948 Geneva Convention)

Denmark
Finland
Guatemala (CC Art 2026)
Iceland
S Korea
Turkey
United States (lien is non-possessory)

The following countries rank the possessory repairers' lien after the mortgage:

Germany (no possessory lien at all?)
Norway
Sweden

Aircraft tort liability

As to tort liability for damages or injury caused by the aircraft, **Colombia**   20–25
(which is not a 1948 Geneva country) is an example of a state which ranks
the lien ahead of the mortgagee if not covered by insurance. **Italy** gives
priority to liability for damage to third parties on the surface, for collision,
for death or personal injury to passengers and crew and for loss of or
damage to cargo – this is wider than the Geneva optional tort lien. The presence of this lien emphasises the importance of insurance from a mortgagee's
point of view.

General aircraft priority creditors

It needs to be recalled that some states place certain privileged claims ahead   20–26
of all mortgages, notably taxes and general employee claims and benefits.
This appears to be the case in **Brazil** (see BL Decree Law No 7,661 145 Art
124), **Mexico** and **Peru**. **Turkey** and **Venezuela** put general taxes ahead. In
France these claims rank after aircraft mortgages.

Aircraft charterers

As to the rights of charterers, the position is probably similar to that pertaining to ships: para 20–17 *et seq*. The 1948 Geneva Convention provides   20–27
for the honouring of recorded lease rights: para 19–16. Thus in **Denmark**
and **Germany**, lease rights can be recorded on the aircraft register and the
effect is that a prior recorded lease right must be respected by a later mort-

gagee. In Mexico a mortgagee cannot override leases and must respect his rights.

Governing law of maritime and aircraft liens generally

20–28　As to governing law of liens, there are two questions.

- What law governs whether the claim confers a lien at all?
- What law governs the priority of the lien, notably whether it ranks before or after a mortgage? (This is a more important question in practice than availability).

Law governing lien availability

20–29　As to the availability of liens, the main possible systems of law are the law of the flag, the lex fori where the proceedings to enforce the lien take place or the law with which the lien is most closely connected, except where a convention applies. The flag law is the most stable, permanent and easily ascertainable. The lex fori is the most unstable – a lien on Monday in harbour A but not on Tuesday in harbour B. The law of closest connection is unpredictable but may do the greatest justice because it will often result in the law of the place where the lien was incurred and therefore meet legitimate expectations. Further, the local suppliers will know their own law.

The summary below relates primarily to maritime liens, but aircraft liens may adopt similar rules. Note the priority rules in the Brussels 1926 Ship Convention (para 20–14) and the Geneva 1948 Aircraft Convention (para 19–29).

20–30　**Flag** In the following countries, maritime liens will be recognised only if recognised by flag law (subject to applicable convention):

- Finland – but the foreign lien cannot have a higher priority than the Finnish lien (broadly the 1967 Brussels Convention liens)
- Greece – Code of Maritime Law Art 9
- Italy
- Sweden – but Swedish liens (based on the 1967 Brussels Convention) rank ahead of foreign liens. In other words, priorities not known to Swedish law follow the flag but rank after the liens known to Swedish law.

20–31　**Lex fori** In the following countries, maritime liens will be recognised only if recognised by **law of the forum** (subject to applicable convention):

Bahamas

Belgium
England: *The Halcyon Isle* [1981] AC 221
Germany
France
Japan (probably)
Norway (possibly)
Singapore: *The Halcyon Isle* [1981] AC 221
South Africa: see *The Andrico Unity* (1987) 3 SALR 794; *The Kalantiao* (1987) 4 SALR 250
Turkey

Governing law In the following countries, the court applies the **law of   20-32 closest connection** to a maritime lien (subject to applicable convention):

Canada: *The Ioannis Daskelilis* [1974] SCR 128; *The Har Rai* [1984] AMC 1649, CA; [1987] 1 SCR 52
Denmark (possibly)
Malta (possibly)
The Netherlands
United States: *The Leah* (1984) AMC 2089 (4th Cir CA); *The Seisho Maru*, 744 F 2d 461 (5th Cir CA) but subject to a lien for US-supplied necessaries

In **Thailand**, foreign liens are not recognised at all.

Law governing priority of liens

As to the priority of the liens between themselves and as against a registered   20-33 mortgage, the choice lies between the law of the flag, the lex fori, the lex situs, or the governing law (closest connection), except where a convention applies. The flag is the most stable, but many states adopt the lexi fori, presumably to stop foreign claimants from getting priority over the mortgage if they would not have had it locally.

The following countries apply the **flag** priorities to maritime liens: 20-34

Greece
Japan (possibly)
Italy
Taiwan: Conflict of Laws Act Art 10(4)

The following countries apply the **lex fori** priorities (subject to applicable convention):

Bahamas

Belgium
Canada: *The Ioannis Daskelilis* [1974] SCR 128
Denmark
England: *The Halcyon Isle* [1981] AC 221
Germany
Finland
France
Malta
The Netherlands
Norway
Panama
Turkey

20–35   In **Denmark,** the law of the flag decides whether a maritime lien ranks before or after the mortgage, otherwise the lex fori governs priority.

In **South Africa,** it seems that foreign maritime liens rank after South African registered ship mortgages on liquidation, but not if enforced prior to liquidation.

In **Venezuela** foreign vessels are not subject to attachment except for debts contracted in Venezuela for the benefit of those vessels: CC Art 621. This also applies to foreign mortgages.

Priorities of foreign liens in English-based countries As to the priorities of foreign liens, the English courts have applied the law of the forum: see *The Colorado* [1923] P 102. English-based countries are in conflict on the recognition and priority of maritime liens.

> In *The Ioannis Daskalelis* [1974] SCR 128, decided by the Supreme Court of Canada, a Panamanian company had in 1961 granted a Greek mortgage over a Greek flag vessel to a Panamanian mortgagee. In 1963 a shipyard in the United States carried out repairs. In 1964 the vessel was sold by court order in Vancouver. An unpaid repairer does not have a maritime lien under Canadian law (the repairer having given up possession) but he does under American law. *Held:* the court applied American law as the proper law of the repair contract to decide whether or not there was a maritime lien. Having found that American law granted a lien, Canadian law, as the lex fori, was applied to determine whether a right of that nature has priority over a mortgage. Since Canadian law grants priority to maritime liens, it was held that the repairers had priority over the mortgage.

> In *The Halcyon Isle* [1981] AC 221, PC, on appeal from Singapore, the Privy Council refused to follow the Canadian approach. New York repairers executed repairs on the vessel in March 1974. In May 1974 a British mortgage over the vessel was registered in favour of an English bank. The vessel was

arrested by the mortgagees in September 1974 in Singapore. Under American law, the repairer had a maritime lien, but under Singapore law (which is virtually identical to English law in this matter), the repairer had no lien. *Held* by a majority: "the question as to the right to proceed *in rem* against a ship as well as priorities in the distribution between competing claimants of the proceeds of its sale in an action *in rem* in the High Court of Singapore falls to be determined by the lex fori, as if the events that gave rise to the claim had occurred in Singapore." The mortgagee therefore had priority. The basis of the decision was that a maritime lien is a procedural, not a substantive, right.

Priorities of foreign liens in the United States As to the priority of the American necessaries liens on foreign vessels, see para 20–13. **20–36**

Apart from this, the American courts have followed *The Colorado* (1923) P 102 and determined priorities according to the law of the forum. However a more flexible approach was signalled in *Rainbow Line Inc v M/V Tequila*, 480 F 2d 1024, 1973 AMC 1431 (2d Cir 1973):

> While the ship was registered as a British ship, the English owners wrongfully withdrew her from service under the charterparty. Such a breach gave rise to a lien under American maritime law but not under English law. The ship was then transferred to Liberian registry and a mortgage created in favour of an American mortgagee. After the transfer an American salvor acquired a claim for salvage and there were claims for unpaid wages of the crew. *Held* that the maritime law of the United States applied to determine the existence of the liens and their priority. However Judge Anderson concluded that the choice of law question in cases involving foreign ship mortgages should be decided in the light of the governmental interest guidelines laid down by the Supreme Court in *Lauritzen v Larsen*, 345 US 571, 73 S Ct 921, 1953 AMC 1210 (1953). Conceivably the adoption of a more flexible approach might result in the determination of lien priorities according to the law of some foreign country in a case not involving any American contacts or claims.

See also *The Leah* (1984) AMC 2089 (4th Cir CA); *The Seisho Maru*, 744 F 2d 461 (5th Cir CA).

CHAPTER 21

SECURITY OVER SHIP AND AIRCRAFT EARNINGS AND CHARTERS

Generally

21–1   It is the invariable practice for lenders taking security over a ship also to take an assignment of earnings – at least outside the liner trade. The object is to safeguard priorities on the earnings, both on insolvency and as against competing assignees and attaching creditors.

Much of what is said as to ships here also applies to aircraft.

Practice differs as to whether the assignment of the earnings is contained in the mortgage or in a separate document. Among the reasons for the occasional preference for separate documents one might include, first, a ship or aircraft mortgage is generally subject to the law of the flag whereas the lender may prefer that the assignments be subject to a different system of law, such as the law of his own jurisdiction. Secondly, in order to perfect assignments of claims, many jurisdictions require that notice of the assignment be given to the debtor – this may be facilitated if the assignment is in a separate document. Thirdly, it may not be necessary to translate the assignment for registration purposes.

The earnings of the mortgaged vessel generally form the main or only source of cash flow for debt service. However a time charterparty is not to be treated as an unimpeachable source of cash flow. It often happens that in a falling market, a shipowner who is financially embarrassed will suffer difficulties in servicing a charterparty and thereby give the charterer a right to repudiate the charterparty for a breach by the owner. Hence the lender would lose the benefit of the security and of the cash flow at the time he needs it most. Further off-hire risks and escalating operating costs increase the vulnerability of the security. The same applies to aircraft charters. Security assignments of contractual claims were discussed generally in chapter 4.

Types of contracts of affreightment

21–2   There are basically two forms of maritime contract of affreightment, the charterparty and the bill of lading. A bill of lading is used in relation to a smaller parcel of goods and functions as evidence of the contract of affreightment, as a receipt and as evidence that the holder owns the goods. Bills of lading do not cover the whole vessel and need concern us no further. A charterparty, on the other hand, is a contract between the shipowner and the charterer by which the charterer hires the use of the whole ship from the shipowner either for a fixed period, such as 12 months (a time charter), or for a voyage or series of voyages (a voyage or consecutive voyage charterparty).

The charter may take the form of ordinary hire or it may be a lease of the vessel or aircraft. The latter is a charter by demise or a bareboat charter. The principal difference is that under an ordinary charter the master and crew are appointed by the shipowner or aircraft owner while under a demise charter they are the employees of the demise charterer and not of the owner. One might broadly describe the difference as that between taking a hotel room and leasing an unfurnished apartment, or between hiring a cab and leasing a self-drive car.

Validity of assignments of earnings on bankruptcy

Usually there is a general non-notified assignment of present and future   21–3
earnings to the mortgagee on the basis that until a default occurs the earnings are to be paid direct to the owner of the ship or aircraft.

Possessory pledge required In some jurisdictions, notably in the Franco-Latin group, an assignment of earnings by way of security is not effective against the creditors of the owner in bankruptcy in the following cases:

– The assignment is of future claims: para 4–13.

– The assignment does not identify the claims precisely (because of the doctrine of specificity): para 1–6.

– The assignment is not a possessory pledge of the earnings which in practice means that the assignee must have a full legal transfer of the earnings and must retain full dominion over the earnings (see para 4–5). Thus, (1) the assignment must be notified to the debtors for validity against the owner's creditors (as opposed to notification to preserve priorities against competing assignees and to tell the debtor who to pay), (2) the assignee must take possession of all documents evidencing the claim assigned, e.g. charterparties, and (3) the assignee must not allow the earnings to be paid to the owner (but the owner needs to use the earnings to operate the ship or aircraft). In England the loss of control over the earnings may simply convert the assignment into a floating charge, but not in the case of the assignment of a specific charterparty.

 – The assignment is not registered in a public registry.

All of these rules are primarily designed to avoid the somewhat obsolete objection to "false wealth", i.e. the debtor has many possessions but few assets and thereby falsely includes creditors into giving the debtor credit: para 19–8. According to this doctrine, there is no false wealth if the assignee effectively has a full possessory pledge of the earnings – the possession has to be artificial since one cannot take possession of an intangible in the same way as goods.

21–4   **Public registration** Public notice can sometimes be achieved by registration at a public office: see chapter 9. In England, registration of an assignment of earnings will be required at the Companies Registry in the case of English companies and foreign companies having an established place of business in England if, in the latter case, the earnings are "property in England": see para 9–34 *et seq.*

In the United States a general assignment may require registration pursuant to the provisions of Art 9 of the Uniform Commercial Code in order to be perfected, but there is a foreign exception: para 9–24. As to aircraft, in the US if there is an assignment of a lease, (1) file at the central Oklahoma City FAA Registry because it may be a "conveyance" of an interest in an aircraft perfectible only by filing at the FAA Registry, and (2) file at the UCC location if applicable. The mortgagee should take possession of the original counterparty lease as chattel paper since if the lease is chattel paper within the UCC, then perfection is by possession. A financial lessor should file under the UCC against the lessee naming the aircraft as collateral in case the lease is construed as a security interest. This is a precautionary filing.

21–5   **Earnings as an accessory to the ship** Alternatively, the earnings may be treated as accessory to the ship or aircraft and follow the mortgage of the ship or aircraft without further formality. Countries arrive at different solutions as to whether freight earned by a ship is deemed part of the mortgaged vessel or whether it must be separately assigned to the mortgagee and the publicity formalities observed. The following paragraphs apply only to ships, but the principles might apply to aircraft as well.

In **England**, freight in the course of being earned belongs to the mortgagee as from the time he enforces his mortgage by taking possession: *Keith v Burrows* (1877) 2 App Cas 636. It does not need to be separately assigned, although it commonly is. A corporate charge over "book debts" requires public registration, as does a floating charge: para 9–34 *et seq.*

In **Turkey** freight belongs to the mortgagee as from the date of filing of a forced sale demand.

In **Belgium** freight is treated as an accessory to the mortgage and in **Spain** the freight of the last voyage is an accessory.

But in **Greece** and **Italy** freight is not an accessory and must be separately   21-6
assigned and the appropriate assignment formalities observed.

The position in **France** is strict. Bareboats and time charterparties of ships must be registered if they are to be valid against third parties (including the insolvency administrator): Law of January 3, 1967 on the status of ships, Decree October 3, 1967. Assignments of freight for more than one year must also be registered to be valid against third parties. Assignments of charterhire must be notified in the prescribed manner to the charterer if the assignment is to be effective on the insolvency of the shipowner-assignor. Registration of charters is permissive in **Denmark**, but excluded in **Norway**: s 20 of the Maritime Code.

Forms of assignment

The earnings which are assigned may be defined as follows: 21-7

" 'Earnings' means all present and future moneys and claims which are earned by or become payable to or for the account of the owner in connection with the ownership or operation of the vessel and includes (i) freights, hires and passage moneys, (ii) remuneration for salvage and towage services, (iii) demurrage and detention moneys, (iv) all present and future moneys and claims payable to the owner in respect of any breach of a charterparty or contract of affreightment in respect of the vessel, (v) all moneys and claims in respect of the actual, constructive, agreed, compromised or arranged total loss of the vessel or the requisition of title to or use or compulsory acquisition of the vessel."

Where a specific charterparty is assigned, it will often be provided as follows:

"1. The owner will:
   (a) perform the charterparty;
   (b) not amend or terminate the charterparty;
   (c) not make or agree any claim that the charterparty is frustrated;
   (d) not waive or release any of the charterer's obligations.
2. The mortgagee:
   (a) is excused from liability in respect of obligations under the charterparty;
   (b) need not return any moneys if the charterparty is frustrated or hire must be refunded [see *The Trident Beauty* [1994] 1 All ER 470, HL (assignee lender not liable to charterers to return advance hire paid to lenders even though charterer entitled to reduction because of non-repair of vessel)];
   (c) is not obliged to enforce any of the terms of the charterparty or to enquire into the sufficiency of any payment;
   (d) has power to demand and give receipts for the earnings and to institute collection proceedings."

21–8   Generally, all assigned earnings must be paid into a retention account maintained by the mortgagee bank on terms that a certain amount is retained each month to meet the next principal and interest repayment. Security over this account may be by way of set-off or charge-back (if available): chapter 5.

There should be warranties from the owners as to the charter, e.g. full copy supplied, validity, no set-offs, etc.

Often the assignment is of proceeds, not of the contracts themselves. In the case of demise charters, the mortgagee should also take an assignment from the demise charterer of sub-charters and earnings: para 17–5.

Terms of charterparty

21–9   Where a specific charterparty is assigned, the mortgagee should in particular check:

 — whether there is a restriction on assignments without consent;

 — whether there is a provision which allows the owner to substitute another ship (the new owner may have a lien on sub-freights ranking ahead of the assignment);

 — whether there are provisions for the refund of charterhire retroactively according to performance criteria;

 — whether the charterer has a contractual lien on ship for breach of the charterparty;

 — the charterer's termination rights;

 — the stringency of performance tests;

 — any right of the charterer to withhold disputed hire;

 — and rate step-downs (standby rates, force majeure rates, off-hire rates and deductions).

Much of the above also applies to aircraft charters.

The lender may be prejudiced if a full copy of the charter is not supplied, but not always.

> In *The Oldenfeld* [1978] 2 Lloyds Rep 357, the owner mortgaged the vessel and assigned a charter to the financier. The charter had been amended by a side-letter reducing the hire. *Held*: the financier was entitled to the full hire from the charterer and could ignore the side-letter. The charterer knew that the charterparty was to be used to raise the loan, but took no steps to inform the financier of the side-letter.

Charterer's undertakings

Mortgagees sometimes request specific undertakings from charterers **21–10** designed to ensure payment of the full face amount of the charter-hire. However in the case of ordinary operating charterparties (as compared with demise charterparties), charterers are not usually willing to waive set-offs and counterclaims that they may acquire as against the owner (e.g. because the vessel does not perform as warranted or because of non-compliance by the shipowner), nor will they generally agree that they will not terminate the charter if the mortgagee agrees to perform, e.g. by taking possession of the vessel in those countries where possessory management is allowed.

The owner should be required to direct the charterer's agent to pay bills of lading freights to the mortgagee. The owner is usually entitled to the freights in the first instance (because the owner's employee, the master, signs the bill of lading), subject to a duty to account to the charterer. But in practice the charterer's agent usually collects and keeps the balance after payment of hire.

Priority of assignment of earnings

The main priority contests in relation to assignments of earnings and char- **21–11** terparties relate to:

– priority of general preferred creditors on insolvency: para 12–5

– super-priority insolvency loans to the insolvency administrator to finance the rescue proceedings: chapter 11

– prior and subsequent sales or mortgages of the earnings: para 12–19

– prior and subsequent liens on the freight by maritime lienholders. Thus in Panama, prior liens on the freight include court costs, salvage, crews wages, general average, insurance premiums, charterers and shippers: ComC Art 1510.

– prior contractual restrictions, e.g. a negative pledge

– the priority of future advances made by the first mortgagee over a subsequently created second mortgage: para 12–21.

In **England**, if the mortgagee does not take a security assignment there are special rules where a mortgagee takes possession. A mortgagee who takes possession of the vessel on a default or where the security is impaired has a right to take over the earnings: *Keith v Burrows* (1877) 2 App Cas 636. However, where there has been a legal assignment of the freight prior to the mortgage, or the mortgagee had notice of an equitable assignment, the mortgagee's rights will be defeated: *Wilson v Wilson* (1872) LR 14 Eq 32.

Airline clearing systems

21–12 The International Air Transport Association is a private organisation of airlines which provides a clearing-house in London for the periodic settlement of debts between its members for carrier and other services. The Airline Clearing House Inc provides a clearing system for US airlines similar to that provided globally by IATA.

  An assignment of the general earnings of an aircraft (apart from specific charters) is usually of limited value since the clearing may take priority so that an airline's claims are netted. On default an airline will often be a net debtor.

CHAPTER 22

SECURITY OVER SHIP AND AIRCRAFT INSURANCES

Generally

The normal forms of maritime insurance policy are extraordinary docu- 22–1
ments. This may be attributable to the fact that the Lloyds standard policy
form which was originated in the seventeenth century was itself based upon
a form of policy imported from Italy some 200 years earlier. Buller J said
that "a policy of assurance has at all times been considered in courts of law
as an absurd and incoherent instrument but it is founded on usage": *Brough
v Whitmore* (1791) 4 TR 206, 210.

This section deals primarily with marine insurance, but the principles
governing aircraft insurance are similar.

Categories of marine insurance

It may be useful to summarise the main classes of marine insurance with 22–2
which a lender is likely to be concerned. The classes are:

– **Hull and machinery cover**

– **Protection and indemnity insurance and war risk insurance.** These insurances are provided by associations of ship-owners formed for the
   purpose of mutual insurance to enable owners entered in the association
   or club to insure against risks which Lloyds either do not insure at all or
   only on very unfavourable terms. Examples of such risks are: liability to
   officers and crew, especially in respect of loss of life and personal injury;
   one-quarter of collision liability; damage from war risks; and loss
   through strikes of dock workers. Members of clubs enter their ships for
   a certain amount for an advance premium and agree to pay supplemen-
   tary calls if there is a deficit.

– **Loss of hire.** Such insurance, covering off-hire risks, is generally expensive and is often not required by lenders.

– **Mortgagee's interest protection insurance.** This is not insurance against
   the loss of interest payable to the mortgagee. The insurance is designed

---

to protect the mortgagee against the avoidance of the policy by reason of some act or default of the shipowner who originally takes out the policy. Thus a policy may be avoided for misrepresentation or non-disclosure of a material fact by the shipowner, by breach of warranty or by intentional loss such as scuttling. Mortgagee interest protection policies will not necessarily provide protection against all these risks. Some Norwegian and German policies in any event contain a clause protecting the mortgagee in certain events.

Assignments of insurances

22–3 The common practice is to include an express assignment of insurances so as to take the insurances out of the hands of the unsecured creditors of the owner. Insurance assignments may cover the following ground (in outline only):

"1. 'Insurances' means the policies and contracts of insurance and all entries in a protection and indemnity or war risk association which are now or may hereafter be taken out or effected in respect of the vessel, her freights, disbursements, profits or otherwise howsoever and all benefits thereof including all claims and returns of premiums.

2. The owner will:
   (a) Effect and maintain the prescribed insurances with insurers, through brokers, in the names, under policies, in the currency and in amounts approved by the mortgagee and will enter the vessel in such war risk and protection and indemnity associations as may be approved by the mortgagee in respect of risks approved by the mortgagee.
   (b) Pay the premiums, calls and contributions and will ensure that nothing is done or omitted whereby the insurances may become void or voidable and will not alter any of the insurances.
   (c) Not operate the vessel outside the cover provided by the insurances or in conflict with any of the terms of the insurances or engage in any voyage or trade not permitted by the insurances.
   (d) Provide details of the insurances and up-to-date reports including an independent broker's estimation of the adequacy of the insurances.
   (e) Ensure that prescribed notices of assignment, loss payable clauses and cancellation clauses are endorsed on the policies.
   (f) Not settle, compromise or abandon any claims in respect of the insurances.
   (g) Ensure that the insurers, managers of war risk or protection and indemnity associations or brokers issue to the mortgagee an undertaking to hold the insurance documents to the order of the mortgagee and to advise the mortgagee of cancellations or

variations of the insurances, default in payment of premiums or other sums payable in respect of the insurances or in the provision of guarantees, failures to renew and events known to them which may render void or voidable any of the insurances. See para 22–7.

3. If the owner does not comply with the above undertakings the mortgagee may itself take out the insurances and add the cost of doing so to the amount secured."

It was held in *The Basildon* (1867) 1 LR 19 that a ship mortgagee not in possession may add the cost of premiums paid by him to the mortgage debt only if an express clause in the mortgage entitles him to do so.

"4. Insurance proceeds will be applied as follows:
    (a) After a default, all insurance proceeds are payable to the mortgagee for application against the mortgage debt.
    (b) Before a default, insurance proceeds are to be applied as follows:
        (i) In the case of an actual, constructive, agreed, compromised or arranged total loss, all insurance proceeds are to be applied against the mortgage debt.
        (ii) In the case of a major casualty (namely, one in excess of a certain figure), all proceeds are to be payable to the mortgagee who may retain them by way of security until the damage has been repaired or liability paid.
        (iii) In the case of a minor loss (namely, a loss below the threshold figure), all proceeds may be payable to the owner who is obliged to apply them in the repair of the damage concerned.
        (iv) Third party liability insurance proceeds are to be paid direct to the third party."

Validity of assignment on owner's bankruptcy

Similar rules outlined in para 21–3 *et seq* in relation to assignments of earnings may apply to assignments of insurances, except that a registration requirement is infrequent.   22–4

The rigour of these rules may be mitigated by the fact that in many countries (not England) asset insurance follows the asset without a specific assignment.

In the case of ships and aircraft or both, the following are examples of states which treat the insurance of the asset as being an accessory which is automatically mortgaged along with the asset without a separate assignment (thereby obviating "notice to the debtor" rules):

Argentina (including indemnities for third parties injured by the aircraft)

Bolivia
Denmark
Finland (at least for aircraft, but possibly not ships)
France (unless the policy otherwise provides)
Germany
Greece – Private Maritime Code, Art 198 (but maritime liens do not attach to the proceeds)
Italy
Japan
Luxembourg
Malta
Norway
Denmark
Peru
Portugal – CC 794
Spain
Sweden – Insurance Art 1925, s 54
Turkey
Uruguay
Venezuela

But in other states the policy or its proceeds must generally be separately assigned and, if it is not so assigned, the proceeds fall into the pool of assets available to unsecured creditors. These states include England and English-influenced states, and South Africa.

Priorities

22–5 In general, the normal priorities rules for the assignment of contracts apply. For a list see para 12–1, to which one may add the potential priority lien of brokers and insurers for unpaid premiums.

As to competing assignments, in England priorities rank according to the date that the insurers receive notice of the assignment. In practice it is thought that in the London market brokers do not give notices of assignment to all the underwriters accepting the risk and at most to the lead underwriters only. Compliance may also be required with the terms of the policy. For example, clause 23 of the Institutes' Time Clauses (Hulls) provides that no assignment of or interest in the policy is binding on underwriters unless a dated notice of such assignment signed by the assured is endorsed on the policy. P&I clubs may avoid the coverage if the vessel is mortgaged without the agreement of the club unless an undertaking is given to cover future assessments. The mortgagee should obtain a waiver of this rule.

Avoidance of policy

An assignee of a policy is in the same position as the assignor. In principle   22–6
(and by s 50(2) of the Marine Insurance Act 1906) an insurer is entitled to
raise as against the assignee lender any defence arising out of the insurance
contract that he would have been entitled to raise as against the owner who
took out the insurance, e.g. non-disclosure or breach of warranty (sea
worthiness, trading limits)

> In *William Pickersgill & Sons Ltd v London & Marine Provincial Insurance
> Co Ltd* [1912] KB 614, the assignors of the marine insurance policy failed to
> disclose a material fact to the insurance company. The insured vessel was lost
> and the assignee of the policy, who did not know of the non-disclosure, claimed
> against the insurance company. *Held*: the insurer was entitled to avoid liability
> under the policy on the grounds of non-disclosure, even against an innocent
> assignee.

> In *Graham Joint Stock Shipping Co v Merchants' Marine Shipping* [1924] AC
> 294, a ship was scuttled by the master and crew with the connivance of the
> shipowner. The mortgagees brought an action on the policy against the
> insurers. *Held*: the insurers could avoid the policy against the shipowner and
> the mortgagees as assignees could be in no better position. They were not joint
> insured or parties to the policy.

Insurance brokers

In the London market, insurances are commonly effected through the   22–7
owner's brokers who deliver an undertaking to the mortgagee regarding the
insurances.

The undertakings are usually in a standard form. The brokers may confirm that they have effected the specified insurances and undertake: (1) to
hold the insurances and renewals and substitutions to the order of the mortgagee in accordance with the loss payable clause, (2) to arrange for the loss
payable clauses to be endorsed on the policies when issued, (3) to have
notices of assignment endorsed on the policies when issued and acknowledged by underwriters in accordance with market practice, and (4) to
advise the mortgagee immediately of material changes to the insurances
and, on application by the mortgagee not later than one month before the
expiry of the insurances, to notify the mortgagee whether renewal instructions have been received. The undertakings are usually expressed to be subject to the brokers lien for premiums. The brokers may reserve the right,
until notice is received to the contrary, to arrange for collision or salvage

guarantees to be given in the event of bail being required to prevent the arrest of the vessel or to secure the release of the vessel following a casualty. Any payments under the guarantee can be reimbursed out of the proceeds of the policies.

Where insurances are effected through brokers the mortgagee runs the risk that the brokers might fail to comply with the terms of the undertaking in which event the brokers may be unable to discharge any damages suffered, subject to any statutory indemnity scheme.

In England, brokers undertakings must, as with any other contract, be supported by consideration: see *Amalgamated General Finance Co Ltd v C E Golding & Co* [1964] 2 Lloyd's Rep 163. Practice is to satisfy this requirement by an arrangement whereby the broker agrees with the mortgagee that, in consideration of the mortgagee approving the broker for the purposes of the ship's insurances, the broker will issue his undertaking in the prescribed form. If this is to be effective for consideration purposes, the mortgagee must have a future right in the mortgage to approve the brokers.

Brokers (and insurers) may have a prior lien on the policies for any unpaid premium – see s 53 (2) of the Marine Insurance Act 1906. If the shipowner owns a large number of ships held by separate companies and has taken out a floating policy covering all of the ships, the mortgagee is exposed to the risk that the broker may deduct claims for unpaid premiums in respect of other ships from the proceeds relating to the mortgaged ship, unless otherwise agreed. Brokers often give owners credit for premiums.

Joint insurance

22–8 There is some advantage to a mortgagee in procuring that the insurances are taken out in the joint names of the owner and the bank. Under s 14(1) of the Marine Insurances Act 1906 a mortgagee has an insurable interest in respect of any sum due or to become due under the mortgage.

The advantages of joint insurance are: (1) both joint assureds must give a receipt for any claims, thereby reducing the risk of a misapplication of the proceeds (but this advantage may be partially vitiated if the proceeds are collectible by the brokers only); (2) the consent of the mortgagee would normally be required to a variation of the insurances (which may not be the case if the insurances are taken out by the owner alone); and (3) a breach of warranty by the owner, e.g. seaworthiness, trading limits, could probably not be set up against the mortgagee by the insurers so as to avoid the claim unless the mortgagee were privy to the breach.

A disadvantage is that the mortgagee may be liable for unpaid premiums. The policy can waive that liability.

Captives and reinsurance

If the insurance is arranged with a captive insurance company within the   22–9
shipowner's group or with insurance companies of low credit standing, the
mortgagee should require reinsurance with an acceptable reinsurer. If the
initial insurer fails, it is usually the case that the mortgagor cannot claim
direct from reinsurers, although cut-throughs for third party liability insurance may be possible by statute. The mortgagee should require the captive
or other initial insurer to assign the benefit of the reinsurance by way of
collateral and require the usual notices of assignment to be given plus, if
possible, waivers of lien and set-off. Guarantee protection clauses should be
inserted: para 25–10 *et seq*. But the reinsurance should specifically match
the initial insurance.

CHAPTER 23

SHIP CONSTRUCTION FINANCE

23–1   Construction finance is often risky because the security is unlikely to be worth much in the builder's yard unless the mortgagee is willing to complete the construction. Construction loans are therefore often supported by other security until completion. In essence, ship construction finance is similar to project finance generally.

If the builder is being financed, the security will generally comprise the benefit of the building contract (principally, the right to payment from the buyer) together with any accompanying guarantees, and if the title in the uncompleted vessel remains in the builder until delivery, a mortgage on the unfinished vessel and materials on site (if non-possessory chattel mortgages are available).

If the buyer is being financed, the security will comprise the same elements except that the main rights assigned under the building contract will be the right to delivery, any damages for failure to perform and the benefit of the warranties. The availability of a mortgage over the unfinished vessel depends upon whether title is passed to the buyer as the vessel is constructed. Insurances will also be assigned. If there is a guarantee from a bank of the obligations of the builder to refund advance instalments of the contract price if the vessel is rejected, this too will be assigned.

For comments on the security assignment of contracts, see chapter 4.

23–2   In many countries mortgages over unfinished ships can (and sometimes must) be registered, e.g. Italy, Greece, Belgium, Norway and Denmark. These mortgages may mature into a preferred mortgage on completion if the vessel is, on completion, to be registered in the same state as that in which it is built. These rules are of limited value from this point of view where the vessel on completion is registered under a foreign flag.

The 1967 Brussels Convention relating to registration of rights in respect of vessels under construction required that contracting states establish a public register for the registration of title to and mortgages and "hypothe-ques" over vessels being or to be constructed. The ranking between the registered mortgages and liens was to be determined according to the rules laid down in the Convention. De-registration required the consent of the holder of the right. Although this Convention never came into force, it is believed that the rules were absorbed in Germany and Scandinavia, but this would be a matter for investigation.

In Britain, a maritime mortgage on an uncompleted vessel is not possible since an unfinished vessel is not a "ship" within the Merchant Shipping Act 1894 as it cannot be used in navigation. It is necessary to use ordinary security such as a floating charge or a corporate chattel mortgage. Registration will usually be required under the Companies Act 1985: para 9–34 *et seq.*

Similarly in the United States the preferred ship mortgage is not available for construction finance and a chattel mortgage must be employed. A statement must generally be filed under Art 9 of the Uniform Commercial Code: para 9–14 *et seq.*

PART III

GUARANTEES

CHAPTER 24

GUARANTEES: INTRODUCTION

Protection of guarantors

To the layman a guarantee is a baffling document. The main obligation, **24-1** namely to pay if the borrower does not pay, is expressed in two or three lines. Why then does there have to be a long document bristling with curious legalese?

In fact many of the technical provisions are vital to the protection of a lender. Some are so fundamental that if they are not there, the lender could find himself with a useless guarantee by reason of some seemingly trivial action on his part. Guarantees are encrusted with law. This is no doubt attributable to the fact that guarantors have, historically, sought every available legal means to avoid a liability which, human nature being what it is, they did not expect to have to meet when they gave the guarantee. The guarantor usually does not receive the money; it follows that courts must be jealous to safeguard the interests of guarantors. Therefore guarantors are the darlings of the courts. Lawyers have drafted provisions into guarantees to counter the vulnerability of the obligation and to redress the balance.

Purpose of guarantees

Guarantees are usually taken to provide a second pocket to pay if the first **24-2** should be empty. However guarantees sometimes have other purposes.

Responsibility of controller   Where the borrower is under the control of a third party who may be the real beneficiary of the loan in economic terms, then the guarantee of the controller may be taken, not so much for credit reasons, but to ensure that the borrower is operated with the interests of the lender in mind. An example at the corporate level is the personal guarantee commonly called for from the owners of private companies, e.g. guarantees given by individuals to support loans to one-ship companies owned by them, or guarantees by a parent company or by trading companies in the group. These guarantees in commercial effect strip away the veil of incorporation.

A state may be requested to guarantee a loan to a state entity or subordinate administrative division in order to protect the lender against changes in state policy which may disable the borrower from meeting its obligations, e.g. the removal of the taxing power of a municipality, interference with the ability of a public utility to set its tariffs at a commercial level sufficient to enable it to service its obligations, or the revocation of an exchange control consent or of an exemption from a withholding tax. In project finance the guarantee of the state may be required in order to strengthen the protections against an expropriation of the concession upon which the project is based. In such cases the state guarantor may be called upon to honour an obligation which by its own act it prevented the borrower from fulfilling.

Special cases Sometimes the identity of the borrower may be determined for special reasons and a "guarantee" required of the "real" borrower. A parent company may arrange for a bond issue to be made by a financing subsidiary in a tax haven in order to avoid a withholding tax which would be leviable if the parent were to be the borrower: the proceeds are on-lent to the parent which guarantees the bonds. A central bank may be substituted as the borrower of record under the guarantee of the state in order to bring the foreign currency reserves of the state (which may be technically owned by the central bank as a separate legal entity) within the scope of the covenant.

A guarantee may be required to establish mutuality for set-off purposes, as when a bank agrees with a group of companies to net all accounts of the group: to enable the set-off to operate, each company must guarantee the debit balances of all the others, so that the bank can set off a credit balance against the mutual guarantee liability.

Initial legal checks

24–3   This section reviews some of the main initial legal checks which should be made when a guarantee is taken.

Corporate powers and benefit

Like any other corporate transaction, a legal entity must have corporate power to give a guarantee. A perennial, though dwindling, problem in relation to corporate guarantees arises from the rule, historically applicable in most jurisdictions, whereby it is ultra vires a corporation and a fraud upon its shareholders and creditors if it gives away its assets without receiving some benefit in return: if the guarantee is called, the company is paying the debt of a third party. See *Re Lee, Behrens & Co* [1932] 2 Ch 46 (a pension case); *Rolled Steel Products Holdings Ltd v British Steel Corp* [1982] 3 All ER 1057 (guarantee set aside as ultra vires because there was no benefit to the guarantor company). Charity has no place at board meetings: "there are to be no cakes and ale except such as are required for the benefit of the company" per Bowen LJ in *Hutton v West Cork Rly* (1883) 23 Ch D 654, 673, CA.

Where there are minority shareholders in a subsidiary which is called upon to guarantee the parent's debt, a local corporate concept that the parent has a fiduciary duty to the minority not to operate the subsidiary solely in the selfish interests of the parent may come into play. United States case law is fertile on the subject.

There is generally no objection on this count to downstream guarantees (e.g. where a parent guarantees a subsidiary) because the parent presumably derives benefit from the increased financial strength of the subsidiary. The position is different with cross-stream guarantees (where one subsidiary guarantees a co-subsidiary), upstream guarantees (where a subsidiary guarantees a parent) and brother-and-sister guarantees (where the borrower and guarantor are in the common ownership of the same individual or a consortium).

This rule has however been steadily eroded in commercial jurisdictions in 24–4 keeping with the general tendency to limit the scope of the ultra vires doctrine, which has little to commend it.

In a number of countries statute has intervened. The ultra vires rule for ordinary companies has been virtually abolished in EU jurisdictions as regards third parties by virtue of European company law directives, reflected in the British Companies Act 1985 s 35A (inserted in 1989). But shareholders can enjoin ultra vires acts and directors continue to be liable for ultra vires acts so that if there is no benefit or no corporate power, they are unlikely to enter into the transaction.

The US Revised Model Business Corporation Act provides that the validity of corporate action may not be challenged on the grounds of lack of power unless the claim is asserted, for example, by (a) a shareholder to enjoin the doing of the act; or (b) the corporation or its representative against the officers or directors: s 3.04. Identical or similar provisions have been enacted in most US states including New York.

Courts in the United States have relaxed the benefit requirement and recognised benefits which are indirect and intangible, e.g. the indirect benefit accruing to a subsidiary from being part of a strong group especially where the subsidiary is dependent on the parent for various matters such as advertising, publicity, supplies or finance: see, e.g. the brother-sister case of *Stromgberg-Carlson T Mfg Co v George C Beckwith Co*, 193 Minn 255, 258 NW 314 (1935).

German law has the novel concept of a "domination contract" whereby a parent and its subsidiaries can, upon fulfilment of certain conditions, elect to be treated as an integrated corporate system. In this event no question of separate corporate benefit can arise because the group is legally a single economic unit. As a condition of this arrangement, the parent is responsible for the losses of subsidiaries.

Authorisations

24–5   The guarantee must be authorised by the directors. There may be limits on guarantees in the guarantor's constitutional documents, e.g. in a borrowing limit. A further question is whether the directors were in conflict of interest, as where a director of the guarantor is also a director of the debtor which may prevent a disinterested quorum entitled to vote. The impact of these internal matters on the third party creditor is decided by local corporate law.

Financial assistance ⊢ to abolished

One should check whether the guarantee is prohibited financial assistance for the purchase of the company's shares within the Companies Act 1985 s 151 or other local equivalent, as where, for example, a company guarantees a loan made to another company to buy the guaranteeing company's shares in a take-over.

Transaction at an undervalue

24–6   A guarantee may amount to a gift liable to be set aside as a preference on insolvency if it is granted in the suspect period and the guarantor is insolvent. Thus the guarantee may be a transaction at an undervalue within the British Insolvency Act 1986 s 238. There is a two-year suspect period (five for individuals), and a defence if the company transacted "in good faith and for the purpose of carrying on its business" and at the time "there were reasonable grounds for believing the transaction would benefit the company". This defence does not apply to individuals and, being objective, is difficult for banks to prove affirmatively. The potential avoidance of gifts or undervalue transactions by an insolvent company in the relevant suspect period is universal: para 31–3 *et seq*.

Contractual restrictions

There may be limits on guarantees in the loan agreements, etc., of the guarantor or its parent. Financial ratios might be breached. A breach might trigger an acceleration by the lender where a credit agreement covenant is broken or expose the creditor taking the guarantee to the tort of inducing a breach of contract if the creditor knew of the breach.

Undue influence

The problem of undue influence is of a minimum importance in international finance. It generally arises, e.g. where a wife or aged mother is asked to guarantee an impecunious family member without understanding the implications. 24–7

Misrepresentation inducing guarantee

Under English law, full disclosure by the creditor to the guarantor of all material facts is, outside the consumer context, required only in special cases (e.g. credit insurance, or clear unconscionability). But omissions are a misrepresentation if some facts are disclosed since a half-truth is as bad as a lie. Thus partial disclosure may attract full disclosure. Any actual misrepresentation by the creditor, e.g. as to the credit status of the debtor guaranteed or the presence of non-existent security for the guaranteed debt, may lead to the avoidance of the guarantee on normal principles of contract law. The risk is of greater relevance where the guarantor is independent of the debtor guaranteed, e.g. a surety or insurance company or a bank. Surety companies may make their guarantee conditional on full disclosure of all material facts known to the creditor – a condition which may be dangerous for creditors since, if the guarantee is called, this must usually be because the credit of the debtor, thought to be sound, turns out to be unsound.

Tax and stamp duties

The usual checks should be carried out to ensure that there are no withholding taxes on payments by the guarantor and no stamp duties or other documentary taxes on the guarantor (none in the UK). 24–8

Unfair Contract Terms Act 1977

This – mainly consumer – statute avoids unfair contract terms if (in the business context) they are unreasonable. Similar statutes are common in developed jurisdictions. It will be seen below that standard form guarantees contain extensive protections to preserve the guarantee and which weaken the favourable position of the guarantor. But in England, standard guarantee clauses are unlikely to be unfair contract terms in the business context.

CHAPTER 25

TERMS OF GUARANTEES

General

Guarantee law is by no means uniform in commercial jurisdictions although **25–1** there are marked similarities especially in common law countries. The following discussion briefly reviews the provisions which are commonly found in an English guarantee. It is not intended to explore all the twists and turns of guarantee law (which are readily discoverable from the books), but rather to indicate the usual terms of guarantees and briefly why they are there.

Consideration clause

Like any other contract in English law, a guarantee requires consideration if **25–2** it is to be valid, i.e. some benefit or promise given by the lender to the guarantor in return for the guarantee. The doctrine of consideration is replaced in civil code countries by other indicia of seriousness of intent and is sometimes only partially applied by other common law jurisdictions. The rule is to be distinguished from the principles discussed above relating to corporate benefit. Consideration is a rule applying to any contract; corporate benefit applies only to corporations. Consideration may be nominal, e.g. £1, but corporate benefit must be commercially justifiable. Voidable transactions at an undervalue under insolvency preference law involve a material element of gift. The consideration does not have to be stated (Mercantile Law Amendment Act 1856 s 3), but it usually is.

In England, if there is no consideration the guarantee must be executed under seal.

Usually the consideration for a guarantee is the agreement of the lender to make the loan to the borrower if the guarantor agrees to give his guarantee. However, there are two traps:

— The consideration must not be past. In English-based systems, past consideration is no consideration. Hence, if a guarantee, expressed to be granted in consideration of the lender making the loan, is given after the loan has been made or after the lender is already committed, the consideration is past (i.e. has already been performed) and the guarantee will lapse for failure of consideration. Guarantees are often entered into at the time the loan agreement is signed. However, if they are given at a subsequent date, the agreement of the lender to waive a default by the borrower, to extend the time for payment in return for the guarantee or to treat a condition precedent as satisfied, can constitute good consideration. In those cases, the consideration should, as a matter of prudence, be documented.

- The fulfilment of the stated consideration may be construed as a condition precedent to the guarantor's liability. For example, if the guarantee is given in consideration of the bank lending the borrower US$5 million and the bank in the event lends only US$4 million, then the guarantee may be ineffective. The bank has not performed its side of the bargain: see *Burton v Gray* (1873) 8 Ch App 932.

Guaranteed sums

25–3 The guarantee should clarify what is guaranteed, e.g. all liabilities or those under a particular agreement (which should extend to variations of that agreement). Does it cover future liabilities? Does it cover obligations of the debtor incurred in favour of a third party and assigned to the guaranteed creditor?

Limited amount guarantees

25–4 The liability of a guarantor may be limited to a specific sum. This may be because the guarantor is prevented by law or its constitution from issuing unlimited guarantees; the guarantee is not of the whole amount of the loan; the guarantor wishes to safeguard himself against the possibility that the lender will increase the facilities to be made available to the borrower; the guaranteed loan agreement contains provisions which could substantially increase the guarantor's liabilities over and above principal plus interest, such as indemnity or damages clauses or obligations on the borrower to pay stamp duties or taxes.

The limit affects the right of subrogation: para 25–15 *et seq*. The guarantee should clarify whether the limit includes interest, default interest, costs, tax gross-ups under the guarantee, default interest against the guarantor, stamp duties on the guarantee and currency indemnities under both the guaranteed loan agreement and the guarantee itself, and the rate at which one converts guaranteed sums in a foreign currency into the currency in which the limit is expressed.

Guarantees of interest

A guarantee may be only of the interest on a loan. Like all partial guaran- 25–5
tees, the most important questions are whether the guarantor is subrogated
on payment of his part, in which event he dilutes the assets available to the
creditor (para 25–15 *et seq*), and whether the creditor can appropriate
recoveries to the unguaranteed principal first so as to preserve the claim for
the guaranteed interest.

The guarantee should make it clear whether default interest, capitalised
interest added to principal, tax grossing-up, and interest accruing after the
debtor's insolvency (not normally provable) are covered.

Demand

The guarantee should be payable on demand so as to establish clearly (what 25–6
is probably the law) that the statute of limitations runs from the demand,
not the date of the giving of the guarantee.

Multiple demands should be expressly allowed, e.g. to cover future liabilities not caught by the initial demand.

First demand guarantees

A provision that the guarantee is payable on first demand approximates the
guarantee to a letter of credit. Under a letter of credit the beneficiary is, in
the absence of fraud, entitled to draw on the credit upon presenting the
documents called for by the credit: the issuer of the credit must pay, regardless of a dispute in relation to the underlying transaction. This is helpful to a
lender if the borrower should dispute, say, the validity of an acceleration,
but naturally the clause exposes the guarantor to a wrongful call on the
guarantee. For a review of first demand bank guarantees, see para 26–18 *et
seq*.

Joint and several guarantees

Where there is more than one guarantor, the guarantee is expressed to be 25–7
the joint and several obligation of the guarantors. "Several" does not mean
that each is liable for only a proportionate share. Two of the many technical
differences between joint liability and several liability are as follows:

(a) When an individual guarantor is jointly bound with a co-guarantor, the
    guarantor's liability (probably) terminates with his death. The survivor
    becomes liable. But where his liability is joint and several, his liability
    passes to his estate.

(b) Where the liability is joint there is only one cause of action. This means that, although each guarantor is liable for the full amount, the lender can only bring one suit. He can bring an action against all the joint guarantors or he can bring an action against one of them. But if he brings an action against one of them and the judgment is unsatisfied, he cannot afterwards bring an action against the others. On the other hand, several liability results in there being as many causes of action as there are obligors.

If it is intended to limit each guarantor's several liability, a specific limit should be included in the guarantee.

If the lender agrees with one guarantor to vary the guarantee without the consent of the others, the others cease to be bound: *Ellesmere Brewery Company v Cooper* [1896] 1 QB 75.

If the guarantee envisages that all will sign, but one guarantor does not, the guarantee may be ineffective against the others: *James Graham & Co (Timber) Ltd v Southgate Sands* [1986] QB 80, CA; *Marston v Griffith & Co Pty Ltd* (1985) 2 NSWLR 294. The guarantee should expressly counter this result.

Continuing guarantee

25–8   An English guarantee is often expressed to be a "continuing" guarantee. This does not mean that the liability under the guarantee goes on and on. The word "continuing" is a legal term of art used to avoid a technical rule of English law, known as the Rule in *Clayton's Case* (1816) 1 Mer 572, whereby the liability of a guarantor is reduced by payments into a current account by the borrower so that subsequent drawings out are not protected. Thus a guarantee of an overdraft which is not stated to be a continuing guarantee will be extinguished by repayments of the overdraft and further advances up to the overdraft limit will not be covered. While the provision may not be strictly necessary if it is clear from the guarantee that the guarantor is liable for all the obligations of the borrower which may arise under a loan agreement or bond, common practice is to include the phrase "this is a continuing guarantee".

Limited duration guarantees and expiry

25–9   The guarantee may be limited as to duration. In this connection a distinction must be made between the crystallisation of liability and the termination of liability.

In the case of a continuing guarantee covering all present and future moneys from time to time due to the creditor, the continuing nature of the guarantee may be determined and the liability crystallised on the occurrence of certain events, e.g. on a notice given by the guarantor (usually resulting in the bank withdrawing the debtor's facilities) or automatically by operation of law, as on the bankruptcy, liquidation or death of the guarantor. On cessation of the guarantee as a continuing security, future voluntary advances are not covered but the guarantor still remains liable for the amounts outstanding on the cessation.

In the case of a specific guarantee covering a particular loan or all the liabilities of the borrower arising under a term loan agreement or bonds, the liability extends to the loans expressed to be covered and no case for crystallisation arises.

Termination of liability after a specified period is a different matter. For example, a guarantor may require that any claims must be made within, say, 30 days of the date the sum became due from the principal debtor. If no date were fixed, the creditor could reserve his rights against the guarantor for as long as he wished, subject only to the statutory period of limitation, thereby leaving the guarantor in suspense. However a guarantor may have a legal right to pay out the creditor without waiting for a demand once the guaranteed sum has become due (but not before). He may wish to do this in order to take over the creditor's security by subrogation to prevent its erosion.

If there is an expiry date, this should relate only to the period within which demands must be made, and should not cancel the guarantor's liability. There should be plenty of time to serve a demand after the guaranteed claim matures. Ideally, the expiry should stretch after the preference period in case the payment of the guarantee is deemed a preferential transfer by the guarantor and must be disgorged by the creditor – this may be after the expiry so that the creditor can no longer claim, unless the court is empowered to extend the expiry date when it orders a return of a preferential payment.

Extensions and variations of guaranteed debt

Certain acts by a lender will automatically release a guarantor from liability.   25–10

Extensions If the lender agrees to give the borrower extra time to pay, the guarantor is automatically released even if he is not prejudiced: *Nisbet v Smith* (1789) 2 Bro C C 579. Sometimes, of course, the guarantor is prejudiced, e.g. because the extension results in an increase in liability on account of extra interest, or because the financial position of the borrower worsens during the extension with the result that when the guarantor is ultimately called upon to pay the guarantor's claim for reimbursement from the borrower may be worthless. Often, however, the guarantor is not prejudiced. Quite the reverse in many cases: guarantors do not lie awake at night, dreading that the bank may give the debtor extra time to pay. But the rule is inflexible and is applied even if mercy shown to the borrower is also mercy to the guarantor.

Variations If the lender materially alters the loan agreement, the guarantor is discharged: *Holmes v Brunskill* (1878) 3 Q B D 495. The guaranteed obligation has been changed.

Compositions If the lender agrees to reduce the borrower's liability or to enter into a composition with the borrower, the guarantor is discharged. Thus, if the lender enters into a binding agreement with the borrower and other creditors of the borrower outside bankruptcy law whereby the creditors agree to accept a reduction of their claims as an alternative to a liquidation, the guarantee would lapse. A creditor's arrangement, by allowing the borrower to carry on business, may offer the best available chance of at least a partial pay-out, but, unless otherwise provided, the guarantor's consent is required: *Ex parte Smith* (1789) 3 Bro CC 1.

25–11   The effect of the above rules is so cataclysmic that guarantees invariably include a protective clause to the effect that the guarantee is not to be prejudiced by relaxations of the terms of the loan agreement, waivers, compositions with the borrower or variations of the credit, such as increases in the amount, or extensions of payment dates.

> In *American Bank & Trust Company v Koplik*, 87 A D 2d 351 (NY App Div 1st Dep't 1982), it was held that guarantors were not released from their guarantees by an agreement between debtor and creditor extending the time for payment since the guarantee agreement expressly permitted the creditor, without notice to the guarantors, to change the manner or terms of payment or to change or extend the time of payment.

> In *Chemical Bank v PIC Motors*, 87 A D 2d 447 (NY App Div 1st Dep't 1982), it was held that the failure of a creditor, negligent or otherwise, to preserve or protect collateral while it was in the possession of the debtor did not release a guarantor which has executed a waiver of the creditor's obligation not to impair the security.

Where a variation is significant, a prudent lender should not rely on a clause giving him power to change the guaranteed obligation without the consent of the guarantor but should obtain the guarantor's concurrence before the variation is effected: there may be a difference between a varied obligation and a new obligation.

Release of securities and co-guarantors

Once a guarantor has paid the debt guaranteed, the guarantor can step into   **25–12**
the shoes of the lender and take over any security the lender may have for
the loan and also claim contribution from any other co-guarantors of the
same debt. The law requires that a lender must not prejudice this right, for
example, by releasing a mortgage or excusing a co-guarantor from liability.
If the lender does so, the guarantor's liability is reduced by the value of the
protection lost to him, namely the value of the security released or the value
of the claim against the co-guarantor: *Carter v White* (1883) 25 Ch D 666.
This rule applies even if the security or co-guarantees were taken after the
guarantee was given and even if the guarantor did not know of the other
security or co-guarantees. A release of one joint and several guarantor
releases the other from liability: *Mercantile Bank of Sydney v Taylor* (1893)
AC 317.

A clause is commonly inserted giving the lender a free hand to deal with
the other security and other guarantors, e.g. by releasing or varying security
or other guarantees. The waiver is also extended to cover certain other
circumstances which might prejudice the guarantor's right of reimbursement once he has paid off the debt, such as failure by the lender to perfect
the security, variations of the security or failure to carry out the necessary
formalities on dishonour of a note by the borrower.

Invalidity of guaranteed debt

A guarantee is generally expressed to be in respect of sums "payable" by the   **25–13**
borrower. If those sums are not legally payable, there is nothing to pay
under the guarantee. There are any number of reasons why a debt may not
be legally payable, e.g. the loan may have been borrowed in excess of the
constitutional powers of the borrower or its directors; interest may contra-
vene usury law; post-insolvency interest may not be payable on the insolvency of the principal debtor (as is usually the case); the principal debt may
be discharged, e.g. on winding-up or dissolution of the principal debtor, or
by a foreclosure order for security.

It is therefore standard to provide that the obligations of the guarantor
are not to be affected by any unenforceability, non-provability or invalidity
of the principal debt. The clause is sometimes extended to oblige the guarantor to pay the loan as it falls due in accordance with its expressed terms even
though the borrower may not be liable to pay, e.g. because of a local moratorium law or a local law reducing the interest rate.

A clause providing that the guarantee is to remain on foot notwithstanding any illegality affecting the principal debt may not be enforceable if the

same illegality taints the guarantee. Wider considerations of public policy may prevent the enforcement of a guarantee for a debt which is illegal.

Subrogation

25–14   **Guarantor's right of subrogation** As soon as the guarantor has paid his guarantee in full, he acquires an immediate right to seek reimbursement from the borrower. He can also take over all the securities for the loan and claims against co-guarantors even though the guarantor did not know of the existence of the security or the security was given after the guarantee was entered into. He can claim rateable contribution from co-guarantors. If the liability of the guarantor does not cover the whole claim, the guarantor acquires a proportionate interest in the securities and the claims against the co-guarantors: *Goodwin v Gray* (1874) 22 WR 312.

The right of subrogation can have an unfortunate effect upon the position of the lender who has not been fully paid: the lender's security has to be shared pro rata with the guarantor; the dividends the lender might receive in the liquidation of the borrower would be reduced by the fact that the guarantor is claiming as well. Where the guarantee is joint and several, a guarantor who has paid his share can claim alongside the creditor against those co-guarantors who have not paid. In effect, the guarantor gives with one hand and takes with the other.

Guarantees, accordingly, should include a clause excluding this right of subrogation and all rights of indemnity against the debtor or contribution from co-guarantors until the loan and interest are fully paid. Sometimes the clause goes further by providing that, after the guarantee has been called, the guarantor is not to compete in any way with the lender against the guarantor, e.g. by claiming or receiving some separate debt due from the borrower to the guarantor or by exercising a set-off or realising any security. In short, all claims of the guarantor against the borrower are sought to be subordinated to the claims of the lender, not merely the claim for reimbursement. In appropriate cases (e.g. where a parent guarantees a subsidiary) an express subordination agreement may be better adapted to cover the intricacies of subordination.

25–15   **Rule against double proof and partial guarantees** As mentioned, the guarantor's right of subrogation arises only when the guarantor has paid the guaranteed liability in full. Difficult questions arise if the guarantor has paid only part of the claim or if there is a limit in the guarantee on the total amount recoverable from the guarantor. These intricacies require an appreciation of "the rule against double proof".

Where a guarantor is claiming reimbursement from an insolvent principal debtor, but has not paid the principal creditor in full, the rule against double proof or its equivalent may prevent both creditor and guarantor proving at the same time for what is substantially the same debt.

It is obvious that, if there are ten guarantors, and if each could claim the contingent reimbursement liability of the principal debtor to them before any guarantor has paid anything to the principal creditor, the principal debtor's estate would be liable for the same debt 11 times. To prevent this, the principal creditor has the senior right of claim and, if he is claiming, none of the guarantors can claim.

The English attitude to guarantors who pay only part of the debt guaranteed is complex but is of great practical importance, Broadly, the guarantor or issuer of the letter of credit must have paid the full claim guaranteed before he can claim reimbursement from the principal debtor. A quirky sidestream flowing from this is, if the guarantor's liability is subject to a lesser limit and the guarantor has paid up to that limit, e.g. if the guarantor guarantees 100 subject to a limit of 60, the guarantor must pay 100 before he is entitled to claim reimbursement from the principal debtor in bankruptcy. It is not enough if he pays up to his limit of 60. He has guaranteed 100, albeit subject to a limit of 60.

On the other hand, if he guarantees only 60 and pays 60, then he has a right of reimbursement, subject to any prohibition in the guarantee to the contrary.

The object of the rule that the guarantor must pay in full the amount he has guaranteed is to maximise the claim of the creditor against the principal debtor. If the guarantor pays only 60 out of a guaranteed debt of 100 and if the recovering creditor must then reduce his claim against the principal debtor by the 60 he has received from the guarantor, he can claim only for 40 and must compete with the guarantor who is now claiming reimbursement from the principal debtor for the 60 which the guarantor has paid. The result is that the creditor will receive less dividends. If on the other hand the creditor can insist that the guarantor cannot claim in competition with the creditor until the guarantor has paid the full 100, then the creditor can put in a claim against the principal debtor for 100 on which he will receive much greater dividends than if he had put in a claim for a mere 40.

This is one case where English guarantee law favours the creditor as opposed to the guarantor – usually the hapless guarantor is seen as the victim deserving of the law's benevolent protection and indulgence. The reason for the reversal of the guarantor's fortunes in this case is the contrary policy that it is unreasonable that a guarantor who is still in default should diminish the creditor's claim against the principal debtor – that he should give with one hand and take with the other. Usually the guarantor is also insolvent and so forfeits the sympathy of the law: the competition is now

25–16

between the solvent creditor and the creditors of a defaulting guarantor. In any event, the rule is well established by case law: see, e.g. *Re Rees* (1881) 17 Ch D 98; *Re Sass* [1896] 2 QB 12 and numerous cases since then.

25-17   There is however one English exception which relates to negotiable instruments. The general rule for negotiable instruments, such as bills of exchange and promissory notes, is that the original holder and all subsequent indorsers who transfer the instrument by indorsement are liable to the ultimate holder of the instrument if the principal debtor – the acceptor or maker or issuer – does not pay the ultimate holder. Effectively, they guarantee it unless otherwise agreed, e.g. by the words "*sans recours*". The rule here is that, if a prior indorser is called upon to pay, but pays only in part, e.g. 60 out of 100, then the holder must apply that 60 towards the 100 so as to reduce his claim to 40. This would typically happen when the indorser is also insolvent and pays only a dividend. For some unexplained reason, the holder of a negotiable instrument is not favoured in the same way as the holder of an ordinary guarantee and he has to compete with the paying indorser, notwithstanding that the latter is still in default: *Re Houghton, ex p Tayler* (1857) 26 LJ Bank 58. But the English courts resent the exception and have cut it down: if the holder receives the partial payment from the indorser after the holder has put in his claim (proof) in the principal debtor's insolvency (acceptor, or maker of the note), then the holder does not have to reduce his claim by the receipt, and correspondingly the indorser is too late to claim against the principal debtor for the amount the indorser has paid. In other words, the cut-off point shutting out the indorser's right of reimbursement is payment prior to holder's proof: *Re London, Bombay & Mediterranean Bank, ex p Cama* (1874) LR 9 Ch 686; *Re Fothergill, ex p Turquand* (1876) 3 Ch D 445.

In any event, the special rule applying to negotiable instruments is one reason for the "suspense account clause" discussed below.

25-18   The United States position under the Bankruptcy Code of 1978 appears to be similar to the double-proof analysis discussed above in the case of guarantees of ordinary creditors. The effect of ss 502(e) and 509(b) is that a surety or other co-debtor has no claim for reimbursement or subrogation until he has paid the creditors in full: he is then entitled to be subrogated. If he pays in part only, he is not permitted to compete with the creditor and is subordinated to that creditor. This codifies previous case law and echoes a Bankruptcy Act amendment in 1962 to make it clear that a surety cannot share in dividends until the creditor is paid in full. The principle applies also to the subrogation of third parties who have deposited collateral with the creditor to secure the debtor but without personal liability on the part of the third party. Note that the sections apply only to payments made by the surety and other co-debtor after the commencement of the case. The position with regard to prior payments is left to the general law – usually state law.

The double-proof analysis has been applied elsewhere, e.g. in Scotland: *Henderson v Mackinnon* (1876) 3 R 608.

Suspense account for guarantor's partial payments

Guarantees sometimes include a provision that the lender is entitled to hold all partial payments by the guarantor in suspense until the full amount of the loan is paid. A partial payment will then be held in a separate account "on the shelf" and not applied in reduction of the guaranteed amount so that the lender can prove for the whole amount of the loan in the liquidation of the borrower: *Commercial Bank of Australia v Wilson* [1893] AC 181, PC. This normally increases the dividend payable in the liquidation and maximises the creditor's claim. If the payments received from the guarantor plus the distribution paid in the liquidation of the borrower exceed the amounts guaranteed, the lender would have to return the surplus to the guarantor.

25–19

Immediate recourse to guarantee

If a borrower defaults in payment of the loan, the lender does not have to exhaust his remedies against the borrower before claiming under the guarantee. But it is nevertheless common practice to provide expressly that any such right of the guarantor is excluded.

25–20

> In *Republic National Bank of New York v Sabet*, 681 F 2d 802 (2nd Cir 1981) cert denied 102 S Ct 2241 (1982), an Iranian company guaranteed the debt of another Iranian company in favour of a New York bank. Following a revolution in Iran, the assets of the Iranian debtor company were expropriated. Subsequently the US Government entered into an accord with the Iranian Government which barred expropriation claims which were to be referred to international arbitration. The bank sought to recover under the guarantee. *Held*: the bank was entitled to recover from the guarantor and under New York law did not have to proceed against the Iranian debtor first.

In other systems of law, the answer may not be so clear-cut. Plainly the worth of the guarantee could be substantially eroded if it were necessary first to recover from the borrower. Such recovery, particularly if it involved a liquidation of the borrower or the realisation of security, might involve substantial delays during which the lender could be exposed to a possible deterioration of the credit of the guarantor.

Appropriation of payments by creditor

25–21　The creditor should be expressly entitled to appropriate payments from the principal debtor (including set-offs and the proceeds of realisation of security) towards an unguaranteed debt owed by the principal debtor to the creditor so as to preserve the guarantor's liability for the guaranteed debt and to maximise recoveries. Without an express right of appropriation, it seems that the creditor does not have to apply these recoveries. But an express clause is prudent to ensure payment of the guaranteed debt first so that the safe debt is reduced, but the unsafe debt left at its full amount.

Reinstatement of avoided guarantee and security

25–22　A payment by the guarantor may subsequently be set aside as a preference on the insolvency of the guarantor. Similarly, a payment by the principal debtor of the guaranteed debt may be set aside as a preference of the guarantor on the principal debtor's insolvency. On the faith of the payment, the creditor may release the guarantee and security granted by the principal debtor or the guarantor.

If the payment is recovered from the creditor (as opposed to the guarantor), there should be provision for the guarantee to spring up again. A court may so order. But if there was an express expiry date in the guarantee, that expiry date may have passed: the expiry date should take this into account.

If security from the guarantor has been released, it is too late unless the assets still exist and the court is prepared to order reinstatement of the security. Ditto for released security from the principal debtor. Ideally the security should restrict the right of release by providing that it is not redeemable unless the party granting the security can establish that the payment on the faith of which the security is released is not liable to avoidance, e.g. by production of an auditor's certificate showing the payer or principal debtor was not insolvent so that the suspect period has not begun. This should be tested against rules outlawing restrictions (or clogs) on a debtor's right of redemption: para 8–14 *et seq.*

Additional security

25–23　Guarantees often state that the guarantee is additional to any other guarantee or security the creditor may have. This is to avoid any implication that the creditor's action in taking other security is an implied waiver of the guarantee.

Certificate of amount owing

It is usual to state in an English guarantee that a certificate from the lender   **25–24**
stating the amount due from the borrower is to be conclusive evidence of
that amount as against the guarantor. The origin of this provision was to
obviate a technical rule of evidence to the effect that a judgment against the
borrower is not evidence of the amount owing from the borrower in proceedings against the guarantor for recovery under the guarantee: *Ex parte
Young* (1881) 17 Ch D 668. If the guarantor were to dispute the amount
owing, then, without the clause, it would be necessary to re-prove the
amount of the debt in the proceedings against the guarantor. The provision
may also be helpful in approximating the guarantee to a "first demand"
guarantee.

"Unconditional and irrevocable" guarantees

That the guarantee is "unconditional and irrevocable" appears as a catch-   **25–25**
phrase in a great many international guarantees.

"Unconditional" might describe a guarantee which can be enforced
immediately on a default without a requirement that the creditor first
exhausts his remedies against the debtor. It is prudent to include a specific
"immediate recourse" clause: para 25–20. Or it might be intended to
strengthen the independence of the guarantee from the obligation guaranteed so as to give it "first demand" status: para 26–13 *et seq.*

"Irrevocable" possibly derives from the old rule that letters of credit were
revocable unless expressed to be irrevocable under pre-1994 versions of the
Uniform Customs and Practice for Documentary Credits. It might be hoped
that the word excludes certain defences which a surety might otherwise
have, e.g. if the lender extends the time for payment of a sum due from the
borrower, releases security or grants a waiver. Again, specific protections
should be included.

In short, this usage of the phrase probably stems from the desire for
vehement emphasis and should not be a substitute for clarity of intention.

Guarantor as "primary obligor"

The guarantor is often expressed to undertake liability as "primary obligor"   **25–26**
or as "principal debtor". There is no reason in principle why the guarantor
should not, as against the creditor, be in the position of a principal debtor,
while continuing to act as surety against the debtor (in order, for example,
to maintain rights of reimbursement). The "primary obligor" language may

be construed so as to establish liability even if the principal debt is invalid, to support the independence of the guarantee from the underlying obligation, to establish immediate recourse, to avoid certain of the technical rules under which the guarantor may become discharged (e.g. if the creditor grants waivers to the debtor) and to import into the guarantee certain of the terms of the principal debt, e.g. as to the place and currency of payment. It has been said that in such a case the creditor can treat the guarantor as principal debtor in every respect: *Duncan, Fox & Co v North and South Wales Bank* (1880) 6 App Cas 1. However, the phrase is vague short-hand and does not obviate the desirability of express protective clauses.

General terms of guarantees

25–27   The credit of the guarantor is often the basis of the whole loan. Hence, in addition to guarantee protective clauses, guarantees frequently contain provisions which would have been found in a loan agreement with the guarantor if the guarantor had been the direct borrower.

Both the loan agreement and the guarantee are generally expressed to be subject to a common system of law and a common forum for disputes. Although unity is not legally necessary, a uniform proper law is more convenient. A common forum would have the advantage of facilitating a single set of actions in the chosen forum.

If the guarantee omits an express choice of law, the law may impliedly be that of the principal debt by attraction or tacit intent. The principles are reviewed in another work in this series.

Whether the guarantee is included in the loan agreement or as a separate document is purely a matter of form and convenience. In the case of bond issues, the guarantee is generally endorsed on the bond itself or, occasionally, contained in a trust deed constituting the issue in which event the guarantee is merely referred to on the face of the bond. A guarantee endorsed on the bond does not prejudice its negotiability in English law.

Other clauses include: place, manner and currency of payments; payments to be made without set-off or counterclaim (as to when a guarantor can use a set-off available to the principal debtor, see Wood, *English & International Set-Off* (1989) Sweet & Maxwell, paras 10–193 *et seq*); tax grossing-up; representations and warranties; covenants, e.g. information and accounts, compliance certificates, negative pledge, no substantial disposals, pari passu clause, maintenance of consents, financial ratios, no change of business; general boiler-plate, e.g. stamp duties, costs, default interest, set-off, waivers, remedies cumulative, currency indemnity, assignments, notices, jurisdiction, waiver of immunity, governing law; and pro rata sharing in guarantees of syndicated loans. These general provisions are reviewed in relation to term loan agreements in another work in this series. If a term loan is guaranteed, the loan agreement should contain events of default relating to the guarantor and the guarantee so that, on a guarantor default, the lender should be able to accelerate the loan, cancel further draw downs and call the guarantee.

CHAPTER 26

INDEPENDENT GUARANTORS: BANK AND EXPORT CREDIT GUARANTEES

Generally

26–1 Where the guarantor controls the borrower, there is usually no difficulty in negotiating a guarantee which excludes defences which might normally be available to a guarantor and permits the creditor to agree extensions and variations, etc. However where the guarantor is independent of the borrower and has no control over the borrower's operations, the position is different. Typical examples are guarantees given by banks of a customer's liability or by national export credit agencies or other governmental or public institutions which do not have control of the borrower guaranteed. The practice naturally depends upon the circumstances but there are a number of provisions which, severally or wholly, are commonly found in guarantees given by independent guarantors.

First demand

A "first demand" guarantee without proof of liability is preferred by bank guarantors, see para 26–13 *et seq.*

Expiry

26–2 Banks will generally require the guarantee to have an express expiry date by which claims must be made. Apart from the obvious prudence of such a provision, regulatory authorities may require this. Where the claim guaranteed is payable by instalments, e.g. a term loan or hire under a lease or charterparty, the bank may also require the insertion of an inner limit, i.e. a time within which claims must be made in respect of each instalment of principal and interest. The liability of the guarantor is therefore reduced after the expiry of each inner limit. The inner limit assists certainty and also provides a predictable means of reducing the commission payable by the customer which is usually calculated on the maximum contingent liability of the bank guarantor under its guarantee.

Grace period

Independent guarantees sometimes provide that the guarantor will pay valid   26–3
claims only after a specified period after their maturity such as 60 days,
especially guarantees of export credit agencies. The purpose of this provision is (among other things) to establish that the default is permanent and
to enable the guarantor to cure the default.

Scheduled maturities

Under a normal guarantee when the loan is accelerated and unpaid then the
lender can claim the accelerated amount from the guarantor. However independent guarantors often stipulate that they will pay out only according to
the original scheduled maturities and will not meet a lump sum due on an
acceleration.

Limitation of claims guaranteed

Independent guarantors commonly limit the sums guaranteed only to, say,   26–4
principal and interest and insert a maximum liability. Commissions, fees,
expenses, penalties, payments under indemnity clauses, currency indemnity
clauses and tax grossing-up clauses may not be covered. For the effect of this
limit in relation to the rule against double-proof, see para 26–9.

Application of recoveries

The guarantee may require that, where partial payments are received from
the borrower in default (or any other source which is available for use in
reduction or satisfaction of the guaranteed claims), those payments must
first be appropriated towards the guaranteed obligations in a specified order
of priority so that in effect the claims which are not covered by the guarantee cannot be claimed from the borrower until the guaranteed claims are
met. The independent guarantor thereby achieves the recovery of its own
obligations first. In the absence of such a provision, a guarantor normally
has no right to compel the principal creditor to appropriate receipts from
the debtor to the guaranteed part.

No waiver of defences

Normal forms of guarantee used in international finance exclude a number   26–5
of defences which might be available to a guarantor, such as the ability of a
guarantor to cancel the guarantee if the creditor should change the under-

lying obligation or agree to extend a time for payment: para 25–10. Independent guarantors are naturally reluctant to agree to the waiver of these defences since they have no manner of controlling the release of underlying security or extensions of the time for payment or any other action between the lender and the borrower which might increase the guarantor's obligations or otherwise prejudice its position. From the point of view of a lender however the absence of these waivers increases the legal risk of the revocability of the guarantee for some relatively trivial matter.

Control

26–6   An independent guarantor may insist upon the ability to control the underlying loan agreement in return for the guarantee support. Effectively the guarantor adopts the position that the real creditor is the guarantor and that, as the guarantor would step into the shoes of the lender on a default, the loan agreement is in reality the guarantor's loan agreement. This control may include a right of the guarantor to decide whether or not the loan is to be accelerated on a default (so long as the guarantor pays overdue scheduled payments), a requirement that the creditor first exhaust his remedies against the borrower as directed by the guarantor before claiming under the guarantee (which might oblige the creditor to force a final liquidation lasting many years) and (dangerous) requirements that the lender should endeavour to minimise the loss and should keep the guarantor fully informed about matters which might affect its interests, such as the occurrence of events of default, so as to throw the monitoring risk on to the creditor (and so that, if the creditor failed to notify some technical default, the guarantor may complain that, if he had known, he could have compelled an acceleration leading to full recovery). The burden of these duties may be intensified by the complexity of the financing. If the lender were to fail to comply, then the guarantee might be reduced by the damages suffered by the guarantor or revoked altogether. Export credit agencies employing standard form documentation commonly insist on these restrictions and insurance and surety companies often seek them.

Assignments

26–7   The guarantee may prohibit assignments of the loan agreement or the guarantee without the consent of the guarantor so that the guarantor can keep control over the identity of the beneficiary of the guarantee.

The integrity of the beneficiary is relevant for "first demand" guarantees payable against the certificate of default because of the ease with which the beneficiary can make a wrongful drawing. Assignments may also affect the guarantor's tax liability if there is a tax grossing-up clause in the guarantee.

Retirement of guarantee

A problem in relation to bank guarantees is the difficulty faced by the guar- 26–8 antor in accelerating its liability under the guarantee. The bank may wish to do this because the financial position of its customer as indemnifying party is deteriorating, because an event of default has occurred under the back-up indemnity given by the debtor to the guarantor, such as a cross-default and the bank wishes to be able to be represented as a creditor at negotiations between the customer and its creditors, or because the guarantee is secured and the bank wishes to be able to enforce this security by reason of a breach of covenant or other creditor claims against the security, e.g. lienors. Nevertheless it is probably the case in common law countries that a guarantor cannot accelerate its liability by paying out the credit in advance of the claim becoming due. The bank cannot thus achieve an accrued claim against its customer but has to wait until a payment falls due (in which case the guarantor can pay the claim with or without a demand) or until the beneficiary of the guarantee accelerates sums payable.

A number of techniques may be employed to obviate this difficulty. The guarantor could insert a requirement in the indemnity with the customer that upon specified events of default the customer is to provide full cash cover, thereby creating an accrued debt owing by the customer to the bank guarantor. Some old English cases uphold the ability of a guarantor to accelerate the indemnity against the customer in this way. The accrual of the contingency may be treated as an agreement to provide cash collateral which, if the customer is insolvent, may run foul of fraudulent preference doctrines.

The guarantor could agree with the creditor that the guarantor will have the right to prepay the creditor on the occurrence of the specified events of default. The indemnity from the customer would provide that the customer will reimburse the bank guarantor for any prepayment made. Alternatively, the guarantor could agree with the creditor that the guarantor may at any time purchase the creditor's claim on the customer for a sum equal to principal plus interest. The guarantor could then agree with its customer that, notwithstanding the terms of the claim guaranteed, the bank on such purchase is to be entitled to call in the claim guaranteed on specified events of default.

Usually of course, the occasion for a call on the principal debtor is also an occasion for the calling of the guarantee.

Subrogation and rule against double-proof

26–9 As mentioned, if the guarantor has guaranteed the whole claim of the creditor but the amount claimable from the guarantor is subject to a lesser maximum liability and the guarantor pays up to its maximum liability, the guarantor is not entitled to prove against the bankrupt debtor and the creditor can prove for the full amount without giving credit for the part payment: *Re Rees* (1881) 17 Ch D 98, CA; *Re Sass* [1896] 2 QB 12: para 25–15. In such case the guarantor should seek to agree in advance with the creditor that the guarantor is entitled to be subrogated to such part of the creditor's claim as has been paid, that the creditor is not to be permitted to put the partial payment on suspense account and that the guarantor is to be entitled to take over a pro rata benefit of the creditor's proof. This naturally erodes the creditor's returns. Independent guarantors commonly require the creditor to assign to the guarantor the sum guaranteed upon payment of the guarantee as a reinforcement of the right of subrogation.

Set-off against cash cover

26–10 If the guarantor is relying on a set-off of the customer's reimbursement liability against a deposit owed by the guarantor to the customer, i.e. cash cover, the guarantee should state that the creditor will not submit a proof or claim in the insolvency of the customer without first calling the guarantee and giving the guarantor a grace period within which to pay. This is to protect the guarantor's loss of set-off against the insolvent customer because of the rule against double-proof: para. 25–15 *et seq*. The guarantor's claim is excluded (and hence his set-off) so long as the creditor is proving against the customer. In practice the creditor is unlikely to go to the trouble of claiming against the debtor without first calling the guarantee.

Indemnity from customer

26–11 Where a bank gives a guarantee, it is desirable that the bank should take a full form of indemnity from the customer to amplify the right of subrogation. This should entitle the bank to claim reimbursement from the customer if the bank pays out (or sets off) against a demand appearing to be in order on its face, notwithstanding that the claim guaranteed is not legally due. Without such a provision, if the bank paid out the guarantee when it was strictly not legally liable to do so, then it would not normally be able to claim an indemnity from the customer. Whether a bank can contract out of its duty to take reasonable care in paying a demand is a matter for applicable law. The English courts uphold conclusivity clauses in counter-indemnities: see, e.g. *Bache & Co (London) Ltd v Banque Vernes et Commerciale de Paris SA* [1973] 2 Lloyds Rep 437, CA. The indemnity should also contain rights on events of default, notably acceleration of the indemnity against the debtor, a right to call for cash cover and a right to compromise the guarantee, prepay the guaranteed debt, prepay the guarantee or purchase the guaranteed debt: see para 26–8.

Insurance

Where banks issue guarantees, investigation should be made first as to 26–12
whether the bank has the necessary power under applicable banking law and also whether the giving of guarantees constitutes pecuniary loss insurance business requiring special regulatory approval. Insurance business is heavily regulated in most commercial jurisdictions but often it will be found that there is an exemption for ordinary course of business banking transactions including bank guarantees.

First demand bank guarantees

Definition

A first demand bank guarantee is a guarantee issued by a bank which makes 26–13
it clear that the bank must pay under the guarantee on first demand by the beneficiary, whether or not the guaranteed claim is legally due and unpaid. The guarantee is autonomous and independent and, to a degree, is not an accessory or collateral obligation which hangs on the principal claim and stands or falls according to the existence of the principal claim.

In common law countries these are called "first demand" guarantees or indemnities; *Garantie* in Germany, as opposed to *Bürgschaft*; *garantie de banque* in France, as opposed to *cautionnement*.

The aim is that all the beneficiary has to do is to present a complying demand and, if that is on its face in order and in the absence of manifest fraud, the bank pays.

These guarantees may take the form of a documentary letter of credit guaranteeing the payment of the price of goods by buyer to seller (or constituting the means of payment), or a standby letter of credit guaranteeing a loan or equipment lease rentals, or a first demand bank guarantee making it clear that it is independent, or a contract bond or guarantee used primarily in relation to construction contracts, e.g. a performance guarantee, a bid bond, or a maintenance bond.

Policies

26–14   The objective of the beneficiary of the guarantee is to be absolutely certain that he will be paid regardless of objections by the principal. For example, a seller of goods must know that a bank letter of credit has been opened in his favour for the price before he ships the goods. The employer of construction works wishes to be sure that he is protected against the insolvency of the contractor or against defective work and that a claim for payment of damages will not be postponed indefinitely by litigation or not paid at all. An equipment lessor wishes to be sure that rentals under a finance lease will be paid, regardless of a dispute by the lessee that the equipment is defective.

The objective of banks is to be able to pay against a demand appearing on its face to be in order. They do not wish to become involved in disputes as to whether the amount is legally payable since they could as a result be forever an unwilling protagonist in commercial disputes which are nothing to do with them. If they paid wrongfully, there might be a question as to whether they could recover from their customer. They have no means of ascertaining in most cases whether the guaranteed debt is legally due. In addition, non-payment might erode public confidence in banks.

From the principal's point of view, the issue of a bank guarantee is often a convenient substitute for the provision of real security, such as a cash deposit, or a financial surcharge in the contract to compensate the other party for the increased risk.

The main risk is the abusive drawing, i.e. the beneficiary calls the guarantee and is paid, notwithstanding that the beneficiary is not entitled to be paid because the guaranteed sum is not legally due from the principal. If the bank must pay, then the effect is that the beneficiary must pay because the beneficiary must reimburse the bank. The principal is then left with a right to claim restitution from the beneficiary ("pay first, litigate later") which may be prevented, e.g. because the beneficiary is insolvent or is located in a hostile country. The obligation to reimburse the bank may itself bankrupt the principal.

The international consensus in developed countries seems to be that the international trade is fostered by enhancing the liquidity and certainty of bank guarantees, and that the only exception should be clear fraud on the part of the beneficiary. This consensus is well-documented in a study by Professors Norbert Horn and Eddy Wymeersch in "Bank Guarantees, Standby Letters of Credit and Performance Bonds in International Trade" in Horn (ed), *The Law of International Trade Finance* (1989) Kluwer, pp 455–529.

Whether guarantee is independent

Whether the guarantee is independent of the guaranted debt is entirely a 26–15
matter of contract construction. If the Uniform Customs and Practice for
Documentary Credits apply or if it is stated that the guarantee is a "letter of
credit", then the guarantee will usually be construed as being documentary
only. In other cases, the parties by the use of terms of art connoting the type
of obligation or the language, may make its status clear, e.g. "This guarantee is payable on first demand without proof of liability or evidence" or "is
payable unconditionally on presentation of a statement stating that the
guaranteed sum is due". Thus in France the Court of Appeals (November
24, 1981, D 1982 II 196) held that a "first demand" guarantee has to be
paid, irrespective of language requiring a justified request confirming that
the seller had not been performing its obligations. The court held that such a
requirement was merely to assist the seller in a dispute so that the phrase
"on first demand" effectively overrode any requirement that a valid claim be
stated.

Abusive drawings

The ready availability of the guarantee has frequently led to drawings on the 26–16
guarantee by the beneficiary when no money was due or to menacing threats
to draw unless the expiry date is extended ("pay or extend"). In some cases
the beneficiary drew on the guarantee even though the guaranteed contract
had not come into force because an authorisation had not been granted, or
the contract had been varied, or the contractor had duly completed and
obtained a completion certificate, or there were no delays or defects as
alleged, or the beneficiary was responsible for the delays, e.g. by not providing a ship or not obtaining a consent or blocking the employment of foreign
management, or the delay was caused by permitted force majeure. Often it
was clear that the drawing was simply a method of reducing the price, or
extorting other advantages in a contract dispute, or was politically motivated, as during the Iranian revolution in the late 1970s, when Iranian
entities drew on as many US guarantees as were available. In one case an
Egyptian buyer drew on a guarantee alleging a defective machine: the
machine did not work because it had not been filled with the right fuel.

  The Horn/Wymeersch study shows that developed countries recognise a
fraud exception – *abus de droit*, *Rechtmissbrauch* – on the basis that *fraus
omnia corrumpit*: "fraud unravels all". But the fraud must be manifest and
obvious and it must be known to the bank before payment so that it is, in
the words of a Dutch court, "as clear as the sun". It must be provable on the
spot (*pronta e liquide*) or "manifestly arbitrary" or "a manifest abuse on

first glance" or a "blatant and serious breach" (*offensichtlich und schwer*). The reason for immediate obviousness is that the integrity of payouts would be eroded if payments were delayed beyond a few days. This is broadly the position taken by the courts of Belgium, England, France, Italy, Luxembourg, the Netherlands and the United States.

26–17   The usual chain of events is that the principal, fearing an abusive draw, brings an action against the bank for an interim injunction restraining the bank from making a payment. Most developed countries allow temporary injunctions on the basis of limited proof and without a full hearing of both sides provided that a clear case is made out and there is a risk of irreparable harm if the injunction is not granted: the tests are elaborated in the United States in *Caulfield v Board of Education*, 583 F 2d 605 (2d Cir 1978), in England in *American Cyanamid Co v Ethicon Ltd* [1975] AC 396, in Germany in decisions under ZPO Art 935 *et seq* (*einstweilige Verfügung* – the interim injunction), in Belgium under Art 584 of the Code of Civil Procedure, in Italy under Art 700 of the Italian Code of Civil Procedure, and in Switzerland under Cantonal law (where the claim must be *rigoureusement vraisemblable*).

A few case law examples will suffice. In the United States, it has frequently been held than an account party can enjoin an issuer from paying out only if he can show fraud or forgery: see *Sztein v J Henry Schroder Banking Corporation*, 117 Misc 719, 31 NYS 2d 631 (1941). The English case of *Discount Records Ltd v Barclays Bank Ltd* [1975] 1 WLR 315 is to the same effect. The fraud exception has been codified in s 5–114 of the Uniform Commercial Code. This entitles the issuer to decline payment where a required document "is forged or fraudulent or there is fraud in the transaction".

> A leading American case is *Dynamics Corporation of America v Citizens & Southern National Bank*, 356 F Supp 991 (ND Cal 1973). The case involved a sale of defence-related equipment to India. The letter of credit required a certification signed by the President of India that the plaintiff corporation had not carried out its obligations under the sales contract. The plaintiff contended that the certification was fraudulent because the plaintiff had in fact fully performed the contract. *Held*: the court would grant a preliminary injunction. India was entitled to be paid if "India has a bona fide legal claim of breach of contract to assert" even if that claim was in fact wrong in law. On the other hand, India would "not be allowed to take unconscientious advantage of the situation and run off with the plaintiff's money on a pro forma declaration which has absolutely no basis in fact".

In the United States, the beneficiary can therefore claim if he is in good faith and has some factual basis for the claim but not where there is obviously no factual or legal basis for the claim so that the claim is inevitably fraudulent. In numerous cases following the Iranian revolution, the courts ordered injunctions and were clearly influenced by the fact that any actions for recovery by American exporters against the Iranian beneficiaries in Iran would be useless, e.g. *Itek Corp v First National Bank of Boston*, 511 F Supp 1341 (D Mass 1981); *Wyle v Bank Melli*, 577 F Supp 1148 (1983) (case was based on "evil intent"); *Rockwell International Systems Inc v Citibank NA*, 719 F 2d 583 (1983 USCA 2d Cir).

> In *KMW International v The Chase Manhattan, Bank NA*, 606 F 2d 10 (2d Cir 1979), a bank opened an irrevocable letter of credit for the account of KMW in favour of an Iranian bank. KMW sought a temporary restraining order enjoining the bank from making any payment on the ground that, as a result of the Iranian revolution in 1979, the underlying contract had been wholly frustrated and therefore any drawing on the credit would of necessity be fraudulent. *Held*: there was nothing in the UCC or the UCP excusing an issuing bank from paying a letter of credit because of supervening illegality, impossibility, war or insurrection. These were not the equivalent of fraud.

However, during the litigation following on the 1979 Iranian revolution some US courts were prepared to issue a "notice" injunction imposing a short delay period so as to give the party time to produce evidence of fraud since, under Art 8(d) of the UCP, an issuer as a matter of commercial practice has a "reasonable time" to examine documents without incurring liability for non-payment.

The English courts limit the fraud exception and probably adopt one of   **26–18**
the most stringent attitudes internationally.

> In *Edward Owen Engineering Ltd v Barclays Bank International Ltd* [1978] 1 Lloyds Rep 166, Browne LJ said (at 172): "[I]t is well-established that . . . the confirming bank is not in any way concerned with disputes between the buyers and the sellers under the contract of sale which underlies the credit. But I agree also that it is established that there is at any rate one exception to this rule . . . That exception is that where the documents under the credit are presented by the beneficiary himself and the bank knows when the documents are presented that they are forged or fraudulent, the bank is entitled to refuse payment. But it is certainly not enough to allege fraud; it must be 'established' and in such circumstances I should say very clearly 'established'." See also *Bolivinter Oil SA v The Chase Manhattan Bank, NA* [1984] 1 All ER 351n, CA.

> In *United City Merchants (Investments) Ltd v Royal Bank of Canada* [1982] 2 All ER 720, HL, a shipping agent falsely and fraudulently entered the wrong date of shipment on the bill of lading so as to bring it within the presentation date prescribed by the letter of credit. At the time of presentation, the beneficiary of the credit did not know of the fraud. *Held* by the House of Lords: letters

of credits must be paid subject to the one established exception, that is "where the seller, for the purpose of drawing on the credit, fraudulently presents to the confirming bank documents that contain, expressly or by implication, material representations of fact that to his knowledge are untrue" (p 725). However, as the beneficiary of the credit did not know of the fraud, the exception did not apply and the bank was bound to pay.

The Ontario case of *Rosen v Pullen* (1981) 126 DLR (3d) 62 illustrates the sweet uses to which a standby letter of credit can be put.

Mr Rosen issued a letter of credit to Ms Pullen. It was alleged that the underlying agreement was that the letter of credit could only be drawn if Ms Pullen resided with Mr Rosen and Mr Rosen failed to marry Ms Pullen by March 1982. Ms Pullen purported to draw US$100,000 on the letter of credit. *Held*: Mr Rosen had made out a good prima facie case of fraud because Ms Pullen knew that she was not entitled to those proceeds and this, if proved, would constitute fraud.

Attachment of proceeds

26–19   A device sometimes attempted where the seller has defaulted on the underlying contract is for the buyer to obtain judgment against the seller and attach the proceeds of the letter of credit. If successful, the attachment would frustrate the purpose of a letter of credit as an irrevocable means of payment notwithstanding the underlying contract.

The English courts will not usually order an attachment or Mareva injunction.

In the English case of *Power Curber International Ltd v National Bank of Kuwait SAK* [1981] 3 All ER 607, CA, Kuwaiti buyers gave instructions for the opening of an irrevocable letter of credit to the National Bank of Kuwait which issued the letter of credit through a bank in North Carolina. The Kuwait buyers obtained from a Kuwaiti court an order for provisional attachment of the sums payable by National Bank of Kuwait under the credit. The beneficiary of the credit started proceedings in England against the National Bank of Kuwait irrespective of the Kuwaiti order forbidding the bank to pay. *Held*: the bank must pay. Lord Denning MR said that "it is part of the law of international trade that letters of credit should be honoured and not nullified by attachment order at the suit of the buyer . . . the buyer himself by his conduct has precluded himself from asking for an attachment order . . . He has contracted under the terms of the Uniform Customs and Practice by which he promises that the bank will pay without regard to any set-off or counterclaim and implicitly that he will not seek an attachment order."

In France, any creditor may exercise a *saisie-arret* in order to attach   **26–20**
personal property of his debtor in the hands of third parties if the creditor's
rights are based on documentary evidence: CCP Art 557–8. Where such
evidence is missing an order of attachment may nevertheless be granted at
the court's discretion. Previous French cases had been contrary to the view
taken by the courts of most other commercial countries as to the inviolabi-
lity of letters of credit but later decisions changed the French position.

> In the decision of the French Court of Cassation of October 14, 1981; JCP
> 1982, 19815, the buyer alleged breach of the underlying sale contract and on
> the basis of the claim attached, by means of a *saisie-arret* issued against the
> bank, the amount accrued under the letter of credit. *Held*: when an issuing
> bank receives documents complying with the terms of a letter of credit it must
> make payment to the beneficiary. The buyer is not entitled to obtain a *saisie-
> arret* or a sequestration order in order to preclude payment. When the buyer
> furnishes an irrevocable credit in the beneficiary's name, he agrees not to inter-
> fere with the rights accrued by the beneficiary under the letter of credit.

> In the decision of the Court of Appeal of Paris of October 27, 1981 (JCP 1981.
> II.19702) the court refused to uphold a *saisie conservatoire* whereby the appli-
> cant for the credit sought to attach the proceeds of a standby letter of credit
> issued in respect of a charterparty. See also Cass, March 18, 1986, JCP 1986
> 20624.

According to the Horn/Wymeersch study, the refusal to allow the principal to block the payment by the side-wind of a seizure (the German *Arrest*,
the French *saisie-arret*, the US prejudgment attachment) is more or less
adopted by many courts – in Belgium, England, France, Germany, Italy, the
Netherlands and Switzerland.

CHAPTER 27

COMFORT LETTERS

Meaning of comfort letters

27–1   A comfort letter is a letter, written usually by a parent company or even by a government, to the lender giving comfort to the lender about a loan made to a subsidiary or a public entity.

Comfort letters are commonly taken where the "guarantor" is not willing to accept a legal commitment. This may be, e.g. because a guarantee would infringe guarantee limits in its constitution or borrowing instruments or because it does not wish a contingent liability to appear on its balance sheet, or simply because the only support on offer is this comfort.

A commercial agreement is deemed to be legally binding unless otherwise clearly stated: see *Edwards v Skyways Ltd* [1964] 1 All ER 494; however, it is open to the parties to state that an agreement is binding in honour only: *Jones v Vernon's Pools Ltd* [1938] 2 All ER 626. If an agreement states that it is not legally binding, then a liquidator would be bound to disregard it.

Even if the letter is legally binding, its terms are often so woolly and the commitments of such limited effect that the letter does not give rise to substantial rights. Although a comfort letter is sometimes thought to enable a parent to justify a payment to a lender to protect its reputation, a company which pays out money to meet a non-legally binding obligation may be wasting corporate assets in breach of duty to shareholders and creditors. Comfort letters also do not usually contain the protective clauses appearing in formal guarantees.

In essence, comfort letters are only of use where a shadow of a guarantee is considered better than nothing at all (only just). They are inappropriate for lenders who require a serious legal claim.

Terms of comfort letters

27–2   The points usually covered are (a) a statement of awareness of the financing, (b) a commitment to maintain ownership interest, and (c) the degree of support required by the lender.

Awareness of financing The parent states that it is aware of the proposed loan and approves of it. Such a statement is intended to prevent the parent, morally speaking, from afterwards objecting that the subsidiary went off on a frolic on its own with the connivance of the lender thereby absolving the parent from commercial responsibility. The statement has no legal effect in guarantee terms. But the statement may estop the parent from afterwards objecting that the directors of the subsidiary were guilty of misfeasance in giving the guarantee.

The parent may state that it has complete confidence in the management of the subsidiary: this must be judged according to the usual principles of misrepresentation law.

Maintenance of ownership interest The parent agrees to maintain a speci- 27–3 fied percentage interest in the share capital of the borrower so long as the loan is outstanding. Although an injunction may possibly be available to prevent a threatened breach, such a commitment would not normally give rise to a right to damages if ownership were lost and subsequently the subsidiary became insolvent since a shareholder is not liable for the debts of the company. There might conceivably be liability if in the particular circumstances the sale caused a termination of lines of credit available to the subsidiary and the insolvency resulted directly from that termination. It would have to be proved that these results were in the contemplation of the parties at the time the comfort letter was given and that they were a direct result of the sale.

Normally the ownership statement merely confers commercial comfort in the expectation that parent companies usually do not allow their subsidiaries to sink.

Sometimes it is stated that, if the parent ceases to own the borrowing subsidiary, it will give a guarantee to the lender of the subsidiary's obligations. If the terms of the guarantee were not clearly stated, the statement may be merely an unenforceable agreement to agree. A contract to give a guarantee should be buttressed by the same protective clauses as a guarantee itself.

Support The terms of the financial support vary widely and their legal effect 27–4 depends upon ordinary principles of contract law and rules of construction. Usual general defects, however, are that: the language is too vague to give rise to enforceable obligations; the remedy is usually a right of damages rather than a claim for a liquidated sum and there may be difficulties and delays in proving these; it may be difficult to show that the loss was directly caused by the breach; sometimes it may be necessary to wind up the borrower to see whether or not it is insolvent in order to show a breach of the undertaking; the undertaking is generally weakened by the absence of protective "guarantee" clauses on the lines discussed above; all commercial contracts of this type are more vulnerable to the defence of force majeure.

The assurance is often expressed as an intention, e.g. "it is our intention" that the subsidiary will meet its financial obligations or "it is our policy that our subsidiaries' obligations will be met", or that "it is our present policy that no group company should become bankrupt". An expression of present intention gives no assurances as to the future: intentions may change. While there might be liability for misrepresentation if the parent never had such an intention or policy, then, even if this could be proved, it would normally be difficult to show that the loss of the loan flowed from the absence of the parent's intention as at a particular date. See the case law cited below.

27–5   The following are common formulations:

Management   The parent states that it will "do everything in its power to ensure that the subsidiary is properly managed in accordance with prudent fiscal policies" or that the parent will "exercise its share capital voting rights to ensure that the subsidiary pay its creditors when due". Apart from the woolliness of the obligation, the lender may be unable to prove that his loss flowed from a breach: insolvency may not result from bad management.

No asset-stripping   The parent states that "we shall not receive moneys from our subsidiary if as a result it would not be able to meet its obligations". The parent agrees not to take money out: but it does not agree to put money in. Proving that a dividend or intercompany loan results in the subsidiary's insolvency and that the loss was not caused by, say, a drop in market, bad management or governmental policies, might be difficult, especially where there is a time-lag between the payment out and the insolvency.

Funding   The parent agrees that it will "provide our subsidiary with the necessary means to fulfil its financial obligations". Substantive damages would flow from breach of this obligation, which is similar to a full guarantee, albeit without protective "guarantee" clauses.

Case law on comfort letters

27–6   Cases on comfort letters are of interest. The English courts treat them as intended to create a contract but lean against converting comfort letters into guarantees and construe them against the creditor: no doubt the reason is that, if the creditor wanted a formal guarantee, he should have asked for one.

In *Chemco Leasing SpA v Rediffusion plc* (1987) 1 FTLR 201, CA, a parent company stated in a letter of comfort to Chemco that, if it disposed of its interest in its subsidiary, "we undertake to take over the remaining liabilities to Chemco of [the subsidiary] should the new shareholders be unacceptable to Chemco". *Held*: these words made the parent liable as guarantor, but the parent escaped liability because Chemco had failed to comply with an implied obligation to give reasonable notice that the new shareholders were not acceptable to it.

In *Kleinwort Benson Ltd v Malaysian Mining Corpn Bhd* [1989] 1 All ER 785, [1989] 1 WLR 379, CA, the parent stated in its comfort letter: "It is our policy to ensure that the business of [our subsidiary] is at all times in a position to meet its liabilities to you." *Held*: the parent was not liable. It merely stated its present policy which could be changed at any time in the future.

In *Re Augustus Barnett & Son Ltd* (1986) 2 BCC 98,904 the company was a wholly-owned subsidiary of a Spanish company. The subsidiary traded at a loss for some time, but the parent company issued statements to the effect that it would continue to support the subsidiary. These statements appeared in "comfort letters" sent to the subsidiary's auditors and published in its annual accounts for three successive years. The subsidiary went into liquidation. *Held*: the parent company had an honest intent to support the subsidiary at the time the statements were made. It later changed its mind, but its early "comfort letter" statements were not fraudulent.

Contrast *Banque Brussels Lambert v Australian National Industries Ltd* (1989) NSW S Ct, in which the parent company said in its comfort letter to the banks that "it is our practice to ensure that our affiliate . . . will at all times be in a position to meet its financial obligations as they fall due", including repayment of obligations to the bank. *Held*: the parent company was liable. See also *Capital Financial Group Ltd v Rothwells Ltd* (1993) 30 NSWLR 619.

In the United States, the familiar process of construing the terms of the   27–7
engagement meticulously was followed in *Hernado Bank v Bryant Electric Co Inc*, 357 F Supp 575 (DC Miss 1973).

Bryant partially took over a company which was indebted to the bank. Bryant gave notice of its new ownership and said, with respect to outstanding loans, that it would "do everything possible to see that this is settled as per agreement". *Held*: Bryant had not guaranteed the debts of the company.

In the Washington case of *Exchange National Bank of Spokane v Pantages*, 133 P 1025 (SC Wash 1913) the shareholder of a company asked the bank for a loan and sent a telegram to the bank's officer: "tell bank I request them to renew the note . . . I will arrange things satisfactory to them upon my return . . . " *Held*: the shareholder guaranteed the loan. The bank relied on the assurance in renewing the loan instead of enforcing it and the shareholder was aware of the bank's expectation. See also *Nimrod Marketing (Overseas) Ltd v Texas Energy Investment Corp*, 769 F 2d 1076 (5th Cir 1985).

27–8   In France and Germany, there has been much discussion in the literature as to whether comfort letters strictly fall within the definition of a proper guarantee in the civil code, but it would appear that the discussion is not of great relevance since the letter is a contract, usually, and has to be construed like any other contract. For example, a Stuttgart court upheld the obligation of the issuer of a letter to supply sufficient funds to a group company when the group company became bankrupt: OLG Stuttgart (1985) WM at 455.
There have been a number of decisions in France.

> In a 1979 decision of the Court of Appeal of Paris (Vasseur DS 1980, IR 55) a company wrote to the bank and said that it would "do everything necessary in order that the subsidiary would have available sufficient assets to permit it to meet its obligations which it contracted towards the bank". *Held*: the company was responsible in damages if the subsidiary did not pay the bank.

> In 1985 the Court of Appeal of Montpellier (DS 1985, IR 341) came to a similar conclusion where a majority shareholder informed the bank that "we confirm our intention to follow and to support our affiliate in its financial needs and, if it becomes necessary, to substitute ourselves for it in order to meet all its engagements that it may undertake towards you, our care being to ensure in permanent fashion its total solvency. We confirm our intention, in case of necessity, immediately to effect the necessary steps . . . to obtain authorisation for the transfer of the funds". *Held*: the majority shareholder was liable. Indeed one could hardly have had a clearer expression of obligation.

Some of the above decisions are cited in an article by Georg Wittuhn, 35 *Revue de Droit de McGill* 490 (1990).

CHAPTER 28

STANDBY LETTERS OF CREDIT

Generally

A letter of credit is a letter issued by one party (the issuer) to another (the   **28–1** beneficiary) at the request of a third party (the account party) whereby the issuer must pay the beneficiary a stipulated sum (or accept a draft) upon presentation of specified documents. Instead of issuing a guarantee therefore a guarantor can at the request of the borrower issue a standby letter of credit to the lender under which the lender may draw on presentation of a certificate that the loan is in default.

The oldest form of letter of credit was probably the traveller's letter of credit which was issued by the Kings of England in the thirteenth century to emissaries travelling to Rome to enable the traveller to draw funds without having to carry large amounts of money with him. The commercial letter of credit appeared at the beginning of the nineteenth century and the standby credit as an offshoot probably in the middle of the twentieth century.

The standby credit has been extensively used in the United States by banks because of the limited powers of banks under the National Bank Act to give guarantees, even though the instrument is almost identical in economic substance to a first demand guarantee. Generally guarantees issued by United States banks are ultra vires although there are exemptions in favour of overseas branches if banking practice in the jurisdiction concerned permits guarantee business. A ruling of the Controller of Currency of the United States (12 CFR Art 7.7016 (1975)) requires the following characteristics to establish the obligation as an intra vires letter of credit:

> "[T]he bank must receive a fee or other valid business consideration for the issuance of its undertaking; (b) the bank's undertaking must contain a specified expiration date or be for a definite term; (c) the bank's undertaking must not be unlimited but be up to a stated amount; (d) the bank's obligation to pay must arise only upon the presentation of specific documents and the bank must not be called upon to determine disputed questions of fact or law; (e) the bank's customer must have an unqualified obligation to reimburse the bank on the same condition as the bank has paid."

The essential characteristic of a standby letter of credit is that it is independent from the underlying loan contract, i.e. it pays against provision

---

of documents, such as a certificate of default, and does not require the issuer to examine whether or not there has actually been a default under the loan agreement: see the leading United States case of *Barclays Bank DCO v Mercantile National Bank*, 339 F Supp 457 (1972), affirmed 481 F 2d 1224 (5th Cir 1973).

> In *Wichita Eagle and Beacon Publishing Co Inc v Pacific National Bank*, 343 F Supp 332 (1971), reversed 493 F, 2d 1285 (9th Cir 1974), it was held that a credit payable on default by the account party under a contract to erect a building was a guarantee but would not have been a guarantee if payment were dependent upon the provision of a certificate stating that there had been a default.

Application of Codes

28–2 The Uniform Customs and Practice for Documentary Credits (1993 Revision), produced by the International Chamber of Commerce, is a code of rules applying to documentary letters of credit which parties are free to incorporate into their documents. However, the UCP can apparently apply only where the payment is made against "stipulated document(s)" (i.e. the credit must be documentary: the UCP is not concerned with "clean" credits) and only if the issuer is a "bank" (see Art 2), although plainly the parties can modify this. Standby letters of credit are specifically contemplated: Art 1.

In the United States, Art 5 of the Uniform Commercial Code (which has been adopted with local modifications by most states in the United States) partially codifies some of the rules relating to letters of credit, although generally these may be excluded by agreement.

Consideration

28–3 Consideration is required for a guarantee but not for a letter of credit: see *Malas v British Imex Industries Ltd* [1958] 2 QB 127. The United States authority is *Barclays Bank DCO v Mercantile National Bank*, 339 F Supp 457 (1972), affirmed 481 F 2d 1224 (5th Cir 1973), where it was held that Art 5 of the UCC excluded the consideration requirement.

Revocability

28–4 A letter of credit will usually state whether it is revocable or irrevocable. A revocable credit is a useless security from the point of view of a lender. If the instrument is silent on revocability then in the normal case the document will be construed as irrevocable in order to give it business efficacy: *West Virginia Housing Development Fund v Sroka*, 415 F Supp 1107 (1976).

If the Uniform Customs are incorporated into the instrument, the credit will be deemed irrevocable: Art 6c.

Primary obligation

Since the letter of credit is independent of the underlying transaction, the   28–5
issuer has a primary obligation which is binding even if the underlying transaction is void: see *Savage v First National Bank and Trust Co*, 413 F Supp 447 (1976). But the beneficiary might in such a case have difficulty in presenting a valid claim.

Wrongful drawings

Under the UCP, letters of credit are separate transactions from the contracts   28–6
on which they may be based and the obligation of the bank to pay is not subject to claims or defences of the applicant resulting from his relationship with the beneficiary. The parties deal only with documents: Arts 3 and 4. Because a standby letter of credit is usually payable, not on the provision of shipping and other documents indicating performance by a seller, but on a simple certificate of the beneficiary that there has been a default on the claim covered by the standby, there is a risk of a wrongful draw by a beneficiary who is determined to be paid even though he is not entitled to be paid under the underlying contract. As a general rule, case law in many jurisdictions has insisted that, in the interests of the commercial stability of letters of credit, standby credits must be honoured if the document presented is on its face in order unless there is a clear showing of fraud. Courts have differed as to the scope of the fraud and the onus is upon the parties seeking relief to make out a clear showing of fraud in order to obtain relief, e.g. the money is clearly not payable or a document is a forgery. There has been much litigation on the subject. See para 26–16 *et seq*.

Conformity of documents

Strict compliance by the documents furnished with those required by the   28–7
standby letter of credit is one of the fundamental doctrines of commercial credits. However, the issuer merely has to establish that the documents are correct "on their face" and does not have to establish their truth or falsity. This rule is not likely to be of great importance in relation to standby credits

used in this context because the document usually required to be tendered, e.g. a certificate of default, will usually be simple enough not to give rise to questions of compliance.

Application of guarantee law

28–8　Consideration should be given as to whether the general doctrines of suretyship apply in relation to standby letters of credit, e.g. lapse because of extensions of time or variations and diminution on account of release of security. Consideration should also be given, in the case of standbys which do not cover the whole of the beneficiary's claim, as to whether the insolvency rule against double-proof would prevent a bank, which has paid up to its maximum liability under the standby, from proving in the insolvency of its customer so long as the beneficiary were proving in the insolvency: para 25–15. In principle, suretyship law should continue to apply to a transaction which is in substance a contract of suretyship, except as modified by the terms of the contract, e.g. the bank must pay against a conforming document and the principle that these obligations are to a degree independent of the obligation guaranteed.

Assignments

The UCP contemplates only assignments of proceeds (Art 49) and transfers (see Art 48). A transfer is different from an assignment. A specific assignment clause should be inserted, if appropriate.

CHAPTER 29

OTHER FORMS OF GUARANTEE

Project finance "guarantees"

Contracts showing some features of guarantees are commonly found in   **29–1**
project finance. For example, under a **purchase agreement** the "guarantor"
agrees to purchase the principal debt on default. The main difference is that
breach results in damages, not a liquidated demand for the whole debt.
Under a **completion guarantee** the "guarantor" guarantees that the works
will be completed by a specified date. Breach results in damages, not specific
performance. The damages are the real loss, e.g. there would be no damages
if the debtor would not be able to pay even if the project had been completed on time. Under an **investment agreement**, the "guarantor" agrees to
invest in the debtor by subordinated loan or equity subscription, e.g. if there
is a cost overrun. Again the remedy for breach is damages and usually there
is no right to compel the "guarantor" to invest. The obligation may not be
performable if the debtor is in liquidation because the debtor can no longer
borrow or issue shares. Under a **take-or-pay contract**, the "guarantor"
agrees to pay a stipulated minimum sum for goods or services from the project, whether or not he takes them, regardless of defects or non-supply and
regardless of force majeure.

These quasi-guarantees are described in more detail in a chapter on project finance in another work in this series on financial law.

Avals on negotiable instruments

A negotiable instrument may be guaranteed by an "*aval*" which is a simple   **29–2**
signature on the instrument by the "guarantor", with the addition of the
words "*bon pour aval*" or other equivalent phrase and (although not
necessarily) with the identity of the party guaranteed. These avals are
restricted in English law because guarantees must be in writing (Statute of

Frauds 1877 s 4) and there is obscure case law as to when a simple signature is enough.

Contract bonds and guarantees

29–3　These are guarantees issued by a bank or surety company to guarantee the performance of a commercial contract, e.g. the sale of goods or for construction work, as opposed to a loan or other financial contract. Examples are:

- a **performance bond** whereby the guarantor guarantees that the seller or contractor will perform the contract in favour of the buyer or employer;

- a **bid or tender bond** whereby the guarantor guarantees to an employer for construction work that the contractor bidding or tendering for the contract will enter into the contract if it is granted to that contractor – so as to cover the employer's expenses of the tendering and negotiation process;

- an **advance payment bond** whereby the guarantor guarantees to a buyer or employer that any advance payment, which is made by the latter to the seller or contractor, of the price for the goods or works will be repaid if the seller does not deliver the goods or the contractor does not carry out the works;

- a **retention money bond** whereby the guarantor gives a guarantee to an employer that any retention from the price which the employer is entitled to withhold until the work is completed but which is paid in advance to the contractor, will be repaid if the work is not completed;

- a **maintenance bond** whereby the guarantor gives a guarantee to the employer that any maintenance and repair work which the contractor must carry out during the post-completion warranty period, will be duly carried out by the contractor.

These bonds may be made subject to the Uniform Rules for Contract Guarantees of 1978 published by the International Chamber of Commerce (No 325), the ICC Uniform Rules of Contract Bonds of 1993 (No 524), or the Uniform Rules for Demand Guarantees (No 458).

In each case one of the most important questions is whether the beneficiary can call the bond on first demand without proof of a default in the absence of manifest fraud: para 26–14 *et seq*. Some bonds are of the "first demand without proof of liability" type, while others are accessory to the principal contract, and require the beneficiary to prove a default by the contractor or require the submission of a court or arbitral award as a condition of a drawing.

Residual value guarantees

Under a residual value guarantee, a manufacturer agrees to pay to the lessor   29–4
of the equipment who has purchased the equipment from the manufacturer
and leased it to an operator, any shortfall in the value of the equipment on
the expiry or earlier termination of the lease. These guarantees were developed primarily by aircraft manufacturers to support the sales of their aircraft. These residual value guarantees specify the amount of the guarantee,
the time at which the residual value is determined, how it is determined
(actual sale or valuation), the exclusion of the guarantor's responsibility for
reduction in the sale price by reason of sales taxes, currency losses, the
lessee's failure to maintain, liens and the like, and the position if the equipment cannot be sold, e.g. because it is destroyed, or frozen by a bankruptcy
order against the lessee, or is expropriated or requisitioned.

Guarantees by deed poll

In most systems of law, guarantees are unilateral contracts which do not   29–5
have to be signed by the beneficiaries of the contract, and in English law a
bank which agrees to make a loan in reliance on a guarantee addressed to
the bank can rely on the guarantee if it makes the loan. In the case of note or
commercial paper issues, it is English market practice for any guarantee to
be given by a deed poll which is a unilateral guarantee given by the guarantor in favour of the noteholders and executed under seal (historically to indicate seriousness of contractual intent). The noteholders do not sign the
guarantee. They can take advantage of the guarantee without being named
provided that they can be identified with sufficient particularity even though
they are future noteholders. This ancient but useful process obviates the
need to endorse the guarantee on the notes or to assign it separately. A deed
poll is so called because the parchment on which it was written was shaved
even or polled at the top, as compared to an indenture which was cut with a
waving or indented line at the top. But shaving the paper is not a legal
requirement and it is not necessary to bring along a pair of scissors to the
completion meeting.

Syndicated guarantees

Generally

A guarantee may be syndicated amongst a group of banks to spread the risk.   29–6
A syndicated guarantee follows conventional syndication principles, namely

syndicate severality, syndicate democracy, pro rata sharing, and the appointment of an agent bank. The agreement will contain a commitment to issue the guarantee, conditions precedent, guarantee commission, the principal's reimbursement indemnity, payments clause, tax grossing-up, increased cost clause, illegality clause, representations and warranties, covenants, events of default, agency clause, and the usual boiler-plate, e.g. notices, default interest, set-off, assignments, governing law, jurisdiction and waiver of any immunity. These clauses are discussed in another work in this series.

Severability of obligations

29–7   The guarantee is commonly expressed to be the several obligation of the banks in the stated shares so that each bank is responsible only for its own portion: the banks do not underwrite each other. But sometimes the guarantee is issued by one bank which is counter-indemnified by the other banks who are in turn counter-indemnified by the principal: in this case the bank issuing the guarantee takes a risk on the other banks which should be reflected in its risk-asset ratio for capital adequacy purposes (and which is not a favoured structure).

Prepayments of guarantee

29–8   In the case of a syndicated loan, the borrower can usually prepay the banks pro rata, can prepay individual banks under the increased cost and tax grossing-up clauses and must prepay an individual bank under the illegality clause. These clauses are discussed in another work in this series. But in the case of a syndicated guarantee, these "prepayments" are not possible since a release of a syndicate member requires the consent of the beneficiary of the guarantee to the release: a compulsory release would not appear in the guarantee. Hence the principal bears a greater risk on tax grossing-up and increased costs and the banks bear a greater risk on the illegality clause (although the risks in practice are small). Whether a right of the principal to deposit cash collateral would help is a matter for consideration. Cash deposited with a guarantor which is a bank would raise questions of whether the guarantor relies on set-off or a charge-back: see chapter 5. Prepayment of the guaranteed debt could also be considered.

Cash cover on default

29–9   If an event of default occurs, the banks should have the right to call for cash cover from the principal and should in the guarantee have the right to retire the guarantee by payment: see para 25–15 for the background to this.

Subsequent participations

A guarantee may be subsequently syndicated without the involvement of the   29–10
borrower. Severalising the guarantee itself would require the consent of the
guarantor, but novation clauses have appeared which set out a procedure
whereby banks can novate their obligations to other banks without consent,
but usually only to incoming banks satisfying prescribed eligibility qualifications, e.g. as to credit-rating and location. Aside from pre-agreed syndica-
tions, any incoming bank would typically give a proportionate counter-
indemnity to the bank which has issued the guarantee.

If the principal has not requested the incoming bank to give the guarantee, the bank may not be entitled to an indemnity from the principal by
reason of the inconvenient decision in *Owen v Tate* [1976] QB 402, CA,
that an uninvited payment of another's debt by a third party does not give
rise to a right of indemnity – he is a busy bystander who should not have
interfered. While it is considered likely that the bank would have a statutory
right of subrogation if the lead bank accepts the payment under the Mercantile Law Amendments Act 1856 s 5, the safe course is for the lead bank to
agree to assign the appropriate portion of its rights against the principal to
the incoming bank when the lead bank pays. There must be no express or
implied restriction on assignability, e.g. a requirement for the express consent of the principal, or an implied prohibition springing from the banker's
duty of confidentiality.

Guarantees of financial leases

Where a lessor leases big-ticket equipment, such as an aircraft or ship, under   29–11
a financial lease, it is relatively common for the obligations of the lessee to
the lessor to be guaranteed by a bank guarantee.

Thus, in project finance, part of the capital may be provided by bank
loans and another part by a financial lease of heavy equipment or plant and
the main lending banks then give a guarantee to the lessor.

The usual structure is that a bank or syndicate of banks gives a guarantee
to the lessor of the obligations of the lessee to the lessor under the financial
lease. The guarantee is usually of the "first demand bank guarantee" type or
a standby letter of credit which is drawable on simple submission of a certificate that the lessee is in default in stating the amount payable, i.e. it is not
an accessory guarantee: see para 26–13 *et seq* for a discussion.

The lessee agrees in normal form to indemnify the bank guarantor in case
the bank guarantor should be obliged to pay under the guarantee and, as
security for its liability to reimburse the bank, assigns its rights under the

lease to the bank. The lessee may also give other security, e.g. fixed and floating charges over all its other assets. The main right which the lessee has under the lease, apart from the right to use the equipment, is a right to any surplus of the proceeds of sale if the lessor should, on a default by the lessee, sell the equipment. Most financial leases provide that on such a sale the lessor must, after paying itself any outstanding rentals and the present value of future rentals, pay any surplus to the lessee by way of rebate of rental (less a commission) so that in effect the lessee gets back the surplus value of the equipment, just as he would if he actually owned the equipment and had mortgaged it to the lessor.

The guarantee agreement between the bank guarantor and the lessor will usually contain provisions as to the exercise of this right of sale on default by the lessee and sometimes give the guarantor a right to compel the lessor to exercise his rights on a default.

29–12   One possible weakness of this structure is that the bank guarantor takes the risk of liens imposed on the equipment (flowing either from unpaid debts of the lessor or the lessee) which would dilute the proceeds of sale. The bank guarantor is also exposed to the bankruptcy of the lessor, in which event the enforcement of the duty to sell and account for proceeds may be somewhat complicated. These risks can be obviated if the lessor grants to the bank guarantor a mortgage over the equipment (which it owns) by way of collateral security, without personal liability, for the liabilities of the lessee to the bank under the reimbursement indemnity. But many financial lessors are not willing to grant security over their assets and furthermore they may argue that they require access to the unencumbered equipment which they own in order to have a fund out of which to recover any liabilities of the lessee which are not covered by the guarantee. For example, lease guarantees commonly cover only the fixed amount of the rentals, plus the stipulated termination sum, and do not cover indemnities given by the lessee to the lessor in respect of taxes imposed on the lessor or other owner liabilities imposed on the lessor, e.g. for pollution or personal injury or death caused by the equipment to third parties. Bank guarantors could not provide unlimited guarantees against these risks, since either by practice or bank regulation, bank guarantees must be limited in amount.

The awkwardness of this structure illustrates one of the differences between title finance and ordinary security. If, instead of a financial lease, the lessee acquired the equipment, borrowed money from the lessor and mortgaged the equipment to the lessor to secure the loan, then the bank guarantee would be a guarantee of the loan and, on payment, the bank guarantor would be subrogated to the lessor's rights against the lessee together with the benefit of the mortgage over the equipment. In the case of a financial lease, the lessor is the owner of the equipment and the lessee has no beneficial ownership to mortgage to the creditor. Further, it seems doubtful that the doctrine of subrogation would permit the bank guarantor, on payment, to take over the lessor's beneficial ownership of the equipment leased, but only to take over the lessor's rights against the lessee under the lease by subrogation. The lessor could of course agree to transfer title to the equipment to the bank guarantor on payment, but the impact of this on the tax treatment of the lease would have to be considered and further the lessor may be unwilling to transfer title so long as it was unsure whether or not its potential liabilities as owner of the equipment and the responsibilities of the lessee under the various indemnities had completely disappeared.

PART IV

PREFERENCES

CHAPTER 30

AVOIDANCE OF SECURITY AND GUARANTEES AS PREFERENCES: INTRODUCTION

Introduction

These chapters select material from chapters in another work (on inter- **30–1**
national insolvency) in this series of books on international financial law –
chapters which discuss the comparative law of insolvency preferences and
which cover most of the world's jurisdictions. The focus in this chapter is
purely on security and guarantees and not, for example, on the application
of preference doctrines to payments, set-offs, compensating contracts,
transfers of a business, judicial executions or the like. The review here does
not deal with the application of preference doctrines to financial assistance
given by a company for the purpose of acquiring its own shares. The reader
is referred to the other work on the principles of international insolvency
law for a treatment of these topics and for a fuller treatment of the areas
summarised below.

Policies

All developed bankruptcy laws provide for the recapture of assets trans- **30–2**
ferred by the debtor in the twilight suspect period prior to the commencement of formal insolvency proceedings.

The fundamental and universal requirements qualifying a transaction as
preferential are that the transaction:

— prejudices other creditors of the debtor, and

— occurs while the debtor is actually insolvent or renders him insolvent,
and

— occurs in a suspect period prior to the formal opening of insolvency proceedings.

The first item is always required. The other two are usually required but there are exceptions, e.g. in the case of deliberate concealment.

30–3   The objectives are as follows:

- **Fraud** The main and original object is to prevent the debtor from fraudulently concealing or transferring his assets beyond the reach of his creditors when he knows that his own insolvency is looming. This is the true fraudulent conveyance or transfer and often carries an element of dishonesty.

- **Equality** The second object is that, if the debtor is in fact insolvent, he ought to treat his creditors equally even though formal insolvency proceedings have not yet begun. Other creditors should not be prejudiced by a preferential payment or transfer to one of them, thereby diminishing the assets of the estate available to creditors generally.

- **Debtor harassment** Finally, the rules against preferences are designed to discourage creditors with special leverage or who are specially diligent from harassing the debtor in financial difficulties to pay them off or secure them in priority to the others.

30–4   These policies are everywhere espoused, more or less. However there are other policies which may on occasion conflict with the above objectives.

- **Predictability** The first is the need for the predictability and certainty that transactions with a party will be inviolable and be upheld in favour of third parties dealing with the party in good faith and for value. If all transactions could be unwound if they took place in the suspect period regardless of guilty participation or lack of value given by the third party, there would be no safety in commercial and financial transactions. The preference rules impose the theory of equality at some uncertain date long before the formal insolvency proceedings have already begun and therefore back-date the guillotine.

- **Avoidance of insolvency** The second policy mitigating against an over-broad recapture is the need on occasion to permit the debtor opportunity to trade out of his difficulties. If the debtor and its directors are potentially exposed to penalties or disqualification if they do prefer creditors, then the debtor may be pressurised into shutting up shop prematurely to the likely detriment of his creditors generally. Insolvency proceedings generally have a catastrophic effect upon the value of a company's assets and usually destroy its goodwill, even if euphemistically dressed up as a rehabilitation. This contrary policy illustrates the tension which always exists between encouraging debtors to stop before it is too late and allowing them to continue so as to rescue both themselves and their creditors.

– **Honouring commitments** Finally, there is a conflict between the bankruptcy policy of equality of distribution and the policy that debtors should honour their obligations, e.g. the payment of matured debts.

Whilst nobody objects to the avoidance of the intentional dissipation of assets, the reach of preference laws to catch the more ordinary transaction has always been unpopular and the massive international case law reflects this hostility by creditors called upon to disgorge.

Terminology

The transactions under review enjoy no common universal terminology. In 30–5 common law states they are referred to as preferences (or fraudulent preferences or fraudulent transfers, even though the transaction may not be dishonestly fraudulent) any many include the "relation back" doctrine whereby the bankruptcy is deemed to relate back to actual insolvency so as to recapture transfers in that period. In French-based jurisdictions they are often termed transactions inopposable to the mass of creditors (now in France a nullity). In South Africa, they are impeachable transactions. In this study, the transactions will collectively be called "preferences".

Outline of preference law

In developed jurisdictions, the preference rules may be grouped into broad 30–6 categories as follows:

1. **Intentionally prejudicial transfers** The first category comprises transfers by the debtor which are intended to prejudice or defeat creditors by removing assets otherwise available to them on insolvency. This is the original Actio Pauliana, stemming from Rome in the second century BC and rediscovered in Europe in the eleventh century, and is reflected in all developed bankruptcy laws. Its hallmark is a deliberate intention to defraud creditors. Commonly there is no suspect period and the transaction is vulnerable whenever made. Examples are:

   Austria BA s 28; Belgium CC Art 448; Denmark BA Art 74; England IA 1986 s 423 stemming from an Elizabethan Act of 1571; France CC 1167; Greece CC Arts 939–945; Italy CC Arts 2901–4; Netherlands CC Bk3 ss 45–48; South Africa IA 1936 s 31; Sweden BA s 5; Switzerland Federal Debt Collection and Bankruptcy Act 1889 s 288; United States BC 1978 s 548.

The doctrine has been used to avoid gifts and the grant of a mortgage for pre-existing debt.

The English version stems back to an Elizabethan Act of 1571 which, though changed in England, continues to apply in many English-based jurisdictions. The statute generally provides that every conveyance made with intent to hinder, delay or defraud creditors is voidable at the instance of any person thereby prejudiced. This applies to any transfer of property, including (probably) payments. Insolvency at the time of the transfer need not be proved. There is an unlimited suspect period. Actual intent to deprive creditors must be proved – but deceit is not necessary. Any prejudiced creditor can theoretically apply for avoidance. Innocent transferees in good faith for valuable consideration and without notice of intent to defraud are protected. Bona fide transferees from bad faith transferees are also protected. This version of the Actio Pauliana applies to both companies and individuals.

The 1571 Act was replaced and recast in England in 1925 by s 172 of the Law of Property Act 1925 which in turn was replaced by IA 1986 s 423 to similar effect. The 1986 version now applies to all transactions at an undervalue (not just dispositions of property) entered into for the purpose of putting the assets beyond the reach of creditors or potential creditors or otherwise prejudicing such creditors. The victim can apply for an avoidance order and the company debtor need not be in financial difficulties. Transferees from the transferee are protected if they acquire the property in good faith, for value and without notice of the undervalue and the evasive or prejudicial intention: IA 1986 s 425. In many civil code countries such as Austria, Belgium, Greece and Switzerland, the creditor must be aware of the prejudice to creditors and also (often) the fraudulent intent of the debtor. This makes the Pauline action more difficult to use in these countries when compared to the deemed avoidance of certain transactions, such as security for pre-existing debt and gifts.

The English version only applies to transactions at an undervalue and so will not apply to the grant of security. This is not true of the US version. The action is often resorted to because the suspect period is longer (or, as in England, unlimited) and so is used where the usual suspect period has expired.

2. **Gifts** The second category comprises the avoidance of gifts by the debtor since these must clearly reduce the assets available to creditors. This category also generally includes transactions at an undervalue where there is an element of gift, such as a guarantee for no commensurate return. There may or may not be a suspect period for gifts.

3. **General preferences** The third category comprises a general provision attacking all payments and transfers by the debtor which prejudice creditors by depleting the debtor's assets or improve the position of the preferential creditor by placing him in a better position than he would have been on the insolvency of the debtor in the absence of the transfer, e.g. security for pre-existing debt.

Almost invariably, these general preferences in class (3) must occur within a specified suspect period prior to the commencement of insolvency proceedings at a time when the debtor was actually insolvent.

There is a further category (amongst others), namely the timely publication of security granted by the debtor, which is sometimes treated as within the scope of the preference rules but is more properly a matter pertaining to the avoidance of apparent wealth undercut by a secret lien.

Main issues

The main issues in determining where a jurisdiction's corporate insolvency   30–7
law (ignoring individuals) is pro-creditor or pro-debtor in the matter of preferences include: the extent of creditor protections for general preferences, notably whether the transaction is saved if the debtor had no intent to prefer or if the creditor did not know of the debtor's insolvency at the time of the transfer; the protection of ordinary course of business payments; the validity of security for pre-existing debt (the main litmus test); and the length of the suspect period.

The main factor in ranking jurisdictions is probably the presence of creditor protections, such as the requirement for debtor intent to prefer which, it will be seen, significantly emasculates the preference doctrine in the interests of the favoured creditor as against the bankruptcy estate. The second chief factor is the length of the suspect period, but in this case the comparison is unsafe by reason of the presence of numerous suspect periods for different types of preference, e.g. one for gifts, another for general preferences and a third for insiders, and the presence of parallel and overlapping grounds of avoidance.

The pro-creditor jurisdictions include the English-based countries, the Netherlands and Switzerland. Traditional French countries take a middle position. The United States is pro-debtor as regards preferences, largely because of the absence of creditor safe-harbours.

Before discussing the comparative approach to particular issues, it is proposed briefly to summarise the statutory provisions in English-based and Franco-Latin jurisdictions and in the United States but only so far as they affect security and guarantees (not, e.g. payments). A representative sampling of preference laws are summarised elsewhere in this series of works.

English-based jurisdictions

30–8   The chief features of the English-based approach relevant to the present topics are set out below and will be found in similar form in numerous English-based jurisdictions, although significantly altered in Australia, Canada and New Zealand.

Corporate and individual bankruptcies In traditional English countries, the bankruptcy preference rules applying to individuals are generally applied to companies by cross-reference in Companies Act sections relating to liquidations. But there remain significant differences between the rules applying to individuals and those applying to companies: in the interests of commerce, many corporate transactions are not invalidated where they would be invalidated if done by an individual.

Actio Pauliana – fraudulent conveyances This catches transactions made with intent to hinder, delay or defraud creditors: para 30–6 *et seq.*

30–9   **Gifts** It is generally provided that gifts (i.e. transactions in favour of a transferee without reasonably equivalent value or in favour of transferee acting in bad faith – which could include guarantees) are voidable if (see the old BA 1914 s 42 based on BA 1969 and BA 1883 s 91):

–   made within (usually) two years of the commencement of the bankruptcy, regardless of the solvency of the debtor; or

–   made within (usually) 10 years of the commencement of the bankruptcy unless the donee can prove that the debtor was able to pay all his debts (liability/asset test) without the aid of the gift and that the donee received the full interest of the debtor (i.e. no rights retained).

The English insolvency legislation of 1986 made substantial changes to these rules by introducing the concept of a transaction at an undervalue and a requirement of insolvency in all cases. Transactions at an undervalue are voidable on insolvent corporate liquidation and individual bankruptcy, and on corporate administration: IA 1986 ss 238, 240 and 241 for companies; ss 339, 341 and 342 for individuals.

The present English tests for avoidance are (1) a transaction for no value or significant undervalue; (2) the debtor is insolvent (widely defined to include excess of liabilities over assets – see s 123) at the time of the transaction (or becomes insolvent as a result of the transaction), (3) suspect period of two years for companies; five years for individuals. The onus is on the insolvency representative to prove insolvency, except in the case of transactions with connected persons and associates when the onus is on the transferee. Connected persons include directors, shadow directors and associates of directors, such as those with close family ties, controllers and associated companies: IA 1986 s 435.

Under IA 1986 it is a defence if the company transacted "in good faith and for the purpose of carrying on its business" and at the time there were "reasonable grounds for believing that the transaction would benefit the company". Note that "reasonable grounds" is an objective test, and the debtor's or creditor's bona fide belief in reasonable grounds is irrelevant. This defence does not apply to individuals.

The court may restore the position to what it would have been if the transaction has not occurred. This generally means that the transaction is avoided.

Transactions at an undervalue and preferences are badges of unfitness for purposes of the disqualification of directors from acting as a director.

Case law holds that the grant of security is not a transaction at an undervalue, so that the less stringent tests of ordinary preferences apply instead of the tougher undervalue tests.

Preferences Under the usual traditional English provision, a disposition is 30–10 voidable if (a) the debtor is unable to pay his debts as they fall due out of his own money, (b) the disposition is made in favour of a creditor, (c) the disposition is made "with a view to" giving the creditor or any guarantor for a creditor a preference over other creditors; (d) three- or six-month suspect period. Transferees from the preferred creditor are protected if they acted in good faith and for valuable consideration. The provision was first introduced in BA 1969 s 92 codifying common law, adapted in BA 1883 s 48, repeated in BA 1914, s 44 and extended to companies by successive Companies Acts.

The chief feature of the English preference doctrine distinguishing it from the traditional French model is that the debtor's factual intent to prefer must be proved: the onus is on the insolvency administrator. The intent must be the dominant intention. Intent is negated by pressure.

The main lines of this preference rule were preserved in the English Insolvency Act 1986 except that the "dominant intent" motive was replaced by the motive that the debtor was merely "influenced" by a desire to put the preferred creditor in a better position: IA 1986 s 239 (for companies); s 340 (for individuals). But the creditor's knowledge or otherwise of the insolvency or of the intent remains irrelevant.

The English suspect period is six months. A two-year suspect period for connected persons was also introduced in 1986. Connected persons included directors, shadow directors and associates of directors or of the company – associates are defined to include those with close family ties, controllers and certain associated companies: IA 1986 s 435. The company is presumed to be influenced by a desire to put the preferred creditor in a better position in the case of connected persons unless the contrary is proved, i.e. the onus of proof is reversed in the case of insiders.

30–11   **Floating charges** Special rules apply to the avoidance of floating charges on insolvent corporate liquidations and (now in England) corporate administrations. They do not apply to individuals since bankruptcy law generally prevents floating charges by individuals, at least over receivables and goods.

The present English tests are (IA 1986 s 245): (1) the company is insolvent at the time of the creation of the charge (or insolvent as a result of the transaction) – but insolvency at the time of the creation of the charge is not a requirement for charges to connected persons (such as directors and close family of directors and associated companies); (2) suspect period of 12 months (two years for connected persons), but (3) the charge is valid for money paid, value of goods and services supplied or the discharge or reduction of a debt, at or after the creation and in consideration of the charge (meaning "by reason of" or "having regard to the existence" of the charge), plus contractual interest.

In traditional English countries based on previous English law, there is commonly no time extension for connected persons, and the validation is permitted only for new money (not other new value) after the creation of the charge plus interest at a prescribed rate, e.g. 5 per cent.

Franco-Latin jurisdictions

30–12   The basic Franco-Latin model is followed, though with numerous detailed differences, by the central Napoleonic group (France, Belgium and Luxembourg) together with former French dominions (such as the Dominican Republic, Egypt and Haiti) and a large number of Latin American countries, including Argentina, Brazil, Chile and Venezuela. The law in countries like Denmark, Norway, Sweden and Greece is influenced by this approach. Spain and Portugal appear to be distinctive.

The main lines of the approach were substantially settled in the bankruptcy law in the third Book of the French Commercial Code of 1807 promulgated in 1808 – see Arts 443–447 – and modified in 1838. The changes since then have been at the edges. The chief features relevant to security and guarantees are set out below.

Actio Pauliana All intentionally fraudulent transfers by the debtor are void regardless of their date and regardless of insolvency. The creditor must generally be aware of the damage to creditors. See para 30–6.

30–13   **Transactions automatically void** Some transactions are generally automatically void if within a suspect period commencing on the date the debtor became insolvent (cessation of payments) as determined by the bankruptcy judge in the bankruptcy order, plus (sometimes) a period of 10 days prior to that date or even longer. Apart from certain payments, these include:

– gifts and transactions at a significant undervalue;

– security granted to secure existing debts.

The transferee's knowledge of the insolvency or the preferential intent of the debtor are irrelevant.

General preferences Other payments and dispositions may be declared void if made during the suspect period and the transferee knew of the insolvency (cessation of payments) of the debtor. Preferential intent is usually not relevant.

United States law

The US Federal preference rules are continued in ss 547, 548 and 550 of the   **30–14** Bankruptcy Code of 1978 as amended.

Preferences: s 547 The trustee in bankruptcy (including a Chapter 11 debtor-in-possession) may avoid any transfer of an interest of the debtor in property if the following tests are met: the transfer (which includes involuntary transfers, executions, such as foreclosure of the debtor's equity of redemption) is:

1. to or for the benefit of a creditor;

2. for or on account of an antecedent debt owed by the debtor before the transfer was made;

3. made while the debtor is insolvent (balance-sheet test – s 101);

4. made within 90 days before the filing of the petition (or one year if the creditor was an insider – e.g. relative, affiliate, director, controller of debtor); and

5. enables the creditor to receive more than he would otherwise have received in a Chapter 7 case (i.e. distributive liquidation).

The intent of the debtor is irrelevant. The debtor is presumed to have been insolvent during the 90-day suspect period, but this is rebuttable by the transferee. The onus of proving the above elements is on the trustee.

30–15   The trustee may not avoid in the following main cases relevant to security and guarantees (the burden of proof usually falling on the transferee):

1. the transfer was in substantially contemporaneous exchange for new value (defined to include money, goods, services, new credit, releases), e.g. security against new loans;

2. the transfer creates a perfected security interest to secure new value to enable the debtor to acquire the property used as collateral for the security interest (subject to conditions), e.g. loans to acquire property after the loan is made;

3. the transfer is after-acquired inventory or receivables or proceeds covered by a perfected security interest if either the creditor's position is not improved or if the creditor's improvement did not prejudice unsecured creditors. This is intended to cover floating liens catching after-acquired property of the debtor.

If the creditor and the debtor have more than one exchange during the 90-day period, the exchanges are netted out in accordance with a formula in s 547(c)(4). The netting out only applies to transfers after the preferential transfer. To the extent the new value that the creditor advances is unsecured, that value qualifies under this exemption. This applies notably to running trading accounts.

30–16   **Fraudulent transfers: s 548**   The trustee may avoid a transfer of the debtor's property or any obligation incurred by the debtor voluntarily or involuntarily where:

1. the transaction took place within one year of the filing of the petition;

2. (a) the transaction was with actual intent to hinder, delay or defraud any creditor (the Actio Pauliana), or
    (b) (1) the transfer as at an undervalue, and (2) the debtor was insolvent (or became insolvent as a result of the transfer–balance sheet test, not inability to pay debts as they fall due), or the debtor was left with unreasonably small capital for a business or transaction, or the debtor intended to incur debts beyond his ability to pay as they matured.

The transferee has a lien or other appropriate protection for any value given in good faith.

Time limits   The trustee must avoid within two years of his appointment or (if earlier) closure or dismissal of the case. For debtor-in-possession in Chapter 11 rehabilitation proceedings, the authorities are split as to two years from Chapter 11 filing or closure or dismissal of the case. Recovery action in both cases must be commenced within one year of avoidance of transfer or (if earlier) before closure or dismissal of the case. There are different periods under state laws, typically four years or more.

Other protections: s 564 Amongst other protections, the trustee may not   30–17
avoid a transfer if it is a margin payment or a settlement payment made by or to a commodity broker, stockbroker, or financial institution before the commencement of the case (unless there is intent to defraud other creditors and it is not made in good faith).

The trustee may not avoid a margin/settlement payment to a repurchase agreement participant or a swap agreement by or to a swap participant made before the commencement of the case.

State law Most states have additional rules and the trustee can use these: s 544(b). Note especially the Uniform Fraudulent Transfer Act (applying in 50 states with variations and generally having a four-year suspect period) and the Uniform Fraudulent Conveyance Act.

CHAPTER 31

PREFERENCES:
PREJUDICE TO CREDITORS

Introduction

31-1   The basic requirement of all preferences is that other creditors of the debtor are prejudiced. This usually means that the assets of the debtor available to pay his debts are reduced or depleted.

In some countries, e.g. in England and the United States, the test of prejudice to the bankrupt estate is the other way round and provides that the position of the creditor concerned in the transaction is improved in the sense that the transaction puts him in a better position then he would have been on the insolvency of the debtor if the transaction had not taken place.

In most cases it makes no difference which test is adopted. But in at least one situation, there is a difference, namely a substitution of creditor. For example, if a bank pays a creditor of the debtor at the request of the debtor and thereby increases the overdraft of the debtor, the bank becomes a creditor in place of the paid creditor. The net assets of the debtor are not diminished and remain the same. However, the position of the paid creditor is improved because he has been paid in full when he would only have got a dividend on the bankruptcy. This will affect novations of debt and triangle schemes whereby one lender makes a new loan which the debtor uses to pay off another lender. These transactions prejudice creditors only where the incoming creditor has greater recovery powers than the outgoing creditor, e.g. because the incoming creditor has security.

31-2   International case law shows that there is no prejudice to creditors if:

– The debtor pays a fully secured debt, because the creditor could realise the security for that debt on insolvency. Case law in many jurisdictions so holds, e.g. Denmark, the United States and Germany: BGHZ 90212. If the creditor is only partially secured, the payment ought to be applied to the unsecured portion and US case law so presumes.

– Substitutions of equal security, e.g. *Roy's Trustees v Colville & Drysdale*, 1903 5F 769 (Scotland), because there is no change in position unless the creditor's security is improved.

- realisation of security unless at an undervalue: see *Durrett v Washington National Insurance Co*, 621 F 2d 201 (5th Cir 1980)—70 per cent of market value is reasonably equivalent value.

- security for contemporaneous new money: para 31–6.

What follows is an analysis of some typical situations involving security and guarantees from the point of view of this test, it being remembered that, even if a transaction fails on the prejudice test, it may nevertheless be protected by some other defence, e.g. it was outside the suspect period, or was granted without intent to prefer, or was validated by a safe harbour rule in favour of a good faith creditor unaware of the insolvency.

Prejudice to creditors: undervalue transactions

Gifts and transactions at an undervalue

A gift of assets by an embarrassed debtor will always satisfy the test of   **31–3** prejudice to creditors because it involves a diminution of assets without equal return: less assets will be available to the bankrupt estate on insolvency.

The doctrine commonly extends to transactions at an undervalue where there is a significant element of gift. Only the gift element is voidable.

Corporate gifts would sometimes be ultra vires or, if protected against ultra vires by safe harbours for third parties, be a misfeasance by the directors for which they are liable. The ultra vires doctrine is partly an investor protection and partly a creditor protection and is distinguishable from preference rules.

Examples of undervalue transaction or gifts relevant to our topic might   **31–4** include:

- the surrender of security held by the debtor for an obligation owed to the debtor by the creditor;

- the release by the creditor of an invalid security in return for a payment by the debtor (the debtor is paying for nothing);

- collusive judgments whereby the debtor allows the creditor to enter a judgment against him for more than the creditor is entitled to or where the debtor has a good defence or where the debtor allows creditor application to the court to register security out of time in circumstances where the debtor could have opposed the application.

Some jurisdictions stigmatise gifts as preferential regardless of the insolvency of the debtor if they are made within a fixed suspect period. These countries appear to include Austria, Denmark, Japan, Norway, Sweden, Switzerland and traditional English countries, but not England or Australia (where the transaction is referred to as an "uncommercial transaction" under s 588 of the Corporate Law Reform Act 1992).

Others stigmatise the gift only if it occurs after (or a short time before) the suspension of payments or when the debtor is insolvent. These include traditional French and Latin countries, South Africa and the United States (one-year suspect period, but often longer periods under state law).

Guarantees as undervalue transactions

31–5 A perennial problem is whether a corporate guarantee of another's debt is granted for an adequate return. This issue arises also under doctrines of corporate law which forbid directors from giving away assets of the company – there must be corporate benefit. As mentioned, the "corporate benefit" doctrine is partly intended to protect shareholders against an improper depletion of the assets – an investor protection – and is partly intended to protect creditors for the same reason – a creditor protection.

Where a parent guarantees a loan made by a lender to a subsidiary, the benefit will often be the improvement in the value of the shares held by the parent in its subsidiary by virtue of additional finance put to profitable ends or the on-lending of the proceeds to finance the parent or the rest of the group. But the corresponding return will often be more difficult to prove where one subsidiary guarantees a sister-subsidiary or guarantees its own parent, unless the guaranteeing company receives a market rate of commission for the guarantee or other corporate benefit, such as an on-lending of loan proceeds or a tangible enhancement of its trading position by virtue of the financing of the group as a whole.

In England, corporate guarantees (and other transactions) which do amount to a transaction at an undervalue during the relevant suspect period when the debtor is insolvent are saved if the guaranteeing company acted in good faith and for the purpose of *its* business and also at the time of the transaction there were reasonable grounds for believing that the transaction would benefit the company – an objective test: IA 1986 s 238(5). It can be difficult, if not impossible, for banks and others receiving corporate guarantees to establish these essentially commercial benefits with complete certainty and so the safe harbour is not as safe as it should be. The defence does not apply to individuals and hence would not protect guarantees given by individuals.

Similar principles apply to collateral security given by one party to secure the debt of another (in substance a guarantee with recourse limited to the collateral).

In the United States "upstream" and "cross-stream" guarantees and pledges among related corporate entities have been successfully avoided because the guarantor or pledgor did not receive reasonable equivalent value for the transfer. Some courts have expanded avoidance to "downstream" guarantees and pledges when the relevant transfer did not actually increase the value of the subsidiary on a balance sheet basis or otherwise.

Prejudice to creditors: security

Security for new money

Security granted by the debtor for new money paid at or about the time the security is granted is usually not treated as prejudicial to creditors: e.g. *Re Conn*, 9 Bankr 431 (Bankr ND Ohio 1981). There is an equivalent exchange of value, like a cash sale. This factor should protect new money mortgages, purchase money mortgages, initial margin deposited in connection with trading in organised markets and possessory liens arising by operation of law (though the US position on liens is complex – see BC 1978 s 545). But collateral mortgages to secure the debt of third parties may amount to transactions at an undervalue: para 31–3 *et seq*. 31–6

The US has a specific exemption in favour of contemporaneous exchanges for new value in BC 1978 s 547. There are numerous US cases on whether a delayed grant of security is substantially contemporaneous, each turning on the length of the delay and the circumstances, e.g. whether the delay was administrative or inadvertent or usual, or was intentional.

Secured loans to pay off existing creditors

Triangle transactions or indirect security, where a debtor borrows money from a new lender against security in order to pay off an existing unsecured creditor have often been treated as a preference of the paid creditor in the US to the extent of the security granted to the new creditor: *Re Hartley*, 825 F 2d 1067, 17 CBC 2d 550 (6th Cir 1987). 31–7

> In *Re Beerman* 112 F 663 (ND Ga 1981), the creditor got a third party to lend money to the debtor secured by a mortgage and the loan was used to pay the creditor's claim, with the creditor indemnifying the lender against any loss the lender might suffer. *Held*: preferential.

In *Kellogg v Blue Quail Energy*, 831 F 2d 556, 17 CBC 2d 987 (5th Cir 1987), a third party issued a letter of credit to an existing creditor in return for a pledge by the debtor. *Held*: the issuance of the letter of credit was an indirect preference of the existing creditor who was the beneficiary of the letter of credit.

The economic result of the combined transactions substituting one new secured creditor for the old paid creditors is that the debtor has granted security for pre-existing debt: see below. Similar principles have been applied in England to floating charges: see para 31–12 *et seq*.

Although the payment to the third party creditors may be caught by the ordinary preference rules in BC 1978 s 547, the mortgage would not be – in the US because of the s 547 exemption in favour of contemporaneous exchanges of value unless it is caught by the Actio Pauliana, as in BC 1978 s 548 (actual intent to hinder, defraud or delay creditors by an insolvent debtor): *Coleman American Moving Services Inc v First National Bank & Trust Co*, 5 CBC 2d 410, (B Ct D Kan 1981).

Security for pre-existing debt

31–8 Generally the grant by the debtor of security for an existing unsecured debt is regarded as prejudicial to creditors: otherwise the pari passu treatment of creditors might be thwarted by creditors harassing the debtor into granting security in the twilight period and the race would go to the most pressing.

The availability of security for pre-existing debt is one of the leading litmus tests of the pro-creditor or pro-debtor bias of a jurisdiction. The international attitude may be summarised as set out below:

– **Deliberate intent** In most developed countries the Pauline action is available but this generally requires the debtor's intent to prejudice creditors and creditor collusion, both of which may be difficult to prove: see para 31–6.

– **Automatically void** In a large group of countries, security for pre-existing debt by an insolvent debtor in the suspect period is automatically void, regardless of the creditor's knowledge of the insolvency. These countries include the Franco-Latin jurisdictions, Denmark, Norway and the United States. The Franco-Latin jurisdictions treat this as on the same footing as gifts. Some shorten the suspect period – e.g. Norway (three months).

– **Not void if intent negated** In the English-based countries, security for pre-existing debt is void only if the debtor had intent to prefer, which will often be negated if there is pressure or a desire to keep the business going by maintaining the goodwill of the bank and the hope of future credit or the bank's forbearance. The *quid pro quo* is keeping the debtor alive.

In *Re M C Bacon Ltd* [1990] BCLC 324, a company in financial difficulties granted security to its bank for existing debt and went into liquidation eight months later. *Held*: the security was not preferential because the directors were not influenced by a positive desire to improve the bank's position on liquidation by granting the security. They were motivated only by the desire to retain the bank's support for the company.

– **Valid if pursuant to previous obligation** In another group of jurisdic-   31–9
tions, security granted pursuant to a pre-existing obligation is saved provided that the debtor undertook the obligation outside the suspect period or, more usually, the obligation was entered into when the debt was incurred and was therefore part of the consideration for the loan. This group includes Switzerland (BA s 287) and, more hesitantly, the Netherlands: see BA ss 42, 43. Sweden might be in this group: see BA s 12. But in all cases the security may be caught by the Pauline action, although here the safe harbours in favour of the creditor are generally more protective so that it is more difficult for the estate to avoid.

One argument is that the obligation to secure on request was part of the original consideration for the loan. The contrary argument is that the creditor is reserving to himself the power to be preferred. In England security granted pursuant to a legal obligation to do so may negative intent which is an English requirement, e.g. where the debtor agreed to grant the security as part of the original deal – as in *Re Bent* (1873) 42 LJ Bcy 25, LJ (security granted a year after debt incurred and six weeks after the creditor's requirement for the security); *Re Softley* (1875) LR 20 Eq 746 (security granted pursuant to a previous undertaking to the bank to grant security); *Bulteel & Colmore v Parker & Bulteel's Trustee* (1916) 32 TLR 661. But in other cases the grant of security pursuant to an obligation entered into at the time of the initial advance has been struck down as an agreement to prefer.

In *Re Eric Holmes (Property) Ltd* [1965] Ch 1052, the security was granted to secure a director's advances pursuant to an agreement to grant the security. *Held*: this was an agreement to prefer on request. But the result was probably influenced by the fact that it was an insider who was preferred and by the fact that the company got no advantage from the security.

The point is important in relation to the validity of variation margin in organised markets. Initial margin (i.e. collateral or cash deposits) is generally given by the trader to the market clearing house at the inception of trading and variation margin is called when the debtor's exposure on his existing trades is increased by reason of market fluctuations. It is crucial to the safety and integrity of markets that the variation margin should be valid and certain. But only the increase in collateral value should be vulnerable.

Both the United States and Britain have special statutory protections for security given in certain organised markets and in certain other cases. In the United States, BC 1978 s 546 provides that, the trustee may not avoid a transfer if it is a margin payment or a settlement payment made by or to a commodity broker, stockbroker or financial institution before the commencement of the case (unless there is intent to defraud other creditors and it is not made in good faith). Also the trustee may not avoid a margin/settlement payment to a repurchase agreement participant or a swap agreement by or to a swap participant made before the commencement of the case. In Britain, Part VII of the Companies Act 1989 protects margin and certain other security given to secure obligations under market contracts in connection with various recognised investment exchanges and clearing-houses: s 165.

–   **No knowledge of insolvency** In the final group, the creditor may be protected if he did not know of the insolvency of the debtor (Italy, Japan, it seems). This does not help rescues of companies obviously in difficulties.

Roll-over of secured current accounts

31–10   In England security given to secure an existing overdraft on current account will be whitewashed by subsequent payments in and payments out on the current account on the FIFO basis of *Clayton's Case* so that all payments out of the current account by the bank after the creation of the security are treated as new advances and thereafter are not pre-existing debt: *Re Yeovil Glove Co Ltd* [1965] Ch 148. But an artificial roll-over will not achieve this result.

In France and Belgium, the case law has adopted three solutions to the question of whether a current account which continues to be operated after the grant of the security can constitute new money. For Belgium, see Cloquet, *Droit Commercial* (3rd ed) vol IV para 539 *et seq*; for France, see Ripert/Roblot, *Traite de Droit Commercial* (11th ed) vol 2 para 2344. The older, more conservative, cases decided that, if the balance on the current account at the date of the final closure of the account exceeded the balance when the security was granted, then the excess must be new money advanced after the date of the security and hence the security would not be avoidable under this head to the extent of the excess. But if the balance on final closure was equal to or less than the balance on the security-date, the whole security was automatically void as security for pre-existing debt.

Subsequent decisions in both countries introduced the refinement that the protected excess was the excess of the final balance over the lowest balance after the security-date.

More recent decisions have, it seems, adopted the *Clayton's Case* analysis that any payments into the account by the debtor are imputed to the oldest payments out so as to operate to repay those oldest advances. Hence new advances after the security-date are capable of being treated as new money regardless of the account balance. It does not seem unfair that post-security advances should be protected: they are given in return for the security and the bank could instead have closed the accounts at once. Hence there is commonly a real *quid pro quo*.

Security over after-acquired assets

Where security covers future assets, then when the future asset comes into existence, the effect is that the security over the future asset secures pre-existing debt. Examples are floating charges covering all future assets, buildings added to mortgaged land, and engines fixed to aircraft (usually an exempt substitution).

The capture of after-acquired assets by a floating charge is not treated as preferential in England even though the after-acquired assets were acquired in the suspect period. Other creditors are forewarned by registration of the security.

In the United States the Bankruptcy Code of 1978 preserves the power of a floating lien over after-acquired property, but only if the "two-point net improvement" test in s 547(c)(5) is satisfied. A security interest in inventory or receivables is protected against avoidance to the extent that the secured party either does not improve his position during the preference period (e.g. inventory collateral increases without an increase in the debt) or can show that his improvement in position was not "to the prejudice of other creditors holding unsecured claims".

The question often arises in those countries (mainly outside the common law group) which prohibit the grant of security over future unidentified assets by reason of the doctrine of specificity: para 1–6. For example, a pledgor who has pledged investment securities may substitute securities in order to trade them, provided the margin of cover is maintained: the new substituted securities are effectively newly pledged. In the Netherlands, the non-possessory pledge over inventory or receivables may cover future assets and the practice is for the pledgor to send "pledge forms" from time to time to the pledgee covering those new assets. Strictly these new pledges are now security for pre-existing debt, but they ought not to be treated as such to the extent that the value of the collateral is not improved, e.g. where the new inventory replaces old inventory or the new receivables replace old receivables which have been paid, or the new securities replace old securities. This is believed to be the solution adopted in Belgium, for example, and is paralleled by the US approach. The English-based approach is much more favourable to the creditor: if after-acquired assets are specified in the original charge, even if generically, there is no preference even if the value of the collateral is thereby improved.

Floating charges for pre-existing debt

31–12   Floating charges receive specially stringent treatment in English-based jurisdictions by reason of the fact that they are a monopolistic security. Ordinarily the floating charge is invalid if created while the company is insolvent (widely defined in the English IA 1986 s 123) in a suspect period of one year except to the extent of cash received by the company for the charge at or about the time of the creation of the charge and interest thereon at a maximum prescribed rate, e.g. 5 per cent. It is not a defence that the company had no intent to prefer or granted the charge under pressure. The object is to allow floating charges only for new money received when the charge is created and to prevent creditors calling for subsequent floating charges for existing debts. In England the concept of new money in cash was widened in 1986 to include the market value (objectively ascertained) of goods or services supplied and the reduction of debts of the company and the allowable interest is at the contractual rate, not a prescribed rate: see IA 1986 s 245.

Guarantees are not protected because they do not result in the injection of new money into the guaranteeing company so that floating charges by insolvent companies to secure guarantees must survive the one-year period.

31–13   But if the charge secures an existing current account, payments out following payments in after the charge may "purify" the floating charge because the payments out are treated as new money even though the level of debt remains the same: *Re Yeovil Glove Co Ltd* [1965] Ch 148.

The new money cannot be created by a transparent subterfuge as where the lender rolls over his loan, nor does the company have new money if it never has the use or control of the money because it must immediately be used to pay other creditors under the terms of the loan: *Re Destone Fabrics Ltd* [1941] Ch 319. The effect here is purely to substitute a secured debt for an unsecured debt: *Re GT Whyte & Co Ltd* [1983] BCLC 311.

In *Re Orleans Motor Co* [1911] 2 Ch 41, a bank pressed directors for payment on their guarantee of the company's overdraft. The directors paid the company and the company immediately paid the bank and issued a floating charge to the directors. *Held*: the payment was not new money in return for the charge since the company had no benefit from the transaction.

The invalidation does not have retrospective effect so any recoveries on a pre-liquidation enforcement are not recoverable from the chargee: *Mace Builders v Lunn* [1985] 3 WLR 465.

In England, in order to attack mainly inter-company floating charges effectively putting shareholders monopolistically ahead of unsecured creditors, charges to insiders must survive for two years and are invalidated even though the company was not insolvent at the time of the creation of the charge. This was a 1986 innovation.

Simultaneity is not essential provided that the new money was reasonably contemporaneous. A gap of a fortnight has been validated where it was always intended that the charge would be given in consideration of the advances: *Re Columbian Fire-proofing Co* [1910] 2 Ch 120, CA. But later case law has narrowed this time-gap.

In order to avoid the rigors of the 12–month avoidance rule, it is common in English-based jurisdictions to convert the floating charge into a fixed charge over as many assets as is practicable having regard to the company's need to be able to deal with its trading assets, e.g. inventory. The fixed charges would then be subject to a six-month suspect period instead of 12 months and the additional requirement that prejudicial intent by the debtor be proved. The fixed charges could apply, for example, to land, buildings, shares in subsidiaries, intellectual property rights, goodwill, major contracts and receivables (but not the working bank account).

Late registration of security

The usual position for security requiring public registration is either that it   31–14 must be registered within a prescribed time or, if not, it is treated as constituted when it is registered so that, if this is in the suspect period, it is potentially void as security for pre-existing debt. In many French-based and Latin American countries, registration of non-possessory chattel mortgages, including over ships and aircraft is constitutive and hence the time of registration determines the time when the security is created for the purposes of the preference rule. Commonly there is a grace period, e.g. 15 days. In Denmark, for example, failure to file the particulars of a mortgage in the appropriate public registry without undue delay renders the security liable to be set aside. When the filing takes place within three months of the commencement of bankruptcy proceedings, undue delay is presumed.

In numerous English-based countries, failure to register corporate security within the 21-day (or 30-day) period generally invalidates the security against creditors (since the object is to prevent the secret lien from deceiving creditors), but it is possible to apply for registration out of time if the non-registration was through inadvertence or other sufficient cause. But the court will not permit late registration if liquidation proceedings have commenced or, usually, if the company is in fact insolvent. The English position was altered by the Companies Act 1989 (provision not yet in force), but the effect remains substantially similar.

31–15   In England, the replacement of a void security by a valid security has been held not to be preferential because the object of the debtor was not to prefer but rather to undo an error.

> In *Re FLE Holdings Ltd* [1967] 3 All ER 553, a company granted a charge to its bank over the company's factory. The charge was void for inadvertent lack of registration. The bank repeatedly required a valid charge and this was granted when the company was insolvent. *Held*: the charge was good because the company's dominant motive was to keep on good terms with the bankers in the hope of future advances, not to confer an advantage on the bank. Similar facts arose in *Peat v Gresham Trust* [1934] AC 252, HL, where the company did not oppose a creditor application to the court to register a void charge out of time even though the company was insolvent. *Held*: the liquidator failed to produce evidence showing an intent to prefer and the court would not infer such an intent.

> In *Re Tweedale* [1892] 2 QB 216, a debtor created a chattel mortgage over furniture to secure advances made by his wife. The mortgage was void because it covered after-acquired property. Immediately before his bankruptcy, the debtor corrected the error by a fresh chattel mortgage over the identical furniture. He believed himself under an obligation to create this security. *Held*: the correction of the initial blunder negated the intent to prefer.

In the United States, on the other hand, the intent doctrine does not apply. Hence the absence of continuous perfection of a security interest, as where the filing lapses or the creditor temporarily gives up possession of the collateral, means that the transfer is deemed to take place when the creditor cures the position by a second filing: the second filing does not relate back: see BC 1978 s 547(e) and *Re Abell*, 66 BR 375 (B Ct, ND Miss 1968).

Late notification of assignments

31–16   In many countries, the assignment of a debt is invalid on the seller's bankruptcy (subject to various exceptions) if the assignment is not notified to the debtor, often in some formal manner. These countries include France, Luxembourg, Italy, Portugal, Japan and South Korea, but not the English-based countries (at least in the case of assignments by companies as opposed to individuals), Belgium, Germany or the United States.

In the nullifying countries, notification within the suspect period may be treated as preferential in the same way that late registration of security is preferential because the notification is effectively constitutive of the security assignment.

> In a Danish Supreme Court decision (U 1986, p 508), a bank financed the purchase of goods by a company which intended to resell the goods. The company pledged the resale price to the bank on August 26. The bank issued a guarantee for the purchase. The bank's pledge was notified to the ultimate purchaser of the goods by a notice in an invoice sent with the goods on September 2. *Held*: the notice was unduly delayed and the pledge was set aside. A stringent view.

Purchase of unsecured claims by secured creditor

If a secured creditor with security for all moneys purchases an unsecured   31–17
claim or is an assignee of the security, the effect is that an unsecured debt of the lender becomes secured. This transaction will usually escape because the debtor is not involved unless he participated in the assignment, e.g. by giving a necessary consent to the assignment.

Prejudice to creditors: preferment of guarantors

If a company pays a creditor a loan which is guaranteed by a third party   31–18
guarantor, the effect may be to prefer the guarantor. The guarantor's position is improved because, if the company failed, he would have to pay the creditor under his guarantee and be left with a mere right to a dividend on the insolvency of the company. Other creditors are prejudiced because the assets of the company are diminished by the payment in full.

Cases in many jurisdictions stigmatise this as preferential. The payment of the guaranteed credit is often made at the instance of directors of the company who have guaranteed a loan by the bank to the company: they are preferring themselves.

> In *Re M Kushler Ltd* [1943] Ch 248, CA, a director in sole control of a company guaranteed the company's overdraft at the bank. During the run up to liquidation, the director paid all the company's receipts into the bank to reduce the overdraft, but the company did not pay any trade creditors. *Held*: the company through its director intended to prefer the director as guarantor. But the mere fact that payments in fact prefer the guarantor is insufficient without the

necessary intent, as where payments of trade receivables are made to the bank in the ordinary course of business: *Re Lyons* [1935] 51 TLR 24.

In *Re Conley* [1938] 2 All ER 127, the wife and mother of a debtor deposited shares with his bank by way of collateral to secure his overdraft. Just before his bankruptcy, the debtor paid off the bank loan to release his family's security. *Held*: fraudulent preference of the collateral sureties.

For the United States, see, e.g. *Herman Cantor Corp v Central Fidelity Bank*, 15 BR 747 (B Ct, ED Va 1981) where it was held that a payment to a creditor which discharged the guarantor is a preferential transfer for the benefit of the guarantor. For South Africa see, e.g. *Roussouw v Hodgson*, 1925 AD 97.

Presumably there can be no preference of the guarantor if the guarantor has no recourse to the debtor or his recourse is limited to the net worth of the debtor, i.e. any surplus.

CHAPTER 32

PREFERENCES: SUSPECT PERIOD AND OTHER MATTERS

Actual insolvency of debtor

The first test of a preference is prejudice to creditors: this has been discussed   32–1
above. The second main test of a preference is that the debtor was insolvent
when he granted the preference or was rendered insolvent by the transaction, e.g. by the gift or the guarantee. The reach-back applies because it is
insolvency which crystallises the equality principle and the collective
proceeding.

Insolvency may be defined for this purposes as inability to pay debts as
they fall due, or the balance sheet test of excess of liabilities over assets, or
both, and commonly includes other indicia of insolvency, e.g. unsatisfied
judgments.

The test of inability to pay debts as they fall due is more protective of
creditors since there is at least some chance of their learning of the financial
difficulties. The balance sheet test is uncertain for creditors since they may
have no means of valuing the assets except by financial statements which
may be out-of-date. The balance sheet test also poses problems for directors
who may incur misfeasance liability or other penalties for granting preferences – assets can be difficult to value precisely and may fetch much less on a
break-up than on a going-concern basis. There are obvious evidential
obstacles. England applies both tests: see IA 1986 s 240.

Length of suspect period

Except for the Pauline action, it is generally true that the transaction must   32–2
have taken place in a prescribed period prior to the commencement of the
formal insolvency proceedings. The object of a suspect period is to give certainty to transactions which outlive the period concerned, even though on
occasion the period may turn out to be too short. Fixed periods also recognise the practicalities of the matter that, in most cases, an actual insolvency

is swiftly followed by a formal insolvency and that, the longer the period, the more formidable the evidential problems.

Everybody has a different idea on how long the suspect period for particular preferences should be and one simply has to look it up in each case.

Commonly there are different suspect periods for different classes of preference, with the more culpable meriting the longest, e.g. gifts, with no suspect period at all in the case of culpable fraud.

The traditional English approach is to fix a period of generally three or six months – so that transactions outside that period are saved, apart from the special rules for intentional fraud and gifts. Apart from these situations, the Franco-Latin rule back-dates the suspect period to the time the debtor actually becomes insolvent, as determined by the judge, and often with a further back-dating of 10 days or more, so that there is no upper limit. Here and there, there is a maximum period of back-dating (sometimes only for some transactions, e.g. non-gifts) – six months in Belgium and Luxembourg, 18 months in France. Pro-creditor countries in this group, such as Norway and Switzerland, generally fix up an upper limit. But there is a bewildering variety of periods.

The United States has a basic 90-day period (lengthened by state statutes) whereas six months is the international norm for the ordinary non-gift non-fraudulent preference.

Insiders and connected persons

32–3   The preference rules are frequently tougher for insiders. Older statutes have often stigmatised transfers to spouses and other relations. More modern versions extend the concept of insiders to co-directors, controlling shareholders or commonly-controlled corporations or affiliates. The reason for the tougher rules for insiders is that manipulation by those in control is more likely (they are more likely to have advance knowledge of the debtor's demise), that the temptation to prefer themselves is greater and that insiders should be subordinate to external creditors.

The trends are: (1) a longer suspect period; (2) reversal of the onus of proof, e.g. as to insolvency or creditor-awareness of the insolvency; and (3) insolvency at the time of the transaction may not be an essential element (e.g. in England for floating charges granted to connected persons).

In the context of groups of companies, the insider doctrine affects, for example, security granted to a parent by a subsidiary, asset-stripping, shuffling assets around the group at an undervalue, the payment by a group company of an inter-company debt during the suspect period and guarantees by an affiliate or a director.

Composition proceedings

Apart from the Pauliana (which can apply outside formal insolvency pro-   32–4
ceedings), always the preference doctrines apply to final bankruptcy proceedings or insolvent liquidations. They also often apply to composition or
rehabilitation proceedings.

The argument is that, if a company is insolvent, the principle of non-dis-
criminatory treatment of creditors, which is at the heart of these avoidance
powers, ought to come into play and can do so without damaging legitimate
expectations, regardless of whether the proceeding is final or rehabilitative.

The normal insolvency powers to avoid pre-commencement transactions
as preferences or otherwise apply in an **English administration**, a US
Chapter 11 case (see BC 1928 s 1107(a) – powers exercisable by the debtor
in possession), a **French** *redressement* and a **Japanese reorganisation** (being
the avoidance powers set out in the Corporate Reorganisation Law, Art 78
et seq).

Where the preference rules do not apply on a composition or rehabilitation proceeding, but the composition fails, e.g. because the debtor does
not comply with his reduced obligations, and the debtor is bankrupted
instead, it is sometimes the case that the suspect period is calculated up to
the application for or promulgation of the composition as opposed to the
subsequent bankruptcy. The purpose of this is to maintain the suspect
period up to the commencement of insolvency proceedings, albeit of a com-
pository sort, e.g. in Belgium, Denmark and Luxembourg. Where the preference rules do apply to a composition, it is for investigation whether time
stops during the composition.

Defences

Summary

The defences available to the preferred creditor are influenced primarily by: 32–5
(a) the pro-creditor or pro-debtor orientation of the bankruptcy laws, i.e.
the policy of protecting creditors and enhancing the predictability of transactions as against the policy of enlarging the debtor's estate and protecting
him and his creditors or, more commonly, priority creditors, such as taxes
and employees; (b) the culpability of the preference, e.g. intentional preferences and gifts enjoy less favour than ordinary course of business payments;
and (c) the proximity of the transaction to the opening of the insolvency
proceedings.

The prime dividing line between jurisdictions, ranking in importance far ahead of such matters as what is deemed preferential and the length of the suspect period, is the availability of creditor defences, even though objectively the creditor has improved his position in the suspect period to the detriment of other creditors.

The two main defences internationally are as follows:

1.   The debtor did not intend to prefer.

2.   The creditor did not know that the debtor was insolvent.

Of course, there are other defences in particular situations, such as the frequent requirement for creditor collusion in the case of fraudulent transfers within the Pauliana, and the protection of ordinary course of business payments. But the above two are the fundamental protections and may now be examined in turn.

Preferential intent

32–6   A characteristic of England and many English-based jurisdictions is the moral culpability or wrongful intent of the debtor – he must have intended to prefer the creditor. In England, since 1986 the intent need be only one of the motives influencing the transaction, but in many other English-based countries it must still be the dominant motive. This intent requirement does not apply to gifts or transactions at an undervalue where preferential intent is presumed. Creditor knowledge of the debtor's preferential intent is irrelevant. These countries belong to the subjective school.

Classification of "intent" jurisdictions Apart from the Pauline action (deliberate prejudicial intent by the debtor, usually with creditor collusion) and apart from gifts, the "intent" doctrine applies, as mentioned, in **England** and many (but not all) English-influenced countries. In **Austria**, in the case of the grant of security or payments by the debtor, no debtor preferential intent need be shown if the creditor was not entitled to the security or payments or not in that form, but in other cases debtor intent is necessary when the security or payment is to non-insiders: there is only a preference if the transferor was aware or should have been aware of the intent of the bankrupt to prefer: BA s 30(3).

In **Switzerland** creditor collusion is also required except (amongst others) in the case of (1) gifts and (2) pledges for pre-existing debt otherwise than pursuant to obligation to do so. In the case of pledges, the transaction is protected if the beneficiary proves he was unaware of the insolvency. Hence

Switzerland appears protective of creditors in this respect. **Spain** requires intent in some cases: see Act 881.

Apart from the Pauliana, the intent doctrine does not apply in the following countries and is usually (but not always) replaced by a requirement that the creditor knew of the debtor's insolvency: these countries may be classed as the objective school:

Australia
Denmark
Italy
Japan
S Korea (probably)
Netherlands
Norway
South Africa and probably related countries, like Botswana, Lesotho and Zimbabwe
Sweden
Traditional French group (e.g. Belgium, France, Greece, Luxembourg, Egypt, former French colonies and many Latin American countries)
United States (where even creditor knowledge of the insolvency is not a defence)

Advantages and disadvantages of intent doctrine The advantage of the   32–7
intent test is that it can be used by courts to validate transactions so as to protect creditors. It also helps protect ordinary course of business transactions, security for pre-existing debt (*Re MC Bacon Ltd* [1990] BCLC 324), the correction of errors in the original void security (*Re Tweedale* [1892] 2 QB 216), even discriminatory payments where the motives of the debtor may simply have been to do a deal or to finance the business or to keep the business going or to secure further supplies or otherwise to benefit himself: see *Re FLE Holdings Ltd* [1967] 3 All ER 553. It has also validated security for pre-existing debt if there was an obligation to grant it: the debtor intends to perform his obligations, not to prefer. Effectively the "intent" test, regardless of its logic, is a leading creditor protection.

But a disposition made where the motive is to favour a creditor who is himself in difficulties or to whom the debtor feels he owes a moral obligation or where the motive is to favour all creditors except a hated creditor is with intent to prefer in England: there is a deliberate intention to discriminate and the fact that one creditor is regarded as more deserving than another is immaterial: *Re Fletcher* (1891) 9 Mor 8.

The disadvantages are that the motives of the debtor are irrelevant to other creditors who are actually prejudiced, that proof is often difficult, and that the preferred creditor cannot necessarily know the debtor's subjective state of mind so that the doctrine is unpredictable. These disadvantages can lead to a requirement for creditor collusion or for notice to the creditor of the preferential intent, but this is not a requirement in England. But for the above reasons, the intent doctrine has been abandoned in the United States and in Australia for some of the preference tests. The net effect is greatly to increase creditor exposure to the avoidance of transactions. The argument therefore is not whether the debtor's intent is logically relevant, but whether the preference doctrine should be broad or narrow.

In the English-based jurisdictions there are numerous cases on the intent doctrine, all of which turn on the particular facts of the cases.

32–8   **Pressure negates intent**   A leading feature of the intent doctrine is that a disposition which is not voluntary but is made under pressure is not made with intent to prefer but with intent to escape the pressure.

There are many English cases on this point, but just as there are cases where the threat of legal proceedings was sufficient, so also are there many cases where creditor pressure did not negative intent. The general trend seems to be that mere pressure is not enough to negative intent but is enough if coupled with some other motive, such as the debtor's expectation of maintaining financial or commercial relationships with the creditor. The courts do not encourage creditor bullying.

> In *Re Ramsay* [1913] 2 KB 80, the creditor threatened to "make it hot" for the debtor unless he was paid. The debtor returned goods to cover debts due and also those not yet due. *Held*: fraudulent preference.

> Compare *Re Wilkinson* [1864] 1 Morr 65. A judgment creditor threatened the debtor with execution. The debtor gave the creditor security. The creditor agreed to pay off the debtor's existing mortgage and to pay arrears of rent. *Held*: not a fraudulent preference. The creditor gave something in return.

> In *Re Wrigley* [1875] LR 20 Eq 763, a creditor pressurised an insolvent debtor into buying goods from others on credit and then using the proceeds of sale to pay the creditor, instead of the supplier. *Held*: notwithstanding the pressure, the transaction was fraudulent in its inception.

32–9   **Onus of proof**   The onus in the traditional English jurisdictions is on the party seeking to avoid the transfer to show that there was intent to prefer. The effect therefore is an initial presumption in favour of the validity of the disposition. This proof is somewhat difficult because the bankrupt himself will often be disinclined to admit an intention to prefer since this will disfavour the creditor and will potentially exposure the bankrupt to penalties.

In such a case the court may, in view of the circumstantial evidence, be drawn to disbelieving the bankrupt: *Re M Kushler Ltd* [1943] Ch 248, CA.

Creditor ignorance of the insolvency

Jurisdictions inclined to favour the predictability of transactions give the **32–10** creditor a defence if he did not know of the insolvency—this may be knowledge of a stoppage of payments, or of balance-sheet insolvency, or of the commencement of proceedings by the filing of a petition.

The countries which espouse the "creditor knowledge" rule are in the "objective" school, as opposed to those who require debtor intent to prefer – the subjective school described above.

The objective school generally excludes the countries listed above as requiring debtor intent, e.g. England and the traditional English countries, and includes the following states:

Franco-Latin countries
Italy
Japan
S Korea (probably)
Netherlands, where the test is commonly that the creditor knew that the act prejudiced creditors. The satisfaction of a material obligation is preferential if the satisfaction is made pursuant to consultation between the debtor and the creditor with a view to a preference.

In the **United States**, the test of a preference is wholly objective (apart **32–11** from fraudulent conveyances) and creditor knowledge of the debtor's financial state is irrelevant.

The advantages of the awareness rule is that, if the awareness is actual and obvious awareness, creditors know where they are, i.e. that further dealings with the debtor may be vulnerable. The disadvantage is that the effect of the rule is that, once creditors know of the debtor's embarrassment, his further dealings are frozen and he is no longer in a position to trade out of his difficulties. He has little chance of recovery. This is not because of creditor disincentive to carry out transactions which may be set aside (creditors prefer a potentially voidable payment to no payment at all), but because the debtor and his controllers may be exposed to penalties if they do prefer creditors. In practice, many attempts to save major groups in difficulties, e.g. by a private bank restructuring exercise, are carried out at a time when the bank and other creditors are fully aware of the debtor's financial state in which even the sole defence of creditors lack of knowledge of the insolvency is of no assistance. The English-based "intent" doctrine tends to avoid this difficulty. Hence an "intent" doctrine favours a policy of helping debtors to survive, but a pure "awareness" doctrine is less effective to this end.

From the point of view of the disappointed creditors, it is irrelevant to them that a particular creditor did not know of the insolvency if he was in fact preferred and so theoretical logic would point to the elimination of the knowledge defence. But against this logic is the wider policy of whether or not to confer predictability on transactions and whether or not to back-date the insolvency to some date prior to the actual formal commencement.

The state of insolvency may be inferred. Thus in Belgium the creditor's knowledge that the debtor is insolvent will be inferred where, for example, the creditor has issued proceedings asking for the debtor to be declared bankrupt, or a creditor has refused to grant further credit to the debtor, or a creditor has made advances to the debtor to help him overcome a liquidity crisis.

Avoidance and recapture

Avoidance procedure

32–12   Commonly the transactions may be either automatically void or merely voidable. The importance of the distinction is that, where a transaction is only voidable, this may allow the court to exercise a discretion.

Whether the avoidance is initiated by the insolvency administrator or a committee of creditors or is supervised by the court is a procedural matter for which there are many solutions. But, except for the Paulian action, the recovery is usually an asset of the estate available to all creditors.

Recapture

32–13   The basic principle of the recapture is to put the parties in the position they would have been in if the transaction had not occurred and tends to follow the broadly traditional pattern of avoidance procedures in other contexts, e.g. the restoration of a party induced into a contract by misrepresentation or in the case of a contract collapsing by frustration or *force majeure*. In view of the complexity of the circumstances, some countries, including England and the United States, give the court broad discretions as to the manner of recovery (though, in the case of England, the statute sets out a range of specific options without prejudice to the generality of the discretion), while others, like Norway, attempt some specific rules: Debt Recovery Act 1984 ss 5–11, 5–12.

Revival of guarantees

If the debtor paid off a guaranteed debt in order to prefer the guarantors, **32–14** the paid creditor may have released the guarantee. If the creditor is obliged to restore the amount paid, the debt owing to him springs up again – but with the guarantee gone. One solution is to treat the guarantor as the creditor who is preferred – he is a creditor because he has a contingent right of reimbursement against the debtor – and to order him to repay the estate. The other more logical solution is to cause the creditor to disgorge and to resurrect the guarantee so that the creditor is in the same position he was before, e.g. if the guarantor is bankrupt or the guarantor is prevented from competing with the creditor. In any event, in England the insolvency statute allows the court to order a revival of the guarantee and any security for the guarantee as well as security granted to the creditor for the debt which was paid off: IA 1986 s 241. Where this is in question, the beneficiary of the guarantor should expressly condition the release of the guarantee on the validity of the payment by the principal debtor and many guarantees contain an express provision to this effect. If the guarantee contained an expiry date for demands, that expiry date may have passed when the guarantee resurrects. Whether the court can extend the expiry date depends upon its powers to reform the original transaction.

Revival of security

A similar problem arises where a secured creditor is paid off preferentially **32–15** and releases his security. The English courts are authorised to reinstate the security on recovery of the preferential payment by the debtor's estate. Security documents often contain a provision that the security-holder can retain the security for the applicable preference periods despite a redemption of the debt, but this may conflict with a rule that the debtor is entitled to have his security back once he pays the secured debt. One possible solution is to provide that the security covers debts resurrected on an invalidation of a payment as a preference and to require the debtor to show at the time of the payment that the payment is not preferential. There are obvious practical problems. The saving for many of these situations is that, as has been shown, the payment off of a fully secured creditor is not generally in itself preferential because there is no improvement in position.

Security over after-acquired assets

32–16   Where security validly extends to after-acquired assets, such as an English-based floating charge covering all present and future assets, the asset recovered by the estate may fall within the clutch of the charge in favour of the secured creditor. The objection to this is that the secured creditor is effectively improving his security after the insolvency which ought to be the cut-off date. The policy in favour is that the holder of a general business charge ought to have everything so that the business can be sold as a whole and that the right to possessory management through a receiver must include future income produced by the assets and should also include assets which would have been included in the charge but for the preferential transfer by the creditor: the secured creditor should not be deprived of his rightful security and the unsecured creditors should not receive a windfall as a result of the wrongful act of the debtor.

Norway comes down in favour of the secured creditor as does Sweden: see the Swedish Supreme Court *Minitube case* (NJA 1982, p 900), which gave the holder of a Swedish floating charge the benefit of the recovered asset. England however took a contrary view in *Re Yagerphone Ltd* [1935] Ch 392.

Deterrence and penalties

32–17   The penalty suffered by transferees who have been preferred is that they are liable to return the property or its equivalent. This may not be a great deterrence in some cases, because the hope of retention of an asset may be better than no asset at all. This is a view which banks may take when insisting on security for pre-existing debt.

Nevertheless it is not generally considered appropriate to penalise transferees further, except in the case of clear fraudulent collusion involving actual dishonesty. The business of bankruptcy law is not the punishment of creditors nor would the criminalisation of creditor conduct be generally acceptable: society has more usually tended to punish the defaulter than his hapless creditors.

It is otherwise with the debtor who confers the preference. Everywhere it is thought that dishonest fraudulent transfers and concealments of assets will meet with bankruptcy penalties. Thus in Italy preferential payments to creditors with intent to favour them are within the group of bankruptcy offences entailing imprisonment from three to 10 years. But ordinary preferences, not involving true fraud or deceit, merit a range of sanctions. It is of the essence of criminal penalties that the criminal must have criminal intent or *mens rea* and this is generally true of the bankruptcy penalties. How the courts interpret this in practice in relation to transfers deemed preferential, e.g. security for pre-existing debt, where the debtor acted honestly or under pressure, is a matter for investigation: criminalisation without *mens rea* would reveal an intense hostility to preferential transfers and a vestige of the old idea that debtors ought to be punished.

In England a director participating in a corporate preference may be liable for misfeasance proceedings and the conduct is a factor to be taken into account in disqualification proceedings under the Company Directors Disqualification Act 1986. Paying one creditor preferentially out of moneys received is not criminal fraud except in unusual circumstances: *Re EB Tractors Ltd* [1987] PCC 313.

APPENDIX

CHECK-LISTS, OUTLINES, PRECEDENTS

Appendix

CHECK-LISTS, OUTLINES, PRECEDENTS

Part I: General

1. General check-list of main issues in relation to security
2. General check-list of main priority questions in relation to security
3. Outline general summary of terms of security agreements
4. Charging clauses in English fixed and floating charge
5. Outline form of security over investment securities with margin requirement
6. Guarantee-type clauses in security for third party's debt

Part II: Ship Finance

7. British Ship Mortgage Form
8. British Ship Mortgage Deed of Covenants
9. Cyprus Ship Mortgage Form
10. Greek Ship Mortgage
11. Liberian Ship Mortgage
12. Norwegian Ship Mortgage Deed
13. Panamanian Ship Mortgage

Part III: Guarantees

14. Outline of guarantee of term loan
15. List of main terms in guarantee by bank or other independent guarantor
16. Short form guarantee of facility agreement

APPENDIX: PART I

GENERAL

1. General check-list of main issues in relation to security

- The **scope of assets** which may be mortgaged, e.g. the availability of floating charges or other general business charges over all assets of a corporate debtor; the availability of non-possessory chattel mortgages, of security over receivables without notification to the debtor, and of security over future or after-acquired property.

- The **publication** of the security; whether the security must be publicly registered or protected by a public filing and whether the registration must be periodically renewed; whether the creditor must take possession of the asset or (in the case of debts) notify the debtor or (in the case of investment securities) be registered as the holder in the books of the issuer, and take possession of any certificates.

- The **formalities** for the grant of security; whether the security must be notarised or in writing or in other formal form or can be created orally or informally by deposit of title deeds, share certificates or other indicia of ownership or paper representing the asset; whether the contents of the security document are prescribed.

- Whether any **right of the debtor to deal with the collateral** (including rights of substitution) destroys a possessory pledge or (in English-based countries) results in the security becoming a floating charge.

- The scope of the **debt which may be secured**; whether there are any limitations on secured debt, such as exclusions for future debt (affecting current accounts, revolving loans and currency convertibles) or for damages (i.e. only liquidated sums); whether a maximum amount must be specified; whether foreign currency mortgages are possible; whether there are any limitations on interest; and whether junior priority debt secured on the same asset (a second mortgage) is possible.

- Any **limitations on the creditors** entitled to the security, e.g. domiciliaries or nationals only, or non-recognition of trustees holding security for several creditors, or restrictions limiting the grant of security to banks or other financial institutions.

- The scope of the **remedies** of the secured creditor, including any limitation of remedies, such as public auction only (as opposed to a private sale or temporary receivership or possession), compulsory grace periods on enforcement rights, or sale only to nationals or in local currency; and the costs of enforcement; delays in judicial enforcement leading to pile up of interest and fall in value of the collateral.

- Whether there are any **bankruptcy freezes** on enforcement of the security or a moratorium on secured debt; whether the insolvency administrator can use the secured asset or substitute security in the event of insolvency rescue proceedings.

- Whether the insolvency administrator of the debtor in an insolvency rehabilitation can raise **super-priority moratorium loans** to finance the rehabilitation but which prime existing security.

- Whether the security is capable of being avoided as a **preference** on insolvency and the length of the suspect period and any safe harbours in favour of the creditor.

- Whether the secured creditor can check the debtor's **title** to the asset, e.g. whether the debtor owns the asset and whether there are any encumbrances over the asset.

- The certainty and predictability of the creditor's **priority** over competing interests: see the next check-list.

- Whether the creditor may **restrict redemption** of the security, e.g. by a restriction on prepayments, or by prepayment penalties, or by insisting on the consolidation of mortgages (a doctrine which insists that the debtor redeem both mortgages or neither).

- Whether there are any **stamp duties** and other documentary taxes on the security.

- The **recognition** by local insolvency law of foreign security.

- Whether the secured creditor is subject to any **liabilities** in relation to the secured asset, e.g. taxes, obligations on contracts and leases affecting the asset, preservation duties, environmental liabilities, duties to notify the interest to the issuer of shares.

- Whether the security violates any rules prohibiting a company from giving **financial assistance** in connection with the purchase of its shares, e.g. where an acquired company charges its assets to secure a bank loan made to the acquiror of the shares of the company to finance the acquisition.

- Whether the security conflicts with any **contractual restrictions** binding on the debtor, e.g. a negative pledge, pari passu clause or clause prohibiting disposals in the debtor's bank loan agreements or bond issues; whether there are any contractual restrictions in the asset itself prohibiting security, e.g. prohibitions on assignments in contracts or concessions, or pre-emption provisions on a sale of shares. The restriction may prevent the security itself or the sale of the collateral on enforcement.

- Whether a contract, lease or licence which is covered by the security can be **cancelled** on a default by the debtor in which event the secured creditor would be left with nothing.

- Whether a corporate debtor has the **power** to grant security and what **authorisations** are necessary.

- Where **insolvency proceedings** have been commenced against the debtor, which would render the security void.

2. General check-list of main priority questions in relation to security

The chief competing claimants include:

— **Preferential creditors** on bankruptcy, e.g. for taxes and wages

— **Prior attaching creditors** who attached or levied execution over the collateral prior to the grant of the security

— **Subsequent attaching creditors** after the grant of the security. The security is valueless if it is ineffective against unsecured creditors

— **Prior mortgagees** of the asset or its proceeds

— **Subsequent mortgagees** of the asset or its proceeds

— **Prior purchasers** of the asset (or those with an option to purchase)

— **Subsequent purchasers** of the asset (or those with an option to purchase)

— **Beneficiaries under a trust** of the asset or its proceeds held by the debtor as trustee, e.g. retention of title sellers entitled to the proceeds

— **Principals** who have given possession of the asset or the documents of title or evidence of ownership (land deeds, bills of lading, bills of sale, warehouse receipts, certificated securities) to their agent, such as a broker, who purports to grant the security as if the asset were his own

— **Unpaid sellers** of the asset to the debtor who have a retention of title clause

— Holders of a prior **lien** over the asset, e.g. a repairman's lien, a maritime lien or an unpaid vendor's lien

— Holders of a **subsequent lien** over the asset

— Subsequent second priority secured creditor over the same asset who claims to rank ahead of **future advances** made to the debtor by the first secured creditor

— **Prior lessees**, charterers and licencees of the asset, e.g. a lessee of land, the charterer or a ship or the licencee of a patent

— **Subsequent lessees**, charterers and licencees of the asset

— Owners or mortgagees of other assets (a) to which the collateral is attached as a **fixture or accession** such as materials incorporated in a building or an engine fitted to an aircraft, or (b) into which the collateral is **commingled** or processed, such as glue incorporated in chipboard or such as proceeds of the collateral deposited in a mixed bank account

–   Holders of **prior contractual restrictions** on the grant of security, e.g. a negative pledge in a loan agreement

–   Debtors with a **set-off** against a secured receivable.

3. Outline general summary of terms of security agreements

This summary contains a compendious list of clauses which might be considered for a particular security document, depending on the asset and the jurisdiction.

Debtor and secured creditor

Any restrictions on secured creditor? No trustee? Only nationals or credit institutions?

Secured liabilities

All present and future liabilities and obligations owing by debtor to creditor, including contingent obligations, unliquidated obligations, those owing jointly, those acquired by the creditor from a third party; *or* all liabilities and obligations owing by debtor to the creditor under a specified agreement (and under any changes or supplements to the agreement), plus those designated by the creditor and the debtor as secured liabilities, and plus those arising under the security agreement itself, e.g. costs.
   Consider applicability of the following:

- Security for future debt (current account, revolving credit?)
- Maximum amount to be stated? Split between principal, interest and costs?
- Security available for foreign currency debt?
- Limits on interest rate, capitalised interest, penalty interest, recoverable back-interest?

Payment of secured liabilities

- Debtor covenants to pay secured liabilities to creditor
- Security is continuing security and extends to ultimate balance, notwithstanding interim payments.
- Creditor has first right of appropriation in the case of partial payments, e.g. to interest before principal.

– Creditor's certificate of amount owing is conclusive in absence of manifest error.

Secured assets

Land To include accessories, buildings, fixtures and fittings, covenants for title, leases, licences, rights of way and other easements, compensation for compulsory purchase. Fixed security. Assign leases, licences, etc.

Goods To include accessories, e.g. engines, communications equipment, leases, charters, licences. Fixed security on plant and equipment. Assign leases, licences, etc.

Contracts To include: variations, rights of action, rights to terminate, security and guarantees, damages, arbitration awards. Fixed security on major contracts. Assign any security and guarantees in required form

Debts To include: interest, security and guarantees; bank deposits. Fixed security, e.g. on investment holdings of loan claims against subsidiaries, affiliates and joint venture companies

Negotiable instruments See also next heading

Investment securities To include: dividends, interest and other income; property resulting from substitution, consolidations, sub-divisions; property in right of the investment security, e.g. bonuses, capital redemptions, new issues, conversions and exchanges, options, warrants; right to exercise powers; claims against custodians holding fungible securities; deposit accounts into which income and capital proceeds are deposited. Fixed security on shareholdings in subsidiaries, affiliates and joint ventures

Insurances To include: return of premiums

Nationalisation Compensation for nationalisation, requisition and expropriation and other compulsory acquisitions or cancellations. Fixed security

Intellectual property To include: royalties and other income; licences; rights to apply for registration or other protection

Other Interest in pension funds, letters of credit, goodwill, uncalled capital

Proceeds All proceeds of the above and any bank account into which they may be paid

In each case, consider:

- whether security over principal asset extends automatically to accessories, leases, licences, insurances;
- the degree of specific identification required;
- availability of security over future assets without a new security.

Floating charge

- Floating charge over all present and future assets which are not subject to fixed security
- Fixed charge on: land; plant and large equipment; major contracts; non-trading claims against affiliates; shareholdings in affiliates; compulsory acquisition compensation; intellectual property and licences; uncalled capital; insurance proceeds in respect of all assets (except third party liability)
- Restrictions on rights to deal outside ordinary course of business
- Conversion of floating charge to fixed charge
    - by creditor notice if event of default or potential default has occurred or assets in jeopardy, e.g. attachments or seizures
    - automatically on presentation of insolvency petition or calling of meeting to resolve to wind up.

Collateral clauses (if third party collateral security)

Guarantee-type clauses, e.g. waiver of defences, security remains valid if secured obligation is invalid; immediate recourse, appropriation of recoveries by creditor first to unsecured debt; non-competition, certificate of amount owing.

Representations and warranties

Basic Status; powers; authorisations; validity and enforceability; non-conflict with laws, contracts, constitution; official consents; no litigation; no default; financial statements and information correct; no documentary taxes

Security generally Security is first priority, security ranking ahead of all other creditors and not pari passu with any other creditors; security is not liable to avoidance on debtor's insolvency; debtor has title to and beneficial ownership of secured assets, free of other security interests, liens, encumbrances, options, rights of others; assets are saleable on enforcement (no prohibitions).

Warranties for particular security, consider:

Land Title duly registered; no leases, rights of occupation, rights of way, restrictions, covenants or other adverse rights or interests affecting property; environmental compliance; no breach of planning or other laws, laws in relation to the land and buildings.

Goods No leases or adverse rights

Contracts Full copies supplied, no unnotified variations; contracts are assignable by security and on realisation; validity and enforceability of the contracts (including any security or guarantees for the contracts); no set-offs or defences of obligors who are liable on the contracts.

Investment securities Fully-paid, no liabilities; secured party and any purchaser on enforcement has right to be registered as holder.

Debts Full disclosure of terms; no set-offs or defences of debtors owing the debts; validity and enforceability of the debts (including any security or guarantees for the debts)

Intellectual property No licences or encumbrances; no known actual or pending claim for infringement of the intellectual property rights; compliance with terms; due registration

Covenants

Debtor will:

– supply information about its financial condition and the secured assets;

– supply financial statements;

– allow creditor access and inspection rights;

– notify litigation, liabilities, official notices, defaults on contracts, and claims affecting the secured asset;

– permit investigation of title (especially land) and provide report on title;

- supply compliance certificates and notify defaults;
- maintain security, notably:
    - maintain and renew registration;
    - grant formal security over after-acquired property and accessions;
    - grant further assurance to validate and perfect security;
    - grant security over foreign assets in required local form;
    - give creditor possession of land title deeds, documents relating to goods, major contracts, investments, negotiable instruments, insurance policies and intellectual property rights;
    - assist creditor to be registered as legal holder of investments and other intangibles;
    - notice to obligors on claims covered by the security;
- not grant or permit other security over the secured assets;
- prevent liens;
- not sell or dispose of all or part of secured assets (except dealing with assets covered by the floating charge in the ordinary course of business);
- not grant leases, licences, or charters of the assets, nor accept surrenders of leases or licences (land, ship, aircraft, large chattels, intellectual property);
- keep assets in repair;
- not make alterations to the asset:
    - no land development, construction or change of user (compliance with development and zoning laws);
    - no alterations to ship, aircraft, large chattels;
    - no variations or waivers or terminations of specific contracts covered by the security or grants of consents thereunder;
    - not submit contract disputes to arbitration;
- as to insurance:
    - maintain insurance against specified risks in approved amounts, subject to approved deductibles, in approved terms, with approved insurers, and through approved brokers;
    - apply insurances towards reinstatement if required (otherwise towards secured debt), or after default, towards the secured liabilities (but third party liability insurance to be paid direct to third parties concerned);
    - ensure insurances do not become void or voidable, comply with warranties and conditions;
    - pay premiums and notify renewals to creditor;

- notify assignment of insurances to insurers;
- provide insurance broker reports;
- procure brokers undertakings to waive their lien on the policies, notify revocation of cover or non-renewal;
- deposit policies with secured creditor;
- procure that insurers will not cancel policy, reduce the cover or change the deductibles without prior written notice to the secured creditor;
- (where the secured creditor is joint insured) procure that insurers agree in scheduled form that (1) the insurers waive all rights of subrogation against the secured creditor, (2) the secured creditor is additional insured, (3) the insurers waive rights of contribution against other insurances effected by the secured creditor, (4) the secured creditor is not liable for premiums or other policy obligations, (5) the secured creditor is under no duty of disclosure to the insurers, (6) as against the secured creditor, the insurance will not be avoided by reason of misrepresentation, absence of due diligence, cancellation by the debtor, or breach of any warranty or condition in the policy;

- comply with contracts, charters, leases, licences, obligations affecting the secured asset;

- comply with contracts covered by the security;

- endeavour to procure compliance by other contracting parties, prevent infringements of intellectual property rights;

- pay taxes, rents, royalties, liabilities, rights issue subscriptions, exchange prices and registration fees applicable to the secured asset;

- maintain intellectual property rights (fees, registration);

- comply with environmental and other laws applicable to the secured asset;

- defend assets against adverse claims;

- exercise voting and other rights in respect of investment securities so as not to prejudice security value and, after event of default or potential event of default, as directed by the creditor; provide proxies to secured creditor (if secured creditor not registered holder).

Consider other credit covenants: no change in business, financial ratios, no large capital expenditure or large investments; limitation on borrowings and guarantees, etc.

Maintenance of value

Debtor will provide extra eligible security or prepay secured debt if the value of the secured assets falls below percentage of secured debt, e.g. 130 per cent. Frequency and method of valuation. Payment of costs of valuations.

Retention accounts

Debtor will pay the following into retention account of bank creditor:

- rentals and hire on leases, licences and charters;
- royalties;
- commercial receivables;
- proceeds under contracts;
- dividends, interest, redemption and sale proceeds on investment securities;
- insurance proceeds;
- nationalisation, expropriation, requisition and other compensation proceeds.

Events of default

Non-payment; non-compliance with covenants; incorrect representation or warranty; cross-default; insolvency events; other security enforcement creditors execution and other process; material adverse change. Apply appropriate events of default to subsidiaries, guarantors, other parties providing security, lessees, other contracting parties, as appropriate.

Enforcement

- Creditor has right to remedy breach of covenant at expense of debtor, e.g. repairs, insurance, pay taxes.
- Enforcement powers: sale privately, or by public auction, in whole or in parts, in any currency, on deferred terms, for cash or property; possession; receivership (receiver's powers, remuneration, removal and protections, agent of debtor). Waiver of appraisal in some civil code countries

- Application of proceeds: prior claims, costs, interest, principal

- Protection of third parties, e.g. purchasers on enforcement (not concerned to see if enforcement is valid or price sufficient or as to application of realisation proceeds)

- Creditor right to delegate powers

- Power of attorney, e.g. to transfer the property on forced sale, implement covenants

- Creditor right to consolidate securities

- Debtor liable for shortfall

- Right to collect and compromise claims on enforcement and terminate contracts

- Powers of floating charge receiver in English-based countries: see next form

Creditor protections

- Standard of care in relation to deposited documents, secured assets held by creditor or registered in his name, voting and conversion rights

- No duty to enforce contracts or other rights

- No liability to return sums paid under unenforceable or invalidated contracts, e.g. for *force majeure*

- Standard of care in relation to enforced sale

- No liability as mortgagee in possession

- Indemnity to creditor, his receivers and agents

- Right to disclose interests, e.g. in shares

Miscellaneous

Expenses; assignments; currency indemnity; waivers; remedies cumulative; set-off; notices; severability; counterparts; language; governing law; jurisdiction; waiver of sovereign immunity. Syndicate agent or trustee clauses where appropriate.

4. Charging clauses in English fixed and floating charge

This form illustrates typical provisions in an English universal fixed and floating charge over all a company's assets for the creation of the charges.

The objective of the charging clause is to impose a fixed charge on as many assets as possible since a fixed charge has a better priority and other advantages when compared to a floating charge, especially priority over preferential creditors (taxes and employees): see para 2.6. But if the company is able to deal with any fixed charge assets in the ordinary course of business, then – even if the charge is expressly stated to be a floating charge – it may be treated as a floating charge. This will be most likely to occur in relation to fixed charges over working bank accounts and possibly temporary investment securities, but case law shows that a restriction on dealings with commercial receivables, other than by paying them into the company's bank account, will generally be upheld, even though the proceeds, once in the bank account, are inevitably subject only to a floating charge. But if the moneys paid into a particular bank account are frozen (even though those in another bank account are not), the bank account may be subject to a fixed charge. Restrictions on dealing with other fixed assets should be considered, e.g. plant and machinery, and investment securities. It is impracticable to impose a fixed charge on assets which the company must be able to use and dispose of in the ordinary course of business, e.g. inventory and manufactured products.

This form does not contain a provision for the automatic crystallisation of a floating charge (i.e. its conversion into a fixed charge) over assets which are in danger of being seized by another creditor, but such a provision could be considered.

CHARGING CLAUSES

1. Creation of fixed security
The chargor charges and agrees to charge in favour of the Bank, as security for the payment of all the secured liabilities, all its present and future interests in the following:

(a) by way of a first legal mortgage:

- all the property specified in the schedule;
- all other estates or interests in any freehold or leasehold property now belonging to it;

    – all shares in any subsidiaries of the chargor and all income and capital moneys, securities or other property and rights arising in relation to those shares; and

(b) by way of a first fixed charge:

    – (to the extent that they are not the subject of a mortgage under paragraph (a) above) all estates or interests in any freehold or leasehold property;

    – all buildings, fixtures, and fittings, and all plant and machinery attached to any property hereby specifically charged;

    – the benefit of any covenants for title given or entered into by any predecessor in title of the chargor in respect of that property or any moneys paid or payable in respect of those covenants;

    – all plant and machinery;

    – (to the extent that they are not the subject of a mortgage under paragraph (a) above) shares, bonds, debentures, and other securities and investments;

    – all moneys standing to the creditor of any account with any bank or other person and the debts represented by them;

    – all contracts and policies of insurance and all benefits in respect of the insurances and all claims and returns of premiums in respect of them;

    – all of the chargor's book and other debts, the proceeds of the same and all other moneys due and owing to the chargor and the benefit of all rights, securities and guarantees of any nature in relation to any of the foregoing;

    – all of the chargor's rights and benefits under the agreements listed in the schedule, any distributorship or similar agreements entered into by it, any letters of credit issued in its favour and all bills of exchange and other negotiable instruments held by it;

    – any beneficial interest, claim or entitlement of the chargor in any pension fund;

    – its goodwill;

    – the benefit of all licences, consents and authorisations (statutory or otherwise) held in connection with its business or the use of any asset specified in any other paragraph in this clause and the right to recover and receive all compensation which may be payable to it in respect of them;

    – its uncalled capital;

    – all know-how, patents, trade marks, service marks, designs, business names, topographical or similar rights, copyrights and other intellectual property monopoly rights and any interests (including by way of licence) in any of the foregoing (in each case whether registered or not and including all applications for the same), together with the patents and trademarks specified in the schedule.

2. Creation of floating charge

The chargor charges in favour of the Bank by way of a first floating charge all its assets not otherwise effectively mortgaged or charged by way of fixed mortgage or charge by Clause 1.

3. Conversion

The Bank may by notice to the chargor convert the floating charge created by this Deed into a fixed charge as regards all or any of the chargor's assets specified in the notice if:

(a) an Event of Default is outstanding; or

(b) the Bank considers those assets to be in danger of being seized or sold under any form of distress, attachment, execution or other legal process or otherwise to be in jeopardy.

4. Restrictions on dealing

4.1 General The chargor shall not:

(a) create or permit to subsist any mortgage, charge, lien or other security interest on any asset covered by this Deed other than any security interest created by this Deed; or

(b) sell, transfer, grant, or lease or otherwise dispose of any asset covered by this Deed, except for the disposal in the ordinary course of trade of any asset subject to the floating charge created under Clause 2.

4.2 Book debts and receipts The chargor shall:

(a) get in and realise the chargor's:

- securities to the extent held by way of temporary investment;
- book and other debts and other moneys; and
- royalties, fees and income of like nature in relation to any intellectual property right owned by it,

in the ordinary course of its business and hold the proceeds of the getting in and realisation (until payment into a bank account) upon trust for the Bank; and

(b) save to the extent that the Bank otherwise agrees, pay the proceeds of the getting in and realisation into a bank account in the name of the chargor.

5. Outline form of security over investment securities with margin requirement

Note on the form

This form sets out outline suggestions for a security agreement over marketable investment securities, notably debt securities including those held by depositories. The form would have to be adapted to meet the requirements of the relevant jurisdiction. Security over investment securities is described in chapter 6.

The chargor is required to maintain the collateral at a minimum value and has a right of substitution.

Particular points to check include (1) whether the secured party must be the legal holder of the securities as possessory pledgee, (2) whether any rights of substitution destroy the possessory pledge in those jurisdiction where absolute possession is required or converts the security into a floating charge in English-based jurisdictions, and (3) whether deposits of cash held by the secured party can be charged-back: see chapter 5. If not, they must be placed with a third party bank or be eligible for set-off on the insolvency of the chargor. For other points, see the checklists in this Appendix (nos. 1 and 2).

Controlling interests in equity securities would raise additional problems: see para 6–25. A sale of these securities, if 30 per cent or more of the total equity, might attract a mandatory offer for all the equity under the UK Takeover Code.

This form is inappropriate for a case where the secured creditor wishes to treat the securities as its own and to return equivalent securities or cash. In that event, the appropriate form would be a sale and repurchase agreement or equivalent title finance agreement. These are reviewed in another book in this series.

Outline form

Parties

— The debtor/borrower as chargor

— The bank/lender/contract counterparty as secured party

1. Secured obligations

1.1 Meaning The secured obligations are (for example):

1. all present and future liabilities and obligations owing by the chargor to the secured party, including contingent liabilities, damages, those owing jointly, and those acquired by the secured party from a third party; or

2. all liabilities and obligations owing by the debtor to the creditor under a specified credit or other agreement (as amended from time to time) plus those designated by the chargor to the secured party plus those arising under this security agreement.

1.2 Payment The chargor will pay the secured obligations when due.

1.3 Appropriation The secured party may appropriate payments received towards the secured obligations in such order as it wishes, or towards other obligations owed by the chargor to the secured party.

1.4 Ultimate balance The security created by this security agreement is continuing and extends to the ultimate balance of the secured obligations, regardless of any earlier payment of the secured obligations in whole or in part.

2. Grant of security

The chargor mortgages and charges and agrees to mortgage and charge the collateral defined below to the secured party as fixed security for the secured obligations.

3. Meaning of collateral

The collateral is all the present and future right, title and interest of the chargor in the following, present and future:

- all cash deposits at banks specified by the chargor from time to time for the purposes of this security agreement;

- all certificated securities specified by the chargor from time to time for the purposes of this agreement or held in the name of or from time to time deposited with the secured party or its nominee or the certificates or other documentary evidence of which is held by the secured party or its nominee;

- all book-entry securities specified by the chargor from time to time for the purposes of this security agreement or held in the name of the secured party or its nominee;

- all claims, proprietary or otherwise, against depositories, custodians, clearing systems, investment managers and the like ("depositories") in respect of securities, fungible or specific, specified by the chargor from time to time for the purposes of this security agreement or credited to an account of the chargor with the Euroclear System or Cedel S.A. or other depository or held in the name of the secured party or its nominee, together with those securities;

- all cash accounts maintained by the above depositories for the chargor in respect of the securities specified above;

- all claims under contracts for the sale or other disposal or any collateral or other contracts for the purchase of assets intended to form part of the collateral;

- all distributions as defined below, with respect to all of the above and all accounts to which they are credited;

- all cash deposits owed by the secured party to the chargor;

- all substitutions, sub-divisions and variations of the above;

- all rights and powers in respect of the above assets.

4. Meaning of distributions

Distributions means:

- all dividends, interest, repayment or redemption proceeds paid or payable in respect of the collateral, whether capital or income;

- all securities or other property paid, distributed, accruing or offered in respect of the collateral or any exchanges of the collateral or any conversion of the collateral;

- the proceeds of sale or other realisation of any of the collateral or the above.

5. Transfer of collateral

5.1   Method of transfer The chargor will transfer the collateral to the secured party as follows:

- in the case of cash or deposits, by procuring that the cash or deposits are held by a bank specified by the secured party in an account in the name of the secured party;

- in the case of certificated securities, by delivery of the certificates or other paper to the secured party, accompanied by appropriate duly executed instruments of transfer or assignments, and any other documents necessary to confer legal title on the secured party;

- in the case of book-entry securities, by procuring that the entity maintaining the register or other record of the securities records the secured party as the legal holder of the securities or as pledgee if applicable;

- in the case of claims in respect of securities (and distributions in relation to those securities) against depositories, by procuring that the depository records the secured party as the legal holder of the claims;

- in all cases by such other action as is necessary to give the secured party full legal title and possession of the collateral and a valid pledge.

5.2 Documentary taxes The chargor will ensure that all stamp duties and other documentary taxes are paid in respect of the above transfers of the collateral.

5.3 Agents The secured party may appoint an agent to hold the collateral in the name of the agent. Subject to clause 9.1, the secured party will be responsible for the acts and omissions of the agent to the same extent that the secured party is responsible for its own acts and omissions under the security agreement.

6. Margin of value

6.1 Minimum value The chargor will ensure that eligible collateral has at all times a minimum value of not less than 125 per cent of the amount of the secured obligations.

6.2 Eligible collateral Eligible collateral is [specify eligible securities by reference for example to type, issuer, currency, maturity, listing, fully-paid and rating by approved rating agencies; specify eligible cash by reference to the currency].

6.3 Valuation of collateral Eligible collateral will be valued as follows:

- in the case of cash, its nominal amount;

- in the case of securities, the market value quoted on the relevant exchange or, if there is no quotation or, in the opinion of the secured party, the quotation does not reflect the then market value of the security, the market value estimated by the secured party in its good faith opinion.

6.4 Currency conversion For valuation purposes, cash and securities denominated in a currency other than the currency of the secured obligations will be converted into the currency of the secured obligations at the market spot rate of exchange in the specified international market for the purchase of the currency of the secured obligations with the currency of the relevant cash or securities as determined by the secured party in good faith.

6.5 Valuation of secured obligations Where the secured obligation arises under an interest swap, collar or cap or futures option or derivative agreement or an agreement for the sale or purchase of property, or the like, the secured obligation will be valued on any day by the secured party in a commercially reasonable manner as the total of all net sums payable under the agreement by the chargor to the secured party on that day plus the net sum which would be payable by the chargor to the secured party on that day if the secured party were to terminate or close-out the transactions concerned on that day in accordance with the relevant agreement. (Note: This formula assumes that netting is available on the insolvency of the chargor. Netting is reviewed on another work in this series on international financial law. If netting is not available, the secured sum would be gross, not net.)

6.6 Shortfalls If the value of eligible collateral falls short of the minimum value, the chargor will not later than one business day of telephonic or other request by the secured party either pay the secured obligations or transfer additional eligible collateral to the secured party in the manner described in clause 5 having a value not less than the shortfall.

6.7 Excesses If the value of eligible collateral exceeds the minimum value for not less than [one] business day, the secured party will, so long as no event of default or pending event of default has occurred, transfer the excess or hold the excess to the order of the chargor, but only if thereafter the minimum value would be maintained. The cash or securities representing the excess will be as specified by the chargor.

7. Substitutions

7.1 Notice of substitution The chargor may, not less than two business days in advance, notify the secured party in writing that the chargor wishes to substitute the collateral specified in the notice with other collateral.

7.2   Release and substitution The secured party will, not later than two business days after the notice release the collateral to be replaced by transfer in the manner described in clause 18.2 but only if:

- the new collateral is eligible collateral having a value not less than the value of the replaced collateral;

- the minimum value should be maintained immediately after the release;

- the new collateral has been transferred to the secured party in the manner described in clause 5 and the secured party is satisfied that it is covered by this security agreement;

- no event of default or pending event of default has occurred or is continuing or may occur on the release;

- the chargor has executed such documents and done such things as are necessary to ensure that the new collateral is covered by the security contemplated by this security agreement;

- the secured party is satisfied that the security over the new collateral is not liable to be set aside on the insolvency of the chargor.

7.3   Springing security The security interests created by this security agreement will continue over the collateral to be replaced until it is actually released and will cover the new collateral immediately without any further act.

8.   Distributions on the collateral

8.1   Cash distributions The secured party will credit all distributions in respect of the collateral which the secured party receives in cash to an account in its own books or with a bank selected by the secured party in its discretion. The chargor will be entitled to withdraw the moneys if:

- the minimum value would be maintained after the withdrawal;

- no event of default or pending event of default has occurred or is continuing or would occur on the withdrawal.

8.2   Other distributions All non-cash distributions received by the secured party in respect of the collateral will be added to the collateral.

8.3   Distributions received by chargor If the chargor receives direct any distributions in cash or property in respect of the collateral, they will be subject to this security and the chargor will hold them in trust for the secured party and at once transfer them to the secured party unless the chargor would have been entitled to withdraw them.

9.   Responsibilities in relation to collateral

9.1   Standard of care The secured party will exercise reasonable care to ensure the safe custody of the collateral to the extent required by applicable law and will be deemed to have exercised reasonable care if it exercises the same care as it would exercise in relation to its own property, but the secured party will have no liability:

— to insure the collateral;

— to collect any distributions in relation to the collateral;

— to enforce or monitor or preserve any rights or make claims pertaining to the collateral or distributions in respect of the collateral;

— to sell any collateral which may fall in value;

— for the insolvency of any bank or depository holding any cash or collateral;

— to exercise any voting, conversion, redemption or other rights in relation to the collateral except as specified below;

— to monitor the value of the collateral;

— to perform any obligations arising from securities included in the collateral.

9.2   Statements The secured party will provide periodic statements of the collateral appearing to it to be covered by this security agreement. These statements are not binding.

9.3   Bank accounts The secured party may operate all bank accounts covered by this security agreement. The chargor will give such mandates as are necessary to this end.

9.4   Notification duties The secured party may notify any person of the interest of the secured party or the chargor in the collateral when required to do so by law, regulation, official directive, or terms applying to the collateral concerned. The chargor will supply all information necessary to enable the secured party to comply with the above.

9.5   Voting and other rights The chargor may exercise, or direct the secured party to exercise, all voting and other rights in respect of the collateral but only if:

— the direction is in writing;

— no event of default or pending event of default has occurred and is continuing (when the secured party may exercise those rights without responsibility to the chargor);

— the exercise is consistent with this security agreement;

— the exercise will not, in the opinion of the secured party, adversely affect or diminish the value of the collateral;

— the exercise would not result in the minimum value not being maintained;

— the exercise would not, in the good faith opinion of the secured party, expose the secured party to any liability or other prejudice.

9.6   Proxies The chargor will provide the secured party with all proxies and other authorities which are necessary or desirable to enable the secured party to exercise those rights and powers in relation to the collateral which it is required or entitled to exercise.

9.7   Responsibilities for exercise of rights The secured party is not responsible for any exercise of rights required by the chargor. The chargor will indemnify the secured party against the same. The secured party will send to the chargor all notices and other communications it actually receives in respect of the collateral. The chargor is responsible for monitoring and for the exercise of all rights in respect of the collateral, including voting, options and conversion rights. In the absence of a complying direction as to exercise, the secured party may refrain from exercise or exercise as it sees fit, without liability to the chargor.

9.8   Interest The secured party will pay interest on credits to accounts owing by it to the chargor and included in the collateral in accordance with its usual practice for similar accounts.

9.9   Obligations on collateral The chargor will promptly pay all costs, subscription moneys, and other payments, perform all obligations and give all notifications it is required to give in relation to the collateral. If the chargor does not do so, the secured party may do so (without obligation) and the costs of so doing will be payable by the chargor immediately on demand and will be added to the secured obligations.

10. General covenants of chargor

The chargor will:

- supply financial statements and information about its financial condition;

- at its own cost, register and protect the security and file financing statements and the like where desirable;

- do acts, serve notices, execute documents and grant further assurance to validate and perfect the security and to ensure its priority, as requested by the secured party;

- enter into such security agreements in local form as the secured party may require in relation to foreign collateral;

- not sell or otherwise dispose of the collateral or any part of it or its proceeds except as permitted by this security agreement;

- no create or permit to subsist any other security interest over all or any of the collateral or its proceeds other than any lien in favour of depositories of any collateral for their charges pursuant to their usual terms of business;

- pay all taxes, stamp duties and levies in relation to the collateral and this security agreement;

- pay the fees and charges of all depositories and agents holding any collateral.

11. Return of equivalent securities

Where the secured party is required to transfer securities to the chargor under this security agreement, the secured party may return securities of an identical type, nominal value, description and amount. The secured party may not use non-cash collateral as its own and may not pay cash in lieu of non-cash collateral. (Note: If the secured party could use the securities as its own, the security may be converted into a sale and the appropriate title finance form should be used. The ability to return equivalent securities is intended to enable the secured party to return equivalents where the securities are held by a depository on a fungible basis.)

12. Representations and warranties

12.1 Main warranties The chargor warrants:

1. Status;

---

2. Powers

3. Authorisations

4. Validity and enforceability

5. Non-conflict with laws, constitution, contracts

6. Official consents

7. No litigation

8. No default on other obligations

9. Financial statements correct and no material adverse change since then

10. Security is a first priority security interest over the collateral ranking ahead of all other creditors and not pari passu with any other creditors and is effective on insolvency and against other creditors, and is not liable to avoidance as a preference or otherwise.

11. The chargor has absolute title to and beneficial ownership of the collateral free of all other security interests, liens and rights of others except for this security agreement.

12. The collateral is freely saleable without prohibitions, consents or prejudice to the secured party.

12.2 Repetition The representations and warranties will remain true so long as any secured obligation is outstanding or may become outstanding.

13. Events of default

The events of default are:

1. Non-payment of secured obligations when due

2. Non-compliance with obligations in the security agreement or in documents evidencing secured obligations

3. Incorrect representation or warranty in this security agreement or in documents evidencing secured obligations or in connection therewith

4. Cross-default

5. Enforcement of other security

6. Insolvency events

7. Creditors execution and other processes

8. Material adverse change. Apply appropriate events of default to guarantors, other providers of security and subsidiaries of the chargor.

14. Enforcement

14.1 Acceleration If an event of default occurs, the secured party may by notice declare the secured obligations immediately due and payable and immediately enforce this security without grace periods.

14.2 Powers of enforcement On enforcement, the secured party may:

- take possession of the collateral and documents in relation to the collateral, place the collateral with custodians or nominees and do all things necessary to this end;

- collect all payments and other property in respect of the collateral and give a good discharge;

- exercise all voting and other rights in respect of the collateral;

- appoint a receiver in respect of the collateral who is an agent of the chargor and for whose liabilities and remuneration the chargor is responsible;

- sell, exchange, convert into money or otherwise realise the collateral, privately or by auction, in whole or in lots, for money in any currency or for property, for immediate cash or on credit;

- convert the currency of recoveries into the currency of the secured obligations;

- generally act in relation to the collateral as if the secured party were the absolute beneficial owner of the collateral;

- exercise all other remedies of a secured creditor available by law.

14.3 Waivers In relation to enforcement, the chargor waives:

- notification or other formality;

- advertisements;

- appraisals and valuations.

14.4 Enforcement liabilities To the extent permissible by law, neither the secured party nor its receivers, depositories or agents or their respective officers or employees are responsible for any act, omission, default, negligence or other defect in the exercise of its powers (other than wilful misconduct). The chargor will indemnify them against liabilities and costs in the exercise of those powers, including any defect in title.

14.5 Delegation The secured party, its receivers, depositories, agents and attornies may delegate and sub-delegate their rights and powers.

14.6   Order of application All proceeds of realisation will be applied in the following order:

1.   to any claims having priority by law;

2.   to the secured obligations in such order as the secured party sees fit;

3.   to the chargor or other person entitled thereto.

14.7   Shortfall The chargor is liable for any shortfall.

14.8   Protection of third parties Purchasers and other third parties are protected, regardless of whether the powers of enforcement have become exercisable and regardless of the propriety or price or terms of any realisation or other act.

15.   Power of attorney

The chargor by way of security irrevocably appoints the secured party as its attorney to do anything the secured party may do, in the name of the chargor or the secured party.

16.   Avoidance

16.1   Reinstatement If any security is released on the faith of a payment which is avoided, the security will be reinstated.

16.2   Evidence If the secured obligations are paid, the secured party need not release the collateral unless certain that the payment is not liable to be avoided.

16.3   Compromise The secured party may compromise any avoidance claim.

16.4   Indemnity The chargor will indemnify the secured party against all liabilities and costs in connection with any avoidance.

17.   Set-off

The secured party may set off any secured obligations or other claims owed to the secured party by the chargor when due against any liability owed by the secured party to the chargor and may effect currency conversions to achieve the set-off. The secured party is not bound to set off.

18. Release of security

18.1 Payment in full Subject to the terms of this security agreement, when the secured obligations have been irrevocably paid or discharged in full and the secured party is under no liability which may give rise to a secured obligation, the secured party, will at the request and expense of the chargor release this security and transfer the collateral to the chargor.

18.2 Manner of release The transfer on any release of collateral to the chargor under this security agreement will be as reasonably directed by the chargor and at the expense of the chargor.

19. Miscellaneous

Expenses, assignments, currency indemnity in relation to secured obligations, default interest, secured party certificates as to the amount of the secured obligations conclusive in absence of manifest error, (in English forms) exclusion of s 93 of the Law of Property Act 1925 relating to consolidation, waivers, remedies cumulative, notices, severability of unenforceable or void terms, counterparts, language, (in US forms) waiver by chargor of jury trial, jurisdiction, waiver of sovereign immunity, governing law.

6. Guarantee-type clauses in security for third party's debt

Note on the Form

This form sets out guarantee-type clauses to be inserted in a security agreement where the grantor of the security gives the security as security for the debt of a third party, but does not assume personal liability for the third party's debt which is secured. In substance, the security is like a guarantee but the secured creditor's recourse is limited to the security. Hence the security agreement should contain clauses designed to protect the security along the lines of those found in guarantees. For a discussion of these clauses in relation to guarantees, see chapter 25.

In this form the security is given by a chargor to a bank in respect of the liabilities of a third party borrower which owes the secured liabilities to the bank.

1. Continuing security This security is a continuing security and shall secure the ultimate balance of the secured liabilities.

2. Waiver of defences This security shall not be prejudiced, affected or diminished by any act, omission or circumstance which but for this provision might operate to release or otherwise prejudice this security in whole or in part, including without limitation and whether or not known to the chargor or the Bank:

(a) any time or waiver granted to or composition with the borrower or any other person;

(b) the taking, variation, compromise, renewal or release of or neglect to perfect or enforce any rights, remedies or securities against the borrower or any other person;

(c) any legal limitation, incapacity or other circumstances relating to the borrower or the bankruptcy or liquidation of the borrower or any other person;

(d) any unenforceability, invalidity, non-provability or frustration of the secured liabilities or of any obligations of any other person or security, to the intent that this security hereunder shall remain in full force and this security agreement be construed as if there were no such unenforceability, invalidity, non-provability or frustration.

3. Immediate recourse The chargor waives any right it may have of first requiring the Bank to proceed against or enforce any other rights or security

---

of or claim payment from the borrower or any other person before enforcing this security.

4. Preservation of rights Until all the secured liabilities have been irrevocably paid and discharged in full, the Bank may:

(a) refrain from applying or enforcing any other security, moneys or rights held or received by the Bank in respect of the secured liabilities or apply and enforce the same in such manner and order as the Bank sees fit (whether against the secured liabilities or otherwise) and the chargor shall not be entitled to require that they are applied against the secured liabilities; and

(b) hold in suspense account (without liability to pay interest thereon) any proceeds received in respect of this security.

5. Non-competition Until the secured liabilities have been irrevocably paid in full, the chargor shall not by virtue of any payment made, or enforcement of this security or moneys received in respect of the collateral:

(a) be subrogated to any rights, security or moneys held, received or receivable by the Bank or be entitled to any right of contribution or indemnity;

(b) be entitled and shall not claim to rank as creditor against the estate or in the bankruptcy or liquidation of the borrower or other insolvency proceedings involving the borrower in competition with the Bank;

(c) receive, claim or have the benefit of any payment, distribution or security from or on account of the borrower or exercise any right of set-off as against the borrower or any other person or claim the benefit of any security or moneys held by or for the account of the Bank, and the Bank shall be entitled to apply such security and moneys as it sees fit.

The chargor shall forthwith pay to the Bank an amount equal to any such set-off in fact exercised by it and shall hold in trust for and forthwith pay or transfer, as the case may be, to the Bank any such payment or distribution or benefit of security in fact received by it.

6. Reinstatement Where any discharge (whether in respect of the secured liabilities or this security, or otherwise) is made in whole or in part or any arrangement is made on the faith of any payment, security or other disposition which is avoided or must be repaid on bankruptcy, liquidation, administration or otherwise without limitation, this security shall continue and be reinstated as if there had been no such discharge or arrangement. The Bank shall be entitled to concede or compromise any claim that any such payment, security or other disposition is liable to avoidance or repayment.

7. Additional security This security shall be in addition to and shall not in any way be prejudiced by any other security now or hereafter held by the Bank as security for the secured liabilities.

8. Certificate A certificate of the Bank as to the secured liabilities shall be conclusive as against the chargor.

Appendix: Part II

SHIP FINANCE

7. British Ship Mortgage Form

Note on the Form

The mortgage is in standard form issued by the Department of Transport under the Merchant Shipping (Registration, etc.) Act 1993.

The form is to the following effect and is accompanied by a deed of covenants setting out covenants, assignments of earnings and insurances and the like: see the next form. The deed of covenants is not registered in the ship registry but may have to be registered at the Companies Registry under Companies Act requirements for the public registration of most charges created by companies. The forms in other British-related jurisdictions are often in the pre-1993 form but are to similar effect. There is also usually in these other jurisdictions a form to secure a principal sum plus interest but this is rarely used. For a discussion of British ship mortgages specifically, see para 16–5 *et seq*.

MORTGAGE OF SHIP

to secure Account Current etc./other obligation

Guidance notes on the form state:

* If more than one mortgagor then a separate mortgage is required from each mortgagor, unless shares are jointly held.

* In respect of fishing vessels, mortgages may be registered only against those registered with FULL registration.

* The prompt registration of a mortgage deed with the Registry is essential to establish the priority of the mortgage. This is because the priority of the mortgage is determined by the date on which it is produced for registration and not from the date of the mortgage itself.

* If the mortgagor is a company, the mortgage must also be registered with the Registrar of the Companies within 21 days of its execution.

* It is important that the Registry is informed of any changes.

* Please write in black ink using BLOCK CAPITALS, and tick boxes where appropriate.

The mortgage reference No. (issued by the mortgagee) is:
[   ]

SECTION 1: DETAILS OF THE SHIP

IS THIS MORTGAGE IN RESPECT OF A FISHING VESSEL?
Yes/No

NAME OF SHIP: [   ]

OFFICIAL NUMBER: [   ]

SECTION 2: THE MORTAGE

Whereas there is [state "an account current" or write in a short description of the obligation]

between [give full name and address, with place of business in respect of a company] [as joint mortgagors] (hereinafter called "the mortgagor")

and [give full name and address, with place of business in respect of a company] [as joint mortgagees] (hereinafter called "the mortgagee")

[Describe fully the nature of the liabilities secured. You may refer to another document.]

Complete in respect of "account current":

Now I/we the mortgagor(s) in consideration of the advance made or to be made to me/us by the mortgagee(s), bind myself/ourselves to pay to the mortgagee(s) the sums for the time being due on this security whether by way of principal, interest or otherwise at the time(s) and in the manner mentioned above.

Complete in respect of "other obligation":

Now I/we the mortgagor(s) in consideration of

bind myself/ourselves to

For the purpose of better securing to the mortgagee(s) the sums/obligation mentioned above. I/we hereby mortgage to the mortgagee(s) [   ] (figures in words) shares of which I am/we are the owners in the ship described above and in its appurtenances.

Lastly, I/we for myself/ourselves, hereby declare that I/we have the power to mortgage in the manner aforesaid the above-mentioned shares and that they are free from encumbrances [*save as appears by the registry of the above ship*].

COMPLETE IF THE TRANSFEROR IS A COMPANY

Executed by the mortgagor as a deed on this

_____day of_____19_____by:

(a) the affixing of the common seal of the mortgagor in the presence of the following persons signing; *or*

(b) signing by the following persons;

Director _____

Director/Secretary _____

Authorised Signatory _____   Authorised Signatory _____

NOTE: *IN SCOTLAND – signature may be by:*
two directors; **or**
by a director and the secretary of the company; **or**
by any two persons authorised to sign and subscribe the documents on behalf of the company.

EXCEPT IN SCOTLAND – signature may be by:
two directors; **or**
by a director and the secretary of the company. If the common seal is affixed, any special requirements of the company's articles about signing must be complied with.

SECTION 3: TRANSFER OF MORTGAGE

I/We, the above mentioned mortgagee(s), in consideration of [enter the sum of money or the nature of the obligation]

this day [enter "paid to me/us", or narrative suitable to the obligation]
by [give full name and address of the transferee, with place of business in respect of a company]

hereby transfer to him/her/them the benefit of the within written security.

COMPLETE IF THE TRANSFEROR IS A COMPANY

Executed by the transferor as a deed on this

_____day of_____19_____by:

(a) the affixing of the common seal of the transferor in the presence of the following persons signing; *or*

(b) signing by the following persons

Director _____

Director/Secretary _____

Authorised Signatory _____   Authorised Signatory _____

NOTE: *IN SCOTLAND – signature may*   *EXCEPT IN SCOTLAND – signature may*
       be by: *be by:*
       two directors; **or**   *two directors;* **or**
       by a director and the secretary of   *by a director and the secretary of the com-*
       the company; **or**   *pany. If the common seal is affixed, any*
       by any two persons authorised to   *special requirements of the company's articles*
       sign and subscribe the documents   *about signing must be complied with.*
       on behalf of the company.

SECTION 4: DISCHARGE OF MORTGAGE

Received by the within-mentioned mortgagee(s)/transferee(s) of the mort-gage, [enter "the sum of   ", or narrative suitable to the obligation].

This within written security is now discharged.

The within mentioned mortgagee(s)/transferee(s) have agreed to discharge this within written security, and it is therefore, discharged.

Executed by the morgagee/transferee as a deed on this

_____day of_____19____by:

(a) the affixing of the common seal of the mortgagee/transferee in the presence of the following persons signing; *or*

(b) signing by the following persons

Director _____

Director/Secretary _____

Authorised Signatory _____   Authorised Signatory _____

NOTE: *IN SCOTLAND – signature may*   *EXCEPT IN SCOTLAND – signature may*
       be by: *be by:*
       two directors; **or**   *two directors;* **or**
       by a director and the secretary of   *by a director and the secretary of the com-*
       the company; **or**   *pany. If the common seal is affixed, any*
       by any two persons authorised to   *special requirements of the company's articles*
       sign and subscribe the documents   *about signing must be complied with.*
       on behalf of the company.

When the mortgage is originally executed this deed is sent with the correct fee to:

Registry of Shipping & Seamen
PO Box 165
Cardiff
CF1 5FU

8.   British Ship Mortgage Deed of Covenants

Note on the Form

This deed of covenants amplifies the basic provisions in the British standard form of ship mortgage. The reason for this split is historical. The deed of covenants is not registered at the ship registry but will usually have to be registered at the Companies Registry if the mortgage is created by a company. In this form, the mortgage secures liabilities under a specific loan or other facility agreement. This form will be suitable for most British-related jurisdictions.

In the interests of brevity, this form does not contain representations and warranties or events of default – those would normally appear in the facility agreement. For outline representations and warranties and events of default see the Outline General Summary of Terms of Security Agreements in this Appendix. These are also reviewed in detail in another work in this series on financial law – a book dealing with international loans, bonds and securities regulation. See also:

— as to registration of ships and ship mortgages, para 15–12 *et seq*

— as to covenants in ship mortgages, para 17–1 *et seq*

— as to ship loan events of default, para 18–2 *et seq*

— as to assignments of earnings and charters, chapter 21

— as to assignments of insurances, chapter 22.

Form of Deed of Covenants

THIS DEED OF COVENANTS is made the   day of
199

BETWEEN

1.   [   ] a company incorporated under the laws of
     [   ] whose principal office is at [   ] (the
     "Owner"); and

2.   [   ] carrying on a banking business at its branch
     at [   ] (the "Bank").

WHEREAS:

(A) The Owner is the sole, absolute owner of sixty-four sixty-fourth unen-cumbered shares in the motor vessel m.v. "[   ]" further described in the Appendix hereto.

(B) By a Facility Agreement dated [   ] 199 between (inter alia) [   ], the Owner and the Bank, the Owner has agreed on the terms thereof to execute and deliver and has executed and delivered on the date hereof in favour of the Bank a first priority Statutory Morgage over the whole of the said vessel as security (inter alia) for the due pay-ment of all sums from time to time payable thereunder by the Owner to the Bank.

(C) This Deed is supplemental to the Mortgage and to the security thereby created.

IT IS AGREED as follows:

I   GENERAL

1.   Interpretation

1.1   Incorporated definitions Unless the contrary intention appears any term defined in the Facility Agreement has the same meaning when used in this Mortgage.

1.2   Definitions

(a) In this Deed:

"**Charter**" has the meaning given to it in Clause 7 (Status of Charters).

"**Default Rate**" means the rate specified in Clause [   ] of the Facility Agreement. [This is a conventional default interest clause for overdue sums.]

"**Earnings**" includes all present and future moneys and claims which are earned by or become payable to or for the account of the Owner in connection with the operation or ownership of the Vessel and including but not limited to (i) freights, passage and hire moneys, (ii) remuneration for salvage and towage services, (iii) demurrage and detention moneys, (iv) all present and future moneys and claims payable to the Owner in respect of any breach or variation of a charterparty or contract of affreightment in respect of the Vessel, and (v) all moneys and claims in respect of the requisition for hire of the Vessel.

"Earnings Account" means the account opened and maintained by the Owner under Clause 10 (Payment of Earnings).

"Facility Agreement" means the Facility Agreement referred to in Recital (B) above.

"Insurances" means (a) all contracts and policies of insurance and all entries in clubs and/or associations which are from time to time taken out or effected in respect of the Vessel pursuant to Clause 13 (Insurances) and (b) all benefits thereunder, all claims in respect thereof and return of premiums, and "excess risks" in Clause 13 (Insurances) means (i) the proportion of claims for general average and salvage charges which are not recoverable as a result of the value at which a vessel is assessed for the purpose of such claims exceeding her hull and machinery insured value and (ii) collision liabilities not recoverable in full under the hull and machinery insurance by reason of such liabilities exceeding such proportion of the insured value of a vessel as is covered thereunder.

"Mortgage" means the Mortgage referred to in recital (B) above.

"Permitted Liens" means:

  (a) liens for unpaid crew's wages arising in accordance with usual maritime practice; and
  (b) liens for salvage,

and to the extent they are subordinate to the lien of the Mortgage:

  (i) liens for Master's disbursements incurred in the ordinary course of trading; and
  (ii) any other lien arising in the ordinary course of operation of the Vessel.

"Requisition Compensation" includes all moneys or other compensation payable by reason of requisition for title to or other compulsory acquisition of the Vessel otherwise than by requisition for hire.

"Secured Liabilities" means the sums and liabilities (actual or contingent) which are or may become payable or owing by the Owner to the Bank under or in connection with the Facility Agreement, this Deed, the Mortgage or any other Security Documents.

"**Security Assets**" means the Vessel, each Charter, the Earnings, the Insurances, Requisition Compensation and all other assets the subject of this security.

"**Security Period**" means the period beginning on the date hereof and ending on the date upon which all the Secured Liabilities which have or may arise have been irrevocably paid and discharged.

"**Total Loss**" includes:

(a) actual, constructive, compromised, agreed or arranged total loss of the Vessel;

(b) requisition for title or other compulsory acquisition of the Vessel otherwise than by requisition for hire; and

(c) capture, seizure, arrest, detention or confiscation of the Vessel by any government or by persons acting or purporting to act on behalf of any government unless the Vessel be released from such capture, seizure, arrest, detention or confiscation within one month after the occurrence thereof.

"**Vessel**" means m.v. "[   ]", as described in Recital (A) above and includes each part thereof and interest therein and all her engines, boilers, machinery, masts, spars, sails, boats, anchors, cables, chains, rigging tackle, outfit, spare gear, fuel, consumable and other stores, whether on board or ashore and whether now owned or hereafter acquired and also any and all conditions, improvements and replacements hereafter made in or to the Vessel or any part thereof, including all items and appurtenances aforesaid.

(b) In the Mortgage:

(i) references to "interest" mean interest and commission covenanted to be paid in accordance with the Facility Agreement;

(ii) references to "principal" mean all other sums of money and liabilities for the time being comprised in the Secured Liabilities; and

(iii) the expression "all sums for the time being owing to the Bank" means the whole of the Secured Liabilities.

1.3 Construction

(a) In this Deed, unless the contrary intention appears, a reference to:

(i) a provision of a law or regulation is a reference to that provision as amended or re-enacted;

(ii) a Clause or a Schedule is a reference to a clause of or a schedule to this Deed;

(iii)   any person includes a reference to its successors and assigns;

(iv)   the Facility Agreement, the Mortgage, this Deed, any other Security Document or any other document is a reference to the Facility Agreement, the Mortgage, this Deed, such other Security Document or such other document as amended, novated or supplemented.

(b) The headings in this Deed are for convenience only and are to be ignored in construing this Deed.

2.   Mortgage

As security for payment of the Secured Liabilities the Owner hereby mortgages the Vessel to the Bank by way of first fixed mortgage.

3.   Assignment

(a) The Owner hereby:

(i)   assigns and agrees to assign absolutely to the Bank all its rights, title and interest in or to each Charter, the Earnings, the Insurances, Requisition Compensation and all moneys payable in respect of a Total Loss; and

(ii)   to the fullest extent permitted by law charges as security for the Secured Liabilities in favour of the Bank all its rights, title and interest (if any) in the balance for the time being and from time to time standing to the credit of the Earnings Account, all interest thereon and the debts represented by such credit balance and interest,

PROVIDED THAT upon irrevocable payment in full of the Secured Liabilities the Bank will at the request and expense of the Owner re-assign to the Owner the items assigned by this Clause 3.

(b) The Owner will do or procure the doing of all such things and the execution of all such documents, as the Bank may from time to time require to ensure the payment to the Bank of the items assigned by this Clause 3.

4.   Continuing security

The security constituted by this Deed shall be continuing and not satisfied by any intermediate payment or satisfaction of the whole or any part of the Secured Liabilities but shall secure the ultimate balance of the Secured Liabilities. The security hereby given shall be in addition to and shall not be affected by any other security interest now or hereafter held by the Bank for all or any of the Secured Liabilities.

5. Covenant to pay and perform

The Owner hereby covenants (i) to pay the Secured Liabilities to the Bank promptly when due and (ii) to comply at all times with the terms (express or implied) of this Deed, the Mortgage and the Facility Agreement and any other Security Document to which it is a party.

6. Encumbrances and disposals

The Owner undertakes that (except with the prior written consent of the Bank) during the Security Period it will not except in favour of the Bank:

1. create or permit to subsist any mortgage, charge, lien or other security interest upon all or any part of the Security Assets other than, in the case of the Vessel, Permitted Liens; or

2. assign, sell, transfer or otherwise dispose of or abandon all or any part of the Security Assets or their proceeds.

II   EARNINGS

7. Status of charters

The Owner represents and warrants to the Bank that:

(a) neither it nor any charterer is in default under any charter or other contract for the employment of the Vessel (a "Charter");

(b) there are no pending or threatened actions, suits or proceedings in connection with any Charter.

8. Maintenance of charters

The Owner will:

(a) take all necessary steps to procure the due performance by each charterer or shipper of its obligations under each Charter;

(b) duly perform its obligations under each Charter, notify the Bank of any material default by itself or any charterer or shipper under any Charter and institute and maintain all such proceedings as may be necessary or expedient to preserve or protect the interest of the Owner and the Bank in each Charter.

9. Obligations under charters

Notwithstanding anything concerned herein:

(a) the Owner shall remain liable under each Charter to perform all the obligations assumed by it thereunder;

(b) the Bank shall not be under any obligations or liability under any Charter or liable to make any payment thereunder;

(c) the Bank shall not be obliged to enforce against any charterer or shipper any term of any Charter, or to make any enquiries as to the nature or sufficiency of any payment received by the Bank.

10. Payment of Earnings

The Owner will:

(a) immediately open and thereafter maintain an account (the "Earnings Account") with the Bank for the purpose of receiving the Earnings of the Vessel;

(b) procure that the Earnings are paid directly to the Earnings Account or as the Bank may from time to time direct;

(c) at any time and from time to time upon the written request of the Bank execute and deliver any and all such further instruments and documents as the Bank may require for the purpose of obtaining the full benefit of the assignment of the Earnings effected hereby and of the rights and powers hereby granted;

(d) from time to time at the request of the Bank give notice to any charterer under any Charter which has a duration of more than three months or which by virtue of optional extensions may exceed three months substantially in the following form (duly completed):

"To: [Charterer]

Dear Sirs,

m.v. "[   ]"

We hereby give you notice that by a Deed of Covenants dated [   ] 199
we assigned to [   ] of [   ] (the "Bank") all hire, freights
and other earnings of the above-named Vessel.

Accordingly, we hereby authorise and instruct you to pay to the Bank at its
address aforesaid all payments due to us under the terms of the charter relating to the Vessel dated [   ].

Will you please note that these instructions are not to be revoked or varied
without the prior written consent of the Bank.

Will you please acknowledge receipt of this letter by signing and returning
one copy to us and one copy to the Bank.

Yours faithfully,

We, [   ] of [   ] acknowledge receipt of a notice of
assignment of which this is a copy, confirm that we have not received any
other notices of assignment relating to the charter mentioned above, and
agree that we will pay all sums hereafter to become due under the said
charter to [   ] at the address specified above."

11. Application of earnings

(a) Until the occurrence of an Event of Default or an event which with giving of notice, lapse of time or other condition might constitute an Event
of Default, all Earnings in the Earnings Account may be withdrawn by
the Owner.

(b) On and after the occurrence of an Event of Default or event which
would with giving of notice, lapse of time or other condition might constitute an Event of Default, the Bank may, so long as such Event or event
continues:

(i) retain all amounts credited to the Earnings Account and the Owner
shall not be entitled to withdraw the same;

(ii) set off or otherwise apply all or any part of such retentions in or
towards payment of the Secured Liabilities in such order as the
Bank may decide; or

(iii) combine or consolidate the Earnings Account with any other
account of the Owner (whether sole or joint account) including one
specially opened for that purpose.

III INSURANCES

12. Insurance definitions

In this Deed:

(a) "approved" means approved by the Bank in writing;

(b) "required amount" means the higher of (i) the market value of the Vessel, determined from time to time in accordance with Clause [   ] of the Facility Agreement but without deduction of the amount of any prior or equal ranking security interest or lien thereon and (ii) that amount which at the relevant time is 120 per cent of the Secured Liabilities;

(c) "Insurers" means the underwriters or insurance companies with whom any obligatory insurance is effected and the managers of any protection and indemnity or war risks association in which the Vessel may at any time be entered;

(d) "obligatory insurance" means insurances and entries required by the terms hereof.

13. Insurances

During the Security Period the Owner will:

(a) at all times keep the Vessel insured in the required amount, in US dollars or another approved currency in the name of the Owner or (if the Bank so requires) in the joint names of the Owner and Bank through approved brokers against all risks (including hull and machinery and excess risks) with approved underwriters or insurance companies and by policies in approved form;

(b) at all times keep the Vessel insured in the required amount in the like manner as aforesaid against war risks (including risks of mines and all risks, whether or not regarded as war risks, excepted by the free of capture and seizure clauses in the standard form of Lloyds marine policy) either:

   (i) with approved underwriters or insurance companies and by policies in approved form, or, at its option,

  (ii) by entering the Vessel in an approved war risks association;

(c) at all times keep the Vessel entered in respect of her full value and tonnage in an approved protection and indemnity association against all risks as are normally covered by such protection and indemnity association (including pollution risks and the proportion not recoverable in case of collision under the running down clause inserted in the ordinary Lloyd's policies); and

(d) effect and maintain at all times after a request from the Bank a policy of mortgagee's interest insurance (including an additional perils clause whereby the Bank is indemnified against additional perils that arise as a direct consequence of the Vessel or Owner or the Managers of the Vessel or any Charterers causing a discharge of oil or other hazardous substance for which the total liability amounts payable in compensation for pollution damage and clean up costs exceed the amount, if any, paid and recoverable by the Owner under insurances effected in respect of the Vessel) in approved form and in such amount as the Bank may from time to time stipulate.

14. Insurance covenants

During the Security Period the Owner will:

(a) not without the prior consent of the Bank alter any obligatory insurance nor make, do, consent or agree to any act or omission which would or might render any obligatory insurance invalid, void, voidable or unenforceable or render any sum paid out under any obligatory insurance repayable in whole or in part;

(b) not cause or permit the Vessel to be operated in any way inconsistent with the provisions of warranties of, or implied in, or outside the cover provided by, any obligatory insurance or to be engaged in any voyage or to carry any cargo not permitted by the obligatory insurances without first covering the Vessel in the required amount and her freights for an amount approved by the Bank in US dollars or another approved currency with approved insurers;

(c) duly pay all premiums, calls, contributions or other sums of money from time to time payable in respect of any obligatory insurance;

(d) renew all Insurances at least fourteen days before the relevant policies or contracts expire and procure that the approved brokers and war risks and protection and indemnity clubs and associations shall promptly confirm in writing to the Bank as and when each such renewal is effected;

(e) forthwith upon the effecting of any obligatory insurance, give written notice thereof to the Bank stating the full particulars (including the dates and amounts) thereof, and on request produce the receipts for each sum paid by it pursuant to Clause 14(c) above;

(f) arrange for the execution and delivery of such guarantees as may from time to time be required by any protection and indemnity or war risks club or association;

(g) in the event that the Owner receives payment of any moneys hereby assigned save as provided in the loss payable clauses scheduled hereto, forthwith pay over the same to the Bank and until paid over such moneys shall be held in trust for the Bank by the Owner.

15. Application of insurance proceeds

(a) All sums receivable in respect of the Insurances after the occurrence of an Event of Default which is continuing and all sums receivable in respect of a Total Loss shall be paid to the Bank and the Bank may in its discretion, apply them towards the loss, liability or damage concerned or as permitted by the Security Documents or by law or in or towards payment of the Secured Liabilities in such order as the Bank may decide.

(b) Subject to sub-clause (a):

(i) each sum receivable in respect of a major casualty (that is to say any casualty in respect whereof the claim or the aggregate of the claims exceed US$[ ] (or equivalent)) other than in respect of protection and indemnity risk Insurances shall be paid to the Bank;

(ii) the insurance moneys received by the Bank in respect of any such major casualty shall, at the option of the Bank, be paid (1) to the person to whom the relevant liability shall have been incurred or (2) upon the Owner furnishing evidence satisfactory to the Bank that all loss and damage resulting from the casualty has been properly made good and repaired, to the Owner or, at the option of the Bank, to the person by whom any repairs have been or are to be effected. The receipt of any such person shall be a full and sufficient discharge for the same to the Bank.

(c) Subject to sub-clause (a), each sum receivable referred to in sub-clause (b) which does not exceed US$[ ] (or equivalent) shall be paid in full to the Owner or its order and shall be applied by it for the purpose of making good the loss and fully repairing all damage in respect of which the receivables shall have been collected.

(d) Subject to sub-clause (a), each sum receivable in respect of protection and indemnity risk Insurances shall be paid direct to the person to whom the liability to which such sum relates was incurred, or to the Owner in reimbursement to it of moneys expended in satisfaction of such liability.

16. Notices, undertakings, endorsements

(a) The Owner shall forthwith give notice in the form set out as Schedule I hereto (duly completed) or in such other form as the Bank may require and cause its insurance brokers to give notice of this Assignment in respect of Insurances to all insurers, clubs and associations providing insurance in connection with the Vessel and procure that such notice is endorsed on all policies, entries, slips, cover notes or other instruments of the Insurances (other than in respect of Mortgagee's Interest Insurance) effected in respect of the Vessel.

(b) The Owner shall ensure that (i) all relevant brokers, insurers, underwriters, war risks clubs and protection and indemnity associations will address to the Bank letters of undertaking in the LIBA form in the case of London brokers, in their standard form in the case of London clubs and substantially in the form set out as Schedule II hereto in any other case and (ii) the approved brokers shall retain all instruments of Insurance referred to in Clause 13(a) and supply copies thereof to the Bank.

(c) The Owner shall ensure that a loss payable clause substantially in the form set out as Schedule III hereto (or in their standard form in the case of London clubs) is endorsed on all Insurances, certificates of entry slips, cover notes or other instruments of Insurance (other than mortgage interest insurance) and that the interest of the Bank in the Insurances by virtue of the assignment contained herein ranks in all respects prior to the interest of the Owner.

17. Power of Bank to insure

If the Owner fails to effect and keep in force insurances in accordance with this Deed, it shall be permissible, but not obligatory, for the Bank to effect and keep in force insurance or insurances in the amounts required hereunder and entries in a protection and indemnity association or club and, if it deems necessary or expedient, the war risks upon the Vessel, and the Owner will pay to the Bank the costs of so doing.

IV VESSEL COVENANTS

18. Registration of vessel

The Owner will during the Security Period:

(a) maintain the valid and effective registration of the Vessel under the laws of England and the British flag and ensure nothing is done or omitted whereby such registration of the Vessel would or might be defeated or imperilled; and

(b) not change the name, port of registration or certificate of registry or equivalent document of the Vessel.

19. Classification and repair

The Owner will during the Security Period:

(a) ensure that the Vessel is surveyed from time to time as required by the classification society in which the Vessel is for the time being entered and maintain and preserve the Vessel in good working order and repair, ordinary wear and tear excepted, and in any event in such condition as will entitle her to the classification [   ] with [   ], or to the equivalent classification in another internationally recognised classification society of like standing;

(b) procure that all repairs to or replacement of any damaged, worn or lost parts or equipment shall be effected in such manner (both as regards workmanship and quality of materials) as not to diminish the value of the Vessel;

(c) ensure that the Vessel complies with all laws, regulations and requirements (statutory or otherwise) from time to time applicable to vessels registered under the British flag; and

(d) not without the prior written consent of the Bank cause or permit to be made any change in the structure, type or performance characteristics of the Vessel.

20. Lawful and safe operation

The Owner will during the Security Period:

(a) not cause or permit the Vessel to be operated in any manner contrary to the laws, regulations, treaties and conventions (and all rules and regulations issued thereunder) from time to time applicable to the Vessel;

(b) not cause or permit the Vessel to trade with or within the territorial waters of any country wherein her safety may be imperilled;

(c) not cause or permit the Vessel to be employed in any manner which would render her liable to confiscation, forfeiture, seizure, destruction or condemnation as prize;

(d) ensure that the Vessel is not employed in any trade or business which is forbidden by international law or is illicit or is carrying illicit or prohibited goods;

(e) in the event of hostilities in any part of the world (whether war be declared or not) ensure that the Vessel is not employed in carrying any contraband goods and does not trade in any zone after it has been declared a war zone by any authority or by the Vessel's war risks insurers unless the Bank shall have first given its consent thereto in writing and there shall have been effected by the Owner and at its expense such special insurance cover as the Bank may require; and

(f) not charter the Vessel to or permit the Vessel to serve under any contract of affreightment with a person included within the definition of designated foreign country or national of a designated foreign country being a country from time to time specified by the Bank and such that, if the Earnings or any part thereof were derived therefrom, that fact would render either the Facility Agreement or the security conferred hereby unlawful under government regulations applicable to the Bank. Note: This is designed to cover "trading with the enemy" embargoes and is particularly important for US banks.

21. Chartering, management and repairs

Except as the Bank may otherwise have previously consented in writing, the Owner will during the Security Period:

(a) not let the Vessel (i) on demise charter for any period or (ii) on any time or consecutive voyage charter for a term which exceeds or which by virtue of any optional extensions could exceed [six] months duration or (iii) on terms whereby more than two months hire is payable in advance or (iv) otherwise than on the best commercial terms then available in arm's length transactions;

(b) not enter into any agreement or arrangement whereby the Earnings may be shared with any other person;

(c) ensure that the Vessel is managed only by [   ] of [   ]; and

(d) not put the Vessel into the possession of any person for the purpose of work being done upon her beyond the amount of US$[ ] (or equivalent) unless either (1) such person shall have given an undertaking to the Bank not to exercise any lien on the Vessel or her Earnings or Insurances for the cost of such work or otherwise or (2) the Bank is satisfied in its discretion that by reason of the availability of insurances to meet the cost of such work or by reason of the ability of the Owner to discharge such cost when due or otherwise there is no risk of the Bank being prejudiced by the absence of such an undertaking.

22.   Arrests and liabilities

The Owner will during the Security Period:

(a) pay and discharge all obligations and liabilities whatsoever which have given or may give rise to liens on or claims enforceable against the Vessel and take all other steps necessary to prevent a threatened arrest of the Vessel;

(b) notify the Bank promptly in writing of the levy of any distress on the Vessel or her arrest, detention, seizure, condemnation as prize, compulsory acquisition or requisition for title or use and (save in the case of compulsory acquisition or requisition for title or use) obtain her release within 14 days; and

(c) pay and discharge when due all dues, taxes, assessments, governmental charges, fines and penalties lawfully imposed on or in respect of the Vessel or the Owner.

23.   Information

The Owner will during the Security Period:

(a) promptly notify the Bank of the occurrence of any accident, casualty or other event which has caused or resulted in or may cause or result in the Vessel's being or becoming a Total Loss;

(b) give to the Bank from time to time on request such information as the Bank may require regarding the Vessel, her employment, position and engagements;

(c) provide the Bank on request with copies of the classification certificate of the Vessel and of all periodic, damage or survey reports on the Vessel;

(d) promptly furnish the Bank with full information of any casualty or other accident or damage to the Vessel involving an amount in excess of US$[   ] (or equivalent);

(e) give to the Bank and its duly authorised representatives reasonable access to the Vessel for the purpose of conducting on board inspections and surveys of the Vessel and will pay the reasonable expenses incurred by the Bank in connection with such inspections and surveys. [Such inspection and surveys shall not take place at the expense of the Owner more than once in each calendar year]; and

(f) furnish to the Bank from time to time upon reasonable request certified copies of the ship's log in respect of the Vessel.

24. Protection of security

(a) The Bank shall without prejudice to its other rights and powers here-under be entitled (but not bound) at any time and as often as may be necessary to take any such action as it may in its discretion think fit for the purpose of protecting the security created by this Deed.

(b) Without prejudice to the generality of the foregoing:

  (i) if any of the terms of Clause 13 (Insurances) shall not be complied with the Bank shall be entitled to effect and thereafter to maintain all such Insurances upon the Vessel as the Bank in its discretion may think fit;

  (ii) if any of the terms of Clause 19 (Classification and repair) above shall not be complied with the Bank may arrange for the carrying out of such repairs and surveys as it may deem expedient or necessary;

  (iii) if any of the terms of Clauses 21 (Chartering, management and repairs) and 22 (Arrests and liabilities) shall not be complied with the Bank may pay and discharge all such obligations and liabilities as are therein mentioned and take any such measures as it may deem necessary for the purpose of securing the release of the Vessel.

(c) Each and every expense or liability incurred by the Bank in or about the protection of the security and pursuant to the foregoing sub-clause shall be repayable to it by the Owner on demand together with interest thereon at the Default Rate from the date whereon such expense or liability was incurred by the Bank.

V ENFORCEMENT

25. Enforcement of security

This security shall become immediately enforceable upon the occurrence of an Event of Default [i.e. conventional events of default in the facility agreement] and the Bank shall be entitled without notice immediately or at any time thereafter to put into force and exercise all the powers and remedies possessed by it according to law as mortgagee and chargee of the Security Assets as and when it may see fit (so that ss 93 and 103 of the Law of Property Act, 1925 shall not apply to this security) and in particular:

(a) to demand payment by written notice to the Owner of the Secured Liabilities, whereupon such payment by the Owner to the Bank shall become immediately due and payable;

(b) to exercise all the rights and remedies in foreclosure and otherwise given to the Bank by any applicable law;

(c) to take possession of the Vessel;

(d) to recover and collect all Earnings, Insurances and Requisition Compensation, to give a good receipt therefor on behalf of the Owner, to permit the brokers through whom collection or recovery of any Insurances is effected to charge and retain the usual brokerage therefor and to require that all policies, contracts and other records relating to the Insurances (including details of and correspondence concerning outstanding claims) be immediately delivered to or to the order of the Bank;

(e) to take over or institute all such proceedings in connection with all or any of the Security Assets as the Bank in its absolute discretion thinks fit and to discharge, compound, release or compromise all or any of the Security Assets or claims in respect thereof including without limitation claims in respect of the Vessel which have given or may give rise to any charge or lien on or arrest of the Vessel or which are or may be enforceable by proceedings against the Vessel;

(f) to sell all or any part of the Security Assets, (in the case of the Vessel with or without the benefit of any charterparty or other contract) by public auction or private contract, at any place in the world, with or without advertisement or notice to the Owner, for cash or on credit and otherwise and upon such terms as the Bank in its absolute discretion may determine, and at any such public sale to purchase the Vessel and to set off all or any part of the Secured Liabilities against any purchase price;

(g) to manage the Vessel and to insure, maintain, repair and reclass the Vessel, renew any parts thereof and to put her through survey and to hold, lay up, lease, charter, operate or otherwise use the Vessel in such manner and for such period as the Bank deems necessary and generally to do all such things as an Owner of the Vessel could do in relation thereto, accounting only for the net proceeds (if any) of such use;

(h) to set off any of the Secured Liabilities against any moneys comprised in the Security Assets;

(i) to implement any contracts included in the Security Assets, or to agree with any other party thereto to determine the same on such terms and conditions as the Bank and such party may agree.

26. Receiver

(a) In addition to the powers conferred above, at any time after the security hereby created shall have become enforceable the Bank may appoint in writing a receiver or a receiver and manager (hereafter a "Receiver") of all or any part of the Security Assets and remove any Receiver so appointed and appoint another in his stead and may from time to time fix the remuneration of any such Receiver.

(b) The Bank may by instrument in writing delegate to any such Receiver all or any of the rights, powers and discretions vested in it by this Deed.

(c) The Bank shall not be responsible for misconduct or negligence on the part of such Receiver.

(d) Such Receiver shall be the agent of the Owner and the Owner shall be responsible for his acts, defaults and remuneration and liable on any contracts made by him.

27. Application of proceeds

All moneys received by the Bank or any Receiver in respect of the Security Assets after this security has become enforceable shall be applied by the Bank in or towards payment of the Secured Liabilities in such order as the Bank may decide but without prejudice to the right of the Bank to recover any shortfall from the Owner.

28. Power of attorney

(a) The Owner hereby by way of security for the ultimate balance of the Secured Liabilities irrevocably appoints the Bank and any Receiver appointed by the Bank jointly or severally the attorney(s) of the Owner on its behalf and in the name of the Owner, the Bank or such Receiver as the attorney(s) may decide to do all acts and execute all documents which the Owner could itself do in relation to the Security Assets or in connection with any of the matters provided for in this Deed including, without limitation, the execution of any bill of sale, transfer or other assurance in respect of the Security Assets.

(b) The Bank may:

(i) ask, require, demand, receive and give acquittance for any sum forming part of the Security Assets;

(ii) endorse any cheques or other instruments or orders in connection therewith; and

(iii) make any claims or take any action or institute any proceedings which may be necessary or advisable in the premises to protect the interest of the Bank in all or any part of the Security Assets.

29. Protection of third parties

No purchaser or other person dealing with the Bank or any Receiver appointed by it or with its or his attorneys or agents shall be concerned to enquire (i) whether any power exercised or purported to be exercised by it or him has become exercisable, (ii) whether any money remains due on the security hereby created, (iii) as to the propriety or regularity of any of his, its or their actions or (iv) as to the application of any money paid to him, it or them. In the absence of mala fides on the part of such purchaser or other person such dealings shall be deemed so far as regards the safety and protection of such purchaser or other person to be within the powers hereby conferred and to be valid accordingly. The remedy of the Owner in respect of any impropriety or irregularity whatever in the exercise of such powers shall be in damages only.

30. Delegation

The Bank may at the expense of the Bank at any time or times:

(a) delegate to any person(s) all or any of its rights, powers and discretions hereunder on such terms (including power to subdelegate) as the Bank sees fit;

(b) employ agents, managers, employees, advisers and others on such terms as the Bank sees fit for any of the purposes set out herein.

VI MISCELLANEOUS

31. Indemnity

(a) The Owner will indemnify the Bank and every Receiver or attorney appointed pursuant hereto in respect of all liabilities and expenses incurred by it, him or them in good faith in the execution or purported execution of any rights, powers or discretions vested in it, him or them pursuant hereto.

(b) The Bank shall not be liable for any losses arising in connection with the exercise or purported exercise of any of its rights, powers and discretions in good faith hereunder and in particular without limitation the Bank, and any Receiver, in possession shall not be liable to account as mortgagee in possession or for anything except actual receipts.

32. Governing law

This Deed shall be governed by English law.

33. Jurisdiction

For the benefit of the Bank, the Owner:

(a) agrees that the courts of England or the courts of any jurisdiction where the Vessel may be located have jurisdiction in relation to enforcement of this Deed of Covenants and to settle any disputes in connection with this Deed of Covenants and accordingly submits to the jurisdiction of those courts;

(b) (without prejudice to any other mode of service) appoints [   ] as its agent for service of process relating to any proceedings before those courts in connection with this Deed of Covenants; and

(c) agrees that nothing in this Clause 33 limits the right of the Bank to bring proceedings against the Owner in connection with this Deed of Covenants in any other court of competent jurisdiction.

34. Severability

If any of the terms hereof is or becomes invalid or unenforceable for any reason under the laws of any jurisdiction, such invalidity or unenforceability shall not affect its validity or enforceability in any other jurisdiction or invalidate or make unenforceable any other term hereof.

IN WITNESS whereof this Deed has been duly executed on the date first above written as a Deed.

The Vessel

Official Number:

Name of Ship:

Number, Year and Port of Registry:

Sailing, Steam or Motor Ship:

Horse Power of Engines:

Gross Tons:

Register Tons:

Length:

Main breadth:

Depth:

The Common Seal of)
[   ] was hereunto)
affixed in the presence of:)

Director:

Director/Secretary:

SCHEDULE   I

NOTICE OF ASSIGNMENT

(for attachment by way of endorsement to the Policy)

We, [   ], the Owner of m.v. "[   ]" HEREBY GIVE
NOTICE that by a Deed of Covenants dated [   ], 199[ ] and made by
us in favour of [   ] there has been assigned by us to
[   ] as first priority mortgagee and assignee of the Vessel this
policy and all the Owner's rights, title and interest in and to all insurances

and entries effected and to be effected in respect of the Vessel, including the insurances constituted by the policy or entry whereon this notice is endorsed.

For and on behalf of
[   ]

By:_____
Attorney-in-fact

For and on behalf of
[   ]

By:_____

Dated:

SCHEDULE II(A)

FORM OF LETTER OF UNDERTAKING TO BE DELIVERED BY BROKERS

To: [Bank]

Re: m.v. "[   ]"

We acknowledge receipt of the notice of assignment of the insurances on the above vessel (the "Vessel") for attachment by way of endorsement to the policies and in consideration of your approving our appointment as brokers for the Vessel pursuant to the provisions of the Deed of Covenants made by [   ] (the "**Owner**") in your favour we hereby undertake and confirm:

1. that we have effected insurance of the Vessel for hull and machinery risks and war risks with the underwriters and upon the terms and conditions set forth in Appendix A hereto;

2. that pursuant to instructions received from the Owner to hold the insurance slips or contracts, the policies (when issued), and any renewals of such policies or new policies or any policies substituted (with your consent) therefor and the benefit of the insurances thereunder, to your order as first assignee in accordance with the terms of the loss payable clause set out in Appendix B hereto and to procure that the loss payable clause shall be included in or endorsed on all the insurance slips, contracts, policies, renewals and substitutes as aforesaid;

3.   that the notice of assignment in the form of Appendix C hereto shall be endorsed upon all cover notes, policies and insurance slips or contracts, renewals or substitutes as aforesaid.

Our above undertakings are given subject to our lien on the policies for premiums in respect of effecting the policies for the Vessel only and subject to our rights of cancellation on default in payment of any such premiums, but we undertake with you (until such time as we may receive written notice to the contrary from you) (i) that we shall only exercise our lien for unpaid premiums to the extent that such unpaid premiums are attributable or may be properly allocated to the Vessel, (ii) to advise you immediately if any premiums are not paid to us by the due date and (iii) not to exercise our right of cancellation without giving you fourteen (14) days' prior notice in writing and a reasonable opportunity of paying any outstanding premiums.

We further undertake (until such time as we may receive written notice to the contrary from you) to advise you by written notice not later than fourteen (14) days prior to the expiry of the policies aforesaid and any renewals thereof if instructions have not been received for such renewals or further renewals and in the event of our receiving instructions to renew or further to renew as aforesaid to advise you promptly of the details thereof.

Finally, we undertake to notify you immediately of any material changes which are proposed to be made in the terms of the insurance, or if we cease to be the Owner's brokers for all purposes connected with the hull and machinery risks and war risks insurances of the Vessel, or of any circumstance or event whereby the said insurances may become invalid, voidable or otherwise unenforceable.

Yours faithfully,

Appendix A-attach details of insurances
Appendix B-attach loss payable clause (Sched III)
Appendix C-attach notice of assignment (Sched I)

SCHEDULE   II(B)

DRAFT LETTER OF UNDERTAKING TO BE WRITTEN BY CLUB IN RESPECT OF PROTECTION AND INDEMNITY RISKS INSURANCES. THE CLUB SHOULD INSERT THE RELEVANT RULE NUMBERS BY REFERENCE TO THE NOTES AT THE END OF THIS LETTER

To: [Bank]

Dear Sirs,

Re: m.v. "[ ]"

We note that you have taken an assignment of the insurances on the above ship. So far as this association is concerned, the managers do not consent to such assignment for the purposes of Rule [ ] [see Note 1] other than to give efficacy to the loss payable clause set out below and subject always to the association's rights under Rule [ ] [see Note 1].

We do confirm however that the above ship is entered in this association for protection and indemnity risks on the terms and conditions set out or to be set out in the certificate of entry. Furthermore, in consideration of your agreeing to the entry or continuing entry of the above ship in this association, the managers agree:

(a) that the Owner shall not cease to be insured by the association in respect of the above ship by reason of such assignment (see Rule [ ]) [see Note 2]; and

(b) that, notwithstanding that the above ship is mortgaged to you and that no undertaking or guarantee has been given to the Association to pay all contributions due in respect of the above ship, the Owner does not cease to be insured by reason of the operation of Rule [ ] [see Note 3].

It is further agreed that the following loss payable clause will be included in the certificate of entry:

"Payment of any recovery which the Owner is entitled to make out of the funds of the association in respect of any liability, costs or expenses incurred by it shall be made to the Owner or to its order unless and until the association receives notice from [   ] as first mortgagee of the ship, that the Owner is in default under the Mortgage, in which event all recoveries shall thereafter be paid to [ ] or to its order; provided always that no liability whatsoever shall attach to the association, its managers or their agents for failure to comply with the latter obligation until after the expiry of two (2) clear business days from the receipt of such notice."

The association undertakes:

(a) to inform you if the association gives the Owner of the above ship notice under Rule [ ] [see Note 4] that its insurance in the association in respect of the above ship is to cease at the end of the then current policy year;

(b) to give fourteen (14) days' prior written notice of the association's intention to cancel the insurance of the Owner by reason of its failure to pay when due and demanded any sum due from it to the association.

Yours faithfully,

Notes (the relevant Rule Numbers to be inserted)

1. The Rule relating to prohibition of assignment

2. The Rule stating that the Owner will cease to be insured if the Owner assigns any of its interest in the ship.

3. The Rule stating that the Owner will cease to be insured if the ship is mortgaged without the Bank having given an undertaking to pay all contributions as they fall due.

4. The Rule stating that the directors may give notice to the Owner not later than [   ] that the insurance of the ship will cease at the end of the current policy year.

SCHEDULE III

LOSS PAYABLE CLAUSE

By an assignment of the insurances on the motor vessel "[   ]" (the "**Vessel**") contained in a Deed of Covenants dated [   ] 199[ ] made by [   ] (the "**Owner**") in favour of [   ] of [   ] (the "**Bank**"), the Owner (inter alia) assigned to the Bank this insurance and the benefits thereof, including all claims of whatsoever nature in respect of the Vessel, return of premiums, and each and every right hereunder.

It is further noted and agreed:

(a) that in the event of actual or constructive or compromised or agreed or arranged total loss of the Vessel the proceeds of insurance shall be paid to the Bank;

(b) that all other losses not exceeding US$[   ] shall be paid to the Owner or its order unless and until the Owner shall be in default under a Facility Agreement dated [   ] between the Owner and the Bank and if the underwriters or insurers shall have been so notified by the Bank, then such losses shall be paid to the Bank;

(c) that all other losses exceeding US$[   ] shall be paid to or in accordance with the instructions of the Bank;

(d) that in the event of non-payment of premiums when due, the underwriters or insurers undertake not to exercise any right of cancellation which they may have without giving fourteen (14) days' prior written notice of such cancellation to the Bank and an opportunity of paying such premiums which are in default.

9.   Cyprus Ship Mortgage Form

Note on the Form

The form contains details of the ship, i.e. official number; name; number, year and port of registry; whether sailing, steam or motor ship; horse power of engines; length, breadth, depth; tonnage and as described in more detail in the Certificate of the Surveyor and the Register Book. The form is in "account current" statutory form.

As with the British mortgage, the form is accompanied by a deed of covenants containing covenants, assignments of earnings and insurances, and the like: see the previous form. But, unlike British practice, the Deed is also registered at the shipping registry.

Completed Form of Mortgage for a Specific Loan Agreement

Whereas there is an account current between (1) [Name of company] ("the Mortgagor") a company incorporated under the laws of Cyprus and whose registered office is at [address], Republic of Cyprus and (2) [Name of lender] ("the Mortgagee") a corporation organised under the laws of [   ] [and carrying on a branch business at [   ]] regulated by (a) a Loan Agreement dated the [   ] day of [   ], 199[   ] between, inter alia, the Mortgagor and the Mortgagee and (b) a Deed of Covenants of even date herewith made between the Mortgagor and the Mortgagee (references to the said Loan Agreement and the said Deed of Covenants herein include variations thereof and supplements thereto from time to time in force) and whereas pursuant to the said Loan Agreement the Mortgagor has agreed to execute this Mortgage for the purpose of securing payment by the Mortgagor to the Mortgagee of all sums for the time being due or owing to the Mortgagee in respect of principal and interest and otherwise in the manner and at the times set forth in the said Loan Agreement and Deed of Covenants and whereas the amount of principal and interest and other sums at any given time can be ascertained by reference to the said Loan Agreement, and Deed of Covenants (or to the books of accounts of the Mortgagee).

Now we, [Name of company] in consideration of the premises for ourselves and our successors, covenant with the said [Name of lender] and its assigns to pay to him or them or it the sums for the time being due on this security whether by way of principal or interest at the times and manner aforesaid. And for the purpose of better securing to the Mortgagee the payment of such sums as last aforesaid, we do hereby mortgage to the Mortgagee one-hundred one hundredth shares of which we are the owners in the ship above particularly described and in her boats and appurtenances. Lastly we for ourselves and our successors covenant with the Mortgagee and its assigns that we have power to mortgage in manner aforesaid the above mentioned shares and that the same are free from encumbrance.

IN WITNESS whereof we have caused this mortgage to be duly executed on the [ ] day of [   ], 199[ ].

SIGNED SEALED AND	)
DELIVERED by	)
the duly authorised attorney	)
of [Name of company] [or	)
corporate sealing] in the	)
presence of:	)

10.   Greek Ship Mortgage

Note on the Form

For a discussion of Greek ship mortgages specifically, see para 16–23 et seq. This form will be accompanied by a separate assignment of earnings, insurances and requisition compensation: see the British Ship Mortgage Deed of Covenants in this Appendix.

In the interests of brevity, this form does not contain representations and warranties or events of default – these would normally appear in the facility agreement. For outline representations and warranties and events of default, see the Outline general summary of terms of security agreements in this Appendix. These are also reviewed in detail in another work in this series on financial law – a book dealing with international loans, bonds and securities regulation. See also:

– as to registration of ships and ship mortgages, para 15–12 *et seq*

– as to covenants in ship mortgages, para 17–1 *et seq*

– as to ship loan events of default, para 18–2 *et seq*

– as to assignments of earnings and charters, chapter 21

– as to assignments of insurances, chapter 22.

Form of Mortgage

THIS FIRST PREFERRED MORTGAGE is made the day of 199 BETWEEN

1. [   ] a Company incorporated under the laws of [   ] whose registered office is at [   ] (the "**Owner**"); and

2. [   ] carrying on a banking business at its branch at [   ] (the "**Bank**").

WHEREAS:

(A) The Owner is the sole beneficial owner of the unencumbered motor vessel m.v. ["   "] having acquired title by virtue of a [   ] dated [   ]. The Vessel is [provisionally] registered in the Shipping

Register of [   ] Class ships of the Hellenic Mercantile Marine Service, [Piraeus] [London, under transfer to the port of Piraeus] under Official Number [   ] and of the following dimensions and tonnages: Length [   ] Breadth [   ], Depth [   ], [   ] tons gross and [   ] tons net register, engine [   ], International Call Letters [   ].

(B) By a Facility Agreement dated [   ] between [(inter alia)] the Owner and the Bank, the Bank has agreed to lend up to US$[   ] to the Owner. It is a condition (inter alia) of the Facility Agreement that the Owner shall grant to the Bank this First Preferred Mortgage over the Vessel as security for the payment of the Secured Liabilities (as defined below).

(C) In order to secure the payment to the Bank (inter alia) of all sums payable by the Owner under the Facility Agreement and this Mortgage and the performance and observance of and compliance with all the covenants, terms and conditions contained in this Mortgage and the Facility Agreement, the Owner has duly authorised the execution and delivery of this First Preferred Mortgage.

NOW IT IS HEREBY AGREED and DECLARED as follows:

I GENERAL

1. Interpretation

1.1 Incorporated definitions

(a) Unless the contrary intention appears any term defined in the Facility Agreement has the same meaning when used in this Mortgage.

(b) The terms "Earnings", "Insurances", "Requisition Compensation" and "Total Loss" all have the meaning given to them in the Assignment.

1.2 Definitions In this Mortgage:

"Assignment" means the assignment dated of or about the date of this Mortgage of earnings and insurances of the Vessel granted by the Owner to the Bank. [See the British Deed of Covenants in this Appendix].

"Default Rate" means the rate specified in Clause [ ] of the Facility Agreement. [This is a conventional default interest clause for overdue sums.]

"Facility Agreement" means the Facility Agreement referred to in Recital (B) above.

"Permitted Liens" means,

(a) liens for unpaid crew's wages arising in accordance with usual maritime practice; and

(b) liens for salvage,

and to the extent they are subordinate to the lien of this Mortgage:

(i) liens for Master's disbursements incurred in the ordinary course of trading; and

(ii) any other lien arising in the ordinary course of operation of the Vessel.

"Secured Liabilities" means the sums and liabilities (actual or contingent) which are or may become payable or owing by the Owner to the Bank under or in connection with the Facility Agreement, this Mortgage or any other Security Document.

"Security Period" means the period beginning on the date hereof and ending on the date upon which all the Secured Liabilities which have or may arise have been irrevocably paid and discharged.

"Vessel" means m.v. [   ], as described in recital (A) above and includes each part thereof and interest therein and all her engines, boilers, machinery, masts, spars, sails, boats, anchors, cables, chains, rigging tackle, outfit, spare gear, fuel, consumable and other stores, whether on board or ashore and whether now owned or hereafter acquired and also any and all additions, improvements and replacements hereafter made in or to the Vessel or any part thereof, including all items and appurtenances aforesaid.

1.3   Construction

(a) In this Mortgage, unless the contrary intention appears, a reference to:

(i) a provision of a law or regulation is a reference to that provision as amended or re-enacted;

(ii) a Clause or a Schedule is a reference to a clause of or a schedule to this Mortgage;

(iii) any person includes a reference to its successors and assigns;

(iv) the Facility Agreement, this Mortgage, any other Security Document or any other document is a reference to the Facility Agreement, this Mortgage, such other Security Document or such other document as amended, novated or supplemented.

(b) The headings in this Mortgage are for convenience only and are to be ignored in construing this Mortgage.

2. Status of mortgage

The Owner declares and warrants to the Bank that:

(a) the Vessel belongs to the Owner in her entirety, the Owner acquired title to the Vessel by virtue of [   ] dated [   ] and the Vessel is free from any security interest or encumbrance other than in favour of the Bank;

(b) this Mortgage is in accordance with the provisions of the Greek Code of Private Maritime Law (Act of Parliament Number 3816/1958) as completed by Legislative Decree Number 3899/1958 on Mortgages on Ships (all the provisions whereof benefiting the Bank shall be deemed as being contained herein and as having been expressly agreed by the parties hereto) and the provisions of the Greek Legislative Decree Number 2687/53 on "the Investment and Protection of Capital from Abroad" and of Decision Number [ ] of the Ministers of Co-ordination, Merchant Marine and Finance (the **"Ministerial Decision"**). It is agreed that the Owner may apply for an amendment of the Ministerial Decision only with the prior written consent of the Bank;

(c) this Mortgage has priority above all maritime and any other liens by deviation from the provisions of Article 205 of the Private Maritime Code or any present or future provision of Greek law, except the prior liens provided by the International Convention of Brussels of 1926 "Pour l'unification de certaines regles relatives aux privileges et hypotheques maritimes" provided that such liens are also recognised by Greek law;

(d) this Mortgage will remain in force to secure any new obligations of the Owner if the old obligations are renewed or replaced in accordance with Articles 436 and 439 of the Greek Civil Code.

3. Grant of mortgage

As security for payment of the Secured Liabilities and for performance and observance of the terms of this Mortgage the Owner:

(a) hereby grants to the Bank a First Preferred Mortgage on the Vessel together with the right to register such First Preferred Mortgage on the Vessel in the mortgage register of the competent Greek Maritime Mortgage Office directly and without any action by or on behalf of the Owner up to the total amount of US$[   ] plus interest; and

(b) hereby assigns and agrees to assign to the Bank all its rights and benefits under and deriving from (i) Greek Legislative Decrees Number 2687/1953 and 2928/1954 insofar as they relate to the Vessel and (ii) the Ministerial Decision.

PROVIDED HOWEVER that (i) the Owner shall remain liable to perform the obligations to be performed by it under the Ministerial Decision and any laws or regulations applicable thereto and (ii) the Bank shall be under no obligation thereunder or be under any liability if the Owner fails to perform its obligations thereunder.

4. Amount and maturity of secured liabilities

(a) This Mortgage shall be registered in accordance with the requirements of Greek law as constituting security for the following amounts:

   (i) US$[   ] or the equivalent in any currency which is freely transferable and convertible into dollars in respect of principal at any one time outstanding (whether actual or contingent) together with interest thereon at the rates provided for in the Facility Agreement; and

   (ii) US$[   ] or the equivalent in any currency which is freely transferable and convertible into dollars in respect of all other moneys constituting the Secured Liabilities (including costs and expenses of the Bank and interest thereon)

and the total amount secured by this Mortgage is US$[   ] or the equivalent in any currency which is freely transferable and convertible into dollars plus interest thereon.

(b) The date of maturity of the Secured Liabilities (being the debt secured by this Mortgage) is [   ].

(c) If any of the amounts hereby secured shall be or become invalid for any reason whatsoever, this Mortgage shall secure to the same extent the indebtedness of the Owner for unjustifiable enrichment in accordance with Article 904 *et seq* of the Greek Civil Code.

[(d) No prepayment or repayment of all or any part of the Loan on or prior to the end of the [drawdown period] shall discharge in whole or in part the amount specified in Clause 4(a)(i) above and this Mortgage shall stand as valid security for the repayment of any subsequent part of the Loan made by the Bank in accordance with its obligations as set out in the Facility Agreement.]

[(e) In accordance with Article 19 of Decision Number 54027 of the Ministers of Co-ordination, Merchant Marine and Finance and in deviation from the provisions of the Greek Civil Code and from the Greek Civil Procedure rules, the Owner and the Bank hereby agree that this Mortgage will secure the amount at each time outstanding, whether in US dollars or in an Optional Currency even if the amount of the Loan in that Optional Currency at the time of payment exceeds what would have been the US dollar equivalent had such amount remained in US dollars.]

5. Continuing security

The security constituted by this Mortgage shall be continuing and not satisfied by any intermediate payment or satisfaction of the whole or any part of the Secured Liabilities but shall secure the ultimate balance of the Secured Liabilities. The security hereby given shall be in addition to and shall not be affected by any other security interest or other encumbrance now or hereafter held by the Bank for all or any of the Secured Liabilities.

6. Covenant to pay and perform

The Owner hereby covenants (i) to pay the Secured Liabilities to the Bank promptly when due and (ii) to comply at all times with the terms (express or implied) of this Mortgage, the Facility Agreement and any other Security Document to which it is or becomes a party.

II THE INDEBTEDNESS

7. Acknowledgment of indebtedness

The Owner hereby acknowledges that it is or may become indebted to the Bank under the terms of the Facility Agreement and that it grants this Mortgage as security for the due payment of the Secured Liabilities.

[Insert repayment, prepayment, optional currency, interest period and interest clauses from Facility Agreement and matching definitions].

III VESSEL COVENANTS

8. Registration of vessel

The Owner will during the Security Period:

(a) maintain the valid and effective registration of the Vessel under the laws and flag of Greece and ensure nothing is done or omitted whereby such registration of the Vessel would or might be defeated or imperilled; and

(b) not change the name, port of registration, certificate of registry or other registration documentation of the Vessel.

9. Maintenance of mortgage

The Owner will during the Security Period:

(a) take all such action as may be necessary under the Greek Code of Private Maritime Law and the Greek Legislative Decrees Numbered 2687/1953 and 3899/1958 or otherwise for the purpose of perfecting, registering and maintaining this Mortgage as a good and valid First Preferred Mortgage on the Vessel;

(b) keep on board the Vessel the Mortgage Book referred to in Article 15 of Legislative Decree Number 3899/1958 and cause to be recorded therein the particulars relating to this Mortgage as specified in Article 16 of Legislative Decree Number 3899/1958;

(c) carry on board the Vessel a properly certified copy of this Mortgage pursuant to Article 17 of Legislative Decree Number 3899/1958 and upon request exhibit the same to any parties having a legal interest therein or to anyone having business with the Vessel which might give rise to any lien on the Vessel;

(d) place and keep prominently in the Chart Room and in the Master's Cabin on the Vessel a framed printed notice in plain type of such size that the paragraph of reading matter shall cover a space not less than six inches wide and nine inches high reading as follows:

"NOTICE OF MORTGAGE

This Vessel is covered by a First Preferred Mortgage in favour of [   ] under the authority of Greek Legislative Decree Number 3899/1958. Under the terms of the Mortgage and of Greek law neither the owner(s), any manager, charterer, the Master of the Vessel nor any other person has any right, power or authority to create, incur or permit to be imposed upon this Vessel any lien whatsoever other than (a) liens for unpaid crew's wages arising in accordance with usual maritime practice, (b) liens for salvage and, to the extent they are subordinate to the lien of this Mortgage (i) liens for Master's disbursements incurred in the ordinary course of trading, and (ii) any other lien arising in the ordinary course of operation of the Vessel."

PROVIDED THAT in the event that this Mortgage is assigned by the Bank the details of such assignment and of the assignee shall, at the request of the Bank, be inserted in such notice; and

(e) not without the prior written consent of the Bank (and then only on and subject to such terms as the Bank may agree) cancel, vary or apply for an amendment of the Ministerial Decision and not commit any breach of the Ministerial Decision.

[For clauses 10 to 15, see the corresponding provisions in the British Deed of Covenants in this Appendix].

10. Classification and repair

11. Lawful and safe operation

12. Mortgages, sales, chartering, management and repairs

13. Arrests and liabilities

14. Information

15. Protection of security

IV ENFORCEMENT

16. Enforcement of security

This security shall become immediately enforceable upon the occurrence of an Event of Default and the Bank shall be entitled without notice immediately or at any time thereafter to put into force and exercise all the powers and remedies possessed by it according to law as mortgagee and chargee of the Vessel and the other assets subject to the security constituted by this Mortgage as and when it may see fit and in particular (without limitation):

(a) to demand payment by written notice to the Owner of the Secured Liabilities, whereupon such payment by the Owner to the Bank shall become immediately due and payable;

(b) to exercise all the rights and remedies in foreclosure and otherwise given to the Bank by any applicable law;

(c) to take possession of the Vessel;

(d) to recover and collect all Earnings, Insurances and Requisition Compensation, to give a good receipt therefor on behalf of the Owner, to permit the brokers through whom collection or recovery of any Insurances is effected to charge and retain the usual brokerage therefor and to require that all policies, contracts and other records relating to the Insurances (including details of and correspondence concerning outstanding claims) be immediately delivered to or to the order of the Bank;

(e) to take over or institute all such proceedings in connection with the Vessel as the Bank in its absolute discretion thinks fit and to discharge, compound, release or compromise the Vessel or claims in respect thereof which have given or may give rise to any charge or lien on or arrest of the Vessel or which are or may be enforceable by proceedings against the Vessel;

(f) to sell all or any part of the Vessel, with or without the benefit of any charterparty or other contract by public auction or private contract, at any place in the world, with or without advertisement or notice to the Owner, for cash or on credit and otherwise and upon such terms as the Bank in its absolute discretion may determine, and at any such public sale to purchase the Vessel and to set off any purchase price against all or any part of the Secured Liabilities;

(g) to manage the Vessel and to insure, maintain, repair and reclass the Vessel, renew any parts thereof and to put her through survey and to hold, lay up, lease, charter, operate or otherwise use the Vessel in such manner and for such period as the Bank in its absolute discretion deems expedient and generally to do all such things as an owner of the Vessel could do in relation thereto, accounting only for the net proceeds (if any) of such use.

In accordance with the terms of the Ministerial Decision and the Act No 1687/87 the repayment of the amount secured by this Mortgage shall be made in US dollars (or in an Optional Currency) and if the Vessel is sold by public auction in Greece, all sums of money in relation to such sale, including (without limitation) the demand for repayment, the programme of sale, the offer price and the sale price, shall be expressed in US dollars or at the discretion of the Bank the equivalent in any Optional Currency. If for any reason any such sale is completed in drachmae (which expression shall mean for the purposes of this Clause the lawful currency of Greece) the value of such amount of drachmae shall, notwithstanding Article 917 of the Greek Civil Procedure Code, be determined by reference to the Bank's spot rate of exchange for drachmae with the relevant currency of the Secured Liabilities on the date of receipt of the sale proceeds by the Bank.

17. Receiver

(a) In addition to the powers conferred above, at any time after the security hereby created shall have become enforceable the Bank may appoint in writing a receiver or a receiver and manager (hereafter a "**Receiver**") of all or any part of the Vessel and remove any Receiver so appointed and appoint another in his stead and may from time to time fix the remuneration of any such Receiver.

(b) The Bank may by instrument in writing delegate to any such Receiver all or any of the rights, powers and discretions vested in it by this Mortgage.

(c) The Bank shall not be responsible for misconduct or negligence on the part of such Receiver.

(d) Such Receiver shall be the agent of the Owner and the Owner shall be responsible for his acts, defaults and remuneration and liable on any contracts made by him.

18. Application of proceeds

All moneys received by the Bank or any Receiver in respect of the Vessel after this security has become enforceable shall be applied by the Bank in or towards payment of the Secured Liabilities in such order as the Bank may decide but without prejudice to the right of the Bank to recover any shortfall from the Owner.

19. Power of attorney

The Owner by way of security for the ultimate balance of the Secured Liabilities hereby irrevocably appoints the Bank and any Receiver appointed by the Bank jointly or severally the attorney(s) of the Owner on its behalf and in the name of the Owner, the Bank or such Receiver as the attorney(s) may decide to do all acts and execute all documents which the Owner could itself do in relation to the Vessel or in connection with any of the matters provided for in this Mortgage including without limitation the execution of any bill of sale or other assurance in respect of the Vessel.

20. Protection of third parties

No purchaser or other person dealing with the Bank or any Receiver appointed by it or with its or his attorneys or agents shall be concerned to enquire (i) whether any power exercised or purported to be exercised by it or him has become exercisable, (ii) whether any money remains due on the security hereby created, (iii) as to the propriety or regularity of any of his, its or their actions or (iv) as the the application of any money paid to him, it or them. In the absence of mala fides on the part of such purchaser or other person such dealings shall be deemed so far as regards the safety and protection of such purchaser or other person to be within the powers hereby conferred and to be valid accordingly. The remedy of the Owner in respect of any impropriety or irregularity whatever in the exercise of such powers shall be in damages only.

21. Delegation

The Bank may at the expense of the Bank at any time(s):

(a) delegate to any person(s) all or any of its rights, powers and discretions hereunder on such terms (including power to subdelegate) as the Bank sees fit;

(b) employ agents, managers, employees, advisers and others on such terms as the Bank sees fit for any of the purposes set out herein.

V   MISCELLANEOUS

22. Indemnity

(a) The Owner will indemnify the Bank and every Receiver or attorney appointed pursuant hereto in respect of all liabilities and expenses incurred by it, him or them in good faith in the execution or purported execution of any rights, powers or discretions vested in it, him or them pursuant hereto.

(b) The Bank shall not be liable for any losses arising in connection with the exercise or purported exercise of any of its rights, powers and discretions in good faith hereunder and in particular without limitation the Bank and any Receiver in possession shall not be liable to account as mortgagee in possession or for anything except actual receipts.

23.   Governing law

This Mortgage shall be governed by Greek law, provided that the Bank shall be entitled to the most extensive remedies that are available to or capable of being given to a mortgagee in the jurisdiction where the Vessel may be located or where any proceedings in relation to this Mortgage are brought.

24.   Jurisdiction

For the benefit of the Bank, the Owner:

(a) agrees that the courts of England or the courts of any jurisdiction where the Vessel may be located have jurisdiction in relation to enforcement of this Mortgage and to settle any disputes in connection with this Mortgage and accordingly submits to the jurisdiction of those courts;

(b) (without prejudice to any other mode of service) appoints [   ] as its agent for service of process relating to any proceedings before those courts in connection with this Mortgage; and

(c) agrees that nothing in this Clause 24 limits the right of the Bank to bring proceedings against the Owner in connection with this Mortgage in any other court of competent jurisdiction.

25.   Agents in Greece

Each of the Owner and the Bank hereby appoints the following respectively as its agent and representative in Greece who is authorised to accept on its behalf service of notices or legal process:

(a) The Owner's Agent: [   ].

(b) The Bank's Agent: [   ].

26.   Severability

If any of the terms hereof is or becomes invalid or unenforceable for any reason under the laws of any jurisdiction, such invalidity or unenforceability shall not affect its validity or enforceability in any other jurisdiction or invalidate or make unenforceable any other term hereof.

IN WITNESS whereof this Mortgage has been duty executed as a deed on the date first above written.

SIGNED by [ ]   )
the duly authorised   )
attorney-in-fact of, and   )
SEALED   and
DELIVERED by   )
[   ]   )
in the presence of:)

THE   CORPORATE
SEAL   )
of [
          ]   )
was hereunto affixed in
the   )
presence of:)

11.   Liberian Ship Mortgage

Note on the Form

For a discussion of Liberian ship mortgages specifically, see para 16–11 *et seq*. There will usually be a separate general assignment of earnings, insurances and requisition compensation: see the British Ship Mortgage Deed of Covenants in this Appendix.

In the interests of brevity, this form does not contain representations and warranties or events of default – these would normally appear in the facility agreement. For outline representations and warranties and events of default see the Outline general summary of terms of security agreements in this Appendix. These are also reviewed in detail in another work in this series on financial law – a book dealing with international loans, bonds and securities regulation. See also:

– as to registration of ships and ship mortgages, para 15–12 *et seq*

– as to covenants in ship mortgages, para 17–1 *et seq*

– as to ship loan events of default, para 18–2 *et seq*

– as to assignments of earnings and charters, chapter 21

– as to assignments of insurances, chapter 22.

Form of Mortgage

THIS FIRST PREFERRED MORTGAGE is made the day of 199
BETWEEN

1. [   ] a corporation organised and existing under the laws of Liberia whose registered office is at [80 Broad Street, Monrovia, Liberia] (the "**Owner**"); and
2. [   ] carrying on a banking business at its branch at [ ] (the "**Bank**").

WHEREAS:

(A) The Owner is the sole legal and beneficial owner of the unencumbered motor vessel m.v. "[   ]" having acquired title by virtue of a [Bill of Sale] dated [   ]. The Vessel is duly documented under the laws and flag of the Republic of Liberia at the port of Monrovia,

---

with Official Number [   ], of the following dimensions and tonnages: Length [   ], Breadth [   ], Depth [   ],[   ] gross tons [   ] net tons built in 19[   ] at [   ].

(B) By a Facility Agreement dated [   ] 199[ ] between [(inter alia)] the Owner and the Bank, the Bank has agreed to lend up to US$[   ] to the Owner. A copy of the Facility Agreement (without the Schedules or Annexures thereto, if any) is attached hereto as Annex A.

[(C)The Owner has executed and delivered a guarantee (the **"Guarantee"**) to the Bank contained in Clause [ ] of the Facility Agreement pursuant to which the Owner has agreed to pay to the Bank, on demand, all amounts which may from time to time be due and owing under the Facility Agreement from the Borrowers which are not paid by the Borrowers when due.]

[(D)In order to secure the payment of principal, interest and all other amounts [payable by the Owner under the Facility Agreement] [guaranteed according to the terms of the Guarantee] and payment of all other sums as may be secured by this Mortgage and to secure the performance and observance of and compliance with all the covenants, terms and conditions contained in this Mortgage [, the Guarantee] and the Facility Agreement, the Owner has duly authorised the execution and delivery of this First Preferred Mortgage under and pursuant to the laws of the Republic of Liberia.]

IT IS AGREED as follows:

I GENERAL

1. Interpretation

1.1 Incorporated definitions

(a) Unless the contrary intention appears any term defined in the Facility Agreement has the same meaning when used in this Mortgage.

(b) The terms "Earnings", "Insurances", "Requisition Compensation" and "Total Loss" all have the meaning given to them in the Assignment.

1.2 Definitions In this Mortgage:

"**Assignment**" means the general assignment dated on or about the date of this Mortgage of earnings and insurances of the Vessel granted by the Owner to the Bank. [See the British Deed of Covenants in this Appendix.]

"Default Rate" means the rate specified in Clause [ ] of the Facility Agreement. [This is a conventional default interest provision for overdue sums.]

[Environmental definitions]

"Facility Agreement" means the Facility Agreement referred to in Recital (B) above.

[**"Guarantee"** means the Guarantee contained in the Facility Agreement and referred to in Recital (C) above];

"Permitted Liens" means

(a) liens for unpaid crew's wages arising in accordance with usual maritime practice; and

(b) liens for salvage,

and to the extent they are subordinate to the lien of this Mortgage:

(i) liens for Master's disbursements incurred in the ordinary course of trading; and

(ii) any other lien arising in the ordinary course of operation of the Vessel.

"Secured Liabilities" means the sums and liabilities (actual or contingent) which are or may become payable or owing by the Owner to the Bank under or in connection with the Facility Agreement, [the Guarantee], this Mortgage or any other Security Document.

"Security Period" means the period beginning on the date hereof and ending on the date upon which all the Secured Liabilities which have or may arise have been irrevocably paid and discharged.

"Vessel" means m.v. ["   "], as described in Recital (A) above and includes each part thereof and interest therein and all her engines, boilers, machinery, masts, spars, sails, boats, anchors, cables, chains, rigging tackle, outfit, spare gear, fuel, consumable and other stores, whether on board or ashore and whether now owned or hereafter acquired and also any and all additions, improvements and replacements hereafter made in or to the Vessel or any part thereof, including all items and appurtenances aforesaid.

1.3 Construction

(a) In this Mortgage, unless the contrary intention appears, a reference to:

    (i)   a provision of a law or regulation is a reference to that provision as amended or re-enacted;

   (ii)   a Clause or a Schedule is a reference to a clause of or a schedule to this Mortgage;

  (iii)   any person includes a reference to its successors and assigns;

  (iv)   the Facility Agreement, [the Guarantee,] this Mortgage, any other Security Document or any other document is a reference to the Facility Agreement, [the Guarantee,] this Mortgage, such other Security Document or such other document as amended, novated or supplemented.

(b) The headings in this Mortgage are for convenience only and are to be ignored in construing this Mortgage.

2. Grant of mortgage

(a) As security for payment of the Secured Liabilities and for performance and observance of the terms of this Mortgage the Owner hereby grants, conveys and mortgages to and in favour of the Bank the whole of the Vessel TO HAVE AND TO HOLD the same unto the Bank its successors and assigns upon the terms herein set forth.

(b) Notwithstanding anything to the contrary herein contained, it is not intended that this Mortgage shall cover property other than the Vessel and it shall not cover property other than the Vessel as that term is used in subdivision 2 of Section 106 of Chapter 3 of Title 22 of the Liberian Code of Laws of 1956 as amended.

[(c) In addition, as a protection against currency exchange fluctuations, this Mortgage shall secure any currency exchange obligation payable under Clauses [   ] [Optional currency clauses] of the Facility Agreement of $[   ].]

3. Continuing security

The security constituted by this Mortgage shall be continuing and not satisfied by any intermediate payment or satisfaction of the whole or any part of the Secured Liabilities but shall secure the ultimate balance of the Secured Liabilities. The security hereby given shall be in addition to and shall not be affected by any other Encumbrance now or hereafter held by the Bank for all or any of the Secured Liabilities.

4. Covenant to pay and perform

The Owner hereby covenants (i) to pay the Secured Liabilities to the Bank promptly when due and (ii) to comply at all times with the terms (express or implied) of this Mortgage, [the Guarantee,] the Assignment and the Facility Agreement and any other Security Document to which it is or becomes a party.

II   VESSEL COVENANTS

5. Registration of vessel

The Owner will during the Security Period:

(a) maintain the valid and effective registration of the Vessel under the laws and flag of Liberia and ensure nothing is done or omitted whereby such registration of the Vessel would or might be defeated or imperilled; and

(b) not change the name, port of registration or certificate of registry or equivalent document of the Vessel.

6. Notice of mortgage

The Owner will during the Security Period place and at all times and places retain with the Vessel's marine document a duly certified copy of this Mortgage and of any assignment of this Mortgage (if requested by an assignee) (which shall form a part of the Vessel's documents) on board the Vessel with her papers and cause each such certified copy and such papers to be shown to any and all persons having business therewith which might give rise to any lien thereon other than Permitted Liens and to any representative of the Bank. Neither the Owner, any manager, charterer, the Master of the Vessel nor any other person has or shall have the right, power or authority to create, incur or permit to be placed or imposed or continued upon the Vessel any lien whatsoever other than Permitted Liens. The Owner will place and keep prominently displayed in the Chart Room and in the Master's cabin of the Vessel a framed printed Notice in the following form:

"NOTICE OF MORTGAGE

This Vessel is covered by a First Preferred Mortgage to [   ]
of [   ] under authority of the laws of the Republic of Liberia. Under

the terms of Mortgage neither the owner, any manager, charterer, the Master of the Vessel nor any other person has any right, power or authority to create, incur or permit to be imposed upon this Vessel any lien whatsoever other than (a) liens for unpaid crew's wages arising in accordance with usual maritime practice, (b) liens for salvage and, to the extent they are subordinate to the lien of this Mortgage (i) liens for Master's disbursements incurred in the ordinary course of trading, and (ii) any other lien arising in the ordinary course of operation of the Vessel",

PROVIDED THAT in the event that this Mortgage is assigned by the Bank the details of such assignment and of the assignee shall, at the request of the Bank, be inserted in such notice.

[For clauses 7 to 12, see the corresponding provisions in the British Deed of Covenants in this Appendix.]

7.   **Classification and repair**

8.   **Lawful and safe operation**

9.   **Mortgages, sales, chartering, management and repairs**

10.   **Arrests and liabilities**

11.   **Information**

12.   **Protection of security**

13.   **Recording of mortgage**

The Owner will cause this Mortgage to be duly recorded in accordance with the provisions of Title 22 of the Liberian Code of Laws of 1956 as amended (the "Liberian Maritime Law") and will otherwise comply with and satisfy all of the provisions of the Liberian Maritime Law in order to establish and maintain this Mortgage as a First Preferred Mortgage Lien thereunder upon the Vessel and upon all renewals, replacements and improvements made in or to the Vessel for the amount of the Secured Liabilities.

III   ENFORCEMENT

14.   **Enforcement of security**

This security shall become immediately enforceable upon the occurrence of an Event of Default and the Bank shall be entitled without notice immediately or at any time thereafter to put into force and exercise all the powers and remedies possessed by it according to law as mortgagee and chargee of the Vessel and the other assets subject to the security constituted by this Mortgage as and when it may see fit and in particular (without limitation):

(a) to demand payment by written notice to the Owner of the Secured Liabilities, whereupon such payment by the Owner to the Bank shall become immediately due and payable;

(b) to exercise all the rights and remedies in foreclosure and otherwise given to the Bank by any applicable law, including, without limitation, those under the provisions of Chapter 3 of Title 22 of the Liberian Code of Laws of 1956, as amended;

(c) to take possession of the Vessel;

(d) to recover and collect all Earnings, Insurances and Requisition Compensation, to give a good receipt therefor on behalf of the Owner, and to permit the brokers through whom collection or recovery of any Insurances is effected to charge and retain the usual brokerage therefor and to require that all policies, contracts and other records relating to the Insurances (including details of and correspondence concerning outstanding claims) be immediately delivered to or to the order of the Bank;

(e) to take over or institute all such proceedings in connection with the Vessel as the Bank in its absolute discretion thinks fit and to discharge, compound, release or compromise the Vessel or claims in respect thereof which have given or may give rise to any charge or lien on or arrest of the Vessel or which are or may be enforceable by proceedings against the Vessel;

(f) to sell all or any part of the Vessel, with or without the benefit of any charterparty or other contract by public auction or private contract, at any place in the world, with or without advertisement or notice to the Owner, for cash or on credit and otherwise and upon such terms as the Bank in its absolute discretion may determine, and at any such public sale to purchase the Vessel and to set off any purchase price against all or any part of the Secured Liabilities;

(g) to manage the Vessel and to insure, maintain, repair and reclass the Vessel, renew any parts thereof and to put her through survey and to hold, lay up, lease, charter, operate or otherwise use the Vessel in such manner and for such period as the Bank in its absolute discretion deems expedient and generally to do all such things as an owner of the Vessel could do in relation thereto, accounting only for the net proceeds (if any) of such use.

15. Receiver

(a) In addition to the powers conferred above, at any time after the security hereby created shall have become enforceable the Bank may appoint in writing a receiver or a receiver and manager (a **"Receiver"**) of all or any part of the Vessel and remove any Receiver so appointed and appoint another in his stead and may from time to time fix the remuneration of any such Receiver.

(b) The Bank may by instrument in writing delegate to any such Receiver all or any of the rights, powers and discretions vested in it by this Mortgage.

(c) The Bank shall not be responsible for misconduct or negligence on the part of such Receiver.

(d) Such Receiver shall be the agent of the Owner and the Owner shall be responsible for his acts, defaults and remuneration and liable on any contracts made by him.

16. Application of proceeds

All moneys received by the Bank or any Receiver in respect of the Vessel after this security has become enforceable shall be applied by the Bank in or towards payment of the Secured Liabilities in such order as the Bank may decide but without prejudice to the right of the Bank to recover any shortfall from the Owner.

17. Power of attorney

The Owner by way of security for the ultimate balance of the Secured Liabilities hereby irrevocably appoints the Bank and any Receiver appointed by the Bank jointly or severally the attorney(s) of the Owner on its behalf and in the name of the Owner, the Bank or such Receiver as the attorney(s) may decide to do all acts and execute all documents which the Owner could itself do in relation to the Vessel or in connection with any of the matters provided for in this Mortgage including, without limitation, the execution of any bill of sale or other assurance in respect of the Vessel.

18. Protection of third parties

No purchaser or other person dealing with the Bank or any Receiver appointed by it or with its or his attorneys or agents shall be concerned to enquire (i) whether any power exercised or purported to be exercised by it or him has become exercisable, (ii) whether any money remains due on the security hereby created, (iii) as to the propriety or regularity or any of his, its or their actions or (iv) as to the application of any money paid to him, it or them. In the absence of mala fides on the part of such purchaser or other person such dealings shall be deemed so far as regards the safety and protection of such purchaser or other person to be within the powers hereby conferred and to be valid accordingly. The remedy of the Owner in respect of any impropriety or irregularity whatever in the exercise of such powers shall be in damages only.

19. Delegation

The Bank may at the expense of the Bank at any time(s):

(a) delegate to any person(s) all or any of its rights, powers and discretions hereunder on such terms (including power to subdelegate) as the Bank sees fit;

(b) employ agents, managers, employees, advisers and others on such terms as the Bank sees fit for any of the purposes set out herein.

IV   MISCELLANEOUS

20.   Indemnity

(a) The Owner will indemnify the Bank and every Receiver or attorney appointed pursuant hereto in respect of all liabilities and expenses incurred by it, him or them in good faith in the execution or purported execution of any rights, powers or discretions vested in it, him or them pursuant hereto.

(b) The Bank shall not be liable for any losses arising in connection with the exercise or purported exercise of any of its rights, powers and discretions in good faith hereunder and in particular without limitation the Bank, and any Receiver, in possession shall not be liable to account as mortgagee in possession or for anything except actual receipts.

21.   Governing law

This Mortgage is governed by the law of the Republic of Liberia to the extent that it is necessary to make it a valid preferred mortgage provided that the Bank shall be entitled to the most extensive remedies that are available to or capable of being given to a mortgagee in the jurisdiction where the Vessel may be located or where any proceedings in relation to this Mortgage are brought.

22. Jurisdiction

For the benefit of the Bank, the Owner:

(a) agrees that the courts of England or the courts of any jurisdiction where the Vessel may be located have jurisdiction in relation to enforcement of this Mortgage and to settle any disputes in connection with this Mortgage and accordingly submits to the jurisdiction of those courts;

(b) (without prejudice to any other mode of service) appoints [   ] as its agent for service of process relating to any proceedings before those courts in connection with this Mortgage; and

(c) agrees that nothing in this Clause 22 limits the right of the Bank to bring proceedings against the Owner in connection with this Mortgage in any other court of competent jurisdiction.

23. No waiver of preferred status

(a) If any provision of this Mortgage shall be deemed invalid and shall be deemed to affect adversely the preferred status of this Mortgage under any applicable law, such provision shall cease to be a part of this Mortgage without affecting any other provisions, which shall remain in full force and effect.

(b) If this Mortgage [the Guarantee] or the Facility Agreement or any of the documents or instruments which may from time to time be delivered hereunder or thereunder or any provision hereof or thereof shall be deemed invalidated by present or future law of any nation or by decision of any court, or if any third party shall fail or refuse to recognise any of the powers granted to the Bank under this Mortgage when it is sought to exercise them, this shall not affect the validity or enforceability of all or any part of the Facility Agreement [, the Guarantee] or this Mortgage or such documents or instruments and, in any such case, the Owner covenants and agrees that, on demand, it will execute and deliver such other and further agreements and instruments and do such things as the Bank in its discretion may deem to be necessary to carry out the true intent of this Mortgage.

(c) Notwithstanding anything to the contrary in this Mortgage, it is intended that nothing in this Mortgage shall waive the preferred status of this Mortgage and that, if any provision shall be construed by any court of competent jurisdiction to waive the preferred status of this Mortgage, then such provision, to that extent, shall be of no effect.

24. Severability

If any of the terms hereof is or becomes invalid or unenforceable for any reason under the laws of any jurisdiction, such invalidity or unenforceability shall not affect its validity or enforceability in any other jurisdiction or invalidate or make unenforceable any other term hereof.

25. Recordation

For the purpose of recording this First Preferred Mortgage as required by Chapter 3 of Title 22 of the Liberian Code of Laws of 1956, as amended, the total amount is [X-Y] United States dollars (US$[X-Y]) or the equivalent amount in any alternative unit of account or accounts of which US$[X] represents the principal amount of the Loans and US$[Y] represents the optional currency excess amount together with interest and performance of mortgage covenants. The date of maturity is [on demand]. For property other than the Vessel, if any should be determined to be covered by this Mortgage, the separate discharge amount is zero point zero one per cent (0.01 per cent) of the total amount.

IN WITNESS whereof this Mortgage has been duly executed as a deed and has been delivered by a duly authorised representative of the Owner on the date first above written.

SIGNED by [   ]   )
the duly authorised   )
attorney-in-fact of, and   )
SEALED   and
DELIVERED by   )
[   ]   )
in the presence of:)

....
Notary Public
State of New York

ACKNOWLEDGEMENT

STATE OF   )
      :   SS. :
COUNTY OF)

On this   day of   , 199 before me personally appeared   , to me known and known to me to be the person who executed the foregoing instrument, who being by me duly sworn, deposes and says that he/she resides at   ; that he/she is the   of the Corporation described in and which executed the foregoing instrument, and that he/she signed his/her name thereto by order of board of directors of said Corporation and that the foregoing instrument is the act and deed of said corporation.

....
Notary Public

12.   Norwegian Ship Mortgage Deed

Norwegian ship mortgages are on a standard form which is usually substantially modified. See para 16–27 *et seq*.

The standard from provides:

[Amount]

Name of debtor   Identity No/Enterprise No.

HEREBY ACKNOWLEDGE(S) TO BE INDEBTED TO

Mortgagee/Creditor

Amount   Amount in words

The principal (the amount) to be repaid

The principal to carry interest from . . . . at the rate of. . . . .% per annum

Interest to be prepaid/postpaid on each . . . . and . . . ., the first payment to be effected on . . . . 19 . . . .

On any overdue, unpaid interests, instalments or principal, interest will be charged at the rate of . . . .% per annum over the normal rate of interest.

As security for payment of:

> Principal, interest and charges, etc. and costs incurred to safeguard the mortgaged ship and other costs to safeguard the security and all other claims which may arise from the loan under the following conditions

I/WE HEREBY MORTGAGE

Name of the ship:

Signal letters: entered in the   Register of ships

Built in the year: Home port:

The mortgage comprises the ship's various parts and appurtenances of whatever kind including future acquisitions, cf. the Maritime Act (Norway) Section 260.

If the ship has been entered in the Shipbuilding Register, this mortgage also comprises the main engines and major sections of the hull whether or not they are being built outside the principal builder's yard. It is the responsibility of the debtor to provide for the necessary marking or other identification of materials and equipment in the possession of the principal builder's yard, or in the possession of other builders who are building the main engines or major sections of the hull, cf. the Maritime Act (Norway) Section 257.

Other builders are:

The mortgage also comprises all insurance sums for the ship.

This mortgage has right of succession as and when claims of equal or prior rank are paid off or redeemed, and at present this mortgage ranks after:

The mortgaged ship shall not be sold or further encumbered without the consent of the mortgagee.

In addition to disposing of the mortgaged ship by forced sale or by taking possession of the ship, the repayment of the debt together with interest and all costs and expenses incurred may be enforced without prior legal proceedings, according to the Enforcement Act (Norway) Section 7–2.

Furthermore, the mortgage is subject to the following:

CONDITIONS

Clause 1

Without the written consent of the creditor the mortgaged ship shall not be chartered for a continuous period exceeding 12 months or on bareboat terms.

The creditor's consent in writing shall be obtained in advance, if it is intended to break up the mortgaged ship, to alter its nature or to incur major costs on it.

The mortgaged ship shall not be employed in defiance of current laws, rules, international conventions or insurance terms which have been accepted by the creditor.

Clause 2

The debtor undertakes to take out such insurances as required at any time by the creditor.

Hull and risk insurances shall cover full value, on full terms.

Other insurances shall cover the amounts customary for the type of ship concerned and shall comprise those risks which it is customary to cover in connection with the use of the mortgaged ship and its trading area or as the creditor deems necessary to protect his interests as mortgagee.

The insurance terms, choice of currency and the underwriters covering the insurances are subject to the approval of the creditor.

The debtor shall ensure that the creditor receives insurance documents which contain the insurance terms and which confirm that the creditor's interests as mortgagees are co-insured or noted. Notation or assignment of the insurances shall be effected in the manner required by the creditor.

If the debtor does not fulfil his obligation to insure, the creditor has the right to cover the insurances for the debtor's account.

Clause 3

In the event of any salvage claim or if anyone takes legal steps to obtain any right in or disposal of the mortgaged ship, the debtor shall promptly notify the creditor thereof. The same applies in the event of major damage or capture or if for any other reason the debtor's control of the mortgaged ship is lost or restricted, or if he resolves to lay up the mortgaged ship.

The debtor shall send to the creditor, undemanded, the annual financial statement, annual report and auditor's report as soon as they are available.

Clause 4

The creditor or his representative may at any time inspect the ship and have it valued for the debtor's account.

If renewed valuation of the mortgaged ship indicates in the judgment of the creditor that the security has diminished substantially, the creditor may require extraordinary repayment of the debt.

Clause 5

The debt is deemed to have fallen due by default if:

(a) The debtor substantially defaults on his obligations under this ship mortgage deed.

(b) The debtor has given the creditor incorrect information.

(c) The debtor, the guarantor or the owner of the mortgaged ship dies, suspends payment, seeks composition or other debt settlements, is declared bankrupt or is subject to enforcement proceedings.

(d) The management of the mortgaged ship is changed or there is any partial or complete change in the equity interest of this ship through the assignment of stocks, shares or otherwise.

(e) The mortgaged ship is lost or broken up.

(f) The security is substantially diminished as a consequence of damage to the mortgaged ship.

(g) The mortgaged ship loses its nationality.

(h) The mortgaged ship is subject to temporary enforcement proceedings or there is taken possession of the mortgaged ship, or it is seized, requisitioned, captured or if the debtor for any other reason wholly or partially loses control of the mortgaged ship.

(i) The mortgaged ship is sold by forced sale, is encumbered by any distraint, or if any claim secured by maritime lien is not paid when due.

In the event of such default the creditor may require the whole debt to be paid immediately without any notice.

Clause 6

In the event of default the creditor may require the debtor promptly to bring the mortgaged ship to any port designated by the creditor.

Clause 7

For any legal proceedings the undersigned and subsequent owners of the mortgaged ship accept
. . . . as venue.

Clause 8

The debtor shall pay all costs and expenses arising in connection with the loan.

Place, date

Signature of debtor   Repeated in type or block letters

I/We confirm that the signer(s) being over 18 years of age, has/have signed this document or acknowledged his/their signature(s) hereto in my/our presence. I am/We are of age and resident in Norway.

1st Signature   Repeated in type or block letters

Address (typed or in block letters)

2nd Signature   Repeated in type or block letters

Address (typed or in block letters)

13. Panamanian Ship Mortgage

Note on the Form

Panamanian ship mortgages are discussed specifically at para 16–21 *et seq*.

In the interests of brevity, this form does not contain representations and warranties or events of default – these would normally appear in the facility agreement. For outline representations and warranties and events of default, see the Outline general summary of terms of security agreements in this Appendix. These are also reviewed in detail in another work in this series on financial law – a book dealing with international loans, bonds and securities regulation. See also:

– as to registration of ships and ship mortgages, para 15–12 *et seq*

– as to covenants in ship mortgages, para 17–1 *et seq*

– as to ship loan events of default, para 18–2 *et seq*

– as to assignments of earnings and charters, chapter 21

– as to assignments of insurances, chapter 22.

Form of Mortgage

THIS FIRST PRIORITY MORTGAGE is made the   day of
      199 **BETWEEN**

1. [   ] a company incorporated under the laws of [   ]
    whose principal office is at [   ] (the "**Owner**"); and

2. [   ] carrying on a banking business at its branch at
    [   ] (the "**Bank**").

WHEREAS:

(A) The Owner is the sole and absolute owner of the whole of the unencumbered vessel m.v. "[   ]" further described in Schedule I hereto.

(B) By a Facility Agreement dated [   ] 199[ ] between (inter alia)
    [   ], the Owner and the Bank, the Owner has agreed on the terms thereof to execute and deliver in favour of the Bank a First Preferred Mortgage over the whole of the said vessel as security (inter alia)

---

for the due payment of all sums from time to time payable thereunder by the Owner to the Bank.

NOW IT IS HEREBY AGREED AND DECLARED as follows.

I GENERAL

1. Interpretation

1.1 Incorporated definitions Unless the contrary intention appears any term defined in the Facility Agreement has the same meaning when used in this Mortgage.

1.2 Definitions

(a) In this Mortgage:

"**Charter**" has the meaning given to it in Clause 8 (Status of Charters).

"**Default Rate**" means the rate specified in Clause [ ] of the Facility Agreement. [This is a conventional default interest clause for overdue sums.]

"**Earnings**" includes all present and future moneys and claims which are earned by or become payable to or for the account of the Owner in connection with the operation or ownership of the Vessel and including but not limited to (i) freights, passage and hire moneys, (ii) remuneration for salvage and towage services, (iii) demurrage and detention moneys, (iv) all present and future moneys and claims payable to the Owner in respect of any breach or variation of a charterparty or contract of affreightment in respect of the Vessel, and (v) all moneys and claims in respect of the requisition for hire of the Vessel.

"**Earnings Account**" means the account opened and maintained by the Owner under Clause 11 (Payment of Earnings).

"**Facility Agreement**" means the Facility Agreement referred to in recital (B) above.

"**Insurances**" means (a) all contracts and policies of insurance and all entries in clubs and/or associations which are from time to time taken out or effected in respect of the Vessel pursuant to Clause 14 (Insurances) below and (b) all benefits thereunder, all claims in respect thereof and return of premiums, and "excess risks" in Clause 14 (Insurances) means (i) the proportion of claims for general average and salvage charges which are not recoverable as a result of the value at which a vessel is assessed for the purpose of such claims exceeding her hull and machinery insured value and (ii) collision liabilities not recoverable in full under the hull and machinery insurance by reason of such liabilities exceeding such proportion of the insured value of a vessel as is covered thereunder.

"**Permitted Liens**" means:

(a) liens for unpaid crew's wages arising in accordance with usual maritime practice; and
(b) liens for salvage,

and to the extent they are subordinate to the lien of this Mortgage:

(i) liens for Master's disbursements incurred in the ordinary course of trading; and
(ii) any other lien arising in the ordinary course of operation of the Vessel.

"**Requisition Compensation**" includes all moneys or other compensation payable by reason of requisition for title to or other compulsory acquisition of the Vessel otherwise than by requisition for hire.

"**Secured Liabilities**" means the sums and liabilities (actual or contingent) which are or may become payable or owing by the Owner to the Bank under or in connection with the Facility Agreement, this Mortgage or any other Security Document.

"**Security Assets**" means the Vessel, each Charter, the Earnings, the Insurances, Requisition Compensation and all other assets the subject of this security.

"**Security Period**" means the period beginning on the date hereof and ending on the date upon which all the Secured Liabilities which have or may arise have been irrevocably paid and discharged.

"**Total Loss**" includes:

(a) actual, constructive, compromised, agreed or arranged total loss of the Vessel;
(b) requisition for title or other compulsory acquisition of the Vessel otherwise than by requisition for hire; and
(c) capture, seizure, arrest, detention or confiscation of the Vessel by

any government or by persons acting or purporting to act on behalf of any government unless the Vessel be released from such capture, seizure, arrest, detention or confiscation within one month after the occurrence thereof.

"**Vessel**" means m.v. "[   ]", as described in Recital (A) above and includes each part thereof and interest therein and all her engines, boilers, machinery, masts, spars, sails, boats, anchors, cables, chains, rigging tackle, outfit, spare gear, fuel, consumable and other stores, whether on board or ashore and whether now owned or hereafter acquired and also any and all additions, improvements and replacements hereafter made in or to the Vessel or any part thereof, including all items and appurtenances aforesaid.

1.3   Construction

(a) In this Mortgage, unless the contrary intention appears, a reference to:

   (i)   a provision of a law or regulation is a reference to that provision as amended or re-enacted;

  (ii)   a Clause or a Schedule is a reference to a clause of or a schedule to this Mortgage;

 (iii)   any person includes a reference to its successors and assigns;

 (iv)   the Facility Agreement, this Mortgage, any other Security Document or any other document is a reference to the Facility Agreement, this Mortgage, such other Security Document or such other document as amended, novated or supplemented.

(b) The headings in this Mortgage are for convenience only and are to be ignored in construing this Mortgage.

2.   Grant of mortgage

(a) As security for payment of the Secured Liabilities the Owner hereby executes and constitutes in favour of the Bank a first and absolute mortgage on the Vessel in accordance with the provisions of Chapter V Title IV of Second Book of the Code of Commerce and of the pertinent provisions of the Civil Code and other legislation of the Republic of Panama.

(b) Forthwith upon the execution of this Mortgage and the acceptance thereof by the Bank, the Owner will procure due and proper legalisation and recordation thereof against the Vessel by recording this Mortgage in the [Public Registry of the City of Panama] OR [Panamanian Consulate in London by way of provisional recordation and for immediate transfer to the Public Registry of the City of Panama] pursuant to the pertinent legislation of the Republic of Panama.

3. Assignment

(a) The Owner as beneficial owner hereby:

    (i)   assigns and agrees to assign absolutely to the Bank all its rights, title and interest in or to each Charter, the Earnings, the Insurances, Requisition Compensation and all moneys payable in respect of a Total Loss; and

    (ii) to the fullest extent permitted by law charges as security for the Secured Liabilities in favour of the Bank all its rights, title and interest (if any) in the balance for the time being and from time to time standing to the credit of the Earnings Account, all interest thereon and the debts represented by such credit balance and interest,

PROVIDED THAT upon irrevocable payment in full of the Secured Liabilities the Bank will at the request and expense of the Owner re-assign to the Owner the items assigned by this Clause.

(b) The Owner will do or procure the doing of all such things and the execution of all such documents, as the Bank may from time to time require to ensure the payment to the Bank of the items assigned by this Clause.

4. Continuing security

The security constituted by this Mortgage shall be continuing and not satisfied by any intermediate payment or satisfaction of the whole or any part of the Secured Liabilities but shall secure the ultimate balance of the Secured Liabilities. The security hereby given shall be in addition to and shall not be affected by any other security now or hereafter held by the Bank for all or any of the Secured Liabilities.

5. Covenant to pay and perform

The Owner hereby covenants (i) to pay the Secured Liabilities to the Bank promptly when due and (ii) to comply at all times with the terms (express or implied) of this Mortgage, the Facility Agreement and any other Security Document to which it is a party.

6. Acknowledgement of indebtedness

Pursuant to the provisions of Article 1515 of the Code of Commerce of the Republic of Panama the Owner acknowledges that it is, or may become, indebted to the Bank pursuant to the terms of the Facility Agreement or otherwise howsoever in the principal amount of up to US$[   ] and that it grants this Mortgage as security for the payment when due of the Secured Liabilities as the same are (inter alia) set out in the following paragraphs:

[Insert repayment, prepayment, optional currency, interest period, interest, substitute basis, payments, taxes, increased costs, illegality, fees, indemnities and expenses clauses from Facility Agreement and matching definitions].

7. Encumbrances and disposals

The Owner undertakes that (except with the prior written consent of the Bank) during the Security Period it will not except in favour of the Bank:

(a) create or permit to subsist any mortgage, charge, pledge, lien or other security interest upon all or any part of the Security Assets other than, in the case of the Vessel, Permitted Liens; or

(b) assign, sell, transfer or otherwise dispose of or abandon all or any part of the Security Assets.

II EARNINGS

[For these clauses, see the corresponding clauses in the British Ship Mortgage Deed of Covenants in this Appendix.]

8. Status of charters

9. Maintenance of charters

10. Obligations under charters

11. Payment of earnings

12. Application of earnings

III   INSURANCES

[For clauses 13 to 18, see the corresponding provisions in the British Ship Mortgage Deed of Covenants in this Appendix.]

13.   **Insurance definitions**

14.   **Insurances**

15.   **Insurance covenants**

16.   **Application of insurance proceeds**

17.   **Notices, Undertakings, Endorsements**

18.   **Power of bank to insure**

IV   VESSEL COVENANTS

19.   **Registration of vessel and mortgage**

The Owner will during the Security Period:

(a) maintain the valid and effective registration of the Vessel under the laws and flag of the Republic of Panama and ensure nothing is done or omitted whereby such registration of the Vessel would or might be defeated or imperilled;

(b) not change the name, port of registration or certificate of registry or equivalent document of the Vessel;

(c) [procure permanent registration of and] keep this Mortgage registered as a first preferred mortgage on the Vessel and for this purpose execute and record in the Public Registry of the Republic of Panama in due time all such instruments as may be necessary or desirable to preserve this Mortgage as a valid first preferred mortgage and deliver to the Bank forthwith on request at the Owner's expense all appropriate certificates and evidence thereof.

20. Notice of mortgage

The Owner will during the Security Period place and at all times and places retain with the Vessel's marine document a duly certified copy of this Mortgage and of any assignment of this Mortgage (if requested by an assignee) (which shall form a part of the Vessel's documents) on board the Vessel with her papers and cause each such certified copy and such papers to be shown to any and all persons having business therewith which might give rise to any lien thereon other than Permitted Liens and to any representative of the Bank. Neither the Owner, any manager, charterer, the Master of the Vessel nor any other person has or shall have the right, power or authority to create, incur or permit to be placed or imposed or continued upon the Vessel any lien whatsoever other than Permitted Liens. The Owner will place and maintain in a conspicuous place in the navigation room and in the Master's cabin of the Vessel a framed printed notice in the following form:

"NOTICE OF NAVAL MORTGAGE

This Vessel is mortgaged by the Owner thereof [   ] whose registered office is situated in Panama City, Panama to [   ] through its branch at [   ] pursuant to the provisions of Chapter V Title IV of Book Second of the Code of Commerce of the Republic of Panama and other pertinent legislation and pursuant also to the terms of the said Mortgage a certified copy of which is preserved with the Vessel's papers. Under the terms of the Mortgage, neither the owner, any manager, charterer, the Master of the Vessel nor any other person has any right, power or authority to create, incur or permit to be imposed on this Vessel any lien whatsoever other than (a) liens for unpaid crew's wages arising in accordance with usual maritime practice, (b) liens for salvage and, to the extent they are subordinate to the lien of this Mortgage (i) liens for Master's disbursements incurred in the ordinary course of trading, and (ii) any other lien arising in the ordinary course of operation of the Vessel."

[For clauses 21 to 26, see the corresponding provisions in the British Ship Mortgage Deed of Covenants in this Appendix.]

21. Classification and repair

22. Lawful and safe operation

23. Chartering, management and repairs

24. Arrests and Liabilities

25. Information

26. Protection of security

V ENFORCEMENT

27. Enforcement of security

This security shall become immediately enforceable upon the occurrence of an Event of Default and the Bank shall be entitled without notice immediately or at any time thereafter to put into force and exercise all the powers and remedies possessed by it according to law as mortgagee and chargee of the Security Assets as and when it may see fit and in particular (without limitation):

(a) to demand payment by written notice to the Owner of the Secured Liabilities, whereupon such payment by the Owner to the Bank shall become immediately due and payable;

(b) to exercise all the rights and remedies in foreclosure and otherwise given to the Bank by any applicable law;

(c) to take possession of the Vessel;

(d) to recover and collect all Earnings, Insurances and Requisition Compensation, to give a good receipt therefor on behalf of the Owner, and to permit the brokers through whom collection or recovery of any Insurances is effected to charge and retain the usual brokerage therefor and to require that all policies, contracts and other records relating to the Insurances (including details of and correspondence concerning outstanding claims) be immediately delivered to or to the order of the Bank;

(e) to take over or institute all such proceedings in connection with all or any of the Security Assets as the Bank in its absolute discretion thinks fit and to discharge, compound, release or compromise all or any of the Security Assets or claims in respect thereof including without limitation claims in respect of the Vessel which have given or may give rise to any charge or lien on or arrest of the Vessel or which are or may be enforceable by proceedings against the Vessel;

(f) to sell all or any part of the Security Assets, (in the case of the Vessel with or without the benefit of any charterparty or other contract) by public auction or private contract, at any place in the world, with or without advertisement or notice to the Owner except, in the case of a private sale, subject to not less than 20 days' prior written notice having been given to the Owner, for cash or on credit and otherwise and upon such terms as the Bank in its absolute discretion may determine, and at any such public sale to purchase the Vessel and to set off any purchase price against all or any part of the Secured Liabilities;

(g) to manage the Vessel and to insure, maintain, repair and reclass the Vessel, renew any parts thereof and to put her through survey and to hold, lay up, lease, charter, operate or otherwise use the Vessel in such manner and for such period as the Bank deems necessary and generally to do all such things as an Owner of the Vessel could do in relation thereto, accounting only for the net proceeds (if any) of such use;

(h) to set off any moneys comprised in the Security Assets against all or any of the Secured Liabilities;

(i) to implement any contracts included in the Security Assets, or to agree with any other party thereto to determine the same on such terms and conditions as the Bank and such party may agree.

28. Receiver

(a) In addition to the powers conferred above, at any time after the security hereby created shall have become enforceable the Bank may appoint in writing a receiver or a receiver and manager (hereafter a "**Receiver**") of all or any part of the Security Assets and remove any Receiver so appointed and appoint another in his stead and may from time to time fix the remuneration of any such Receiver.

(b) The Bank may by instrument in writing delegate to any such Receiver all or any of the rights, powers and discretions vested in it by this Mortgage.

(c) The Bank shall not be responsible for misconduct or negligence on the part of such Receiver.

(d) Such Receiver shall be the agent of the Owner and the Owner shall be responsible for his acts, defaults and remuneration and liable on any contracts made by him.

29. Application of proceeds

All moneys received by the Bank or any Receiver in respect of the Security Assets after this security has become enforceable shall be applied by the

Bank in or towards payment of the Secured Liabilities in such order as the Bank may decide but without prejudice to the right of the Bank to recover any shortfall from the Owner.

30. Power of attorney

(a) The Owner by way of security for the ultimate balance of the Secured Liabilities hereby irrevocably appoints the Bank and any Receiver appointed by the Bank jointly or severally the attorney(s) of the Owner on its behalf and in the name of the Owner, the Bank or such Receiver as the attorney(s) may decide to do all acts and execute all documents which the Owner could itself do in relation to the Security Assets or in connection with any of the matters provided for in this Mortgage including without limitation the execution of any bill of sale, transfer or other assurance in respect of the Security Assets.

(b) The Bank may:

  (i) ask, require, demand, receive and give acquittance for any sum forming part of the Security Assets;
  (ii) endorse any cheques or other instruments or orders in connection therewith; and
  (iii) make any claims or take any action or institute any proceedings which may be necessary or advisable in the premises to protect the interest of the Bank in all or any part of the Security Assets.

31. Protection of third parties

No purchaser or other person dealing with the Bank or any Receiver appointed by it or with its or his attorneys or agents shall be concerned to enquire (i) whether any power exercised or purported to be exercised by it or him has become exercisable, (ii) whether any money remains due on the security hereby created, (iii) as to the propriety or regularity of any of his, its or their actions or (iv) as to the application of any money paid to him, it or them. In the absence of mala fides on the part of such purchaser or other person such dealings shall be deemed so far as regards the safety and protection of such purchaser or other person to be within the powers hereby conferred and to be valid accordingly. The remedy of the Owner in respect of any impropriety or irregularity whatever in the exercise of such powers shall be in damages only.

32. Delegation

The Bank may at the expense of the Bank at any time(s):

(a) delegate to any person(s) all or any of its rights, powers and discretions hereunder on such terms (including power to subdelegate) as the Bank sees fit;

(b) employ agents, managers, employees, advisers and others on such terms as the Bank sees fit for any of the purposes set out herein.

VI   MISCELLANEOUS

33.   Indemnity

(a) The Owner will indemnify the Bank and every Receiver or attorney appointed pursuant hereto in respect of all liabilities and expenses incurred by it, him or them in good faith in the execution or purported execution of any rights, powers or discretions vested in it, him or them pursuant hereto;

(b) The Bank shall not be liable for any losses arising in connection with the exercise or purported exercise of any of its rights, powers and discretions in good faith hereunder and in particular without limitation the Bank and any Receiver in possession shall not be liable to account as mortgagee in possession or for anything except actual receipts.

34.   Governing law

This Mortgage shall be governed by English law but, in matters relating to the enforcement of rights against the Vessel, Panamanian law shall apply as far as necessary.

35.   Jurisdiction

For the benefit of the Bank, the Owner:

(a) agrees that the courts of England or the courts of any jurisdiction where the Vessel may be located have jurisdiction in relation to enforcement of this Mortgage and to settle any disputes in connection with this Mortgage and accordingly submits to the jurisdiction of those courts;

(b) (without prejudice to any other mode of service) appoints [   ] as its agent for service of process relating to any proceedings before those courts in connection with this Mortgage; and

(c) agrees that nothing in this Clause 35 limits the right of the Bank to bring proceedings against the Owner in connection with this Mortgage in any other court of competent jurisdiction.

36. Severability

(a) If any of the terms hereof is or becomes invalid or unenforceable for any reason under the laws of any jurisdiction, such invalidity or unenforceability shall not affect its validity or enforceability in any other jurisdiction or invalidate or make unenforceable any other term hereof.

(b) If any provision of this Mortgage or the first priority security conferred hereby for all of the sums intended to be secured hereby should be or become invalid or defective in any respect, such provision or security shall have the fullest effect, validity and enforceability that it would have had if it had been contained in or conferred by a British statutory mortgage and Deed of Covenants.

37. Maturity date

The maturity date of the Secured Liabilities is [   ].

38. Agents in Panama

(a) The Owner's representatives and agents in Panama are [   ].

(b) The Owner and the Bank each confer a special power of attorney with right of substitution upon [   ] and any partner in that firm empowering such firm or any such partner to take all necessary steps to record this instrument or mortgage in the appropriate registry of the Republic of Panama.

[Clauses relating to Expenses, Stamp Duties, Accounts, Notices, Assignment, Set-off, Currency Indemnity, Waivers]

IN WITNESS whereof this Mortgage has been duly executed as a deed on the date first above written.

SIGNED by [   ]   )
the duly authorised   )
attorney-in-fact of, and   )
SEALED   and   )
DELIVERED   )
by [   ]   )
in the presence of:)

SCHEDULE   I

Name of Vessel:

Use:

Owner:

Built In:

Length:

Breadth

Depth:

Gross Tons:

Net Tons:

Call Sign:

Official Number:

Local Representatives:

ACCEPTANCE OF MORTGAGE

[   ] through its branch at [   ] HEREBY ACCEPTS the annexed First Preferred Mortgage executed in its favour by [   ] a [Panamanian] Company under the date of [   ] covering the Panamanian Vessel [   ] AND DOES HEREBY ACCEPT the Mortgage in all respects and agrees to all terms and conditions of the Mortgage.

IN WITNESS whereof the said [   ] has caused this Mortgage to be executed this [   ] day of [   ] One thousand nine hundred and ninety [   ].

SIGNED by   )
[   ]   )
on behalf of [   )
          ] in the   )
presence of:)   Authorised Signatory

APPENDIX: PART III

GUARANTEES

14. Outline of guarantee of term loan

This outline summarises the main provisions in a guarantee of a term loan. The provisions are discussed in detail in chapter 25.

Initial checks

Check:

- corporate powers and authorities of guarantor
- disinterested quorum of guarantor's directors approving the guarantee
- whether the guarantee is prohibited financial assistance to purchase guarantor's shares (e.g. British Companies Act 1985 s 151)
- whether the guarantee is transaction at an undervalue or insolvency preference
- contractual restrictions in guarantor's credit agreements, etc.
- disclosure and misrepresentation inducing guarantee
- guarantor's duty to notify material commitments to stock exchange
- withholding taxes on payments by the guarantor
- stamp duties on the guarantee
- exchange controls on payments by the guarantor
- unfair contract terms in the guarantee.

For these checks, see para 24–3 *et seq.*

Outline terms of guarantee

1. The guarantor as primary obligor guarantees all sums payable by the debtor under or in connection with the facility agreement (as varied from time to time) and will pay overdue sums on first demand(s) from time to time. The sums payable include damages and sums payable on rescission of the facility agreement.

2. This is a continuing guarantee and extends to the ultimate balance owing under the facility agreement.

3. Liability of guarantor is not affected by:

   – waivers, variations, compositions, releases, failure to perfect and other circumstances in relation to principal debt or debtor, co-obligors or security;
   – liquidation, dissolution or merger of debtor;
   – any invalidity, non-provability, or unenforceability of the principal debt; the guarantee will be construed as if that debt were valid etc.

4. The bank may apply recoveries as it sees fit from debtor, security or co-obligors, and need not apply them first to the guaranteed debt.

5. After demand and so long as the full amount demanded is unpaid, the guarantor will not claim against the debtor or other person in competition with the bank, or exercise any remedy or receive any moneys in respect of the sums paid. The bank need not apply partial recoveries towards the principal debt until it is fully paid.

6. If any payment must be restored on the insolvency of the debtor, the guarantee will revive.

7. The bank need not claim or exhaust recourse against the debtor or security before claiming under this guarantee.

8. The guarantee is additional to other rights and security available to the bank.

9. The bank's certificate of amount owing under the facility agreement is conclusive against the guarantor.

10. Place, manner and currency of payments; payments without set-off or counterclaim; tax grossing-up; representations and warranties; covenants; stamp duties; costs; default interest; bank's right of set-off; waivers; remedies cumulative; currency indemnity; assignments; notices; governing law; jurisdiction; waiver of immunity.

15. List of main terms in guarantee given by bank or other independent guarantor

This note lists the main points to be taken into account in drafting a guarantee by a bank or other guarantor which is independent of the debtor. The topic is discussed in chapter 26 where the issues listed below are reviewed.

1. Guarantee is payable on first demand without proof of liability.

2. Expiry date for demands by creditor.

3. Maximum amount guaranteed.

4. No variations of principal debt or release of co-obligors or security?

5. Creditor to exhaust recourse against principal debtor first?

6. Guarantor's right to pay by originally scheduled instalments?

7. Creditor will disclose all material facts known to him prior to and during guarantee and will notify known defaults to guarantor?

8. Creditor will assign guaranteed debt to guarantor after payment, plus security, etc.

9. Creditor to appropriate recoveries to guaranteed debt first?

10. Guarantor can pay guaranteed debt on demand at any time, or purchase guaranteed debt. Creditor will not claim in debtor's insolvency without first calling the guarantee.

11. Restrictions on assignment of guarantee?

16. Short form guarantee of facility agreement

From: The Guarantor

To: The Bank

Dear Sirs,

1. We (the "**Guarantor**") refer to the facility letter from the Bank to
    [   ] (the "**Borrower**") dated [   ] (the "**Facility Letter**") which
    term includes all variations thereof from time to time in force) in rela-
    tion to a proposed loan facility of [   ].

2. In consideration of the Bank at the request of the Guarantor granting
    any credit facilities to the Borrower (or for other valuable consideration
    receipt whereof as hereby acknowledged), the Guarantor as primary
    obligor unconditionally and irrevocably (i) guarantees to the Bank by
    way of continuing guarantee the payment when due of all amounts
    payable by the Borrower under the Facility Letter, and (ii) agrees that if
    and each time that the Borrower shall fail to make any payments as and
    when the same become due under the Facility Letter the Guarantor will
    on demand (without requiring the Bank first to take steps against the
    Borrower or any other person) pay to the Bank such amounts (as to
    which the certificate of the Bank shall in the absence of manifest error
    be conclusive) in the currency in which such amounts are payable by
    the Borrower free of all deductions whatsoever together with interest
    thereon from the date of demand until the date of payment at the rate
    specified in the Facility Letter. If deductions must be made by law then
    the Guarantor will pay such additional amounts as may be necessary to
    ensure that the Bank receives the full amount provided for.

3. The obligations of the Guarantor hereunder shall not be affected by
    any matter of thing which but for this provision might operate to affect
    such obligations including without limitation (i) any time or indulgence
    granted to or composition with the Borrower or any other person, (ii)
    the taking, variation, renewal or release of, or neglect to perfect or
    enforce, any rights, remedies or securities against the Borrower or any
    other person or (iii) any unenforceability or invalidity of any obli-
    gations of the Borrower so that this Guarantee shall be construed as if
    there were no such unenforceability or invalidity.

4. The Guarantor warrants that this Guarantee is its legally binding obli-
    gation enforceable in accordance with its terms and that all necessary

governmental consents and authorisations for the giving and implementation of this Guarantee have been obtained.

5. Until all amounts which may be or become payable under the Facility Letter have been irrevocably paid in full, the Guarantor shall not by virtue of this Guarantee be subrogated to any rights of the Bank or claim in competition with the Bank against the Borrower or any other person.

6. The Guarantor will reimburse the Bank all costs incurred by the Bank in connection with the preparation and the enforcement of this Guarantee.

7. This Guarantee shall be governed by with the laws of England. For the benefit of the Bank solely, the Guarantor hereby submits to the non-exclusive jurisdiction of the English courts and appoints [   ] as its agent for service of process.

Yours faithfully,

....
For and on behalf of
the Guarantor

SELECT BIBLIOGRAPHY

Articles from the journals are not listed. The main English journals on international finance include *International Financial Law Review* (Euromoney), *Journal of International Banking Law* (ESC Publishing Ltd/Sweet & Maxwell), and *Butterworths Journal of International Banking and Financial Law*. In the main, this short list only includes works which contain comparative or international law and not standard works on the domestic law of a jurisdiction.

1. Security

There are very few books on the comparative law of security. See the 11-volume series *Credit and Security* by David Allen, Mary Hiscock and Derek Roebuck, 1970s, University of Queensland Press/Crane, Russak & Company, Inc, covering Pacific rim and Asian countries. Also useful is Michael G Dickson, Wolfgang Rosener, Paul M Storm (eds), *Security on Movable Property and Receivables in Europe* (1988) ESC Publishing Ltd.

2. Ship and aircraft finance

The Greek Code of Private Maritime Law, translation by Theodoros Karatzas and Nigel Ready (1982) Nijhoff

JD Buchan,	*Mortgages of Ships*: *Marine Security in Canada* (1986) Butterworths
John Cahillane	*Cross-Border Aircraft Leasing*: *an industry report* (1992) Lloyd's of London Press
Benjamin Constant	*The Law Relating to the Mortgage of Ships* (1920)
Lennary Hagberg (ed)	*Maritime Law*, Kluwer/IBA, Several volumes published in the 1970s and 1980s
Simon Hall (ed)	*Aircraft Financing* (2nd ed 1993) Euromoney
Richard Hames and Graham S McBain	*Aircraft Finance: registration, security and enforcement* (1988) Longman

David C Jackson	*Enforcement of Maritime Claims* (1985) Lloyd's of London Press
David C Jackson	*Civil Jurisdiction and Judgements – Maritime Claims* (1987) Lloyd's of London Press
Nigel Meeson	*Ship and Aircraft Mortgages* (1989) Lloyd's of London Press
Stephenson Harwood	*Shipping Finance* (1991) Euromoney
W Tetley	*Maritime Liens and Claims* (1985) Business Law Communications
D Rhidian Thomas	*Maritime Liens* (1980) Stevens

Numerous articles on aircraft finance are to be found in the legal journals, e.g. the *Journal of Air Law & Commerce*.

LIST OF RESEARCH TOPICS

This list contains topics which could be considered for a research thesis or a shorter article. The topics relate to the areas covered by this book. Research topics in relation to the areas covered by other books in this series on international financial law will be found in the volume concerned.

The selection is based on relative originality and usefulness. Topics which have already been extensively covered by the legal literature are not included. In many cases there is an existing literature on the listed topics, but further work is considered worthwhile to develop what has already been achieved or to explore a new approach. If the chosen titles do not appeal, it is hoped that they will be suggestive of those which do. Some of the titles are no more than pointers which would have to be developed into a proper topic.

The author would be very glad to receive a copy of any essays which may be written and which are derived from this list. See the address after the Preface.

Principles of security

- Legal theory of security

- Economic theory of security

- Security and creditor equality on bankruptcy

- Security and the doctrine of specificity (see para 1–6)

- Debtor protection in the law of non-consumer security

- Security and corporate rehabilitation proceedings

- History of security law

- Security interests by groups of jurisdictions (for these and other groups, see the lists in *Comparative Financial Law* in this series)

    – Security interest in common law jurisdictions

    – Security interests in Germanic jurisdictions

    – Security interests in Scandinavian jurisdictions

- – Security interests in Franco-Latin jurisdictions
- – Security interests in Islamic jurisdictions
- – Security interests in emerging (former communist) jurisdictions
- Floating and other universal business charges: comparative law
- Security interests over future property
- Registration of security interests over goods (tangible movables): comparative law
- Registration of security interests over contracts, investment securities and other intangible movables: comparative survey
- Extraterritoriality of registration systems for security interests
- Registration as a non-bankruptcy priority system
- Security, dispossession of the debtor and the false wealth doctrine: publicity of security interests (see para 1–5)
- Permissible secured debt: comparative law
- Trustees for security: comparative law
- Limitations of security to financial institutions and other approved creditors: comparative law
- Enforcement remedies of the secured creditor: comparative law
- Comparative land registration systems: ownership title and mortgages
- Comparative law of fiduciary transfers: Germany, Japan, the Netherlands, Switzerland
- Non-possessory chattel mortgages and trade finance: international survey
- Security assignments of contract debts: comparative survey
- Purchase money security interests: comparative survey
- Security interests and accessories to the collateral (fixtures to land, engines to aircraft, ship freight, etc.)
- Liabilities of secured creditors in respect of the collateral: international survey
- Set-off, charge-backs and flawed assets: comparative law
- Possessory and other liens: comparative law
- Security interests over fungible investment securities deposited with custodians and clearance systems

- Security interests over intellectual property: comparative survey
- Classification of priority contests
- Comparative law of priority of security interests
- Priority rights of lessees, licensees and charterers of collateral (land, goods, intellectual property, etc.) comparative survey
- Priority of security interests over investment securities: international survey
- Priority of liens over security interests
- Effect on security of debtor rights to deal with the collateral or to substitute collateral: comparative survey
- Priority over proceeds of security interests (sale, dividends, rentals, etc.)
- Comparative law of marshalling
- Conflict of laws and security interests: international survey
- Conflict of laws and security interests over contract debts
- Conflict of laws and security interests over investment securities
- Judicial jurisdiction over security interests

Ship and aircraft finance

- Comparative law of ship and aircraft finance
- Comparison of ownership and mortgage registration systems for land, ships and aircraft
- Security interests over aircraft engines, spare parts and other accessories: comparative law
- International conventions relating to ship and aircraft mortgages
- History of law of ship mortgages
- Comparative law of priority between charterers and mortgagees
- Security interests over ship and aircraft charters and earnings
- Security interests over ship and aircraft insurances
- Ship and aircraft finance in groups of jurisdictions (see the listing of these and other groups in *Comparative Financial Law* in this series):

- Ship and aircraft finance in common law jurisdictions
- Ship and aircraft finance in Germanic jurisdictions
- Ship and aircraft finance in Scandinavian jurisdictions
- Ship and aircraft finance in Franco-Latin jurisdictions
- Ship and aircraft finance in Islamic jurisdictions
- Ship and aircraft finance in emerging (former communist) jurisdictions

Guarantees

- Comparative law of guarantees of commercial (non-consumer) finance
- Guarantor and creditor protection in guarantee law
- Comparative law of guarantor subrogation and the insolvency rule against double-proof
- Export credit guarantees: comparative legal characteristics

INDEX

All references are to paragraph number

Abusive drawings,
  generally, 26–16 to 26–18
Advance payment bond,
  generally, 29–3
Affreightment,
  contracts of, 21–2
Africa. *See* **Algeria; Botswana;**
  Cameroon; Central African
  Republic; Chad; Ethiopia; Gabon;
  Gambia; Islamic countries; Ivory
  Coast; Kenya; Lesotho; Malawi;
  Niger; Nigeria; Rwanda; Sierra
  Leone; South Africa; Togo;
  Tunisia; Zambia; Zimbabwe
Aircraft finance,
  airline clearing system, 21–12
  charterers, registration of, 15–11
  de-registration of title, 15–24
  earnings, assignment of, 21–1, 21–12
  generally, 14–2
  hovercraft, 15–9
  insurance,
    assignment on owner's bankruptcy,
      22–4
    generally, 22–1
  liens. *See* **Aircraft liens**
  mortgages. *See* **Aircraft mortgages**
  registration of title, 15–20, 15–22
    charterers, 15–11
    Chicago Convention 1994, 15–8
    eligible aircraft, 15–9
    eligible owners, 15–10
    ineligibility, 15–18
  security structures, 14–6
Aircraft liens,
  generally, 20–23
  governing law, 20–28
  possessory repairer's lien, 20–24
  priority, 15–27
    aircraft charterers, 20–27

Aircraft liens—*cont.*
  priority—*cont.*
    general aircraft priority creditors,
      20–26
    possessory repairer's lien, 20–24
    statutory rights of detention, 20–24
    tort liability for damages, 20–25
Aircraft mortgages,
  certificate of deletion, 10–8
  covenants, 17–1
  de-registration of title, 15–23, 15–24
  enforcement,
    arrest jurisdiction, 18–32
      Rome Aircraft Convention 1933,
        18–33
    events of default,
      generally, 18–2 to 18–3
      restrictions on, 18–4
    generally, 18–1
    jurisdiction,
      arrest jurisdiction, 18–11 to
        18–33
      generally, 18–11
      jurisdiction clauses, 18–12
    Mareva injunction, 18–32
    remedies,
      express, 18–5
      judicial sale, 10–11, 18–6,
        19–26 to 19–28
      possession, 10–7, 18–8 to 18–10
      private sales, 10–8, 10–10, 18–6
      public auction, 10–9
      sale, 18–6 to 18–7
      summary, 18–4
  engine,
    removed, 15–29
    replacement, 15–32
      mortgaged to third party, where,
        15–34
      owned by third party, where,
        15–33
    spare, 15–30

Charge-backs—*cont.*
international reception of, 5–6 to
5–10
set-offs distinguished, 5–2
theoretical objections to, 5–5
Charterparties. *See* **Ship finance**
Chicago Convention 1944, 15–8
Chile. *See also* **Franco-Latin
jurisdictions; Latin America**
aircraft mortgages,
recognition of foreign,
Geneva Aircraft Convention
1948, 19–14
lex situs, 19–11
registration of, 9–6
spare parts, 15–30
contract debts, 4–6
enforcement of security,
judicial sale, 10–11
possessory management, 10–7
lex situs, 19–11
non-possessory chattel mortgages,
3–4
possessory management, 10–7
priorities, mortgages registered on
same day, 12–12, 15–26
registration of security, 9–6
ship mortgages, 15–26
China,
aircraft mortgages,
registration, 15–15
title of owner, 15–22
mortgages, generally, 1–8
security, attitude to, 1–8
Special Economic Zones, 1–8
Colombia. *See also* **Latin America**
aircraft finance,
liens, priority, 20–25
mortgages, title of owner, 15–22
contract debts, 4–6
enforcement of security,
judicial sale, 10–11
possessory management, 10–7
floating charges, 2–10
non-possessory chattel mortgages,
3–4
possessory management, 10–7
Comfort letters,
awareness of financing, 27–2
funding, 27–5

Comfort letters—*cont.*
management, 27–5
meaning of, 27–1
no asset-stripping, 27–5
ownership interest, maintenance of,
27–3
support required by lender, 27–4
terms of, 27–2 to 27–5
Confidential information. *See*
Intellectual property
Conflict of laws,
aircraft mortgages, validity of, 13–15
bankruptcy,
policies, enforcement by home
forum, 13–12
rules, 13–8 to 13–9
categorisation of issues, 13–3
contractual aspects, 13–4
false wealth and publicity, 13–5 to
13–7
floating charges, recognition of,
13–26 to 13–29
not recognised by home state,
13–26
not recognised where assets are
situate, 13–27 to 13–28
recognition of receiver, 13–29
freeze on enforcement, 13–30 to
13–31
interference with security, 13–30
investment securities, 13–25
land mortgages, 13–13 to 13–14
lex situs, 13–11, 13–16
main issues, 13–1 to 13–2
priorities, 13–8
preferential creditors, 13–32
title registration, impact of, 13–10
validity of security,
goods, over,
aircraft, 13–15
generally, 13–15
goods in transit, 13–15
ships, 13–15
stationary goods, 13–15, 13–16
to 13–18
priority, 13–19
intangible movables,
contract debts, 13–21
generally, 13–20
priority, 13–24

Consolidation,
  secured creditors, 8–19
Construction finance,
  ships, 23–1 to 23–2
Contract debts, security over,
  assignment, prohibitions on, 4–9
  cancellation clauses, 4–10
  categories of, 4–2
  conflict of laws and, 13–21 to 13–23
  enforcement remedies, 4–21
  future debts, 4–13 to 4–16
  generally, 4–1
  guaranteed debts, 4–11
  jurisdictional classifications, 4–4 to
    4–6
    "pledge",
      countries not requiring, 4–4
      countries requiring, 4–5 to 4–6
  negotiable instruments, 4–7
  objections to, 4–3
  preferences, 4–20
  priorities, 4–22
  secured creditors. *See* **Secured
    creditors**
  secured debt, 4–11
    permissible, 4–17, 8–3
  specificity doctrine and, 4–13
  sub-mortgages, 4–11
  validity of, 13–21 to 13–23
Contracts,
  cancellation clauses, 4–10
  cancellation of, 1–11
  negative pledge, 1–11
  pari passu clauses, 1–11
  Rome Convention 1980, 13–4, 13–7,
    13–22, 13–24
  take-or-pay, 29–1
Copyright. *See* **Intellectual property
  Corporate rehabilitation**. *See also*
  Judicial rescue proceedings
  administration. *See* **England**
  examples of proceedings, 11–6
  mild proceedings, 11–6
  security,
    impact on, 11–7 to 11–8
    stays on enforcement, 11–7
  tough proceedings, 11–6

Costa Rica. *See also* **Latin America**
  Brussels Arrest Convention 1952,
    18–21
  contract debts, 4–6
  enforcement of security,
    possessory management, 10–7
    stages auctions, 10–11
  non-possessory chattel mortgages,
    3–4
  possessory management, 10–7
  ships, registration of title to, 15–5
Custodians. *See* **Investment securities**
Cyprus,
  aircraft mortgages,
    registration of, 15–15
    title of owner, 15–22
  company charges, registration of,
    9–35
  floating charge, 2–8
  registration of title to ships, 15–5
  ship mortgages,
    deed of covenants, 16–7
    legislation, 16–5
Czech Republic,
  contract debts, 4–4
  fiduciary transfers, 2–11

Damages,
  mortgage securing, 8–10
Debentures. *See also* **Investment
  securities**
  charge-backs, 5–1
  general floating lien, with, 3–6
  registration of security, 9–13
Denmark. *See also* **Scandinavia**
  aircraft finance,
    liens, priority, 20–24, 20–27
    mortgages,
      Geneva Aircraft Convention
        1948, 19–14
      spare parts, 15–30
      title of owner, 15–22
  assignment of mortgages, 4–11
  contract debts, 4–6
  enforcement of security,
    events of default, 10–16
    grace periods, 10–15
    possessory management, 10–7
    summary bailiff sale, 10–11
  fiduciary transfers and, 2–11

Flags of convenience,
  generally, 15–5
Floating charge,
  aircraft mortgage, 15–13
    spare parts, 15–31
  conflict of laws. *See* **Conflict of laws**
  converted into fixed charge, 31–13
  enforcement of security, stay on
    11–10
  English-based,
    characteristics of, 2–5
    crystallisation, 2–5
    enforcement, 2–4, 2–5
    generally, 2–4
    insolvency administration, impact
      of, 2–7
    jurisdictions adopting, 2–8
    justification for, 2–4
  false wealth rule and, 1–5, 2–5
  fiduciary transfers compared, 2–12,
    2–13
  generally, 2–1, 2–3
  non-English-based, 2–10
  part of assets, over, 2–7, 11–10
  pre-existing debt, for, 31–12 to
    31–13
  preferences rules, 2–6, 30–11
  priority of,
    attaching creditors, 2–6, 12–25
    execution creditor, 2–6
    garnishee orders, 12–25
    generally, 2–6
    lien creditors, 12–25
    Mareva injunctions, 12–25
    mortgagees, 12–24
    possessory liens, 2–6
    preferential creditors, 12–22
    purchasers, 12–23
    retention of title, 12–23
    set-off, 2–6, 12–25
    subsequent fixed charges, 2–6,
      12–24
  recognition of, 2–6
    conflict of laws. *See* **Conflict of
      laws**
  ship mortgage, 15–13
  stay on enforcement, 11–10
  US security interest compared, 2–9
  weaknesses of, 2–6
Forfeiture,
  ships, of, 15–19

Formalities,
  aircraft mortgages, 16–1
  disadvantages of, 8–2
  intellectual property, 7–8
  investment securities, 6–17
  objectives of, 8–1
  security agreements, 4–12, 8–1, *et
    seq.*
  ship mortgages, 16–1
France. *See also* **Franco-Latin
  jurisdictions,**
  abusive drawings, 26–16
  aircraft finance,
    liens, priority, 20–26
    mortgages,
      arrest jurisdiction, 18–32
      recognition of foreign,
        flag law, 19–11
        Geneva Aircraft Convention
          1948, 19–14
      registration of, 9–6
        renewal of, 9–7
      replacement engine, 15–32
      spare parts, 15–31
      title of owner, 15–22
    registration of title, 15–9
      eligible owners, 15–10
  antichrèse, 3–1
  back-interest, limitation period, 8–8
  charge-backs, 5–4, 5–10
  charterhire, assignments of, 4–8
  comfort letters, 27–8
  contract debts, 4–5, 4–6, 13–23
    income-producing property, 4–8
  contracts, cancellation clauses, 4–10
  corporate rehabilitation. *See*
    redressement judiciaire, *infra*
  enforcement of security,
    events of default, efficacy of, 10–16
    judicial sale, 10–11
    possessory management, 10–7
    stay on, 11–17
  fiduciary transfers and, 2–11
  flag law, 19–3, 19–11
  foreign currency mortgages, 8–5
  freight, assignment of, 4–8
  future assets, security over, 4–16
  insolvency set-off, attitude to, 5–4
  interest, 8–8

Greece—*cont.*
  ship finance—*cont.*
    construction finance, 23–2
    earnings, assignment of, 21–6
    insurance, assignment of, 22–4
    maritime liens,
      priority of,
        flag law, 20–34
        supplier's lien, 20–15
      recognition, flag law, 20–30
    mortgages,
      agent banks, 16–26
      de-registration of title, 15–24
      formal requirements, 16–24
      generally, 16–23
      official consents, 16–26
      possession, 18–10
      priority,
        registered on same day, where, 15–26
        supplier's lien, 20–15
      recordation, 16–25
      registration, 15–14
        provisional, 15–14
        unfinished ships, 23–2
      title of owner, 15–21
      trustees, 16–26
    registration of title, 15–21
    ships, registration of title, 15–4
    trusts, attitude to, 16–26
    usury laws, 8–8
Guarantees,
  abusive drawings, 26–16 to 26–18
  additional security, 25–23
  advance payment bond, 29–3
  appropriation of payments by creditor, 25–21
  assignments, 26–7
  authorisations, 24–5
  avals on negotiable instruments, 29–2
  avoided, reinstatement of, 25–22
  bank guarantees. *See* first demand bank guarantees; independent guarantors, *infra*
  bid bond, 29–3
  certificate of amount owing, 25–24
  co-guarantors, release of, 25–12
  comfort letters. *See* **Comfort letters**
  completion guarantee, 29–1
  compositions of guaranteed debt, 25–10

Guarantees—*cont.*
  consideration clause, 25–2
  continuing guarantee, 25–8
  contract bonds, 29–3
  contractual restrictions, 24–6
  corporate powers and benefit, 24–3 to 24–4
  "cross-stream" guarantees, 31–5
  deed poll, by, 29–5
  demand, 25–6
  double proof rule, 5–3, 25–15 to 25–18, 26–9
  expiry, 25–9, 26–2
  export credit guarantees. *See* independent guarantors, *infra*
  extensions of guaranteed debt, 25–10
  financial assistance to purchase own shares, 24–5
  financial lease guarantees, 29–11 to 29–12
  first demand guarantees, 25–6, 26–1
    abusive drawings, 26–16 to 26–18
    attachment of proceeds, 26–19 to 26–20
    definition, 26–13
    independence of, 26–15
    policies, 26–14
  general terms of, 25–27
  grace periods, 26–3
  guaranteed sums, 25–3
  immediate recourse to guarantee, 25–20
  independent guarantors, 26–1 to 26–20
    application of recoveries, 26–4
    assignments of guarantees, 26–7
    control, 26–6
    defences, no waiver of, 26–5
    expiry, 26–2
    first demand, 26–1. *See also* first demand bank guarantees, *supra*
    grace period, 26–3
    indemnity from customer, 26–11
    insurance, 26–12
    limitation of claims guaranteed, 26–4
    retirement of guarantee, 26–8
    scheduled maturities, 26–3

International Convention for the
   Prevention of Pollution from Ships
   1973 and 1978 Protocol, 20–22
Investment securities,
   accessories, 6–14
   charges over
      formalities, 6–17
      international availability of, 6–6
      perfection of, 6–8
         disadvantages of non-
            registration, 6–12
         possessory pledge, 6–8 to 6–11
         registration, 6–8 to 6–11
      restrictions on, 6–7
         financial assistance for purchase
            of own shares, 1–11, 6–7,
            24–5
      use of, 6–5
   conflict of laws, 13–25
   controllers, liability of, 6–25
   custodians,
      depositories,
         central, 6–39
         claims against, types of, 6–31
         legal aspects, 6–32 to 6–33
         reasons for 6–30
      Euroclear System. See Euroclear
         System
      ownership of securities held by see
         trusts below,
   documentation of, 6–2
   enforcement remedies, 6–28
   fungibility,
      custodian using securities as his
         own, 6–40, 6–41 to 6–43
      generally, 6–16, 6–40
      ownership, 6–40
      partial redemption, 6–40
      securities lost, destroyed or
         counterfeit, 6–40
   fungible securities, 6–16
   future securities, 6–14
   generally, 4–1
   identity of issuer, 6–3
   liabilities on, 6–22
      controllers, 6–25
      duty to take care of charged
         property, 6–22 to 6–23
      insider dealing, 6–26
      notification duties, 6–24

Investment securities—*cont.*
   liabilities on—*cont.*
      preferential transfers, 6–27
   pledges over,
      civil code securities, 6–45
      common law countries, 6–44
   priority, 6–29
   secured creditors,
      liabilities of, 6–21
      permissible, 6–19
   secured debts, permissible, 6–18
   securities, permissible, 6–20
   specificity, doctrine of, 6–17
   substitution rights, 6–13
   trusts. *See also* **Trusts,**
      forms of, 6–35
      recognition of, 6–34
      statutory custodian trusts, 6–36 to
         6–39
   types of, 6–4
   voting rights, 6–15
Ireland. *See* **Northern Ireland; Republic
   of Ireland Islamic countries.** *See
   also* **Algeria; Bahrain, Egypt;
   Pakistan; Oatar; Saudi Arabia;
   Shariah law; Syria; United Arab
   Emirates**
   security, attitude to, 1–9
   Shariah law. *See* **Shariah law**
Isle of Man. *See also* **Britain**
   registration of title to ships, 15–5
Israel,
   aircraft mortgages,
      registration, 15–15
      renewal of, 9–7
      title of owner, 15–22
   company charges, registration of,
      9–35
   contract debts, 4–4
   enforcement of security,
      judicial sale, 10–11
      post-mortgage agreement to private
         sale, 10–13
      quick summary procedure, 10–12
   flag law, 19–3
   floating charge, 2–8
   maximum amount mortgages, 8–4
   prepayment, restrictions on, 8–16
   priorities, mortgages registered on
      same day, 12–12, 15–26

Israel—*cont.*
  registration of security, renewal of,
    9–7
  ship finance,
    mortgages,
      priority,
        registered on same day, where,
          15–26
        repairer's lien, 20–16
        supplier's lien, 20–15
        recognition of foreign, flag law,
          19–3
        title of owner, 15–21
    registration of title, 15–21
Italy,
  abusive drawings, 26–16
  aircraft finance,
    liens, priority, 20–25
    mortgages,
      registration of, 9–6
      renewal of, 9–7
      replacement engine, 15–32
      spare parts, 15–30
  assignment of mortgages, 4–11
  back-interest, limitation period, 8–8
  charge-back, 5–10
  contract debts, 4–6
    income-producing property, 4–8
  corporate rehabilitation, 11–6
  enforcement of security,
    events of default, efficacy of, 10–16
    judicial sale, 10–11
    possessory management, 10–7
    public auction, 10–9
  extraordinary administration, 11–6
  fiduciary transfers and, 2–11
  flag law, 19–3, 20–30, 20–34
  foreign currency mortgages, 8–5
  frieght, assignment of, 4–8
  future receivables, security over, 4–16
  interest, 8–8
  machinery, non-possessory lien over,
    3–7
  non-possessory chattel mortgages,
    3–7
  possessory management, 10–7
  preferences,
    Actio Pauliana, 30–6
    defences,
      creditor ignorance of insolvency,
        32–10
      preferential intent, 32–6

Italy—*cont.*
  preferences—*cont.*
    security,
      assignments, late registration of,
        31–16
      pre-existing debt, for, 31–9
  prepayment, restrictions on, 8–16
  preventive composition proceedings,
    11–5
  priority, registered on same day,
    where, 15–26
  privilegio speciale, 2–20
  registered non-possessory lien, 3–7
  registration of security, 9–6
    re-registration of movable assets,
      9–8
    renewal of, 9–7
  restricted business charge, 2–20
  security, attitude to, 1–7, 11–7
  ship finance,
    construction finance, 23–2
    earnings, assignment of, 21–6
    insurance, assignment of, 22–4
    maritime liens,
      priority of, flag law, 20–34
      recognition, flag law, 20–30
    mortgages,
      jurisdiction,
        attachment jurisdiction over
          ship but not debtor,
          18–16
        final judgment, 18–18
        "ready to sail" rule, 18–17
      priority, registered on same day,
        where, 15–26
      recognition of foreign, flag law,
        19–3
    unfinished ships, 23–2
    shares, division of ship into, 15–6
  usury laws, 8–8
Ivory Coast,
  Geneva Aircraft Convention 1948,
    19–14

Jamaica,
  aircraft mortgages, registration,
    15–15
  company charges, registration of,
    9–35
  floating charge, 2–8

Japan,
aircraft finance,
mortgages, title of owner, 15–22
registration of title, 15–9
eligible owners, 15–10
assignment of mortgages, 4–11
contract debts, 4–4, 4–6, 13–23
corporate reorganisation, 11–6,
11–20, 32–4
enforcement of security,
judicial sale, 10–11
possessory management, 10–7
private sales, 10–10
ship finance, 18–17
stay on, 11–20
fiduciary transfers, 2–11
over-security and, 2–14
flag law, 19–3, 20–34
foreign currency mortgages, 8–5
judicial rescue proceedings, 11–6,
11–20
lex fori, 20–31
non-possessory chattel mortgages,
3–4
possessory management, 10–7
preferences,
defences,
creditor ignorance of insolvency,
32–10
preferential intent, 32–6
prejudice to creditors,
gifts, 31–4
security,
assignments, late registration
of, 31–16
pre-existing debt, for, 31–9
undervalue transactions, 31–4
priorities, prior and subsequent
purchasers and mortgages,
12–18
private sales, 10–10
security,
attitude to, 1–7, 11–7
registration of, attitude to, 9–12
ship finance,
flag law, 19–3, 20–34
insurance, assignment of, 22–4
maritime liens,
lex fori, 20–31

Japan—*cont.*
ship finance—*cont.*
maritime liens—*cont.*
priority of, 20–34
repairer's lien, 20–16
supplier's lien, 20–15
recognition, 20–30
mortgages,
enforcement, jurisdiction "ready
to sail" rule, 18–17
forced sale of ship, 15–25
in rem jurisdiction over ship and
debtor, 18–14, 18–15
priority,
repairer's lien, 20–16
supplier's lien, 20–15
recognition of foreign, 19–3
registration, 15–12
title of owner, 15–21
registration of title, 15–21
offshore international registers,
15–5
trustees, 8–23
Judicial rescue proceedings,
classification of proceedings, 11–3
compositions and moratoriums,
moratoriums, 11–5
preventive composition
proceedings, 11–5
voluntary compositions, 11–4
corporate rehabilitation. *See*
Corporate rehabilitation
generally, 11–1
private debt restructuring, 11–2
work-out, 11–2

Kenya,
company charges, registration of,
9–35
floating charge, 2–8
Kerguelen,
registration of title to ships, 15–5
Korea,
aircraft finance,
liens, priority, 20–24
mortgages,
recognition of foreign, flag law,
19–11
registration of, 9–6
replacement engine, 15–32

Middle East. *See* Algeria; Bahrain;
    Cyprus; Egypt; Islamic countries;
    Isreal; Kuwait; Libyan Arab
    Republic; Pakistan; Qatar; Saudi
    Arabia; Syria; Turkey; United
    Arab Emirates
Moratoriums,
    preventive compositions and, 11–5
    super-priority moratorium loans,
        1–10
Morocco,
    contract debts, 4–6
Mortgages. *See also* Security; *see under*
    individual countries, *e.g.* **France**
    agricultural, 3–3
    aircraft mortgages. *See* **Aircraft**
        mortgages,
    assignment of, 4–11
    damages, securing, 8–10
    foreign currency, 8–5
    land, of,
        corporate, 3–1
        generally, 3–1
        registration of, 3–1
    maximum amount, 8–4
    moveables, of, 3–1
        Shariah law and 1–9
    non-possessory chattel mortgages. *See*
        Non-possessory chattel
        mortgages
    "owner's mortgage", 8–13
    purchase money chattel, 2–19
    second priority security, 8–11
    ship mortgages. *See* **Ship mortgages**
    sub-mortgages, 4–11

Natal. *See* **South Africa**
Negotiable instruments,
    avals on, 29–2
    contract debts, 4–7
    generally, 4–1, 4–7
    guarantees and, 25–17, 29–2
    priority, 12–20
    registration of security, 9–13
    validity of security over, 13–20
Netherlands,
    abusive drawings, 26–16
    aircraft finance,
        mortgages,
            arrest jurisdiction, 18–32

Netherlands—*cont.*
    aircraft finance—*cont.*
        mortgages—*cont.*
            Geneva Aricraft Convention
                1948, 19–14
            replacement engine, 15–32
            spare parts, 15–30
            registration of title, 15–9
                eligible owners, 15–10
                lessee, 15–11
    charge-backs, 5–10
    contract debts, 4–4
    enforcement of security, events of
        default, 10–16
    fiduciary transfers, 2–11, 2–12, 2–15
        over-security, 2–14
        practice, 2–15
    future debts, security over, 4–16, 8–3
    lex fori, 20–34
    non-possessory chattel mortgages,
        3–4
    non-possessory pledge, 2–15, 31–11
        conversion to possessory pledge,
            2–15
    preferences,
        Actio Pauliana, 30–6
        defences,
            creditor ignorance of insolvency,
                32–10
            preferential intent, 32–6
        generally, 30–7
        security,
            after-acquired assets, over,
                31–11
            pre-existing debt, for, 31–9
    preventive composition proceedings,
        11–5
    priorities,
        mortgages registered on same day,
            12–12, 15–26
        prior and subsequent purchasers
            and mortgages, 12–18
    registration of security, 9–12
    Rome Aircraft Convention 1933,
        18–33
    security, attitude to, 1–7, 11–7
    ship finance,
        maritime liens,
            priority of, lex fori, 20–34
            recognition, law of closest
                connection, 20–32

Secured debt—*cont.*
  permissible—*cont.*
    prepayment—*cont.*
      restrictions on, 8–15
      redemption, restriction on, 8–14
      second priority security, 8–11
      third party security, 8–12
    restrictions on,
      aircraft mortgages, 16–2
      ship mortgages, 16–2
    ship mortgages, 16–2, 16–9, 16–14
Security. *See also* **Mortgages; Secured**
    creditors; Secured debt
  after-acquired assets, over, 1–6,
    4–14, 31–11, 32–16
  aircraft finance. *See* **Aircraft finance**
  assets, scope of, 1–10
  assignments of debts by creditor to
    debtor. *See* **Charge-backs**
  attitudes to, 1–7 to 1–9, 11–7
  charge-backs. *See* **Charge-backs**
  conflict of laws, and. *See* **Conflict of**
    laws
  contract, cancellation of, 1–11
  contract debts, over. *See* **Contract**
    debts
  contractual restrictions, 1–11
  countries hostile to, 11–7
  countries sympathetic to, 11–7
  debt, scope of, 1–10
  enforcement of. *See* **Enforcement of**
    security
  essence of, 1–4
  false wealth objection. *See* **False**
    wealth,
  foreign, recognition of, 1–10
  formalities, 1–10, 4–12
  future assets, over, 1–6, 4–14, 31–11,
    32–16
  future debts, over. *See* **Future debts**
  guaranteed debts, over, 4–11
  income-producing property, 4–8
  insolvency proceedings, 1–11
  jurisdictional classification, 1–7
    hostile, 11–7
    main issues, 1–10
    sympathetic, 11–7
    undeveloped security, where, 1–8,
      1–9
  lease, cancellation of, 1–11
  liabilities, 1–10
  licence, cancellation of, 1–11

Security—*cont.*
  limitations on creditors, 1–10
  main issues on, 1–10
  meaning of, 1–4
  mortgages. *See* **Mortgages**
  objections to, 1–3
    false wealth, 1–5
  over-security, 2–14
  perfection of, 1–10
  policies of, 1–2
  power to grant, 1–11
  preferences. *See* **Preferences**
  principles of, 1–1 to 1–11
  priority, predictability of, 1–10
  public registration of. *See*
    Registration of security
  purposes of, 1–2
  rationale of, 1–2
  recognition of foreign security, 1–10
  redemption, restricting, 1–10
  registration of. *See* **Registration of**
    security
  remedies of secured creditor, 1–10
  safe harbours, 1–10
  second priority, 8–11
  secured creditors. *See* **Secured**
    creditors
  secured debt. *See* **Secured debt**
  ship finance. *See* **Ship finance**
  specificity, doctrine, of 1–6
  stamp duties, 1–10, 3–6, 24–8
  stays on enforcement, 11–7
  sub-mortgages, 4–11
  super-priority moratorium loans,
    1–10
  third party, 8–12
  title, 1–10
    transfer of, as, 1–4
  universal business charges. *See*
    Universal business charges
Senegal,
  Rome Aircraft Convention 1933,
    18–33
Set-off,
  cash cover, against, 26–10
  charge-back distinguished, 5–2
  collateral security, 5–3
  floating charge, priority of, 2–6,
    12–25
  generally, 5–2 to 5–4

South Africa—*cont.*
  preferences—*cont.*
    undervalue transactions, 31–4
  priorities, mortgages registered on
    same day, 12–12, 15–26
  security,
    attitude to, 1–7
    place of registration, 9–8
  ship finance,
    insurance, assignment of, 22–4
    maritime liens,
      priority of, 20–16, 20–35
      recognition, lex fori, 20–31
    mortgages,
      in rem jurisdiction over ship and
        debtor, 18–14, 18–15
      priority,
        registered on same day, where,
          15–26
      repairer's lien, 20–16
    trustees, 8–23
South America. *See* **Latin America**
South Korea. *See* **Korea**
Spain,
  aircraft mortgages,
    flag law, 19–11
    foreign, recognition of, 19–11
    registration of, 9–6
  assignment of mortgages, 4–11
  charge-backs, 5–4, 5–10
  contract debt, income-producing
    property, 4–8
  corporate rehabilitation, 11–6
  enforcement of security,
    foreclosure, 10–3
    grace periods, 10–15
    judicial sale, 10–11
    notary auction, 10–11
    possessory management, 10–7
    ship finance, 10–7, 18–17, 18–21
    ships, 10–7
  fiduciary transfers and, 2–11
  flag law, 19–11
  foreclosure, 10–3
  foreign currency mortgages, 8–5
  freight, 4–8
  goods in transit, 13–15
  insolvency set-off, attitude to, 5–4
  mortgages,
    aircraft. *See* aircraft mortgages,
      supra

Spain—*cont.*
  mortgages—*cont.*
    assignment of, 4–11
    non-possessory chattel mortgages,
      2–22, 8–11
    ship. *See* ship finance, *infra*
  pledge, 2–22
  possessory management, 10–7
  preferences, defences, preferential
    intent, 32–6
  priorities,
    mortgage registration, 12–11
      registered on same day, 12–12,
        15–26
    ship mortgages. *See* ship finance,
      infra
  registration of security, 9–6
  restricted business charges, 2–22
  security, attitude to, 1–7, 11–7
  security agreements, formalities,
    4–12, 8–2
  ship finance,
    demise charterers, registration of,
      15–7
    insurance, assignment of, 22–4
    maritime liens, priority, 20–15
    mortgages,
      enforcement, 10–7
      jurisdiction,
        Brussels Arrest Convention
          1952, 18–21
        "ready to sail" rule, 18–17
        possession, 10–7, 18–10
      priority,
        registered on same day, where,
          15–26
        supplier's lien, 20–15
        title of owner, 15–21
      registration of title, 15–21
  suspension of payments, 11–6
Specificity, doctrine of,
  assignment of future debts, 4–13
  generally, 1–6, 31–11
  investment securities, 6–17
Stamp duties,
  generally, 1–10, 3–6
  guarantees, 24–8
Stays on enforcement. *See* **Enforcement
  of security**
Sweden. See also **Scandinavia**
  aircraft finance,
    liens, priority, 20–24

Turkey—*cont.*
  non-possessory chattel mortgages
    and, 15–16
  registration of security, renewal of,
    9–7
  ship finance,
    earnings, assignment of, 21–5
    insurance, assignment of, 22–4
    lex fori, 20–31
    maritime liens,
      lex fori,
        priority under, 20–34
        recognition under, 20–31
      priority,
        lex fiori, 20–34
        supplier's lien, 20–15
    mortgages,
      non-recognition of foreign, 19–4
      priority, supplier's lien, 20–15
      title of owner, 15–21
    registration of title, 15–21

United Arab Emirates. *See also* **Islamic
  countries**
  commercial code, 1–9
  security, attitude to, 1–9
United Kingdom. *See* **Britain; Channel
  Islands; England; English-based
  countries; Isle of Man; Northern
  Ireland; Scotland**
United States,
  after-acquired collateral, security
    over, 4–14
  aircraft finance,
    liens, priority, 20–24
    mortgages,
      arrest jurisdiction, 18–32
      floating charge, spare parts,
        15–30
      Geneva Aircraft Convention
        1948, 19–14
      registration,
        ineligibility for title
          registration, 15–18
        renewal of, 9–7
      spare parts, 15–30
        floating charge, 15–30
      title of owner, 15–22
    registration of title, 15–22
    charterers, 15–11

United States—*cont.*
  aircraft finance—*cont.*
    registration of title—*cont.*
      eligible owners, 15–10
      ineligibility, 15–18
  California, charge-backs, 5–9
  central depository, 6–39
  CERCLA, 20–22
  charge-backs, 5–8 to 5–9
  comfort letters, 27–7
  contract debts, 4–4, 4–5
    liabilities of secured creditors, 4–19
    negotiable instruments, 4–7
    secured debts, 4–11
  contracts,
    cancellation clauses, 4–10
    prohibition on assignment, 4–9
  corporate rehabilitation,
    adequate protection, 11–12
    debtor's use of collateral, 11–13
    generally, 11–6
    plan, 11–16
    post-commencement property,
      11–15
    post-petition interest, 11–15
    priority, 11–14
    stay on enforcement of security,
      11–11 to 11–16
  enforcement of security,
    grace periods, 10–15
    marshalling, 10–17
    methods of, 10–2
    private sales, 10–10
    stay on, corporate rehabilitation,
      11–11 to 11–16
  financial assistance for acquisition of
    own shares, 6–7
  flag law, 19–3
  floating charge. *See* **Floating charge**
  future debts, security over, 4–14
  general enterprise security interest,
    2–9
    English floating-charge compared,
      2–9
    formalities, 4–12
  guarantees,
    abusive drawings, 26–16, 26–17
    corporate powers and benefit, 24–4
    "cross-stream", 31–5
    standby letters of credit, 28–1,
      28–2
    subrogation, 25–17, 25–18

United States—*cont.*
  ship finance—*cont.*
    mortgages—*cont.*
      registration, 15–14
        ineligibility for title
          registration, 15–18
      unfinished ships, 23–2
      registration of title, 15–4
        ineligibility, 15–18
    trusts, 6–35
    universal business charges. *See*
      general enterprises security
      interest, *supra*
Universal business charges,
  definition, 2–1
  false wealth rule and, 1–5
  fiduciary transfer. *See* **Fiduciary transfer**
  floating charge. *See* **Floating charge,**
  generally, 2–1 to 2–3
  notarial bond, 2–1, 2–16
  restricted business charges,
    characterisitics of, 2–17
    examples, 2–18 to 2–22
    generally, 2–17
  stay on enforcement of security and, 11–10
  US general enterprise security interest, 2–9, 4–12
Uruguay. *See also* **Latin America**
  aircraft mortgages,
    recognition of foreign, lex situs, 19–11
    renewal of registration, 9–7
    spare parts, 15–30
  contract debts, 4–6
  enforcement of security,
    judicial sale, 10–11
    possessory management, 10–7
  lex situs, 19–11
  non-possessory chattel mortgages, 3–4
  possessory management, 10–7
  ship finance,
    insurance, assignment of, 22–4
    registration of title, 15–5
Usury,
  back-interest, 8–8
  historical hostility to, 1–3
  laws, 8–7 to 8–8

Vanuata,
  ship finance,
    demise charterers, registration of, 15–7
    registration of title, 15–5
Venezuela. *See also* **Franco-Latin jurisdictions; Latin America**
  aircraft finance,
    liens, priority, 20–26
    mortgages,
      foreign, non-recognition, 19–12
      renewal of registration, 9–7
      title of owner, 15–22
  contract debts, 4–6
  enforcement of security,
    judicial sale, 10–8, 10–11
    possessory management, 10–7
  financial institutions, securities granted to, 8–24
  foreign currency mortgages, 8–5
  non-possessory mortgages, 3–8
  possessory management, 10–7
  registration of security, renewal of, 9–7
  ship finance,
    insurance, assignment of, 22–4
    maritime liens, 20–35
    mortgages,
      foreign, 19–4
      title of owner, 15–21
    registration of title, 15–21
  statutory custodian trusts, 6–38
  trustees, 8–23

Work-out. *See* **Judicial rescue proceedings**

Yugoslavia,
  Brussels Arrest Convention 1952, 18–21

Zaire,
  Rome Aircraft Convention 1933, 18–33